BURGHLEY

STEPHEN ALFORD was educated at the University of St Andrews, Scotland, and is university lecturer in history at Cambridge University and a Fellow of King's College. He is the author of *The Early Elizabethan Polity* (1998) and *Kingship and Politics in the Reign of Edward VI* (2002).

BURGHLEY

WILLIAM CECIL AT THE COURT OF ELIZABETH I

STEPHEN ALFORD

YALE UNIVERSITY PRESS
NEW HAVEN AND LONDON

Published with assistance from the foundation established in memory of Oliver Baty Cunningham of the Class of 1917, Yale College.

For information about this and other Yale University Press publications, please contact:
U.S. Office: sales.press@yale.edu   www.yalebooks.com
Europe Office: sales@yaleup.co.uk   www.yaleup.co.uk

Set in Minion by SX Composing, Rayleigh, Essex
Printed in Great Britain by TJ International, Padstow, Cornwall

Library of Congress Cataloging-in-Publication Data

Alford, Stephen, 1970–
    Burghley:William Cecil at the court of Elizabeth I/Stephen Alford.
        p. cm.
    Includes bibliographical references and index.
    ISBN 978–0–300–11896–4 (alk. paper)
1. Burghley, William Cecil, Baron, 1520–1598. 2. Great Britain—History—Elizabeth, 1558–1603—Biography. 3. Statesmen—Great Britain—Biography. 4. Great Britain—Politics and government—1558–1603. 5. Elizabeth I, Queen of England, 1533–1603—Relations with statesmen. I. Title.
DA358.B9.A66 2008
942.05'5092—dc22
[B]
2007042537

A catalogue record for this book is available from the British Library.

ISBN 978–0–300–17088–7 (pbk)

The paper used for the text pages of this book is FSC certified. FSC (The Forest Stewardship Council) is an international network to promote responsible management of the world's forests.

10 9 8 7 6 5 4 3 2 1

For Max, with love

Contents

You see I am in a mixture of divinity and policy, preferring in policy Her Majesty afore all others on the earth, and in divinity the King of Heaven above all, betwixt alpha and omega.

William Cecil, Lord Burghley to Sir Robert Cecil, 13 March 1596

Illustrations

Preface

To imagine the court of Elizabeth I is to perceive a world of glamour and intrigue. Elizabeth is a queen we can understand. We feel we know her. We have read about her in books and seen her on television and in films. She was decisive and commanding, possessed of the heart and stomach of a king. She was a monarch who knew her own mind, a war leader, even a visionary. We can imagine how she lived at court, attended by her ladies and gentlewomen, and surrounded by dashing courtiers: the Earl of Leicester, perhaps, or Sir Christopher Hatton, or the Earl of Essex. In our little reverie everybody is richly and fashionably dressed, wonderfully glamorous. This is, after all, a time of glorious stability, of exploration, of the triumph of Protestant England, of victory over Spain.

Somewhere in the background there is someone else. It is easy not to notice him. He slips easily out of mind. He is a bureaucrat dressed in sombre black. He lives for paper, not people. He is elderly and conservative. He fusses over the Queen. He pours cold water on courtly ambition. He is the Polonius of Elizabeth's court, worthy, dull, old-fashioned and silly. Doubtless, we might think, Elizabeth and her courtiers tolerate and humour him: the brilliant cannot be brilliant without someone to throw their brilliance into relief. He is the man who can reduce everything to grey. This master bureaucrat is William Cecil, first Baron of Burghley, Queen Elizabeth's Secretary and later her Lord Treasurer.

But there is a problem here. Our cosy and familiar picture of Elizabeth's reign is a carefully contrived fiction. This book gives a quite different version of the Elizabethan age. It is Lord Burghley's story. It is not a stodgy monograph on Tudor government administration; it is instead the life of the most powerful man in Elizabethan England.

Burghley was brilliant, controlled and to his enemies terrifying. He dominated everything. He believed it was his mission to save Elizabeth from those at home and abroad who wished to destroy her. He looked round about him and saw danger everywhere. He believed to the core of his being that the Protestant England he had helped to build was engaged in a great war against the Antichrist of the Roman Catholic Church. He helped rebels abroad to resist Spanish tyranny. He fought subversion and brought traitors to justice. His great enemy was Mary, Queen of Scots; at the end of a battle of wills with Mary that lasted for nearly thirty years, he saw to it that she went to the executioner's block. He was obsessive, passionate and driven, a master politician who, when colleagues stood in his way, had an uncanny ability to prevail.

If history remembers Lord Burghley as a dull bureaucrat, the servant of the Queen who did only what he was told, then this was because Burghley wanted it that way. It suited him to say that he was merely a humble functionary. He made his reputation on it: powerful men often do. Anyone who knew anything about the Elizabethan court, who met the Queen in her Privy Chamber or sat with the Privy Council or understood how government worked, saw through the pose in an instant. Burghley professed moderation and self-discipline. But he also built three fabulous houses and planted beautiful gardens. He was a collector of fine things. He loved expensive clothes and lived as grandly as any other courtier.

An Elizabethan insider would have seen also the fascinating relationship between Elizabeth and Burghley. This was not the stuff of soft-focus biography. It was tough and uncompromising, with hard words spoken on both sides. But it was, above all things, extraordinarily subtle. For forty years Burghley worked to save Elizabeth from herself. He thought he saw clearly where she at times did not. While Elizabeth prevaricated and hesitated, Burghley sought decisive action. He believed he had a mission from God to protect his monarch, even if this meant disobeying her direct commands. He had the self-assurance of someone who is absolutely convinced of the rightness of his actions. He risked everything to make sure that the Queen of Scots was executed. He went to his tomb believing that God was on his side, however many wretched things he had done to defend religion, realm and Queen.

To get to the truth of Burghley's life we have to cut through four hundred years of propaganda. The first paragraphs of this preface are full of it. Biographers like Sir John Neale, who professed to be in love with Elizabeth, have made it their living. So do today's movie directors. Elizabeth and her court speak to our modern condition, to the cult of fashionable celebrity as well as to the instinctively attractive notion of a powerful woman winning through in a world dominated by men. The age of Gloriana looks sparkling and glorious. Burghley, for too long written off as a dull administrator, gave a very different account of life at court. He lived and breathed politics. No one else knew Elizabeth and her kingdoms as well as he did. No one is a better guide to the real story of Elizabeth I's reign.

William Cecil has looked over my shoulder for the whole of my professional life. Over the years I have found it impossible to escape from him. So this book is my effort to make sense of William Cecil, even to make my peace with him. I cannot pretend that it is exhaustive. It does not cover every aspect of Burghley's administrative career and it is not a technical monograph. That is not the kind of book I wanted to write. It is my account of his life: this is my Burghley, as I have come to understand him, for better or worse.

What follows is the story of a man who believed that everything he did was necessary for a greater good, for God and Queen. That may have been true, it may have been self-delusion. I have tried to tell Burghley's story as simply and as clearly as I can, but I do not believe for a moment that William Cecil was a simple man.

Like any of us, Burghley's personality was staggeringly complex, a mass of contradictions. We face paradoxes at every turn. He was a humble servant of the monarch who possessed an overwhelming sense of what had to be done. He lived with immense riches in three magnificent houses, yet he once called himself 'the poorest lord in England'. He protested conscience at all times but he could be a ruthless political operator. He was the assured public servant who struggled to discipline his adolescent son. He was the devoted husband whose marriage is almost entirely hidden from view because of the massive weight of government business he bore.

And so the layers of Burghley's character, so often awkward and contradictory, begin to be exposed. I have no doubt that many other layers have been lost to history. A man as careful as he was knew how to keep a secret. But the sources he left tell a compelling story of politics at its toughest, of wealth, power and the joys and sadnesses of family life.

In this book I have tried to allow Burghley to speak for himself. His voice is direct and plain, often urgent in its tone, but, as we should expect from a craftsman with words, always very subtle. One of the finest examples of this is the short extract I have used to introduce my book: 'You see I am in a mixture of divinity and policy, preferring in policy Her Majesty afore all others on the earth, and in divinity the King of Heaven above all, betwixt alpha and omega.'

In this sentence, which he wrote half a century after entering political life, Burghley captured the subtlety of his service to God and Queen. In strict theory there was no conflict between the two: the Queen, as any one of her councillors knew, was God's representative on earth. But politics was never that simple in the sixteenth century. Burghley always said that he was merely a servant, a humble official, yet we know that he was also the most powerful and capable politician of the Tudor century. To work at the highest levels of politics for as long as he did took great intelligence, resolution, stamina and cunning. This book tries to capture the man. It is Burghley's story.

Acknowledgements

This book has been a long time in the making, and over the years of thinking about it, and then writing it, I have profited from the advice and wisdom of many friends and colleagues. As the great map-maker John Speed wrote in 1612, 'I have put my sickle into other men's corn, and have laid my building upon other men's foundations.' I feel and acknowledge some deep obligations.

John Guy trained me as a professional historian and for many years now I have been extraordinarily blessed with his kindness and friendship. Peter Robinson's sharp eyes helped to turn a proposal into a book and I am deeply grateful to him for his support and encouragement. Robert Baldock of Yale University Press has never once shown anything but the warmest enthusiasm for the project, and I am lucky indeed to have so experienced and wise an editor. I must thank Tom Buhler, Robert's colleague, for his perceptive comments on the manuscript of the book. I should salute also the generous and frank counsel of the two readers asked by the Press to read the book before copy-editing.

Many friends have taken time and trouble to read drafts of the manuscript. John Cramsie, my oldest comrade, worked at it heroically in a busy teaching term. Matthew Clark, Leanda de Lisle, Wallace MacCaffrey, Ellen Rossiter and Sue Williams have seen chapters of the book at various stages of its evolution. Tom Freeman and Liz Evenden have given freely and generously of their great knowledge. Simon Goldhill translated Burghley's Greek from my eccentric scribbles. Members of seminars in London, Cambridge, Oxford, St Andrews and Bangor have helped me to test lots of ideas. So, too, have my friends and colleagues in the Faculty of History at Cambridge and at King's, and I am very grateful to them all. Needless to say, any mistakes in the book are my own and no one else's.

I have had the great privilege to work in wonderful libraries and archives. The staffs of the Manuscripts Room, the Munby Rare Books Room, the Official Publications Room and the Map Room of Cambridge University

Library have been, as they always are, both courteous and expert. The same is true of the staff of the Manuscripts Room of the British Library and the National Archives in London; Duke Humfrey's Library in the Bodleian Library, Oxford; the National Library of Scotland in Edinburgh; and St Andrews University Library. I must thank especially Malcolm Underwood for the help he gave me in the archives of St John's College, Cambridge; Richard Rex for showing me the earliest dated specimen we have of Burghley's handwriting; and Glyn Redworth for his advice on a Spanish source. At Burghley House Lady Victoria Leatham, Carolyn Crookall and Jon Culverhouse have all shown me great kindness and hospitality. It is to Lady Victoria that I owe thanks for being able to read Lord Burghley's copy of Abraham Ortelius's *Theatrum orbis terrarum* on a beautiful summer's day in 2006.

My greatest debt is to Max. No one should have to live with Burghley for as long as she has done. She has smiled through it all with serene patience. If this book has any kind of balance, insight or humanity it is, in all kinds of subtle ways, her doing. There was nothing to do but to dedicate it to her.

Albert, Flash and Zorro have been frankly ambivalent about the book. At times they really haven't seen the point of it, though they have enjoyed the warmth of the piles of paper that sit in my study. And quite right, too: cats keep all kinds of things in right perspective.

Albert died before I finished the book. If Burghley was the *éminence grise* of Elizabeth I's court, then Albert was always the dark brooding presence on our sofa. I am sure it was no accident that the great cat so often rested himself on transcripts of the papers of the great man. I imagine Albert now in the fine mead-hall that old warrior cats journey to in the end: long may he feast with the great giver of tuna.

Stephen Alford
Chatton, Northumberland, April 2007

1. The Cecils

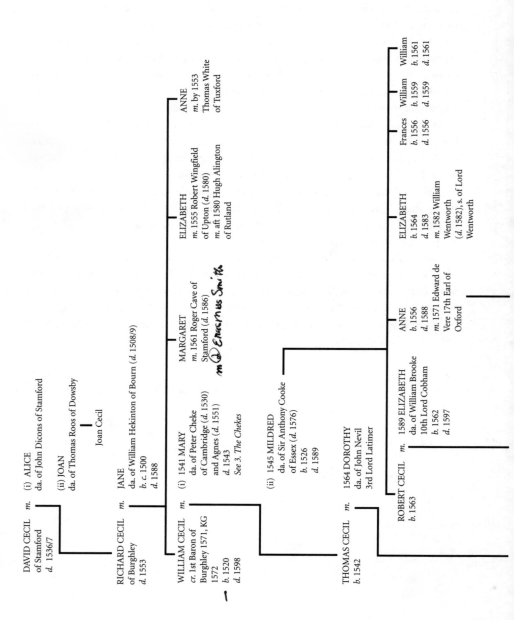

DAVID CECIL *m.* (i) ALICE
of Stamford   da. of John Dicons of Stamford
d. 1536/7

      (ii) JOAN
      da. of Thomas Roos of Dowsby

          Joan Cecil

RICHARD CECIL *m.*   JANE
of Burghley   da. of William Hekinton of Bourn (*d.* 1508/9)
d. 1553   *b. c.* 1500
            d. 1588

MARGARET	ELIZABETH	ANNE	
m. 1561 Roger Cave of Stamford (*d.* 1586)	*m.* 1555 Robert Wingfield of Upton (*d.* 1580)	*m.* by 1553 Thomas White of Tuxford	
m. ① Erasmus Smith	*m.* aft 1580 Hugh Alington of Rutland		

WILLIAM CECIL *m.* (i) 1541 MARY
cr. 1st Baron of   da. of Peter Cheke (*d.* 1530)
Burghley 1571, KG   of Cambridge (*d.* 1551)
1572   and Agnes (*d.* 1551)
b. 1520   *d.* 1543
d. 1598   *See 3. The Chekes*

       (ii) 1545 MILDRED
           da. of Sir Anthony Cooke
           of Essex (*d.* 1576)
           b. 1526
           d. 1589

THOMAS CECIL *m.*   1564 DOROTHY
b. 1542   da. of John Nevil
           3rd Lord Latimer

ROBERT CECIL *m.*   1589 ELIZABETH
b. 1563   da. of William Brooke
           10th Lord Cobham
           b. 1562
           d. 1597

ANNE	ELIZABETH	Frances	William	William
b. 1556	*b.* 1564	*b.* 1556	*b.* 1559	*b.* 1561
d. 1588	*d.* 1583	*d.* 1556	*d.* 1559	*d.* 1561
m. 1571 Edward de Vere 17th Earl of Oxford	*m.* 1582 William Wentworth (*d.* 1582), s. of Lord Wentworth			

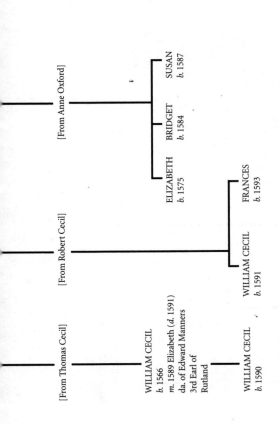

[From Thomas Cecil] [From Robert Cecil] [From Anne Oxford]

ELIZABETH
b. 1575

BRIDGET
b. 1584

SUSAN
b. 1587

WILLIAM CECIL
b. 1566
m. 1589 Elizabeth (*d.* 1591)
da. of Edward Manners
3rd Earl of
Rutland

WILLIAM CECIL
b. 1591

FRANCES
b. 1593

WILLIAM CECIL
b. 1590

2. The Cookes

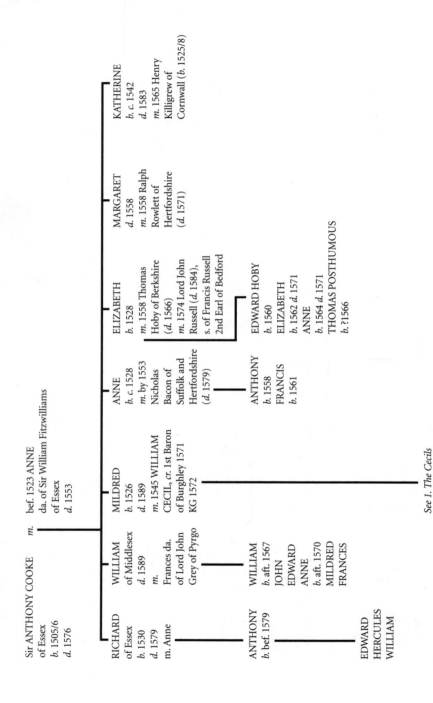

Sir ANTHONY COOKE   *m.*   bef. 1523 ANNE
of Essex   da. of Sir William Fitzwilliams
b. 1505/6   of Essex
d. 1576   *d.* 1553

RICHARD
of Essex
b. 1530
d. 1579
m. Anne

WILLIAM
of Middlesex
d. 1589
m.
Frances da.
of Lord John
Grey of Pyrgo

MILDRED
b. 1526
d. 1589
m. 1545 WILLIAM
CECIL, *cr.* 1st Baron
of Burghley 1571
KG 1572

ANNE
b. c. 1528
m. by 1553
Nicholas
Bacon of
Suffolk and
Hertfordshire
(*d.* 1579)

ELIZABETH
b. 1528
m. 1558 Thomas
Hoby of Berkshire
(*d.* 1566)
m. 1574 Lord John
Russell (*d.* 1584),
s. of Francis Russell
2nd Earl of Bedford

MARGARET
d. 1558
m. 1558 Ralph
Rowlett of
Hertfordshire
(*d.* 1571)

KATHERINE
b. c. 1542
d. 1583
m. 1565 Henry
Killigrew of
Cornwall (*b.* 1525/8)

ANTHONY
b. bef. 1579

WILLIAM
b. aft. 1567
JOHN
EDWARD
ANNE
b. aft. 1570
MILDRED
FRANCES

ANTHONY
b. 1558
FRANCIS
b. 1561

EDWARD HOBY
b. 1560
ELIZABETH
b. 1562 *d.* 1571
ANNE
b. 1564 *d.* 1571
THOMAS POSTHUMOUS
b. ?1566

EDWARD
HERCULES
WILLIAM

See 1. The Cecils

3. The Chekes

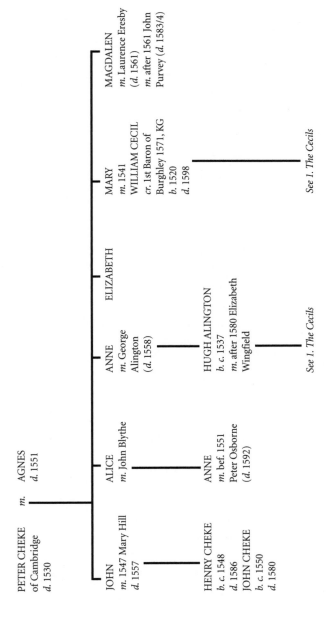

PETER CHEKE *m.* AGNES
of Cambridge *d.* 1551
d. 1530

ALICE
m. John Blythe

JOHN
m. 1547 Mary Hill
d. 1557

ANNE
m. bef. 1551
Peter Osborne
(*d.* 1592)

HENRY CHEKE
b. c. 1548
d. 1586
JOHN CHEKE
b. c. 1550
d. 1580

ANNE
m. George
Alington
(*d.* 1558)

HUGH ALINGTON
b. c. 1537
m. after 1580 Elizabeth
Wingfield

See 1. The Cecils

ELIZABETH

MARY
m. 1541
WILLIAM CECIL
cr. 1st Baron of
Burghley 1571, KG
b. 1520
d. 1598

See 1. The Cecils

MAGDALEN
m. Laurence Eresby
(*d.* 1561)
m. after 1561 John
Purvey (*d.* 1583/4)

PART ONE

Apprenticeships

1

The Cyssylls of Stamford

It was an unobtrusive arrival into the world. He was born in the second half of September 1520, 'the sun entering into Libra', in the small town of Bourne in Lincolnshire in the east of England, a wild sort of county of low-lying fens and wide skies, a land that did daily battle with water. His mother, Jane, was a gentleman's daughter. His father, Richard, was a gentleman with a coat of arms, if not quite in 1520 a manor of his own. Richard was about twenty-five, a humble servant at the court of King Henry VIII. Jane was probably twenty. William was their first child and only son.[1]

The world into which William Cecil was born was one he would later help to tear to pieces bit by bit. It was the world of his grandfather, William Hekington, Jane's father, a man of conventional piety who had died in 1508. In 1520 Hekington was lying with his first wife under a stone slab under the choir of the Church of St Peter and St Paul in Bourne. It was here, in a small monastic foundation of Augustinian canons, that Cecil, a very Protestant Elizabethan, was given a Catholic baptism. It would have been an elaborate ritual performed to resist the power of the Devil. The priest would have immersed baby William in the church font and made the sign of the cross on his forehead, breast and hands. Probably on the same day in the same church a chantry priest sang Mass for the soul of William's grandfather Hekington.

William Hekington had made his will on the Friday before Whitsunday in 1508 in the presence of the vicar of St Peter and St Paul and many of his friends. He contemplated death and made his peace with God. He was a man of his time, a generous benefactor and friend to the people of Bourne, and a Christian with a care for his immortal soul. He provided for a priest to sing Mass for his soul in the Lady Chapel of the church. He bequeathed a few pence to the clergy and officials of the parish: to the vicar and deacons, to the parish clerks and to three local children. He gave the abbey £5 to glaze its cloister.[2]

But Hekington was hardly content to leave it at that. He left money to the priory of Augustinian canons at Newstead near Stamford; to the small Cistercian abbey of Vaudey; to the four orders of friars in Stamford; and to Dame Margaret Walcot, a kinswoman, of the nunnery of Sempringham. This was over a decade before the suppression of the monasteries. It was a time of parish churches richly decorated with wall paintings and statues and altars to saints and chantry chapels like Hekington's own in Bourne. Today the Norman and late medieval walls of the abbey Church of St Peter and St Paul are neatly scrubbed, but in 1520 they would have been anything but. We can imagine the elaborate wall paintings and the sweet smell of incense in the air. At the eastern end of the church perhaps a painted doom, a scene of hell; at the western end the medieval font, still in place, probably the very font William Cecil was baptised in, with its Latin inscription 'Jesus the name above all names'.

Religion was about community, and grandfather Hekington was a man who loved the society of early Tudor Bourne. He was a great supporter of the town's religious guilds. These were small societies, or fraternities, whose members, men and women, came together for worship and friendship. They paid for candles to burn before the images of saints and engaged priests to say prayers for the souls of the departed. And of course they met to eat, drink and gossip.

William Hekington was a brother of the guilds of the Trinity, St John, St Margaret and St Anne. He left money to them all. Trinity guild was especially favoured. He left it one of his houses in Bourne, on the condition that every year a dirge and a Mass were sung for him and his brothers and sisters in the guild. So far as he knew and believed, prayers for the dead would be said for ever. They would not: Hekington's grandson would help to see to that.

So in 1520 it was the sacrifice of the Mass, rather than the words of the Prayer Book or the English Bible, which gave meaning to worship. England was a province of the Roman Catholic Church. Men and women went on pilgrimage to shrines, to Thomas Becket at Canterbury, perhaps, or St Etheldreda at Ely; they prayed for the souls of the dead; and they celebrated the holy days of saints. Henry VIII, a young king still, was a good Catholic. A year after William Cecil was born, Pope Leo X conferred upon Henry the title of *Fidei defensor*, 'Defender of the Faith', for the King's defence of good Catholic faith against Martin Luther.

In the year of William's birth, Henry VIII was married to his first queen, Katherine of Aragon. They had a young daughter, Mary, not yet five. A year older than William was Henry Fitzroy, later Duke of Richmond, the King's illegitimate son by his mistress, Elizabeth Blount. Anne Boleyn was not yet on the scene. With Anne would come the break with the Church of Rome. But in

1520 there was as yet no sign of the revolution in church and state that would determine the course of William Cecil's life. It would come soon enough.

*

When William Hekington made his will in 1508 he made sure to look to his family's future. His widow would be Alice, his second wife. His only child, from his first marriage, was Jane, who was just a young girl.

Hekington was a wealthy man. He owned land in and around Bourne and near Spalding not far away, in Dyke, Hanthorpe and Morton and at Pinchbeck and Surfleet, all small fenland villages. He owned three houses in Bourne. One was in Star Lane, a second on Potter Lane. Most of this estate would go to Alice Hekington.

Hekington wanted to make sure that Jane was well set up for marriage. That was some way off, of course; she was about eight years old. Once Alice was dead everything would be Jane's. But if Jane married before her stepmother's death then she had to have marriage money. Hekington left £50 for her dowry. This may not sound like much today, but it might be useful to compare it to the salary of one of the most skilled craftsmen and architects of the day, John Wastell, who created the fan vaulting of King's College Chapel in Cambridge. In 1508 Wastell was paid £13 6s. 8d. Hekington was rich enough to leave his little daughter another £10 to furnish her chamber as a married woman. And with all this money came a house. It was to be Jane's as soon as she married, and it had lands and pastures and meadows. This was where William Cecil was born. Tradition has it that it stood in Bourne's market place.[3]

We cannot be sure how Jane Hekington met her husband Richard. Certainly in 1519, probably just before they married, Richard was leased royal lands near Bourne which had once belonged to the Countess of Richmond, Henry VIII's grandmother. The match must have satisfied Alice Hekington, if she was still alive, and also Richard Cecil's father, David, who was an important gentleman in the town of Stamford a few miles from Bourne. Jane was a very respectable young gentlewoman and Richard was a man with good prospects.[4]

Richard was a page of the King's Chamber. True, this was not a glamorous office. With eight other pages it was his job to keep the outer chambers of the royal palaces clean and tidy. But he was close to the centre of a magnificent court, richly decorated, physical, martial, presided over by a king who loved 'pastime in good company'. Certainly Richard saw one of the most sparkling events of the sixteenth century. In June 1520, when Jane would have been about six months pregnant with William, Richard Cecil was one man in a vast train of six thousand who went with Henry VIII to the fabulous tournament in France known as the Field of the Cloth of Gold. Here Henry met his great rival and contemporary, King Francis I. Henry resided in a temporary palace, Francis in a city of golden tents. The kings' knights and noblemen jousted and fought. The message of the great tournament was peace between England and France, and the foundation stone was laid for a chapel of Our Lady of Friendship. Cardinal Wolsey, Henry's minister, sang a solemn Mass. It was one of the great moments of the Tudor century and William Cecil's father was there.[5]

The Cecils served: it was their fortune. David Cecil, Richard's father and a former soldier, had served the royal family since at least the 1490s. Father and son were known to be the King's men. In 1520 they were joint keepers of the royal manor of King's Cliffe Park in Northamptonshire. They were firmly planted in the eastern counties of the English midlands. Their local area of interest – they would have called it their 'country' – was a sort of triangle that ran south-west from Bourne into the very small county of Rutland and then east near to the cathedral city of Peterborough. At the centre of this triangle was Stamford, a beautiful town that straddled the borders of Lincolnshire, Northamptonshire and Rutland.[6]

David Cecil was Welsh. He was born on the other side of the country at the foot of the Black Mountains, on the border of Herefordshire and Monmouthshire. He wrote his name as 'David Cecyll' or 'David Cyssyll'. It was pronounced like 'Sicily' without the y. William, too, began with 'Cicyll'. He only began to write his surname as 'Cecill' (always with two l's) when he was in his thirties.[7]

It is hard to be certain about the genealogy of David Cecil's Welsh ancestry. He was a younger son of Richard Seyceld (or Seycill or Syssell) of the manor of Allt Yr Ynys. His father died about 1508. Beyond that the family's history is very confused, in good part because of William Cecil's own researches and dubious findings. One of the themes of this book is Cecil's passion for nobility and lineage. He was determined to trace his Welsh ancestry back to 'the very old princes of Wales themselves', and much of the work done on this subject in the sixteenth century, by Cecil and others, was pure fantasy.[8]

David Cecil did not inherit his father's estate and he did not stay in Wales. Instead he made his own fortune. As a soldier he appears to have been tough and resourceful. He did well in Stamford and soon became one of the town's leading citizens. He also prospered in royal service, a yeoman of the King's Chamber by 1509 and then a serjeant-at-arms to Henry VIII in 1513. By the time William was born David Cecil was in his sixties, still active and spry.[9]

David Cecil did very well for himself in Stamford and at court. He had the help of his godfather, Sir David Philip, who was a kinsman of his mother's. If the Cecils' fortune was service to the royal family of the Tudors, then they had Sir David to thank for it. Philip was squire of the body to Henry VII and he was also one of the chief household officers of the King's mother, the Lady Margaret Beaufort, Countess of Richmond. Where Philip went, his godson David followed. From 1506 they kept the royal park of King's Cliffe, the very same manor that David and Richard Cecil managed when William was born in 1520. Philip made David Cecil one of the executors of his will, and after Philip's death it was David who went to Henry VII to ask for a licence to found a chantry of two chaplains to pray for the souls of Philip and his family and the King and his late Queen Elizabeth.[10]

Sir David Philip's patroness, the Lady Margaret Beaufort, was a powerful woman in English politics. She was the King's mother, shrewd and vigorous, a conspirator against Richard III in the Wars of the Roses as well as the wealthy and pious foundress of religious houses and Cambridge colleges. It was no accident that her heraldic badges of the portcullis and greyhound were so often shown with the early Tudors' coats of arms. They told King Henry's subjects that his royal family went back to John of Gaunt, Earl of Lancaster and Earl of Derby, the fourth son of King Edward III. Everything about the Lady Margaret was royal: her blood, her wealth and her power.

Lady Margaret was Lincolnshire's great landowner. She had the manor of Maxey, just a few miles to the west of Stamford, where Sir David Philip also had a house, which was necessary given that he had some responsibility for the castle and the estate. Philip also had property in Stamford, just like his godson David Cecil, whose house was right by St George's Church.[11]

The Lady Margaret was a sister of the guild of the Holy and Blessed Virgin and Martyr St Catherine in Stamford. In this she had something in common with David Cecil and his wife, Alice. The guild was a Who's Who of the town's most important citizens. Local priors, abbots and priests, wealthy international merchants and local tradesmen, shoemakers, butchers, bakers, chandlers and their wives were all fellow members of the guild.[12]

The brothers and sisters of St Catherine's guild met in the chapel over the church door of St Paul's in Stamford. Every year they came together for a service of evensong on the eve of St Catherine's Day in November. On the day itself they worshipped at matins, Mass and evensong. Then new members of the guild swore their oaths to be true to God Almighty, to Our Lady St Mary and to the Holy Virgin and Martyr St Catherine. They paid their shillings and pence for 'wax-shot', a subscription for candles to burn before the saint's statue in the chapel. And then there was a great feast. All of this was governed by a constitution, and each year there was a kind of annual general meeting of the members to 'provide and ordain for the worship, profit and all things necessary at that time for the welfare of the said guild'.[13]

David Cecil paid his wax-shot for over thirty years. He was a reliable member of the guild of St Catherine. He was also a good Catholic. Both of William Cecil's grandfathers believed in purgatory, the place where souls rested temporarily after death for the expiation of their venial sins. When David made his will in 1535 he made it clear that he wanted a priest, Sir William Huddeston, to sing for his soul for one year in St George's Church in Stamford.[14]

All of this – the guild, the proper provisions for a chantry, the public belonging to a closely knit town community – was important to David. He was a member of Stamford's council and served three terms as its chief officer, the Alderman. Five times between 1515 and 1523 he went off to Westminster to sit for Stamford in Henry VIII's parliaments. When David married Alice Dicons it was no surprise that her father, John, was one of David's colleagues in the town council and a brother of St Catherine's guild. It was through Dicons that David got his interest in the Tabard inn in Stamford, probably a good and thriving business in a town that was on the main road from London to York. But many years later David's association with the Tabard caused William Cecil all sorts of trouble. Enemies jibed that David, the grandfather of the great Lord Burghley, had been merely a humble innkeeper.[15]

William Cecil was brought up in this small world of local rank and privilege. Stamford was provincial, certainly; but it was also a beautiful town that had done very well out of the wool trade in the fifteenth century. Wealthy bene-factors had built hospitals and rebuilt great churches like St Mary's and St John's. The country around Stamford was in William Cecil's blood. It shaped him and defined him. It told him who he was. It gave him a sense of local duty that he remembered to his dying day. It was the town he wanted to be buried in. It was his first apprenticeship.

The early life of anyone can be hard to judge. This is true even for someone as important as William Cecil. We can guess that his father was often away from home. Richard Cecil never played a big part in the life of Stamford, for the good reason that his duties lay elsewhere. The royal court of Henry VIII was generally a hundred miles from Stamford, moving from palace to palace along the River Thames. Richard was needed at court. But he was doing well for himself. From page of the chamber he was promoted by 1536 to a groom of the royal Wardrobe and then its yeoman. Humble, routine service, perhaps, but Richard was close to the King.

Probably the most important man in young William Cecil's life was his grandfather. David Cecil's service at court was long over. But he was still the King's man in Stamford and in 1532, when William was twelve, David served as the sheriff of Northamptonshire. He was a justice of the peace and the keeper of royal manors. The old soldier did good service for the King, something that did not go unnoticed by Henry's advisers. David had a wealth of experience and a long memory. William would have learned so much from a grandfather who remembered the Wars of the Roses and the first of the Tudor kings; who had seen military service and been at the royal court; who was part of the fabric of the place where he grew up. David knew and understood Stamford, just as he knew some of the most powerful men in the kingdom. When William was a very small boy it was David Cecil who entertained the young Duke of Richmond at King's Cliffe, by then the duke's manor, and 'made him good cheer'.[16]

As a powerful councillor at the court of Elizabeth I, William Cecil carefully policed the social distinctions of rank and order. He was a keen genealogist. He wanted to know all about families and he loved heraldry. There was surely something of his childhood here. He was raised to know his place in society. William Hekington, David Cecil and Richard Cecil all called themselves esquires and they had coats of arms. They were 'masters' and gentlemen, men of land, property and tenants. Land was everything. God had created a world in which there were all sorts of ranks of people, from the highest to the lowest, set in order for the smooth working of human society.

There is every reason to think that William's religious upbringing was very traditional. At the end of his life he wrote that his parents had instructed him in good religion. Jane Cecil had a great reputation for piety and generosity to the poor, and certainly her father had made many elaborate provisions in his will for charitable and religious causes in and around Bourne. William Cecil was raised as a pious Christian who was used to traditional Catholic worship in parish church, guild and chantry.

In the last years of the 1520s William's world became steadily bigger. There was a settling down for his family, even if his father was still often away at the royal court. Richard Cecil bought the manors of Burghley and Little Burghley, very near Stamford, between 1526 and 1528. William had close family who lived near Stamford. These were his grandfather and David's second wife, Joan. They had a daughter, also called Joan, who was Richard Cecil's half-sister. William's uncle David, Richard Cecil's brother, may at this time have lived quite close to Bourne at Witham on the Hill. By the 1530s William may have had a sister too; in the end he had three, Margaret, Elizabeth and Anne, but no brothers. And there would have been other people in this growing social world: the gentlemen of Stamford and the surrounding villages and estates and their families, the servants of his grandfather and the household servants of his own family. Eventually there were school friends too.[17]

William went to school first in Grantham and then, from about 1532, in Stamford. Both of these foundations were chantry schools whose founders had left lands to support priests to pray for their souls and to teach local boys.

Late in the fifteenth century the Grantham merchant Henry Curteys and his son Richard had provided for two chaplains, of whom one was to instruct boys 'in good manners and the art of grammar'. At about the time William was a pupil there the school's great patron was Bishop Richard Fox of Winchester, a powerful man at the courts of Henry VII and Henry VIII, who gave lands for the foundation and money for a schoolhouse and a house for the master.[18]

The chantry school at Grantham was probably not very convenient for William and his family. Grantham is about fifteen miles from Bourne and twenty from Stamford. The school day would have begun very early in the morning. William could hardly have gone from home to school every day, and his parents must have come to some arrangement about his lodging and board. So when a small school opened in Stamford, founded in 1532 by the will of William Radcliffe, a brother of St Catherine's guild, William moved much closer to his home at Burghley.

It is hard to know what his father, mother and grandfather wanted from William's education. There was no predestined path to greatness for William Cecil. In all likelihood he was a very bright little boy who would follow his family's footsteps into royal service. David Cecil knew Latin and considered himself to be a good judge of penmanship. Probably Richard Cecil felt the same about his own academic abilities. Neither David nor Richard had served Henry VII or Henry VIII by their scholarship. Perhaps William was different: perhaps they noticed a spark.

It is interesting that his family did not send him to one of the great schools of the day: St Paul's in London, for example, with its advanced curriculum of the ancient classics, or Westminster, or Winchester, or Eton. His school, in contrast to all of these august institutions, was positively humble. It had one teacher, a young priest called Libeus Byard, twenty-one years old, whose principal duty was to celebrate Mass and pray for the soul of Radcliffe. His other job was to teach Latin to the boys of Stamford and the local villages. This teaching he did for free. His income as chaplain of Radcliffe's chantry, which was not very large, came from lands left to trustees. The school had no building of its own. Byard taught the boys in the chapel of the guild of Corpus Christi in the medieval Church of St Mary the Virgin.[19]

Who was Libeus Byard, the young man who gave William Cecil some of his first lessons? It is hard to know: Byard is a determinedly obscure character. He may not have been a university graduate. He probably was local, for Byard is a good Lincolnshire name. Certainly he was a good teacher. Years later Cecil would call him 'an honest and learned schoolmaster', and that was high praise indeed.[20]

So William Cecil was not educated at a great school. He was not even a grammar school boy. He was taught by a young Catholic priest in a chapel lit by candles to saints. Above him was a beautiful late medieval wooden ceiling carved forty years before he was born. Nearby, between the altar of the chapel and the high altar in the chancel was a great tomb chest. Nothing could have reminded William more of what his family meant to Stamford. The tomb is that of Sir David Philip, David Cecil's godfather. There, while Byard taught his pupils, was Philip in effigy, in plate armour and a servant's collar. His life was celebrated for all to see in a tomb decorated with the crowned Tudor rose and the Welsh dragons and greyhounds of Lady Margaret Beaufort and her royal family. A priest would have sung for his soul.[21]

In those first couple of years of Radcliffe's chantry school, Byard taught two bright boys who went off to university. One was Ralph Robinson, who had moved with William Cecil from Grantham to Stamford at about the same time. In 1536 Robinson began to study at Corpus Christi College in Oxford. Later he would distinguish himself as the first English translator of Thomas More's *Utopia*. It was a work he dedicated to Cecil as a mark of 'the old acquaintance that was between you and me in the time of our childhood, being then schoolfellows together'.[22]

Cecil left Stamford for university in 1535. His family chose Cambridge and a very appropriate college, St John's. Through Sir David Philip, whose tomb young William saw every day, the Cecils had served the Tudors. The Lady Margaret Beaufort was Philip's noble mistress. David Cecil owed her a great debt, too. St John the Evangelist was a modern college with a strong reputation and it was founded in Lady Margaret's memory. Her arms and badges decorated the college's great brick gatehouse. When fourteen-year-old William Cecil saw it in 1535 he, more than anyone else, would have known what those arms stood for.

2

St John the Evangelist

William Cecil had the best political mind of his generation. He was shrewd and perceptive. To the end of his life he had a sharp eye and a penetrating intellect. If he could analyse the problems facing Elizabeth's government, which he did every day of his life, it was because he could apply to them the rigorous skills of the trained scholar. For these essential instruments of rule he could thank his teachers at St John's College, Cambridge.

St John's was more than a college to Cecil. It became his family. He was, he wrote as an old man, 'wholly brought up' there 'from my age of fourteen years'. The fellows and boys were surrogate fathers, uncles and brothers. He thrived in a close community of brilliant scholars. But St John's was also a lesson in life, because, as in most families, it was not plain sailing all the time. For a bright teenager from Stamford this was a second apprenticeship in the often hard ways of the world.[1]

*

Early Tudor Cambridge was filthy. The streets of the town were dark and dirty, its houses low and dingy, strewn with soiled straw and infested with fleas. The town's western boundary was the River Cam, which came in from the south and flowed north into the fens, where the men and women of the islands around Ely were believed to be hardly human. Running like a crescent scar to the east of Cambridge was the King's Ditch, little more than an open sewer. Plague visited the town so often that some of the university's colleges had places of refuge in the surrounding countryside. Natives and visitors complained about the seeping cold of long winters.

Cambridge would have been a whole new world to fourteen-year-old William. Since its foundation in the thirteenth century the university had attracted the patronage of kings and queens, noblemen and noblewomen. Only a few years before Cecil was born Erasmus of Rotterdam, the greatest northern European scholar of his day, had given lectures in the university. Its buildings stood for power as well as learning – great towers and walls of brick and stone protecting halls, chapels, gardens and fishponds. The town and the university lived together in a kind of forced unequal marriage. The scholars of Cambridge had all sorts of rights and privileges which were denied to the town, and these were resented by the locals. It was no wonder that even by the time Cecil arrived there was a long unpleasant history of violence between scholars and townspeople.

In the middle years of the 1530s there were about six hundred teachers and students in Cambridge. Many students arrived at their colleges in their middle teens, just like William. They began their studies for the Bachelor of Arts in grammar, rhetoric and logic before proceeding to music and mathematics, the philosophies and theology. More study led to the degree of Master of Arts, and beyond this were higher degrees in theology, law and medicine, all awarded at ceremonies in the Church of St Mary the Great on the High Street. Many students became priests, and this was really the purpose of a university education in the early sixteenth century. Some were elected as fellows of their colleges and began to teach undergraduates. The university had its own officers and lecture halls, or 'Schools', for teaching.

There were fourteen colleges in Tudor Cambridge. Peterhouse was the oldest, founded in the late thirteenth century. The other medieval colleges were Benet Hall, Clare Hall, Gonville Hall, King's Hall, Michaelhouse, Pembroke Hall, Queens' College and Trinity Hall. Over the centuries their names have changed a little and old buildings, sometimes old colleges, have been replaced by new ones; but a walk around these colleges today still gives some sense of how Cambridge was laid out in the 1530s.

The great royal foundation of Cecil's day was King's College, for which Henry VI had flattened a good part of the west of the town – lanes, churches, hostels, tenements, gardens – in the early 1440s. King's was never completed as Henry had intended and even the Chapel had to be finished off by the Tudors, which gave Henry VII and Henry VIII a good opportunity to advertise their power with badges of dynasty carved in stone. Cecil would have seen King's Chapel much as we see it today. The magnificent stained-glass window which shows King Henry VIII as King Solomon, receiving the Queen of Sheba, was put in at about the time William arrived in Cambridge. When Cecil was a student, St Catharine's College and Jesus College were barely forty years old. In 1535 Christ's, a re-foundation of a medieval college called Godshouse, was celebrating its thirtieth anniversary. William's own college, St John's, was just a few years younger, founded in 1511.[2]

Like Christ's, the College of St John the Evangelist was founded by, or at least in the name of, Lady Margaret Beaufort. For a family that had done so well out of its association with the Lady Margaret and her family, St John's was an excellent place for Richard Cecil's heir. The education the college offered to its students was of the best quality. St John's was carefully conservative in its society and religion, but it was also an enterprising and entrepreneurial place, much larger and wealthier than Christ's. It was flourishing because of its Master, Dr Nicholas Metcalfe, who was an enthusiastic supporter of learning. Cecil's friend Roger Ascham, a fellow of St John's and one of William's teachers, wrote of Metcalfe that he was 'a man meanly learned himself, but not meanly affectioned to set forward learning in others'.[3]

St John's was well off because Metcalfe was a great fundraiser. Only King's was richer. Because of its reputation St John's attracted wealthy benefactors who gave money for scholarships and fellowships. And the college also welcomed paying students. William was probably one of these 'pensioners' rather than a scholar whose education was paid for by the college. Scholars were generally poor: with Richard Cecil doing well in royal service his family was comfortably off. But, pensioner or scholar, William was still under the discipline of Metcalfe as Master, the deans and the seven senior fellows of the college, and he would have followed the same course of study as the other students.[4]

The great patron of St John's was Bishop John Fisher of Rochester, who had used the provisions of Lady Margaret Beaufort's will to build a new college on the site of the old Hospital of St John. Fisher dominated the early college. He wrote its statutes and provided for the teaching of its students. He funded fellowships and scholarships. But by the time William Cecil arrived at St John's in 1535 Fisher's patronage of the college was a mixed blessing. The year before, Henry VIII had declared his royal supremacy over the English Church. Fisher, like Thomas More, refused to accept that supremacy and the King's plans for his royal succession. William was an eyewitness to a revolution in church and state. Even if he saw only fragments in Cambridge, they were enough. His political education had begun. And so had his scholarly studies.

Throughout his life Cecil believed in institutions, in their discipline, routine and order. All of these things he would have found at St John's, carefully set out by Bishop Fisher. A boy who went on to become a passionate Protestant councillor to Elizabeth I was taught at school by a young Catholic priest and shaped by a Cambridge college given life by a Catholic martyr. The irony is hard to miss.

To a modern eye St John's in 1535 would have looked a lot like a religious community. Its physical shape was clear enough. The college was a single court, or quadrangle, of buildings. Some of these buildings had been part of St John's Hospital and dated back to the thirteenth century. This was the case with the college's chapel and the range of buildings used as a storehouse and stables. The rest of the court was built in neat red brick for the new college after 1511. There were chambers for fellows and students, a gatehouse, a library, a treasury, kitchens and a hall.

The hall was the only part of St John's heated by a good fire, and it was the place where students and fellows met to teach and to learn as well as to eat. In hall fellows, students and servants entertained one another by telling stories, reciting poems and singing songs. College life could be hard and cold, particularly when the day began with the ringing of the bell at four o'clock in the morning. In the winter much of the day would have been spent in very little light: candles were expensive. Cold feet were often a concern to the college authorities. Feasts, especially the celebrations at Christmas, could be grand and boisterous; though most of the time fellows and students lived on a more sober diet of bread, meat, fish and beer.[5]

St John's had a fishpond and a meadow near the River Cam; here students were allowed to play in small groups. Bishop Fisher was careful to regulate the behaviour of his fellows and scholars. They were forbidden to play at dice. They were not allowed to keep ferrets or hounds or song birds. Brightly coloured shoes of green, red or blue were forbidden. Singing, dancing and other noisy pastimes were not allowed in fellows' and students' rooms. Only doctors of divinity and college preachers had rooms of their own. All fellows and students of St John's had to wear sober academic gowns. Everyone in the college, even its servants, had to have a monk-like tonsure. Students could leave the college only with the permission of the Master and the deans, and there were punishments for those who were caught outside the walls without good reason. A student's food could be stopped for a day or, if an offence was serious enough, he could be expelled from the college. Some colleges in Cambridge had stocks and some flogged students for their misbehaviour.

So the life of a student at St John's was one of disciplined privilege. Cecil was not a poor scholar, but he was still under the watchful eye of his college. He lived in a close community. With his friends and teachers he ate, drank, studied, played, worshipped, prayed and slept. He could not escape from them, nor they from him. The friends he made in this close society were his friends for life.

Cambridge colleges gave their students security. The towers and the walls and the gates kept the world out as much as they held students in, for the streets of Cambridge could be dangerous for scholars. Members of colleges could be sure of good food, clean clothes and the care of physicians when they were sick. And every time William looked up at the gate tower of St John's on his way back from lectures in the Schools he, perhaps more than most, would have been struck by the colourful badges of the royal family that supported his college, the same family his grandfather and father served. Over the main gate of St John's were the two-horned yales, the mythical beasts that also decorated the gatehouse of Christ's College; the red and white Tudor double rose of Lancaster and York; the Beaufort portcullises; and the daisies of the Countess of Richmond, the Lady Margaret's *marguerites*.[6]

At St John's the day was one of prayerful routine and order. Bishop Fisher wrote one prayer to be said by members of the college privately in the morning and a second for the evening. William prayed, too, for the Lady Margaret and the members of her royal family. Every day he would have said Psalm 130. 'De profundis clamavi ad te, Domine: Domine, exaudi vocem meam. Fiant aures tuae intendentes, in vocem deprecationis meae.' 'Out of the depths have I cried unto thee, O Lord. Lord, hear my voice: let thine ears be attentive to the voice of my supplications.'

Teaching began at six o'clock after morning Mass. Classes in college and in the Schools went on for most of the day, generally in blocks of one or two hours, with breaks for food and drink in hall and perhaps an hour or two in the early afternoon for leisure or private study in the library. Fisher's timetable of teaching for the college suggests that there would have been a meal between ten o'clock and noon, probably the main meal of the day, and another at about five o'clock in the afternoon. At meal times the college's preachers would take it in turns to read either lessons from the Bible or the works of the ancient Church Fathers.

The teaching at St John's was done by oral training and examination. Subjects like logic, rhetoric, philosophy and theology were taught by means of public disputations and orations with and before other students and fellows. It was the ability to speak in public, and not fluency on paper in silent examinations, that made the successful student and fellow. Some of the fellows of St John's were paid specially to lecture and hear students. They were called 'lectors', or lecturers, and they were helped by other fellows called 'sublectors'. The college also employed examiners to test students on what they had learned in the Schools. The subjects Cecil studied were taught in all the other colleges in Cambridge, but at St John's Bishop Fisher had made special arrangements for the teaching of Greek and Hebrew, and in the 1520s the royal physician Thomas Linacre gave money for a medical lectureship. In these disciplines St John's had an especially strong reputation.

Many of the college's fellows were interested in mathematics, and so they lectured on the related subjects of arithmetic, geometry and perspective, the study of the behaviour of light rays. Cecil would have read Euclid on geometry and Ptolemy's works on astronomy. One of his great passions was 'cosmography', the study of the earth, of maps and of what today we would call geography. It was the mathematicians who lectured on cosmography and in their teaching they used the books of the ancient authors Plato, Pliny,

Strabo and Pomponius Mela. Some of the earliest purchases for the library of St John's were 'a book of cosmographia' and a 'mappa mundi with a table' (here table probably means index or legend). One of Cecil's contemporaries at Cambridge, Richard Eden of Christ's and Queens', became an alchemist and a cosmographer and an expert on exploration. Richard Buller of Christ's also owned a 'mappa mundi' and other maps. There is every reason to think that Cecil's later passion for maps and plans and charts came from his lessons as a teenager on cosmography.[7]

We know the names of William's teachers in his first years at St John's. They were Roger Brough and John Hatcher; John Cheke, Alban Langdale, Richard Cumberforth and Roger Ascham; Robert Pember and John Redman. Most of these were fairly young men in their early twenties or even in their very late teens, but Pember and Redman, the lecturers in Greek and Hebrew, were a little older, and they were scholars of great intellect and reputation. Both later moved from St John's to Henry VIII's new college, Trinity. From 1538 Redman was Lady Margaret's Professor of Divinity. Hatcher was a young fellow when he taught Cecil; he became a physician and an influential man in the university. Cheke and Ascham were just as accomplished. Cheke was later tutor to Prince Edward Tudor, and he also became the Provost of King's College. Ascham taught Edward's sister, Princess Elizabeth, and he wrote *The Scholemaster*, one of the most important English books on education of its day.[8]

In 1535 Cheke was barely twenty-one; Ascham was twenty. Both men became William's mentors and friends. To a boy from Stamford they must have seemed heroic in their passion for learning. In the year Cecil went to Cambridge Cheke and his friend Thomas Smith, of Queens' College, began to introduce to their colleagues and students a controversial new pronunciation of classical Greek. This was a cause championed by the great Erasmus of Rotterdam, who had written a book on it, but in Cambridge there was some resistance to these new principles. Cecil doubtless heard the first of Cheke's lectures using Erasmus's pronunciation of Greek vowels. Smith and Cheke's great project was talked about in Cambridge. Soon Cheke was in trouble for it with the university's authorities: it was undoubtedly the cause of excitement and discussion at St John's.[9]

In Cheke, Redman and Ascham, St John's had three of the best Greek scholars in the kingdom. The young Ascham was encouraged by Redman and Cheke to read the works of authors like Aristotle, Demosthenes, Isocrates, Plato and Thucydides. He also studied the Latin authors Caesar and Cicero. Another of Ascham's mentors was Walter Haddon, famed as a Latin scholar, and a fellow of King's. By the time Cecil had settled in at St John's, in the late 1530s, he was also part of Cheke's and Ascham's circle, an elite group of academics sharing new and exciting ideas. This was why St John's was so important to Cecil: he was one of a club of young, energetic and clever men who loved scholarship and learned from one another. This small community of scholars made Cecil a formidable classicist, and it gave him friends for life.[10]

Smith and Cheke's principles for the correct pronunciation of ancient Greek annoyed the university's establishment. Young men were challenging their elders. When he was in a position of authority himself, Cheke wrote about 'the lightness of young heads': that was exactly what the university's authorities made of Cheke. But the Cambridge establishment had another, greater worry, and that was Lutheran heresy.[11]

For probably a decade before Cecil arrived in Cambridge the writings of Martin Luther and other European reformers had been quietly talked about, and almost certainly read, in the university. The group which met at the White Horse Inn, between King's College and St Catharine's College, was known as 'Little Germany' because of its discussions of Luther's works. The early English reformer Hugh Latimer was a Cambridge man, a fellow of Clare. A few years before Cecil arrived in Cambridge, Latimer had fallen out with some of the fellows of St John's. Among Latimer's great opponents was Thomas Greenwood, one of the most senior fellows of the college when Cecil was a student there. In the 1530s the air still crackled with the energy of dissent and disagreement.

Latimer was not a lone voice of reform. Nicholas Ridley, later burned at the stake in the reign of Mary, was a fellow of Pembroke Hall when Cecil was at St John's. We know that Cambridge scholars owned some of the books and pamphlets of these years of Reformation. Philip Wogan of Christ's had a copy of Thomas More's *Confutation* of William Tyndale, the reformer and translator of the Bible. George Fowlbery of Clare owned an edition of Luther's sermons.[12]

At St John's fellows like Cheke, Ascham and Ascham's pupil William Bill leaned towards reform, but others were more traditionally Catholic in their religious beliefs. Many of these more conservatively minded men were Cecil's teachers, like Alban Langdale, Robert Pember, John Seton and Thomas Watson and also John Young.

It was impossible by the middle 1530s to ignore the national politics of Henry VIII's break with Rome. In 1534 Roger Ascham spoke against the Pope and so was disciplined by the senior fellows of St John's. But, as he wrote years later, the matter of the King and the Pope was 'then in every man's mouth'. That same year Simon Heynes of Queens' College and the university's Vice-Chancellor, John Skip, took part in a debate on papal authority. Cambridge could not escape from the greatest political topic of the day.

Oxford and Cambridge were dragged into the King's 'great matter' of the annulment of his marriage to Queen Katherine of Aragon. Henry and his advisers claimed that his marriage to Katherine was invalid by church law because her first marriage to Henry's brother, Arthur, had been consummated. Cambridge, like other universities in Europe, was asked for its opinion. This was given in 1530. Cambridge agreed with the King, but the university was split.

It was little easier three years later, when Henry declared England an empire and himself an emperor beholden to no other power. Within four years Henry VIII was 'the only supreme head in earth of the Church of England'. No longer did he need a pope to determine on the question of his marriage to Katherine. On this Cambridge was asked for its opinion. Officially it agreed with the King. But the university was divided. Some strongly disagreed with the official line. Others, of whom Roger Ascham was one, wholeheartedly supported it.[13]

We cannot really expect fourteen-year-old William Cecil to have taken a position on all of this. But a clever boy with an observant eye and a clear brain must have been struck by the passion of the debate as it rumbled through Cambridge. And no student of St John's could have failed to miss the horror of what happened to Bishop Fisher, the college's greatest friend and also a strong supporter of Katherine of Aragon. In the spring of 1534 Fisher went to the Tower. He was executed as a traitor in June 1535. Thomas Cromwell, the King's minister and one of the architects of Henry's break from Rome, soon became the Chancellor of the university. He made sure that St John's suffered. After Fisher's execution Cromwell ordered that any reference to the bishop in the chapel of St John's should be defaced. The beautiful tomb that had been built there for Fisher was wrecked.

Everything was changing, even the curriculum. In the year Cecil arrived at Cambridge royal injunctions permitted students to read the Bible privately and to attend lectures on it. All ceremonies and observances in religion that hindered 'polite learning' had to be abolished. There were even fears that the colleges, with all their lands and estates, would be dissolved, just like the religious houses. All that was certain and solid about the world of John Fisher was swept away in a revolution that changed the politics of England for ever.[14]

So though we might think of quiet and pleasant studies in beautiful college buildings, of peace and learning away from the bustle of the world, William Cecil's time at St John's was a political education. St John's was hit very hard indeed. The college could not hide from the malice of Thomas Cromwell. Its patron – its inspiration – had died a traitor on Tower Hill and his head had been set up on London Bridge. Thomas Greenwood, the old opponent of Latimer, refused to accept the royal supremacy. He was put in prison, where he probably died in 1537. Nicholas Metcalfe was broken, too. He was called to

London for an interview with Thomas Cromwell. When he returned he met the fellows in the chapel and resigned his mastership, 'saying that he was commanded so to do, which he did with weeping tears'.[15]

It was a terrible time at St John's and the college went into a kind of flat spin. There were tussles with Cromwell about the next Master. Fellows argued amongst themselves. Morale and confidence slowly eroded away. The College of St John the Evangelist, a place of learning and brilliance, was at a low ebb.[16]

By now William Cecil was in his late teens. He was not a fellow of St John's and he would have taken no direct part in college politics. But he would have seen and heard, for scholars always have something to bicker about and in small communities gossip travels quickly. Later perhaps he reflected that Cambridge colleges were not so unlike royal courts. Politics was shifting and fluid. Strong personalities could dominate. One had to be mindful of friends and enemies. And who was to say who was a friend and who an enemy?

*

For all of the febrile politics of St John's College, Cambridge, some men prospered. Clever, confident and supremely able, John Cheke, William's teacher, began to do very well for himself.

In 1540 Henry VIII appointed Cheke, still only in his middle twenties, the first Regius professor of Greek in Cambridge on the comfortable salary of £40 a year. He was by now one of the most senior fellows of St John's. Two years later Cheke became the university's public orator. This meant that Cheke now spoke for the university to the King and his advisers. He was well set for a career at the royal court. His moment came in 1544 when Henry VIII appointed Cheke tutor to his six-year-old son Prince Edward.

John Cheke was William Cecil's teacher and mentor; he was also about to become family. A few months after leaving St John's, in 1540, William married John's sister, Mary. The sad story of William's first marriage properly belongs to the next part of his life in London. But the Chekes were a Cambridge family – in many ways they were a family of the university – and it makes good sense to think of William's relationship with them as something rooted in his days as a student.

I wish we knew much more about William Cecil and Mary Cheke. There are hints here and there, mere fragments. It was probably a love match. There is evidence from a reliable source that Richard Cecil seriously disapproved of the marriage. Unfortunately we really know nothing of the courtship of Mary and William, but given the discipline of life at St John's the couple must have met through John. Probably William visited the Chekes at their house on the corner of Market Hill and Petty Cury, very close to the market square and a short walk from St John's.

William never met Peter Cheke, Mary's father, who had died in January 1530. Peter had been an esquire bedell in Cambridge, working for the disciplinary officers of the university, the proctors. He attended all the formal ceremonies of the university, kept the Schools in order, collected fees from students and announced the decrees of the Chancellor. Peter Cheke was not a graduate, but his office was important and it came with a salary of £35 a year. Peter's wife, Agnes, was a vintner who made a good living by selling wine to the colleges. The family lived in the parish of St Mary the Great and they were very busy in the life of their church.[17]

When Peter died he left Agnes to look after John and John's five sisters Alice, Anne, Elizabeth, Mary and Magdalen. John was already a fellow of St John's. In his will Peter left money to his daughters, who were each to receive £10 on their nineteenth birthday. Peter also left his son £10, though John had to wait till he was twenty-one to get it. John Cheke celebrated that birthday a month after young William Cecil arrived at St John's.[18]

So what would Cecil have known of the Chekes? Their mother was an astute businesswoman who owned property in and around Cambridge. Agnes was also a devout parishioner of St Mary the Great. John he knew as his teacher. Alice was married to a fellow of King's College called John Blythe. Blythe must have been nearly ten years older than his wife and when Cecil first came to Cambridge he was probably in Italy studying medicine. George Blythe, John and Alice's son, would have been born at about the time Cecil arrived at St John's. Anne Cheke was married to George Alington of Norfolk. Their son, Hugh, was born in 1537. Years later Hugh would be Cecil's private secretary. Of the younger Chekes Elizabeth and Mary must have been the nearest in age to William. And there were friends who were also important to the family, particularly after Peter Cheke's death. One was Dr William Butts, a physician to Henry VIII. Another friend was George Day of St John's, one of the college's most senior fellows.

It seems that Richard Cecil 'conceived displeasure' towards William's marriage to Mary. Probably Richard had not liked the idea of his son and heir, away from home and the guidance of his parents, marrying someone he had happened to fall in love with. With a clever and capable son who had had the best education of any member of his family, perhaps Richard had ambitions to marry William to a promising family at court. David and Richard Cecil, however well they had done for themselves in royal service, would never have been able to advance much beyond the practical uses to the King of supervising the running of his estates and fetching and carrying his gowns. William's education in Cambridge fitted him for something greater. Had he thrown it all away by making an imprudent marriage? It may be that he was removed from Cambridge in 1540 for his own good.[19]

William married Mary anyway. He was nineteen years old, and Cambridge had done its job. William Cecil was the son and heir of an esquire in royal service. There was no good reason to think that he was ever going to be either a priest or a professional scholar. He did not take his degrees, but there again he did not need to. His mind was trained. If his family had some kind of plan in mind for him, then it was time for the next phase of it. But plan or not, and married or not, it was no wonder that someone as bright as William Cecil felt the magnetic pull of London.

The fourteen-year-old boy who had come to St John's College from provincial Stamford left half a decade later drilled in logic, rhetoric and philosophy. In 1540 William would have been as familiar with mathematics as he was with the great orators and philosophers of ancient Greece and Rome. He would have had the experience of standing before his friends and teachers to deliver arguments and orations. He had been taught by some of the best minds in England. It was a tough and rigorous intellectual training. Cecil always knew that he was probably brighter than anyone he worked with. If there was one thing that never plagued him, it was a feeling of intellectual inferiority. He was ferociously and forensically learned.

At Cambridge Cecil had acquired some of the tools of what would be his chosen trade. He had learned to love scholarship. It was a retreat from busyness, a refuge from the day-to-day grind of politics at court. At St John's he also made great friends. In a political career of fifty years Cecil would work with many men he had known as boys at Cambridge.

What Cecil had also seen at St John's was how the world worked. Life in college in the second half of the 1530s was hardly cosy. He saw at first hand a revolution. He saw men who loved St John's broken by politics. In the chapel he worshipped in every day he saw the tomb prepared for Bishop Fisher smashed to pieces. He knew, even by the age of nineteen, what kings and powerful ministers could do when they put their minds to it. He had seen men conform and others resist. This was quite an apprenticeship.

*

Roger Ascham began his *Scholemaster* with a scene in Cecil's chamber at court early in Elizabeth's reign. At dinner with Cecil were Ascham and some old friends from Cambridge and government. Ascham died before his book was published, and so it was his widow who dedicated it to Cecil. Margaret Ascham remembered how good he had been to her husband. She praised the way Cecil, by then the university's Chancellor, still worked to promote learning in Cambridge. 'How happily you have spent your time in such studies,' she wrote, 'and carried the use thereof to the right end.'[20]

In 1540 his apprenticeship continued as Cecil moved from Cambridge to London.

3

London and Court

William Cecil always said he was a man of his country. Stamford and Burghley were in his blood. He had all the instincts of a landed gentleman and nobleman. His country was who he was. And yet from the age of fourteen he moved away from home almost for good. First of all there was Cambridge and the close community of St John's College, Cecil's second family. Then in 1540 the Great North Road took him south to London. It was here, whether he knew it or not, that his future lay.

London was another new world for Cecil. It was like nowhere else in England. For all its old medieval grandeur Stamford was a small provincial town. At Cambridge Cecil had sensed power beyond the walls of the university and colleges, but the discipline of student life inevitably put limits on a teenage boy. Cecil arrived in London at nineteen. He had a great city to explore. And for the first time in his life he was able to see power up close, at Henry VIII's court, in the lawcourts, even in the public punishments meted out to criminals.

These were first steps in his public career. London changed William Cecil's life for ever. It led to the royal court, and the court to office and power. They were years that were incredibly important in Cecil's life. They are also some of the most difficult to piece together. But what is clear as day is that this was the time Cecil came to the notice of powerful people at court. He began to navigate the hard road of politics and religion. It was perhaps the most important phase of his apprenticeship so far.

*

In 1540 Cecil began to study the law. He worked and lived at Gray's Inn, one of the inns of court clustered round Holborn and Chancery Lane. This was lawyers' London, slightly away from the walled city proper and from Westminster. It ran along Holborn east of Drury Lane as far as the Church of

St Andrew; and then south of Holborn down to Fleet Street and beyond to the River Thames, from Temple Bar in the west to Shoe Lane and Water Lane in the east. Gray's Inn was the northernmost of all the main inns of court, away from the bustle of the city.[1]

Doubtless Richard Cecil had some kind of plan for his son. Probably William had a good idea of what he wanted to do, too. Five years at Cambridge had given him a formidable academic training. He was bright and able. Gray's Inn was another stepping-stone to royal service. At St John's College it had seemed hardly likely that the son of an esquire in the King's service would become either a priest or a college fellow. The same is probably true of Gray's Inn. Though he became interested in legal theory and history, Cecil did not want to become a professional lawyer. As it was for many of the young men at the inns of court the law was a preparation for the life of a gentleman. It was also an introduction to a world of court connection. It would have been very plain to Richard Cecil that many of the men of influence at Henry VIII's court had studied at the inns of court. Cambridge and Gray's Inn would set William up for life.

Gray's Inn was very much of the world. Cecil was not cloistered away in the few years after 1540: he would have spent his days talking to men who had sat in parliaments and been members of royal commissions, just as he would have shadowed professional barristers pleading their cases in Westminster Hall, the great Norman building into which the various courts of King's Bench, Common Pleas, Exchequer, and others, were crammed.

There was more to life than the professional grind of the law. Inside Westminster Hall and out, in the precincts of the ancient palace of Westminster, there were throngs of people ready to share news and gossip. Whitehall, the most important of all the royal palaces, was very close by. Many noblemen and councillors, archbishops and bishops had houses on Cannon Row near the River Thames and grand residences on the Strand. On the streets as well as in the hall and chambers of Gray's Inn, Cecil would have heard all the news about the comings and goings of the King and his court. William Cecil's London was a city crammed with people; it bustled with business, wealth, trade and power. It was an education all of its own.

So what, in 1540, would a wandering young lawyer have been able to see of the city? From Gray's Inn a moderate constitutional would have taken twenty-year-old William Cecil down Chancery Lane and Middle Temple Lane to the Temple Stairs. Here he would have hired a boat on the Thames. This was the best way to get about London and Westminster. There were steps, landing stages, and wharves all along the banks of the river. The Thames would have been busy with boats carrying passengers and freight. If Cecil wanted to visit, say, his father at Whitehall Palace, or go to Lambeth or

Southwark on the south bank of the Thames, then he would have travelled by water.

Near the southern end of Chancery Lane and the Church of St Dunstan was the Temple Bar. West of this was the Strand, and eventually the great Charing Cross and the King's palace of Whitehall. East of the Temple Bar was Fleet Street, which was one of the ways into the walled city of London proper. This was the most ancient part of London, packed with shops and houses and churches and the great municipal buildings and halls. We are lucky to have the beautiful sketches of London by Anthonis van den Wyngaerde. They show a cityscape of two- and three-storey buildings, of palaces and halls, of towers and churches, hugging the Thames as far west as the palace of Westminster and Westminster Abbey and as far east as the great battlements of the Tower of London. London Bridge joined the city to Southwark on the south side of the Thames. Even the bridge was piled high with buildings. Well above the skyline of Wyngaerde's and Cecil's London, visible for miles, was the great spire of St Paul's Cathedral.[2]

The easiest route on foot from Gray's Inn to the centre of London was east along Holborn Bars, over the Fleet River at Holborn Bridge and on to Snow Hill and then to the gate in the city wall on Newgate Street. A walk from Newgate market along the Shambles went past many of the halls of the wealthy trade guilds and led eventually to Cheapside. Before Cheapside, at the end of the Shambles and near the Church of St Michael le Querne, was Paternoster Row, in the shadow of St Paul's Cathedral.

On the other side of the cathedral lay St Paul's Churchyard. This was the place where Cecil would have visited the workshops of London's printers and booksellers. Here he could have bought books on almost any subject under the sun, from the shops of William Bonham at the sign of the King's Arms or John Reynes at the sign of St George or from many other booksellers. The printers did good business. They produced great chronicles, almanacs, legal texts and works of cosmography. If Cecil wanted the official publications of the King's printer, Thomas Berthelet, he would have bought them in Paul's Churchyard. In 1540, the year Cecil arrived in London, Richard Grafton and Edward Whitchurch printed Thomas Cranmer's Great Bible. This was the official Bible in English, a vast work which had as its title-page a stunning woodcut derived from Holbein of King Henry handing the word of God to his subjects.

These were the years of Henry's revolution in church and state. William Cecil knew that well enough. He had seen the power of Henry and Thomas Cromwell, the King's chief minister, at work in Cambridge. Politics and religion were impossible to separate in Cecil's London: evidence of the King and his authority were everywhere he turned. He must have heard Henry's proclamations and perhaps bought copies of them from Paul's Churchyard.

He would have seen criminals punished by order of the King's justice. This was done in public, not hidden away behind prison walls. At Smithfield, not very far from Gray's Inn, a woman was boiled to death in 1542 for poisoning her employers' families. In the same year two people were hanged for a murder in Lincoln's Inn. Criminals were whipped and branded. In 1545 a priest was punished because he had feigned a miracle.

This priest did public penance at St Paul's Cross. The Cross was the most important pulpit in London and it was in the shadow of St Paul's Cathedral. From here Henry VIII's government spoke to the people of London. At St Paul's Cross Cecil would have heard for himself the great sermons of the day preached by the likes of Bishop Stephen Gardiner of Winchester and Archbishop Thomas Cranmer of Canterbury. Years later, as Elizabeth's Secretary, Cecil took great care to find the right men to preach at Paul's Cross. There was no more important place in London to get the government's message across to the people.[3]

No one, however powerful, could escape the dizzying twists and turns of royal politics in the 1540s. This was a decade in which a queen was executed: Katherine Howard, Henry's fifth wife, went to the block in 1542. More spectacular in many ways was the rise and fall of Thomas Cromwell, the man who had broken Nicholas Metcalfe of St John's and who had dominated the King's court for a decade. In April 1540 Cromwell was made Earl of Essex and Chamberlain of England. In July he felt the sharp blow of the executioner's axe on his neck. Political fortunes could change as quickly as that. It was something the Cecils would have known all about. The day before Cromwell was executed, it was Richard Cecil who received into his charge the 'stuff' of the soon to be late Earl of Essex.[4]

Among Thomas Cromwell's crimes were treason and heresy. The complicated religious politics of the 1540s certainly had something to do with his death. Cecil would have seen as clearly as anyone that Henry's revolution was strange and unpredictable. It had all kinds of oddities and unintended consequences, as of course revolutions often do. At St John's College he had seen the calculated destruction of Bishop Fisher's tomb by Thomas Cromwell. In the 1530s all the signs were that old corruptions in Catholic worship would be done away with. The monasteries and other religious houses were dissolved. There is no doubt that the Cecils prospered from all of this. In the year William went to London his father was granted some of the former religious lands in Stamford. In almost no time at all the world had been turned upside down.[5]

If the 1530s had been a decade for the reformers, for Cromwell and Cranmer, the atmosphere was very different a decade later. At court there was a backlash against reform. It was quite possible for conservative theologians to support Henry's supremacy over the Church. An act of parliament was used to reaffirm Catholic doctrine. Heretical books were burned. At St Paul's Cross Cecil would have been able to hear for himself the recantations of men who held absolutely different opinions: those who still professed loyalty to the Pope, and who were made to declare their belief in the King's supremacy; and those who no longer professed Catholic theology, the 'sacramentarians', deniers of the Mass, accused by the government of heresy.

This was a tricky time to navigate the ways of politics and religion. William Cecil knew that as well as anyone, and it was why he took no chances. In 1545 'Gulielmus Cicyll' donated a book probably to St John's or to someone in the college. It was by Bishop Fisher on the real presence in the Eucharist, one of the most controversial topics of the moment. Anything by Fisher was an appropriate donation for a former student of the bishop's beloved college. In his neatest handwriting Cecil wrote that he hoped Fisher's work would be used against the 'impious sacramentarians'.[6]

What should we make of this? Is it a plain declaration that at twenty-five years old Cecil was still a pious Catholic who hated heresy? Certainly it was what a good scholar of St John's College might be expected to say. Or was it subtle code, a way of saying one thing by writing precisely the opposite? Was Cecil already a secret reformer, long influenced by John Cheke and others at Cambridge? As an old man he wrote something very interesting, in its own way a special code: 'I did come to the years of discretion to have knowledge of the gospel of our saviour Jesus Christ, the knowledge whereof began about that time to be more clearly revealed here in England than it had been many years before.'[7]

Faith was a secret which, for the time being at least, William Cecil kept to himself. But this was not a self-indulgent game. Cecil's life would have depended on being known to be of good religion. In the year Cecil presented his book to St John's, a gentlewoman called Anne Askew was arrested because she had spoken against the sacrament of the Mass. A year later she was burned to death for heresy. William Cecil would spend a lifetime walking the hard paths of loyalty and conscience, belief and politics. This was an essential apprenticeship.

*

William Cecil lived by his brain. He did not live secluded from the world; he was never a career scholar, however much he had enjoyed Cambridge and loved scholarly pursuits. His business was with the world, in the courts of princes. It was clear that his mind, like his pen, was a precision instrument of his service to the Tudor monarchs.

At St John's College, Cambridge he had been taught by some of the best scholars in Europe. Men like Cheke, Roger Ascham and Thomas Smith were inspiring teachers, pushing the boundaries of knowledge. At St John's Cecil had thrived on intellectual rigour and self-discipline.

Gray's Inn was different. The world of the Tudor lawyer was an arcane one. The English common law was complicated. Conducted in law French, and constrained by generations of tradition and method, the law probably seemed pretty dull after the brightness and clarity of the oratory of Demosthenes or Cicero, or even Cecil's lessons on cosmography. But the law had a discipline and rigour all of its own; and it was a vocational training, in the courts at Westminster and in long debates, or 'moots', at Gray's Inn, that gave Cecil skills essential to the future royal servant. For a Tudor Secretary the training was invaluable. He was taught to examine points of law with forensic rigour. Cecil always had a lawyer's eye for detail. For the rest of his life, at court or in the Privy Council, he argued policy effectively and robustly. Here he could thank the teachers who had worked him hard at St John's and Gray's Inn.

If Cecil aspired to service at court, then his family had given him a perfect start. His father and grandfather knew what service was all about. They had had nothing like William's training or education and must have had high hopes of a student of a royal foundation in Cambridge and a barrister in one of the most exclusive professional clubs in London. There was no doubt that William Cecil was one of the elite of Tudor society.

Cecil was bright and talented. He also, no less importantly, knew people who mattered. At Gray's Inn he made some good friends, just as he had done at St John's. Richard Goodrich and John Gosnold were two talented lawyers of the inn. William would have known Nicholas Bacon, a very bright prospect in the 1540s who had come to the attention of the King. Much grander, and much older, was Edward Hall, one of the senior lawyers of Gray's Inn in the 1540s.

Hall was a veteran of the Tudor parliaments and an eyewitness of the revolution of the 1530s. He was the author of *The Union of the Two Noble and Illustre Families of Lancaster and York*, often known as 'Hall's Chronicle', a massive book published after his death in 1547. It was such an important account of the Wars of the Roses that Shakespeare used it extensively for his history plays. When Hall died, the manuscript of his 'chronicle late made' was found in his chamber at Gray's Inn. It is perfectly possible that Hall had spoken to young William Cecil about one of the greatest Tudor histories.[8]

Cecil later wrote of Gray's Inn as the 'the place where myself came forth unto service'. It was a means to an end. In spring 1540 Cecil was a young man of nineteen newly arrived from the fens. Seven years later he wrote a preface for a book written by Queen Katherine Parr, Henry VIII's sixth and last wife. By 1547 Cecil was part of Katherine's circle. His career at court was launched.

But in telling the story of Cecil's arrival at court, education can take us only so far. What also mattered was a very political marriage.[9]

Here we have to make sense of one of the mysteries of Cecil's early life: his marriage to Mary Cheke of Cambridge. They married, with or without Richard Cecil's blessing, in August 1541. Mary was dead within two years. She died in Cambridge in the icy winter of 1543. She was buried by Agnes, her mother, in the churchyard of St Mary the Great on Cambridge High Street. Agnes paid 6s. 8d. for the service. It was of course a Catholic burial. Mary's family gave 16d. for four wax torches to burn at the funeral.[10]

Mary in Cambridge, William in London; one son, Thomas, born in Cambridge in May 1542; Richard Cecil unhappy at the marriage, for whatever reason. These are something like the bare facts of William and Mary's married life together. We have to wonder whether they were happy; there is no way to tell.[11]

So in 1543 William was a twenty-two-year-old widower with a baby son. Less than two years later he was married again. This time it was an astute match which put him close to the heart of Henry VIII's court. Surely this time Richard Cecil left little to chance. William's marriage to Mildred Cooke in December 1545 was just as much a part of his political rise as his training at St John's College and Gray's Inn.

Mildred was six years younger than William. Her father, Sir Anthony Cooke of Essex, was in many ways a conventional Tudor gentleman. He had started out as a lawyer of the Inner Temple in the early 1520s. After travel and military service abroad he went to court in 1539 to serve as one of fifty 'Spears', a bodyguard to Henry VIII. He took on duties at court and in Essex. When William married Mildred, Cooke had just served as sheriff of Essex and Hertfordshire.

What was more unusual about Sir Anthony Cooke was his learning. He was a self-taught scholar who gave all his children, daughters as well as sons, a rigorous education in the classics. Mildred Cooke was not a decorative wife for an ambitious young man: she was clever, scholarly and formidable, quite William's equal. There was a strong bond between them: they were married for forty-four years.

Marriage to Mildred was for Cecil the first step to gentlemanly independence. In 1544 he appointed a couple of servants. A month before the wedding Richard Cecil gave Mildred and William some of his land in Rutland and Lincolnshire; Anthony Cooke must have done the same sort of thing for Mildred's dowry. They began to live as an established married couple. In 1545 William even took on a secretary called Francis Yaxley, of Gray's Inn, the first of a long line of confidential secretaries and clerks who served him.[12]

Sir Anthony Cooke was a scholar-courtier close to Queen Katherine Parr. In 1541 he translated St Cyprian's Latin sermon on prayer and dedicated it to the King. This was a decade in which scholarship could not easily remain politically neutral. In Cooke's translation of St Cyprian, for example, he denounced the Church of Rome. Cooke was not explicitly Protestant in his beliefs – that would have been too dangerous. But in a mild and conservative way he showed himself a supporter of reform, writing in the tradition of the northern European humanists like Erasmus and the French reformer Guillaume Budé. There was really nothing in Cooke's writings to cause any suspicion of his religious orthodoxy: we should not expect there to be. But what it is important to say here is that Cooke was strongly associated with men and women at the court who, once Henry VIII was dead, supported a thoroughgoing Protestant Reformation in the Church. After 1545, even by association, Cecil was one of these people.[13]

The most important person of all in this court circle of those moving carefully but purposefully in the direction of reform was Queen Katherine Parr. As the stepmother of Princess Mary, Princess Elizabeth and Prince Edward, Katherine had much to do with the royal nursery, and with Prince Edward's tutors. William's brother-in-law, John Cheke, was one of these. Sir Anthony Cooke helped to teach Edward, too. Queen Katherine gave support to those of pronounced reformed tendencies, a dangerous business indeed. The interrogations of Anne Askew, a leading Protestant, in 1545 and 1546 suggested to the King that there were associations between those who spoke against the Catholic sacraments and some royal courtiers. Henry nearly ordered an investigation; it was only avoided because Katherine took part in what was probably a staged interview with her husband in which she 'submitted' herself to his direction in matters of religion.

So Cecil may have looked like a court reformer in the last years of Henry VIII's reign. He was a clever and supremely subtle man: we can guess that he navigated the tricky politics of religion with great care and ingenuity. The nearest we have is that coded reference in the book dedication in 1545. But if Cecil really hated heresy when he wrote in Bishop Fisher's book, did he begin to change his ideas with his marriage to Mildred Cooke? Was this the time when he came, as he later put it, to an understanding of Christ's knowledge? This was a secret he kept to himself.

What we can say is that William Cecil surveyed the difficult landscape of politics and religion with an already experienced eye. Even by his late twenties he had seen so much. His training was nearly complete. He was very able, and it would not be long before his talents were recognised at court. He had all the right connections. In the last days of Henry VIII young William Cecil had put down some very sound foundations for a political career.

*

Cecil was not caught up in the power struggles of Henry's last days, and that was just as well. But we can be sure that his powers of observation were as acute as ever. And there were at least two men of his family who, in their different ways, would have been able to tell him something of the arrangements being made in secret for the succession of King Henry's heir, Prince Edward, only nine years old. Sir Anthony Cooke was an influential man, Richard Cecil less so. Richard, the experienced royal servant, would have had his eyes open. Powerful men were preparing themselves for the first royal minority in many decades.

In a small clause of Henry VIII's will, the King left one hundred marks to Richard Cecil, yeoman of the Wardrobe of the Robes. Henry never knew, but his servant Richard by then perhaps had realised, that it would be another Cecil who would make a much deeper impression on the reign of the next Tudor king.[14]

4

Servant and Secretary

At the age of twenty-six William Cecil was ready for the life of a public servant. At Cambridge he had studied classical rhetoric, with its art of persuasion that trained the mind of a counsellor to princes. He knew the law and how to think like a lawyer. Through friends and kinsmen he was familiar with the ways of court politics. The time had come for Cecil to begin the sort of career his education and the service of his family to the Tudors had always promised. In 1547 he began a public life which saw him to his tomb fifty-one years later.

William's career began, not in the service of the King but in the household of Edward VI's maternal uncle, Edward Seymour, Earl of Hertford and Duke of Somerset. Somerset was the most powerful man in England. He was born about the year 1500, the son of an ancient family from Wiltshire. His power and titles came from his success as a courtier, a soldier and a politician in the reign of Henry VIII, and from the fact that he was the brother of Queen Jane Seymour. When Henry died in January 1547 Seymour, by then Earl of Hertford, was a man to be reckoned with. He became Lord Protector and Governor of the King's Person during the royal minority of his nine-year-old nephew Edward. Hertford was king in all but name. A month after Henry's death he became a duke with the title of Somerset.

As the Duke of Somerset's servant, Cecil moved with his master. He was with Somerset from very early in the new reign, a clever young man close to where power lay in government. Cecil's name began to appear in the duke's correspondence in the spring of 1547. In April one correspondent called Cecil the duke's 'agent', and by July he was known to be 'with my Lord Protector's grace'. A year later Cecil was 'Master of Requests' to the Protector, dealing with all the petitioners who sought Somerset's help and influence. It was Cecil's job to pass the petitions to the appropriate court at Westminster. By this time Cecil was probably also one of the Protector's secretaries.[1]

In the early days of Protector Somerset's rule William Cecil's good word and influence could help to get favours from the most powerful man in the realm. Earls, knights and even gentlemen of the King's Privy Chamber knew that Somerset's permission or indulgence had to be sought before they could get offices or favours or land. They also knew that Cecil was the Protector's man. Papers could be moved to the top of the pile, quiet words said in private. Cecil began to get to know some of the most important people in the kingdom, and often they were very grateful for his help in their suits, and gave him gifts as tokens of their appreciation.

Cecil was the Protector's man first, but he would always do what he could for other men and women of influence. As he wrote to the Earl of Shrewsbury in 1548, 'in any service next to my Lord's grace I will not fail to declare. And therefore I heartily desire your Lordship to make proof thereof at all times.' From the beginning Cecil knew how to build up his credit with men of influence.[2]

One regular writer of letters to Cecil at this time was John Dudley, Earl of Warwick. He was a prolific seeker after patronage and a powerful man in Edwardian politics. He was also, like Protector Somerset, a soldier. When Warwick was chosen as one of the leaders of a military expedition into Scotland in the autumn of 1547, he appointed Cecil as a judge of the Marshalsea Court. The Marshalsea heard cases of law that involved the royal household, and in 1547 its two judges for the campaign, Cecil and a Londoner called William Patten, travelled into Scotland with the English forces.

On his first journey outside England, Cecil wanted to see and record as much as he could. Patten wanted to do the same, 'whereby we both,' Patten wrote, 'not being bound so straightly in days of travel to order of march: nor other while, but when we sat in court, to any great affairs, had liberty to ride, to see things that were done, and leisure to note occurrences that came'. They kept journals of what they had seen; and after they returned home Patten borrowed Cecil's journal and used it to write an account of the campaign. When his book, *The Expedition into Scotland*, was published in London in January 1548, Patten thanked Cecil for his 'gentleness' and help.[3]

What Cecil witnessed in Scotland in the autumn of 1547 was the most effective military operation ever put together by the English crown. It was part of what are known as the 'Rough Wooings', the wars against Scotland started by Henry VIII in the early 1540s after the failure of the negotiations to marry his son Prince Edward to Mary, Queen of Scots, the baby daughter of King James V. In 1547 Cecil could only have guessed at how completely Mary Stuart would come to dominate his political career.

In Somerset's campaign Cecil saw his first battle, Pinkie Cleugh, the decisive encounter of the expedition. On Saturday, 10 September the armies of England and Scotland met near the town of Musselburgh, east of Edinburgh, where Protector Somerset's force of about fifteen thousand troops, some of them foreign mercenaries, supported by a large fleet of royal warships, engaged Scottish troops led by the Earl of Huntly and the Earl of Arran. At first the Scots looked as if they had the better of Protector Somerset's army, but a charge by the English heavy horse and constant gunfire by the English artillery broke Huntly and Arran's men. About ten thousand Scots were killed.

In *The Expedition into Scotland* Patten gave a graphic account of terrible slaughter. William Cecil was not a soldier, but he saw at first hand one of the most important battles fought in the sixteenth century between England and Scotland. He also saw the worst of what battles could be.

Already it was clear that Cecil's natural habitat was the Tudor palace. He had an easy ability to do well in political life. Others struggled in Somerset's household, like Thomas Smith, one of Cecil's old teachers from Cambridge. Smith's prickly personality led to a bruising encounter with the Protector's wife, Anne, a formidable woman. There was a whiff of corruption. Smith was accused of making some unscrupulous land deals. He was shocked by the allegation. So he tried, ever so subtly, to deflect some of the charges. The same, he suggested, could be said of Cecil, who was also doing very well financially out of his service. Perhaps Smith gently resented Cecil's success in the Protector's employment. But if he did, he denied it: 'Master Cecil is a great mote to be cast against me, that he poor man, is none such. Surely, for Master Cecil, I take him to be an honest and a worthy man, nor I see no cause why he should be brought and used to my displeasure, whom I have ever loved.'[4]

Where his old friend Smith struggled, Cecil strode forward purposefully. He prospered. His household grew, from four servants in September 1546 to eight at Christmas 1547. He even cultivated a public profile, showing how close he was to powerful men and women in the government. In November 1547 he wrote an introduction to *The Lamentation of a Sinner*, the religious contemplations of the Dowager Queen Katherine Parr. Cecil did not spare Katherine's blushes. His praise of the book was effusive and courtly. There was a second printing of the *Lamentation*, with Cecil's introduction, in the following March.[5]

Katherine Parr's *Lamentation* was printed 'at the instant desire' and 'earnest request' of two people, her brother William, Marquess of Northampton, and Katherine Brandon, Duchess of Suffolk. Katherine Brandon was one of Cecil's close friends in Edward's reign. She lived as a widow at Grimsthorpe, near Stamford, in the house built by her late husband, Charles Brandon, Duke of Suffolk. Katherine and Cecil had known each other since about 1545. Both were members of the Parr circle. They were also much the same age, Katherine a shade older than her friend.

Katherine Brandon valued Cecil's position near the Protector. The letters she wrote to him were friendly, even playful and gently teasing. She was rich and independent and used her money to further her religious interests, which were Protestant. But Katherine Brandon was just one of a number of talented, clever and powerful women Cecil knew.

There was, of course, Queen Katherine Parr. The Protector's wife, Anne, Duchess of Somerset, was another woman of great influence. Around Anne clustered Cecil's sisters-in-law, the Cookes, and the wives of his friends Thomas Smith and John Cheke. Mildred Cecil showed both her learning and the influence of Anne Seymour's patronage when she translated from Greek St Basil the Great's sermon on the book of Deuteronomy and dedicated it to the duchess. The Duchess of Somerset was Mildred's 'right good lady and mistress', and Mildred was the duchess's 'humble servant and debtor' and 'your grace's in service'.[6]

What many of these women had in common was strong religious faith. That faith was Protestant, though at the time they would have used words like 'evangelical' or 'godly' to describe their beliefs. And as with the women at or near court, so with the men, who were more obviously able to change the ways of the Church. Women like Katherine Brandon supported Protestant preachers and new scholarship and books on religion. Edward's councillors and male courtiers did this sort of thing too, but they also made and changed laws and introduced new ways of doings things. And what the men of Edward VI's government began to do very early in the reign was to sweep away centuries of Catholic belief and practice. After the reign of Edward, England would never be the same again. As a boy William Cecil had seen Henry VIII's revolution in church and state. Now he would help to see it to its second phase.

Henry's was not a Protestant Reformation, but there had been men around the King, like Thomas Cromwell and Archbishop Thomas Cranmer of Canterbury, who used Henry's newly declared royal supremacy to purge what they saw as abuses and corruptions in worship. In the King's title of supreme head of the Church was the promise of reform in religion.

Now the men around Edward VI used Henry's supremacy to engineer vastly more radical change. Royal injunctions were issued in July 1547 and commissioners went out into the realm to enforce them. The injunctions reminded the clergy that they should keep all the laws made 'as well for the abolishing and extirpation of the Bishop of Rome, his pretenced and usurped power and jurisdiction, as for the establishment and confirmation of the King's authority, jurisdiction and supremacy of the Church of England and Ireland'. Bibles in English translation were to be placed in churches, as were copies of Erasmus's *Paraphrases* on the Gospels. The injunctions allowed the royal commissioners to take away anything that tended to idolatry and abuse. So already, within months of the accession of Edward the boy-king, religious images began to disappear from churches and cathedrals. The iconoclasm had begun.[7]

Cecil sat as MP for Stamford in the first parliament of Edward's reign. It was this parliament which began to put the revolution into law. In the months before and after Christmas 1547 treason and heresy acts were repealed, and so were statutes that gave Catholic belief the force of law. Parliament outlawed chantry chapels and guilds and fraternities. They no longer served a purpose: purgatory and prayers for the dead were superstitious and had to be stopped. Edward's Council ordered the destruction of all religious images and the depictions of saints in stained-glass windows. Medieval wall paintings were covered over with whitewash.

There is no doubt that this revolution affected Cecil's own family. Prayers were no longer sung for the soul of his grandfather, William Hekington. Cecil's old schoolmaster, Libeus Byard, was out of a job, at least as a chantry priest. He was thirty-six in 1548, still celebrating Mass and instructing the boys of Stamford in the art of grammar. Luckily for Byard he was able to continue to teach. That year, 1548, Cecil managed to get an act of parliament to re-found the old chantry foundation as a grammar school. The purpose of this new school was 'to educate and bring up children and youth as well in learning as also in civil manners'. Byard became the senior master. His school had a clear income and a new formal affiliation with Cecil's old Cambridge college, St John's.[8]

Officially this great Reformation was Edward's. He was cast by Archbishop Cranmer as a second Josiah, the young king of Judah who had instructed that the word of God be read to his people and ordered the destruction of idols (2 Kings:22–23). The authority of a boy-king who could not yet rule for himself was being used to justify Protestant Reformation. Catholics insisted that it was Protector Somerset's duty merely to keep the kingdom as he had found it on Henry VIII's death: he had to preserve religion, not destroy it.

One of the greatest thorns in the side of Edward's government was Bishop Stephen Gardiner of Winchester. It was Gardiner who, more than anyone else, poked and prodded at what Protector Somerset and his colleagues claimed they could do in the time of the King's minority. Gardiner was dangerous. He was a talented and articulate scholar, lawyer, diplomat, politician and bishop.

Gardiner believed that the evangelical Reformation was illegal, and he was not afraid to expose what Protector Somerset's government was up to. Gardiner was subtle, clever and persistent, and it was clear to Somerset that he had to be stopped. What the government tried to do was to force Gardiner to support it publicly in an important sermon at the royal court on St Peter's Day, 29 June, in 1548. This was a spectacular risk.

It was obvious in the early summer of 1548 that Stephen Gardiner had to be persuaded to say the right things in his sermon. But who could persuade one of the cleverest and most experienced politicians of the day to preach what

Protector Somerset wanted to hear? Somerset sent as his personal emissary twenty-seven-year-old William Cecil.

Of course it was an impossible mission. Gardiner knew exactly what was going on. And so as soon as Cecil visited him at his palace in Southwark, he went on the attack. Cecil, politely but firmly, set out what the bishop could and could not say in the St Peter's Day sermon. Gardiner exploded. Too dignified to go to Somerset himself, he sent one of his chaplains, Thomas Watson, to complain about Cecil's rudeness. Gardiner and Watson believed that Cecil had gone beyond his orders. Watson, one of Cecil's former teachers at St John's in Cambridge, met Somerset in the King's garden at Whitehall Palace, only to be told that Gardiner 'should not suspect the said duke's trusty servants whom he used to send unto him'. For Cecil it must have been a delicious moment.[9]

On that day Cecil won a small victory. He was a loyal servant of the Protector, and now the government's critics, as well as its friends, knew that fact. But if Cecil's job was to encourage Gardiner to preach the right kind of sermon, he failed. For a young and talented man it was an instructive lesson. The sermon was a masterpiece of subtlety, a beautifully crafted demolition of everything Somerset and his men were doing in the Church. Gardiner managed to defend the 'liberty' of rulers to reform or remove abuses in the Church but almost in the same breath he condemned a government that smashed images. Cecil listened carefully to the sermon. In his hands he had a copy of the 'articles' he had given to the bishop at Southwark. Gardiner paid not one jot of attention to them. It was a public relations catastrophe for the government.[10]

Cecil had not managed to tame Stephen Gardiner. From the beginning it was never likely that he would. But perhaps at least part of Cecil acknowledged the power of Gardiner's sermon. Like Cecil, Gardiner was a craftsman with words.

Cecil was one of the stars of Protector Somerset's household and government. He was trusted by his master to handle difficult and sensitive business. He was Somerset's right hand, and by 1549 the duke wanted Cecil to live 'nigh unto him' at his palace of Syon in Middlesex on the River Thames. Within months Cecil and his family settled at the parsonage in Wimbledon. It was to be their home until the early years of Elizabeth's reign.[11]

Such closeness to Somerset came, in the end, with a cost. The year 1549 was a bitter-sweet one for Cecil. Bishop Gardiner was not the only subject of Edward VI who resisted Reformation. There were others who found their voices in rebellion, and there were uprisings right across England in the summer of 1549. These were put down, but within the government stresses and strains were beginning to show.

Somerset had tried to do too much too quickly. The economy was fragile. Many people were opposed to war abroad and Reformation at home. Somerset was not temperamentally suited to good government in difficult times. Even his political allies advised him to think very carefully about how he ruled. Colleagues had doubts about his temper. William Paget, once Secretary to Henry VIII and a man close to the Protector, reminded Somerset that even a king who did not hear frank counsel put his realm in danger. In a subject the fault was greater: a man who was 'in great authority (as your grace is) using such fashion is like to fall into great danger and peril of his own person, beside that to the commonwealth'.[12]

By October 1549 many of Protector Somerset's colleagues felt they could no longer support him. Some of them broke away from Somerset, Paget and Archbishop Cranmer, who were at Windsor Castle with the King. For days there was a standoff between those of the Council who were in London and those at Windsor. Somerset's opponents claimed he had misused his office, and Somerset defended himself robustly. But in the end, isolated, Somerset gave in, and he and his most senior household servants were detained. Somerset's protectorate was finally at an end and so, it seemed, was William Cecil's flourishing career.

It took a month for Edward's newly fashioned Council to do anything about Cecil. These were anxious weeks, and his prospects did not look good. At least one friend, Katherine Brandon, tried to console him. She offered as much help, support and encouragement as she could. It would not be enough, that she knew; but she imagined that Cecil was in fact well armed against what she called 'froward fortune'. She wrote a letter to clear herself of 'the common infection of fained friendship'. It is a powerful and intimate piece of writing:

> For your troubles as I cannot be but sorry, yet when I consider you I find some comfort. It grieveth me to see your burden but causeth me to think how little you have deserved . . . . I am sorry contrary fortune doth put you to the trial of your friends . . . . I am most sorry that my power serveth me no better for the show of my will towards you. Good Cecil mistrust not but you shall have all that I can do ye, and if there be anything which you think I may do forbear me not, use me as I have been bold to use you.

Katherine Brandon wrote that letter as William's 'very friend' on 16 November 1549. Eight days later, on Sunday, 24 November, at night, Cecil was taken into custody and sent to the Tower of London.[13]

*

The day following his arrest Cecil was moved to the house of John Cornelius, a gun-founder in the Tower. Whatever the comforts of Cornelius's lodgings, the Tower had irresistible associations of imprisonment and state execution. Cecil probably never thought his life was in danger: Somerset and his household men were imprisoned to make a point. Still, it must have been a sobering experience. At the age of twenty-nine William was taught a hard but important lesson about fickle fortune in Tudor politics. On Christmas Day 1549, with his fellow prisoners, he heard a sermon by John Hooper, a future bishop and friend, who spoke about what happened to rulers who 'misordered their vocations': they were punished by God. This was the lesson of the Tower of London.[14]

Cecil spent eight weeks in the Tower. He was released on 25 January 1550 on payment of a very large fine. He was free. But he had to come to terms with the fact that his political career was ruined. True, he was still a servant in the household of the Duke of Somerset, but Somerset was out in the cold. The new power in Council and realm was John Dudley, Earl of Warwick. Within a year Cecil would be as close to Warwick as he had been thus far to Somerset.[15]

Warwick was in his middle forties. He was the son of Edmund Dudley, one of the lawyers and enforcers of the government of Henry VII, executed for treason when John was about five. As a boy John Dudley was brought up in noble households to learn the skills of the courtier. He did well at the famously physical and chivalric court of Henry VIII. In 1523 he was on the Duke of Suffolk's expedition to France, as also was Edward Seymour. Charles Brandon knighted Seymour and Dudley within a week of each other. Dudley continued to do well at the royal court, and he was made Viscount Lisle in 1542. By the time of Henry VIII's death, five years later, Lisle was a powerful player, though lacking Edward Seymour's tie of marriage to the royal family. At the beginning of Edward VI's reign he became the Earl of Warwick.

Warwick was a tough politician, but even he needed help to secure his position as the most important of King Edward's councillors in 1550. In the first months of his pre-eminence Somerset was still a danger to him. It was just as well that William Cecil was willing to help Warwick outmanoeuvre the earl's greatest opponent.

The *coup* of late 1549 was neither a bloody revolution nor a violent purge of political opponents. Somerset's fall was temporary. He was the King's uncle: even the men who had stood up to him in October 1549 knew that it would be very difficult to keep him out of politics and government for long. There was every sign that he would return to Edward's court. Indeed in early April 1550 he was taken back into the Council. That month security was tightened in the King's Privy Chamber. Men close to the Earl of Warwick were given positions of authority in the most private rooms of the royal court. Young Edward noted how gentlemen of his Privy Chamber slept on pallet beds outside his door and a groom kept watch in his bedchamber. Warwick's worry was that Somerset would try to snatch the King.[16]

At the end of April one report said that 'all men seeketh upon' Somerset. Warwick was sick and away from court, and he was plainly worried by Somerset's influence. In the middle of May the Council debated whether Somerset should be given access to the Privy Chamber. This was probably all but inevitable. At the same meeting Edward's councillors agreed that the King should be protected by a force of gentlemen-at-arms and footmen commanded by men close to the Earl of Warwick.[17]

It was a tense spring. There were rumours that Warwick was to be made Duke of Gloucester: they were without substance. Warwick suggested a marriage between one of the Duchess of Suffolk's sons, Charles or Henry, and Somerset's daughter Anne. But Katherine Brandon told her good friend Cecil that she did not want to push them into marriage. The plan came to nothing. This was at the end of the first week of May. Less than a month later Lady Anne Seymour married Warwick's eldest son, John, Lord Lisle at Richmond in the presence of the King. In the end the Earl of Warwick had to ally his own family with Somerset. But he spoiled the moment by missing the wedding.[18]

Warwick was in retreat on his estate at Hatfield. Somerset was apparently the most important man at court and Warwick's fear was that Somerset wanted to return to power. He was irritated and worried by Somerset's new popularity, but what really disturbed him was the strange alliance the duke appeared to be forming with Stephen Gardiner, the man Somerset had once tried to silence. It seemed that Somerset wanted to get Gardiner out of the Tower of London, where he had been sent after his sermon on St Peter's Day 1548. Perhaps it was a way for the duke to show his power, influence and skills of negotiation. So what could be done to stop Somerset and Gardiner?

The Earl of Warwick spoke to two men in the Duke of Somerset's household, Richard Whalley, Somerset's chamberlain, and William Cecil. Surely those eight weeks in the Tower had taught Cecil that service in Somerset's household was no longer the best path to career advancement. Whatever the reason, in late spring and early summer Cecil helped Warwick to lever the Duke of Somerset away from Gardiner.

Secretly Cecil prepared a case against the bishop. Warwick was very grateful for Cecil's work: he wrote to Whalley to say that Cecil was 'such a faithful servant and by that term most witty* counsellor, as unto the King's Majesty and his proceedings, as was scarce the like within this his realm'. This was high praise, and for good reason: Cecil had written articles that would lead to Gardiner's prosecution.[19]

* Having good judgement and discernment.

The articles Cecil sent to Warwick in June 1550 were the making of his political career. They gave Warwick just what he needed to stop Somerset in his tracks. And certainly Somerset seemed to be making good progress in his negotiations with Gardiner. The bishop looked ready to come to an agreement with the Council. On 14 June there was some sort of breakthrough. The King wrote in his journal that Gardiner had at last acquiesced to the Book of Common Prayer which had become law the year before, and which before this moment the bishop had never seemed likely to support.[20]

Gardiner was never allowed to make his peace with Edward and his Council. Within days Warwick was back in London. In early July he struck. A letter was written to Gardiner in the King's name that referred to the bishop's 'insolent wilfulness' and 'notorious and apparent contempts'. Four councillors, of whom Warwick was one, went to see Gardiner in the Tower. Somerset did not go with them. They took 'certain articles' to the bishop. Gardiner subscribed to those articles which had to do with the King's supremacy, the Book of Common Prayer, and the authority of Edward in his minority. But Gardiner would not sign a confession that he was sorry for his opposition to the King's proceedings in religion.

More of the King's councillors went to see Gardiner. The Council decided to commission a new book of articles, this time with the help of Bishop Nicholas Ridley of London and Richard Goodrich of Gray's Inn, one of Cecil's good friends. Cecil helped to prepare the revised articles but probably he did not go to see Gardiner. Those who did got nowhere with the bishop.

The next day the Council agreed to send for Gardiner to come before them. If he still would not confess his offence to the King then the Council would, as the minutes put it, 'denounce unto him the sequestration of his benefice': in other words Gardiner's bishopric would be taken away from him. His days as a bishop were finally coming to an end. Gardiner had fallen and Somerset, who must have loved the importance of his great negotiations with Stephen Gardiner, was simply outmanoeuvred and pushed into the background. The Earl of Warwick had won. It was a private victory for Cecil also: he had shown himself to be a 'witty counsellor' indeed.[21]

*

Within months Cecil was promoted to one of the most important jobs in royal government. At the palace of Oatlands, on Friday, 5 September, he was appointed as Secretary to the King, an office which came with a seat on the board of the Privy Council and which gave him influence at court and significant powers of patronage. Cecil became both a humble servant of the

King and a powerful political player, 'an artificer of practices and counsels', as he put it later in his career.

With intelligence and cunning, Cecil had moved from the political wilderness to being one of the elite at court. He had come a long way since his imprisonment in the Tower of London. Katherine Brandon told him that he had at last 'come to a good market' where his wares were 'so good and saleable'. Katherine was absolutely right. Cecil's useful service to the Earl of Warwick in July had paid off. It is hard to think of anyone else whose career had gone from near disaster to sparkling success in so short a time.[22]

A good Tudor Secretary had to be a scholar as well as an administrator. Ideally he was learned in the law, in languages and in the subtleties of international diplomacy. Words were his weapons, words in speech and on paper. The King ruled his kingdom personally and the Secretary was an instrument of that rule. He made sure that royal government worked and he did this in consultation with his master the King and, in the second half of Edward's reign, with Warwick too. The best Secretaries were cultured and sophisticated men. Often they had had brilliant careers in the universities or in the law. Actually most of them had been, and were still in their bones, scholars or lawyers whose talents were so great that they could be put to the higher service of the King. When William Cecil became a Secretary he could count as his predecessors brilliant, powerful, obsessive and difficult men like Thomas Wolsey, Thomas More, Thomas Cromwell and even Stephen Gardiner. The expectations of a young man who was barely thirty must have been enormous.

The work was punishing. The best of Cecil's predecessors had often stayed at their desks well after midnight. It is hard to imagine that Cecil could spend much time with his family. Like his father, Richard, he now began to move with the court, though he did so with a rank and importance no other member of his family had ever had before.

Cecil had to stay close to Westminster. Just a few weeks after his appointment as Secretary, Richard Goodrich found two houses he thought might interest his friend. They were on Cannon Row, very close indeed to Westminster Abbey and Whitehall Palace, and just set back from the River Thames. They had belonged to Lord Paget, and Goodrich thought they would cost £400 cash. He offered to negotiate the deal for Cecil and was making progress in early October. It seems he was successful: Cannon Row became Cecil's residence in Westminster till Elizabeth's reign.[23]

From the earliest days of his new job he was very busy. With Sir William Petre, the senior Secretary, Cecil shared the burden of administering the government of the kingdom. Cecil also worked, in effect, as the Earl of Warwick's private secretary in government, his agent and representative, and someone who could be trusted to get things done, particularly when Warwick was away from court. Other men within government recognised Cecil's influence and asked him for his assistance in matters of patronage, just as they had done in the years of Protector Somerset. And, more important, William worked with the young King, helping to introduce him to the day-to-day affairs of his kingdom.

All of this meant that Cecil was involved more than ever in some of the most sensitive politics of Edward's reign. He gave evidence at the trial of Stephen Gardiner, at which Gardiner was finally stripped of his bishopric. But the government aimed even higher than Gardiner, and confronted the King's half-sister, Mary, a vigorous opponent of the new religious settlement. Mary was a Catholic who saw no need to practise anything else but the faith of her youth. She was flatly opposed to the forced eradication of Catholicism in England, and for the government it was annoying and embarrassing that the King's sister was one of those who refused to accept the Reformation that was being done in Edward's name.

It was in August 1551, just short of the first anniversary of Cecil's appointment as Secretary, that the Council decided to do something about Mary. She shrugged off the effort by the Council to intimidate her senior household officers. She stuck to her private Mass and she resisted any effort to make her conform to the new church settlement. She also, more worryingly, questioned the ability of so young a king as her brother to determine such complicated matters of belief and doctrine.

The Council met to debate Mary's continuing refusal to conform. It seems Cecil attended very few of these meetings, but he was clearly hard at work behind the scenes. The evidence for this comes from Princess Mary herself. At the end of August a delegation of councillors delivered to Mary a letter from the King which required her finally to conform. At this meeting Mary made a show of loyalty to Edward, receiving the letter on her knees and 'saying that for the honour of the King's Majesty's hand wherewith the letters were signed she could kiss the letter'. But the 'matter contained in them' was quite different. This, she believed, came not from Edward but from his councillors. After reading the letter to herself privately she thought she knew its author. 'Ah!', the official account of the meeting records her as saying, 'Good Master Cecil took much pain here.'[24]

Edward's government never forced Mary to conform to its new church settlement. Controversies about religion refused to go away, and in these 1551 was an important year. God's providence was seen by Cecil and his friends in the deaths of two boys fêted by their contemporaries as young Protestant heroes. They were Charles and Henry Brandon, the sons of Cecil's friend Katherine, Duchess of Suffolk, both victims of what was known as the 'sweating sickness' which struck Cambridge in the summer of 1551. Their

deaths greatly affected Katherine, who wrote a private and moving letter to
Cecil that September, giving thanks for the benefits of God. In what she
described as God's 'punishment' she wrote that she had 'never been so well
taught by any other before to know his power, his love and mercy'. As a
memorial to her sons Katherine set up a scholarship for four poor boys at St
John's College in Cambridge. Cecil and many of his friends in government
paid their respects in Greek and Latin verse to honour the Brandon boys.[25]

Cecil believed in the Edwardian project. He was not merely a time-serving
bureaucrat. He was committed ideologically to the evangelical Reformation
being pursued by the regime. In November 1551, for example, fourteen men
met at his house on Cannon Row to debate the Mass. Five spoke against the
Catholic sacrament, of whom Cecil was one, his brother-in-law Cheke
another, and Edmund Grindal, a future archbishop of Canterbury, a third.
Two speakers defended the Mass: a former monk called John Feckenham; and
John Young, a fellow of St John's College, Cambridge when Cecil was a
student there. Important men came to listen: Lord Francis Russell, the son of
the Earl of Bedford; Thomas Wroth of Edward's Privy Chamber; and Sir
Anthony Cooke, Cecil's father-in-law.

The debate at Cannon Row, and one that followed it just over a week later
at the house of a royal diplomat, Sir Richard Morison, set down some of the
foundations for a document which affected the lives of every one of Edward
VI's subjects. This was the Book of Common Prayer of 1552, which set out to
the letter how God was to be worshipped. There had been a Prayer Book in
1549 which, in some of its more sensitive passages about belief and ritual, had
been perhaps ambiguous enough to keep Catholics happy. There were few
such concessions in the Prayer Book of 1552. It became for Cecil a standard. A
few years later, when the world of Tudor politics had been upside down and
then set right again, it was the Prayer Book of 1552 that Cecil put back into law
at the beginning of Elizabeth's reign.[26]

William Cecil was one of the leading lights of Edward's reign. He believed
in Reformation. He was close to Archbishop Cranmer of Canterbury, who had
masterminded England's return to the 'true religion'. The notion of the King
as God's reforming agent on earth, as an Old Testament Josiah bringing the
word of God back to his people, was one that would stay with Cecil for the rest
of his life.

By the autumn of 1551 Cecil was firmly set on the path to preferment. On 11
October, a Sunday, at Hampton Court, he was knighted by the King in a short
ceremony. Three other men received the same honour that day: Henry Sidney
and Henry Neville, both gentlemen of Edward's Privy Chamber, and John
Cheke, the King's tutor and Cecil's brother-in-law. Just before Cecil received
his knighthood the Earl of Warwick was made Duke of Northumberland.[27]

But where some rose, others fell. The Duke of Somerset, always a worry to Northumberland, was rumoured to be plotting against the government. Cecil met Somerset, probably for the last time, on 14 October. Cecil must have told the young King about the meeting, because Edward noted it in his journal. Somerset, it seems, sent for Cecil 'to tell him he suspected some ill': in other words, that there was a conspiracy afoot. Cecil told Somerset that if he was not guilty he might be of good courage; but if Somerset was guilty, Cecil had nothing to say but to lament him. The last exchange between them was a defiant letter Somerset sent to his young protégé. Whatever else was said, it was clear that Cecil had at last broken his ties with his old master.[28]

The Duke of Somerset was sentenced to death for the felony of bringing together men for a riot. He was beheaded on Tower Hill in January 1552. It was the end of an era.

*

By 1552 Cecil was settling nicely into his office of Secretary. The work was hard and constant and he rarely had time to leave court. But in the early summer of 1552 he was just able to snatch a fortnight at Burghley before that year's royal progress. Cecil, ever a stickler for detail, produced a rigorous itinerary for the trip and spent some time carefully allocating horses for himself, Lady Mildred and their servants.

The party of fourteen set out from London on 14 June 1552. They travelled straight up the Great North Road, planning to be in Royston the next day and at Burghley the day after that. On 19 June, a Sunday, the family had the honour of entertaining the Duke of Northumberland at Burghley. The next day Cecil set out for Sempringham, a few miles from Stamford, to visit his neighbour, Lord Admiral Clinton. He went to Grimsthorpe to call briefly on his good friend the Duchess of Suffolk. The same day he toured some of his estates. On Sunday, 26 June the family went to St Martin's Church in Stamford, where since 1536 Richard Cecil had held the right to appoint the priest. At St Martin's they heard a sermon preached by Cecil's old schoolmaster, Libeus Byard. There followed a methodical tour of estates. On St Peter's Day, exactly four years since Stephen Gardiner had preached his famous sermon at court, Cecil sat with other local justices at the sessions of the peace. It was a reminder to everyone in Stamford that he was still a power in his country, however much his duties as the King's Secretary kept him away from Burghley.

Cecil and his family servants meandered back to London in early July. They went through Northamptonshire, then south-east to Huntingdon, and finally through Cambridgeshire, Suffolk and Essex. On 9 July they were in Cambridge, but that same day continued east into Suffolk. They stayed the night of 11 July at Ingatestone Hall in Essex, where Sir William and Lady Mildred dined with Secretary Petre and Lady Norwich. The Cecils' servants ate in the hall with the haymakers and labourers who had been working in the fields. The next day the party was at Romford, on 13 July in London, and a day after that back home at Wimbledon. On 15 July Richard Goodrich came to visit the Cecils at the parsonage. The next day Cecil went to Archbishop Cranmer's palace at Croydon. On the 18th he was at Nonsuch Palace with Goodrich and their friend Sir Philip Hoby. Cecil was back at court at Guildford just in time to go on the royal progress in August and early September.[29]

Cecil's break at Burghley was exceptional. He was a very busy man who was rarely away from court and service. But even so there was always hospitality for friends and family. Sir Anthony Cooke visited in August. He wrote to Cecil with 'most hearty thanks as well for the pains ye took with me at the court as for the good relief that I found at Wimbledon'. With Cooke were Richard Goodrich and ten-year-old Thomas Cecil, 'in whose towardness* ye have good cause to rejoice'.[30]

Goodrich himself wrote to Cecil two days later because he understood from Lady Mildred 'that you be minded to go to Bath for the benefit of the bath and that you are desirous to have me with you'. Goodrich was too busy to go, and he wondered whether it was really wise for his friend to travel to Bath, because the year was dangerous for fevers and the plague was in Bristol. 'Defer your journey thither unto the beginning of the year,' Goodrich carried on, 'at which time I will be glad to wait upon you, for I assure you ye cannot be without peril at Bath, where there is daily resort from Bristol and specially of beggars and poor folks.'[31]

In the spring of 1553 there was a great family upset. On 19 March Richard Cecil died in William's house on Cannon Row. His body was buried close by in St Margaret's Church near Westminster Abbey. Only Richard's coat armour was carried in procession back to Burghley, for which William lent his mother Jane £8 8s. It was the beginning of some delicate family negotiations.

Richard Cecil had not made a will. There were rumours of something he had set down on paper, but nothing for certain. So Cecil sent Roger Alford, his confidential secretary, to Burghley to find out as much as he could and to talk to Jane Cecil about the estate. It was a sensitive embassy.[32] Alford found Cecil's sisters and their husbands at Burghley. There was a family conference, and already there were tensions. Thomas White, Anne's husband, told Alford that he felt he should withdraw from any discussions about the will because Jane 'had no confidence in him nor did not trust him'. But at least two neighbours,

* Promise or aptitude.

Robert Harington and the Earl of Rutland, were standing by to help the family.

Alford conducted his own investigations. He discovered that in about September 1552 Richard Cecil had written fifteen or sixteen lines on a parchment as 'his will of his goods'. But no one knew anything about Richard's testament because he had said that 'no man should know his mind before his death'. Alford knew the case would go to a hearing before a jury. And so it did. The inquisition found that William Cecil was Richard's son and heir, and Alford delivered its verdict to the royal court. It was the King who in early June gave William a licence to enter on the inheritance of Richard Cecil.[33]

All of this had been difficult enough. But by spring Cecil was sick. His friends thought it was overwork: he was simply doing too much. The illness, which may have been aggravated by the strain of his father's death, came on quickly, he told the Duke of Northumberland. It was known at court by 9 May, when John, Lord Audley sent William some remedies for his sickness.[34]

Audley clearly fancied himself as an amateur physician, encouraged, for better or worse, by Lord Admiral Clinton, who had praised his 'physic'. Audley's first recipe for Cecil's recovery was for what he called 'weakness'. It involved putting a slaughtered nine-day-old sow in a still with spearmint, red fennel, liverwort, turnip, celery, dates, raisins, mace and cinnamon. The mixture was to be heated and distilled, left in the sun for nine days and then nine spoonfuls of it drunk one after the other. The second recipe Audley sent, surely not much more digestible, was a 'compost', or mixture, of a quarter of a hedgehog put in a still with a quart of red wine, a pint of rose water, a quart of sugar, cinnamon and great raisins, one date and twelve turnips. 'Tell me of any disease you have,' Audley ended, ' and I will send you a proved remedy.'

The worst of the illness was over by 14 May, when Cecil felt well enough to write a letter to Northumberland, hoping that the duke would be pleased with 'a little writing from me that could neither write nor read within these few days'. The King wanted to know whether he would be able to attend the next meeting of the Order of the Garter, of which Cecil had recently been appointed Chancellor. 'True it is,' replied Cecil, 'I have good desire to be there then, as at a place of my pilgrimage after my sickness; and for a day or two with some foresight of safe coming I am in hope to be able, if I grow from sickness but half so speedily as I fell into it.' He especially wanted to know about the shape of the satin gown he would have to wear as Chancellor, 'not knowing what manner of sleeves nor what colour'. Considering that the young King had worked so hard to have the Order 'purged of superstition and made of a religious order a military order', Cecil thought 'the less congruence be of this apparel with priestly, the better it is'. He signed the letter with a 'weary hand'.[35]

Cecil was back at court towards the end of May. On 11 June he went to his first Council meeting in seven weeks. Everything was normal, or so it seemed. But in June 1553 the calm stability of Edward's reign was an illusion.

The fifteen-year-old King was dying. In May the Imperial ambassador to Edward's court, Jehan Scheyfve, reported that the physicians thought the King had a suppurating tumour on his lung. On the day Cecil returned to the Council Edward suffered a violent fever. By the end of June all hope for the King's life appeared lost.[36]

The studied normality of the Privy Council and the routine business of royal government hid secret conversations in the private rooms of the court. What would happen after Edward's death? His half-sister Mary was his lawful successor. But given that she had so stoutly resisted the evangelical Reformation, could the Edwardian establishment allow her to succeed Edward?

The politics of all of this was worked out over the next six weeks, when William Cecil had to tread very carefully between loyalty and conscience, King and God. He was about to have to fight for his life and liberty in a test harder even than the one he had survived in the Tower of London three years before.

5

Conscience or Treason?

At the age of thirty-two William Cecil faced the greatest crisis of his short but sparkling political career. In June and July 1553 he was caught up in the most spectacular *coup d'état* of the Tudor century. He put his name to a plan to subvert the will of King Henry VIII by setting Lady Jane Grey on the English throne instead of Henry's eldest daughter, Mary. Everything Cecil had worked so hard to achieve for over half a decade rested on the fragile life of a dying boy-king and on the success of what, however it was dressed up, was pure treason. In the hard school of Tudor politics, this was the toughest lesson of all.

To enter Cecil's life in June and July 1553 is to walk through a hall of mirrors. Bias, perception, distortion, memory: all these are problems. If we hope for a neat, objective account of the *coup* we will not find one. All the sources we have are in some way self-serving. And who can blame their authors?

We have Cecil's own account of what happened, delivered to Mary when it was all over. Can we believe him? We have a rich compelling narrative by Roger Alford, Cecil's confidential secretary. But Alford wrote his account in 1573 when his old master, for whatever reason, was revisiting the events of twenty years before. Should we trust him? There are other sources, too, of course. One, by a senior judge caught up in the affair, was once again a petition to Queen Mary for leniency and mercy. So we have the same kind of problem. The evidence is complicated.

We also have Cecil looking over our shoulder. There is a sense from what survives, a subtle hint, that he went through and pruned his own archive. He kept the documents that showed him to be a loyal subject; there is little in his papers that suggests otherwise. He may have done this before he made his peace with Mary in 1553, or even in 1573 when he commissioned Roger Alford's narrative. Perhaps we can imagine the fifty-three-year-old statesman trying to recapture what it had been like to be an ambitious young man fighting for life and career. We shall probably never know.

So everywhere, and in everything, there are problems. What follows in this chapter might only be a version of the events as they happened. Perhaps it is, in a sense, the authorised story Cecil wanted to be told. Readers will have to judge for themselves.

*

Lady Jane Grey married Lord Guildford Dudley, the Duke of Northumberland's son, on 21 May 1553. For Northumberland it was the perfect dynastic marriage. Fifteen-year-old Jane had a claim to the English throne. She, more than Elizabeth Tudor, was the best alternative to Mary.

By the Succession Act of 1544 and his will of 1546 Henry VIII had determined that the crown would pass to Edward, his son, and then to Edward's legitimate heirs. But Henry had looked to the future with extraordinary care. What would happen if Edward died without an heir? His father had thought about this. Then the crown would go to any heir of Henry and Katherine Parr, his last queen, or to the heir of Henry and 'of any other our lawful wife that we shall hereafter marry'. If there were none, the crown would pass to Henry's eldest daughter, Mary. If Mary died without issue, then her half-sister Elizabeth would become queen.

But the Succession Act did not leave it at that. Henry had even looked beyond Elizabeth. If she ever came to the throne but died without a legitimate heir, or broke the conditions of the act relating to any marriage she made, law and royal will determined that the imperial crown of King Henry would 'wholly remain and come to the heirs of the body of the Lady Frances'.

This was Frances Grey, Henry's niece, the daughter of his sister Mary by her second husband Charles Brandon, Duke of Suffolk. Frances married Henry Grey, who himself became Duke of Suffolk after Charles Brandon's death. Frances and Henry had three daughters: Jane, who was born in 1537, in the same year and month as Edward VI; Katherine, about a year younger than Jane; and Mary, who was born about 1540. These three women were distant heirs to the crown of England.

That any of the Grey sisters would inherit the throne was very unlikely, or so it must have looked to Henry VIII in 1546. By law the heir of Lady Frances Grey was fifth in the line of royal succession. A Grey would surely rule only in fairly desperate circumstances. But in seven years, time and politics changed everything. In 1553 Edward VI believed that Princess Mary could not be trusted to rule: his tussles with her over his reforms in the Church were evidence of that. Even Princess Elizabeth could be ignored. Lady Jane Dudley, formidably educated, dependably Protestant, young and already married, could be relied on. In 1553 it seemed that the succession of a Grey was Protestant England's hope and protection.[1]

If we believe Cecil, the first he heard of the notion of Jane Grey as queen was soon after he returned from his sickbed to the court at Greenwich. Roger Alford had been at Greenwich for a while and his master wanted to know what was going on. They went for a walk in Greenwich Park and talked about Jane and 'a device of King Edward's whereby the succession of the crown should be settled in her'.[2]

There is no way to tell what Cecil and Alford really knew. Their accounts of these weeks tell us that 'a very few' of the King's councillors wanted to make Lady Jane queen. Cecil, so the official story goes, was not one of them. He would have us believe that he found out what was going on from a secret source, a 'friend' who was one of the inner circle of trusted initiates. That, of course, is what he later wanted Queen Mary to think.

But Cecil's political antennae were always finely tuned. He may have been sick at Wimbledon in late May, but he was not in quarantine. Letters passed to and from the court, and it is easy enough to burn a letter that deals with secret business. Doubtless he had visitors, too. If the conspiracy was being planned at court there is no good reason to think that Cecil could not have been part of it.

And there would have been some very good reasons to trust Cecil. He was no political outsider, a neutral civil servant; he was instead a realist and a politician. Cecil rarely allowed himself the luxury of sentiment. By nature he measured, calculated and judged. But he did believe in the Edwardian project. He knew Edward well: he had worked with the young King in 1552 and 1553 and taught him the business of government. Together they wrote papers on some of the big political topics of the day. He was close to Archbishop Cranmer. And of course he was the Duke of Northumberland's right hand, his trusted fixer at court and in Council. He was clever, discreet and able, the outstanding politician of his generation.

It is easy to overlook another important fact. William Cecil was a kinsman of the Greys. The clever political marriage he made to Mildred Cooke in 1545 had opened up all kinds of grand connections of kinship. Mildred's brother, William, was married to Lady Jane's first cousin. In letters to Cecil in Edward's reign the Marquess of Dorset, Jane's father, called the King's young Secretary cousin. There can be few doubts that Cecil would have preferred a queen of the 'true religion', even a Grey, to a Catholic Tudor.

We may imagine that the plan to put Jane Grey on the throne was a dastardly scheme cooked up by the Duke of Northumberland. The timing of the marriage of Jane and Guildford seems evidence enough of that. And it is hard to deny that the whole thing was in Northumberland's interest. He was a tough politician who enjoyed power. If the plan worked, he would have his young daughter-in-law on the throne.

But we should not overlook Edward. It is easy to think that he was a mere cipher. He was not. At fifteen Edward was beginning to sound very much like his father, wilful and commanding. He knew his own mind. It seems he really did want Jane to succeed him. It was Edward who wrote the paper in favour of Jane's claim, 'My device for the succession'. Secretary Petre made a fair copy of it and Edward added his royal sign manual, or royal signature, to each of the six paragraphs.

Edward's 'Device' set out the following. First, he proposed to leave the crown to any male heirs of Lady Frances Grey, Jane's mother, and then in order to the sons of Lady Jane, the sons of Lady Katherine and the sons of Lady Mary. Then a few strokes of the pen changed everything. When he made the change is not clear: perhaps Edward had drafted his 'Device' months before his last illness and then altered it for the last time when he was dying. We shall never know. But in a few seconds Edward altered English history for ever. Part of a sentence that read 'to the Lady Jane's heir males' was changed to read 'to the Lady Jane and her heir males'. Lady Frances had no sons. Nor did Lady Jane, though that was perhaps just a matter of time. But the plain, unmistakable, breathtaking fact was that Jane would be queen.[3]

Nothing could have been more politically explosive. It was a blunt denial of the authority of Henry VIII's Succession Act. It would put Jane on the English throne and it would disinherit Mary. Tudor rule would be at an end. The Greys would be England's new royal family.

The political calculations must have begun as soon as the inner caucus knew of the King's 'Device'. Once he was dead, his councillors would have to defend Mary's exclusion from the royal succession. To say that she did not quite fit the bill as queen would not be good enough. So the argument would be that she was illegitimate, the product of a royal marriage that had been no marriage at all, declared invalid and never to have existed. But here, as Edward and his men would have known all too well, the law was against them. What they ran into from the beginning was the Succession Act.

So how, in early June, did William Cecil begin to come to terms with the secret plan to disinherit Mary? The official memory, which he set down after the *coup* and Roger Alford dutifully confirmed years later, was that he wanted to have nothing to do with it. Cecil made plans to run. He told Alford that he would never subscribe to the conspiracy. He stayed away from the ordinary business meetings of the Privy Council. He made his dispositions, travelling by water from Greenwich to London at night, armed and 'in awe of violence'. One afternoon, probably in the second week of June, he expected to be sent for by the Council, and so he set out some books and his night clothes. He thought he was going to prison. He was called to Council, but nothing was done about the succession at that meeting. He sent Alford to Cannon Row to remove money, plate and papers. These were hidden in the London houses of William Seres, a household servant, and a man called Nelson, clearly someone who was trusted. Cecil did not know whether to flee or to submit himself to what Alford called, quaintly, the Council's 'courtesy'.[4]

So was it pure accident that Cecil happened to be at Council for a very important meeting? This was on 11 June, a Sunday. The Council sent a letter to Sir Edward Montagu, Lord Chief Justice of the Court of Common Pleas, commanding him to attend on them at nine o'clock the next morning. The Marquess of Winchester, the Duke of Northumberland, the earls of Bedford, Shrewsbury and Pembroke, Lord Admiral Clinton, Sir Thomas Darcy, Sir John Gates, Sir William Petre and Sir John Cheke all signed the letter. So did Sir William Cecil.[5]

Montagu was at Greenwich the next day. With him came a small deputation of senior lawyers. They met Winchester, Northampton and Gates. Montagu later remembered that a couple of other councillors attended: Cecil may have been one of them.

Montagu and his colleagues also met the King. Edward, who must have been very frail, spoke to them all. He explained why he did not want his sisters Mary and Elizabeth to succeed him. A 'bill of articles' was then read out. Most likely this was the 'Device' prepared by Secretary Petre. There were six articles covering everything from the new order of the royal succession to the provisions for government in a minority. Edward made it clear to the lawyers that he wanted his 'Device' turned into a proper legal document.

Montagu's position from the beginning was that the King's instructions were against the law, and here he was right. The Succession Act made it very clear that anyone who tampered with the order of succession as it was laid out by Henry VIII was guilty of high treason. There was no question that Edward's successor was Mary. She was named very clearly in the Act of Succession and in Henry's will. The meeting ended awkwardly and abruptly with the opinion of Chief Justice Montagu that the provisions of the 'Device' could not replace the clauses of the Succession Act.[6]

Montagu and the lawyers were ordered to look at the act, which they did the next day, Tuesday, 13 June. What they read only confirmed their first opinion. It would be treason after Edward's death to execute the provisions of the King's 'Device'. But there was worse news for Edward's councillors. It was also treason to make any plan to alter the succession even before the King died. They were in an impossible position. If the councillors obeyed Edward, they were traitors. If nothing was done about the succession, Mary would inherit the throne. The plain fact was that law and politics were facing Edward's councillors in opposite directions.

Of course the secret caucus persisted: they were hardly going to give up. Montagu was prodded to work quickly to produce the document he had been asked to write. Once again the lawyers were called before the Council. Montagu again made it clear that the 'Device' was treason. Tempers were frayed. Northumberland was furious and called Montagu a traitor for refusing to do what the King had commanded.[7]

Cecil was torn. He knew full well that the next couple of days would either make or break the plan to put Jane on the throne. He knew that his life was in danger. What could he do to satisfy his colleagues and protect himself? If he had ever believed that there would be an easy way to put Jane on the throne, then he understood by now that this would be the hardest test of his political career.

As Secretary Cecil had taken the oath prescribed by the Succession Act which bound him to defend the line of succession as Henry VIII had set it out. He knew exactly what the words of the statute meant and what the law demanded of him. He must have known that Montagu was right, however much he believed in Jane's succession. He was frankly being invited to commit treason.

And so from that Tuesday on he followed the only path open to him. He went with his colleagues but watched his back very carefully. He agreed to obey the King, but on special conditions. He protected himself as best he could but professed conscience before all things. With great care he prepared himself for the trial ahead. He talked to close family and trusted servants. To Sir Anthony Cooke, Nicholas Bacon, Lawrence Eresby and Roger Alford and William Caywood he spoke of his determination to suffer – or that is what he later said with great piety to Mary. At the very least he sought the support of old friends he could trust.[8]

To Bacon, by now the husband of Mildred's sister, Anne, he gave a letter. It survives only as a copy, but it reads very much like one of Cecil's compositions. It was for Mildred. In it he asked her to look after young Thomas Cecil. If she wanted to marry again he hoped she would find a husband of good religion. Above all he wanted Mildred to pray for him. Now he had found just the tone of voice he would use over the coming weeks. Torn between what God and men expected of him, he would obey God. He would suffer for conscience. 'And seeing great perils threatened upon us by the likeness of the time, I do make choice to avoid the peril of God's displeasure.'[9]

Cecil's mind may have been on God and conscience, but he knew well enough that events at Greenwich were moving quickly. The next day, Wednesday, 14 June, Chief Justice Montagu and his colleagues were again commanded by the Council to be at court the following day. On Thursday they met the Council at one o'clock.

This was the most important meeting so far. The lawyers were led to a room behind the dining chamber. As they walked in, the King's councillors stared at them. It was a cold, frosty, difficult meeting. Montagu and his colleagues were now expected to do their duty, to make things easy, to come up with the right answers, to give the King what he wanted.[10]

Edward spoke to Montagu and the lawyers. He must have been weak; but he was also angry. Why had a legal document not been drawn up? Montagu maintained his position. Any plan to alter the succession, he said, would be of no force once the King was dead. The Act of Succession held. The only way to untie the knot was to have a new act of parliament to put the King's wishes into law. Edward replied that he was minded to have a parliament shortly. Montagu, seizing on this, suggested that it would be much better to wait for parliament. A new act would solve the problem, 'all dangers and perils saved'. Edward disagreed: the 'Device' should be put into action now, he said. The new order of succession could be ratified by parliament when it met.

Montagu really had no choice. In the end he gave in. At last he agreed to obey the King's commandment to write the legal document Edward needed to alter the line of succession. But he wanted from the King a licence under the Great Seal to do this and a general pardon for all the lawyers involved. In other words, Montagu wanted clear evidence that Edward had formally instructed him to draw up the 'Book'; he also wanted protection from any charge of treason.

We have to imagine Cecil trying to make sense of all this. In that room in Greenwich Palace were the most powerful men in the kingdom. Some of them were strong supporters of the plan, others probably were not. Many must have been plain frightened, thinking of ways to avoid making a commitment. Cecil was somewhere in the middle. Perhaps he was happy to be led by the others. He wanted to do the right thing – but he had his conscience to take into account. Years later Roger Alford remembered that Cecil had complained about the way Montagu and the judges had just crumbled before the Council. But actually Montagu had given the lead for a practical man with a sensitive conscience: obey the King, certainly, but first buy the necessary protection.

There was now no legal objection to Edward's 'Device' – or rather there were no lawyers who were brave enough to tell the King that he could not have what he wanted. Cecil carefully followed his conscience. He told John Cheke and William Petre that he was determined to stand against the plan, or so he later said to Mary. Others knew too; he hoped in fact that because his objections were known he would not be called on to consent to the legal document now being drawn up by Montagu. But here we can choose to believe Cecil only if we want to.[11]

Within probably a day or two of that critical meeting between the King and his councillors and lawyers on 15 June, a statement of common intent was produced. It bound the King's councillors and judges to subscribe to Edward's 'earnest desire and express commandment touching the limitation of the succession in the imperial crown of this realm'. Each man who put his signature to the text promised not to 'vary from this agreement or any part thereof', under threat of 'most sharp punishment'.[12]

At a meeting of the Council on 16 or 17 June Cecil was at last invited to sign the statement. If we believe Cecil and Alford, he refused. The King asked to see him. He was offered the perfect way out. He agreed to put his hand to the document. He did this, not as any kind of supporter of Jane's claim, but merely as a witness of what Edward wanted to have set down on paper. It was indeed convenient that like every other councillor he could sign a document that turned the English succession upside down but preserve intact his delicate conscience.[13]

Twenty-three others signed the common agreement, councillors and lawyers. The King applied his sign manual. The thing was done. There was really nothing Cecil could now do. If Edward died before September, when parliament would meet to pass a new act of succession, Cecil must have known that he had committed treason. He and his colleagues could now only hope that after Edward's death Jane and her Council would be able to hold on to power. It may have helped his conscience to believe that he was merely a witness of these actions rather than an active perpetrator of them, but in practice this was a meaningless distinction. He was as much a supporter of Edward and his 'Device' as anyone else.[14]

By 21 June Montagu's letters patent for the limitation of the succession were ready. The document said everything Edward had wanted to say for weeks. Mary would be disinherited, the crown would go to Jane. Cecil signed it. He and his colleagues could now only wait.[15]

*

King Edward VI died on Thursday, 6 July 1553 between eight and nine o'clock at night. The hope was that his death could be kept secret for a few days, but it was not to be. From this time on the councillors of the King, now members of Jane's government, had to stick to the commitment they had made to one another in June.

The first to hear of the King's death, officially but confidentially, were the Lord Mayor of London and some of his colleagues who were summoned to Greenwich on the afternoon of Saturday, 8 July. They were told about the King's letters patent for the succession. The Mayor and the others added their signatures to the document and were sworn to secrecy. But there had been a leak and the news was out. The next day Princess Mary wrote to the Council from her manor of Kenninghall in Norfolk, asserting her right to the throne. Mary showed herself ready to claim the crown. The battle of wills had begun.[16]

On Sunday, 9 July Edward's old councillors swore their oaths to Queen Jane. By the 10th Jane's Council was at the Tower of London, the customary place of retreat and protection on the accession of a new monarch. At three o'clock that afternoon Jane arrived at the Tower by water from Greenwich. Two hours later she was proclaimed queen by the sheriff of London and the royal heralds. Jane's councillors then put their minds to answering Mary's letter.

They defended Jane's title as just and right and told Mary that she was 'justly made illegitimate, and uninheritable to the crown imperial of this realm'. Cecil claimed he refused to write the letter. Instead the job fell to Sir John Cheke, Cecil's brother-in-law, sworn a councillor in early June and now a third royal Secretary. But certainly Cecil signed the letter.[17]

Cecil began now to play a subtle game. He stood with his colleagues at the Tower. He had sworn the oath to Jane as queen. But, doubtless for reasons of conscience, he refused to do any of the new government's administrative work. This is what he later said to Mary, and it seems to be supported by the papers he kept in his archive – though what he destroyed we shall never know. Already he had refused to draft the proclamation of Jane as queen. Ever keen to protect himself, he suggested that it should be done by Attorney-General Hales or by his good friend Solicitor-General Gosnold. It ended up as the work of Sir John Throckmorton. When Jane's Council arrived at the Tower, Cecil would not write a circular letter to the military lieutenants of the counties because he knew that if he did this he would incriminate himself. And so indeed he would have done: the letter referred to 'the fained and untrue claim of the Lady Mary, bastard daughter' of Henry VIII. The Duke of Northumberland wrote the draft of it himself, in a hurried, almost furious hand.[18]

So Cecil hedged his bets. He also planned to escape from the Tower. In the week before Edward's death he had given instructions to one of his servants in Lincolnshire, Richard Troughton, to come to him when he sent word. Cecil wanted an easy escape route from London to Stamford. Alford found two safe houses, the house of Nelson near the River Thames at Aveley and Alford's mother's house in London. Alford also gathered together blank passports that had already been signed by members of the Council, which would help their escape.

Cecil was worried about his son, Thomas. Once in the Tower Alford advised William to protect Thomas Cecil's inheritance. Cecil took advice from three friends, all lawyers. John Walpole and Gilbert Gerrard, both of Gray's Inn, gave him their opinions; John Gosnold, the Solicitor-General, counselled against giving property to Thomas, 'saying it would be construed as a thing done of a set will in you'.[19]

Cecil doubtless saw very early on that Jane's new government was deeply unstable. For all the bluff and bluster of the Council's letter to Mary, the common agreement of June and even the King's letters patent were worthless. Jane's men had good reason to be terrified, particularly now that Mary was determined to claim the throne. Cecil later said to Mary that he sabotaged Jane's government, wrecking it from the inside. We can choose to believe him or not. But if Jane's regime looked shaky, then why should we not think that Cecil, ready to run for his life, was happy to give it a push?

What follows is pure Cecil: it is his story. He went about to recruit supporters. First of all he talked to his friend and colleague Sir William Petre. Others had to be approached more carefully. He began with Lord Treasurer Winchester, who was sympathetic. Through Winchester Cecil tried to win the support of the Earl of Bedford. Bedford was the key to the West Country. The big plan was for the earl's eldest son, Lord Francis Russell, to deliver Windsor Castle to Mary. Cecil carried with him a letter of credit written by the Marquess of Winchester addressed to Winchester's son, Lord St John, just in case what Cecil called 'the enterprise' of Windsor Castle should fail. In these secret dealings Cecil went under the name of Harding.

Cecil's conspiracy grew: first Winchester and the Russells, then the Earl of Arundel and Lord Darcy. Arundel, it seems, was a supporter; Darcy heard Cecil's plan with 'good contentation'. All this was good news, and Cecil shared it with Petre 'for both our comforts'.[20]

But if all this happened as Cecil said it did, there was in the end no time to put the plan into action. The new government was crumbling too quickly – quite possibly, of course, because of Cecil's secret briefings. In the nine days between Jane's arrival at the Tower and the proclamation of Mary as queen, the cause looked ever more hopeless.

Mary had stood up to Jane's government with an energy that surprised everybody. Northumberland had to go off to fight her in East Anglia. He was not at the Tower to keep an eye on his colleagues and this probably helped to hasten the collapse of the regime. Northumberland was not popular with the people. The day he left London, Thursday, 13 July, a book appeared that called him the 'great devil, Dudley'. Sound Protestants, just as much as Catholics, were deeply offended by the disinheritance of Mary: Henry VIII's law carried some weight. At a time when Northumberland and the other members of Jane's government needed all the support they could get, this was not a good sign.

Formerly loyal colleagues must have been horribly worried about whether a government many people thought was being run by the duke could survive. We can only imagine the whispered conversations in the dark corners and private chambers of the Tower, the contents of the hidden letters of credence and the secret plans of betrayal that occupied Jane's councillors that week. On the evening of 16 July there was a panic that the Marquess of Winchester had left the Tower to go to his house. The keys to the Tower were taken to Queen Jane, but all was well. At midnight Winchester was brought back to the Tower. The uncertainty and the suspicions about loyalty destroyed the morale of Jane's councillors.[21]

Support for Jane and the government established in her name slowly corroded. Failure was all but inevitable, unless of course Northumberland, the experienced soldier, beat Mary in the field. So there had to be a way out. Cecil wanted another route of escape. If Winchester, Arundel and the others decided in the end not to support Cecil's plan – if he was left without a friend – he would go to Mary. He told Petre about this. Cecil had horses ready at Lambeth to take him into East Anglia although he did not know how to get to Mary. But his friend John Gosnold knew the way, and offered to take Cecil to the Princess. There were also Alford's safe houses in London and Essex and the arrangement with Richard Troughton. Alford's cache of blank passports was ready, and Cecil had money and servants who would move on his word. There were ways of escape if he needed them.[22]

Timing was everything. There was no need for Cecil to run for the sake of it. Support for the cause was dying; Jane's government looked as if it would collapse in on itself. Cecil had to be able to predict when that would happen. And he had to be able to judge whether it was better to stay or to go. If he went, would Jane's government be able to catch him and hold him to the common engagement he had signed back in June? How could he convince Mary of his loyalty? Would it look better in the end to have stayed in London or to have cut his ties with Jane? He had allies: Winchester, Bedford, Arundel, Darcy, all powerful men. His most trusted friends were Petre, Cheke and Gosnold. But the escape to Stamford he had planned was for just himself and a few servants. He was probably more alone than he had ever been in his life. And his life depended on the judgement he was about to make.

After five days at the Tower Cecil decided to run. We can be fairly sure that he came to this decision over the weekend of 15 and 16 July. Richard Troughton had heard nothing from his master on Friday, 14 July. But by Monday, the 17th he had, and the next day he was travelling down Ermine Street to Huntingdon to meet Cecil. Given that it took about two days for news from London to reach Lincolnshire, the message must have arrived over the weekend. Troughton's instructions were to meet Cecil at Royston, in Hertfordshire, at noon on Wednesday, 19 July. The message was probably very short. In it Cecil said nothing about whether he was now for or against Jane. Troughton set out with two men and some horses.

Cecil's planned route of escape was simple. It was the shortest and straightest road back home to Stamford. It would have taken him up through the post towns of Ware, Royston, Huntingdon and Stilton to Burghley. But in the end he did not run. Troughton was at Royston, as arranged, at noon on the 19th. Cecil did not arrive: instead he sent Bernard Martyn, a servant, to tell Troughton that their master would not be coming, but that all was well. Quite possibly Martyn had set out from London at first light on a long summer's day. So though we know that Cecil had decided to leave the Tower probably on the Saturday, he had revised his judgement and changed his plans by late on Tuesday, or perhaps in the very small hours of Wednesday morning.[23]

On Wednesday, 19 July it was better for Cecil to be in London than on the road back to Burghley. He realised the game was over and that Jane's government was about to fall. He must have had some faith in Mary and her forgiveness. Or perhaps he knew that there was nothing more he could do: the best thing was to stay where he was and make the best of his situation.

Cecil was right about the end of Jane's government. On Tuesday, 18 July, probably the day he decided not to run, it was very near. Jane the Queen still ruled on Wednesday morning. Her Council even wrote a letter to Lord Rich in Essex asking him to 'remain in that promise and steadfastness to our sovereign lady Queen Jane's service'. It was a letter Cecil did not sign, and those who did must have regretted it. Hours later Jane's Council gave up.[24]

At nine o'clock in the evening they proclaimed Mary Queen. Cecil and the rest of Jane's councillors, now Queen Mary's obedient subjects, removed themselves to Baynard's Castle, the residence of the Earl of Pembroke. The Earl of Arundel was heard to say that he did not like the air at the Tower.[25]

For the councillors to leave their fortress was symbolic: there was simply nothing left to defend. Symbolic too was the journey Arundel and Lord Paget set out on that day. They went to East Anglia to meet Queen Mary, and they carried with them a letter in which the councillors most humbly beseeched her to pardon and remit their 'former infirmities'. A letter was also sent to the Duke of Northumberland, by then in Cambridge, commanding him to disarm, which Cecil signed. All in all it was a spectacular about-face.[26]

So Jane's government fell away. Mary heard the news at Framlingham Castle at about seven o'clock on the evening of Thursday, 20 July. Only three hours earlier she had inspected her army, mustered to fight Northumberland. Now there began a trickle of visitors to the Queen. The Earl of Oxford, Lord Rich, and Edward, Lord Clinton all arrived on 20 July. And so, perhaps within a day or two, did Roger Alford. Cecil sent Alford into East Anglia a little before he himself set off from London with Nicholas Bacon.

It was clever of Cecil to send Alford to the court of the new Queen. Alford was able to dismiss all kinds of rumours, one (which was perfectly true) that Cecil had ordered armed horsemen against her. Alford 'laughed and told her the matter': yes, the horses had been sent, but Cecil had countermanded the orders the next day.

It was useful too for Cecil to have a kinswoman close to Mary. She was Anne Bacon, the wife of Nicholas, one of Mary's ladies-in-waiting. Anne and Mary talked about Cecil. Alford remembered that the Queen had told Anne she thought very well of her brother Cecil and believed him to be an honest man. This was all well and good. But how Cecil navigated these difficult first days of Mary's reign meant everything. He had to have a plan.[27]

Cecil and his brother-in-law Bacon arrived at Mary's court probably on the day she left Framlingham for Ipswich. Cecil was free, at least for the time being. On 25 July the Earl of Arundel escorted Northumberland, his sons and others to the Tower. Friends and colleagues followed: the Marquess of Northampton, Lord Guildford Dudley, Jane's father the Duke of Suffolk, Chief Justice Montagu, and Sir John Cheke. Could Cecil now convince Mary that he was not a traitor?[28]

*

It was nearly a week before Cecil could make his peace with Mary, to explain to her how she could forgive him for anything he had apparently done against her interest. He had to convince her of his innocence; of his principled opposition to the plan to put Jane on the throne; of his careful sabotage of Jane's government. Mary's court moved closer to London, from Ipswich to Colchester and the palace of Newhall in Essex, and then, on Monday, 31 July 1553, to Sir William Petre's house, Ingatestone Hall, for a night. Cecil spent these days thinking about how to defend himself.

At some time between Wednesday, 26 July and Sunday, 30 July Cecil 'exhibited' a defence of his actions to the Queen. It was his great apologia. These were the most important words of his life, and we can imagine that he spent hours crafting them. After his meeting with the Queen, Alford wrote a minute of the submission, a record of the audience. Cecil made his own copy which went into the Privy Council's archive. Ever the careful Secretary, he wanted his private actions set down and preserved in a public record. If he had destroyed any incriminating papers, which quite possibly he had done, he wanted his official narrative to be kept by the new government.[29]

Cecil submitted himself to the Queen 'with all lowliness that any heart can conceive'. His paper ends with a paragraph that perhaps was spoken to Mary much as it was written down after Cecil's audience. The lines must have been carefully rehearsed, the emphases and accents put in all the right places. Cecil beseeched Mary that he might 'feel some difference from others that have more plainly offended and yet be partakers of her highness's bountifulness and grace'. Others were guilty: he was an innocent man and a loyal subject.

Mary must have believed him – or at least she then saw no point in throwing him in prison. Perhaps she really did think he was an honest man.

At Ingatestone Hall on 31 July Cecil kissed the Queen's hand. He was the first member of Edward's old Council to do so. It was a simple act, but it meant everything. William Cecil had survived the reigns of Edward and of Jane.[30]

So in June and July 1553 Sir William Cecil acted according to his conscience, and his conscience brought him at last to a place of safety. He was untainted by disloyalty. He merely witnessed the will of Edward VI in determining the line of royal succession. When he was in the Tower he did his duty by sabotaging Jane's government. He refused to stain his pristine conscience by writing letters for a bogus regime. Or so Cecil wanted everyone to believe.

The truth is more complicated. Cecil stayed with Jane's government until he could see that it was crumbling. He stood with his colleagues in the Tower but wrote and signed as few of the new government's documents as he could. He appears to have been quite happy to volunteer friends to write papers instead. In all likelihood he believed that he was doing the right thing: so long as everything was properly reconciled with his conscience, all was well. He believed in the power of words to make things right. Above all, he believed in himself.

These six or so weeks had been the most testing of Cecil's entire life. He had survived. And doubtless he had learned lessons about politics. Legitimacy, or at least the perception of legitimacy, was everything; and legitimacy to Cecil and his colleagues meant parliament. This was something he would remember for the rest of his career.

Cecil's delicate conscience would have been easy enough with Jane Grey on the throne. If Jane's government had been able to stand up for itself, or more dramatically if Northumberland had actually defeated Mary in battle, surely Cecil would have been happy to say that he had been a witness of Edward VI's resolve to hand the crown to Lady Jane. He would have had a kinswoman on the throne; the Queen and her father would have called him cousin; who knows what honours and offices would have been his? But it was probably obvious early on that the pact Edward's councillors had signed would break. Cecil was very good at reading people; he knew, no doubt, that their hearts were not in it, however much godly Jane was a worthy successor to King Edward.

So by the last day of July it suited him to say what by then he may have truly believed: he had been a reluctant witness, merely a bystander invited to act against his conscience to break the law. He had never actually written that

Mary was a bastard. He had not taken arms against the monarch. He was a loyal subject. And, he may have reflected privately, he liked to back winners. That terrible summer of 1553 was the making of Cecil's political career. He had shown that he was a survivor. His political antennae, his instincts, were superb; self-belief, careful preparation, and a quiet ruthlessness helped to save him from prison or the executioner's block. He would not now be out in the cold in Mary's reign. He was not one of her trusted supporters; but his family, his property and his reputation were safe, and he knew some very powerful people.

Five years in the future his conduct in 1553 would recommend him to the young Elizabeth Tudor. This is one of the oddities of his relationship with Elizabeth. In 1553 Cecil had helped to disinherit her as well as Mary. To outsiders who followed the official line, Cecil had put law and dynasty before political or family self-interest, even before religion. He had shown that he had the qualities of a trusted royal Secretary.

But so far as Cecil knew, Mary would reign for years, and the fact of her rule must have been much on his mind when he returned to London with the new court and Nicholas Bacon in early August 1553. Who could tell what kind of life he would lead from now on?

6

'Some Fruit Made of an Evil Time'

William Cecil came close to treason in the summer of 1553. He had survived by his wits. He had an instinct for survival. He could exercise exceptionally fine judgement. He was able above all to watch his own back. These talents made him the most powerful man in Elizabethan England. But if we imagine for one moment that he decided to hide away in Mary's reign we would be mistaken. Cecil was determined to prosper.

We find two William Cecils in Mary's reign: one is a secret critic of the Queen and her government; the other is a loyal subject who is happy to live with a Catholic monarch. The passionate believer in the Edwardian project conformed. He did not make a heroic stand against the Catholic enemy. He lived comfortably with his family close to the royal court. But of course, ever subtle, he kept his options open. Cecil's story in Mary's reign, which has never been told fully before, reveals to us much about the man who would go on to serve Elizabeth with energy and passion.

*

In August 1553 Cecil travelled from Essex to London with Mary's court. He was instructed to tie up some loose ends of business for the new government. This was a transition time. Cecil, out of a job, had to hand his duties to new men. Mary entered London on 4 August at Aldgate, where she was met by her sister Princess Elizabeth. Three days later Cecil was at Sir Nicholas Bacon's house on Thames Street. It was probably there that he prepared himself for the funeral the next day of his king and former master.[1]

King Edward VI was buried at last on 8 August in Westminster Abbey. The funeral procession moved slowly through streets lined with people weeping for their dead king. Edward's coffin was carried on a chariot pulled by seven horses and covered with cloth of gold. There was an effigy of the dead king as he had been in life, full and complete in his royal powers, wearing a crown imperial of fine gold and a great collar, holding a sceptre, and bearing the ribbon of the Order of the Garter round his leg. Over the chariot was a canopy of blue velvet. The royal heralds carried Edward's armour.

King Edward's servants processed that day in the offices and ranks they had held during their master's life. Cecil was Master Secretary once again, allowed ten yards of cloth at the expense of the royal Exchequer, and some more for eight of his household servants who were to accompany him. With Cecil were Sir William Petre and Sir John Cheke, old friends and colleagues. Also in this great procession was William's father-in-law Sir Anthony Cooke, formerly a gentleman of the King's Privy Chamber. It had the flavour of a last reunion before difficult partings.[2]

Edward VI's funeral was the symbolic end to his reign, the public passing over of his majesty and authority to his sister Mary. The King was dead: long live the Queen. Like the effigy of Edward Tudor as a monarch still living and powerful, the procession of his royal officers on 8 August was a stylised fiction. For Cecil office and authority had vanished. Tentatively he began to adjust to the new ways.

If Cecil hid it was in plain sight. Archbishop Cranmer saw him at Richmond Palace in early August but did not dare speak to him. Cheke was under suspicion and Lord Francis Russell was in trouble too – or so Cranmer had heard. The archbishop felt utterly alone and under suspicion. His nerves probably were not helped by the treason trials of the Duke of Northumberland and other supporters of Queen Jane that were heard at Westminster over the next few days.[3]

There was no job for Cecil in the new government. He probably had not expected one. Still, he had been quick enough to make his peace with Mary and to show his loyalty and obedience. He had many friends still in high places; and his sister-in-law Anne, Sir Nicholas Bacon's wife, was in the Queen's service at court. Also Cecil had received the royal pardon customary before a monarch's coronation. If he was out of office he was also safe, and that, for the time being, was the most important thing.

But Cecil had a secret. On land he owned in the tiny Lincolnshire village of Barholm, five miles from Stamford, a printer called John Day set up a press in the early months of the new reign. Day had been one of the great printers of the Edwardian years, close to the government and a firm Protestant. As a prosperous businessman with a print shop near St Paul's Cathedral he had worked with another printer called William Seres. Seres was a member of Cecil's household. The reason Day was now printing in Lincolnshire rather than in bustling London was simple: he had gone underground.[4]

Day worked to print books against Mary. The first one appeared on the day of the Queen's coronation. Its target was Stephen Gardiner. When it came to

Day's activities, Cecil probably worked on the principle of plausible deniability: he was neither Day's boss nor his editor. There were only two connections of real substance between Day's secret press and Sir William Cecil. The first was the land on which John Day printed. The second is that William Cooke, Lady Mildred's brother, who wore the livery of the Cecil household, played some part in Day's work underground.[5] And for a time Day printed with impunity. But his luck would not last for ever.

While John Day poked and prodded at Mary's government, Cecil and his family and most of his servants lived at the parsonage in Wimbledon. The eldest members of the family were Cecil, Lady Mildred, her sister, Elizabeth, and Cecil's sister, Margaret. There were three boys in the house: Thomas Cecil, by now eleven years old; John Stanhope, about thirteen, who was one of Mildred's relations; and Arthur Hall, Cecil's ward, who was much the same age as Stanhope.[6]

The family's first Christmas of the new reign was made comfortable by the well-stocked kitchens and store rooms of the parsonage. Cecil carefully wrote out what he called his 'diet', and it was the job of his cook, James Unswick, to prepare the family's meals. They ate beef and other roasted and boiled meats, wildfowl and small birds like larks. There were lots of other dishes on the table: pigeon, rabbit, duck, oysters, salads, eggs and fresh fish from the market. Malmsey, sack, other white and red wines and claret were stored away in the cellars. James Unswick could flavour the meals with figs and raisins, sugar, nutmeg and liquorice. All of these provisions were brought to Wimbledon by two other servants, George Williams and William Haddon, who supervised their delivery by boat from the warehouses and wharves of London.[7]

Cecil continued to keep a large household. Even out of office the number of his servants grew. He was still an important gentleman. His priest, Henry Watkyns, had been recruited at Easter 1553. His steward was William Cayworth, who had overall responsibility for the smooth running of the household. Roger Alford remained Cecil's secretary; George Burden of Cambridge taught the boys of the house; and Henry Stephenson looked after Cecil's chamber, as he had done since about 1549. Lady Mildred, her sister and her sister-in-law were attended to by Margaret Browne, Agnes Short, Margaret White and another woman known as Elizabeth.[8]

Cecil was very much a metropolitan gentleman in Mary's reign. He and his family divided their time between Wimbledon and Westminster. But Cecil still had strong ties to the country round Stamford and Burghley. By now he had an impressive portfolio of property. He knew every acre he owned and every penny of rent he got from them. For a gentleman like Cecil, land was everything.

The most senior of his agents at Burghley was John Abraham. Abraham had once been the priest of Sir David Philip's chantry in Stamford. Philip, who had died years before Cecil was born, was godfather and mentor of Cecil's grandfather, David. Abraham lost his position when the chantries were suppressed in 1548; and so in Mary's reign, in a kind of tribute to the memory of Sir David Philip and David Cecil, generations long gone, Abraham served David's grandson, keeping a close eye on Burghley House and reporting regularly to Cecil on his lands and estates.[9]

William Cecil carried on the traditions of his family in Lincolnshire and Northamptonshire. This meant that he could serve Elizabeth Tudor. Here we can begin to see something of Cecil's relationship with Queen Mary's heir. Princess Elizabeth owned lands near Stamford that had once belonged to her great-grandmother, Lady Margaret Beaufort. She had known Cecil since 1549 when he was Protector Somerset's Secretary. A year later she had appointed him the surveyor of her lands. In Mary's reign, for the modest fee of £20 a year, Cecil still advised her on matters to do with property and acted as the steward and constable of some of her estates near to his house at Burghley. This was a good way for Cecil to stay close to Elizabeth without appearing to live in her pocket: it was the perfect business arrangement.[10]

The blunt fact was that any association with Elizabeth in Mary's reign was risky. Mary considered her sister the greatest threat to the security of her realm. Her fears were confirmed, it seemed, when early in 1554 there was an armed uprising in support of Elizabeth's claim to the throne. It was a close-run thing: the forces of Sir Thomas Wyatt, one of the conspirators, came near to defeating Mary's troops on the streets of Westminster, not so far from Cannon Row.

There is nothing even to hint that Cecil had anything to do with the rebellion. It would be remarkable if there was, given how strenuously he had declared his loyalty to Mary in the febrile days of summer 1553. The nearest he ever came to making a political statement came in fact from John Day's press in Barholm. It was a book about Lady Jane Dudley that gave an account of her death and cast her as a Protestant heroine. Yet really everything about Cecil's life in the early months of Mary's reign suggested that in his affairs with the new regime he favoured the path of least resistance. He had nothing to hide from the royal government, or so he would have said. He lived much as any other important and prosperous gentlemen would have done.

Yet, subtle and careful as ever, Cecil was able to maintain a delicate balance in his affairs. If he kept in touch with Elizabeth Tudor it was through her man Thomas Parry, whose name comes up every so often in Cecil's household accounts; but he stayed far enough away from the princess and her household to avoid suspicion.

In the months and years that followed there is no evidence of Cecil's attending Elizabeth in person, except just once: and that visit was in 1558, only a few months before Elizabeth became queen. Incredibly, it is a meeting no one has noticed in 450 years.

*

If Cecil was content to live with his family in Surrey and Westminster, the steady course of his conformity did not suit everyone, even close friends and relations. By the spring of 1554 some of them had left Mary's England. On 14 April Sir John Cheke, freed at last from the Tower and travelling with the Queen's licence, arrived in Strasburg with Sir Anthony Cooke. Nine days later, even with hundreds of miles between them, money still changed hands between Cooke and his son-in-law Cecil. The sum was £14 10s., paid by Cecil for two of Sir Anthony's silver pots. Though in touch with each other by letter, the lives of Cecil and his friends went off in different directions.[11]

But Cecil was not the only one of Edward VI's old servants to remain in England. Sir Nicholas and Lady Anne Bacon often stayed at their house on Thames Street in London and Sir Nicholas was busy at Gray's Inn. Richard Goodrich, lawyer and close friend of the family, lived at the Whitefriars. Sir Anthony Cooke's son, Richard, and his daughter, Elizabeth, by now lived with Sir William and Lady Mildred. Roger Ascham, Cecil's old friend from Cambridge, even entered Queen Mary's service as her Latin secretary.

So journeying abroad was by no means the only choice for old evangelicals from Edward's reign. Cecil was a practical man not given to acts of self-immolation. He had fought hard to convince Mary of his innocence and loyalty to her as queen. There was no obvious need for him to go abroad, and few good reasons for him to leave behind his estates and his livelihood. What would have been the point of throwing away everything when there was no need to? Others, it seems, felt the same way. But the fact is that as early as spring 1554 Cecil was beginning to reconcile himself to Mary's rule. His conformity was incremental, coming upon him a little at a time.

There was no doubt that the days of Edward VI were long over. In May there was a Mass at Westminster offered for the souls of Henry VII and his Queen Elizabeth, for Henry VIII and Katherine of Aragon, and even for Edward. Prayers for the dead had made their return: Edward's reign might never have happened.

There was also a new international alliance to get used to. Mary proposed to marry Philip of Spain, and that summer Philip arrived in London with his retinue. Cecil, the young gentleman of rank and connection, was called on to act as a host. Gonzalo Pérez, one of Philip's secretaries, lodged with him, probably at Cannon Row. It was a wonderful match: Pérez, in his middle fifties, the experienced secretary to one of the most powerful men in Europe, and Cecil sometime agent to Protector Somerset and Secretary of Edward VI. It would be fascinating to know what they talked about, and particularly what Cecil learned of Philip of Spain, later the Most Christian King who would be one of Elizabeth I's great enemies.[12]

So it is clear already that for Cecil these were not years of retreat. He lived at Wimbledon and in Westminster much as he had done before 1553. Life in a bustling household went on. He made provisions for the future by looking to the education of his heir, Thomas, and in September 1554 he engaged Gabriel Goodman, a fellow of Christ's College, Cambridge, as schoolmaster. Cecil presided over a scholarly household. He bought lots of books for his library. He always employed bright young men like Goodman. And then there were the highly educated women of the house, Lady Mildred and her sister Elizabeth. Roger Ascham wrote that Cecil always found time to talk 'most gladly of some matter of learning: wherein, he will courteously hear the mind of the meanest at his table'.[13]

Still, there is just a sense that he missed politics, the buzz of life at court and the excitement of power. All the energy that had once gone into serving Edward VI had to go somewhere. For these years we have a scribbling book kept by Cecil called 'Notes of divers kinds' in which he recorded provisions for the household, the contents of his wardrobe, even the weights of all his family and servants. He became an obsessive collector of facts and data. It is from the book that we happen to know that in 1555 he weighed 136lb. or just over nine and a half stones. By today's standards he was a slight man. But politically he carried a good deal more weight.[14]

Politics had a magnetic attraction for Cecil: the pull of the court was hard to resist. By the autumn of 1554 Cecil had given in to it, if indeed he had put up any resistance at all. In late October Henry Stephenson, the keeper of Cecil's chamber, was busy buying 'the necessaries' for a journey across the English Channel that his master had been recruited to make a few weeks before.[15] It was to be one of the great symbolic moments of Mary's years as queen. For Cecil, servant to the evangelical King Edward, the irony would have been hard to miss. Cecil was chosen to be one of a party sent to Brussels to meet Cardinal Reginald Pole and escort him back to England.

Reginald Pole stood for everything Cecil had helped to destroy in Edward's reign. For years a passionate opponent of the break with Rome, in 1554 Pole was on a mission to absolve England of the terrible sin of schism. If we believe in simple characters and straightforward motives then we might think that Pole and Cecil hated each other. They did not. Over the course of Mary's reign they became friends and often dined together. Pole possessed a spirit of enquiry. He was a reformer in the Church and, like Cecil, a natural scholar. It was a peculiar and important association between two men who were not as different as they appeared on the surface.

There was another reason why, in the autumn of 1554, Cecil felt he should go across the Channel to meet Pole. He had to make a conspicuous show of loyalty to Mary's government. In the middle of October John Day, who for months had been printing secretly in Lincolnshire, was arrested in Norfolk and brought back to the Tower of London. It would not have taken his interrogators very long to make the connection between Day and Cecil. Day was not punished very severely for his offence and Cecil was not disciplined at all. But now Cecil had to show his loyalty and so he went to Brussels.

Cecil took with him his keen brain and sharp eyes. There is no evidence that he played an active part in the mission, but the visit to Brussels meant that he could take a sounding of international politics. Mary's ambassadors had an audience with Philip of Spain's father, the Holy Roman Emperor Charles V. The Emperor thanked God for his daughter-in-law, Mary, and for the hope of succession: Mary, by now Philip of Spain's wife, was pregnant. Pole returned to England with the party. They were at Dover on 20 November. Two days later the Cardinal was received at Whitehall Palace by Mary and Philip in a mood of great celebration. On 28 November Pole addressed parliament. On St Andrew's Day, 30 November, he finally and definitively reconciled England to the papacy. The realm was once again part of the Church of Rome.

There were rumours at this time that Cecil was going to take a job in government. There were signs of his growing cosiness with the regime. Sir Thomas Pope, one of Mary's privy councillors, gave Cecil a very expensive new year's gift in gold. Cecil rewarded Pope's servant with six silver Spanish rials. On 1 January 1555 Cecil sent his own gift of gold to the Queen.[16]

For all his skills and talents, Sir William Cecil was not clairvoyant. He had no way to tell how long Mary's reign would last. We have the luxury of perspective: Cecil of course did not. He was the most naturally gifted and able young politician of his day. Keeping a careful record of the provisions in his kitchens or the weights of his household servants was a waste of his energies.

Mary could have lived for thirty more years. By now she was pregnant. The Catholic Church in England was being built again. England was tied to the Spanish Habsburgs. We are used to the great old Protestant narrative of English history which has Mary's reign as a monstrous aberration. For Cecil, in 1555, there was no triumph of Tudor Protestantism. It may have depressed him that in the history of his country the break with Rome and the reign of godly Edward VI looked like horrible anomalies, a decade and a half of schism and heresy, healed by Pole's return to England. But Cecil was a pragmatist, whatever he believed privately. When he sent his gift to the Queen he probably imagined that the future lay with Mary and a Tudor line united with Spain.

So Cecil flirted with office. He stayed close to the court. He began to build up credit with powerful men like Cardinal Pole. He was no hero of the resistance against Mary, and he had no intention of throwing himself into the flames of martyrdom.

Life went on. In February 1555 Cecil subscribed, like many of his friends in London, to the company of Merchant Adventurers in their quest for the discovery of unknown lands. He also invested £15 in the Muscovy Company, the 'Society of Adventurers of Russia'. In these months of Mary's pregnancy, Cecil was out and about in London and Westminster. He did business with his old colleague, Lord Paget. He was at Cannon Row on Lady Day, 25 March. Perhaps he went the short distance to Whitehall Palace to see a colourful tournament of Spanish and English knights. This seemed to capture the optimism of the moment, the King and the Queen with an heir on the way. Yet by now, as Cecil would have known, men and women were being burned for heresy at Smithfield just outside the city walls.[17]

In fact Mary was not pregnant. By late April she had withdrawn into her private rooms at court and only her women were allowed to attend her. She still believed that she was going to have a baby and London buzzed with rumour and speculation. On 30 April the bells of the city rang in celebration of the birth of a prince; the next day the truth was known that there was no baby for the Queen. The child was due in May. Then it was to be June. As the days passed it was surely less likely that Mary was going to have the heir she wanted so desperately. Sir William and Lady Mildred Cecil were near enough to the royal court to be able to read the signs for themselves, and for the Queen those signs were not good.[18]

The doubts about Mary's pregnancy did not dampen Cecil's political ambitions. In May 1555 he went abroad for the second time in Mary's reign. It was a diplomatic mission to a peace conference between the Empire and France, held at the village of La Marque, between Calais and Gravelines.[19] We cannot be sure what Cecil did at the conference. He was not an official ambassador. He may have wanted merely to keep his hand in. He had been a royal Secretary. He was close to two of the English delegates, Lord Paget and Cardinal Pole. His learning and reputation stood in his favour. The oddest travelling companion for Cecil was Stephen Gardiner, his old adversary, now restored to the bishopric of Winchester.

Probably what Cecil really wanted to do was to travel. He had never been on a grand tour abroad. Other than the short mission to Brussels in 1554 he had only ever been to Scotland. So when Cardinal Pole and the other ambassadors set out for home, Cecil and three of his servants parted company with them.

Sir William went into the Low Countries. He saw towns and cities like Louvain, Antwerp, Ypres, Bruges and Lille. He enjoyed himself. At Menin, in Flanders, he wrote an account of how to plant elm, oak and walnut trees: already he was a keen gardener. He also bought canvas, books and hats for the children at Wimbledon.[20]

By late June he was home. In July he prepared for the marriage of his sister, Elizabeth, to Robert Wingfield of Upton in Rutland. Elizabeth's dowry was £66 13s. 4d., which came from her brother's pocket. Cecil was at Burghley on 27 July to handle the money business personally. They married that September. Cecil paid 5s. for a puppet show and hired minstrels to play for the guests, and the musicians received the handsome reward of 20s. The food was prepared in the kitchens at Burghley, where James Unswick was in charge, helped by his assistant Richard and Robert Wingfield's own cook.[21]

Sir William, Lady Mildred and the family stayed at Burghley till the middle of October. On the 15th they set out for Surrey, travelling down the Great North Road through Huntingdon. They were all back at Wimbledon four days later. By this time Cecil had had his writ to sit as MP for Lincolnshire in the forthcoming parliament. Work in the Commons, mainly on bills for agriculture and land reform, kept him busy from the end of October till early December.[22]

Cecil probably knew early on in the parliament that the government wanted to do something about the exiles, people like Sir Anthony Cooke who had chosen to leave England either to tour Italy or to spend time in centres of Protestant learning such as Zurich or Strasburg. A bill was introduced in the House of Lords that threatened to take away the exiles' land. It was known informally as 'the Duchess of Suffolk's bill', a reference to Katherine, Cecil's close friend and the most prominent of all the exiles, who had gone abroad in February 1555.[23]

In early December the bill finally arrived in the Commons for its first reading. It was defeated in extraordinary circumstances. Opponents of the bill barricaded and locked the door of the chamber and forced the Speaker to put it to the vote. Its opponents knew they were in the majority. The exiles bill was defeated.

Cecil was one of the bill's opponents. Of course his opposition was subtle. He was not thrown into the Tower like the leader of the parliamentary *coup*: that was a lesson he had learned a long time before. But he was given a stern warning by two old friends, Lord Paget and Sir William Petre. Petre had not long before received from Cecil a gift of a half haunch of hind, which turned out to be a nicely timed reminder of their friendship. Only Cecil recorded the words he claimed to have said to Paget and Petre. 'Although with danger to myself,' he wrote, 'I spoke my opinion freely and brought upon me some ill will thereby; but it is better to serve God than man.'[24]

Once again we hear the voice of the man of conscience standing up for what is right. The fact is that Cecil was given nothing more than a mild warning. He was a free man, his feathers barely ruffled. On the day parliament ended he travelled by boat from Wimbledon to Cannon Row. In the following days he relaxed by playing cards and seeing the Earl and Countess of Bedford at their house on the Strand. He even lost money at cards: 12*d*. at Mary's court on 15 December, a Monday, and 4*d*. the next day. On the Tuesday he gave a penny in alms to a poor man. In the New Year Sir Thomas Pope, ever generous, gave him a gift of gold coins.[25]

Cecil had no intention of giving up his comfortable metropolitan life. But there was a wrinkle. In the middle of March Queen Mary granted Cardinal Pole the manor of Wimbledon. Cecil may have worried that his family's home, the parsonage, might be taken away from him. With his wife he set out to make sure that it was not.

In February, quite possibly hearing of Mary's intentions, Sir William and Lady Mildred visited the Lord Chancellor, Nicholas Heath. For the following fortnight they stayed close to Wimbledon and Westminster and Lady Mildred made sure that she was seen in all the right places. On 22 March she took a boat to the court at Whitehall; this was the weekend Thomas Cranmer, Cecil's old friend, was burned to death in Oxford. In Westminster the Cecils had other business in hand. Reginald Pole was about to preach the first of his English sermons. On Lady Day, 25 March, Lady Mildred was rowed down the Thames to Three Cranes stairs, from which she went up into the city to the Church of St Mary Arches. For Pole's sermon the church was hung with cloth of gold and rich arras and decorated with cushions. This was a great and grand occasion. And there to hear Pole preach was Sir William Cecil's clever wife.[26]

It was probably no great surprise to Cecil, or perhaps to anyone else, that he was appointed high steward of Cardinal Pole's manor of Wimbledon. On Easter Day, 5 April, the whole family and household received the sacrament of the Mass at Wimbledon and a priest heard their confessions. Cecil paid for everything that was needed for this Mass: wine, bread, wax, tapers, oil and cream, and for the hire of a boat to bring them from London. Days after Cranmer's death in Oxford, it was a public declaration of conformity and obedience. The evangelical revolution of Edward's reign was a mere memory.[27]

*

Older biographers liked to think that Cecil retired to his estates at Burghley. He did not. He stuck close to London and Westminster and enjoyed himself with his family. In the early summer of 1556 he practised archery with fourteen-year-old Thomas Cecil. In the same week Cecil went off to

Wandsworth to visit his barber for a 'polling'. The haircut cost 8*d*., the boat ride there 12*d*. more.[28]

Burghley was not forgotten in these months spent by the River Thames. Cecil was a keen amateur architect and he had plans for the improvement of his father's old house: garret windows in the inner court and a new bay window, with stairs from the base court to the terrace. There was also work to be done on the roof of the great kitchen where less than a year before James Unswick had prepared the feast for Elizabeth Cecil's wedding. Cecil worked out all the details with his mason, Roger Warde, and John Abraham kept a sharp eye on Warde's progress.[29]

It could be hard to prise Cecil from home. Sir Philip Hoby, an old friend from Edward's reign, tried every possible way to get the Cecils to visit his house at Bisham in Berkshire. Hoby's letters to Cecil were always cheerful and teasing. In July 1556 Hoby even offered his coach for Lady Mildred; she was pregnant and Sir Philip guessed this would be Cecil's excuse not to come to see his friends.[30] Mary's reign was a bitter-sweet time for Cecil. Lady Mildred probably saw her husband more often in these years than she did at any other time in their marriage. They met friends, bought clothes and books, played games and went to see plays in London. It was a period of peace in their lives and, with a baby on the way, hope too.

But set against all of this was the politics of religion. Two weeks after Sir Philip Hoby's generous offer to the Cecils of a carriage to take them to Bisham, John Cheke, Cecil's old teacher and brother-in-law, formally recanted his Protestant beliefs. He told the Queen that he was at last 'glad to serve and obey' her laws in religion. He wanted his liberty. He was in the Tower, put there after being arrested by English agents on the continent, tied to a cart and brought back to England. He had done too much abroad to irritate Mary's government. In the Tower he was given the choice to recant or to burn. Cheke chose to recant: he did so before the whole royal court.[31]

Only months earlier, in February 1556, Cheke had written a letter to Cecil about the dangers of conformity. He had been breathtakingly frank. He was 'as glad to hear tell' of Cecil's 'well doing' as he was sorry many times when he heard the contrary. He wanted Cecil to ignore 'the dazed zeal of the ignorant'. He should not deceive himself: 'whatsoever ye know to be evil indeed,' Cheke wrote, 'so judge it and take it always. And let neither your own doings whatsoever, nor common usage nor favour of any friendship carry you away to deceive yourself in error.' 'I would be glad to see some fruit made of an evil time,' he continued, 'if not for the remedy of an outgrown evil, yet for the forwardness of some common good.'

There is something timeless about Cheke's letter. It is the appeal to a good man in evil days: a man who, though still able to stand up for what is right, has been seduced into mistaking bad for good and good for bad. The letter is a passionate entreaty from a man who is trying to understand his own new life as an exile, 'learning', as Cheke put it, 'how to live and imagining by what occupation I shall be able to feed myself'. Cheke, like Cecil, had been an influential man in Edward's reign. Now 'a new living' had replaced 'this old ending of life'. Cheke finished his letter with commendations to Lady Mildred. 'Fare thee well,' he ended, 'and bring up your son in the true fear of God.'[32]

Within months Cheke too had conformed. But his conformity was of a quite different kind to Cecil's. Cheke had been broken: Cecil had adapted. And, while Cheke went off to live in London with his nephew Peter Osborne, Cecil carried on his easy relations with friends and former colleagues. Important lawyers like Sir Roger Cholmley wanted a favour to do with a house Cecil owned in St Paul's Churchyard. The Countess of Bedford asked Cecil to intercede on her behalf with Cardinal Pole. Princess Elizabeth asked, through one of her household officers, for Cecil's advice on some of her Northamptonshire estates.[33]

As ever, life went on. In November Cecil celebrated the baptism of Dr Robert Huick's new baby. Huick was a physician whose patients over the years had included King Edward, Princess Elizabeth and Cecil himself. Cecil also was about to become a father again. A daughter, Anne, was born on 5 December. The baby's godmother was Lady Anne Petre. Her husband Sir William, Mary's Secretary, paid 71s. 6d. for a gift for little Anne. It was a gilt salt, the kind of great salt-cellar that was the centrepiece of any grand Tudor table, and doubtless it was a very fine piece of work by a London craftsman. Sir Philip Hoby wrote with congratulations muted only by the fact that Anne was a girl: 'Of my Lady's daughter (in hope of a son hereafter) I trust ye be now no sorrowful man.' He looked forward to seeing them at Bisham soon enough.[34]

For a time the Cecils stayed close to home. From Cannon Row, on 12 December, Cecil wrote to inform Sir Anthony Cooke of his granddaughter's birth. Lady Mildred was well enough to be out in Westminster by the end of the month. Hoby, never discouraged, invited the Cecils to Bisham. He had heard that Cecil had been as good a nurse to Mildred 'as you would have her to be good nurse to you'. Sir Philip expected Sir John Mason and his wife at Bisham the next day and Lord Paget the day after that, 'to whom as to me you shall be right welcome; but I fear you can make no step hither without the licence of my Lady'.[35]

Instead, the Cecils stayed in London. In early January 1557 they went with their servants in two boats to the Three Cranes stairs, probably to visit the Bacons on Thames Street. They spent the following week at Cannon Row. On 10 January Sir Anthony Cooke wrote from Strasburg to say that he was glad his daughter had been 'well delivered'. A son might have been welcome, he wrote to Cecil, but the birth of Anne gave Sir Anthony 'good hope' that

Mildred would 'increase you with many sons and daughters, though she were not hasty at the beginning'. He had no news from Strasburg other than that he had been 'very ill troubled with a colic'.[36]

By late January the Cecils were back in Westminster society. They went to see a play in London. Lady Mildred travelled regularly to court. Cecil visited Cardinal Pole at Lambeth Palace and met a foreign ambassador at Suffolk Place on the Strand. He dined with Pole on 21 January.

For the next fortnight Sir William and Lady Mildred hardly stayed still. They visited the Lord Mayor of London. Mildred went to the court at Greenwich. Her husband took boats to Lambeth and to the Whitefriars, perhaps to visit his good friend Richard Goodrich. By the end of February Cecil had been to Kew, Mortlake and Cannon Row; he had bought a book at the Temple Bar; he had been to Syon Palace; and he had visited the Duchess of Somerset, the widow of his old master Protector Somerset. That same month Cecil also supervised the conveyance of property between the Earl of Rutland and Sir Philip Hoby. This of course came with an invitation to Bisham by Hoby. 'It were much better to come abroad,' Sir Philip wrote, 'and not to tarry so long with my Lady, and in such a stinking city, the filthiest of the world.'[37]

In early March, still in the cold of winter, Cecil did actually leave London. He went to Essex for the christening of the baby son of Lord John Grey. Grey was a kinsman: his daughter had married Lady Mildred's brother, William Cooke. Lord John was the uncle of Lady Jane Dudley, and at this time in Mary's reign he was exceptionally lucky to be alive. Grey had been tangled up in the Wyatt rebellion of 1554 and was saved from the block only by the petitions of his wife. By early 1557 the Greys were living in comfortable retreat at Walden. Lord John invited Cecil to be godfather to his 'jolly boy'; he was 'half ashamed' at the invitation, 'considering the distance of the way with the coldness of the weather'. But still Cecil went. On 1 March he met another of Lord John's cousins, Thomas Wotton, at the Bull inn on Bishopsgate. On their way out of London Cecil stopped at the hospital of St Mary Spital and gave a penny to the poor there. Lady Mildred stayed at home. The day after her husband had set out for Walden she took a boat to the Temple stairs.[38]

Cecil was settled and comfortable. He enjoyed the society of his friends and it was clear that he still maintained his political connections. He was known, even favoured, at Mary's court. By March 1557 he had made an ally of the Lord Deputy of Calais, Lord Wentworth, who thanked him for his intervention in a legal case involving Wentworth in Westminster Hall. 'This doing of yours is so well accepted,' wrote Sir Thomas Cornwallis, a courtier, 'that my Lordship thinketh himself much in your debt, which (in this time of his credit with the Queen's highness) may stand you in good stead, if ye shall have any occasion to use him.'

It was a game Cecil knew very well; making himself useful to powerful men could build up much-needed credit. But every so often a little of that credit had to be used. In late March Cecil stood by his rights when, at nine o'clock in the morning of the 27th at Cannon Row, he wrote a letter to three JPs in Surrey who had mustered Cardinal Pole's tenants at Wimbledon. Cecil's letter was a stern rebuke: he made the point that only he, as Pole's high steward, had the right to do this.[39]

The bills and accounts kept by Cecil's household servants for this time in Mary's reign give us a good sense of the family's life. As ever there was no clear boundary between politics and private life. Even the family physician who attended to Lady Mildred in April 1557, Dr Robert Huick, was a doctor who for many years had treated members of the Tudor royal family. Huick's professional fee on this occasion was 3s. 4d., exactly the same as the surgeon brought in to bleed Mildred, though Cecil gave Huick another 10s. as a reward.[40]

A couple of weeks later Lady Mildred was well enough to go to the Blackfriars and the Whitefriars. In the week of St George's Day the family was at Cannon Row. Perhaps they saw the Garter procession at Whitehall, with King Philip in his Garter robes and Secretary Petre wearing a gown of crimson velvet. We know for sure that within a few days Cecil was at Lambeth to visit Cardinal Pole. On 1 May he visited Lambeth twice.[41]

By now young Thomas Cecil was, like any future courtier, learning to dance. The Cecils were keeping grand company. In June Cecil visited his friend the Earl of Bedford. He often went by boat from Cannon Row to the Temple stairs, possibly to Gray's Inn. Mildred visited Whitehall Palace. Cecil went on a short break to see Sir Philip Hoby, but was back in Westminster in time for the return of King Philip and Queen Mary to Whitehall after a hunting party at Hampton Court. On the day the King and Queen were at Whitehall, Mildred was there too, while Cecil visited Lambeth. Certainly Lady Mildred was at court on 13 June, Trinity Sunday. Perhaps she celebrated Corpus Christi at Whitehall four days later, when Philip and Mary processed through the hall and the great court gate, 'attended with goodly singing as ever was heard'.[42]

When Philip of Spain had returned to Mary's court in March 1557, it was to bring Mary and England into his war against France. Though many opposed it, Mary supported her husband. War was declared at the beginning of June, but there is no obvious sign of it in the Cecils' accounts. William practised his archery, but for pleasure and money: between 20 and 27 June he lost 2d. to Arthur Hall. He paid ten times that sum in reward to a man who played the lute and gave 2s. to 'one that turned the virginals'. Arthur and young Thomas Cecil had had seven weeks of tuition on the virginal given by one Master Ellys.

Mildred and William went to Bisham with Sir Philip Hoby, Lady Bourne and Elizabeth Cooke. With the party was Sir Thomas Hoby, Philip's brother and the translator from Italian of *The Courtier* by Baldassare Castiglione, a handbook of court manners and behaviour. If there was anyone who was qualified to comment on the importance of music to the courtly gentleman it was Thomas Hoby. On 25 June Cecil paid for beer and a manchet loaf for Sir Philip and was back in London the same day, going by boat to visit the Earl of Bedford and to stay at Cannon Row.[43]

Cecil did not fight in Mary's wars. But he was entrusted with the care of the family of a friend who crossed the Channel to fight the French. This was Francis Russell, Earl of Bedford. On 26 July Bedford, in Calais, sent a letter to his 'singular good friend' Cecil. 'I pray you have me in your remembrance,' wrote the earl, 'and be good to my wife and children, under whose protection I do altogether commit them.'

Cecil was true to his promise. In early August the Countess of Bedford wrote to William with news that her husband was in good health and merry. And he was valiant too, or so she had heard from Susan Clarencius, one of the Queen's ladies, with whom she was going to Chelsea the next day 'to see stuff and jewels, that is there to be sold, where I would wish I might meet my Lady your wife although I think she will not bestow very much money there nor more will I'. The Russells' son had an ague, or head cold, and the countess proposed to put him to Lady Mildred's 'order'.[44]

There were some worries that summer about illness, as there were throughout the kingdom: this was a time of dearth and sickness. Margaret Cooke fell ill, but she was well enough by the middle of August for her sister, Anne, and Anne's husband, Sir Nicholas Bacon, to write of her recovery. Margaret may have been cheered by the two gowns Cecil bought for her that month, one of crimson (at £6) and other, at £8, of blue velvet. One of the Bacons' little daughters was sick with a fever, but she had recovered enough by the 18th for Sir Nicholas to travel to London. He planned to be at Cannon Row by ten o'clock the next morning, and hoped to be with Cecil in time to see a hanging.

Lady Anne Bacon ended the letter with thoughts of baby Anne Cecil, known to the family as Nan. 'We at Bedford are no less glad of Wimbledon's welfare, and specially of little Nan's, trusting for all this shrewd* fever to see her and mine playfellows many times. Thus wishing continuance of all good things to you all at once because your man hasteth away and my husband to dinner.'[45]

In the weeks just before Christmas 1557 the Cecils were rowed up and down the Thames to familiar places: to Bedford House; to the Blackfriars; to the

---

* Grievous or serious.

Bacons on Thames Street; to the Whitefriars; to the Duchess of Somerset. In January 1558 the visits continued, with dinners, suppers and cards. But this year was different: after it Sir William Cecil's life would never be the same again.

*

Cecil had no way of knowing that soon the Queen would be dead. But he was clever and acute and his political contacts were impeccable. He knew in early 1558 that the world was changing. He was close to Cardinal Pole, and Pole was very close indeed to the Queen. In the last week of January Cecil visited Lord Paget, the most politically experienced and seasoned of all Mary's advisers. This was a meeting of two former royal secretaries, and it is hard to imagine that they did not talk about the most important news of the moment: the fall of Calais. The town had been lost to the French just weeks before. It was the Tudors' last toehold in continental Europe and its fall was a disaster.[46]

The loss of Calais was known in London on 10 January, but Cecil's sources were better. He had written about Calais to Sir Anthony Cooke a fortnight earlier. Cooke, even hundreds of miles away in Strasburg, knew that it would shake the English political world. 'I was much troubled with the ill news of the taking of Calais,' Cooke wrote to Cecil, 'yet I received some comfort in reading your letter so friendly and lovingly as I had not received from you long before. I see not but friends shall have more cause every day to help and comfort one another.' Cooke was almost glad he was away from England. 'The grief that I find in hearing of these storms maketh me understand my weakness to bear them, if I [were] at the sight and doings of them.'[47]

As much of a worry was the royal succession. Mary was sure she was pregnant: few really believed her. By the end of March she had made a will in preparation for the trial of childbirth. She refused even the possibility that on her death Elizabeth would become queen. As ever, the politics of succession in Tudor England was dangerously and delicately balanced.

It was at exactly this moment in Mary's reign, when anyone who had anything to do with the court was thinking about the future, that Cecil met Princess Elizabeth: the cleverest young man in Tudor politics had an interview at Somerset House with the heir to the throne. Cecil was on good terms with Mary's government. But it was clear, too, that he maintained close touch with Elizabeth's household. And so when the Princess came to London in late February with 'a great company of lords and noblemen and noblewomen' he took his chance. It was a meeting that helped to shape the course of her reign and his life.[48]

There are no great papers for this meeting. Perhaps Cecil had good reason to put nothing down for the future. But we are lucky that one of his household servants, Quentin Sneynton, kept a careful record of his master's boat journeys up and down the Thames. It was Sneynton who noted the visit to and from Elizabeth at the cost of 3*d*. there and 2*d*. back.

This was a critical time for Elizabeth. King Philip wanted her to be married off to a good Catholic prince; this at the very least was something to talk about. What seems very unlikely is that it was a dull business meeting between Elizabeth and the surveyor of her estates. The questions of the moment were many and insistent. Was Mary really pregnant? What would happen if she was not? What if Mary's health deteriorated even further? What then for Elizabeth and the succession?

If Cecil had kept in touch with Elizabeth since 1553 he had done so carefully, even covertly. The meeting in late February 1558 may have been confidential. But there can be little doubt that from this time on Cecil played an important part in Elizabeth's plans for the future.[49]

Mary's health was indeed failing. In May one of King Philip's most trusted councillors, the Count of Feria, reported that the Queen was weak and melancholy and sleeping badly. She was 'worse than usual' in early June, and had developed a fever by the middle of August. In early September she recovered a little; but at the end of the month her health was once again a worry. Philip planned to travel to England but was prevented from doing so by the death of his father, the Emperor Charles V. He would never see his wife again.

In late October 1558 Mary, by now very ill, understood that her sister Elizabeth would succeed her as Queen. On the 28th Mary added a codicil to her will. At last she recognised that the Tudor crown would go to Elizabeth as their father had intended it to in the event of Mary's dying without a legitimate heir. Philip of Spain would 'have no further government' in England; Elizabeth would be queen in her own right, though Mary could not bring herself to mention her sister by name.[50]

So the law stood. Henry VIII's Succession Act, which only a few years before had brought Cecil to within a cat's whisker of treason, now secured his political career. Elizabeth would rule, and there was every sign that Cecil was going to be back in government. The intelligence from the Count of Feria in the weeks before Mary's death was that Cecil would be Secretary again.

By early November Elizabeth was Queen-in-waiting. She knew she was popular with the people: she told the Count of Feria so in a private interview at Brocket Hall, very close to her estate at Hatfield, on 10 November. Mary had lost the support of her subjects, Elizabeth said, by marrying a foreigner.

Feria's judgement of Elizabeth was not a flattering one: 'She is a very vain and clever woman,' he wrote. 'She must have been thoroughly schooled in the manner in which her father conducted his affairs, and I am very much afraid that she will not be well-disposed in matters of religion, for I see her inclined to govern through men who are believed to be heretics.' Keen to brief King Philip, Feria began to identify the men Elizabeth favoured and would probably promote to government office. Cecil was prominent among them. 'He is said to be an able and virtuous man,' wrote Feria dismissively, 'but a heretic.'[51]

Sir William Cecil was at Hatfield on the day Mary died, Thursday, 17 November 1558. He was already working as Elizabeth's Secretary, though the twenty-five-year-old Queen would not formally appoint him to the job for another three days. He had never really been away from the world of politics, even in Mary's reign. But now he was, once again, right at the heart of government: and so he would be till the day he died.

PART TWO

'A Shop for Cunning Men'

7

Master Secretary's Device

On that Thursday Elizabeth became Queen by rightful succession, by law and above all by blood. She was Henry VIII's daughter and she would rule. There was no contest for the throne, nothing like the febrile summer months of 1553. This was cold calm November.

Tudor theory held that monarchs were sacred beings who possessed two bodies conjoined in a mystical union. Any king or queen had a physical body that was fragile and mortal but they also carried the 'body politic', the body of their kingdom, the authority and rule that never died and which passed on death to their successor. There was a powerful mystery to all of this. In an instant Elizabeth Tudor's whole being was transformed. Her 'I' became 'We' in a regal style that would not leave her till the day she died.

William Cecil's life, too, was changed for ever. For every day of the next forty years he would think about the public business of the realm. He would guide and direct it in ways which seemed to him compelling. He would dominate Elizabethan politics. It is hard to imagine that any of this would have happened in Mary's reign, even if she had ruled for another thirty years. He had been close to the governing circle. But he would never have had the same influence in Mary's government that he would now in Elizabeth's.

So why did Elizabeth choose Cecil to be her Secretary? This is perhaps the question of questions, and there are some good practical answers to it. He was, first of all, a man of experience and knowledge. He had been one of the brightest lights of Edward VI's government, and even in Mary's reign he had never moved far away from the world of Westminster and the royal court. He was an instinctive politician, supremely able, and still, at thirty-eight, fairly young. His youth and his ability marked him out. Even in 1558 he was still something of a prodigy.

But there was something else, which historians find hard to measure. Power and authority are so often captured in the moment, in the person, in their eyes and manner, in their confidence and self-belief. There was something about William Cecil. Look at his eyes in any of the early portraits: they are steady and penetrating, calm and confident. He was frighteningly controlled and precise. These qualities never left him. There was from the beginning a promise of the great creative tension that would shape his political career. He never tired of telling people that he was merely a minister and a servant. Yet there was also his clarity of belief, his unshakeable sense of what had to be done.

So here was the consummate royal servant, loyal and efficient, and also the man who knew his own mind, clever, confident and commanding. Formed by a life at court that had taken him to the palaces of kings and queens, cardinals and archbishops, as well as to the Tower of London and close to treason, he was a formidable politician.

Cecil was simply the best man for the job of Secretary. He had recommended himself to Elizabeth in Mary's reign. His meeting with the Princess in the late winter of 1558 is very suggestive. She may have recruited him there and then to a shadow government. But there is something, too, about the way he conducted himself more generally. Perhaps his loyalty to Mary stood in his favour. This sounds like a paradox, but of course people are rarely straightforward. Elizabeth had accepted the Mass after 1553, yet she was never trusted by Mary. Cecil too had gone to Mass, though in Mary's last illness the Count of Feria called him a heretic.

The other knot to unpick in the relationship between Elizabeth and Cecil is his support for Jane Grey. Cecil had sworn his oath to Jane. In 1553 he had cut Elizabeth out of the royal succession. Perhaps Elizabeth believed the story he had told to Mary, when he had protested conscience and proved himself to be a loyal subject. He had, so it seemed, put lawful dynastic succession before politics, even before religion. So perhaps some things were best forgotten. Sir William Cecil was a man Elizabeth, the rightful monarch by blood and the law of succession, could trust.

If Cecil was tested and tempered by the politics of the Tudor court, the same was true of Elizabeth Tudor. She was born in 1533, the daughter of Henry VIII by his second wife Anne Boleyn. From the moment of her birth she was caught up in the complicated and often dangerous politics of dynasty. As a baby she was heir presumptive to the Tudor throne, displacing her seventeen-year-old half-sister Mary. Both Mary and Elizabeth were declared illegitimate by an act of parliament when Henry at last had a son, Edward, by Jane Seymour, though by 1544 Elizabeth was once again a lawful successor to the crown.

In the reigns of Edward and Mary she was the object of the dubious attentions of Thomas Seymour, Protector Somerset's brother, and in the eyes of Philip of Spain she was a princess who needed to be married to a good Catholic. Princess Elizabeth was rich, guaranteed an annual income of £3,000 by the will of her father, with more houses and lands than she could ever need, and a household of between 120 and 130 servants. But as a woman suspected of dabbling in plots and conspiracies against her sister, Elizabeth also knew what it was like to be interrogated by Mary's Council and to live as a prisoner in the Tower of London and under house arrest in Woodstock in Oxfordshire. To put it simply, by 1558 Elizabeth had pretty much seen it all.[1]

The Count of Feria believed Elizabeth was clever and vain. But who could blame her? In November 1558 she had every reason to think that providence had led her almost miraculously to the Tudor throne, and probably that confidence, and surely relief too, came across in her interview with the Count at Brocket Hall in Hertfordshire a week before her accession.

Feria was right to say that she was clever. From a little girl Elizabeth had been given a rigorous education, taught Latin, Italian, French and ancient and New Testament Greek, first by John Astley, a trusted servant, and then by William Grindal, a pupil of Cecil's friend and teacher Roger Ascham. This was the sort of education Cecil knew very well: he had been trained that way himself. Cecil and Elizabeth had a bond that, directly for one and indirectly for the other, went back to the College of St John the Evangelist in Cambridge in the 1530s.

What we will see in the rest of this book is evidence of a fascinating relationship between a queen and her minister. Elizabeth can be elusive: for the public role she performed she guarded her privacy very closely indeed. She was clever, controlled and engaging; but at the same time, for reasons which made perfect sense to her even if they did not to Cecil, she often preferred to follow a policy of masterly inactivity. The result was a professional relationship that often crackled with the electricity of raw politics.

*

From the first hours of the new reign it was clear that Cecil had an enormous job on his hands. He wrote note after note, trying to set down everything that needed to be done. On 17 November it was Elizabeth's proclamation, the preparation of the Tower of London for her arrival, the security of the realm and its trouble spots, diplomatic embassies to foreign powers to tell them of Elizabeth's accession, the appointment of commissioners to arrange Mary's burial, and of course plans for the Queen's coronation.

Very early on Cecil had formed ideas of the best men to perform the first tasks of the new government. The Marquess of Northampton would handle the business of moving the Queen to London. Northampton, the Marquess of Winchester, Sir Walter Mildmay and Mary's old officers would see to her funeral. The gentlewomen of Mary's Privy Chamber had the jewels which now belonged to her royal sister: those valuables had to be taken into custody. Lord William Howard and Sir Edward Rogers dealt with the royal Chamber. Cecil noted that Sir Henry Bedingfield, Vice-Chamberlain of Mary's household and Elizabeth's gaoler at Woodstock, should be discharged from his office. And so it went on, note after note, in mind-boggling detail.[2]

There was also a new Council to appoint. This had to be done quickly. By the second day of the reign Elizabeth and Cecil had a good idea of the best men to recruit. Some were Elizabeth's natural supporters; others were for the moment useful men to have at court. On 18 November Cecil scribbled notes on what he called the 'admittance of the Council at London', and these show that Archbishop Heath of York, the three powerful noblemen the Marquess of Winchester, the Earl of Shrewsbury and the Earl of Derby, Sir Thomas Cheyney and Sir William Petre were in Elizabeth's and Cecil's minds almost right from the beginning. A great friend of the new regime was the Earl of Bedford, who was at Hatfield by the 21st. Other new councillors had loyally served King Edward or Elizabeth as princess. They were the Earl of Pembroke, Edward, Lord Clinton, Lord Howard of Effingham, Sir Thomas Parry, Sir Ambrose Cave, Sir Richard Sackville, the Earl of Bedford and Sir Ralph Sadler.[3]

Some of the key men of the new regime were those privy councillors who held office at Elizabeth's fledgling court. Cecil believed the important offices in the royal household should be given to men who were fit to serve in the Privy Council. Here he thought back to the reign of Edward VI. In the early 1550s the King's councillors, the officers of the royal household and the gentlemen of Edward's Privy Chamber had formed a tightly knit group around the King: they saw to his education, to his entertainment, to the running of his court, to finance, to the making of policy. Cecil had been one of these men.

Because she was a woman, Elizabeth's court would have to work in a different way to a man's or even a boy's. Her Privy Chamber could not be staffed by men, so some of the administrative jobs the gentlemen of the Privy Chamber had taken upon themselves in Edward's reign would have to be done in different ways. Here Elizabeth's Secretary would be important. So, too, would the Queen's Council.

The key offices in the royal household that Cecil believed should 'be bestowed upon men meet for counsel' were those of the Lord Chamberlain of the Household, the Vice-Chamberlain, the Comptroller and the Secretary. Cecil wanted to make absolutely sure that he would sit at the Council table, just as he had done as Secretary in Edward's reign; there was no other way for him to co-ordinate policy and government.[4]

The most important thing to notice is that he wrote Secretary, not Secretaries: sweeping away years of practice and convention there would be no second Secretary. The huge burden of the job, and all the power that went with it, would be Cecil's alone. He was sworn a privy councillor at Hatfield on 20 November.[5]

Each one of Elizabeth's councillors swore to bear true faith and allegiance to the Queen's Majesty Elizabeth, by the grace of God Queen of England, France and Ireland, defender of the faith. In all matters a councillor promised, to the best of his power and wit, to 'give such counsel to Her Majesty as may best seem' in his conscience 'to the safety of Her Majesty's person, and to the common weal of this realm'. This was an oath of obedience, loyalty and frank speech.[6]

Elizabeth had special words for her Secretary:

I give you this charge, that you shall be of my Privy Council and content yourself to take pains for me and my realm. This judgement I have of you, that you will not be corrupted with any manner of gift, and that you will be faithful to the state, and that without respect of my private will you will give me that counsel that you think best. And if you know anything necessary to be declared to me of secrecy, you shall show it to myself only, and assure yourself I will not fail to keep taciturnity therein, and therefore herewith I charge you.[7]

He took these words very seriously. His job was to speak his mind as freely and frankly as he could. It was something he did for the next forty years.

*

Elizabeth did not race for the Tower of London as a place of refuge. Instead she arrived in her capital city after a leisurely progress through Hertfordshire and Middlesex. Even then she did not go straight to the Tower. By 25 November Elizabeth and her court were at the Charterhouse, Lord North's house on the outskirts of London just off Aldersgate Street. Only on the 28th did Elizabeth arrive at the Tower after a grand procession through the Barbican and Cripplegate to Bishopsgate, along Leadenhall and Gracechurch Street and Fenchurch Street.

Cecil understood how important it was to get royal ceremonial right. He was behind the scenes, making sure that everything ran properly and smoothly. All in all it was a perfect accession, popular with the people and done with just the right amount of ceremony.[8]

Yet for all of this, it would have been hard in the winter of 1558 for Elizabeth's new privy councillors to be cheerful. They knew that Europe was a hostile place. War with Spain against France had come with enormous costs, to the armed forces, to the economy and government finances. Calais was lost, a terrible psychological blow to the English governing elite. Spain professed friendship; but King Philip was an uncertain ally who only really cared about his larger strategic interests. If observers like the Count of Feria were right, and Elizabeth's supporters were heretics, then Cecil and his colleagues had a job on their hands to build a Protestant English Church. Mary had thrown away Henry VIII's and Edward VI's royal supremacy, and so they would have to break with the Church of Rome all over again. But if Elizabeth's government wanted to go back to the Church of Edward VI, in structure and in belief, the Catholic powers of Spain and France, and of course the Pope, would be deeply hostile.

There was also the matter of the Queen's sex. She would have to marry as quickly as possible. Marriage would bring an heir, an heir would mean security for her people. But who was Elizabeth to marry? And what was to stop any dynastic match with a foreign prince turning, like Mary's, to disaster?

Money, European politics, religion, marriage, succession and security: already Sir William Cecil could see stretching out before him matters that were to keep him busy for the rest of his life.

*

By early December 1558 Cecil had decided to recruit some experts to examine the problems Elizabeth's government faced and to suggest ways to proceed. The first experts he approached were lawyers. One was John Eyre, whom Cecil asked to come to London from Norwich if (as Eyre put it) 'I were in health and might possibly'. But Eyre was not in health: he was very sick and unable to travel, and so he sent his apologies.

Another lawyer was Richard Goodrich of Gray's Inn, Cecil's old personal friend. Goodrich was the perfect man to give Cecil confidential legal counsel. In December 1558 Cecil consulted him as a trusted friend, as a professional lawyer of long experience, and as a supporter of the new government.[9]

Goodrich wrote a paper about the Church in England and the power of the Pope. These matters may not have been to do with the day-to-day business of the accession, but in the first weeks of Elizabeth's reign they clearly concerned Cecil very deeply. How could England return to the 'true religion' of Edward's reign?

Here Goodrich had some good news for the government. His reading of the law and its authorities told him that English monarchs did not have to put up with popes. What Goodrich called 'the Pope's curse' was of no value in the realm, even though from time to time kings had been 'grieved with the continual usurpation of the Pope and his clergy'. So much was clear: years before 'the Pope was banished with his authority' from England.

But Goodrich believed that to take on the power and authority of the Pope was a dangerous business. It all had to be considered very carefully before a parliament could act. Nothing should be done, he argued, except to repeal some laws that had to do with the powers of bishops. The safest way was to go back to the religious practices of the reign of Henry VIII. Goodrich advised that Elizabeth could use the Mass without the elevation of the Host, that unambiguous mark of the Catholic sacrament. Goodrich urged conservative caution. His advice was careful and balanced. Certainly it was too moderate for Cecil's taste.[10]

Here we come to one of the most intriguing and important government papers of the first years of Elizabeth's reign, 'The Device for the alteration of religion'. For a long time historians have wondered about its authorship. Clearly it came from the heart of government. But who wrote it? There are very good reasons to think that it was the work of Master Secretary Cecil.[11]

The paper was a bold, confident and frank analysis of the state England was in. It offered a plan for Reformation. The 'Device' is uncompromisingly radical. In the winter of 1558, with things still so uncertain for Elizabeth and the future, it gave substance to a plan for revolution in church and state. It would have been easy to counsel caution and restraint, as Goodrich had done. Cecil had no way of knowing that Elizabeth's reign would last for over forty years: he had to make sure that it could survive its first weeks. Slow and careful change could have taken account of all the early dangers. France and other Catholic powers were not Elizabeth's friends; Philip II of Spain was at best polite. Richard Goodrich had flinched at the technical problems of breaking with the Church of Rome all over again. But for Cecil the best way to defend was to attack.

Change had to come quickly. There was to be nothing of Goodrich's caution. In the first parliament of the new reign there would be an 'alteration of religion': the sooner religion was restored, the sooner God would be glorified, and the more chance there was of divine protection for Elizabeth. It always paid to err on the side of providence.

Cecil and his friends were in the habit of writing and talking about 'true religion'. True religion stood four square against the errors of the Church of Rome, and it had so far found its most perfect form in England in the Church of Edward VI. In Edward's reign truth had triumphed over the lies of Rome; the Pope had been sent packing; the Temple had been purged of superstition and idolatry. In all sorts of coded ways, here was the point of reference of Cecil's paper, the lodestone of his compass.

But to defend true religion came of course with a cost, and that was the enmity of the Catholic superpowers of Europe like Spain and France and the papacy itself. Spain was not mentioned in the paper probably because Spain, though uncertain, was still a friend. This so-called friendship was something Cecil would soon see for what it really was. But before the Christmas of 1558 France was more obviously hostile, and Cecil imagined that when England went back to 'religion', as he called it in the 'Device', the French would fight the English as heretics as well as enemies. The Pope would be angry: he would excommunicate Elizabeth, put the realm under an interdict, 'and give it to prey to all princes that will enter upon it'. Scotland, an ally of France, would be used by the French to invade England. It would be difficult to control Ireland 'by reason of the clergy that is so addicted to Rome'.

Internally there would be enemies of any new settlement of religion. The governors Mary had chosen because of their religion would do all they could to hold on to power. The bishops and the clergy would persuade the people to oppose it. Mary's judges and justices of the peace would conspire with the bishops and clergy. Some people would rise up when Elizabeth's government needed money. And then there would be those on the other side of the fence, hot Protestants, who would think the new Church imperfectly reformed and would complain about it.

So Cecil's paper was hard reading. He had no illusions about how difficult it would be to break with Rome all over again. This was anything but Richard Goodrich's cautious middle way. But the 'Device' shows that Cecil had a plan.

The first thing to do was to seek peace with France after Mary's war, though Cecil was no innocent in the ways of international politics. He saw that there were good reasons for Elizabeth's government to stir up trouble in France: 'If controversy of religion be there among them, to help to kindle it.' Nothing good could be expected to come from Rome, 'but evil will, cursing and practising'. This was such a given that there was no obvious remedy for it. Scotland would follow France in any peace with England. 'But', Cecil wrote, 'there may be practised to help forward their divisions, and especially to augment the hope of them who incline to good religion.' In 1558 Scotland was governed by a French regent, Mary of Guise, the mother of Mary, Queen of Scots, who was doing her best to defeat the forces of Protestant Scots noble-men. Already Cecil appeared to want to support the rebels; certainly he wanted to fortify the border between England and Scotland, just as he wanted to spend money to secure Ireland.

It was clear to Cecil that those of Mary's Council who had been chosen 'only or chiefly for being of the Pope's religion, and earnest in the same' had to be discredited. If they remained in positions of authority they would give hope to Catholics in England. Only Elizabeth's 'sure servants, who have tarried with her, and not shrunk in the last storms' could be trusted. So it was to be out with the Catholics and in with the new Queen's Protestant supporters. 'Good' religion was to be the principal test of loyalty in public office. 'And throughout all England such persons as are known to be sure in religion, every one, according to his ability to serve in the commonwealth, to be set in place.'

Only someone who really knew what was going on could have written a paper like the 'Device'. There are other position papers from these months, written by enthusiasts close to government. Not one has the authority or the precision of the 'Device'. It came from the highest levels of power and it spoke to an inner caucus of Cecil's friends in government.

The 'Device' was part political analysis, part manifesto. It set out aims and objectives that Cecil pursued for the next tens of years. But here is the knot. How could Sir William Cecil, the man who had conformed so effortlessly to Catholic Mary, write with such passion about the true religion? Here we come to the paradox of William Cecil.

How he understood himself, of course, is not how others necessarily viewed him. He felt he was one of Elizabeth's 'sure servants' even in Mary's reign. This may say something about his careful links with Princess Elizabeth's household. Certainly he was one of her most subtle and supple supporters. In 1558 he was a like a man reborn, the true believer newly invigorated after a time of doubt and dryness of faith. All the moral ambiguities of Mary's reign were gone. Elizabeth's was a new start. There had to be a single loyalty to God and Queen: to true religion, to Elizabeth, to dynasty. At last Cecil could show himself for what he was. He was for the English Church as it had been in the years of Edward VI and wholeheartedly against the Bishop of Rome. He was for Elizabeth and her preservation.

Cecil proposed to leave the mechanics of his 'Device' to others. He referred his paper to a small group of friends and to 'such learned men as be meet to show their minds herein'. This was a hand-picked committee of men who saw the world as Cecil saw it. They were churchmen, academics and exiles from Cambridge, some of them former servants of Edward VI. All were close to Cecil.

The job of this committee of experts was to draw up a 'plat' (a proposal or plan) for the new Church. This would be shown to the Queen and then put to parliament. The group was to be chaired by Cecil's old friend, teacher and colleague, Sir Thomas Smith. Other 'grave and learned' men would be brought in to offer their opinions. Cecil thought they would meet in Smith's lodgings on Cannon Row. He even thought of the provisions they, with all their servants, would need: meat, drink, wood and coal. It was a wonderful piece of in-house private enterprise.

The 'Device' tells us about how Cecil went about tackling the great political topics of the day. He consulted men he trusted. He thought about the problems Elizabeth faced and about ways to deal with those problems, and he put his ideas down on paper. Like a good student of St John's College and Gray's Inn he wanted his ideas to be examined by clever men from the universities and the law, each one bringing skills, talents and insight. The details had to be right, the consultation thorough, the atmosphere scholarly but convivial, with meat and drink for all.

So in the first days of Elizabeth's reign, Cecil had a plan. There was going to be a Reformation. He knew it would shake European politics and diplomacy to their foundations.

*

In Christmas week scaffolds were put up in London for pageants to celebrate Elizabeth's coronation. This had been on Cecil's mind since the day of her accession. It promised to be a sumptuous event. In fact its elaborate ritual and splendour would cost the royal treasury nearly £20,000. But this staggering sum of money was worth paying. Everyone would be able to see what Elizabeth stood for. Nothing could be left to chance: the least thing would send out all sorts of important diplomatic signals.[12]

Slowly the religious leanings of the Queen and her government began to show themselves. After supper on Twelfth Night, 6 January, a masque was performed before Elizabeth and her court. In it were actors who played crows in the character of Roman cardinals. A statue of St Thomas was stoned, beheaded and then finally removed. These were goings-on to make Catholics fear for the future.[13]

Actually the government came down hard on people who believed that the days of Mary's Catholicism were gone. Until parliament met, men and women had to obey the law: the Mass stood, with all its Latin ritual, protected by statutes from the reign of Mary. But now there were some coded hints about an alteration of religion. For all the care the government took to obey the law, it was possible to imagine that Reformation was on the way again.

On Twelfth Night Elizabeth and her courtiers colluded in a thinly disguised attack on the Catholic Church. Just as subtle in their messages were the pageants on the day before the Queen's coronation and the coronation service itself. Care and attention were given to law and propriety, but the court and the city must have been fizzing with the anticipation of Reformation. Perhaps the days of King Edward had come again.[14]

Little of this was surprising at the time. Elizabeth was known to be a Protestant, though she did not have very much of the passion of her brother,

Edward. If she favoured one or other of the Books of Common Prayer, it was almost certainly the Prayer Book of 1549, rather more traditional and ambiguous than its more stridently evangelical successor of 1552. Put very simply, Elizabeth was for 1549; her Secretary Cecil, and many other councillors, for 1552. She was probably also less convinced than many of the men who served her of her standing as a 'godly prince' – a monarch whose duties were defined and described in terms of enthusiastic Protestant reform. But there is no doubt that she believed she was God's lieutenant on earth and that all subjects owed to her unconditional obedience.

The notion of the godly prince had its roots in the 1530s, in the supremacy of Henry VIII, in Henry's sense of authority existing 'on earth next under God'. That had been taken up and marketed, very cleverly, by the advisers of Edward VI, who had put a decidedly Protestant spin on the Tudor royal supremacy. The monarch had become an agent of Reformation and revolution, God's instrument in the great cosmic battle of Christ against the Antichrist of the Church of Rome. Elizabeth would go on to believe in her own supremacy, which was constructed in the few months after her coronation, but she interpreted her power much more conservatively than her advisers did. Here she was out of step with Cecil and his colleagues.

The pageants of 1559 were at once celebrations of Elizabeth's rule and reminders for her to do her duty as Queen. They were deeply symbolic and very elaborate. Significantly, they were planned by her advisers. Elizabeth saw them on Saturday, 14 January 1559, when she went out from the Tower of London at about two o'clock in the afternoon to go to Westminster.

She set out on the procession 'richly furnished and most honourably accompanied, as well with gentlemen, barons and other the nobility of this realm, as also with a notable train of goodly and beautiful ladies, richly appointed'. Elizabeth travelled in an open litter trimmed with gold brocade and pulled by two mules. Rows of footmen walked either side of the Queen. They wore crimson velvet jerkins studded with gilt silver and decorated front and back with the Tudor rose of Lancaster and York and with the letters ER, *Elisabetha Regina*. Flanking the footmen were two lines of the Queen's Gentlemen Pensioners, in crimson damask, carrying their poll axes. It was a superb spectacle.

In this way Elizabeth processed through her city of London, followed by her councillors and courtiers. Cecil would have been prominent among them. On the streets and roads Elizabeth went along there were wooden barriers to hold back spectators. The only thing that dulled the colour and splendour of the procession was the mud in the streets, caused by filthy winter weather, and churned up by thousands of hoofs and feet. But even deep mud and January cold did not deter the people from seeing their new Queen, dressed in a robe of cloth of gold, a coif on her head and wearing a plain gold crown.

At Gracechurch Street, in the heart of the city, Elizabeth came to the first pageant of the day. It was a celebration of her family, and of peace and reconciliation after war, and it had the name 'The uniting of the two houses of Lancaster and York'. Across the street was a great triumphal arch, moving from figures of Elizabeth's royal grandfather Henry VII and his wife Elizabeth of York, to Henry VIII and Anne Boleyn and finally, on the highest level, a queen shown in majesty. This was the dynasty of the Tudors, the double rose of red and white, unity out of civil war, the majesty of royalty.

But true religion was just as important as the rightful rule of Elizabeth Tudor. A second arch showed the Queen wearing her imperial crown, surrounded by 'four personages' who stood for the virtues of pure religion, love of subjects, wisdom and justice. Pure religion stamped out superstition and ignorance; love of subjects trod on rebellion and insolence; wisdom defeated folly and vainglory; and justice trod on adulation and bribery. The message was that the future lay in true religion protected by a rightful queen. A pageant on Fleet Street made the point even more forcefully. Elizabeth was shown as Deborah of the Old Testament, 'the judge and restorer of the house of Israel', the hope of her people.[15]

The next day, Sunday, 15 January Elizabeth bound herself to her people. In Westminster Abbey she acknowledged their requests to protect the kingdom, the Church and the law. As form and tradition expected, the people were asked if they wished Elizabeth to be crowned their queen. They shouted 'Yes', wrote one observer, 'and the organs, fifes, trumpets, and drums playing, the bells also ringing, it seemed as if the world were come to an end'. The oath Elizabeth swore was the one Archbishop Cranmer had specially written for godly Edward VI in 1547. But an extra clause was added in 1559: she undertook to rule 'according to the Laws of God, [and] the true profession of the Gospel established in this Kingdom'.[16]

Just before this, there was a breathtaking piece of theatre in the abbey. For some strange reason, whether by accident or design, the text of the coronation oath was not in the hands of the officiating bishop, Owen Oglethorpe of Carlisle, when he began the ceremony. When the time came for the oath to be administered to Elizabeth, Secretary Cecil emerged from the side of the stage to hand it to Oglethorpe. We can only imagine why. But it is difficult to overstate the symbolism of Elizabeth's Secretary delivering the oath to the Queen in full view of her court and nobility.[17]

The pageant and the coronation were parts in an unfolding scheme of revolution in church and state, chapters of a manifesto for profound change. But like any manifesto, practical things had to be done to turn a vision into reality. The first chance Elizabeth's government had to get down to serious business was the first parliament of the new reign. It was only in parliament that something could be done about the laws on religion that had caused such deft manoeuvrings and careful wordings so far in the reign.

*

Elizabeth's first parliament began on 25 January 1559. It was opened by Sir Nicholas Bacon, Cecil's brother-in-law and recently appointed Lord Keeper of the Great Seal, who told parliament what the Queen wanted her subjects to do. The first matter of business was religion, 'the well making of laws for the according and uniting of the people of this realm into an uniform order of religion, to the honour and glory of God, the establishment of his Church and tranquillity of the realm'.[18]

Parliament was the first public test of the government's resolution. It was also the first public test of Cecil. Sitting in the Commons, Cecil was able to guide, persuade, cajole and bully other MPs into following the government's plan. One of his most hostile critics, the Spanish diplomat Feria, called the effort to push through a new royal supremacy 'his iniquitous scheme'. And surely Feria was right. There is no doubt that in St Stephen's Chapel in the Palace of Westminster, the chamber where the Commons met; on the corridors of Westminster and in its hall; and in the most private apartments of Whitehall with the Queen and her Privy Council, Cecil was a strong, constant and forceful presence.[19]

For the government it was important to remind everyone of reform. In the first hours of Elizabeth's reign, Cecil had written about the need to make sure that there was a suitable preacher to preach at London's great public pulpit, Paul's Cross. For the next few weeks of Lent the preachers at Paul's Cross, and preachers before the Queen at Whitehall, were the cream of the Edwardian church and the Marian exiles. They thumped home the message of the moment: the days of the Pope were over and true religion would banish idolatry and superstition. The day before a bill for the royal supremacy was introduced into the House of Commons, Dr Richard Cox, one of Edward VI's tutors and an exile in Mary's reign, preached before Elizabeth. The symbolism of Cox's return to the pulpit was clear. It was followed the next day, Thursday, 9 February, by the first move in the effort by the government to give Elizabeth I the kind of authority in spiritual matters that had been exercised by her father and brother.[20]

On that Thursday morning, MPs in the Commons heard the reading of a bill for the Queen's supremacy. It was given to Sir Anthony Cooke, Cecil's father-in-law, to refine. Cooke was impatient for reform: 'we are moving far too slowly'. On the day Cooke wrote those words there was a sermon at Whitehall Palace before 5,000 people at which Dr John Scory, another exile in

Mary's reign, railed against the Pope, the Catholic bishops and the Mass. But the sheer scale and legal complexity of what the government was attempting to do was staggering. After all, it had taken Henry VIII six years to do away with the Pope.[21]

Richard Goodrich had foreseen terrible technical difficulties in bringing back the supremacy. Indeed MPs spent three days on the second reading of the supremacy bill. It was given once again to Sir Anthony Cooke and also to Sir Francis Knollys, the Vice-Chamberlain of Elizabeth's household and the Queen's cousin by marriage. They would revise it. The bill's bumpy ride in the Commons so far would not have cheered Cecil, but at least it was in the safe hands of two firm champions of reform, both former exiles and both close to the Secretary.

By late February the government had introduced, more or less successfully, a workable bill for the Queen's supremacy. The Count of Feria, hostile to a fault, blamed Cecil for its success. He wrote that 'it was necessary, in order to succeed with his iniquitous scheme, for Secretary Cecil to throw the matter into confusion'. What this 'confusion' was Feria did not say. But we have to imagine Cecil using all his considerable skills to persuade the Commons to pass the bill to the House of Lords. It must have been quite a performance.[22]

When this second supremacy bill was read for the first time in the Lords on 28 February, the effect was something like water hitting a live wire. There was uproar. Conservative bishops and peers began to fight it in every way they could. The bishops produced a statement of their faith, insisting that only the Church could determine matters of belief. On 3 March the Bishop of London gave the statement to Lord Keeper Bacon. Bacon did nothing. Any opposition was ignored. Ten days later the Lords once again began to debate the bill.

The words of Anthony Browne, Viscount Montague in the Lords' chamber give some sense of the energy and anger of the debate. He believed that the bill would repeal 'all that ever was made for the defence of the faith against the malignity of wicked heresies'. Montague spoke from the heart, for the saving of his soul 'at the terrible day of God'. But one of the bill's supporters, the Earl of Bedford, Cecil's great friend, goaded him. Was it right, asked Bedford, that when Montague had been in Rome with the Bishop of Ely in Mary's reign, the Roman cardinals had offered to get them whores? Montague, furious, swore before God and the angels that what Bedford said was a lie.[23]

The supporters of the supremacy did not give up. They spoke against the power of the Pope in England. Their script came straight from the reigns of Henry VIII and Edward VI, from Goodrich's legal brief and from Cecil's 'Device'. Kings of England and their parliaments had always resisted popes.

Elizabeth, they said, had as much authority in spiritual matters as any of her predecessors had had. Not to recognise this would put at risk the security of the realm.

Precedent, the bill's supporters were saying, was on their side. No, the opponents of supremacy replied: precedent was on *their* side. Hundreds of years of church history were used by the government's opponents to argue that royal supremacy was unthinkable. Archbishop Heath of York tackled the greatest knot of all. The bill called Elizabeth the 'supreme head of the Church of England next and immediately under God'. He was blunt. '[T]o preach or minister the holy sacraments a woman may not, neither may she be Supreme Head of the Church of Christ.'[24]

Easter was by now days away, and it was expected that parliament would be prorogued at the end of the month. This was not the lightning strike of Reformation Cecil had wanted. So what to do next? The government rushed through a bill that 'no persons shall be punished for using the religion used in King Edward's last year'. This was merely a sticking plaster. At nine o'clock on the morning of Good Friday, 24 March, Elizabeth prepared to go to Westminster to assent to the bills that had been passed by parliament. But very quickly she changed her mind and instructed the Lords and the Commons to reconvene on 3 April. There was a change of plan. We can imagine Cecil busily advising the Queen. What he and the Council devised was a plan to wreck Catholic opposition to the church settlement.[25]

It sounded innocent enough. There was to be a debate in Westminster Abbey. Lords and MPs would be able to come along to listen to supporters and opponents of reform setting out their positions and objections. In fact it turned out to be a rather subtle trap for the Catholics.

The disputation in the abbey was presided over by Cecil's brother-in-law Sir Nicholas Bacon, hardly a disinterested chair of the proceedings. It was great theatre, electric and passionate, in which there were hard words on both sides. William Day, a young servant of Cecil, hoped that God would help all the world to see the ignorance and malice of the Catholics and 'shall hiss them out of place'.

Cecil was busy at work in the abbey. William Day wrote that his master had no leisure to answer letters. 'His business,' Day wrote to Matthew Parker in Cambridge, 'albeit you can easily conjecture how many and great they be when they be but ordinary, and of course, yet for the better satisfying of you in this behalf you shall understand he hath been letted this day from writing with the great disputation kept in Westminster Church.'[26]

The debate collapsed. The Catholic disputants refused to follow Bacon's directions and so, with little warning, he dissolved it. This was probably what Bacon and Cecil had expected all along. Certainly the Privy Council acted with remarkable speed. Just hours after the end of the debate two bishops, Winchester and Lincoln, were charged with disobedience to common authority and sent to the Tower of London by warrant of the Privy Council. The same afternoon the Council ordered a search of the bishops' London houses 'to peruse their studies and writings'. If the Catholics had been able to stall reform in parliament, then Cecil and the Council had found another way to wreck their opposition.[27]

Two tough and articulate opponents of the supremacy bill were now in the Tower. The other Catholic disputants were bound to appear before the Council every day and to pay fines for their 'contempt . . . of late committed against the Queen's Majesty'. The Council took great care to prepare an official account of the Catholic disputants' disloyalty to the Queen. At St Paul's Cross on 9 April Dr William Bill defended the bishops' imprisonment for seditious behaviour. Bill was one of Cecil's oldest friends from Cambridge.[28]

On Monday, 10 April Cecil brought a new bill of supremacy to the House of Commons. He was determined to keep MPs on their toes. He told the Commons that, out of humility, the Queen was unwilling to accept the title of 'supreme head' of the Church; instead this latest bill had the new formula of 'supreme governor'. The new bill proposed to revive an old act of parliament for the reception of the communion in both kinds. It also proposed to repeal Mary's heresy laws. So what it did, by concentrating on the authority of the Queen, was to give good legal shape to Elizabeth's powers, and it also made sure that Protestants would be free to worship.[29]

This time Cecil had found a formula that looked as if it would work. He was helped by the fact that former opponents began to soften a little bit. When this latest bill was sent by the Lords to a committee on 17 April there was no serious effort to sabotage it. The government's opponents in the committee, of which there were only a few, merely altered the wording of the bill to protect Catholics like themselves from severe punishment. The thing was nearly done. By 29 April it was ready for Elizabeth's assent.

All of this went hand in hand with the government's effort to revive the Prayer Book of 1552. Those Catholics still left in the House of Lords put up a spirited defence of their faith. Feckenham, the Abbot of Westminster, was blunt. With a swipe at Cecil's co-ordinated series of Protestant sermons of February and March – at the 'preachers and scaffold players of this new religion' – he saw in this Reformation the end of decent society as he knew it. Obedience was gone, humility and meekness abolished. Virtuous and chaste living had been abandoned. Society was in uproar, turned upside down, 'the subjects disobedient unto God and all superior powers'. Feckenham called on the Lords 'to avoid and expel out of this realm this new religion, whose fruits are already too manifestly known'.[30]

Some peers listened to Feckenham. Eighteen voted against the bill for the Prayer Book. The government won by three votes. If the two bishops had not been locked away in the Tower, or if Feckenham himself had been in the chamber for the vote (strangely he was absent), or if a few lay peers had decided to oppose the bill, then the story would have been very different. As it was, a law that affected worship in the Church of England was passed without a single vote from any of the churchmen in the House of Lords. A close-run thing, certainly; but it was a breathtaking revolution, too.

We will probably never know how Cecil, Bacon and the other councillors persuaded, bullied, flattered and cajoled opponents and friends in this parliament. There had been weeks of desperate negotiations, back-room deals and hard politics. Still, when we consider what the government finally achieved in the face of such determined opposition, it is hard not to be impressed by what Cecil and his colleagues had brought off.

Abbot Feckenham was right to see in this law the victory of Protestantism. The Act of Uniformity explained that Edward VI's second Prayer Book had been repealed by Mary 'to the great decay of the due honour of God and discomfiture to the professors of the truth of Christ's religion'. This was the language of the coronation pageant and of Feckenham's 'preachers and scaffold players'. And now it was the doctrine of the Church of England, enforceable by law and prosecution. Ministers of the Church (the Act of Uniformity did not call them priests) could be removed from office if they refused to use the new Prayer Book. Indeed anyone who in any way criticised the Prayer Book, in plays or songs or poems or 'other open words', could be prosecuted. People had to go to church: there were punishments if they refused. And so, in this way, a Protestant religious service in English was put into law for the first time since 1553.[31]

It is hard to exaggerate the significance of Supremacy and Uniformity. What the parliament of 1559 did was revolutionary. Just another look at Richard Goodrich's legal brief of December 1558 reminds us that even a committed Protestant and experienced lawyer believed that to use parliament to reject the Pope was a terribly dangerous thing to do. Of course Cecil's 'Device' gave a quite different plan to Goodrich's. What Cecil and his colleagues did, very much in line with the 'Device', was to force into law a political and religious settlement that set Elizabeth's England apart from the Catholic powers of Europe.

In the revolution the royal supremacy became the absolute test of loyalty. Anyone who held office in government or Church had to accept in his conscience that Elizabeth was 'the only supreme governor of this realm'. For many it would be an impossible test. Yet the law coolly set out the punishments for anyone, whether or not they had to swear the oath, who maintained 'foreign and usurped power and authority'. For a first offence he would forfeit his goods and property or be put in prison for a year. A third offence was high treason.

Cecil had always known that Reformation would fracture England's relations with the Catholic powers of Europe. He carried on regardless. The parliament of 1559 and the revolution it produced have his fingerprints all over them. Every so often we catch a fleeting glimpse of him in St Stephen's Chapel and in Westminster Abbey and in the Council's chamber at Whitehall. Now the hard work to preserve and protect that revolution was about to begin.

8

'This Famous Isle'

He was everywhere and everything in Elizabethan government. No piece of paper, no report, no policy, no event or panic or crisis at home or abroad could escape his attention. By design and by instinct he was at the heart of Elizabeth's court. He controlled the machinery of power. He ran the royal secretariat and chaired meetings of the Privy Council. He advised the Queen daily and read every piece of paper that was sent to her. He was Elizabeth's voice to the world, for he wrote her letters and proclamations and drafted the instructions to her ambassadors. With ready access to Elizabeth in her private rooms and a mastery of the government machine, he saw and heard all that went on at court.

The royal Secretary who walked the corridors of the Queen's palaces worked harder than anyone else and he knew it. He was the master of every detail on any policy. Elizabeth had an instinctive understanding of his ability. Their working relationship was exceptionally close. She trusted him as her servant, and his unique position within her government was a mark of that trust. He believed absolutely in her rule. He was tough, passionate and uncompromising. He felt that sometimes Elizabeth had to be protected from herself. As an old saying has it, he spoke truth unto power. But this was the way of the world: Cecil knew in his bones that everything was at stake, even the mere survival of a realm beset by its enemies.

It was a punishing professional life. Cecil knew that no one else at Elizabeth's court could do it. With power came the sacrifice of painful service. As Cecil once said to his brother-in-law, Sir Nicholas Bacon, he had 'forborne wife, children, friends, house, yea all mine own to serve, which I know not that any other hath done in this time'. He felt the strains and anxieties of a life consumed by politics. He was often frustrated by his long hours and painful workload. At times he felt isolated and under-appreciated. He was irritated by disagreements with the Queen and his colleagues, particularly when she or they would not see things his way. The politics of the court could be raw – but so we should expect them to be, given the dangers to Elizabeth's throne.[1]

Strip away the febrile politics of the court and we are left with the beliefs Cecil held with great passion and commitment. He believed in England's 'true religion'. He never doubted that the Catholic superpowers of Europe wanted to usurp Elizabeth. He recognised that to survive was to fight, even if this meant helping the rebel subjects of other princes. He believed above all that the only solutions to England's predicament were marriage for Elizabeth and the fact of a sure royal succession. On most of these matters, however, the Queen's view was quite different.

*

Right from the beginning it was clear to Cecil that Catholic Europe wanted to destroy Protestant England. He saw that Elizabeth was surrounded by enemies who believed that another young woman, Mary Stuart, Queen of Scots, was Mary I's rightful heir. These enemies hated the settlement of 'true religion' Cecil had fought so hard to establish in 1559. He believed that Protestant England was fighting for its life. This struggle was Cecil's mission for the rest of his career: light against dark, truth against lies, Christ against Antichrist. His was a personal and passionate war to protect the realm from its enemies.

As early as 1559 he knew there was a conspiracy afoot. At the root of this conspiracy were the negotiations for peace between England, France and Spain at Câteau-Cambrésis in the spring of 1559. The peace of Câteau confirmed the shame of the loss of Calais. And it suggested to Cecil an effort by the Catholics to rob Elizabeth of her crown and give it to Mary, Queen of Scots.[2]

Mary Stuart was sixteen years old in 1559. In a life just as remarkable as Elizabeth's, she had become a queen at the age of one week and had been taken to France five years later. At fifteen she was betrothed and married to the Dauphin of France, Francis. Her French family, the Guises, were ultra-Catholic. But it was the fact of her Tudor blood that was really significant in 1559. As well as being the daughter of Mary of Guise, she was the great-grand-daughter of Henry VII through her father, James V of Scotland and James's mother, Margaret Tudor. Margaret was Henry VIII's sister, and so Mary, Queen of Scots was Henry's great-niece and Elizabeth's cousin.

Cecil had a nervous horror of what the Catholic powers of Europe would do to get their way. Other monarchs treated Elizabeth's right to sit on the English throne with contempt. Catholic princes looked to Mary's Stuart claim. She was, Cecil believed, the instrument of the ambitious and powerful Guises. What made her really dangerous, in Cecil's mind, was that Elizabeth had no husband,

and so as yet no prospect of an heir. No heir made for a dangerously uncertain future. Though Henry VIII's Act of Succession excluded the Stuarts from the English throne, Catholic rulers in Europe and Catholics at home believed, so Cecil thought, that the Queen of Scots was England's rightful monarch.

Cecil quickly began to assemble evidence of the international conspiracy against England. He was outraged by what he read. Elizabeth's ambassador in France, Sir Nicholas Throckmorton, began to send reports that confirmed everything Cecil feared. By the early summer of 1559 he had proof of something that would obsess him for nearly thirty years: Mary and Francis were using the royal arms of Elizabeth as their own. They had the English arms in their seals and they were even having them stamped on their dinnerware. With the Guises behind them, Francis and Mary were claiming the English crown as their own. This was tantamount to a declaration of war.[3]

Cecil feared France because of Mary Stuart's supposed claim to the English royal succession. But his other great worry was a strategic one. Mary was Queen of Scotland as well as the wife of the heir to the French throne. In Mary's minority and absence Scotland was governed by her mother, Mary of Guise. So the power of France lay in the north as well as just across the English Channel. From Scotland French government and garrisons threatened England's troubled northern border.

Here Cecil's hopes in 1559 lay in the rebellion of some Scottish noblemen who called themselves the Lords of the Congregation. The Lords stood against the Regent Mary and the French on the grounds of both religion and patriotism. They were, they claimed, the natural-born leaders of Scotland and they wanted to get rid of foreign oppressors; but they were also Protestants who stood against the persecution of the 'true religion', a persecution that had intensified in Scotland in the months before Elizabeth's accession to the English throne. Cecil had written about this war in Scotland in his 'Device' in late 1558. Even before the humiliating Peace of Câteau he had known that the survival of Protestant England would depend on clever and robust English policy in Scotland.[4]

From the beginning Cecil wanted to help the Lords of the Congregation. He valued their beliefs and he saw in their victory the military security of England. He became passionately involved in the Scots' cause. He remembered the time when as a young man he had marched north with Protector Somerset's army with the message of friendship, religion and British unity. He was a natural British imperialist who knew that Elizabeth's survival as queen would depend on her friendship with Protestant Scots. It took him months to win colleagues to his cause. It took him even longer to convince Elizabeth to do three things to which she was instinctively opposed: help rebels, spend money and commit troops.

Military help for the Congregation was out of the question in the summer of 1559, but Cecil was very keen to give the Scottish Lords all the encouragement he could. At this delicate time, Elizabeth sent a number of agents and ambassadors north to the border with Scotland, and these men were briefed and instructed by the Privy Council. This is where we can see how Cecil could control the government machine. He gathered together a caucus of supporters in the Privy Council. He and they spoke for the Council as a whole. And the Council expressed itself through Cecil's pen: when the rebel Scots read the Council's letter of encouragement, they read Cecil's words.

Cecil assured the Congregation 'that rather than that realm should be with a foreign nation and power oppressed . . . the authority of England would adventure with power and force to aid that realm against any such foreign invasion'. To English diplomats Cecil gave guarded hints of armed support for the Scots: 'The Protestants there shall be assayed with all fair promises first, next with money and last with arms. Wisdom is to look for the worst, and so to provide. Ye may keep them in comfort.' As yet there were no firm promises. But Cecil asked one diplomat, Sir James Croft, 'to kindle the fire'.[5]

The stakes were high enough for England in the early summer of 1559, but Cecil knew as well as anyone that events can change everything. And in July there was a truly tectonic shift in European politics. Mary Stuart's father-in-law, King Henry of France, was killed in a terrible jousting accident. Mary was now Queen of France. Cecil was the first person in England to hear the news, which he broke to Elizabeth privately as soon as he had the letter. That same night he wrote urgently to the Earl of Shrewsbury, the Lord President of the Council in the North at York: 'None yet knoweth this but our mistress only who will break it to her Council anon.' On that Wednesday Cecil was already evaluating, calculating and planning. With Mary's husband as king, and with the aspiring Guises still behind them, surely anything was possible.[6]

We can only imagine Cecil's worry when Sir Nicholas Throckmorton in Paris wrote in late July with more evidence that Francis and Mary, now king and queen of France, were using the English royal arms as their own. So it was no surprise that Cecil threw himself into the business of Scotland. He wrote for the Privy Council a letter of unconditional support for Congregation. It hinted at an ideological purpose, and the old British project: the Council would 'not neglect such godly and honourable enterprises' as may be necessary, and they hoped 'that thereby this famous isle may be conjoined at the last in hearts as it is in continent, land with one sea, and in one uniformity of language, manners and conditions'.[7] Although he was pushing as hard as he could, there was still a long way to go. Cecil had the words; but as yet there were no men and no weapons for the Congregation. This was the next step.

So Cecil put the case for giving military support to the Protestant Scots. At Hampton Court in August he set to work on some important position papers on Scotland. He knew the case had to be well argued and compelling. In his own mind everything was clear. There was, he believed, a deeply rooted international conspiracy against Elizabeth. One way for the Queen to defend herself was to help the Protestant Scots in their patriotic revolution. And here Cecil considered a new way for Scotland to govern itself with the help of England. In this he was influenced deeply by a paper that sat on his desk at Hampton Court. He read it on the last day of August 1559. To judge by its title it was a bland, scholarly piece of work: 'A memorial of certain points meet for restoring the realm of Scotland to the ancient weal'. It is likely that Cecil was its author.

On the surface this 'Memorial' was a proposal for the government of Scotland free from the influence of France. It began with a simple but important premise. The 'best worldly felicity' for Scotland was 'either to continue in a perpetual peace with the kingdom of England or to be made one monarchy with England'. It was a clever proposal to unite two kingdoms into one for the good of Scotland, for the good of true religion, and for the good of England and its security.

The enemy, of course, was France, 'which being an ancient enemy to England seeketh always to make Scotland an instrument to exercise their malice upon England'. Scotland had to be governed by Scots, and while Mary Stuart was in France also by a council. Scotland had to be Protestant, a land 'free from all idolatry like as England is', and this reformation was to be on the English model and enacted by the Scottish parliament. Scotland would rule itself – except of course that it would have the guiding friendship of England.

The sting of the 'Memorial' lay in its recommendation for the deposition of Mary, Queen of Scots. Coolly and calmly the author of the 'Memorial' said that if Francis and Mary were unwilling to agree to any of this, the parliament (or Estates) of Scotland would have the authority to approach the King and Queen with 'their humble requests, and if the same be not effectually granted then finally they [the Estates] may commit the governance thereof to the next heir of that crown, binding the same also to observe the laws and ancient rights of the realm'. Surely Mary would be unwilling to accept this constitution for Scotland 'in respect of the greedy and tyrannous affection of France'. And so, simply, it was apparent that God was 'pleased to transfer from her the rule of that kingdom for the weal of it'. The 'Memorial' set out a constitution for a Protestant Scotland tied for ever to England. Anything that got in the way of this friendship had to be removed: the influence of France and then, almost certainly, the Queen of Scots. In measured constitutional language it proposed simply the disposal of an inconvenient monarch.[8]

Cecil believed in this plan. It was his vision for a united Protestant Britain under English control, and all for one reason: to keep his religion and his Queen and country safe from their desperate enemies.[9]

*

In early September Cecil had leave to spend a few days of much-needed peace away from court at Burghley. He said he felt 'like a bird out of the cage'. But Scotland was never far from his thoughts.[10]

Mary Stuart's offence of taking the royal arms of England still angered Cecil in September 1559. The offence was made even worse by the fact that Mary was now Queen of France as well as Queen of Scots. As autumn arrived he watched and waited, 'being fully occupied with business'. By the end of October Elizabeth finally began to hear advice on what to do about Scotland. Guided by Cecil, she consulted a handful of her advisers. Naturally he was one of them.[11]

He proceeded very carefully. He knew in his bones that something had to be done about Scotland and France, but the Queen had yet to be convinced. And if he could not persuade the Queen that she had to help the Congregation then nothing could be done. He made sure to suppress any letters or reports from Scotland that he felt would offend the Queen. By this time John Knox was the Congregation's secretary and Elizabeth despised Knox for his offensive views on female monarchy. Cecil was alert and careful. He saw everything that arrived on his desk. But he knew better than to share all he knew with Elizabeth.[12]

In December there was a kind of breakthrough when an embassy of Protestant Scots arrived at Elizabeth's court led by William Maitland of Lethington. Maitland was much like Cecil, a scholar as well as a royal servant and a firmly committed Protestant. Cecil briefed and prepared the Scots to make a persuasive case for English aid. Cecil knew that Elizabeth was not interested in arguments about religion or British brotherhood, so he made sure that the ambassadors talked about French violence and oppression in Scotland. They also reminded Elizabeth that French power threatened England. This was the kind of argument she might possibly listen to.[13]

The Congregation's embassy to the English court began the most divisive debate in Elizabeth's government since the tussles in parliament earlier that year. The question was whether it was time to support the Scots in their armed struggle against the French. Cecil had no doubts: the Congregation had to be supported and English troops should help their Scottish allies to destroy French power in Scotland. Elizabeth, he said, would not be aiding rebels to fight against their God-ordained governors: she would merely be helping the natural-born men of Scotland to throw off their foreign oppressors. But the Queen was not yet convinced. Nor indeed were some of Cecil's colleagues. He had a hard political battle on his hands.

On 15 December there was a great debate on Scotland in the Council chamber at Whitehall Palace. Chief among the opponents of intervention was Sir Nicholas Bacon, Cecil's brother-in-law. Bacon's position was everything we should expect of a man whose family motto was 'Safety in moderation'. He did not believe that it was necessary to assist the Congregation openly. They should not be helped directly unless they could fight the French on their own. Bacon argued that England was much too weak to take on a great military power like France. Admittedly he saw no legal objections to war. The French, he said, had behaved outrageously: war was justified. But the plain fact was that England could not stand up to such a powerful enemy.[14]

A speech by such a talented and persuasive speaker as Sir Nicholas Bacon was bound to be compelling. His message was: do nothing for the time being. And in this he was supported by men of rank and experience. Cecil could not move: without a united Council, he could not hope to persuade Elizabeth. But within a fortnight he had in his hands an intelligence report that shattered Bacon's case for care and moderation over Scotland. War was on the way, whether Bacon and his supporters liked it or not.

Even over Christmas Cecil's work had not relented. He was at Whitehall 'almost asleep' at his desk at midnight on 23 December. He had the all-important intelligence report just three days later. It said that the French navy was preparing to put to sea. They had 15,000 German mercenaries ready to move. Cecil acted swiftly. He wrote an urgent letter to the Earl of Shrewsbury. The English garrison at Berwick-upon-Tweed was to be put on alert and horsemen would be sent to Newcastle upon Tyne.[15]

This intelligence changed everything. Now only a single councillor, the Earl of Arundel, opposed war in Scotland. The Privy Council was almost united in the view that the Congregation had to be helped with men, money and munitions. When the councillors met to debate Scotland on 27 December they produced a war plan for a strike against the French army in Scotland. They petitioned the Queen for urgent and speedy action. At the end of a long formal presentation to Elizabeth, Cecil carefully listed the names of fourteen councillors who believed that it was time to send forces to help the Congregation. He explained to Elizabeth that now even the five councillors who had before 'stood doubtful touching any exploit into Scotland' supported war. All they had to do was to wait for the Queen's final decision.[16]

Elizabeth heard Cecil's paper the next day. She refused to do anything: her Secretary noted on the back of his paper simply that it was 'not allowed by Her Majesty'. It was as cut and dried as that. No explanation survives.

Cecil was discouraged but undeterred. That same day he met his inner caucus of supporters in Sir Thomas Parry's chamber at Whitehall. There Cecil once again stated his support for war: 'I cannot for any reason that I yet have heard, think any otherwise than I have done, but that it is meet for the Queen's Majesty to prevent the French possession and conquest of Scotland.' His advocacy of military action was as strong as ever. It was, he believed, a desperate fight for England's survival. As he told the others in the room, 'But yet this and the rest with divers other reasons lead together, make me earnest to think that it is the surest counsel for the Queen's Majesty to prevent this danger of the French and to impeach their conquest of Scotland.'[17]

Still Elizabeth refused to give, however hard Cecil and the Council tried to persuade her of the desperate urgency of the mission. Cecil, too, did not bend: he was sure of his convictions and passionate about what had to be done. This was the greatest test so far of his service to the Queen. He knew he had to obey Elizabeth. After all, he was merely her servant. And yet the oaths he had sworn as a councillor and as her Secretary obliged him to offer advice to the Queen honestly and frankly. This was an impossible knot. So in late December he considered his position and went so far as to draft a letter of resignation.

Cecil wrote that he was Elizabeth's 'poor servant and most lowly subject, an unworthy Secretary'. He could not in conscience give any other advice on Scotland than he had already given. He wanted now to be 'spared to inter-meddle' in that business. He was happy to perform any service for the Queen, even in her kitchens or gardens. He was a servant, sworn 'to be a minister of your Majesty's determinations and not of mine own'. Yet his letter had a keen edge to it. To Cecil it was 'an unprofitable service' to serve Elizabeth 'in anything that myself cannot allow'. These were the tough words of a man who, for all the formalities and flatteries of royal service, felt he had to be listened to.[18]

Did he really want to leave Elizabeth's service? Or is his letter of resignation proof that by now he considered himself indispensable to her rule? Was he confident that she would never accept his resignation? Would she give on Scotland? Only time would tell.

*

Sir William Cecil did not resign over Scotland. His letter, if he ever gave it to the Queen, was a terrific gamble. He risked his whole career on this one policy. But it was a policy he passionately believed in.

And so he continued to press Elizabeth to act. In January 1560 he made it clear to the Queen that if nothing was done the French would conquer Scotland within a month. Then they would prosecute their 'pretence' against

England. Mary Stuart, her husband King Francis and the house of Guise were 'in their hearts mortal enemies' to Elizabeth.[19]

Persistence paid in the end when the Queen finally agreed to military help for the Congregation. At Berwick, in March 1560, a treaty was signed between the English government and the rebel Scots. They would have military assistance in the war against French government. For Cecil it was, at last, evidence of the fact of Protestant solidarity between the two realms. He assured the Scots that he would do 'whatsoever it shall please God to offer to the concord of these two realms being at the creation knit in one isle'.[20]

The English military campaign in Scotland had its setbacks as well as its successes. But by late spring there was at last a chance of a negotiated settlement between England, France and Scotland. The talks were to take place near Edinburgh and Elizabeth sent Cecil as one of her diplomats. With Dr Nicholas Wotton and Thomas Windebank, one of Cecil's servants as well as a lawyer and a fluent French speaker, he set out for Scotland with a large party and twenty-two horses. The negotiations were hard, but by the end of the first week of July Cecil and Wotton and the other diplomats had a workable treaty. It was to be one of Cecil's triumphs, his great revenge for the humiliation of Câteau-Cambrésis.

The text of the treaty of Edinburgh secured many of the things Cecil had wanted for Scotland since the beginning of Elizabeth's reign. It became the touchstone of his career: he would measure everything by it, and judge everything against it, for nearly thirty years.

In the treaty France recognised Elizabeth I's right to be Queen of England. A council of twelve Scottish lords would rule Scotland. The Queen of Scots and the Scottish parliament would choose these councillors, but Mary Stuart's nominations would first be vetted by the parliament. There would be no French office-holders in Scotland. Mary's successors to the throne of Scotland would be the house of Hamilton, the heirs of King James II. The final clause of the treaty bound Mary and her husband, King Francis, to ratify and fulfil all of its conditions. If they failed to do this, England could by the terms of the treaty intervene in Scotland to protect the Protestant religion and keep the French out of the realm.

The treaty of Edinburgh was a triumph, a humiliation for Mary Stuart and for France and a guarantee of England's political and military security. But it all depended on whether Mary and Francis would ratify it.

When Cecil returned to London in late July, he considered the vast amount of money he had spent in Edinburgh. Tudor ambassadors paid for their embassies from their own pockets; they hoped (sometimes vainly) to reclaim the money from the crown. Sir William Cecil was no different. His 'demands' for his allowance at Edinburgh were enormous. The food and other necessaries he would have had as Secretary for free, as 'bouche of court',* but which he had pay for while he was away from London, came to £252. With postage and other expenses, the grand total was £383. This was a huge sum of money.[21]

So for Cecil the diplomatic triumph of Edinburgh came with the costs of time away from the corridors of power at court; the strain of tough negotiations; and, for a man who was very careful with his money, incredible expense.

Events can of course change everything in politics. Even great treaties can be undone by them. And it was once again a royal death in France, this time of Mary's husband King Francis in December 1560, that caused another huge shift in the international affairs of western Europe. Cecil would have recognised this as soon as he read Sir Nicholas Throckmorton's report on the king's death at Orléans on 5 December.[22]

There were more questions than he had adequate answers to. Would the treaty made at Edinburgh ever be ratified? What about Mary herself? Where would she go? Would she stay in France or return to Scotland? She was still the instrument of the dangerous Guises, the greatest weapon Elizabeth's Catholic enemies possessed. Even at best the young widow of eighteen was a nagging uncertainty in Cecil's mind. But at worst she was a terrible danger to England's security. It was Cecil's job to remain vigilant, as he well knew.

*

Sir William Cecil had some good reasons to be cheerful in the new year of 1561. In January Elizabeth appointed him Master of the Court of Wards. The court looked after the orphans of men who owed obligations of service to the crown. It appointed appropriate guardians for these children and arranged their marriages. The Master was a powerful figure in a society where marriage and property determined social standing. He was also close to the Queen, who relied on him for advice on some very sensitive cases. Cecil's promotion to the Wards was mark of royal favour and trust. From now on he would enjoy enormous powers of patronage in Elizabethan government.[23]

Cecil was a power in matters of counsel and policy, a force to be reckoned with at court. All of this showed in the material comfort of Cecil's life of royal service. In the middle of May he received a major grant of lands in Stamford. This takes us all the way back to his early life, for the lands had once belonged to the guild of Corpus Christi in whose chapel he had been taught as a boy. He had by now come a long way from Stamford, yet was always tied by blood and land to his family's old country.[24]

---

* From the French *avoir bouche à cour*, literally 'to have mouth at court'.

Burghley was nearly a hundred miles from London. A powerful man needed a base much closer to the court. And so Cecil bought a grand new house in Westminster near to the royal palace of the Savoy on the Strand. He and his family had outgrown Cannon Row, and Cecil House was worthy of an important man. It was also fit to entertain the Queen, a pleasurable duty for any of her courtiers. Cecil gave a banquet for Elizabeth on 13 July 1561. This meant more to him than a grand dinner: it was one of the great moments of his career.[25]

But not even Sir William Cecil, all-seeing and all-knowing, the master of policy, could control everything in his life. He had great houses and the surety of rank and position. He was also the father of a nineteen-year-old son, and in 1561 the behaviour of Thomas Cecil made him feel wretched and angry. Cecil would have said that he had always done his best for Thomas. He had given him a fine education, hiring only the best tutors from Cambridge. He had made sure that Thomas could dance and play the virginal. Thomas was given the skills to be a courtier. Now it was time to send Thomas to France to complete his education. France was an enemy, certainly; but the French court was great training for young courtiers and Paris a wonderful city. And it was there that the problems for Cecil really began.

The story of Thomas's journey really begins with the sum of three hundred French crowns, or £90, that Cecil's secretary, Hugh Alington, delivered to Thomas Windebank on 30 May. Windebank was Cecil's French expert, a gentleman and a lawyer of Lincoln's Inn, his master's clerk and sometime courier. He had served Cecil well in the negotiations at Edinburgh. Windebank was an urbane and likeable man with a sympathetic understanding of human weakness. This was just as well. In 1561 he was given by Cecil probably the most difficult job in the household: he was to chaperon a lively nineteen-year-old about to taste freedom for the first time in his life.[26]

The money Windebank received from Alington on 30 May 1561 (without a proper receipt, for which Alington was to suffer later) was thought sufficient to cover the expenses of Master Thomas's stay in France. Cecil imagined that his son's time abroad would give Thomas excellent written and spoken French and a good understanding of the families of the French nobility. He would see court life at first hand. Thomas could practise his courtly manners. He would also be able to observe the Queen's ambassador in Paris, Sir Nicholas Throckmorton, who was a cousin of the Marquess of Northampton, and Sir Nicholas's wife Lady Anne. It would be a valuable education for a Secretary's son.

Thomas Cecil's visit to France became one of the great miseries of his father's year. But Cecil had other worries. Even before he began to hear reports of Thomas's misbehaviour in Paris, the intentions of Mary Stuart, the Queen of Scots, were beginning to trouble Cecil.

Now a widow, Mary was going to return to Scotland where she could cause all kinds of mischief. Cecil simply did not trust Mary Stuart. At the end of June he wrote to Thomas Randolph, Elizabeth's ambassador in Scotland, about the harm she could do. Her aim, he believed, was to subvert religion. He felt seriously under-prepared. The clever clauses of the treaty of Edinburgh, which had not yet been ratified by Mary, began to look thin. Would Cecil's great plan for a Protestant Scotland tied by friendship and mutual support to England be able to survive the personal rule of Mary?[27]

What really troubled Cecil was the English royal succession. The Tudor line died with Elizabeth. Catholics believed that Mary Stuart had a claim to the throne and the French government was trying to get its way by aggression. The defence of the realm, the security of the Protestant Church and the protection of the life of Elizabeth I were all matters that were bound up together. Yet what had Elizabeth done to help herself? So far, very little. She was as yet unmarried, and it looked uncomfortably as if this was the way she intended to stay. In 1559 she had even told parliament that 'I happily choose this kind of life in which I yet live'.[28]

Cecil and his colleagues in the Council had no time for this kind of complacency. In July 1561 Cecil wrote frankly of his hopes and fears: 'Well, God send our mistress a husband,' he said to Throckmorton in France, 'and by him a son, that we may hope our posterity shall have a masculine succession. This matter is too big for weak folks and too deep for simple. The Queen's Majesty knoweth of it. And so I will end.' Elizabeth knew very well that it was her first duty as queen to marry and bear a male heir. There can be no doubt that Cecil had told her this to her face. Without a sure succession Elizabeth, her kingdoms and people were exposed to the dangers of foreign invasion and subversion.[29]

Cecil took his grumblings away on royal progress, where he conducted government business on the move. Everything that crossed his desk, on whatever matter, concerned him. From Essex he complained about the 'lack of intelligence' from the Earl of Sussex who was in Ireland trying to put down a worrying insurgency by an Irish chieftain called Shane O'Neill. Always he had one eye on Elizabeth. In a letter to Sussex he wrote that she was in health 'and still far from marriage for aught that I can perceive'.[30] News from abroad was hardly better. In August Cecil heard that Throckmorton had met Mary Stuart. Throckmorton had pressed Mary finally to ratify the treaty of Edinburgh but Mary cleverly refused to do this on a technicality: the clauses of the treaty still bore the name of her dead husband, King Francis, and she said that it could not be ratified 'until it be changed unto my name only'. It was a clever, frustrating and dangerous evasion; it was a sign of things to come.[31]

There were times when even Cecil, consummate politician that he was, felt absolutely hopeless. That summer he was devastated by Sussex's failure to put down the rebellion in Ireland. The news, he wrote back to the earl, 'so appalled me that I had much ado to behave myself in sort to keep close the deep griefs of my heart'. His 'principal grief' was that the Earl of Pembroke, a very old friend in politics, was sick and absent from court and so he had 'not one . . . with whom to break my mind'.[32]

Yet there was a second cause of distress and it had to do with the subject Cecil had been brooding over for weeks: the royal succession. On the day Cecil heard about the bad news from Ireland, he also knew that Lady Katherine Grey, Elizabeth's lawful successor as queen, was pregnant by the Earl of Hertford, the son of Cecil's old master the Duke of Somerset. The Queen was furious.

Katherine Grey's secret marriage and pregnancy constituted a deep offence to Elizabeth. By the Succession Act of 1544 Lady Katherine was heir presumptive to the throne. Her marriage to the Earl of Hertford was secret because the law required the permission of the Queen before it could be performed: it was treason for a person of royal blood to marry without Elizabeth's approval. The fact that Katherine's alleged husband was the nephew of Queen Jane Seymour and the eldest son of a man who had ruled England as Edward VI's Protector aggravated even this grievous offence.

So the news of Lady Katherine's marriage and pregnancy was a dreadful shock; and it shone an uncomfortably hard light on the state of the English succession. Cecil was not helped by the fact that Katherine was family. Lady Mildred's brother, William, was married to the daughter of Katherine's uncle, Lord John Grey of Pyrgo. Lord John called Cecil his cousin; Lord John's brother, the Marquess of Dorset and Lady Katherine's father, had done the same before he was executed for treason in 1554.

Not surprisingly Cecil, at the right hand of the Queen, was immediately caught up in this maelstrom. Lord John Grey sought his help; and so did the Earl of Hertford's mother, who wrote to Cecil of 'the wilfulness of mine unruly child'. But even Cecil could not moderate Elizabeth's fury. Lady Katherine went to the Tower and the earl was summoned from France. 'Thus God is displeased with us', Cecil wrote miserably.[33]

The business of Lady Katherine and Hertford affected Thomas Cecil's tour of France. Already Thomas and Windebank had come across the earl and his entourage in Paris. At first Cecil had imagined that his son might tour with Hertford, but from the beginning Windebank was not sure about the wisdom of this. Ever subtle, he wrote to Cecil to say that he thought Thomas's French would improve away from the company of other Englishmen. Already, he said, the earl's entourage had been 'a great hindrance to Master Thomas, not

only for the tongue, but also other ways, which now I will not declare'. Cecil
was quick to read between the lines. By the time he had Windebank's letter he
knew all about the earl's offence. He sent strict instructions to Windebank: 'I
would not have you keep company with the Earl of Hertford.'[34]

By late August the bad news was coming fast. The Irish campaign was
failing. 'For God's sake, my Lord,' he wrote to the Earl of Sussex, 'bestir you
and recover this mishap as you may.' Away to the east Mary Stuart had finally
landed back in Scotland. Cecil knew within two days of her arrival at Leith.
'She hath no soldiers nor train but a few household; she meaneth to commit
herself to the trust of her own.'[35]

All of this was grim enough. But Cecil was beginning to get reports as well
of Thomas's misbehaviour in France. 'I have a watchword sent me out of
France,' he wrote to Windebank, 'that my son's being there shall serve him to
little purpose, for that he spendeth his time in idleness and not in profiting
himself in learning'. Cecil had expected to be able to read letters written by
Thomas in good Latin and French: hardly any had arrived. And Cecil was
worried, too, about money. 'Will Windebank to advertise me of your
expenses', he wrote to Thomas, 'that I may see how your money passeth away.'
He warned Thomas of the dangers of eating too much too late in the day –
'take heed of surfeits by late suppers' – and asked him to look out for 'any
things meet for my garden'.[36] Cecil was really troubled by the amount of
money his son was spending. By September Thomas had acquired a horse
which needed to be fed and stabled. But why on earth did he need a horse? 'In
my opinion,' Cecil wrote to Windebank, 'I rather covet my son to six or seven
months to live like a scholar, than to be a wanderer in streets.' He trusted
Windebank to inform him plainly of Thomas's faults. And here the father had
few illusions. 'I know some of his old faults were to be slothful in keeping his
bed, negligent and rash in expenses, uncareful or careless of his apparel, an
unordinate lover of unmeet plays, as dice and cards. In study soon weary, in
game never.'

Cecil was a man who valued moderation and self-control. He was so upset
by Thomas's behaviour that he could write no more about it: 'it increaseth my
grief'. And so in the same letter he moved to a happier topic, his new garden
at Cecil House. 'I pray you, Windebank, if ye think that ye can pleasure me
with sending me in the season of the year things meet for my orchard or
garden, help me; and if also ye can procure for me an apt man for mine
orchard or garden.' But before Windebank did anything, Cecil wanted to
know how much it would cost.[37]

As summer moved to autumn there was a whirl of news from abroad. From
France Cecil wanted a full account of how Master Thomas spent his days. 'In
any wise considering his youth,' Cecil wrote to Windebank, 'have great regard

that he may return with a chaste body.' Windebank was to be plain with Thomas about his faults; there was no other way 'to teach him to amend'.[38]

News from Scotland was more cheering. Cecil was very keen to know how Mary, Queen of Scots had been received there. Reports indicated that Scotland's Protestant revolution was intact, and that the man who had 'chief rule' under the young Catholic Queen, and who indeed 'governed' her, was Lord James Stuart, a good Protestant and Mary's half-brother. But there were wrinkles. Already Mary was beginning to speak about the arrangements for Elizabeth's succession. In October her government even questioned the authenticity of Henry VIII's will which, as everyone knew, excluded the Stuarts from the royal succession. This made it more necessary than ever for Elizabeth to marry, though Cecil knew she remained 'still strange to allow of marriage, wherein God alter her mind'.[39]

One moment Cecil would have on his desk a document of great political and diplomatic import, the next he could be dealing with the little local difficulty of a horse in Paris: 1561 was that kind of year. 'The keeping of a horse there I see groweth no small sum', Cecil wrote to Windebank in early November. It became his rank in society well enough, he said, for his son to go about on foot. He told Windebank very plainly that he had sent Thomas to France to learn some useful qualities, not to ride round on a horse. 'But I see in the end,' he added with some force, 'my son shall come home like a spending sot, meet to keep a tennis court.' Windebank quickly got rid of the horse.[40]

Cecil was a demanding master. He was a perfectionist who wanted every detail to be right. Windebank, easygoing and humane, must have been driven nearly to distraction. And it was not only Thomas's behaviour that Windebank had to worry about. Cecil was a great bibliophile, and he looked on Thomas's time in Paris as a way of adding to his library. Windebank was given a list of books to look out for: works of civil law in small and large volumes; the works of Cicero; quarto volumes of church law; 'fair' bibles in Latin and French for Cecil's chapel. And there were the other things Cecil loved: maps and charts, proclamations and edicts, and 'any trifling story or small abridgements' Windebank happened to come across. Windebank dutifully reported what he found, but Cecil sent back a stern letter to say that 'the note of the books which you sent me was imperfect' – Windebank had left out all kinds of details. Meekly he accepted his master's rebuke.[41]

Cecil was very busy at the end of the year. Troubled by sickness he moved between the court at St James's and Whitehall and his new mansion on the Strand. It was at Cecil House that, on 24 November, his sister Margaret married Roger Cave, the nephew of the Chancellor of the Duchy of Lancaster, a sound political match for the two families.[42]

For a time things were peaceful. Cecil wrote to the Earl of Sussex that 'All things appertaining to this estate both abroad and at home to my knowledge be in quiet terms, which I pray God long continue.' They did not. Within weeks Cecil was once more deeply concerned by Ireland and wrote bluntly to Sussex. 'Good my Lord, whether things do well or evil, let me know. I am one that have professed to honour and love you, to further your good meanings.'[43]

Cecil was worried, too, by the Queen. Just before Christmas, from his desk at Whitehall, he wrote frankly on Elizabeth to her ambassador in Paris. He was deeply, painfully frustrated; and behind this frustration was, as always, the royal succession:

> I have carried in my head with care means how Her Majesty should from time to time conduct her affairs. But I do see so little proof of my travails by reason Her Majesty alloweth not of them, that I have left all to the wide world. I do only keep on a course for show, but inwardly I meddle not, leaving things to run in a course as the clock is left when the barrel is wound up.

He wrote in the same letter of 'no small practices in forging' for the succession. 'Some think of the succession if Her Majesty should not marry, or lack issue; this song hath many parts. But for my part I have no skill but in plain song.' Almost worse was the 'great desire' in Elizabeth and the Queen of Scots to have a meeting. Cecil wanted to isolate Mary, to neutralise her influence; Elizabeth wanted to embrace her as a royal cousin. But what did Mary want? Was this a way to help to establish her right to the English throne? 'Knowing the diversity of both their intents,' Cecil wrote, 'although I wish it yet I think it dangerous to be any singular doer therein.'[44]

It was not a happy Christmas for Cecil. 'I am driven in service here into such lack as I never looked for,' he wrote gloomily to Thomas Windebank on 27 December. 'But if I might avoid the court and service I should recover my losses.' The conduct of his son gave him little cause for pleasure. 'Children ought to be as gifts of God, comfort to their parents,' he explained to Thomas that same day. 'But you as the contrary have made me careless of all children. You see how your former misbehaviour hath filled me full of discontentation, and how it will be cured, I leave it to Almighty God . . . God bless you that I may take comfort to give you mine.'[45]

*

Not far away from Cecil House, the young lawyers of the Inner Temple celebrated Christmas by performing a play. It would have suited Secretary

Cecil's glum mood. It was about the disaster that can befall a kingdom which has no properly settled succession. It was called *Gorboduc*, from the name of the mythical British king who unwisely divided his kingdom between his sons. The play ended with civil war and catastrophe. It was performed before Elizabeth on 18 January 1562. We have no idea what she made of it.

Gorboduc showed how princes can destroy their own kingdoms by ignoring good advice. We can imagine some wry smiles on the faces of Elizabeth's courtiers at the closing speech of the play. Eubulus, one of the principal characters, laments the utter ruin of a noble realm, a king dead and a vacant throne. The succession is uncertain. A wretched realm is left an open prey to foreign princes, 'a present spoil by conquest to ensue'. Eubulus was King Gorboduc's Secretary.[46]

The royal succession, the defence of the realm and the protection of Protestant religion were never far from Cecil's mind or pen. He perceived a terrible danger to England. It was clear from Throckmorton's reports that France was in the turmoil of religious civil war, and that the Guises wanted to exterminate the French Protestants, the Huguenots. So once again Cecil tried to persuade Elizabeth to take notice of what to him was a terrible danger. He encouraged her to take advice from some of her councillors.[47]

Cecil never gave up on the Queen. He said that he could not 'complain at all times of all humours, for though Her Majesty be at some time not hasty this way, yet when Her Majesty considereth and heareth reason, she is very well disposed'. But to Cecil's mind Elizabeth persisted in doing the wrong thing. Her policy on Mary Stuart was a case in point.[48]

Instead of isolating Mary, the instrument of Catholic enemies, Elizabeth wanted to embrace her cousin. By the spring and early summer of 1562 it looked as if the two queens would meet. Mary pushed hard for the interview while Cecil did his level best to subvert it. He came up with every reason possible against Elizabeth's going. The Council debated the interview. But in early July the Queen decided that she would meet Mary at York in either August or September. So Cecil was defeated; once again a long battle to make Elizabeth see sense (at least as he understood it) had failed. Yet on this occasion the Queen's habit of changing her mind at a moment's notice came to Cecil's rescue: Elizabeth quickly decided to postpone the meeting for months.[49]

Elizabeth had at last woken up to the persecution of Protestants abroad. France was being torn apart by religious war and, as in Scotland, some of Elizabeth's councillors wanted to help fellow Protestants abroad. Lord Robert Dudley, the Master of Elizabeth's Horse and a star at court, conducted negotiations with Louis of Bourbon, the Prince of Condé and leader of the Huguenots. By late September there was a treaty, and it was at Hampton Court that Elizabeth promised to supply the Huguenots with troops and money. Condé's representatives gave her the port town of Le Havre, or Newhaven, as a pledge till Calais was restored.[50]

It was a tremendously difficult time. In early October Cecil wrote that 'these varieties of the affairs in France . . . have so burned ourselves and our Council here into so many shapes from time to time'. At home things changed daily. The English military expedition began fitfully, yet in Cecil's mind the cause was strong. He wanted an international alliance of Protestants 'to consider how the common cause of religion might be defended against common confederacy of the enemy'.[51]

But as if this was not enough, Cecil and his colleagues had to face their worst nightmare: the possibility of the Queen's death. In October 1562 Elizabeth fell desperately ill with smallpox. Cecil was also sick which, as he wrote, 'happeneth very unseasonably for the affairs here'. But though Elizabeth recovered quickly, Cecil and his colleagues were terrified. For months they had pressed Elizabeth on marriage and succession. Now it was clearer than ever that the security of the kingdom, like Elizabeth's life, hung by a thread.[52] Cecil knew the dangers better than anyone. He read the diplomatic reports every day and it was his job to plan for the worst. He could not afford the luxury of pleasant dreams: his business was with nightmares. He had no doubts that there was a determined conspiracy to destroy Protestant England. War in France, Mary Stuart's manoeuvres in Scotland, the uncertainties at home: everything was connected in his mind. He was deeply anxious for the future and horribly overworked: 'I am so overburdened, and so slenderly helped', he wrote in the few weeks before Christmas 1562.[53]

What could be done about these dangers? In *Gorboduc* Secretary Eubulus had spoken about the appointment by parliament of heirs to the throne. By early November 1562 Cecil knew that Elizabeth was going to hold her second parliament. It was just possible that the Queen might be persuaded by Lords and Commons to act at last for the good of her kingdom.[54]

9

'As Sheep without a Shepherd'

At the beginning of 1563 there were nineteen men who had sworn the oath to counsel the Queen. They met daily wherever the court happened to be. Elizabeth was not present at their private business meetings. So far in the reign they had been 'burned . . . into so many shapes from time to time' by great debates on religion and war that when Elizabeth dragged her feet on policy, they tried to persuade her to act, by hook or by crook. They understood the arts of court politics and they were adept at working with, round and through a queen who was as difficult and stubborn as she was also incisive and controlled.

The two youngest councillors were Thomas Howard, fourth Duke of Norfolk, who was twenty-five years old; and Lord Robert Dudley, who was about thirty. Norfolk and Dudley were brightly painted and brilliant in their elegant courtly manners. Both were Knights of the Garter, members of the elite club of chivalry and royal honour. Both played, with Cecil, very important parts in the story of Elizabeth's reign.

Norfolk was four years older than Cecil's son, Thomas, yet there was a world of difference in how those two young men conducted themselves. The duke was almost a prince, tied by blood to the Queen, and he well knew it. He ruled East Anglia with a nod. At the age of twenty-one he had led a royal army in the North. His rank and title carried enormous weight.

Lord Robert Dudley, though not a duke, was the son of one. From the beginning of the reign he had held court office as Master of the Horse. He had known Elizabeth since she was eight years old, when he would have been eight or nine, and they became friends. His brilliance was dulled for a time by the suspicious death of his wife, Amy, in 1560. But from that time on the young widower was free to spend time with the Queen. In 1561 there was talk of their marriage, though even Cecil, desperate as he was for Elizabeth to find a husband, saw that it would be an imprudent match of queen and subject. But above all Dudley was a sparkling young courtier and a great friend of Elizabeth.

Cecil's feelings towards Lord Robert Dudley were undoubtedly ambivalent. The two men were neither enemies nor close friends. It is too easy to think of political relationships at the court in terms of fixed friendships and hatreds, with Cecil on one side and Dudley on the other. The truth was much more complicated than that. Cecil had once served Dudley's father, the Duke of Northumberland. Sir William and Lord Robert had friends in common, like Roger Ascham, who may have had a hand in Dudley's education. Both Cecil and Dudley were determined Protestants. Yet what must have struck courtiers at the time were their contrasting styles of behaviour at court. Dudley had a special attachment to Elizabeth; they were friends and companions. Cecil's relationship with the Queen was close in a different kind of way, businesslike and formal.

Cecil was at the heart of royal government. He briefed the Privy Council. He knew how to gauge Elizabeth's mood and he understood, as much as anyone could, what made her tick. He was, after all, the man Elizabeth trusted to hold the precious stamp of her sign manual. If Lord Robert Dudley had a deep emotional tie to Elizabeth, then Cecil's professional bond with the Queen was hard for anyone else to match.

Cecil's was a discreet kind of power, appropriate for a royal Secretary in his early forties. He played his part perfectly. It depended very much on his clothes and manner: he was acutely conscious of his image. His clothes were black, quietly expressive of wealth and power. Even in Mary's reign, when he was close to court but out of office, he enjoyed fine tailoring. His coats, jackets, jerkins, cloaks and doublets were of satin, lace, velvet and damask. The economy of the following description of Arnold van Bronckorst's portrait of Cecil from the first decade of the reign captures him very well:

> grey eyes turned toward the spectator; pink complexion with three warts on the right cheek; grey hair and light brown beard and moustache streaked with grey; he wears a flat black cap over a black skull-cap; small white neck and wrist ruffs edged with black stitching; black doublet slashed over black with gold filigree buttons; high-collared black coat with gold mounts as decoration at the collar and shoulders; black silk sleeves; black sword strap with gold buckles and gold sword hilt enamelled with black and white.[1]

This was the man who walked the corridors of power in Elizabeth's court. Cecil's clothes and his pose were absolutely right for his rank and his office as a royal Secretary. It was clear to everyone that he was a formidable man whose humble service had as its foundation a commanding authority.

*

By 1563 it was obvious that something had to be done in parliament about the royal succession, especially about Mary Stuart's claim to the English throne. The news of a plan to exclude Mary had reached the Scottish court by 5 January, when it was reported that William Maitland of Lethington, by now Mary's Secretary, was 'in great choler' because of it. Days later Cecil told Sir Thomas Smith that he thought 'somewhat will be attempted to ascertain the realm of a successor to this crown'. Cecil wrote as though there were very little he could do about it. He was in fact being disingenuous with his old friend and teacher.[2]

The signs were that Elizabeth's councillors had made up their minds to persuade her to settle the succession once and for all. It was no accident that the Dean of St Paul's, Alexander Nowell, whose kinsman Laurence was in Cecil's household, preached before the Queen on the topic of the succession and on the dangers of princes ignoring advice. He repeated a line from a conversation he had overheard: 'Alas what trouble we shall be in, even as great or greater than France, for the succession is so uncertain and such division for religion.' Less than a week later an MP in the House of Commons introduced a 'motion . . . at length for the succession'. It was decided to present a petition to the Queen. Twenty-four MPs met the privy councillors who sat in the Commons, Cecil among them, to draw up the articles.[3] This was an effort to encourage, even to force, the Queen to do something she did not want to do. Cecil was right behind it; they had waited too long. Elizabeth had to plan for the future: it was her duty.

With much formality the petition was read to the Commons by one of the authors of *Gorboduc*, Thomas Norton, who was close to Cecil; the Commons then asked those privy councillors who sat in the House to ask Elizabeth to hear them. She said she would. The Speaker of the Commons duly went off to Whitehall to tell the Queen that by limiting the line of royal succession she could protect herself from a 'faction of heretics and contentious and malicious papists'.

Elizabeth of course had no intention of doing anything. She had established a clear boundary: if she gave in, it would be the thin end of the wedge. So she listened politely but impassively to the Speaker. She accepted the Commons' petition 'with an excellent oration' of her own, 'deferring the answer to further time for the gravity of the cases'.[4]

But parliament was not going to rest. The House of Lords was next. The Lords told Elizabeth that 'surety and preservation' of her person, of the crown and of the realm depended on her marriage and 'some certain limitation' – the succession – of her imperial crown. They reminded her that every prince was the 'living law', and that when the prince died the law died also. Here they spoke to Cecil's greatest fear: the end of government, followed by civil war and invasion. When Protestant England was fighting for its life, government could not afford to come to a standstill. There *had* to be an heir to the throne, or at the very least emergency powers to prevent the realm from falling into the hands of its enemies.[5]

It was the great dilemma of Elizabeth's reign. The Queen could not be forced to do anything she did not want to; but her subjects knew in their bones that she had to act. If she acted, she gave in; if she did not she preserved her authority but made her subjects more desperate than ever. Elizabeth's policy was masterly inactivity. She used fine words and all the best courtly phrases she could. She listened to advice graciously. Then she ignored it and did nothing.

But this second parliament was tenacious. By late March 1563 MPs were debating a succession bill which would have prevented anyone from pretending a claim to the Queen's right or title. It probably also set out the line of succession; certainly there were MPs who supported the claim of Lady Katherine Grey, even after her secret marriage to the Earl of Hertford. Yet the most startling part of the bill had to do with emergency powers for the Privy Council and parliament in the event of Elizabeth's death. Nothing could have been more sensitive. The author of this part of the succession bill was not a fringe radical in parliament. He was Sir William Cecil, the Queen's loyal Secretary.[6]

Today it is hard to conceive just how stunning Cecil's emergency powers were. Like modern governments planning for nuclear apocalypse, it is incredible that he could bring himself to imagine a scenario so horrific. Monarchs were not politicians: they were God's anointed lieutenants who governed with divine sanction and power. They reigned by blood and hereditary right. This was the very soul, the essential logic, of how the Tudors ruled. To think anything else was to turn the world upside down and everything with it.

Cecil had to comprehend a realm without a prince, a notion which may have made him sick with terror. But he had no choice. And so he proposed that if Elizabeth died without a successor the Queen's divine authority to govern would be transferred, not to an heir, but to her Privy Council, and England would become, for a time, an aristocratic republic. Of course a monarch would have to be found. And here was the second part of Cecil's breathtaking plan. Parliament would choose Elizabeth's successor. The republic governed by the Queen's old councillors would be replaced by an elected hereditary monarchy. It was inconceivable that parliament would choose Mary Stuart. But what about Lady Katherine Grey, Elizabeth's heir by the Succession Act? Or perhaps Henry Hastings, the decidedly Protestant third Earl of Huntingdon, with his Plantagenet blood?[7]

What Cecil had done, though of course he never knew it, was to anticipate the Glorious Revolution by 150 years. The notion of a temporary aristocratic government inviting a good Protestant candidate to be king was not entirely original in 1688. Cecil knew he was playing with fire. But government had to go on: there was no choice. He and his colleagues were horribly afraid of the future: they believed they lived in perilous times. Ambition did not drive Cecil to strip away the mystery of hereditary monarchy. This was not about Katherine Grey, though doubtless there were rumours: no plan for the future ever remains entirely theoretical. Probably Cecil and others thought back to the time ten years before when he had sworn his oath to Queen Jane. He knew, more than anyone, how sensitive Elizabeth was to the politics of succession. In 1563 Cecil was not playing games: he acted out of cold despair. Better to have security than uncertainty.

It was the greatest constitutional clash so far of this short reign. It wouldn't be the last. Elizabeth refused to be bounced into doing something she did not want to do. She worried about naming her successor and encouraging a reversionary interest in her heir. She preferred to live with uncertainty than to have a new succession act. So the bill was stifled: either Elizabeth squashed it or it was allowed to fade to nothing.

Yet another effort to get Elizabeth to act had failed: but Cecil refused to give up.

*

In the early summer of 1563 God showed his providence to the Cecil family in the birth of a son, Robert, on 1 June. Lady Mildred was about thirty-seven years old, her husband forty-two. Thomas Cecil was within a year of being married himself: there was a difference of twenty-one years between the brothers. Robert was quite unlike Thomas. He was a sickly child who would grow up with splayed legs and a hunched back. Yet Robert would one day be just like his father, a councillor and a royal Secretary. He was baptised at St Clement Danes on the Strand on 6 June.[8]

Within a month of Robert Cecil's baptism, the godly began to interpret signs of God's punishment. The Newhaven expedition, the English military venture in France, had been a disaster. Those men of the garrison in Le Havre who managed to get back to England brought plague with them. This was held by some to be God's judgment for the sins of Elizabeth's subjects. We can imagine that Cecil saw it also as punishment for parliament's failure to protect the realm and people from the prospect of foreign invasion and civil war.

William Cecil believed with all his heart that God intervened directly in the great affairs of realms and princes and in the lives of ordinary men, women and children. He believed in providence, and in this he was not alone. At the end of July Archbishop Parker of Canterbury wrote to Cecil that England was 'molested universal' by war, by pestilence in London and famine in Canterbury. He had appointed prayers and preaching in his diocese, and wondered why he had had no direction from the Queen or her Council.[9]

Parker's notion seemed to capture the mood of the moment. Bishop Grindal of London wrote to Cecil a week later with the same idea. Already he had commissioned Dean Nowell of St Paul's to write 'an homily meet for the time, which he hath done'. Grindal asked Cecil to look at it before passing it to Parker. Grindal also suggested that Elizabeth's courtiers might set a good example by fasting, and he thought that the food that would be saved by this fast could be sent to the back lanes and alleys of London to feed the poor and the city's Protestant refugees.[10]

Edmund Grindal and Matthew Parker were old friends of the Cecil family. Sir William knew both men from Cambridge. Grindal, who was a year older than Cecil, was a plain-speaking northerner. One of the guests at his palace in Fulham in late July was Lady Mildred, from whom, he wrote, he deserved no thanks for the 'coarse cheer' he had given to her. Matthew Parker was a clever don, a born scholar with a fabulous library, a prickly temperament and a keen eye for status.

It may be a surprise to find out that Cecil, whose desk was always piled so high with urgent government business, should have spent so much time on public prayers for national fasting. But together he, Grindal and Parker produced a full order of service in the time of plague. Grindal did most of the work, but Cecil himself edited Dean Nowell's text (as Grindal had written, one clever academic to another, 'The homily is also not fair written, but of that ye cannot doubt knowing the author') and added some words of his own. Parker, feeling slightly left out, sourly complained that the service was so long it would have the people in prayer till four o'clock in the afternoon.[11]

Cecil's politics was inspired by religious passion. He knew for a fact that God punished people and nations to call them to repentance. In August 1563 the will of God was very much on his mind as he worked from Windsor where the court was virtually in quarantine. So perhaps it was no coincidence that this was the moment Cecil chose to write to his former comrade in Scotland, William Maitland of Lethington, now Mary Stuart's secretary.

Cecil's message was plain: 'the settling of the Gospel of Christ and the dissolution of Antichrist' were more important than anything in politics. Everything else came second, even service to individual monarchs. Maitland's service to Mary had put a great strain on his relationship with Cecil. But both men had to consider British unity, and both had to be aware of what was going on in the world. Cecil wrote of the conspiracy against the international Protestant cause 'conceived in a congregation of Antichrist's soldiers being professedly gathered to destroy the Gospel of Christ'. He promised Maitland that he would never do anything to harm the Protestant cause in England and Scotland, 'For if I shall willingly so do I shall sin against my conscience.' It was a bravura performance, earnest and passionate. Pragmatic, tough and uncompromising he may have been; but he was also a conviction politician who acted with ideological purpose. Still, Cecil was careful in his letter not to refer openly to Mary Stuart's greatest offence, her claim to the English crown.[12]

There was nothing Cecil could do in 1563 to escape the vexed topic of Elizabeth's succession. He, and others, had tried to resolve it in parliament; they had failed. It lay, deeply buried and unspoken, in his letter to Maitland of Lethington. Now, thanks to plague and a family alliance with the Greys, it came in the form of letters written every few days by Lord John Grey and Grey's niece, Lady Katherine, who resolutely signed her name as 'Katherine Hertford'.

In late August 'a burning ague' had already killed the Spanish ambassador in London. It was time to get Katherine out of the city. Lord John thanked Cecil for 'the lively fact of this your great friendship in the delivery of my niece to my custody': Cecil had managed to intercede on Katherine's behalf, and she and her husband were moved at this plague time from the Tower, the Earl of Hertford to Middlesex and his wife to Grey's house at Pyrgo in Essex.

Katherine became a desperate petitioner, emotionally reliant on Cecil and Lord Robert Dudley, her two kinsmen, to plead her case with the Queen; Grey came gradually to despair of a niece who was slowly starving herself. In early November, ill but still probably at court, Cecil looked over a petition Katherine had prepared for the Queen. 'Well, good cousin,' Lord John wrote, 'her chiefest hope consisteth in you, and the Council, for the recovery and full perfecting of the Queen's Majesty's most gracious favour towards her and my Lord, which we daily pray for her to be shortly.' The letter came with a doe from Pyrgo park.[13]

*

Cecil was still at Windsor in early January 1564 and he was in an introspective mood. 'I know the place which I hold hath been of years not long passed, adjudged a shop for cunning men,' he wrote to Sir Thomas Smith in Paris, 'and yet surely I think the opinion commonly conceived thereof, hath been worse than the persons deserved.' As Secretary, he said, he was an 'artificer of practices and counsels'. But though his business was in 'public things of the world' he submitted everything he did to the Christian Gospel.[14]

A few months later there was yet more controversy about the royal succession. The Grey claim refused to go away. It was revealed that John Hales, a man Cecil had known since their service together in the household of

Protector Somerset, had written a book on the Grey succession. In it he defended the secret marriage of Lady Katherine and the Earl of Hertford. Hales had asked some foreign lawyers for their opinions on the book. He had also talked to friends about it; one of them was Lord John Grey. When news of Hales's book broke in spring 1564 Elizabeth was livid. Hales was sent immediately to the Fleet prison in London. Cecil called it 'a troublesome fond matter'.[15]

The Hales affair was a deep offence to Elizabeth. Still, Cecil hoped that some good would come of it: 'God give Her Majesty by this chance a disposition to consider hereof that either by her marriage or by some common order we poor subjects may know where to lean, and aventure our lives with contentation of our consciences' – in other words, Elizabeth had to act for her people. Soon enough Hales went to the Tower and Lord John Grey was in custody at court. Desperate as he was not to get mixed up in the affair, even Cecil was suspected because, as he told Sir Thomas Smith, some of those now in prison 'hath had access to me in their suits'.[16]

In fact the politics of royal succession confronted Cecil wherever he turned in 1564, and he was truly wearied by it. At home there was Hales and in Scotland there was Mary Stuart. But Elizabeth had a plan for Mary, a diplomatic solution all of her own to the tricky problem of succession. It would cause Cecil many months, even years, of trouble.

Elizabeth wanted to play old-fashioned dynastic politics. She thought she would find a good English husband for her cousin. Once Mary was married, she could be controlled. Mary's husband was to be Lord Robert Dudley, whose name was peddled at the Scottish court. The Queen of Scots would have none of it. However, the real danger came from a Scottish family living in England, and it was this family, the Lennox Stewarts, who were used by both Mary and Elizabeth in their diplomatic game. Soon Elizabeth would feel the cost of it.

Matthew Stewart, Earl of Lennox, was a member of one of the most powerful families in Scotland. But it was his wife Margaret, a Douglas, who held the key to the dynastic significance of her family. She was the daughter of Margaret Tudor, Henry VIII's sister, by Margaret's second marriage to the Earl of Angus. Lady Margaret Douglas's eldest surviving son, Henry, Lord Darnley, had Tudor blood. And for an ambitious mother like Margaret Douglas, that blood meant power. In private, after Mary Stuart's return to Scotland, but with spies listening, Margaret made no bones about her son marrying the Queen of Scots and claiming the English throne. That ambition put Margaret in the custody of Sir Richard Sackville and her husband in the Tower of London.[17]

Cecil's secret sources told him what the Lennoxes were up to: he knew how dangerous they were. Together Mary Stuart and Henry Stewart, both great-grandchildren of King Henry VII of England, would be an unstoppable dynastic pairing. What is almost beyond comprehension is that Elizabeth thought that it might be a good idea in 1564 for the Earl of Lennox to return to Scotland. She wanted to cause trouble for Mary and to stir up Scottish politics; Lennox had enemies in Scotland and a long-running feud with the noble house of Hamilton. In late April Elizabeth granted a passport for Lennox to travel to Scotland. He went that September, the same month Lord Robert Dudley was made Earl of Leicester – an earldom was sure to catch Mary's eye. Elizabeth was hopelessly behind the game. But worse was to come: in February 1565, once Lennox was installed in Scotland and had been pardoned by Mary, Elizabeth issued a passport to Lord Darnley to visit his father. Darnley would never return to England and he would die, a few years later, the King of Scots.

It was all a terrible miscalculation. This was really the first time Elizabeth had taken control of her own policy. She had pressed Lord Robert Dudley to marry Mary Stuart, but he did not want to be pushed. Yet she persisted, and she must have overruled Cecil and other councillors of experience who would have told her that to send the Earl of Lennox and his son was to tempt disaster.[18]

The mystery is how it happened. Cecil gives little away. In late September there were rumours that he was on bad terms with Dudley, 'but surely all is well, and so I take myself assured'. He said that the rumours were malicious gossip: both he and Dudley understood that many people were busy trying to stir up trouble between them. Cecil, with the court at St James's, was sick. The trouble was 'an humour fallen into my eyes which the physicians call corisa'; he could neither read nor write. He complained to Sir Thomas Smith that he was 'presently tormented' with a 'medicine of pills' that had lain in his stomach for two days. Feeling truly sorry for himself, he signed the letter with 'a faint sick hand'.[19]

As Cecil gingerly dictated the letter for Smith to Hugh Alington, his confidential secretary and nephew, Elizabeth was writing of the 'labyrinth' she felt she was in over Scotland, desperate for Cecil's advice on what to put in instructions for her ambassador in Edinburgh, Thomas Randolph. This was on 23 September. Cecil was well enough three days later to be at Council. He was busy at St James's in the last week of September. On 4 October he was at Cecil House 'for necessary business' and about to go to bed that evening when his clerk came from St James's with a letter he had to read. The next day he had a routine audience with the Queen. At court the news was of the elevation of Lord Robert Dudley to his earldom: 'his preferment in Scotland is earnestly intended'.[20]

Elizabeth could be tenacious, as she showed in her dogged belief that the new Earl of Leicester could be Mary Stuart's husband. Elizabeth also had a long memory and this, combined with a developed sense of grievance, meant that the Hales affair rumbled on. It even touched Sir Nicholas Bacon, who, suspected to have supported Hales in his views, was in disgrace. 'I have been also noted a favourer of my Lady Katherine's title,' Cecil wrote, 'but my truth therein is tried and so I rest quiet. For surely I am and always have been circumspect to [do] nothing to make offence.' In other words, he kept his head down at a time when the court was jumpy and some tempers were frayed.[21]

In early December the court removed to Whitehall for Christmas and New Year, and it was there that Elizabeth once again fell perilously sick. This was the second time the Queen had been in danger in two years, and it clearly shook Cecil. The illness came on a Saturday, the 9th, just a couple of days after the court's arrival at Whitehall. Her councillors feared what they called a 'flux'; Cecil called it diarrhoea, and it was acute enough over the next five or so days to seem to endanger her life. By the following Friday she was recovering, 'weakened but in health'. Elizabeth's sickness had come and gone quickly. But again her advisers had been terrified: she was 'clearly whole', Cecil wrote on 15 December, 'but for the time she made us sore afraid'. He thanked God that they could take good warning by her sickness and comfort from her recovery.[22]

At best anxiety, at worst sheer despair: and against all of this the business of Scotland and Mary Stuart moved on. In the days before Christmas 1564 intelligence reports told Cecil that the Scottish friends of the Earl of Lennox wanted Darnley to be Mary Stuart's husband. Cecil imagined that some effort would be made 'to bring the Queen's Majesty, not only to allow thereof, but also to move it to the Queen her sister'. Elizabeth was unlikely to do that. Already there had been a meeting between English representatives and Mary's half-brother, the Earl of Moray, and Maitland of Lethington to talk about Leicester as a husband for the Queen of Scots. Elizabeth knew what she wanted, 'but when it cometh to the conditions which are demanded', Cecil thought, 'I see her then remiss of her earnestness'.[23]

Elizabeth suffered through Christmas with a cold, though she was well enough by 30 December to go outside. Cecil was as anxious as ever. He took some comfort from signs he had seen that the Queen was at last considering marriage to a foreign prince. 'If it so may please Almighty God to lead by the hand some meet person to come lay hand on her to her contention,' he mused, 'I could then wish myself more health to endure my years somewhat longer, to enjoy such a world here as I trust would follow.' But it seemed a lost hope: 'as now things hang in desperation, I have no comfort to live'. With things as they were in Scotland, and his brother-in-law Bacon still banished from court, it is easy to see why he felt so wretched.[24]

By the spring of 1565 the greatest danger to Elizabeth's throne and England's safety was the marriage of Mary Stuart to Lord Darnley. Leicester, still being pressed to marry Mary, refused to budge. Suddenly the diplomats realised that Darnley was a serious suitor. This threw the Council into yet another panic. Maitland of Lethington came to London to talk to Elizabeth, and in the last week of May the Council was locked away in 'sundry conferences, long deliberations, and many arguments' about Scotland. The councillors knew that Mary's marriage to Darnley would be a disaster, yet there was nothing they could do about it. Sir Nicholas Throckmorton was sent to Scotland to tell Mary that Elizabeth would be happy for her cousin to marry anyone except Darnley. Mary pointedly ignored the request.[25]

In the end the Queen of Scots had her marriage. On 29 July it was a fact: two claimants to the English succession were husband and wife. But though Mary had played a clever game, Cecil believed by September that she was losing the support of many of her subjects. Scotland was too divided in its politics and religion to be ruled by an openly Catholic Queen and Mary's authority was falling to pieces. The Privy Council considered the case for toppling the Queen of Scots by force. By September there were plans for war. Cecil commissioned a paper on whether Elizabeth could act against Mary. The Council met at least three times to decide what to do. It was briefed by Cecil, who gave a narrative of everything that had happened in Scotland since April that year. But nothing was done: the English government could really do little more than watch events unfold.[26]

So what was the solution to the thorny problem of Mary, Queen of Scots? Sir William Cecil had a very clear idea. It was Elizabeth's marriage and the settlement of the royal succession. Only these things would frustrate the ambitions of a dangerous woman who saw the 'state of this crown to depend only upon the breath of one person, our sovereign lady'.[27]

*

On 24 June 1566 Cecil heard the news that Mary, Queen of Scots had given birth to a baby boy. The courier arrived with the message as he was writing a letter to Sir Henry Sidney in Ireland. Already he understood that Mary had a child but 'whether it be a knave child or a lass, we know not'. He knew soon enough that Mary Stuart had a son.[28]

Mary's succession was now certain. Dynastically she looked secure. But the politics of marriage for Elizabeth were as fraught as ever. There was some notion that the Queen might marry Archduke Charles of Austria, the brother of Emperor Maximilian, but long negotiations conducted by the Earl of Sussex on Elizabeth's behalf came to nothing. They also caused trouble at court because Robert Dudley, the Earl of Leicester, was flatly opposed to the match.

Cecil went on progress with the court that summer. Elizabeth and her household travelled to Northamptonshire where Cecil was looking forward to entertaining her in style at Burghley House. 'God send me my heart's desire,' he wrote to the Marquess of Winchester, 'which is without regard of cost to have Her Majesty see my good will in my service, and all others to find no lack of good cheer.' But plans had to be changed at the last minute when Cecil's ten-year-old daughter, Anne, fell seriously ill. The Queen's health could not be risked. Instead Cecil dined Elizabeth at the old Franciscan friary in Stamford.[29]

By autumn Cecil was hard at work at Whitehall preparing for the second session of the parliament that had sat in 1563. Then Cecil and his colleagues had strongly encouraged the Queen to marry and they had even tried to force through a new act of succession. They had failed; Elizabeth stalled, as she so often did. But Cecil was a persistent man. In the last months of 1566 he would try again to persuade Elizabeth to determine the line of royal succession.

Cecil and his colleagues were the Queen's sworn councillors; they represented her interests and obeyed her instructions; their duty was to make sure that the members of the House of Lords and the House of Commons did the same. Yet there is no doubt that Cecil and the Council were determined to do everything they could to encourage Elizabeth to act. Marriage for the Queen and the settlement of the royal succession were, Cecil wrote, 'the uttermost that can be desired'. It was for Elizabeth 'to determine effectually to marry, and if it succeed not then proceed to discussion of the right of the successor'. This was a private paper and its greatest quality was plain frankness at what Cecil and others were going to do their best to achieve. For the next few months Elizabeth and her Lords and Commons would engage in a kind of constitutional guerrilla warfare.[30]

In the early days of the parliament there was a 'motion' in the Commons for the succession. Elizabeth responded by promising to marry: she wanted to steer MPs away from the issue. But this did not put parliament off the scent. Lords and Commons worked together, as they had done in 1563. And soon enough the Queen was seriously irritated. After the first big debate on the succession in the Lords, Elizabeth forbade the Earl of Pembroke and the Earl of Leicester from entering her Privy Chamber. She was furious that they were meddling, without her consent, in what she believed to be a prerogative matter, private business to be settled by her alone. But if Elizabeth believed that taking such a tough disciplinary line would save her from trouble on the succession, she was to be proved profoundly wrong.

Lords and Commons persisted. It was becoming a familiar story. They went to Whitehall in early November to present a petition to Elizabeth. Her response was polite but cold. She tried to cut them dead. On the subject of her marriage 'she said she thought she had so satisfied by her answer thereto that she looked rather for thanks than for request'. 'The other matter, for limitation of the succession, she said as it was necessary, which she would not deny'; but she also knew that it would be perilous 'to enter into the decision thereof at this present time'. She asked them to trust the word of a prince in a public place.

It was actually Cecil, Elizabeth's loyal Secretary, who was commanded to return to the Commons to read the Queen's reply to parliament's petition. Stoically he did his duty. When MPs heard what the Queen had to say, there was an audible silence in St Stephen's Chapel.[31]

Elizabeth sensed the mood. She realised that her formal answer to parliament's petition might not be enough to still the rumblings, but she was determined not to be subverted in her purpose. So she turned to her lawyers. They gave a legal judgment that if the Queen sent a message to the Commons through one of her councillors it was enough to end debate. But even this did not quieten the Commons. Within days debate began again. An MP called Paul Wentworth went so far as to question the lawyers' judgment. He even wondered whether what the Queen had done was in fact a breach of the old established custom of free speech in the House of Commons.[32]

This was deeply sensitive politics. Wentworth and others had touched an exposed nerve in the Elizabethan body politic. Elizabeth was clear in her own mind: the succession was a matter of royal prerogative. It was not to be touched by subjects. To press the Queen in this way caused her great offence. God's anointed could not be strong-armed by her parliament, however much they believed what they were doing was right.

To the Commons, and actually also to Cecil, the succession *was* public business. It had to do with the future of the realm. Perhaps not everyone was as plain spoken as Paul Wentworth. But the grumbles at Westminster continued in the first fortnight of November, and the Commons began to plan another petition in spite of the Queen's firm prohibition.

So who was behind the petition to force Elizabeth? Who was brave enough to challenge the Queen on a prerogative matter? Radicals, perhaps, who put the interests of the realm before Elizabeth's wishes? In fact the petition's author was Elizabeth's loyal Secretary, who was determined not to lose another chance to press the Queen on marriage and succession.

Cecil worked behind the scenes with what he called 'the thirty committee' of the Commons. He was as subtle as he could be. He called the petition 'thanks' for Elizabeth's promise to marry. It was nothing of the sort: it was a plain effort to bounce the Queen. Cecil and his committee spent hours poring over every word of the new petition; they considered every possible meaning and nuance. Cecil rewrote it three times; and every time he went back to it the petition sounded tougher than it had done the draft before.

The petition put some plain facts before Elizabeth. It said that by ancient and necessary custom the kings of England had always allowed the Commons to 'treat and devise of matters honourable' for the crown and 'profitable for the realm'. In being prevented from debating the succession MPs had been 'sequestered' from what it was their duty to do, 'much to our discomfort and infamy'. This was remarkably strong language to use to God's lieutenant on earth. The petition crafted so carefully by Cecil and the other MPs set the duties of parliament against the express will of the Queen.[33]

Here Cecil was genuinely torn. On the one hand he had a duty of service and obedience to Elizabeth: on the other he had a strong sense of what had to be done. Here were all the tensions of his political career. Duty to the Queen, to the realm, and to God – each pulled at his conscience.

Many years later he perfected a subtle formula to capture this tension, 'preferring in policy Her Majesty afore all others on the earth, and in divinity the King of Heaven above all'. But was not the will of God also the will of the Queen? How could he reconcile the Queen's will with what he knew *had to be done*? Cecil's dilemma found expression in a short prayer he wrote a few weeks after the Commons' petition. 'The Lord God of the spirits of all flesh, set one over this great multitude, which may go out and in before them, and lead them out and in, that the Lord's people be not as sheep without a shepherd.'[34]

While Sir William Cecil patiently and powerfully chipped away at Elizabeth's objections to a debate on the succession, Elizabeth's loyal Secretary went to court and wrote yet another declaration by the Queen to be read to the Commons prohibiting them to hold such a debate. For Cecil it was a controlled political schizophrenia. Elizabeth knew that she was being ignored, and by now she was fuming. She probably did not know that the man responsible was her Secretary. Some MPs, she said, had pressed a suit 'touching the crown of this realm, very unmeet for the time and place, and certainly dangerous for the common quietness of her subjects'. To add force to her statement she consulted her Council and her law officers. Another robust statement of her rights as Queen was read to the Commons by their Speaker.[35]

But there was nothing Elizabeth could do to silence the debate. Try as she might, she could not intimidate her parliament. With Cecil and other councillors behind the MPs, perhaps this is not a great surprise. And parliament went even further. It used a new weapon. This was the subsidy bill, the grant of taxation being prepared by the Commons. Cecil altered the preamble to this tax bill: he gave it an overtly political edge by using it to hold Elizabeth to her promise of marriage: 'for the most comfortable assurances and promise by your Majesty made and declared unto us, that for our weal and surety your Majesty would marry as soon as God should give you opportunity to accomplish the same, whereof we have received infinite comfort'. No chance could be missed to put pressure on the Queen.[36]

When Elizabeth finally ended her second parliament in early January 1567 she said, very pointedly, that the Prince's 'opinion and good will ought in good order [to] have been felt in other sort than in so public a place'. She complained about having heard 'so lip-laboured orations out of such subjects' mouths'. She had nearly said 'wrangling subjects' mouths': she thought better of it. She was livid: she had been disobeyed by men in parliament who felt they had the best interests of the realm at heart. They did not. Only the Queen knew what was best for her kingdoms.[37]

It is true that there were some political mavericks in the Commons who spoke their minds too frankly. Actually the real culprit was Cecil, who all the time was quietly negotiating the tricky path of obedience to the crown and belief in a higher duty to God and realm. Elizabeth believed that her sacred office was all about power and authority. So it was, Cecil would have countered, but power and authority for the public good. And who said what the public good was, Queen or Secretary?

*

The ghost at the feast in Elizabeth's second parliament was Mary, Queen of Scots. In December 1566 Mary celebrated the baptism of her son, Prince James, with a spectacular festival at Stirling. It had a nakedly political purpose. 'Our leader has transposed Mars ablaze with civil war into peace in our time. . . . The importance of kingship is eternal; it will be in the power of the Stewart family; the crown of Mary awaits her grandsons.'

What Mary wanted to communicate to her people and to fellow princes was the power of her family. The spectacle at Stirling was a vision of British unity: but it was about the Stuarts, not the Tudors. It was no accident that Elizabeth's representative at the baptism of Prince James, Cecil's old friend the Earl of Bedford, was placed at an Arthurian round table.[38]

Mary Stuart's spectacular display at Stirling was crafted political spin. The year before, some of Mary's nobility had risen up against her; her half-brother the Earl of Moray (formerly Lord James Stuart) was one of them. In the spring of 1566 Mary's close confidant, David Rizzio, had been brutally murdered in front of her at Holyrood. Mary's husband King Henry, formerly Lord Darnley, was part of that plot. In February 1567 he paid the price for plotting when he was murdered by his confederates.

So the politics of Scotland was desperately unstable: there was a deep structural flaw in Mary Stuart's rule. Mary was the threat to Elizabeth's throne she had always been, yet the authority she exercised in her realm hung by a thread. Cecil, as ever, knew everything that was going on as soon as he could. On the day of Darnley's murder at Kirk O'Field he wrote to Sir Henry Norris, Elizabeth's new ambassador in Paris, about the Earl of Bedford's return from Scotland and gave news of Ireland.

For the time being Cecil took at face value Bedford's report of Mary's intention to keep peace with Elizabeth. But within days, with the report of Darnley's death finally reaching his desk, Cecil knew that Scottish politics was turned upside down again. He had to respond; but he was struggling with poor health. He was forced to use a secretary's hand to write letters (something he hated) because he found it 'somewhat grievous to use mine own at present'. The year before he had had his first attack of what he called gout. But good health or poor, work never went away.[39]

Days later Elizabeth was dealing with the consequences of Darnley's death. The Queen sent Cecil's wife, Lady Mildred, and Lady Margaret Howard to tell the Countess of Lennox about the murder of her son. Cecil wrote that on hearing the news the countess could 'not be by any means kept from such passions of mind, as the horribleness of the fact did require'.[40]

Over the next few days Cecil tried desperately to find out more about the 'strange news of the death of the King of Scots'. He even stopped Sir Henry Norris's son from travelling out to his father in France, on the Queen's command, so that he could gather intelligence on Scotland. Cecil soon heard reports that Darnley had been strangled and his lodgings blown up with gunpowder. There were reports that Darnley's father, the Earl of Lennox, had also been killed, but Cecil knew this intelligence to be false. Yet it was becoming clear to Cecil that Darnley had been murdered as the result of a very large conspiracy against him: 'It is constantly affirmed that there were thirty at the killing of him.' He hoped Elizabeth would show 'some favourable compassion' to the Countess of Lennox, 'whom any humane nature must needs pity'.[41]

By early March Cecil still had no account of Darnley's killing he felt able to trust completely. He knew that on the streets of Edinburgh the Earl of Bothwell was being called one of the 'principal devisors' of the murder. Lennox and his allies searched for the killers. A few weeks later he heard that even the Queen of Scots was implicated in her husband's murder. There was little to be cheerful about. In April Cecil reported to Sir Henry Sidney that Scotland was in a quagmire: 'nobody seemeth to stand still; the most honest desire to go away; the worst tremble with the shaking of their conscience'.[42]

What made the deteriorating political situation in Scotland worse, in Cecil's view, was the international scene. Spain was now conducting a military campaign in its territories in the Low Countries. 'The poor Protestants in

Flanders are brought to worldly desperation, and must trust only to miracles.'
He must have wondered whether the Protestants of England were next.[43]

In Scotland matters only became more complicated. In May 1567 Mary,
Queen of Scots married the Earl of Bothwell, widely regarded as Darnley's
murderer. It was a defining moment in her queenship of Scotland: it was
also, as Cecil probably realised over the coming weeks, the beginning of the
end of Mary's rule. He had had some forewarning of the marriage. Three
days before it happened he had thought that Mary would be 'wooed' to
marry Bothwell. Cecil understood that most of the Scottish nobility was
against it; they were with Prince James at Stirling. By the end of the month
he knew that they openly opposed the Queen. 'What will follow,' he wrote,
'I know not.'[44]

What did follow, as Cecil may have predicted, was civil war. At his desk
Cecil read regular reports on how Scotland was falling to pieces. He knew soon
enough about the standoff between the forces of Mary and Bothwell and their
opponents; about how Bothwell had abandoned his wife on the field of battle;
and about how Mary had been taken by her enemies and locked away in
Lochleven Castle. 'The matters of Scotland grow so great,' he noted, 'as they
draw us to be very careful thereof.' He fought to control the ever growing piles
of paper on his desk, the whole business of government: 'I am pitifully overwhelmed with business.'[45]

Scotland was hugely important to Cecil. A peaceful Scotland sympathetic to
England was an important part of his strategic vision. Together a Protestant
England and a Protestant Scotland could stand against the menaces of
Antichrist's soldiers. This is why the personal rule of Mary, Queen of Scots had
been a disaster. She was by her blood a direct threat to Elizabeth's throne, but
she was also a risk to England's military security. But if Cecil imagined that
Mary in Lochleven was a good thing (which he probably did) he also saw in
the disintegration of orderly Scottish government some terrible dangers to
peace and security. Could Elizabeth help to control and to influence what was
happening in Scotland?

The early signs did not look good. Sir Nicholas Throckmorton, an experienced diplomat, was sent to Scotland to help to negotiate some kind of
agreement between the warring parties. Mary was to be freed, but on strong
conditions. Bothwell would be prosecuted for the murder of Darnley. A Great
Council would govern Scotland. Elizabeth offered herself as a guarantor of any
peace settlement. But Throckmorton got nowhere. The country was in chaos.
Many of Mary's enemies wanted her dead. Throckmorton did his best to argue
moderation but it did no good: near the end of July Mary Stuart was forced to
abdicate her throne. Days later her baby son, James, was crowned King of
Scotland at Stirling.

The English government tried to make sense of what had happened in Scotland. The Queen's sympathies were with Mary: 'how earnestly she is bent in the favour of the Queen of Scots', Cecil wrote. Elizabeth fumed at noblemen who had unseated one of God's anointed, but Cecil and his colleagues, practical politicians as well as firm Protestants, saw that some good could come of Mary's deposition. The man who now ran Scotland's government as regent, James Stuart, Earl of Moray, was a man they had worked with before. He would guarantee the protection of 'true religion' in Scotland and secure England's friendship. Cecil had a high estimate of Moray's abilities and of those of his colleagues in this new revolutionary government: 'I think they are so skilful of other princes' causes and needs, as I think they will remain without fear.'[46]

So was the panic in Scotland over? By the early autumn of 1567 Moray was settling into his regency though Elizabeth remained 'full offended' by the treatment of Mary. The Queen of Scots was well out of the way. 'All things are quiet within this realm', Cecil wrote on 3 September. And so they remained, apparently, for the rest of the year. Cecil noted that the Scottish parliament had formally condemned the Queen of Scots. Regent Moray continued to do well, acquitting himself 'very honourably, to the advancement of religion and justice, without respect of persons'.[47]

It sounds, from these fragments of Cecil's notes and correspondence, like a fairly stable conclusion to a few turbulent years. Cecil had imagined a more conventional solution to the problems of the English succession. In this he had failed. To have the Queen of Scots out of the way was a gift. But it was a gift that would come with a cost. Elizabeth's government was not out of the woods yet.

10

Household and Family

Cecil always said that he sacrificed all for service to the Queen. But in fact he lived as one of the grandest of Elizabeth's courtiers. Often he was on the rack and felt the pain of business and politics, but this made occasional escapes from his public office all the more important for him.

This chapter is concerned with the domestic life of Cecil, his family and household in the early years of Elizabeth's reign. It is a short break from the political narrative of this book. But even here, in a story about wife and children, wards, servants and grand houses, politics runs as a deep seam of continuity. There was nothing politically neutral about any aspect of Cecil's life; this was as true of his time at home as it was of his service at court.

As Secretary he was on call day and night and the hours he worked were punishing. He moved with the court up and down the palaces along the River Thames, and he went on summer progress with the Queen. If he could spend a few precious hours at home, it was because his principal house in the early years of Elizabeth's reign was close to Whitehall Palace and also because this mansion on the Strand served him as an office as well as a home. If we want to know something about Cecil's domestic life, Cecil House is the best place to start.

*

Imagine standing before a great Tudor house in Westminster. Imagine, too, that it is a time in the later 1560s, when it is clear that Sir William Cecil is one of Elizabeth's most trusted councillors. The house in front of you is both a home and a base of operations for the Principal Secretary to the Queen, Master of the Court of Wards and Liveries and High Steward of Westminster. It is the house, therefore, of a powerful and influential man. This is why it is where it is, close to the royal palaces of Whitehall and St James and the palace of Westminster; to the boats and barges of the Thames; and to the busyness of

the city of London. Noblemen, bishops and other councillors live nearby.
York House, the residence of Sir William's brother-in-law, Sir Nicholas
Bacon, Lord Keeper of the Great Seal, is not very far away. No one could fail
to be impressed by all the grand houses and gardens.[1]

There is no doubt that this was the smartest part of Elizabethan
Westminster. But Cecil House had thick walls of brick, and for good reason.
Either side of the house were seedy alleyways and cheap tenement buildings.
These were a worry, particularly because plague and sickness all too often
struck as punishments from God. In fact in the plague time of 1563 Cecil gave
strict orders as Steward of Westminster for the quarantine of the sick and
infected. They had to stay inside their houses and shops and keep their doors
and windows shut tight. All they could rely on was the charity of the local
churches whose curates and churchwardens collected food and fuel for them.
Prayers were said in the city and the Queen and her court stayed at Windsor.
This had happened just outside the gates of Cecil House.[2]

Any visitor standing on the Strand facing Cecil House would have had his
back to the Savoy Hospital, built by Henry VII as a royal palace but by
Elizabeth's reign a hospital for the poor. This was nearest landmark to Cecil
House, and generally when Cecil worked at home he would write 'from my
house near the Savoy' or 'from my house on the Strand'. Before any visitor
stood a rather forbidding wall about 150 feet long with only three small
windows at ground level, impressive but starkly functional, a wall of brick and
timber. To the west a gateway led to a courtyard around which were the service
departments of the household. Across from this was the main gateway to the
southern court of Cecil House monitored by a porter's lodge, such as might be
found at any large house or palace or college. Through this and straight ahead
across the first court was the great southern window of the hall; to the left, the
service side of the house, from where Cecil's servants administered a large and
busy household; and to the right, the family's rooms. In the 1560s the
buildings rose up two storeys; by the 1590s there were at least three.[3]

Before we go on a short tour of Cecil House, the first thing to remember is
that it was both a home for Cecil's family and a place of work close to the court.
By the time he died there in 1598 it was crammed with books and papers. He
interviewed petitioners in his own home, received messages from royal
couriers and worked on government business in his study. At the same time,
Cecil House was a monument to Sir William Cecil's wealth and taste, a
luxurious metropolitan base with beautiful gardens. It was a model, too, for
his other great building projects, Theobalds in Hertfordshire and his father's
house at Burghley.

Cecil House was built in the few years after 1560. There was an old house on
the site which had belonged to one of the Duke of Northumberland's

confederates, Sir Thomas Palmer, executed for treason in 1553. Architecture was one of Cecil's passions, and he spent every spare moment he could planning the kind of house he wanted. It is possible that the plans for Cecil House were made by Lawrence Bradshaw, formerly Surveyor of the Royal Works. It was important for the Secretary to own a house that made a bold statement about his position in Tudor government and society.

Cecil House was a model of architectural symmetry. Its two courts of buildings, as well as its wonderful gardens, sat on an axis running south to north. From the Strand a visitor would have been struck by the rather forbidding exterior to the south. But anyone approaching the house from the north would have had a quite different experience. Through an arched gate in the wall that bounded the open fields of Covent Garden a visitor would enter the gardens of Cecil House. These were large, and they were divided into compartments by brick walls, clipped hedges and gravel walks: they were carefully structured and the walls and pathways gave a feeling of permanence. There was a functional kitchen garden near to the service range on the western side of the house.[4]

The real beauty of this space outside lay in the orchard and the pleasure gardens, with the banqueting house looking out over Covent Garden and a mount rising up from a sunken garden. A busy man like Cecil, always passionate about the outdoors, must have enjoyed walking through the alleyways and along the paths of his gardens. Thomas Hill, in *The Gardeners Labyrinth*, a book dedicated to Cecil, expressed it very well:

> The commodities of these alleys and walks serve to good purposes, the one is that the owner may diligently view the prosperity of his herbs and flowers, the other for the delight and comfort of his wearied mind, which he may by himself, or [in] fellowship of his friends conceive, in the delectable sights and fragrant smells of the flowers, by walking up and down and about the garden in them . . . for the pleasant sights and refreshing of the dull spirits, with the sharpening of memory . . .

Cecil and his guests would have had the pleasure, too, of walking up from the gardens to the house and an elegant loggia built of stone and decorated with marble pillars.[5]

Cecil's study and bedchamber were in the north-east corner of the second courtyard. From these rooms he would have been able to look out over his private garden. This was his space: we know that he kept his papers and books and collections of coins here. These were praised even by Archbishop Parker of Canterbury, himself a discerning bibliophile and collector of great treasures. Cecil was fascinated by Roman history. In 1561 statues of the twelve emperors of Rome were sent to him from Venice. In the gardens at Cecil House there was a Roman inscription from Silchester. He is said to have carried with him at all times a book by the Roman orator Cicero called *On Duties*. He may have imagined himself as a senator of Rome, hearing, as he did, the petitioners who came to him every day.

Lady Mildred also had a suite of rooms in this eastern wing of the house. There would have been accommodation, too, for her children and the young noblemen of the household. To the west, forming the division between the first and second courts, was the hall of Cecil House. The hall had a service end to the west and a high-table end to the east. It was fairly small (about 20 feet by 42 feet) and usually only household servants ate there.

The family and their guests dined in the parlour just to the east of the hall. This was very much their habit. They had done the same at Wimbledon in the 1550s, when the family had eaten in a private room and the senior servants of the household in another room nearby. Dining in the parlour of Cecil House was a more intimate experience than eating in the hall; but the parlour was nevertheless a big room right at the heart of the family range of the house. It was heated by a great fireplace on its southern wall. But perhaps the greatest pleasure of dining there was that family and guests could look out to the private garden through three windows.[6]

Guests leaving by the south door of the parlour would have found a passageway which took them either out to the front court of the house or to a small courtyard. Just off this courtyard was a large tennis court built of brick with a red and white chequerboard floor. Nearby was a bowling alley that was only just shorter than the one at Whitehall Palace. Both tennis and bowling were pursuits of the court. These were just the sorts of sporting amenities that a powerful man like Cecil was expected to provide; and it may be that he offered them to his friends and visiting ambassadors. It seems that there was a way to the tennis court and bowling alley from the Strand, without going through the main porter's lodge. Modern experts on the house and its design have described this as a kind of early private health club. It was certainly a grand and exclusive one.[7]

*

Cecil House was a fine house for a great man. No one who saw it could doubt Cecil's power, wealth and taste. But what Cecil valued above all was his country retreat away from Westminster and London. His great passion was Theobalds.

Theobalds was by the 1580s one of the most spectacular houses in Elizabethan England. The story of what it tells us about Lord Burghley's views on architecture, gardening and dynasty really belongs to a later chapter; but the house should be introduced here. Even in the first few years of Elizabeth's reign, when between 1566 and 1568 £500 was given over to Cecil House, Cecil began to spend quite incredible amounts of money on Theobalds: if the £152 of 1566–67 covered some minor alterations, then the sums of £1,234 a year later and £1,256 in 1568–69 show the vast scale of his new project.[8]

Cecil bought Theobalds in 1564. There, just a little way from the main road between London and Stamford, he found a small old-fashioned moated manor house. It lay fourteen miles from London and its situation was perfect: the road south took Cecil almost directly to the gate of Cecil House in Covent Garden.

Elizabeth visited Theobalds in July 1564 when the court was not far away at Enfield. She may have encouraged Cecil to make something of the house. She did not worry too much about saying exactly what she thought of her courtiers' residences. She famously told Sir Nicholas Bacon that his house near St Albans, Gorhambury, was too small, to which he replied, 'Madam, my house is well, but it is you that have made me too great for my house.' Cecil later defended the grandeur of Theobalds by writing that on one visit Elizabeth had said that her chamber was too small. What could he do, he wrote, but 'to enlarge a room for a larger chamber'?[9]

The house Cecil found in 1564 was unprepossessing, but clearly he thought it had potential. Visitors entered over a bridge and through a gatehouse to a small court. Set round this court were a chapel, chambers and a hall. The hall was separated from the northern range of the house by a small passageway; in this northern range were the pantry, kitchen and kitchen yard. The hall would have had a raised dais at one end for the high table, and from here a doorway led out to the family's quarters on the ground and first floors of the southern wing of the house. To the west was a garden.

Cecil was very much the architect: he always paid close attention to what he wanted his houses to look like. At Theobalds he carefully annotated a plan of the house. By the end of the decade Theobalds had a new hall and kitchen and a great parlour for the family. It was now something like Cecil House, a house fit for an important courtier, really transformed beyond recognition.[10]

Theobalds was a provision for the future. Cecil bought and rebuilt the manor house for his second son, Robert. In the middle years of the 1560s it had a nursery: Cecil noted its position on a plan he had of the house before building work began. It was away from the family's main chambers in the part of the house near the garden, and it was reached by a few steps from the passageway between the hall and the pantry. This nursery would have served for his two small children, Robert and his younger sister Elizabeth.

Both Robert and Elizabeth had been born at Cecil House, Robert on 1 June 1563, and his sister exactly thirteen months later, between seven and eight o'clock in the evening of 1 July 1564. They were late arrivals for a father in his early forties. Before Robert was born Sir William and Lady Mildred had had one daughter, Anne, and three children who died soon after birth: Frances, born at Wimbledon in 1554; and two Williams, one in October 1559 and the second born in May 1561.[11]

Anne Cecil was the apple of her father's eye. He wrote a poem for her in 1567 to accompany his new year's gift of a spinning-wheel, a 'housewife's toy', he wrote, 'to set you on work some thrift to feel'. Two years later she was struck down by a fever that drove Cecil to write a letter thick with emotion. Anne's sickness held her for forty days and it was a terrible time. 'My comfort, my little Nan Cecil, hath been tormented . . . and now continueth in a fever still of unreasonable length, and very doubtful. God comfort me with her amendment, for I knowledge his wrath shall be very burdenous if my sins be avenged with loss of her.'[12]

Behind everything – family, household, life at court and the career in politics – was the marriage of William and Mildred Cecil. Like most marriages its secrets, the good ones as well as the bad, remain deeply buried. After her death Burghley wrote of the 'hearty love' which he bore to a wife 'with whom I lived in the state of matrimony forty and two years, in continual love without any separation or any offence'.[13]

Lady Mildred Cecil was a formidable woman. She came from a political family. She was fiercely intelligent and quite as robust as her husband. There is every reason to think that she was an iron support to his career, as controlled and capable in Elizabeth's reign as she had been in her service to the Duchess of Somerset many years before. There is ample evidence that she was involved in the politics of the court, particularly in the negotiations in the 1560s for Elizabeth's marriage to Archduke Charles of Austria. Two portraits from these years show her richly dressed as a courtier. She has auburn hair and blue eyes. In one of the portraits she is pregnant, probably with Robert; her face is thinner here than in the other picture, her cheekbones and chin keen and drawn.[14]

Lady Mildred was active and vigorous. In 1562 she was presented with an Irish goshawk for hunting. We can imagine her with only the finest bird, a single-minded and determined hunter. 'The signs of a good goshawk', said a Tudor book on falconry, 'are haughty courage, desire and greedy lust to feed, often tiring* and plucking of her meat, sudden snatching of her good upon the fist, good enduring, and great force in assailing her game.'[15]

Mildred, like William, also enjoyed archery. It was a pursuit encouraged by their friend Roger Ascham who, in the year they married, 1545, had published

---

* To pull or tear with the beak.

Toxophilus, the classic English essay on the subject. And also like her husband, Lady Mildred Cecil was an accomplished scholar of Greek and a patroness of learning in Cambridge and Oxford.[16]

The Cecils were one of the leading political families in England. Sir William was an instinctive dynast and the social connections he made through his family's marriage alliances were very important to him. His own sisters, Anne, Elizabeth and Margaret, had all made decent enough matches. Margaret's marriage to Roger Cave at Cecil House in 1561, for example, had established a connection of kinship between her brother and one of his colleagues in the Privy Council.

But it was the Cookes whose relations looked very impressive indeed. William Cooke, Lady Mildred's brother, married Lady Frances Grey, the cousin of Lady Jane Dudley and the daughter of Lord John Grey of Pyrgo: a noble connection indeed, but as we have seen the cause of some awkwardness for Cecil and Sir Nicholas Bacon when the matter of the Grey succession blew up in the 1560s. There was Bacon himself, of course, one of the most senior of the Queen's councillors as Lord Keeper of the Great Seal and the husband of Mildred's sister, Anne. Elizabeth Cooke, who had lived with the Cecils in Mary's reign, married Thomas Hoby in 1558. Hoby was the brother of Sir Philip Hoby, one of Cecil's great friends. Thomas and Elizabeth Hoby had spent their honeymoon at Burghley. Thomas was a brilliant and talented man, a writer and translator and a diplomat. He died very suddenly in 1566 while on embassy in Paris. Elizabeth was pregnant with their son, who was born in England and named Posthumous. Another Cooke sister, Katherine, married Henry Killigrew, a Cornish gentleman, a courtier and a diplomat, in 1565. Cecil did not at first approve of the match, and wrote to Killigrew to say so; his soon-to-be brother-in-law replied with a stinging letter.[17]

It was young Thomas Cecil, the son who had once caused so much worry and anxiety to his father, who made the Cecils' second alliance with the nobility. Thomas made good in the end. In 1564, at the age of twenty-two, Thomas married Dorothy Nevill, the daughter of John, third Lord Latimer. Cecil had met Dorothy three months earlier at her father's house, Belvoir Castle, to talk about marriage to his son. For Cecil it was an important alliance which connected him to the old northern nobility.[18]

Cecil possessed an acute appreciation of political pedigree, and so it is no wonder that when the time came to think about marriage for his daughter, Anne, he looked to a family like the Sidneys. Philip Sidney was the eldest son of Sir Henry Sidney and his wife Lady Mary. Sir Henry had been one of the gentlemen of Edward VI's Privy Chamber, and Cecil had known him for many years. Lady Mary was a daughter of the Duke of Northumberland. She was a Dudley: and an alliance with young Philip

Sidney meant a connection of marriage to Philip's uncle, Robert Dudley, Earl of Leicester.

Contracts for the marriage between Anne and Philip were drawn up in August 1569 and signed a month later. She was twelve, he was fourteen. They never married, for reasons that are not at all clear. But the young man who did marry Anne a few years later, by which time her father was Lord Burghley, had a title even grander than Philip Sidney's: he was the seventeenth Earl of Oxford, Edward de Vere.[19]

Anne Cecil and Edward de Vere must have known each other very well. She and her brother Robert and sister Elizabeth were brought up in the 1560s with Oxford and Edward Manners, the young Earl of Rutland, both of whom were royal wards in the care and keeping of Cecil. Cecil saw to the earls' education: he expected the highest standards of his young protégés.

The Earl of Oxford had come from the household of Sir Thomas Smith and had spent a year at Cambridge. In 1564 Cecil set out plans for his tuition in French and in horsemanship. The earl was thirteen years old. Cecil asked Smith, by then Elizabeth's ambassador in France, to recommend a good native teacher of French: someone who was honest in religion, civil in manners, learned in a science 'and not unpersonable'. Cecil was willing to give him fifty or sixty crowns, about £30 a year, for his trouble. For horsemanship he thought an Italian teacher best, who would have a salary of £20. Once, in July 1567, Oxford's noble pursuits went too far: practising his swordsmanship in the garden of Cecil House he killed an unarmed under-cook. A coroner's jury found, bizarrely, that the under-cook, Thomas Bryncknell, had committed suicide by 'running upon a point of a fence-sword of the said earl'.[20]

The young Earl of Rutland was the son of a family friend who, back in 1553, had stood by to help when Cecil's father, Richard, died very suddenly. The second earl and Sir William Cecil were friends and neighbours, so it was only appropriate that Cecil should help to raise his son. Cecil gave him a sound education and Rutland prospered. In all probability he would have made a less troublesome son-in-law for Cecil than the Earl of Oxford turned out to be. That is a sorry tale waiting to be told in later chapters.

*

The Cecils' household was one of routine and hard work. Sir William Cecil was, after all, the father who gave his daughter a spinning-wheel to impress upon her the value of thrift.

Before everything came God. 'The first, the middest and the last is to continue yourself in your fear of God by daily service of him with prayer,' Cecil wrote in a 'Memorial' for the Earl of Rutland in 1570. The old discipline of St John's College never left him. But now, of course, it was Prayer Book and chaplain, not Mass and priest, that led the way to God. Cecil believed he led a life devoted to the divine. When he came to make his very last will and testament he said that he had trusted in the Holy Spirit always with a desire 'to obey his will and commandments in living religiously and virtuously as far forth as the infirmity of my flesh will suffer'.[21]

But there was plenty of lively scholarly activity and conversation, too. At Wimbledon in the 1550s Cecil had engaged a number of former fellows of Cambridge colleges to teach his son, Thomas. He would one day make the same kind of arrangements for Robert, just as he did now in the 1560s for the young earls and others in his care. We should not imagine that Anne Cecil was left out. It was a tradition in her family that women received the same education as the men. Her mother and her aunt, Lady Anne Bacon, were fine classical scholars and translators.

At Cecil House in the 1560s there were some distinguished academics. Laurence Nowell was one of them, educated at Christ Church, Oxford, and engaged as the Earl of Oxford's tutor. Nowell was a polymath: a mathematician, a cartographer, an Anglo-Saxon scholar. He studied the work of Bede and the *Anglo-Saxon Chronicle*. Like a cryptographer he tried to crack the code of Old English: his work while in Cecil's household was groundbreaking. He owned the only surviving original manuscript of *Beowulf*, one of the greatest jewels of English literature.[22]

As well as studying early British history and language, Nowell was an accomplished cartographer. In 1563 he offered to make for Cecil a map of Britain and Ireland. It survives today, and it is clear that in executing a beautiful piece of penmanship Nowell also produced an invaluable piece of kit for a royal Secretary. On the back of the map, Nowell added the distances between major towns in Europe and the postal routes in England and Scotland. Nowell decorated his map with a wonderful pen sketch of Cecil as the stern master, sitting bolt upright with his arms folded and facing poor Nowell, who was looking harried, held at bay by a dog barking at his feet. Perhaps it was a joke: or indeed perhaps, given Cecil's fiercely high standards, it was not. But there is every reason to think that Cecil appreciated Nowell's craftsmanship. He had a great love of maps and plans that went all the way back to his days as a student of cosmography at Cambridge.[23]

Laurence Nowell was not the only man of Cecil's household staff to write on the English language. John Hart was another. Nowell was about thirty-three when he drew his beautiful map of the British Isles. Hart, at about sixty-two, was a good deal older. He was Cecil's secretary in the Court of Wards and the author of three books on English spelling and pronunciation. These were subjects that had greatly interested two of Cecil's old friends, Sir Thomas

Smith and Sir John Cheke. Like Smith, Cheke and Cecil, Hart was also a talented linguist, who knew Spanish, French, Italian, Dutch and German.

If Hart had Nowell to talk to about English language and literature, then Cecil could turn to William Day for conversation on Greek. Day, probably Thomas Cecil's tutor in the first couple of years of Elizabeth's reign, had taught Greek at King's College, Cambridge. Like other talented men in Cecil's household, having a powerful master helped him to secure a very good job. By 1561 Day was Provost of Eton College.

By the later years of the 1560s, Cecil presided over an elite team of young household servants. His steward from 1566 was Thomas Bellot, a man in his middle thirties, who had the huge job of running the whole household. Bellot supervised everything; but his master still knew all that was going on, particularly when it came to money, which Cecil, busy as he was, personally audited down to the last halfpenny.

Another trusted servant in the 1560s was Hugh Alington. Like William Day, Alington was a former fellow of King's College in Cambridge. He was a few years younger than Day (who was born in 1529; Alington about 1537) and they were good friends. It was Cecil's habit to employ a secretary whom he could trust absolutely: in Edward's reign it had been Roger Alford, now it was Hugh Alington. It is probably significant here that Alington was Cecil's nephew, the son of Sir John Cheke's sister, Anne. Hugh worked for Cecil from at least 1559.

Like his friend Thomas Windebank, Alington helped his master in all kinds of ways. He got into trouble with his uncle for not keeping a proper receipt of the money he gave to Windebank before young Thomas Cecil's visit to Paris. Windebank, too, dealt in ready money, which we know was kept in large amounts in leather and canvas bags in Cecil's study and probably in other secure rooms in Cecil House and at Theobalds.[24]

Alington's principal job, and Windebank's to some degree, was to work as Cecil's amanuensis. This was a delicate task. Cecil always wanted to have control of his own pen: it was a point of professional pride, and frankly also a means of keeping control. He hated having to dictate letters, and any documents that were written for him he made sure to correct very carefully. Cecil derived huge satisfaction from his own penmanship, which was elegant and scholarly. This meant, of course, that he carried a heavy burden of personal correspondence. It is amazing to think that Cecil dealt personally with so much of the paperwork of royal government in Elizabeth's reign and it is no wonder that he felt at times the burden of his office to be utterly crushing.

But if Cecil did not write for himself, generally when he was ill or for very simple matters of business which he did not need to attend to, it was usually Alington who did it for him. Alington was always nearby, his master's trusted shadow; as was Windebank, particularly when the letters were for Elizabeth's ambassador in France. Then Alington would write the address in English and Windebank give it in French in his rather beautiful handwriting. It was a very smooth secretarial operation. But then it had to be, for the weight of business only grew over the course of Elizabeth's reign.

Hugh Alington was discreet and able, clever and educated. To be the private secretary of a man like Secretary Cecil was to work in effect as a public servant: Cecil had done the same himself as Protector Somerset's secretary many years before. Alington did for Cecil what Cecil did for the Queen. He received, opened and read correspondence, and then he carefully filed it away in his master's formidable archive – another piece of paper to add to the collection, always kept, never forgotten.

*

For William Cecil the boundary between work and home was a very blurred one indeed. Sometimes he craved escape, but he was rarely able to hide from business for very long. He was at home in his chambers at court just as he worked on the Queen's business in his study at Cecil House. Although his private houses offered at least some refuge from the daily strains of service at court, what even Cecil's life at home shows is the nature and extent of his power. Of course he was merely a servant of the Queen, a humble official. And yet Cecil's riches and influence were plain for everyone to see, and his household establishment and grand houses reflected his influence at court. Taste combined with wealth to produce on his contemporaries a singular effect of authority and power.

How Cecil viewed the comforts and luxuries of his life is hard to tell. If he sought riches and power for their own sake he never admitted it. Quite the contrary: he professed humility and set service and duty before self. These were the qualities of the true public servant: faithfulness, moderation and magnanimity. This was the part he played at court advising the Queen, or in Westminster Palace as Master of the Court of Wards. It was also the part he played at home, hearing suitors in the hall of Cecil House or fulfilling his obligations as paterfamilias to family and household.

He believed that everything was a gift from God. When he made his last will and testament he spoke of the 'worldly and earthly gifts it hath pleased Almighty God to have given or rather lent unto me' which would have to be left to the world. Like spiritual gifts, their possession was only temporary. This is how he made his peace with God in the last months of his life.[25]

Cecil was always terribly conscious of his image. He played the part of Elizabeth's Secretary to perfection. He was the consummate professional servant, clever, subtle and discreetly grand. He understood the peculiar position he held within the regime, and it is clear that he policed his image very carefully: the habit of control and direction was one he could never give up.

In 1562 he commissioned a design for a family tomb for himself and his wife and children. It is quite possibly the work of Laurence Nowell. It shows Cecil in armour and spurs, kneeling at an altar with his hands on the Bible. Also on the altar sits his plumed helm. He faces Lady Mildred with a steady gaze. The coats of arms of their families are above them. Their children, Anne and Thomas, kneel in prayer behind them. Thomas looks unusually compliant. Cecil carefully added below the names of the three children who had died as babies, the two Williams and Frances.[26]

Here was Sir William Cecil as a Protestant knight in his forties, calm and resolute. He was rich and powerful and built grand houses. But before all things he was God's knight, who fought England's enemies from his study at Cecil House, from the Council table and from the Queen's Privy Chamber. The dangers he knew all too well: Elizabeth's kingdoms were fighting for their survival in a hostile world.

11

Conspiracy and Rebellion

On 2 May 1568 Mary, Queen of Scots escaped from Lochleven Castle. Eleven days later her forces, under the command of the Earl of Argyll, met those of the Earl of Moray. Her soldiers were defeated and scattered at the battle of Langside. On 16 May Mary crossed the Solway Firth in a fishing boat and landed eventually at Workington in Cumberland. The problem of what to do with her would be William Cecil's for the next nineteen years.

Mary could not have arrived in England at a worse time. The cause of international Protestantism was in grave danger. Cecil was deeply troubled by events in France, where once again Huguenots were fighting Catholics. He was worried, too, by what was going on in Flanders; the Prince of Orange, the leader of Protestant resistance to the massive armed force of Spain, was looking increasingly beleaguered.

It was difficult to know how to deal with Mary. Elizabeth had for a while dithered on Scotland: 'But yet we cannot obtain resolution what she will do', Cecil wrote to the Earl of Leicester in the days after Langside. It was clear that the Queen of Scots intended to throw herself on Elizabeth's mercy. And even Cecil, Mary's determined opponent, saw all too clearly that it was possible to make a persuasive case in her favour. She had been made a prisoner by her own subjects; she had not been lawfully tried; she was a monarch and only God could judge her. These were exactly the arguments being used by Mary herself. So it was no surprise that by July she began to play on Elizabeth's natural sympathies as a fellow prince. The Queen of Scots wanted one of two things from her cousin: either help in being restored to her throne or a licence to travel to France. Cecil was in a quandary: 'Hereupon we stand at brawl; she much offended that she hath not her requests; and we much troubled with the difficulties, finding neither her continuance here good nor her departing hence quiet.'[1]

Already by late July Mary had 'long laboured' Elizabeth for her restoration to the throne of Scotland. She agreed that her matter should be heard in

England 'before some good personages to be deputed by the Queen's Majesty'. This was not going to be a trial. Mary would not be present. The purpose of the tribunal was to hear what Mary's opponents could 'allege for themselves' and to allow the Queen of Scots to defend herself through her commissioners. Elizabeth would hear 'the whole matter'. But Cecil understood only too clearly that Elizabeth wanted to fix the tribunal in Mary's favour. She had, he wrote, determined 'with' the Queen of Scots to hear the matter 'and (as it seemeth) to the advantage of that queen'.[2]

It was at this tribunal at York in October that the Earl of Moray produced the famous Casket Letters. This was the evidence, said Moray, of Mary Stuart's complicity in the murder of Lord Darnley and of her adulterous relationship with the Earl of Bothwell. Cecil came to know these documents very well indeed. He pored over the papers, annotated them, and asked searching questions about their provenance. They were the most politically sensitive documents that Cecil had ever read. He knew that if they were genuine Mary could never recover: any hope she had of regaining her throne would surely vanish. He also knew that the Casket Letters had been tampered with: his eyes were too sharp to miss some crude forgeries. It is a mark of his determination to do something about Mary that he ignored obvious fabrications of evidence. Cecil knew this was his best chance yet to draw the poison of the Queen of Scots.[3]

The problem, as Cecil well knew, was the quality of the evidence against Mary. The Duke of Norfolk and the Earl of Sussex, both at York to hear Mary's case, recognised that Mary could subvert the tribunal by simply denying that the letters were really hers. It was also clear that many of Mary Stuart's accusers had themselves been accomplices in Darnley's murder. The tribunal began to look very shaky.

So it was brought south to Westminster, where more commissioners, Cecil among them, sat to hear the cases for and against Mary. Elizabeth instructed her Privy Council and all the earls of the realm to be ready by 18 November, 'at which time Her Majesty meaneth to have this cause of the Queen of Scots fully heard, and therein to take such resolution and end as she shall be advised unto her'. All the parties met in the Painted Chamber in Westminster Palace. Mary's commissioners had made it very clear that they did not want to gather in Westminster Hall: this was not Mary's trial – at least not officially.[4]

It was now Cecil's turn to influence the proceedings. He secured Elizabeth's agreement that if proof of Mary's guilt stood up to scrutiny she would be handed over to Moray and his colleagues. Elizabeth would then formally recognise Moray as regent. Cecil also policed the procedure of this new tribunal in favour of Mary's enemies. Moray and his colleagues produced the original Casket Letters; but they did this only when Mary's commissioners had left the room. The Queen of Scots was not allowed to see the letters till the tribunal had considered them. Elizabeth surely knew exactly what Cecil was trying to pull off. But Cecil was sure-footed and he got his way.

So on 14 December, when the Queen herself presided over a meeting of the tribunal at Hampton Court, it was declared as fact that there was no difference between the copies of the Casket Letters that had been shown to Mary's commissioners and the original documents that had not. Cecil knew very well that this was untrue. But it was a judgment of huge importance.[5]

Cecil gave an account of the final revelation of Mary's guilt to Sir Henry Norris just hours after the final pronouncement on the authenticity of the Casket Letters. He wrote as though Regent Moray had revealed his evidence reluctantly, when forced to defend himself against the vehement charges put to him by Elizabeth. Moray was 'driven' to disclose what Cecil called 'a full fardel of naughty matter tending to convince the queen as devisor of the murder and the Earl of Bothwell her executor'. Mary's commissioners, Cecil said, now found the burden of proof against her to be so great that they wanted the Queen of Scots to come in person to answer the matter for herself. This was 'thought not fit to be granted until the great blots of the marriage with her husband the murderer, and the evident charges by letters of her own to be the devisor of the murder, be somewhat razed or recovered'.

Cecil wrote with injured innocence of the dreadful things he and Elizabeth had heard that day. 'For that as matters are exhibited against her [Mary], it is far unseemly for any prince or chaste ears to be annoyed with the filthy noise thereof.' Yet, he said, he was a commissioner: 'I must and will forbear to pronounce anything herein certainly, although as a private person I cannot but with horror and trembling think thereof'. The private man was horrified: the public man listened disinterestedly to the evidence against Mary. Cecil knew that this meeting at Hampton Court had been a turning point: Mary, Queen of Scots was finished.[6]

*

The tribunals at York and Westminster settled nothing legally. Mary had not been formally tried for the terrible crimes she was alleged to have committed. She was not guilty. But Elizabeth and her Council had seen the evidence against Mary, and it was enough to damage her reputation beyond repair. The tricky knot was that the Scottish Queen was in England as the guest of Elizabeth, though Elizabeth would not see her. Mary's subjects had formally deposed her and had crowned her baby son, James. So what would, or could, now happen to Mary Stuart?

William Cecil believed that Mary was the greatest threat to Elizabeth's throne, to religion and to the security of the Tudor state. There were compelling reasons to keep her locked away in England. But she was still a queen, and this mattered to Elizabeth, who had an instinctive affection for her cousin. The best way to proceed, so it seemed, was to come to a negotiated settlement that would balance Mary's reputation, the interests of England and the protection of the Earl of Moray's Protestant government in Scotland. Either Mary could formally resign her crown to her son, James, and live in England. Or she and James could share the title of the crown but leave government in the regency of Moray. Or she could remain Queen of Scots in name but live in England and allow Moray to govern as regent. Cecil knew that Mary was desperate to come to Elizabeth's presence to prove her innocence. He confessed himself unequal to the problem: 'I find my insufficiency to wade so deep, and the violence of the stream so great, as without good company assisting in counsel, I dare not venture to make any passage.'[7]

Cecil knew that any settlement with Mary Stuart would have to look fair and reasonable to foreign princes. He also believed that although Mary could keep her royal title, Scotland really had to be governed by Regent Moray. And from the beginning he took no chances with the Queen of Scots and her security. She had to be isolated. Cecil planned Mary's imprisonment very carefully. She would be removed to Tutbury Castle in Staffordshire, a place of safe keeping in the English midlands. At Tutbury there would be 'no such free access of persons to her as hath been'. No one would be able to communicate with Mary 'but by the Queen's Majesty's knowledge'. This was Cecil's chance to protect Elizabeth from her dangerous cousin.[8]

Cecil was not being complacent. He knew that England's relations with the foreign Catholic powers, particularly with Spain, were precarious. He was waiting to hear news of the religious wars in France, of 'some great effect to be wrought . . . by some battle stricken betwixt two armies'. Diplomatic relations with Spain had broken down completely. At the time of the tribunal in Westminster, Spanish ships carrying treasure to fund the Duke of Alba's army in the Low Countries were forced to seek shelter in English ports. The English government impounded the treasure. If there had ever been any trust between Elizabeth and Philip II, it began now to ebb away.[9]

Cecil was a deeply experienced politician. He lived in the real world of court politics, which was ever shifting and changing, and to which he adapted and adjusted. But he also had some very fixed ideas about how European politics worked, and a strong sense of who was for and against Elizabeth and her Protestant kingdom. He wrote in early 1569 of the great conspiracy being masterminded against England. Its authors were the Pope and the kings of France and Spain. Their instrument was Mary Stuart. Their patient was Elizabeth. It was a compelling metaphor: the Catholic powers of Europe were operating on Elizabeth like surgeons, using Mary Stuart as their scalpel.

This was Cecil's heartfelt reading of the international scene. The Pope wanted to recover the 'tyranny' of his authority. All true Christian realms were being forced to receive the Catholic faith: here Cecil was thinking of the wars of religion in France and Alba's brutal military campaign in the Netherlands. England, he believed, could not be re-converted to Catholicism without the 'eviction' of Elizabeth's crown, which the conspirators wanted to set upon Mary Stuart's head. And when Cecil looked to the state of England, and its strength to stand up to Catholic aggression, he knew that the kingdom was vulnerable. With Catholic power crushing Protestants in France and the Low Countries, it seemed only a matter of time before there was an open assault on England.[10]

It is easy to think that Cecil was too quick to see conspiracy; that where he looked for it, he found it. But he lived by the words of a young man called Francis Walsingham, who had written to Cecil in late 1568 that 'there is less danger in fearing too much than too little'. To Cecil the politics of 1569 were desperate and dangerous. Security came before everything else.[11]

So in the late winter and spring Cecil looked anxiously to France, to Scotland and to the Low Countries. Mary Stuart was taken to Tutbury at the end of January, where she was put under the supervision of the Earl of Shrewsbury and Henry Knollys, the brother of Elizabeth's Vice-Chamberlain, Sir Francis, and her cousin by marriage. At court there were delicate negotiations with the French and Spanish ambassadors. The French complained that Elizabeth's government was giving succour to the rebel forces of the Prince of Condé, which Cecil denied. Some English ships were being held by the French authorities. The Duke of Alba, in the Low Countries, sent a representative to speak to Elizabeth, but she refused to have anything to do with him. Diplomatic skirmishes between England, France and Spain continued for months. They were evidence of deteriorating relations between Elizabeth and her neighbours. And even Mary Stuart, effectively under lock and key in England, was beginning to cause trouble. Her supporters had published 'sundry false and slanderous things' about Moray 'and to bring the Queen's Majesty's doings into some question'. Cecil blamed Mary personally for this.[12]

In March news came to the court of the death of the Prince of Condé and other French Protestant noblemen at the battle of Jarnac, near Cognac and Angoulême. On 27 March Cecil had more intelligence about Condé's death, but he could not be certain: 'it is thought that either no part was true, or not in such sort as was reported'. Cecil was sick; but he was still at his desk, assessing news from Scotland and looking to Norris for sound information on Condé: 'I shall continually hearken for your letters, to declare to us the truth of this great tale of the battle of Cognac.'[13]

Condé had indeed been killed at Jarnac. It was dreadful news, but it would not have surprised Cecil. Weeks before he had known that the Prince faced powerful Catholic enemies. Elizabeth heard the news formally on the evening of 5 April, when she was told by the French ambassador that God had given the King of France victory in battle. Elizabeth replied that she was glad of any good fortune happening to the King. But she thought she must condole with him 'that it should be counted a victory to have a prince of his blood slain'. The ambassador was anything but impressed by her reply.

Cecil heard the account of the ambassador's audience at second hand: 'I have been, and yet am, not in sure health.' Anne, his twelve-year-old daughter, was desperately ill with a fever. He accepted the determination of providence both in the death of his daughter (though she did recover) and in the affairs of France: 'now the will of God is to be interpreted in this and all things to be best'.[14]

Cecil relied on good regular intelligence; without it he felt helpless to counsel the Queen. In late April he complained to Norris that the Council had not heard from Paris for a long time, 'having in the mean time so many diverse tales, as we were more troubled with the uncertainty than glad of the news'. The politics of the court were as anxious as ever. Cecil understood that Condé's death had upset a delicate agreement in Scotland between the Earl of Moray and the Duke of Châtelherault, a powerful Scots nobleman, in which Châtelherault had agreed to recognise James as king and Moray as regent. 'What will follow I know not; God stay these troubles that increase so near us.' A few days later Cecil went to his desk to write a paper on Scotland, in which he argued that there could be no peace until 'the inward controversy' of that kingdom was settled. Once again, he proposed a negotiated peace treaty to be policed by Elizabeth. But first there would have to be a secret mission to Moray to arrange the settlement.[15]

In the first week of June Cecil was in a resigned and introspective mood. At Cecil House, on the 6th, he reflected on some trying times. He knew not to write too much to Nicholas White, his friend in Ireland, for reasons of security: as he put it, letters were 'casual to be lost and are also permanent to be kept'. White, away in Ireland, had perhaps heard unpleasant rumours; but, Cecil wrote,

I will give you a rule to measure both sorts of reports, be they good or bad. I am, thanked be God, in good health; I am in quietness of mind as feeling the nearness and readiness of God's favour to assist me with his grace to have a disposition to serve him before the world; and therein have I lately proved his mere goodness to preserve me from some clouds or mists, in the midst whereof I trust mine honest actions are proved to have been lightsome and clear.

He found Elizabeth, 'my gracious good lady, without change of any part of her old good meaning towards me'. All his colleagues, he wrote, wished him good will.[16]

This was true in late May and early June. Yet it seems that in the weeks before Cecil had fallen out very seriously with the Duke of Norfolk. A week before his letter to White, Cecil had written of Norfolk's renewal of his 'good favour and allowance of me'. Clearly it had been a bruising encounter. Tempers at court were easily frayed. What Cecil wrote of may have been merely a personal falling out: what Norfolk possessed in social rank Cecil could easily match in political clout. Or it may have been something more serious, an effort to subvert Cecil's tough policy on security and the Queen of Scots. But Cecil made no apologies for the plain language he was using on matters he believed were vital to the preservation of Queen, realm and religion.[17]

To Cecil, Protestant England was fighting for its life. He wrote again about the great conspiracy in the days after his letter to Nicholas White. Captivity, slaughter, murder, spoils, rapes, burnings, drownings and poisonings would follow a Catholic invasion. He balanced himself somewhere between providence and preparation. 'The will of God must be patiently received and obeyed', he wrote to Sir Henry Norris.[18]

And yet there was no way Cecil wanted to tempt destruction. Before the French ambassador in London he had to be more measured. The French had complained about the embassy kept by Norris; he was frankly too Protestant. In July Cecil reassured Norris that 'Your constancy in opinion for the maintenance of God's cause is here of good councillors much liked, and in that respect I assure you I do earnestly commend you'.[19]

Days later Cecil dined with the French ambassador in London. The ambassador explained why Norris was so unpopular in Paris; Cecil recounted it for Norris, 'to be only for the intelligence which you had with his master's rebels; a matter, as he said, if he should attempt the like here, he knew that I would so mislike, as he could not be suffered to remain here as an ambassador'. The ambassador asked Cecil to write to Norris to tell him not to deal with the Huguenot rebels. Cecil's reply was a masterpiece of diplomatic wordcraft. He said that he would write to Norris, and that he could assure the ambassador that Norris would have no dealings with anyone he, Norris, 'could account as rebels'. This was an 'answer answerless' worthy of Elizabeth.[20]

That summer Cecil was very busy. On progress in Surrey and Hampshire he kept in touch with Norris and the war in France and with Moray's government in Scotland. The message of an embassy from Moray in early August was that the nobility of Scotland would not accept the restoration of Mary Stuart to the throne. Elizabeth was annoyed by Moray's letters; she wanted Mary to leave her realm 'with some tolerable conditions to avoid peril'. Cecil was deeply uncomfortable with the idea. It was 'a matter very hard, at the least to me, to compass' and had 'so many weighty circumstances in it, as I wish myself as free from the consideration thereof as I have been from the intelligence of the devising hereof'.[21]

The last part of Cecil's sentence is significant. There was a plan afoot to resolve the problem of Mary Stuart, and he was not directly involved in it. It was the most sensational news of the year: the Duke of Norfolk had proposed to marry the Queen of Scots. There were rumours of this at court in early September. Cecil knew about the proposal, because when he wrote to Nicholas White on 8 September he imagined that White had heard 'plentifully of a marriage intended'. 'I can assure you,' Cecil continued, 'the Queen's Majesty at this present so misliketh it, as I know nobody dare deal therein.' It was the Earl of Leicester who finally told Elizabeth about the plan. He had helped to organise it. Elizabeth was furious. Norfolk left the court without licence, which hardly improved her mood, and he stayed away for a few days against her command, convinced he was going to the Tower. By the end of the month Cecil, Lord Keeper Bacon and other councillors were questioning the conspirators.[22]

The idea for the marriage came from William Maitland of Lethington, at the York tribunal in 1568. It was, perhaps, an unlikely proposal to come from one of the architects of Moray's Protestant regency. But there again it meant different things to different people. For some of the men who supported and encouraged it, it was a way to tame the Queen of Scots. Norfolk is harder to read. His reason was perhaps plain ambition. But the duke had made a disastrous miscalculation and Cecil was not about to let him get away with it. He made sure that Norfolk's reputation was publicly smeared. Thomas Norton, one of Cecil's hired pens, wrote a stinging attack on the proposed marriage. The pamphlet was printed by John Day, who was also very close to Cecil.

Norton did not pull his punches. He went after both Norfolk and Mary together. He wrote that the Queen of Scots was 'in league with the confederate enemies of the Gospel, by the name of the holy league, to root out all such princes and magistrates as are professors of the same'. He alluded to the dreadful things Mary was supposed to have done; surely it was unlikely that any man of good 'would match with one detected of so horrible crimes'? The pamphlet was a wonderful act of ventriloquism. Cecil spoke through Thomas

Norton's pen and John Day's printing press. Norton could say things in public that Cecil could only say in private. It was a damning and effective indictment of the proposed marriage.[23]

Cecil went after Norfolk hard, and the duke barely knew what hit him. He was no match for Cecil's arts. Why is harder to determine. Perhaps their falling out earlier that year still rankled. It may have been the fact that the duke had set out to deal with Mary in a quite different way to Cecil's method of control and isolation, and that this was a chance to cut Norfolk down to size for challenging the Secretary's line.

Whatever the reason, Cecil allowed the duke to dangle. But he held back from suggesting to the Queen that a charge of treason be brought against Norfolk. On 6 October Cecil gave secret counsel to Elizabeth. She was still very angry about what had been done behind her back. Cecil wanted to reassure her: 'your Majesty need not to hinder your health by any care, nor yet impair greatness of your estimation, though this cause be not made so terrible as it seemeth your Majesty would have it'. Although Cecil believed that what Norfolk had done was 'within the compass of treason', he thought that to have the duke so charged would serve little purpose. His reasons were purely practical. First, a treason charge would increase Norfolk's popularity. Secondly, he was bound to be acquitted.

Cecil did not miss this opportunity to force home his advice on Mary Stuart. Here he was uncompromising: 'The Queen of Scots indeed is and shall always be a dangerous person to your estate, yet there be degrees whereby the danger may be more or less.' It would help if Elizabeth married. It would be useful to have Mary 'restrained' either in England or Scotland. If Mary were set free the danger to Elizabeth would be much greater.[24]

By now Norfolk was detained. The Earl of Pembroke, the Earl of Arundel and Lord Lumley had also been questioned and were ordered to keep to their lodgings. Cecil was certain that Pembroke, a good friend, 'meant nothing but well to the Queen's Majesty'. Elizabeth had been 'grievously offended' with the Earl of Leicester, but considering that he had revealed everything to Elizabeth, she had spared her displeasure 'the more' towards him.

'Some disquiets must arise,' Cecil wrote to Norris in Paris, 'but I trust not hurtful, for that Her Majesty saith she will know the truth, so as everyone shall see his own fault and so stay. Thus have I briefly run over a troublesome passage full of fears and jealousies; God send Her Majesty the quietness that she of her goodness desireth.'[25]

But there was still work to do. Cecil supervised an important security operation. The Earl of Shrewsbury and the Earl of Huntingdon searched Mary Stuart's papers. The government wanted to find a letter that had been sent to the Queen of Scots by Pembroke and Leicester, but it seemed that Mary had burned her correspondence, leaving only a couple of ciphers which were sent to London for analysis. On 7 October Cecil and Leicester ordered the arrest of Roberto di Ridolfi, an Italian merchant suspected of bringing money from the Pope to Elizabeth's enemies in England. Days later Pembroke and Throckmorton were interrogated by Cecil and other privy councillors; so, too, were the Duke of Norfolk and John Lesley, Bishop of Ross, Mary's man in England.[26]

So in London Norfolk's secret dealings led to detentions and examinations, disquieting enough for those caught up in them, as colleagues and friends sat facing one another across the interrogator's desk. But in the north of England there was armed rebellion.

The uprising was orchestrated by the Earl of Northumberland and the Earl of Westmorland, two Catholic noblemen tangled up in the Norfolk business. Typical Tudor rebels, they said that they acted to protect Elizabeth from 'certain common enemies of this realm about the Queen's Majesty's person' who had given Elizabeth 'sinister and detestable counsel'. They said that Norfolk, Pembroke and Arundel stood with them; on hearing this the duke and the two earls desperately pleaded their innocence to the Queen.[27]

An army went north to confront the rebel earls and 15,000 men were raised to protect the Queen in the south. Mary Stuart was moved from Tutbury Castle to Coventry. Thomas Cecil went north to serve as an army officer. The Earl of Oxford, Cecil's young charge, was also itching to prove himself in 'the service of my prince and country as at this present troublous time a number are'.[28]

At this dangerous moment Cecil was sick. But there was no time for rest, and he still worked into the night. By late November he had copies of the earls' proclamations. He wrote careful notes on the evidence against the rebels and read the reports of the royal army's successes. In all likelihood he co-ordinated the government's propaganda campaign against the rebel earls, for Thomas Norton, who weeks before had served Cecil so well in denouncing the Norfolk marriage, now addressed a pamphlet 'To the Queen's Majesty's poor deceived subjects of the north': it was an elegant yet terrifying piece of writing which compared the sheer power of Elizabeth and her government to the inadequate and badly supplied forces of Northumberland and Westmorland.[29]

The Northern Rising was the first major rebellion of Elizabeth's reign. It turned out not to be a serious military threat to the regime, but it was a terribly important wake-up call. For months, even years, Cecil had worried about the military deficiencies of England's defences. He was convinced that many of Elizabeth's subjects were not loyal to the Queen. The rebellion showed all too clearly how Mary Stuart and her supporters could take advantage of these weaknesses.

By the end of December Cecil could report, with relief, that 'our northern rebellion is fallen flat to the ground and scattered away'. The earls' 'sorry army' had at last been broken. But he still believed that 'The Queen's Majesty hath had a notable trial of her whole realm and subjects in this time.' And he was determined to learn the lessons of the Northern Rising.[30]

Over Christmas and New Year Cecil set out the terms of a full 'inquisition' into the Rising. He took an extremely tough line on the rebels and their supporters: they had to be made to feel royal justice. 'The vulgar people would be taught how this rebellion was pernicious to the realm, and against the honour of God.' To do this, he carefully planned measured and terrible retribution. Some rebels would be hanged by martial law in market towns and parishes, others executed near to their masters' houses, where their bodies would be left to hang 'for terror'. Wherever bells had been rung to raise rebellion 'there would for a memory be left but one bell in the steeple'. He saw to it personally that the north would remember the cost of disloyalty for a very long time.[31]

*

On 23 January 1570 Regent Moray was shot by an assassin. It was a brutal killing. The earl received a terrible wound and it took hours for him to bleed to death. 'I doubt not but the report of the cruel murder of the Regent in Scotland will be diversely reported in those parts,' Cecil wrote to Sir Henry Norris in Paris, 'and diversely also received, by some with gladness and by some with grief.' Cecil desperately gathered intelligence on what was happening in Scotland. Thomas Randolph, an experienced English ambassador, was sent north.[32]

The murder of Moray, whose regency had given Cecil some hope of security for England, could not have come at a worse time. The French were pressing Elizabeth to give Mary Stuart liberty and to promise not to give comfort to French Protestants. Elizabeth deferred an answer on Mary but the French ambassador kept pestering her for an audience. He had it on 6 February, when Elizabeth and the whole Council met him.

The French King's demand was that Mary should be freed and restored to her throne. Elizabeth said to the ambassador that 'she had used the Queen of Scots with more honour and favour than any prince having like cause would have done; and though she was not bound to make account to any prince of her doings, yet she would impart to the King, her good brother, some reasonable consideration of her doing'. That was all she said: the ambassador left her presence without any kind of answer.[33]

In that first week of February Cecil was kept very busy 'by reason of multitude of other affairs'. He knew about 'the dangerous practices of our adversaries here'. Sir Nicholas Throckmorton was still in disgrace for the part he had played in the secret marriage plan, but hoped on 25 February to have Cecil's favour and friendship. In early March Cecil was occupied by great matters of state: the stability of Scotland still worried him, particularly now that the French supported Mary Stuart's friends.[34]

There were also some unpleasant rumours to face. It was alleged by a gentleman called John Hamford, already a prisoner in the Fleet, that Cecil and Sir Nicholas Bacon, and probably the Earl of Leicester, had conspired together to have the Duke of Norfolk killed in the Tower of London. It was perhaps a wild story, but it would not be the last time that Cecil and Bacon would be accused of this kind of political conspiracy.[35]

However ambivalent Cecil may have felt about Norfolk, the duke was a constant petitioner for his favour. But Cecil was uncovering the full extent of Norfolk's plot. He pursued certain lines of enquiry that led him to believe that the rebel Earl of Northumberland had plotted with John Lesley, Bishop of Ross, Mary's man at Elizabeth's court, and with the French and Spanish ambassadors. Cecil already knew that Lesley had written to Mary of the proposed marriage with Norfolk. On the day Cecil walked with Sir Walter Mildmay in the funeral of the Earl of Pembroke at St Paul's Cathedral, 18 April, he also wrote a list of questions to be put to a man named Hamelyng, who had information about Northumberland's plan to free Mary Stuart. The redoubtable Sir Francis Knollys interrogated Hamelyng and found that the earls had intended 'to provoke the people', but that the 'principal intent' of the Northern Rising 'was to put the Queen of Scots to liberty, and . . . to make her Queen of England'.[36]

Elizabeth was still being pressed diplomatically by France. In late April Sir Henry Norris was instructed what to say to King Charles and his mother, Catherine de Medici, both of whom had been calling for Mary Stuart's restoration. Norris's instructions sounded resolute. Elizabeth recounted all the troubles that the Queen of Scots had caused her, from Mary's failure to ratify the treaty of Edinburgh through to the 'secret dealing of marriage' with Norfolk, and the Northern Rising. '[I]f the requests that are made to us to aid her to our power,' Elizabeth said of her cousin, 'to restore her forthwith to her realm shall be applied to the former things preceding, no indifferent person of any judgement will or can think it in conscience reasonable to move us to commit such a dangerous folly, as to be the author ourself to hazard our own person, our quietness of our realm and people.'[37]

But days later Elizabeth wobbled. She met her councillors at Hampton Court to hear their advice on Scotland and the restoration of Mary. The Privy Council was resolute. 'It was thought,' Cecil wrote, 'that the Queen's Majesty could not have any assurance sufficient for her own safety, if the

Queen of Scots should be restored to liberty and to her crown.' Mary was just too dangerous.[38]

It was clear to Cecil that conspiracies round Mary continued to grow. In early May he knew of a book that had been secretly 'procured' by John Lesley. The book claimed that Mary was not guilty of Darnley's death and that she was the lawful heir to Elizabeth's throne. 'Besides this, a notable lie is there uttered,' Cecil wrote to Sir Henry Norris: 'that all the noblemen that heard her cause did judge her innocent, and that she might marry with my Lord of Norfolk.' 'God send Her Majesty a good issue of this Scottish matter,' Cecil wrote, 'whereinto the entry is easy but the passage within doubtful and I fear the end will be monstrous.' He thought that it would be best 'for the Queen's Majesty to be delivered of the Scottish Queen', but few of his colleagues believed this would be possible.[39]

The definitive proof of the great conspiracy against Elizabeth was nailed to the door of the Bishop of London's house on 25 May. The author of this document was Pope Pius V, and it was the papal bull that excommunicated Elizabeth, declaring her a heretic and schismatic and a bastard. The next day Cecil wrote a wretched letter to Nicholas White in Ireland:

I am as you have known me, if not more, tormented with the blasts of the world, willing to live in calm places, but it pleaseth God otherwise to exercise me in sort as I cannot shun the rages thereof, though his goodness preserveth me as it were with the target of his providence, from the dangers that are gaping upon me.

He desperately wanted 'some intermission from business'. But the burden of work only increased. He had to have one eye on plotting at home as well as his usual command of affairs abroad. He believed Mary Stuart's agents were on the move. On 2 June John Lesley left Elizabeth's court for the Queen of Scots. Within days, Cecil understood that Lesley had had a secret meeting in Lambeth Marsh with the Earl of Southampton, 'a professed papist'.[40]

It was clear to Cecil in the early summer of 1570 that Elizabeth was in terrible danger: she was now the legitimate target of any Catholic plotter, whose conscience would not be stained by her killing. There had been a conspiracy that involved the Queen of Scots and some of Elizabeth's most trusted courtiers. There had been an armed insurrection. And sustained diplomatic pressure was being applied by France in the cause of Mary Stuart.

In late June there were more robust diplomatic exchanges between the English and French governments. Elizabeth wanted the French King to understand that if he sent military forces to Scotland 'she will take herself free from her promise of delivering the Queen of Scots'. That commitment was surely a fragile one: Cecil and the Council did not believe that Mary could really be sent out of England. Cecil reported on 22 June that Elizabeth had hurt her foot and so, 'constrained to keep her bedchamber', she was unable to see the French ambassador. She met him two days later, when he gave her a copy of a letter from his king, 'being of itself long and full of good words purporting his desire to have the Scottish Queen restored and concord established betwixt the two Queens'.[41]

While this difficult diplomacy was going on at the palace of Oatlands, the Duke of Norfolk, in the Tower, wrote to the Queen to declare his error and repentance at what he had done and to give an assurance of his loyalty. He counted Cecil an ally, though a plain-spoken one: 'you have, I thank you, ever advised me to remember that I am in fetters'. But there were rumours that Cecil was not so sympathetic. On 12 July he wrote a furious rebuttal of the allegation that he had in any way 'hindered or altered the Queen's Majesty's disposition or inclination' to get Norfolk out of the Tower. This was a sensitive business; Norfolk petitioned the Council in increasingly strained and desperate language. 'It is no small time for a poor subject to be kept so long in this close air, that never was acquainted with the like before.'[42]

The key to England's security at this tense and difficult time was Scotland. 'If we can be sure of Scotland,' Sir Ralph Sadler wrote to Cecil in August, 'the King of Spain and the French King will do us little harm'. But the real problem was that Mary Stuart remained in England. Cecil was staggered by the complexity of the threat to England. 'I am thrown into a maze at this time,' he wrote in late September, 'that I know not how to walk from dangers.'[43]

Cecil was in a maze because he was being sent on a delicate diplomatic mission to see Mary Stuart in Derbyshire. On 25 September he and Sir Walter Mildmay had their instructions. 'God be our guide,' Cecil wrote, 'for neither of us like the message.' It was for a peace treaty between Mary and Elizabeth and their kingdoms. There had been a time, years before, when one treaty, that of Edinburgh in 1560, had been Cecil's great victory over Mary, but she had never ratified it.[44]

This new proposal was not soft on the Queen of Scots. It expected her to ratify the treaty of Edinburgh 'or the tenor and intention thereof', to prosecute the murderers of Darnley and the Earl of Moray, and to send her son to England as a hostage. But by now Cecil did not believe that Mary should be restored to her throne, and he had little faith that she would keep her assurances. Mildmay and Cecil, with Thomas Windebank, his French expert, were with Mary at Chatsworth, in Derbyshire, on 5 October; they were there for eleven days in hard talks with the Queen of Scots. But would the agreement be worth the paper it was written on? And could it survive the febrile politics of the moment?[45]

When Cecil returned to London he received a very friendly letter from the Duke of Norfolk. The duke imagined that Cecil's visit to Derbyshire had been a hard one, 'considering how lately you were recovered before your journey, and how cold snowy weather you have had in that stormy country since your departure'. And probably the bleak weather suited Cecil's mood.[46]

As autumn turned to winter, Cecil reflected on Mary. He still did not trust her. 'She herself cannot forbear from her continual ardent desire to possess the crown of this realm,' he wrote in December. The Scottish Queen was still being used by Catholic princes who wanted to destroy international Protestantism. If Mary were at liberty, there would be 'continual war to the Queen's Majesty and this realm'. Yet still he did not know what should be done, except that it should be done quickly and justly.[47]

At the end of this memorandum on the Queen of Scots Cecil wrote out the names of 'Dangerous cases', some of them in prison, others abroad and a good number at large at home. Four were earls, a number barons and knights. One was Lord Henry Howard, the Duke of Norfolk's brother, the only nobleman ever to hold a university teaching post in the sixteenth century, a clever and sophisticated opponent of the government. Two of the names on the list, Thomas Watson and John Young, were those of men who had taught Cecil thirty-five years before at St John's College in Cambridge. These people carried weight: that is why Cecil called them dangerous.[48]

The Queen had some formidable enemies. It would be Cecil's job over the next months and years to hunt them down.

*

Nobility was much on Cecil's mind in the new year of 1571. In late January he wrote a 'Memorial' for the young Earl of Rutland, who was about to travel to France to broaden his mind and experience. Rutland was twenty years old. He had been brought up in Cecil's household, and had shown poise and courage as an officer in the army sent to put down the Northern Rising. By habit, Cecil set down on paper exactly what he thought Rutland should do on his travels.[49]

'The first, the middest and the last is to continue yourself in your fear of God by daily service of him with prayer', Cecil wrote to Rutland. The young earl was to look to the French court and royal family; to Roman antiquities; and to the nobility, their families and households and genealogies. Nobility had for a long time fascinated Cecil. He loved family trees and histories. As Master of the Court of Wards he preserved a society founded on rank, lineage and property. And he was himself, by the February of 1571, about to become a nobleman.

The ceremony took place at Windsor. The Council had for days been locked away in hard debate on the future of the Queen of Scots. Cecil threw himself into this work. He had long proved himself to be a masterful, controlling and invaluable servant of the crown: this was as clear to his colleagues in the hours before his elevation to the nobility as it had been in over twelve years of Elizabeth's rule.[50]

On Sunday, 25 February there was an elegant pause before the Council met commissioners from Scotland the next day. Dressed in robe and mantle Sir William Cecil processed with the royal heralds into the Queen's Presence Chamber. The heralds went in pairs, except Garter King of Arms who walked alone carrying the royal charter of Cecil's barony. Behind Garter came Henry Carey, Baron of Hunsdon, Elizabeth's cousin, with a baron's cloak. Cecil followed with two friends either side of him, Edward, Lord Clinton on his right, and on his left Lord Cobham. They entered the Presence Chamber and bowed three times before Elizabeth. Garter King of Arms handed the charter to the Lord Chamberlain, Lord Howard of Effingham, who in turn gave it first to the Queen and then to John Wolley, Elizabeth's Latin secretary, to read out loud. While Wolley read, the Queen put the baron's cloak around Cecil's shoulders. Elizabeth pronounced Sir William Cecil Baron of Burghley and gave him the charter. The new Lord Burghley thanked the Queen for the honour she had shown to him. After his speech, 'a great noise' of trumpets called them all to dinner.[51]

Lord Burghley carefully preserved the patent of his barony. It is a beautiful piece of craftsmanship, a large single sheet of vellum decorated with a miniature of Elizabeth by the court artist Nicholas Hilliard. Attached to the patent was the Great Seal of England in a small pouch on which Burghley wrote the date and regnal year: '25 February 13 Elizabeth Barony of Burghley'. It was a defining moment in his life. Elizabeth rarely gave titles, which made Burghley's all the more valuable. It was recognition of his painful service to the Queen and it meant the world to him.

A couple of weeks after receiving his new title he wrote to his friend Nicholas White in Ireland. It was the first of his letters to White that he signed 'W. Burghley'. 'My style is Lord of Burghley,' he added in a postscript, 'if you mean to know it for your writing, and if you list to write, truly the poorest lord in England.'[52]

12

Vomiting up a Poison

Lord Burghley believed with the strongest conviction that Mary Stuart was the greatest of all the threats to Elizabeth's throne. She had evaded peace treaties, encouraged plotting and stirred up rebellion. She was a menace, even captive in England. Her influence was like mercury, a seeping and persistent poison feeling its way into the cracks of Elizabeth's court, government and realm. It was Burghley's job to be vigilant.

Burghley was something like the chief of the Elizabethan intelligence service. True, there was no secret service in a form that would be recognisable today, with its own buildings, officers and tried methods of gathering and testing intelligence. But nevertheless it was Burghley who received daily reports from diplomats and ambassadors, as well as from a private network of contacts and informants at home and abroad. Diplomatic traffic was protected by codes and ciphers to which Burghley alone held the key. He single-handedly did what many agencies of modern governments do today: he decoded ciphers and codes, collected and collated intelligence, evaluated it, presented it to the Queen and the Privy Council and used it to make policy. He was held by those who worked for him to be especially good at this kind of intelligence work.[1]

In 1571 Burghley uncovered a plot against Elizabeth. It is known as the Ridolfi plot because it was masterminded (if that is quite the right word) by an Italian merchant called Roberto di Ridolfi. In inspiration and execution it was a very murky operation indeed. Painstaking investigations by Burghley revealed what he called the 'branches' of a conspiracy between Mary Stuart, the Catholic powers of Europe and the English nobility.[2]

First, we should begin with the facts about Ridolfi. He was born in 1531 to a wealthy family of Florentine bankers. He had been in London since about 1562, where he was known to the elite of London and Westminster as a respectable businessman. Burghley himself had had dealings with him. But in the late 1560s Ridolfi began to attract the government's attention and he was put under surveillance. Reports indicated that he was 'seen and known very conversant and a practicer with the Bishop of Ross', John Lesley, Mary Stuart's ambassador in London and a fierce supporter of Mary's title to the English throne.

The government noticed that in 1569 he brought huge sums of money into England in bills of exchange which, instead of using to buy merchandise, he gave to the Bishop of Ross and to some servants of the Duke of Norfolk. Ridolfi was a fundraiser for the Catholic cause. He was pulled in for questioning and kept in the custody of Francis Walsingham, Burghley's protégé, at Walsingham's house on Seething Lane in London. The government found out that Ridolfi's twelve thousand crowns, a vast sum of money, had been given to him by Pope Pius V. In November 1569 Ridolfi admitted that he knew the Bishop of Ross; that he had received money for the use of the Queen of Scots; and that he was privy to the proposed secret marriage of Mary Stuart to the Duke of Norfolk. He promised that he would no longer meddle in politics, and he asked, not only to be set free, but to have an audience with Elizabeth and 'to be restored to her favour'.[3]

Ridolfi was released from Walsingham's custody in late January 1570. Just over a year later, in the spring of 1571, Ridolfi made it known that he would like to travel to Italy 'about certain his private business'. At last he got his private interview with Elizabeth in her garden at Greenwich Palace on Sunday, 25 March, 'when he did in like sort make profession of great affection to serve Her Majesty and this crown'. Within a few days he had received 'a very favourable passport' signed by the Queen and a licence to take with him two horses or geldings. And so Ridolfi said goodbye to England. He did indeed go to Italy, to see the Pope about an invasion of Elizabeth's kingdoms; he also went on the same business to Brussels and to the court of King Philip of Spain.[4]

This all sounds straightforward enough. Ridolfi was a conspirator who managed to hoodwink the English government. When he said he wanted to serve Elizabeth, he lied in his teeth. But there is another way to look at Ridolfi's secret career in 1570 and 1571, a quite different interpretation of what he was up to: that Ridolfi was a plant; that the whole conspiracy was a set-up from the start, a plot manufactured by Burghley to expose Mary Stuart for the danger he knew her to be, and to reveal those in England and abroad with whom she had been plotting; and that in the eventual interrogations of Ridolfi's fellow plotters Burghley was merely testing the success of Ridolfi's penetration of the Catholic enemy.

Unfortunately we shall never know the truth. But did Ridolfi himself know the truth, or did Burghley? Ridolfi may indeed have been persuaded by Burghley and Walsingham to work for Elizabeth; it is suggestive, perhaps, that he only began to pester the Bishop of Ross with his credentials from Rome once he was freed from Seething Lane. Who knows what was going on in Ridolfi's mind? He may have conspired for the sheer pleasure of conspiring, for the thrill of being at the centre of a secret world, running between popes, queens and dukes with his secret ciphers, securing audiences and night-time meetings in London, Brussels and Rome.

Yet whatever or whoever Ridolfi was, or believed himself to be, the plot which has taken his name exposed for Lord Burghley a conspiracy against Queen and realm.

*

Any great unravelling often begins with a very small piece of thread. In the story of the Ridolfi plot this small piece of thread is the unlikely figure of Charles Bailly. It was Bailly's capture on 12 April 1571 that led to the unmasking of a traitor who was close indeed to Queen and government. Bailly was small beer, the servant and courier of the Bishop of Ross. But in fact he held the key, literally, to Lesley's secret ciphered correspondence.[5]

Bailly was detained at Dover, where he had just arrived on a ship from the Low Countries. He was searched and found to have in his possession a portmanteau full of English books and some letters addressed to the Bishop of Ross. The port officers were suspicious, so they sent Bailly to Lord Cobham in London. On examining Bailly's books and papers Cobham called for Burghley, and it did not take long for Burghley to recognise that the capture of this courier was very significant indeed.

The books Bailly was carrying with him were copies of *A Treatise concerning the defence of the Honour of . . . Mary Queen of Scotland*, brought from Catholic Louvain. Burghley knew that this was the book John Lesley had tried to have printed secretly at a press in Islington, a small village to the north of London, just a year before. At the very least Bailly was a smuggler of seditious books. But perhaps there was more: the letters for the Bishop of Ross were in cipher. They came, as Burghley may have known, from Roberto di Ridolfi. He ordered that Bailly should be locked up in the Marshalsea prison and kept under close guard.[6]

When Charles Bailly was sent the next day to the Marshalsea, it just so happened that William Herle was there too. Herle was a plant, Burghley's expert intelligencer and informant, and from the moment Bailly arrived Herle watched him keenly. Burghley had instructed that Bailly should be 'kept close' in the Marshalsea, but in fact security was lax enough for Bailly to be able to talk to other prisoners, in particular to an Irish priest and then, secretly at night and communicating through a hole Bailly had found in the wall of his cell, to a secretary of the Spanish ambassador and to two of the Bishop of Ross's household servants. This is precisely what Burghley wanted: he had to find Bailly's contacts. Ciphered letters passed between Bailly and the Bishop of Ross and Burghley had copies made of them. The signs were that Bailly and his master the bishop were hiding a great secret. It was clear soon enough that the secret was about Ridolfi.[7]

Slowly the government went to work on Bailly. His keys were taken from him and the trunk in his chamber at home was searched. He was nervous about this because in the trunk were, he told Lesley, 'certain minutes and other writings that might much hurt me if they did come to their hands'. He also worried about the copies of the *Treatise* that he had in his possession.

And he was right to worry. He was personally questioned by Burghley, a dubious honour and a measure of the value of the information he had to give. He was under constant observation. Every time Bailly wrote a letter to Lesley, the government filed away a copy. Herle listened carefully, though Bailly was suspicious of him and warned the bishop. This may have been a timely warning, because days later Herle was trying to work his way into Lesley's confidences and cast doubt on Bailly's loyalty to the bishop. Dutifully, Herle reported all of this in his letters to Burghley. He also sought from Burghley advice on how to make his imprisonment seem more believable to Bailly.[8]

Burghley quickly began to lose patience with Charles Bailly. He knew that his prisoner was privy to a conspiracy. He had the copies of the prison correspondence between Bailly and his master, but Burghley still could not decipher the letters. So on 26 April Sir Owen Hopton, the Lieutenant of the Tower, and Edmund Tremayne, a clerk of the Privy Council, were given a warrant to torture Bailly. Any method would be used to get information out of him.[9]

It was at first only the threat of torture. Burghley allowed Bailly to dangle. He spoke to Bailly again, this time in the company of Lord Howard of Effingham. Burghley was chillingly blunt. He said to Bailly that 'if they did not cut off his head they would cut off his ears'. And on 29 April Burghley came to see him alone, very early that Sunday morning. Bailly must have been terrified. In the half-light it was made plain to him that if he wanted his liberty he must first decipher the letters he had sent to the bishop. If he refused, Hopton would put him on the rack. It was to be the truth or torture.[10]

At this the Bishop of Ross made an official diplomatic protest. It had no effect. 'I have after travailed as much as is possible for me at this court,' he wrote to Bailly, 'making great exclamations, that it is a cruel and terrible practice to take ambassadors' servants, and to lay them on the rack to confess their masters' secrets, and to decipher their letters.' Leicester and Burghley together told the bishop that Bailly had not yet been racked 'but only put in fear'. The threat was still there.

All this while Burghley was doing his best to crack Lesley's cipher. He was tenacious, and for all the bishop's bluster it was clear within a day or two that Bailly was going to crack. Plainly he was terrified. On 1 May William Herle, who was doing his best to infiltrate Lesley's household, told Burghley that it was well known among the bishop's servants that Bailly had been taken to the rack 'and at his return was scarce able to go, discoloured as pale as ashes'.[11] So it was no great surprise that Bailly wrote on 2 May with an offer of service to Burghley. In return for his freedom, he said, he would tell Burghley everything he knew. 'I should be able to advertise you secretly of all their enterprise, and of the authors. . . . Putting all my confidence in your Lordship and assuring myself that you will keep it secret, as you have promised me, and cause me to have my liberty without stain of mine honour and credit.' Burghley wanted the information but he had no intention of allowing Bailly to go free.

He began to give Burghley the story. He had met Ridolfi in Brussels, where the Italian was trying to negotiate with Philip II's general in the Low Countries, the Duke of Alba; and Ridolfi, knowing that Bailly was Lesley's servant, had asked Bailly to write some letters for him. Two of these letters were for English noblemen 'advertising them of his [Ridolfi's] safe arrival on that side'. The bishop was instructed, through Bailly, to deliver the two letters. They were addressed with numbers only: one was marked 30, the other 40.[12]

Burghley realised that this was vital information. From Bailly's account he could get to Ridolfi, to the Duke of Alba and to their contacts in England. Like any practised interrogator, he made Bailly go over his story again and again, checking, correcting, elaborating; it was painstaking work. Burghley set out 'interrogatories', or written questions, and Bailly replied to them. By 5 May Burghley was beginning to find out more about the meeting in Brussels and the letters addressed to 30 and 40.[13]

But Bailly could only take Burghley so far in his investigations: the Bishop of Ross was next. On 13 May, lying sick in his lodgings near Paul's Wharf on the Thames, Lesley was examined by Burghley, the Earl of Sussex, Sir Ralph Sadler and Sir Walter Mildmay, all experienced and formidable councillors.[14] Burghley knew exactly what information he needed from Ross. He wanted to know more about the bishop's books, where they were printed and how they circulated. He needed to know about the letters Ross had exchanged with Sir Francis Englefield, a prominent English Catholic, just as he wanted to find out about the bishop's correspondence with the Countess of Northumberland, the Earl of Westmorland, Leonard Dacre and other English Catholic rebels. What letters and instructions was Ridolfi carrying with him when he went into Flanders? What letters had Ridolfi sent to Lesley, 'and how many for others, and to whom were they were directed?' Above all, Burghley wanted to discover the identities of 30 and 40.[15]

On 13 May Burghley and his colleagues got as much information as they could. Detail was everything, particularly about the ciphers and patterns of correspondence and communication. They were experienced interrogators, and they well knew that someone as clever as Lesley would put up as many defences as possible. And indeed he parried their questions. He denied ever writing to any of the rebels: he said he had corresponded only with Lady Northumberland, she using a cipher devised by the Scot, Lord Seton. He told Burghley and the others that he had burned all the letters.

But the really important information came near the end. 'He saith', the report of the examination reads, 'that Ridolfi had letters from the Queen of Scots, to the Duke of Alba, the Pope, and the King of Spain; and letters also from himself to the Duke of Alba to have aid and support of men to come into Scotland.' The Pope had given money for Mary. At last they got to the subject of the two coded letters Bailly had mentioned: on 40, 'being demanded who it was, he said, after some long pause, that it was the Queen of Scots; then being pressed to answer to whom was there another, he did deny any second; but being more urged, he said that there was indeed a second, and that was for one noted with the number of 30, who, after some pause, he said was the Spanish ambassador'. It all made sense, and both Mary and the ambassador, Don Guerau de Spes, were duly questioned.[16]

From this time on the government handled Lesley none too delicately. He was left effectively under house arrest in the custody of Henry Skipwith and Henry Kingsmill. Two of his household servants were allowed to stay with him and he was provided with physicians.[17]

But had Bailly and then Lesley told the truth about the letters? Only the next few months would tell.

*

The second unravelling of the conspiracy happened in August of the same year, 1571. Once again it came about by pure accident.

Shrewsbury is a small town on the borders of Wales many miles from London. There, in late summer, a draper called Thomas Browne was given a bag of silver coins by two of the Duke of Norfolk's secretaries, William Barker and Robert Hickford, for delivery to another of the duke's servants, Laurence Bannister, in the north of England.

Or at least Barker and Hickford told Browne the coins were silver: Browne, suspicious of the bag's weight, opened it to find £600 in gold coins and two 'tickets', or slips of paper, written in cipher. Browne reported his find

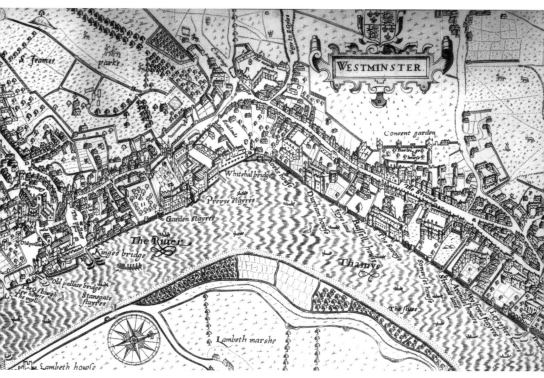

1 Map of Elizabethan Westminster, from John Norden, *Speculum Brittanniae*, 1593. Cecil House on the Strand is shown clearly, as 'Burleige howse', next to Covent Garden. Cannon Row lay near to the King's Bridge, close to Westminster Palace. The Queen's palace of Whitehall can be seen near to the Garden Stairs and the Privy Stairs on the River Thames.

2 The Queen's Secretary: Sir William Cecil in the first years of Elizabeth's reign, probably by Hans Eworth, *c.* 1565.

3 The Secretary's wife: Lady Mildred Cecil in the first years of Elizabeth's reign, probably also by Hans Eworth, *c.* 1565.

4 The Protestant knight and his family: Sir William and Lady Mildred Cecil, and Thomas and Anne Cecil, from a sketch for a family tomb, 1562.

5 A self-portrait of Laurence Nowell, the polymath scholar, held at bay in a corner of the map he drew specially for Sir William Cecil in 1563.

6 Sir William Cecil, arms firmly crossed as Laurence Nowell's stern master, on the map he carried about with him as Elizabeth I's Secretary.

7 The charter of Lord Burghley's barony; the date on the bag containing the royal seal, 25 February 1571, was carefully written out by the new baron.

8 Lord Burghley in his Garter robes, probably painted in the 1580s by Marcus Gheeraerts.

9 Burghley House near Stamford, the only one of William Cecil's great houses to survive.

10 The clock tower at Burghley House, an elaborate show of Lord Burghley's arms and Garter, with the date of 1585.

11 A late Elizabethan woodcut of Lord Burghley's arms and his motto *Cor unum, via una*, 'One heart, one way'.

12 Lord Burghley on his mule, probably painted in the 1590s.

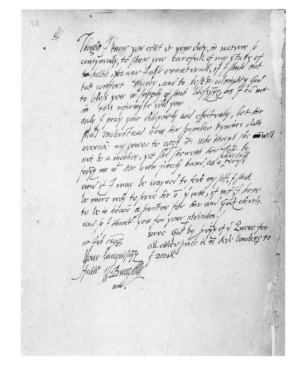

13 A young man's hand: Sir William Cecil's defence of his actions in the affair of Lady Jane Grey in 1553, carefully written out in his delicate scholarly handwriting.

14 An old man's hand: Lord Burghley's last letter to his son, Sir Robert Cecil, in 1598: 'Serve God by serving of the Queen, for all other service is indeed bondage to the Devil.'

immediately to Burghley. So if in spring it had been the arrest of a humble servant of the Bishop of Ross that had promised the solution to a plot, now it was an inquisitive merchant who would open up the conspiracy in a new and stunning way.[18]

Burghley acted with remarkable speed. Browne made his discovery on 29 August. Four days later, on 2 September, Hickford was in the Tower being questioned by Sir Thomas Smith and Dr Thomas Wilson. Smith was an old hand and an experienced interrogator, Wilson a tough lawyer and a former fellow of King's College in Cambridge. For the next few days they worked tirelessly to get Hickford's story. They found very quickly that the key to the cipher in the money bag was hidden at Howard House in London. In fact this 'alphabet' was concealed under a mat in the hallway near the duke's bed-chamber, close to a wall map of England. Thomas Howard, the thirty-three-year-old Duke of Norfolk, was immediately under suspicion.[19]

Smith and Wilson were in London; Burghley was with the court on summer progress in Essex, staying, as chance would have it, at Audley End, another of the duke's houses. So for the next few days couriers galloped up and down the road to London carrying urgent letters between Audley End and the Tower and St Katherine's Hospital next to the prison, where Wilson had chambers. When letters arrived at court Burghley briefed the Queen. From the beginning she was 'very inquisitive' to hear news. The first letter from Smith and Wilson arrived just before nine o'clock on 3 September, and Burghley pored over it, at first missing Smith's transcript of the secret 'ticket' hidden in the bag of gold and only later that morning finding it. Carefully he annotated and filed the letter.[20]

Things were happening very quickly in London. The Duke of Norfolk, not at court but near to Howard House, acted swiftly to cover his tracks. Hickford had already told Smith and Wilson about the hidden cipher key. Before it could be found by investigators, Norfolk had got to it. By three o'clock on the afternoon of the 3rd it was gone. The duke thought he had got away with the deception, believing 'that nothing is known'. But Smith and Wilson, the practised interrogators, knew better: 'your Lordship', they wrote to Burghley, 'may perceive nothing will be long hid.'

The next day Norfolk was detained and kept at Howard House under the watchful and experienced eye of Sir Ralph Sadler. Quickly he was examined. He said he knew nothing about the cipher. At five in the afternoon of 4 September Smith and Wilson sent Burghley the text of Hickford's examination and the questions they had put to the duke and the answers he had given. Norfolk had pointedly refused to put his hand to his statement.[21]

If Norfolk hoped that his interrogators would believe the word of a duke before the evidence of his secretary, he was to be much mistaken. Sadler, a tough and hugely experienced diplomat, was convinced by Hickford's testimony. As early as 5 September Sadler was confident enough to write that if Hickford was telling the truth, which he thought he was, 'then is the duke a devil and no Christian man'. Sadler had planned to stay at the Savoy hospital but he thought it would be safer to lodge at Howard House with Sir Henry Neville, a courtier and royal official, and Henry Skipwith. He was clearly worried about security; he felt 'another place' would be more suitable for the duke, by which he meant the Tower of London.[22]

Sir Ralph's letter was in Burghley's hands that afternoon. He lost no time in setting out to Sadler, Smith and Wilson exactly what the Queen wanted them to do with the Duke of Norfolk. It was clear, Burghley wrote, that the duke's disposition was to maintain his 'manifest unloyalty'. With the help of Sir Henry Neville and Sir Owen Hopton, they were to take Norfolk to the Tower. They were to use their own men to guard the duke and to call on the Mayor and sheriffs of London for help if they needed it. The Tower was to be cleared by Hopton of any prisoners who might have sympathy with the Howard family. The duke was to be watched and monitored very carefully. He could not be allowed to receive any messages from inside or outside the Tower: papers, Burghley wrote, 'will be many ways attempted to be given to him and sent from him to colour and cover the truth of things', smuggled in food, in drink, in clothes and in books. No means were to be spared in uncovering the great conspiracy. The Duke of Norfolk went to the Tower the next day.[23]

Burghley lost no time in confronting the Queen of Scots with the evidence he had found of her part in the Ridolfi conspiracy. Naturally he wanted to give the impression that he had all the proofs he needed to be certain of her complicity in the plot. On the evening of 5 September he wrote a long letter from Elizabeth to the Earl of Shrewsbury, Mary's custodian. In the letter he set out Mary's labours and devices to stir up a new rebellion in this realm, and to have the King of Spain to assist her. Shrewsbury was to provoke Mary, to 'tempt her patience', to press her to give more information. She was also to be kept under close guard, 'very straitly from all conference'. Burghley finished the letter at nine o'clock at night. He gave precise directions that it should go to the post at Doncaster and thence to the earl at Sheffield Castle 'haste post haste, haste, haste, for life, for life, for life, for life'.[24]

On the 5th Burghley was at his desk till midnight. He even began a letter to Smith and Wilson with news from Ireland. He could not finish the letter till next morning when, by nine o'clock, he had worse news: 'I fear the regent in Scotland is slain by a stratagem.' Some reports said that the Earl of Lennox, Regent Moray's successor, was dead. The intelligence was only to go as far as Sir Ralph Sadler, the most experienced Anglo-Scottish diplomat of his generation. Burghley did not want the Regent's wife, Lady Margaret, to hear of her husband's death (if indeed he was dead) till she had been told of it personally by the Queen. He would have remembered the time in 1567 when Lady Mildred had comforted the countess, distraught after the murder of her son, Henry, Lord Darnley.[25]

If Burghley was preoccupied for a few hours by Scotland, he had little time to rest from the interrogations of the Duke of Norfolk and his men. Norfolk was again questioned very closely, and on 8 September, with the report on his desk, Burghley read it carefully and went through every word with the Queen.

They discovered that the alphabet of Norfolk's cipher was written in his bible and was now in the hands of his secretary Hickford: Burghley wanted the bible to be found and Hickford examined again. On the subject of the £600 in gold coins Norfolk was less forthcoming. He thought the money belonged to the French ambassador. But this evasion did not fool Burghley, and Elizabeth also knew that Norfolk was lying. On the secret letters the duke was alleged to have exchanged with the Queen of Scots there was no defence: 'he humbly confesseth his fault and unhappiness, requiring mercy of Her Majesty'. Norfolk told Smith and Wilson that he would give the names of anyone else who knew about his secret dealings when he could 'call them to remembrance'. In Burghley's note to the two interrogators he wrote that 'Her Majesty would have you earnest herein'.[26]

It was clear in all of this that Elizabeth, carefully briefed by Burghley, knew her mind. She felt that William Barker, who had delivered the bag of gold to Hickford, had valuable information to give. Barker was questioned carefully from 5 September, but his early interrogations were not getting to the truth. 'Her Majesty would have you use some extremity with Barker,' Burghley wrote to Smith and Wilson the next day, the 9th, 'to confess more truth, for she thinketh that the money was the duke's, and that this device is a matter accorded betwixt the ambassador, the duke and Barker'. Like Charles Bailly, he was to be put in fear of torture 'if he will not confess the truth voluntarily of all things he knoweth of the Scottish Queen and my Lord'. Norfolk was to be questioned further about his dealings with Mary Stuart and Ridolfi: Smith and Wilson were instructed not to leave the duke till he had answered their questions 'directly'.[27]

By now Norfolk was scared enough to ask for the Queen's mercy. 'O my most dear and dread sovereign Lady Queen and my most gracious mistress,' he wrote, 'when I considered with myself how far I have transgressed my duty to your most excellent Majesty I dare not now presume to look up or hope for your grace's favour.' The plea fell on deaf ears; it had worked in 1569 but by now Elizabeth's patience, and Burghley's, were worn very thin.

Norfolk asked to see Burghley in the Tower on 10 September. But the duke could not hide from the questions, and by the 15th Burghley had prepared the torture warrant for Norfolk's servants, Barker and Bannister. Smith and Wilson were to examine them thoroughly; if they did not 'confess plainly their knowledge' they were to be brought to the rack. If fear of torture did not loosen their tongues, Burghley wrote, Smith and Wilson 'shall cause them to be put to the rack, and to find the taste thereof until they shall deal more plainly, or until you shall think meet'. That afternoon Edmund Tremayne carried the warrant to the Tower.[28]

With care and patience Burghley began to put the pieces of the conspiracy together. So far he had only fragments, but those fragments were suggestive. It began in his mind with Charles Bailly and the associations between Bailly, his master the Bishop of Ross, Roberto di Ridolfi, Mary Stuart, some of the foreign powers of Europe and, so it seemed, two English noblemen. The ciphered ticket found in the bag of gold in August 1571 established a connection between the Duke of Norfolk and Mary, Queen of Scots. The interrogations of William Barker yielded new information. He denied ever having anything to do with any servant of the Spanish ambassador, but he did admit to having had conversations in Islington, at Bankside and in London with servants of the Bishop of Ross. The two lines of enquiry, Bailly and Ridolfi and Norfolk and the Queen of Scots, met in the clever person of John Lesley and led eventually to Ridolfi.

So it is really no wonder that on 16 September, still travelling with the court, Burghley put his mind to two matters. The first had to do with the poor inmates of the Tower: Charles Bailly had to be questioned again about his knowledge of Ridolfi's correspondence with the Bishop of Ross, and the Duke of Norfolk's papers had to be searched afresh. Burghley made it plain to Smith and Wilson that these instructions came directly from the Queen.

The second matter was the political state of Scotland, because Norfolk was clearly tangled up in the politics of civil war north of the border. By now Burghley knew that the Earl of Lennox was dead and that the Earl of Mar, a Protestant and formerly a staunch supporter of Lennox, had been made regent by the Scottish parliament. The supporters of young King James had sworn revenge on Lennox's murderers.[29]

It was now time for Norfolk to give the real story of his plotting. The Privy Council required him in the Queen's name to tell Smith and Wilson everything about his dealings with the Bishop of Ross and Roberto di Ridolfi. How often had Ridolfi visited the duke? What did Ridolfi write to him? What were the names of the noblemen mentioned in his correspondence with Ridolfi? How often had he spoken with the Bishop of Ross and who knew about those conversations? Norfolk answered these questions the next day, he and Smith and Wilson in the Tower of London, while the court was entertained by Burghley at Theobalds. The duke's answers would hardly have satisfied Burghley. Yes, Norfolk had met Ridolfi 'but once'; he had never received any kind of writing from Ridolfi; he had only ever spoken to the bishop at Howard House at about nine o'clock one evening near Christmas 1570; hardly anyone knew of their meeting.[30]

But if Norfolk was still denying that he had done anything untoward, the careful search of his papers by Henry Skipwith was paying off. At last the government had in its possession the duke's bible and concealed therein were cipher alphabets 'in three several places'. A few days later, on 4 October, Burghley set out some questions for the duke on the proposal for marriage with the Queen of Scots. Norfolk was examined again on 10 and 11 October. On the 12th Charles Bailly sent a long account to Burghley of his meetings with Ridolfi and of the letters to 30 and 40 composed by Ridolfi. Once again Burghley was trying to solve his puzzle by coming at it from two directions, from Norfolk's story and from Bailly's: he was trying to make the connections, to find the thread that joined the duke to Mary Stuart and both of them to Ridolfi and the Bishop of Ross.[31]

Burghley was convinced of Norfolk's guilt: the more he and Sir Thomas Smith and Dr Thomas Wilson dug around for evidence, the surer he was of Norfolk's plotting. And by the middle of October he was ready to go public with a piece of anonymous but officially sponsored propaganda. The short pamphlet, *Salutem in Christo*, purported to be a letter from one 'R.G.' to his brother-in-law. It was printed on the press of John Day, who was very close to Burghley; and it bears some of the hallmarks of Burghley's style in official public prose, detailed and informative but rather stodgy, not obviously the work of a professional writer for a popular audience. The date of this letter was supposedly 13 October: this was the date Norfolk appeared before the Privy Council. Two days later, the Recorder of London, William Fleetwood, spoke in London's Guildhall about 'great and dangerous conspiracies' against the Queen. Fleetwood did not mention Norfolk. It was Burghley who put Norfolk's name in print.[32]

Now the whole of London could read about the duke locked away in the Tower. He had planned secretly to marry the Scottish Queen 'without the knowledge of the Queen's Majesty our sovereign lady'. Mary Stuart was the most dangerous enemy to Elizabeth. She had not been able to keep her own kingdom but she wanted Elizabeth's. She could never be trusted, 'nor yet is anything that she should promise, to be holden firm and durable: but as time shall give her cause to keep it or break it'. Once again Burghley wanted to blacken Mary's name, and in *Salutem in Christo* he blamed her personally for the Northern Rising and saw in the destruction of some ancient families of the north, encouraged to rise up against Elizabeth, Mary's 'cunning practice'.[33]

But most important of all, *Salutem in Christo* broke the news of what

Burghley knew so far (or at least was prepared to tell) of the Ridolfi plot. This was an official leak of deeply secret information to which only he and a very small group of indoctrinated councillors and interrogators were privy. Burghley went public. The practices between Norfolk and the Queen of Scots had had 'continuance without interruption by secret means of sundry evil persons'. The plot was discovered by Almighty God: Burghley was calling its discovery an act of providence. There was, he wrote, to have been a rebellion near London. The city would have been taken and held; meanwhile foreign troops from the Low Countries would have landed at an English port. These plans had been communicated in secret letters sent to Norfolk 'and specially to that ungracious priest named the Bishop of Ross', 'the instrument of all the duke's calamity'. Ridolfi's identity was protected: he was referred to only as the 'messenger' who had gone to the Pope for money to fund the rebellion and to King Philip of Spain for men and ships. The messenger had carried letters of credit from the Queen of Scots, the Duke of Norfolk and others. This 'tree of treason and rebellion' had other branches: chief among them were the liberty of Mary Stuart and her proclamation as Queen of England and Scotland and also the kidnap of her son, King James, by her supporters.[34]

Salutem in Christo was a clever and devious way to get the government's message to the people: a fabricated letter that just happened to find its way into print. Its earnest and sensible writer was able to communicate the horror of a terrible plot against Queen and realm without getting dragged into rhetoric or hyperbole; a man who gives nothing away of the source of his information but appeals for corroboration of his story to serious meetings between the Mayor of London and the Privy Council. It was, all things considered, a very nice piece of work, beautifully timed to destroy Norfolk's reputation and to damn the Queen of Scots. This was a sensational revelation from the heart of Elizabeth's government.[35]

The Duke of Norfolk was finished: there was no way back to favour. But Burghley had barely started with the Bishop of Ross, and on 14 October lawyers produced an opinion on whether Lesley, an ambassador, could be proceeded against legally. *Salutem in Christo* made Burghley's view of John Lesley very plain: he was 'an ungracious priest' who had spent years writing attacks on Elizabeth's right to sit on the English throne. The lawyers, too, seemed clear in their opinion: '[W]e do think, that an ambassador, aiding and comforting any traitor in his treason towards the prince with whom he pretendeth to be an ambassador in his realm, knowing the same treason, is punishable by the same prince against whom such treason is committed.'[36]

It was a week before the Privy Council questioned the Bishop of Ross. In the few days before, Elizabeth had stomach pains, relieved only by vomiting. The old fears about her health were as keen as ever. 'You must think such a matter would drive men to the end of their wits,' Burghley wrote to Francis Walsingham, by now ambassador in France, 'but God is the stay of all that put their trust in him.'

Burghley moved between the court at Richmond and Cecil House, and it was from the Strand that he wrote on 23 October to the Earl of Bedford of Lesley's interrogation at Bedford House. The Council grilled the bishop for days. The interrogators were all tough and seasoned veterans of politics and diplomacy, and all were close to Burghley: Lord Admiral Clinton, Sir Francis Knollys and Sir Thomas Smith. Burghley was there for at least two days of close examination.[37]

They took Lesley through his story in painstaking detail. In a sense they covered the territory of *Salutem in Christo*, looking for the details, for the confirmation: Norfolk's secret correspondence, the ciphered letters of the Queen of Scots, the requests to foreign powers for aid; they wanted to know all about Ridolfi's mission, the time he first began to act as an ambassador for the Pope, how he was accepted by the foreign powers. Burghley may have known some of this already. If Ridolfi's mission was a set-up from the beginning, encouraged either directly or indirectly by Burghley, then what Burghley may have been doing in Lesley's interrogation was testing the extent of Ridolfi's penetration of the enemy. Perhaps it is worth remembering here that the name of Roberto di Ridolfi was missing from *Salutem in Christo*: perhaps this was to protect Ridolfi and to allow him to conspire for just a little while longer.[38]

What became apparent in the bishop's examination was just how sympathetic some members of the English nobility had been, and were still, to Ridolfi's plotting. The most important of these were the Howards, principally the Duke of Norfolk himself. Lord Lumley, too, was identified by Lesley as a kindred spirit; indeed Lesley claimed on 26 October that Lumley was 30 and Norfolk was 40. This was, at last, the key Burghley had sought since spring. Now he knew the names of the noblemen mentioned by Charles Bailly. The puzzle was almost solved.

The bishop also gave precise details of Norfolk's 'discourse' with the Duke of Alba, the Spanish general in the Netherlands, and the part Philip of Spain and the Pope had played in a plot to free the Queen of Scots. Lesley's evidence against the Duke of Norfolk was damning: it was Norfolk who had given advice on the size of the invading army, just as it was the duke who had suggested Harwich as the port at which to land. Norfolk's friends, said the bishop, were the Earl of Arundel, Lord Montague, Lord Lumley, Sir John Arundel, Sir Thomas Stanley and others. Everything he said confirmed the sketch of the proposed invasion and *coup d'état* given in *Salutem in Christo*.[39]

Even after two days of close examination the Council had not finished with the Bishop of Ross. A fresh team of interrogators took over on 31 October, led by the Earl of Bedford working with Sir Thomas Smith, Thomas Wilson and another lawyer, Thomas Wilbraham. It was not enough to know the identities of 30 and 40. Lesley was asked about the contents of the letters sent to (so he claimed) Norfolk and Lumley. His examiners wanted to find out more about what the duke had known of Ridolfi's mission abroad; about letters Charles Bailly had brought for Mary Stuart and for the Spanish ambassador in England; and about Ridolfi's standing with the Pope. And so the interrogations continued, by the Earl of Leicester and Burghley on 3 November, and perhaps by Burghley alone on the 6th.

Burghley worked tirelessly through the bishop's answers to identify what he called the branches of the conspiracy. It is these interrogations in November that give us a couple of clues about Ridolfi's putative role as a plant.

First, Lesley claimed that he was constantly pestered by Ridolfi only after Ridolfi's release from Francis Walsingham's custody in 1570. Secondly, Lesley said that the cipher used to write to 40, the Duke of Norfolk, and 30, Lord Lumley, 'was made by Ridolfi in Italian, and served for the said Ridolfi to the Queen of Scots, the Duke of Norfolk' and to himself. This was a ludicrous breach of security: once Burghley had the key to this single alphabet he could read their post with relative ease. Who but an English agent would have made such an obvious mistake?[40]

By November the government had decided to go public again. *Salutem in Christo*, simply and cheaply printed in London and meant to be widely read, was for consumption at home. Now Burghley was planning an altogether more ambitious book that would speak to a European readership as well. On 1 November he wrote to Elizabeth's two representatives at the French court, Francis Walsingham and Henry Killigrew. 'The case of the Duke of Norfolk falleth even out by branches to be more odious', he wrote. 'The Bishop of Ross is in the Tower, where he uttereth many things right plainly . . .'

Burghley sent with his letter 'a little treatise', 'newly printed in Latin', and it concerned Mary Stuart's marriage to the Earl of Bothwell. He did not mention its title but we know the book as *De Maria Scotorum Regina*. 'I hear it is to be translated into English, with addition of many other supplements of like condition.' Burghley was being disingenuous. He knew full well about this translation: he had commissioned it himself and Dr Thomas Wilson, sometime Cambridge scholar, lawyer and interrogator, was hard at work turning it from Latin to mock Lowland Scots.[41]

Ane Detectioun of the duinges of Marie Quene of Scottes was by George Buchanan, the republican theorist who was by then the principal tutor to young King James of Scotland. It was Buchanan's dossier of evidence against Mary Stuart, a vicious attack on the Queen of Scots and her reputation. Burghley had known about it since 1568, when Thomas Randolph, Elizabeth's ambassador in Edinburgh, had sent a copy to him. Now Burghley once again used the London printing press of John Day and the pen of Dr Wilson to publish an edition of Buchanan's uncompromising dossier that would look, at least to the casual reader, as if it came from Scotland and not England.[42]

Wilson had finished his work by 8 November. He was very pleased with himself, and he wrote to Burghley of his translation of Buchanan into 'handsome Scottish'. He was keen to make sure that it would be sent abroad with nothing to indicate 'from whence it cometh'. For Wilson this secret work was entirely justified: he was disgusted by Mary Stuart, the Bishop of Ross and their servants. On the 8th, writing to Burghley, he had just read the latest report of William Barker's interrogation: 'Lord what people are these, what a Queen, and what an ambassador!' Burghley would make sure that Wilson's book was read at the French court to destroy any remaining credit Mary had in France. But it spoke to a domestic audience, too. Wilson concluded *Ane Detectioun* with a few short bitter and provocative statements:

When rude Scotland has vomited up a poison, must fine England lick it up for a restorative? O vile indignity.

While your Queen's enemy liveth, her danger continueth. Desperate necessity will dare the uttermost. O cruel mercy.

O ambition fed with prosperity, strengthened with indulgence, irritated with adversity, not to be neglected, trusted, nor pardoned.

The message to the politicians of Europe, to the people of England and to Queen Elizabeth was unmistakable.[43]

The sheer weight of business pressed down heavily on Burghley. By the middle of November he was sick, a fact we know from an insinuating letter the Bishop of Ross sent to him on the 16th. Lesley was questioned again at the end of the month. By 30 November the bishop recognised that he was neither believed by the English government nor in favour with his mistress the Queen of Scots who, as he wrote to Burghley, 'taketh my proceedings not well, whereof I am sorry . . . I think with myself that I have done but my duty.'

Another plotter desperate to be welcomed back by his mistress was the Duke of Norfolk, still locked away in the Tower. In early November he wrote an urgent letter to Burghley for his intercession in securing Elizabeth's forgiveness. Norfolk even sent a long paper 'of those things' he had forgotten to mention in his interrogations, trying to make a virtue of his reticence. The duke's plea fell on stony ground: he was beyond hope. Days later Elizabeth personally charged him with six offences drawn 'partly from his own confession, partly by others'. It was clear to Elizabeth and to Burghley that the duke had committed treason.[44]

Ane Detectioun of the duinges of Marie Quene of Scottes tells us a great deal about Burghley's beliefs and methods. Just as in *Salutem in Christo*, he was able to use the printing press to defend the government's actions and to convince the Queen's subjects of the rightness of her cause. He was quite happy, for political reasons, for this to be done obliquely and indirectly: this was a politician's art. But he believed, clearly and passionately, that Mary Stuart was a terrible danger to Elizabeth; and in exposing the Ridolfi plot – a plot for which he himself may have put down the foundations – he showed once and for all the seriousness of the vast conspiracy against the Queen and her realm. He had always known that Mary, Queen of Scots was an enemy who had to be rooted out and exposed. He had always recognised that the Catholic powers of Europe were happy to give money and men to destroy Protestant England. But now he had shown that the conspiracy ran so deep that some of Elizabeth's most noble and respectable subjects were up to their eyes in plotting.

So it is no wonder that as Elizabeth's ambassadors distributed copies of George Buchanan's dossier, Burghley set down a long position paper on Scotland for debate by the Privy Council. The civil war in Scotland, he wrote, had to be ended either by treaty or by force. He knew that the political state of Scotland affected the political and military security of England. He knew, too, that Mary Stuart could never be allowed to reign in Scotland again. In Scotland she had ruled as 'a manifest tyrant': in England she had encouraged rebellion and sought secretly to marry the Duke of Norfolk.

And it was Burghley, and the Queen and Council, who had to deal with the consequences of the dangerous politics of 1571: for Burghley personally, when in early November the Countess of Lennox wrote to him of her 'special grief' for her fatherless son Charles, and of her request for Charles to be brought up in Burghley's household; and for Elizabeth and her government, when Don Guerau de Spes, Philip II's ambassador in London, was ordered to depart the realm for 'his practices to disturb our state, to corrupt our subjects, to stir up rebellion'.[45]

It had been a remarkable year for the first Baron of Burghley. He had begun it as Sir William Cecil, rich, powerful and controlling, but without a title. His barony meant the world to him: as an honour it would be surpassed only by his election and installation as a Knight of the Most Noble Order of the Garter, and that would come soon enough. This was the other side to Burghley's life: if his intricate and powerful mind had been able to navigate the twists and turns of the Ridolfi plot, showing him to be a politician of intellect, steady determination and low cunning, then the arrangements he had made while all this was going on round him for the marriage of his daughter to the Earl of Oxford revealed the dynastic ambitions he had for his family. The young earl, who had been raised in Burghley's household after the death of his father, came from an old noble family, the de Veres, who traced their title back to the twelfth century. The wedding of Anne Cecil and Edward de Vere had been postponed from September. At last, on Friday, 19 December 1571, they married.

It is typical of Burghley that on the day of his daughter's wedding he wrote a letter to Elizabeth's ambassador in France, Francis Walsingham. But even Burghley knew that other things mattered that day. 'I can write no more for lack of leisure, being occasioned to write at this time divers ways, and not unoccupied with the feasting of my friends at the marriage of my daughter, who is this day married to the Earl of Oxford, to my comfort, by reason of the Queen's Majesty, who hath very honourably with her presence and great favour accompanied it.'[46]

It was only a temporary respite from business: the security of the realm could never be put to one side for very long.

13

To Kill a Duke

A fortnight after Anne Cecil's wedding to the Earl of Oxford her father received a disquieting letter in the London post. Its writer did not give his name. 'My Lord,' he began, 'of late I have upon discontent entered into a conspiracy with some others to slay your Lordship, and at the time appointed a man with a perfect hand attended you three several times in your garden to have slain your Lordship.' Nothing could be more expressive of Burghley's belief that he stood for the security and preservation of the Elizabethan state: England's enemies had him in their sights.

Touched with remorse, the repentant conspirator described how the Secretary was to be killed. One way was assassination at close quarters, to shoot Burghley on his garden terrace, for the planning of which the conspirators had reconnoitred Cecil House. Another way to kill him was at close range on his return from the royal court. Later Burghley found out that the conspirators intended to shoot him with an arquebus near the Charing Cross.

The writer, who within days was known to be one Kenelm Berney, was sure that Burghley would appreciate the timely warning: 'for the thanks I deserve I shall I doubt not but receive them hereafter at your hands, at more convenient time when these storms are past'. Burghley's thanks would come some months later in Berney's slow and painful death as a traitor.[1]

Kenelm Berney and Edmund Mather, his fellow conspirator, were from Norwich in the east of England. Berney was alleged by someone who knew him to have murdered a man. Mather, strangely enough, had been one of Sir Henry Norris's two secretaries in the Paris embassy. He was the son of a rich Norwich merchant: 'good with his pen, and a well-furnished man', wrote a colleague, but also 'so puffed up with ambition, that unless it were the shaking of a kingdom, nothing could satisfy him, as he was wont oft to say'. By 1572 Berney and Mather were part of the London underworld of criminals and political and religious fantasists.[2]

Berney and Mather were encouraged in their plotting by William Herle, Burghley's informant and agent. Herle was a professional man of the shadows, an expert in coat-trailing for informants and would-be plotters who had infiltrated the household of the Bishop of Ross and helped to trap Charles Bailly. Now to Berney and Mather he posed as a conspirator. They ate together, drank together and plotted together. For all their bravado, Berney and Mather walked straight into a trap expertly set down for them by William Herle.

Within days Berney was under arrest. On the 13th he was interrogated by the Earl of Leicester and Burghley. They quickly fell into routine. Every part of Berney's story was tested for inconsistencies, with questions and answers repeated over again. On 15 January Berney revealed a plan to kidnap Thomas and Robert Cecil; this was an insurance policy on the conspiracy, Burghley's sons to be killed if the plot was aborted. Berney, who probably had no idea that Herle was Burghley's informant, spoke of the conversations in Italian between Herle and Mather. Already Berney was painting Mather as the real villain, but doubtless Burghley and Leicester knew Berney's game – they had heard conspirators shift the blame and claim either innocence or stupidity before – and of course Burghley would have been able to check Berney's story against what Herle told him.[3]

By 28 January Mather himself was being questioned. He admitted that he had spoken secretly to Philip of Spain's disgraced ambassador in England, Don Guerau de Spes, who, said Mather, 'I ever perceived . . . had rooted a grounded malice against my Lord Burghley'. Sitting once at the ambassador's fireside in late October 1571 de Spes and Mather 'grew to talk of my Lord Burghley who the ambassador utterly misliked in all doings, saying that he held the helm, and that he did all in all'. It would not be the last time that Burghley heard that particular allegation from Catholics at home and abroad: that he ruled everything and everybody, including the Queen. It was no wonder, Burghley may have reflected, that conspirators sought to kill him.[4]

It became clear that Berney and Mather had cooked up all kinds of wild schemes in various houses and taverns round London. Quite apart from their plan to kill Burghley, they had other designs. They wanted to raise England's nobility in the cause of the Duke of Norfolk and proposed either to rescue the duke from the Tower using a bridge of canvas and long ropes or to snatch him on the way to his arraignment for treason. Mather certainly wanted to see Mary Stuart Queen of England. On 29 January Berney was questioned on the darkest of all their conspiracies, their plot to kill Elizabeth. From this point on, Berney and Mather were traitors and dead men.[5]

It is easy to see in this conspiracy the imaginings of two men led to their destruction by the cunning of Herle. But the plotting of Berney and Mather, hare-brained though it was, had a significance for Burghley. With everything he knew about politics at home and abroad, he believed that Elizabeth and her government were in mortal danger. The new conspiracy was for him a confirmation of things already known. It tied together the fortunes of Mary, Queen of Scots, the Duke of Norfolk and Elizabeth; Mather's examinations had shown the involvement of Spain. It was absolutely the right time to reflect on Francis Walsingham's aphorism: 'there is less danger in fearing too much than too little'. Dangers lurked everywhere.[6]

To eliminate the threats to Elizabeth's throne was to eliminate the Duke of Norfolk and to destroy the reputation of the Scottish Queen. Burghley made sure that Sir Thomas Smith and Henry Killigrew, both in France, were kept well supplied with copies of *Ane Detectioun of the duinges of Marie Quene of Scottes*. In early January he knew that the book was being eagerly read at the French court. But people at home and abroad had to believe what it said, so Burghley saw to the production of another little pamphlet to publicise *Ane Detectioun*. It appeared, without an author's name anywhere in it, once again from the press of John Day. Its title was *The copie of a letter written by one in London to his frend*; this was Burghley's classic form for official but unattributed pamphlets: he rarely varied successful technique.[7]

The purpose of these fifteen pages of black propaganda was to demonstrate the authenticity of *Ane Detectioun*. Burghley revealed that the author of the Scottish book was the famous George Buchanan. So *Ane Detectioun* was an official document, written on the instructions of the Scottish Privy Council, and it could be trusted to reveal the truth. *The copie of a letter* asserted the authenticity of the Casket Letters, documents Burghley knew full well had been edited and manipulated to convince their readers of Mary Stuart's guilt.[8]

Burghley used *The copie of a letter* to show the obvious guilt of the Duke of Norfolk. The fate of Thomas Howard was intimately tied up with the reputation of the Queen of Scots; Burghley knew that they had plotted together and sought Elizabeth's destruction. Now he enjoyed a grim joke at Norfolk's expense. He said that one of the duke's men had possessed a manuscript copy of Buchanan's *Detectioun*, and so it followed that Norfolk understood exactly what kind of woman Mary Stuart was. Norfolk knew of the Scottish Queen's complicity in the murder of Lord Darnley and of her adultery with the Earl of Bothwell, yet he still conspired to marry a woman who had committed these horrible crimes.[9]

Time was indeed running out for the Duke of Norfolk, and by now he was beyond hope. On 16 January he was taken to be tried for treason in Westminster Hall, where a great stage was set up for the purpose. When Norfolk was brought to the bar of the makeshift court, he had to his right Sir Owen Hopton, the Lieutenant of the Tower, and on his left Sir Peter Carew; next to Carew stood one of the servants of the Tower with the executioner's axe, its cutting edge turned away from the duke, at least for the time being. Before Norfolk was the entire political and legal establishment of Elizabethan England.

Norfolk was caught between confidence in his rank and nervous horror of what faced him. One account of the trial tells us that on entering the hall he surveyed with a 'haughty look' the lords, his judges, ahead of him; but the same observer noted that he did so 'oft biting his lip'. Burghley sat seven places to the right of the Earl of Shrewsbury, who had been appointed High Steward of England just for that day. Burghley had precedence over all the other barons because he was the Queen's Secretary. Now the energetic pursuer of Her Majesty's enemies, the interrogator and the propagandist, was the Duke of Norfolk's dispassionate and disinterested judge.[10]

Norfolk did not have a chance. He was denied legal counsel – standard procedure, the crown's lawyers told him, in cases of treason. 'I must fight without weapons', he told his peers. The evidence that Burghley and his colleagues had pieced together so carefully in the autumn of 1571 was presented to the duke, who answered as well as he could. The senior law officers presented the case but sometimes Burghley interrupted to correct them or to strengthen the prosecution's reading of the evidence. It would have been clear to everyone in Westminster Hall that Burghley had an unrivalled mastery of the evidence of Norfolk's treason.

The duke was found guilty and returned to the Tower. From there, on 22 January, he wrote a pleading letter to Elizabeth which he ended by signing with 'the woeful hand of a dead man, your Majesty's most unworthy subject'. Burghley read the letter, another piece of paper to be noted and filed in the archives. He marked it simply as 'Thomas Howard late Duke of Norfolk'. Within days Howard was ceremonially degraded from the Order of the Garter. His banner of arms, mantles, helm and crest were thrown into the ditch round Windsor Castle. There could not have been a more spectacular fall for a cousin of the Queen and England's premier nobleman.[11]

*

At the end of January Burghley was bothered by three matters that had concerned him almost from the beginning of Elizabeth's reign: the Queen's marriage, the security of her realm, and his own ill health. He wrote to Francis Walsingham about them all on the 23rd. His health, he said, was 'now subject to a combat with a fever'. Just that day he had had 'an assault of a second fit'. 'I must be excused to hold my hand, where my head is not able to command it.' His fits came from 'a great cold and a rheum fallen into my lungs, where it is lodged as yet without moving'.[12]

Burghley was more bothered by the business of the Queen's marriage. This was Walsingham's task as ambassador at the French court. Walsingham, an incredibly able diplomat in his late thirties, had been in Paris since December 1570. All through 1571 negotiations had rumbled on for Elizabeth's marriage to Henry, Duke of Anjou, a son of Catherine de Medici. These negotiations were difficult and intricate, in good part because it was not at all certain that Elizabeth really wanted to marry. Walsingham carried out careful negotiations in Paris while Burghley dealt privately with the French ambassador in London. The great political conundrum of this marriage was that it set the cause of dynasty against the cause of religion. The Queen had to find a husband and she had to produce an heir: yet French Protestants were being persecuted by the family into which it was proposed she should marry. It was a knot that would never be unpicked satisfactorily.

Burghley reflected on Elizabeth's quality of mercy. 'The Queen's Majesty hath been always a merciful lady,' he wrote to Walsingham, 'and by mercy she hath taken more harm than by justice, and yet she thinks that she is more beloved in doing herself harm.' This was a subtle criticism of the Queen; and in writing these words Burghley moved, almost imperceptibly, from saying something about Elizabeth's position on the French negotiations to the way she responded more generally to the terrible dangers she and her country faced. These were the days of Edmund Mather's interrogations, and of Kenelm Berney's admission of a plot to kill the Queen. Burghley was probably also thinking of Thomas Howard.[13]

Burghley was still sick on 2 February. 'I have not been able by a cold to see Her Majesty these eight days,' he wrote again to Walsingham, 'and this day I am in physic thoroughly sick, and I write, as you see, like one unsettled.' The opening of the conspiracy 'to have been rid of the Queen's Majesty', Mather's and Berney's, had made it uncertain whether Thomas Howard would die or remain in the Tower. But a week later the decision was made. On the day that Robert Hickman, the duke's secretary, was tried for treason and found guilty, the Queen signed the warrant for writs to the sheriffs of London for Howard's execution. This she did on Saturday, 9 February. Howard was to die two days later, on the 11th.[14]

Yet Norfolk was not executed that Monday. Thousands of people gathered to see him lose his head on Tower Hill; instead, they witnessed the executions of Mather and Berney. Howard's execution was postponed. Burghley said he did not know 'the inward cause of the stay of the Duke of Norfolk's death', but he recognised that Elizabeth had wobbled: 'sometime when she speaketh of Her Majesty's danger, she concludeth that justice should be done; another time when she speaketh of his nearness of blood, of his superiority in honour etc. she stayeth'.[15]

Burghley was able to tell Walsingham the story of how the postponement of Howard's execution had come about. Late on Sunday night, the 10th, Elizabeth sent for Burghley 'and entered into a great misliking that the duke should die the next day'. She was deeply uneasy. She decided that a new warrant should be drawn up immediately to countermand the order she had given to the sheriffs of London. 'God's will be fulfilled,' Burghley wrote to Walsingham, 'and aid Her Majesty to do herself good.' Elizabeth explained herself to Burghley in a personal letter. The 'hinder part' of her brain would not trust 'the forwards side of the same': she knew very well that her emotions had overruled her reason.[16]

Burghley believed Norfolk should die. He felt that the trials of the duke's servants only confirmed their master's guilt. Robert Hickford revealed that he had both concealed Norfolk's treasons and tried to dissuade him from them. Who knows whether Hickford was telling the truth? But his testimony suited Burghley: 'These two open acts have fortified the duke's condemnation.' Burghley believed that the longer Howard lived, the more dangers Elizabeth would face, both at home and abroad. He wrote a long paper on the subject in which he argued that the execution of Norfolk was essential for the security of the realm.[17]

A stay of execution for Norfolk encouraged Elizabeth's enemies. 'The continuance of the offender's life must needs continue the hope of all such intentions and mischiefs as were intended, and as might probably have ensued if treasons had not been discovered.' The beneficiary would be the Queen of Scots. Burghley did not underestimate the effect on Elizabeth's ordinary subjects of seeing Mary Stuart, the King of Spain and the Duke of Alba with 'a power over-great' over the Queen. When 'the great part of the people of the realm' saw Elizabeth without a husband or any successor, they could be 'easily induced' to give their support to a Scottish queen who had a son and who, if she sat on the English throne, could unite England with Scotland, 'a thing these many hundred years wished for'.

Burghley believed that long imprisonment would make Howard say or promise anything to avoid execution. The duke would be desperate. There was nothing unusual in this, 'for what will not a man's tongue or hand do', Burghley asked, 'to preserve the body in life?' There would be attempts to rescue him (probably here Burghley thought back to Berney and Mather's scheme); and such a rescue would be encouraged by those who were 'greedy to prosecute [i.e. to promote] the Scottish Queen's faction, the papists' longings and the Spanish designs against the Queen's Majesty'.

The great danger for Elizabeth was to carry on as she was doing already: 'Her Majesty can take no more perilous way than as she doth, to keep him in prison desperately . . . to hearten and bolden the adverse faction, to weaken and terrify her own party, and to nourish in her realm such a schism and derision amongst her subjects, as surely no device could have stirred up the like, but the uncertain dealing of Her Majesty.'[18]

In the spring of 1572 Burghley was in a robust mood. He wrote frankly on what he saw to be Elizabeth's failures. The fate of Thomas Howard was still on his mind on 1 April. He truly believed that Elizabeth only encouraged her enemies 'when they see justice forborne against the principal'. 'What more hope can be given to the evil', he continued, 'than to see impunity?' Elizabeth had to act. There was no danger of Burghley putting emotion before reason. His calculations were purely political.

Days later, in a letter to Walsingham, he considered the Anglo-French negotiations for Elizabeth's marriage. In spite of the French King's persecution of the Protestants, 'being of the Queen's religion', she would persevere in a league of peace with the French. Burghley told Walsingham what Elizabeth had asked him to say to the ambassador: first, she could not marry anyone she had not yet seen in the flesh; and secondly, a delicate matter, she could not allow any husband of hers to 'use any manner of religion in outward exercise that is in her conscience contrary and repugnant to the direct word of Almighty God'. Her husband would have to worship according to the English Prayer Book. For a long time, the calculation had been that Anjou would conform in his religion for the sake of a kingdom; but Burghley and Walsingham well knew that this demand was a convenient way for Elizabeth to delay the negotiations.[19]

Burghley believed this marriage to be necessary. The survival of England depended on it. 'You shall understand', he wrote to Walsingham, 'that I see the imminent perils to this state, and namely how long so ever Her Majesty shall by course of nature live and reign, the success of this crown, so manifestly uncertain or rather so manifestly pernicious for the state of religion, that I cannot but persist in seeking for marriage for Her Majesty.'

There was no choice; but the irony of the preservation of Protestant England by an alliance with the Catholic enemy was palpable. Burghley said that he found no way to get Elizabeth to marry 'that is liking to her, but with this duke'; so he 'forced' himself to pursue it – he chose his verb carefully. He flattered his 'fantasy with imaginations' that if Anjou came to England, Elizabeth would still have him. Surely Anjou 'would not lose a Queen with a kingdom for a priest's blessing of a chalice', wrote Burghley in a memorable aphorism.[20]

It was at this point in Elizabeth's reign that Burghley, the Queen's loyal servant, took a long, hard look at what his mistress had and had not so far achieved. It was, like other papers from these months, an uncompromising document; in fact it is by all standards an extraordinary analysis of what

Burghley believed to be the mistakes, errors and miscalculations of the Queen. It is incredible that he put it down in such a permanent record. There was nothing positive in what he wrote. The title of his paper expresses its tone and contents very effectively: 'Certain matters wherein the Queen's Majesty's forbearing and delays hath produced, not only inconveniences and increase of expenses, but also dangers' – not a pretty title but still one that packed a heavy punch.[21]

First of all it was obvious to Burghley that Elizabeth's 'coldness and forbearing from the beginning of her reign to proceed in marriage' had damaged her reputation and weakened her kingdom. This was merely a given, a simple statement of fact. More surprising, perhaps, was Burghley's position on the Queen's religion. Those who opposed the Elizabethan settlement of religion – in many ways Burghley's settlement – had been shown favour by the Queen: its supporters, by contrast, had been 'evil regarded, and in many things slandered, and at the least hindered'. In the thirteen years of Elizabeth's reign opponents in religion had prospered, so much so that there had been an open rebellion in the North and other risings and practices in the north-west and in East Anglia. Many of these opponents, he wrote, favoured Mary Stuart's claim to the English throne. Mary merely lacked force to bring her to the crown: her right to wear it was accepted by many people. The situation was as it was because of Elizabeth's 'continual doubtful dealing with the Queen of Scots'. Mary, Burghley wrote, daily won the hearts of Elizabeth's subjects.

There were two other failings that were especially close to Burghley's heart. The first was Elizabeth's unwillingness to aid directly King James of Scotland 'whose party is wholly for the Queen's Majesty'. This, though Burghley did not mention it, was because James's party had taken Mary Stuart's throne by force: they had usurped an anointed monarch. For Burghley this was nothing to the strategic importance of having Scotland as an ally. But here Elizabeth was failing, and there would one day be a terrible cost: 'The cause of Scotland is by this coldness drawn to such length as truly the calamities thereof, which are many ways bloody, cannot be avoided in the sight of God to be imputed to Her Majesty.' If Scotland should be lost to Spain or France, then the work of thirteen years spent joining Scotland to England in alliance and friendship would be lost and 'to all posterity great shame will be recorded of Her Majesty's lack of conduct'.

The last of Elizabeth's failings was her unwillingness to recruit 'chosen and faithful persons' to serve and protect her. Here Burghley meant the nobility, to which he himself had been only recently elevated. Any monarch needed loyal subjects tied by reciprocal bonds of honour and obligation. Burghley wrote that both Henry VII and Henry VIII had understood this fact: Elizabeth did not. She needed to create more noblemen. In fact their numbers were declining; it was 'some disgrace to the majesty of her time, he explained, 'that seeing the realm lacketh . . . it is disfurnished of principal persons to govern her people'.

This was a damning account of Elizabeth's rule, brutal in its honest evaluation of where the Queen had gone wrong.

It was Burghley's habit to set his thoughts out on paper to clarify his thinking. Sometimes these essays helped him to explain to his colleagues complicated political and diplomatic situations. But often they were written to be read and filed, private compositions perhaps shown to a few close political friends. The paper is not set out in a form common with Burghley, *pro* (for) and *contra* (against); there is no evidence to suggest that he was playing with ideas and arguments in a piece of Tudor rhetoric. It is a stinging critique of Elizabeth's queenship. He may have written it for all kinds of reasons: because of illness, or temper, or anxiety, the cumulative strains of many months of hard work and frustration. He had worked himself into the ground to uncover a conspiracy facing Elizabeth. Yet she appeared to do nothing to help herself and chose the way, not of resolution, but of prevarication and uncertainty.

The deep irony is that Burghley wrote his paper on the failings of the Queen at a time of great royal favour. In late April, on St George's Day, Burghley was nominated a Knight of the Most Noble Order of the Garter. There was no greater mark of his position in Elizabeth's government. This makes his fascinating critique of the Queen's rule all the more remarkable. But for Burghley, loyal service to the crown did not mean silence. He was the master of subtle language; he accepted also that the Queen was God's vicar on earth, a woman set apart from her subjects by her divine mission; and yet he felt he had to talk to her as plainly as he could within the formalities and courtesies of Elizabethan language. He believed it was his job to tell Elizabeth what she did not want to hear.

So if anyone could speak to the Queen about deeply sensitive matters, then it was Burghley, a man she had come to trust. He was secure; in political affairs few men carried his weight or experience. As a rule it is those with position and authority who have the confidence to say things that others dare not. Burghley was above all a counsellor, not a flatterer, and there were many times when what he had to say was not pleasing to delicate ears. It may seem paradoxical that a man who was painfully aware of the Queen's faults counted himself her loyal adviser. But this was the way Burghley made sense of the idea of divinely ordained monarchy. If Elizabeth had to be obeyed unconditionally, she also had to be counselled plainly and encouraged to do the right thing.

*

Elizabeth rarely had a happy time with her parliaments. They had an uncomfortable habit of being spirited and independent. It did not help that Burghley and his colleagues had used most of the parliaments so far in the reign to push the Queen in directions she did not want to go. A new parliament had been summoned for the late spring of 1572. As ever, there was the promise of a tussle between the Queen and her political elite in the House of Lords and the House of Commons.

For Burghley and his colleagues there were two matters of business: first, the fate of the Duke of Norfolk; and secondly, what to do about Mary, Queen of Scots. Howard, as Burghley had predicted weeks before, was doing his best to win Elizabeth's favour. Burghley read a report on 1 May that the duke 'most desireth any way to show himself . . . most thankful to Her Majesty for her Highness' great extraordinary mercies and graces'. Howard now distanced himself from his 'former course with that wretched Queen of Scots'.[22]

Within days the House of Lords appointed a committee on the Scottish Queen, of which Burghley was a member. They met MPs the next day in the Star Chamber. This joint committee set out five 'principal causes' against Mary, from her claim to the English crown to her encouragement of rebellion. They drew up a very detailed case. Much of the information must have come from Burghley, particularly the committee's account of the Ridolfi plot. As ever, he was at the heart of business.[23]

Lords and Commons showed from the beginning an efficient unity of purpose. The Lords' committee on Mary Stuart was composed of the two archbishops, eight earls, five bishops and seven barons. The Attorney-General and the Solicitor-General carried messages between the two houses. By 15 May Sir Francis Knollys, the most senior member of Elizabeth's Council sitting in the Commons, told MPs about the 'plat' 'for their manner of proceeding in the matter concerning the Queen of Scots'. There were passionate debates in the Commons. On the day Knollys spoke to the House, one MP, Sir Thomas Scot, declared that three things should be done: first, cut off the heads of the Scottish Queen and the Duke of Norfolk; secondly, remove Mary Stuart's title; and thirdly, establish a successor for Elizabeth.[24]

These were radical ideas indeed. But Scot was not alone: it is hard to imagine Burghley, or indeed any other member of Elizabeth's Council, finding them objectionable. By 19 May the whole House of Commons resolved to act against the Queen of Scots 'for the better safety and preservation of the Queen's Majesty's person'. This bill would have in its preamble a rehearsal of Mary's treasons and a petition that she might be attainted; in other words, Mary Stuart would be treated as a traitor and excluded from the English throne. Two days later Sir Francis Knollys reported that the Lords were resolved 'in the great cause among themselves, much to the like effect'. There was unanimity.[25]

Elizabeth stalled. She had no intention of being forced to do anything. Already she had her excuses for inaction. The time was not convenient (it so rarely was for Elizabeth); she could not attaint the Scottish Queen without calling Mary to answer for what she was alleged to have done; it was not the best time of year to assemble subjects to hear Mary's case; she wanted parliament to end before the arrival of an important embassy from France, just weeks away.

Burghley saw exactly what was happening. He was hardly surprised. He wrote to Francis Walsingham of the 'soundness' of the Commons in wanting to proceed against the Queen of Scots 'and no lack appearing in the higher house'. But in 'the highest person' there was a total lack of resolution. 'To lament it secretly I cannot forbear,' he wrote, 'and thereby with it and such like I am overthrown in heart.'

He was wonderfully melodramatic: 'I have no spot almost of good spirits left in me to nourish health in my body, being every four days thrown to the ground, so as now I am forced to be carried into the parliament house and to Her Majesty's presence.' Burghley said that he was ashamed that he and his colleagues on the Council were being blamed for Elizabeth's lack of resolve. They had to put up with this 'for saving of the honour of the highest'.[26]

Elizabeth offered a kind of compromise. MPs were told that the Queen wished to defer, not to reject, the proposal to bring a treason bill against the Queen of Scots. She suggested that instead a bill should be drawn up to deny Mary her title to the English throne. But the wording of her message to the Commons was very subtle, and there were still ominous rumblings. The Speaker proposed to tell the Lords that MPs thought a treason bill was still necessary, in spite of the Queen's disposition; and that if the Lords agreed, the two houses should join together to write it.[27]

The Lords and Commons did not abandon their efforts to move against Mary, Queen of Scots. But now they pursued their second objective in this parliament: the execution of the Duke of Norfolk. The House of Commons formally stated its opinion that 'Her Majesty's safety cannot stand without execution of the duke this present session'. MPs were invited by the Speaker to write down their reasons for Howard's execution: at least three of them did so, including Thomas Norton, a man close to Burghley. The Lords indicated that they supported the Commons in its efforts.[28]

In the last week of May there was frantic activity in the chambers and corridors of Westminster Palace. Members of the Lords and Commons, aware that time was quickly running out, gave their reasons for Thomas Howard's execution. They also presented a compelling case for strong action against the Queen of Scots. The arguments given by Elizabeth's bishops were so powerful that they almost had a republican edge to them. Soaked in the Old Testament, they cited instances of kings and princes justly punishing the wicked. But for Elizabeth this had a barbed edge: she had to do something about Mary, or else, like King Saul (1 Samuel 15), she would bring God's punishment upon herself. Saul lost his kingdom because he spared Agag. The case against Mary Stuart was very clear: 'The late Scottish Queen hath heaped up together all the sins of the licentious sons of David, adultery, murder, conspiracy, treasons and blasphemies against God.'[29]

The only effect this had on Elizabeth was to encourage her to dig her heels in even further. Politely she thanked MPs 'in their carefulness' for her safety and preservation. But in some well-chosen words that seemed only on the surface to indicate action, she said she wanted them to do nothing: certainly she did not want 'by any implication or drawing of words' to have Mary Stuart 'either enabled or disabled to or from any manner of title to the crown of this realm or any other title'. The Queen tried to establish very clear boundaries. The bill against Mary, which was now to be a mere shadow of what Burghley and his colleagues wanted, was to be drawn up by the crown's law officers. When it went to the Commons there was to be no debate on it. Parliament fought back by electing committees of Lords and Commons to meet later that day. Burghley was one of the six lords chosen.[30]

If by the end of May 1572 Elizabeth had blocked parliament over Mary Stuart, even she eventually gave way on Thomas Howard. His execution was the political price Elizabeth had to pay to save the Scottish Queen. The death of one cousin was worth the life of another: in any calculation an anointed monarch outranked even a duke. On 31 May Sir Francis Knollys told MPs as clearly as he could that Elizabeth had determined that Howard should at last die. The Earl of Leicester had said only ten days earlier that he thought it unlikely that the duke would be executed. Now, on the last day of the month, Knollys asked the Commons not to petition the Queen for the duke's death 'for that it may be Her Majesty will cause the same to be done of her own disposition'. That night Howard was told to prepare himself for justice; Burghley himself wrote Elizabeth's instructions to the officials in the Tower. On hearing that he was to die, Norfolk said simply 'God his will and Her Majesty's be done.'[31]

Thomas Howard was beheaded on Tower Hill soon after seven o'clock on the morning of 2 June. It was a defining moment in the reign of Elizabeth I. For the Queen it was an agonising choice to have to make; for Burghley it was a necessary act performed in the cause of security. There was no sentiment in what he did or wrote. Later the same day he and the Earl of Leicester were asked for their instructions on the burial of Howard's remains. Burghley spoke to Elizabeth about the duke's death the following evening. He had received a report from Walsingham of the views of important French Protestants on the

Queen of Scots and the Duke of Norfolk. Elizabeth asked Burghley to open the letters, which he did in her presence. He began to read them to her but soon stopped, 'she being somewhat sad for the Duke of Norfolk's death'.[32]

The bill against the Queen of Scots was now the most important piece of business in parliament, and it was given priority over everything else. It was an intricate job: the bill was too long, and members of the Lords and Commons spent days trying to shape it. Teams of experts were hard at work on it, and Burghley was one of them. A powerful committee of five councillors and lawyers produced articles 'wherewith the Queen of Scots may be charged'. But Burghley doubted that Mary Stuart would really feel the effect of any act of parliament: 'it will not', he wrote, 'draw her to any more fear to offend than words will do.' Not even that much was achieved: parliament was adjourned within a few days.

More than this, Mary Stuart put up a vigorous defence of her rights. On 17 June she answered the eleven articles brought against her. She took every advantage of Elizabeth's mercy. Mary refused to submit to her cousin's jurisdiction; she stated that she had 'the honour to be nearest of blood, parentage and right of succession' to the English crown after Elizabeth; and, taking up a point Elizabeth herself had conceded, she asked to be allowed to present herself before parliament to state her case.

After years of effort, and in the spring of 1572 surely the best chance to be rid of Mary Stuart and her claim to the English succession, it was Mary, not Elizabeth, who dictated terms and stated rights.[33]

*

On the day Mary Stuart made her protestation at Sheffield Castle, Lord Burghley, many miles away in Windsor, was installed as the 356th Knight Companion of the Most Noble Order of the Garter. There was no greater honour in Elizabethan England. Four other men joined him that day. Three were English noblemen: Walter Devereux, first Earl of Essex; Edmund Brydges, Baron Chandos; and Arthur Grey, Baron Grey of Wilton. Burghley knew them all well.

The other knight was a French duke, Francis de Montmorency, visiting as an ambassador from the King of France. After frantic days of working on bills in parliament, Burghley took part in high-level meetings with the French delegation. Entertainments for the ambassadors were put on in the Banqueting Hall of Whitehall Palace, with masques and tourneys. The journey to Windsor for the Garter ceremony on Tuesday, 17 June was for Burghley both a break from the punishing routine of government business and an honour that defined him as a nobleman.

The ceremony of installation was presided over by the Earl of Leicester as Lieutenant of the Order. It was a colourful spectacle carefully choreographed. The knights elect entered Windsor Castle at about two o'clock in the afternoon, all but Montmorency on horseback, attended by their servants in full livery. Three hours later Leicester and four other knights went from the castle to St George's Chapel. Burghley and the others were dressed in the beautiful blue robes of the Order; then each was led by two knights to the choir of the chapel. Burghley, like Montmorency before him, was accompanied by the Earl of Bedford and Sir Henry Sidney. Each man took the oath of the Order and then went to his stall in the chapel. After this they went with Leicester, the other knights and the various officers of the Garter to hear Evensong. This was followed by supper in the castle.

The ceremony continued next morning. At nine o'clock the newly installed knights went to hear Morning Prayer. First Leicester, then Burghley and the other knights, accompanied by the royal heralds, paid their respects at the sovereign's stall. Burghley was paired with Lord Grey, and before them were Somerset Herald and Lancaster Herald. All the heralds went with the knights of the Order to the castle. In the great hall they had a grand dinner.[34]

Burghley would have been very familiar with the Garter ceremony. Years before, in the reign of Edward VI, he had been the Chancellor of the Order. But this was something different: he was now a member of a very exclusive club that existed to honour the Queen, the laws of God and the laws of the realm. The Garter gave expression to the very notion of nobility; for someone who was entranced by the genealogies of noble families it was a coming home. It was no accident that many portraits of Burghley from these years show him in his Garter robes, and little wonder either that he made a point of decorating his grand houses with the badge and motto of the Order.

These few days of glamour sparkled in hard weeks of business. Soon enough there were the usual frustrations, disappointments and setbacks of Elizabethan politics. On 24 June, the day Burghley supplied the Duke of Montmorency 'and all his gentlemen with a collation of all things that I could procure', parliament resumed business after its adjournment. The bill to exclude Mary Stuart from the English succession had its third and final reading in the Commons a day later. It denied Mary a right to any estate, dignity, title or interest in Elizabeth's crown. If the Queen of Scots should claim the crown, or do anything to encourage war, rebellion or invasion, then she would be deemed a traitor to Elizabeth. Mary would be tried and judged by the peers of the realm like the wife of an English nobleman. If found guilty of treason she would suffer a traitor's death.[35]

These were tough words. But the bill ignored everything Mary Stuart had already done and it depended for its existence as an act on Elizabeth's assent.

At the end of the parliament, on 30 June, the Queen simply did nothing, deferring any decision till the following November. Burghley wrote to Walsingham with pained and weary resignation: 'I cannot write patiently: all that we laboured for . . . I mean a law to make the Scottish Queen unable and unworthy of succession of the crown, was by Her Majesty neither assented to nor rejected, but deferred until the feast of All Saints; but what all other wise and good men may think thereof you may guess.'[36]

For all his bad humour in the early summer of 1572, Burghley was a force to be reckoned with. He was a baron and the Queen's Secretary, something unique in the Tudor century. For well over thirteen years he had been on call day and night, carrying a huge administrative burden. He was at the centre of everything and his influence was everywhere. But in July Burghley was appointed Lord High Treasurer, an office vacant since the death of the Marquess of Winchester in March. If the Secretary was in theory one of the most junior of the Privy Council, then the Lord Treasurer was virtually its most senior member. He had new responsibilities and enhanced authority. He held the government's purse strings.

Yet he felt, at least at first, that very few things would change. Twelve days after his new appointment he grumbled to Francis Walsingham about the likelihood of Elizabeth's marrying: 'by no marriage,' he wrote, 'all evils must be looked for, and by marriage without liking no good can be hoped. Therefore to God I leave it.' He asked Walsingham to direct letters instead to Sir Thomas Smith, the new Secretary. 'And yet,' Burghley added, 'I am not discharged of mine ordinary cares.'[37]

Burghley was immensely powerful and very rich. For the year 1572 his steward recorded receipts of £5,653, of which the staggering sum of £2,674 was spent on building work at Theobalds. The poorest lord in England possessed riches few could even dream of. This was nothing to his authority in politics; Burghley was at the heart of Elizabethan government, obsessively controlling, the master of detail as well as an architect of policy. He was the voice of the government in proclamations which he drafted or in the semi-official pamphlets printed on John Day's press, the black propaganda used to smear the reputations of Mary, Queen of Scots and the Duke of Norfolk.[38]

There is no doubt that in 1572 Burghley still believed Elizabeth and her kingdoms were in mortal danger. The great Catholic conspiracy against England had not gone away. In April he described the Duke of Alba's military campaign in the Low Countries as 'Pharaoh's cruelties'. But the terrible confirmation of all the fears of persecution came in late August on the eve of St Bartholomew's Day, when some of the leaders of Protestant France, and many others, were murdered in an organised massacre by their Catholic enemies. Francis Walsingham was in the thick of the slaughter; he even sheltered some people fleeing from the killing.[39]

Burghley had heard about the murders by 11 September. 'Sir,' he wrote to Walsingham, 'I see the Devil is suffered by Almighty God for our sins to be strong in following the persecution of Christ's members.' He called for vigilance and repentance. Special prayers were commissioned and printed a few weeks later. More immediately England's sea coasts were prepared for a possible invasion and the navy was put to sea. The whole Council was sent for to meet in emergency session, but those councillors on progress with the Queen in Oxfordshire, of whom Burghley was one, were very busy. Burghley wanted from Walsingham the latest intelligence on those who had been killed in Paris and those who had escaped. 'God keep you,' he wrote, 'and comfort his afflicted church.'[40]

Burghley expected an invasion any day. This was why he had never dropped his guard, and why he had been so determined to hunt down the treasons of the Duke of Norfolk and his accomplices; it was why he could never give up the pursuit of Mary, Queen of Scots. Danger was everywhere, at home and abroad. He saw that the design of the Catholic powers was, as it had been since the treaty of Câteau-Cambrésis in 1559, the destruction of Elizabeth's rule.

All of these ideas were well expressed by a man close to Burghley. He was Robert Beale, Francis Walsingham's brother-in-law and a clerk of the Privy Council. Some time after the massacre in France, Beale composed a position paper for Burghley very much on the model of Burghley's own essays on political topics. Beale wrote of a 'detestable conspiracy' engineered by the Catholic powers of Europe; of the authority of the house of Guise in France; and of the desire by the Queen's enemies to take her life. Pius V's bull had declared Elizabeth a schismatic and a heretic: 'the way is already open to the possession of this crown'. Beale offered a terrifyingly economical summary of England's situation:

The Prince of Condé and Admiral be slain. The Spaniard is placed in the Low Countries. The Prince of Orange's forces be like after this to be so weakened as he shall never be able to lift up his head again. We are left destitute of friends on every side, amazed and divided at home: and consider not that where there is any such irresoluteness and security, that estate cannot in policy upon any foreign invasion (as is intended against this), continue long.

Catholics could not be trusted, for they had no loyalty to the Queen: 'It is unpossible that they should love her, whose religion founded in the Pope's authority maketh her birth and title unlawful.' The cause of this ruin was

Mary, Queen of Scots. And Beale had little time either for Elizabeth's policy on Mary Stuart or the lameness of the actions against Mary in that year's parliament. Wise men throughout Europe, he wrote, marvelled in the Queen's 'over mild dealing' with the Scottish Queen 'in nourishing . . . so pestiferous a viper'. Merely to disable Mary Stuart from the English succession was 'a toy'. There is every reason to believe that Burghley agreed wholeheartedly with Beale's frank assessment.[41]

Burghley had made it his vocation to hunt down Elizabeth's enemies and there were in his perception many of them. But they had teeth of their own, and they could fight back using some of Burghley's methods.

Some months after the massacres in France, in June 1573, Christopher Hatton, a dashing young gentleman of the Queen's Privy Chamber, received an anonymous letter. The writer reminded Hatton of his baptism as a Catholic and appealed to his loyalty to the Queen. Elizabeth had to be saved from wicked men who had usurped her rule. Hatton received with the letter a printed pamphlet called *A table gathered out of a book called A Treatise of treasons*. This short work introduced a much longer book. It identified, if not quite by name, 'the two captain conspirators' who were 'more than barons by office and dignity, more than earls by possessions and wealth, more than dukes in authority'. Hatton was asked to hand the book directly to the Queen.[42]

By the end of July Burghley had seen it. He passed it to Dr Thomas Wilson, the lawyer and practised interrogator. Burghley was in the starring role. To his mind, and to Wilson's, everything was inverted. He was cast, not as the dedicated and hard-working servant of the crown, but as one who governed England tyrannically, 'whereby to bring the Queen in hatred, and to kindle in the hearts of the people a weariness of her subjection'. He was the enemy of Elizabeth, of her people, and of religion.

Wilson was struck by the monstrosity of the claims: 'as the varlet is wicked in his devices, so is he so full of untruths, and so maliciously bent, especially against your honour, as with his overmuch railing, and open lying so often and so apparently, he hath lost all his credit with any wise man of judgement, or godly man of life'. He felt it was important to publish an answer to the book. It was certainly a volume to which Burghley, outraged, gave close attention. It was at once an attack on him personally and an assault on Elizabeth's rule.[43]

*

These nineteen months in Lord Burghley's life were remarkable. They began with an anonymous letter which led him to yet another conspiracy against Elizabeth and her realm. With hindsight and a quite different perspective we might say that someone so obsessed by security was bound to discover plotting wherever he looked; and we might wonder, too, about Burghley's method of using William Herle to flush out two such amateurish conspirators as Kenelm Berney and Edmund Mather. But their plot was for Burghley a confirmation of everything he knew already; and they set him on a course to eliminate two dangerous traitors, the Duke of Norfolk and Mary, Queen of Scots. Only Elizabeth frustrated the efforts of Burghley and his colleagues to deal with Mary Stuart once and for all.

Burghley knew that his efforts came at a cost. He knew that the pamphlet sent secretly to Christopher Hatton was a monstrous libel. He had weathered those accusations before and he would do so again many times. He truly believed he had always done the right thing. And his colleagues told him this too. After *A Treatise of treasons* appeared, Archbishop Parker of Canterbury wrote to Burghley a letter of consolation: 'Your conscience shall be your testimony to Almighty God; it is no new matter for such as take pains for the good government of the commonwealth to be reviled on.'[44]

PART THREE

Burghley's Commonwealth

14

'The Poorest Lord in England'

Soon after he was given his noble title in 1571 the new Baron of Burghley wrote of it to one of his correspondents: 'My style is Lord of Burghley, if you mean to know it for your writing, and if you list to write, truly the poorest lord in England.' Nothing, it would seem, was further from the truth.[1]

This chapter is about the life of Burghley and his family in the middle years of the 1570s. It is, like most of this book, essentially a narrative, running roughly from the late spring of 1574 to the summer of 1576. It is not really a chapter about high politics, or spies, or debates in the Privy Council. It is about the rhythm of family life for the Cecils, about Burghley's passion for building and architecture, about his health, and about the failure of his daughter's marriage. Of course politics is in the background: it always was for Burghley.

Burghley's working habits had changed by these middle years of the 1570s. As Elizabeth's Secretary he found it difficult to be away from court for very long, either because his desk was piled high with papers or because he had little inclination to leave the corridors of power. Sir Francis Walsingham, in so many ways Burghley's protégé, assumed the life of his mentor, as Walsingham's journal attests: the grinding business of the royal secretariat, the political pressures and panics of life in government, the almost constant journeying between the royal palaces. After nearly twelve years of setting exceptionally high standards for his successors to follow, Burghley had perhaps a little more freedom now and then to escape. As time went by, he wanted more and more to retreat to Theobalds, even if what he did there was to work on the Queen's business.

Burghley had the same old compulsion to work. He was often at Elizabeth's court, wherever the court happened to be. He went on progress with the Queen, and had the privilege of entertaining her at Theobalds. During the law terms he spent many of his days in the royal Exchequer or in the Court of Wards at Westminster. He heard endless petitioners in his chambers at Cecil House. John Dee was one such petitioner, ever hopeful of Burghley's help and favour in his various scientific and scholarly projects. In October 1574 he was ready and waiting to catch Burghley's attention when he could. A letter by Dee gives a good sense of how busy Burghley was: 'Considering your marvellous scantiness of leisure from very weighty matters . . . since which time I have some whole days attended at London, hoping for your Lordship's coming thither . . . finding your Lordship at all times of usual access for suitors, so fraught with matters of more importance than any of mine can justly be deemed.' This was the familiar lament of many suitors for Burghley's favour.[2]

The fact that so many people wanted Burghley's help and support was a sure mark of his power. He knew that he could intercede with the Queen in all kinds of business, and that she listened to him. His voice mattered, though he never said as much. There is a good example from May 1575, when Burghley heard that Archbishop Parker of Canterbury was dying. 'This day,' he wrote to Walsingham, 'I heard the danger of the Archbishop of Canterbury's life, being almost speechless.' Matthew Parker had been a friend for many years, but in the letter Burghley spared all preliminaries and got down to business: his successor should, in Burghley's opinion, be the Archbishop of York, Edmund Grindal, and he wanted Walsingham to tell the Queen as much. This was a short note without ceremony and without sentiment. Parker was nearly dead: a successor had to be found. Burghley wrote in that letter about his 'poor voice'. We might reflect that his voice was as poor as his lordship.[3]

Power came with a cost. For too many years Burghley had burned the candle at both ends, working on through sickness and grief, conscious of the pains, literally, of his service to the Queen. Now, entering his middle fifties, he began to feel the effects more and more. At times his health was delicate, as it had been, on and off, for some time.

But was this for a Burghley a deeper worry about a loss of his vitality? It may be significant that in 1576 he wrote of himself as 'an old, worn servant' who could not be compared to the best and the greatest. He was contrasting himself to his twenty-six-year-old son-in-law, Edward de Vere, Earl of Oxford. Of course this may have been rhetorical artifice, a pose. How on earth could anyone seriously favour a lightweight dilettante like Oxford over one of the most powerful men in the kingdom? Yet at that particular time Burghley was feeling especially vulnerable, and Oxford appeared to have the whip hand.[4]

Why Burghley had to stand up to the Earl of Oxford is a story to be told later in this chapter. But it may be as well to give a sketch here of the relations between Oxford, his wife and his father-in-law as an introduction to Burghley's life at court in 1574.

Oxford had been a royal ward under Burghley's guardianship. His father, the sixteenth earl, had died when he was twelve years old, and he was brought up with Burghley's children and another royal ward, the Earl of Rutland. Burghley was effectively Oxford's surrogate father, and saw to the young earl's education, putting him under the tuition of Laurence Nowell, the polymath scholar and cartographer.

Oxford's surviving letters to Burghley suggest a frosty relationship between the young poet with a taste for Chaucer and Plutarch and the driven Secretary to the Queen. There is a certain tone to the letters. It is not a friendly tone: Oxford is resentful, perhaps of Burghley's discipline; proud and sure of himself; able coldly to record perceived sleights and insults to ambition and ability. His companions were young, courtly, clever noblemen like Lord Henry Howard, the brother of the executed Duke of Norfolk. Burghley had long kept a close eye on Howard and the English Catholic network. So even Oxford's choice of friends seemed calculated to annoy. Yet this was the young man who gave Burghley, always a great admirer of nobility and lineage, just the sort of dynastic clout he wanted for his family. It must have been a hard circle for Burghley to square.

The Earl of Oxford could not have been more different to his father-in-law. He had all the talents to play an elegant courtly game. In May 1573, when he was twenty-three years old, it was reported that the Queen 'delighteth more in his personage, and his dancing and valiantness than any other'. But he danced to his own tune, and in July 1574, when the court was on summer progress in Oxfordshire, he left England for Flanders without Elizabeth's licence. The Queen ordered her gentlemen pensioners to bring him back. Burghley was with the court at Bristol in late August and he and Oxford went to see Elizabeth together. For Burghley it must have been an excruciating audience.[5]

This was by no means the end of the Earl of Oxford's career as errant and erring husband and son-in-law. Soon after the interview in Bristol, the earl was given formal licence to go abroad, which he did for over a year. While he was gone his wife gave birth to a girl, who was named Elizabeth. When he finally returned he would have nothing to do with his wife and sent her back to her parents. Burghley was mystified, shocked, hurt; he had to fight rumour and innuendo and feel the shame of a failed marriage. He also had to face the blunt fact that he could not control people as he controlled policy.

Life at court, as Burghley well knew, was never certain, never stable. Sir Francis Walsingham once reminded him 'that the world is made of a round substance, that it cannot stand still'. The same was true of 'our little world'. This was the early spring of 1575, and Burghley, like the Earl of Sussex, was sick. But if Sussex was taking physic, Burghley was instead near the court and busy with matters both public and private. He reflected on the efforts of Walter Devereux, the first Earl of Essex, to colonise Ulster: 'God send him as good speed,' he wrote to Walsingham, 'as if he were mine own son.' Burghley was working, too, on Scotland, dealing with the correspondence of the Regent, the Earl of Morton.

Dynasty was the one reality for Burghley that made sense of his life. This was more than family history, a curiosity about one's ancestors, though Burghley was a keen, if a too creative, genealogist; it was a passion for knowing and celebrating the past but also for looking forward to the generations to come: nurturing children, providing them with estates, building great houses. These were concerns of the present, too, of course, for in the politics of the Elizabethan court there were certain appearances it was important to maintain. But we might say that even Burghley's obsession with work – the careful reading of those papers from Scotland, the thinking about policy in Ireland – was a dynastic urge. Burghley served Elizabeth, just as his father and grandfather had served her predecessors. Burghley felt dynasty: it was a tangible thing to him, a reality of three dimensions.

Indeed dynasty was the reason why, in spring 1575, Burghley did not want his son, Thomas, to travel abroad. Thomas Cecil was a month short of his thirty-third birthday. He had come a long way since his disastrous visit to Paris as a very young man. Now he had asked the Queen for a licence to travel abroad for a year. 'Truly for mine own particular,' Burghley wrote to Walsingham, 'I never did nor do like it.' He could not condemn his son's 'desire to travel to good end'. But he made it plain to Walsingham that he was going to ask Elizabeth to say no which, presumably, she did, for Thomas stayed in England. Burghley's great worry was his succession. 'Indeed,' he explained to Walsingham, 'if he could have left me an heir of full age, I could have assented.' Thomas's son, the second William Cecil, was not yet ten years old. The rhythm of inheritance of generation to generation was too important to be put at risk.[6]

That April Burghley continued to work through sickness. He wrote to Walsingham at court, where Sir Francis was himself wrestling with business. 'I am right glad that you are at the court,' said Burghley, 'where though you cannot find things succeed as were to be desired, yet I doubt not but by your discretion and diligence, either good things will come to effect, or evil fall in defect.' Doubtless he would have said the same of his own life as Elizabeth's Secretary: without his hard work everything was likely to fall to pieces. 'I would gladly help the plough with you,' Burghley continued, 'either in the ridge or furrow, until I had the yoke pulled off from my neck.' But he was hardly fit. In fact he was unsure whether he would be able to get to court later that week for the celebrations on St George's Day of the Order of the Garter. 'I begin to be able to go softly with the help of one staff,' he explained, 'and if the weather shall not hinder me I would hope to do the same with a small staff.' He looked to the advice of 'the Supreme': the Queen herself.[7]

*

The plain truth is that if we want to understand William Cecil, we have to understand Theobalds. To Burghley Theobalds was more than a house: it was an expression in stone of the dynastic ambitions he had for his family.

Burghley was always a keen student of architecture. He kept up a lively and detailed correspondence with the master masons who worked for him. By the 1570s he was spending vast amounts of money on Burghley House in Northamptonshire but principally at Theobalds, importing the best materials from abroad and sparing no expense.

Always he looked for architectural innovation. There is a good example of this from Burghley House. After Richard Cecil's death William commissioned something that was like nothing else in England: a grand Roman staircase which was carved with the arms and badges of half a dozen or so families of his kinship, from the Cecil garb (or wheatsheaf) to the crescent of the Chekes and the cinquefoil of the Cookes. This was dynasty, or at least an element of it. The model for this great staircase came from France, perhaps from the Louvre or from the Hôtel de Ville in Paris: the fact is that even as a young man Burghley wanted to experiment and innovate. Twenty years later he had a very much larger purse and greater ambitions.[8]

Theobalds was Burghley's joy and delight. It was also a project of staggering scale. In the six accounting years after 1567, Burghley spent nearly £10,000 transforming the poky moated manor house he had bought in 1564 into one of the most spectacular houses in Britain. Only in 1575 did the amount of money Burghley spent on Theobalds fall below £1,000, and even then just barely. He personally audited every penny and halfpenny. Everything about the house and its garden was consciously contrived to affect the guest, whether on a casual visit or on progress with Elizabeth's court.

So what, in 1575, would a visitor to Theobalds have seen and experienced? It is hard to be absolutely sure, particularly when it comes to the decorative schemes of the house. Theobalds was still growing, even in the 1570s, and it did not reach its final form until a decade later. Still, with this caveat in mind, we can go on a short tour of the most spectacular house in Elizabethan England.[9]

There were three great central courts at Theobalds. The oldest, Conduit Court, was in the west and the newest, Dial Court, was to the east. Any visitor came first to Dial Court from a long driveway lined with elm and ash trees. Dial Court was really an outer court, with the bake-house, brew-house and laundry on one side of it, and the stables on the other. Straight ahead were the other main courts of the house; to the right, beyond the stables, were the service departments; to the left, though not yet visible, the Great Garden.

At the far end of Dial Court was a gatehouse that served as the main entrance to Theobalds proper. It was a grand affair of two storeys, and in 1575 the stone would have looked very freshly dressed. Through this gate the visitor entered a loggia, an arcade looking out west into Middle Court. At each end of the loggia staircases led up to a glazed long gallery. Here was one of the most talked about features of Burghley's decorative scheme at Theobalds.

In this Green Gallery were painted the coats of arms of all the landed families of the kingdom. The arms were shown to hang on fifty-two trees; between these trees were England's towns, boroughs and rivers. It was an elaborate display, and to any visitor, and certainly to Burghley, it would have had great significance. Here already, before even entering the first main court of Theobalds, was the realm. All at once the visitor saw something of the geography of England and its noble and gentry families. Nothing better illustrated Burghley's passion for nobility and lineage. It showed that he had a close working knowledge of England's landed elite – as Secretary he had made it his business to know all about these families, on whom Elizabeth's security depended.

The gallery said something, too, about his strong visual appreciation of England and its counties. He loved maps and plans. In the few years after Dial Court and its Green Gallery were built, he personally annotated the proofs of Christopher Saxton's maps of England. Burghley was expert enough to comment on the best cartography of the day. Already, in this elegant gallery, the visitor knew something about the man who had built such a splendid house.

Middle Court was Burghley's court: it was probably where he had his private lodgings, over on the northern side. The great hall was at the west of the court, through a gallery specially made in Flanders and brought to Theobalds in 1569, the year of the Northern Rebellion. Rising up behind the gallery was a lantern, on which there was a chiming clock with twelve bells. This was a substantial court, four storeys of brick finished with stone; but it was also beautifully adorned with the gallery and the clock, and right at the heart of the house. It was the Queen's favourite court.

Middle Court was built between 1567 and 1573, the first of the purpose-built courts of Theobalds. Conduit Court, just to the west, was the original court of 1564. Burghley was hardly content to leave it be, and after 1572 it was completely transformed. The hall, which was reached by a passageway between Middle Court and Conduit Court, had also been remodelled. It had a great hammer-beam roof which on the outside was covered in slates imported, like the gallery, from Flanders. The hall was panelled with wood. Its chimneypiece was of blue marble, its floor paved with Purbeck.

At the four corners of Conduit Court stood great square towers, each with a turret roofed with blue slates probably imported from abroad. Four door-ways in the corners of the court led to the grandest state rooms of Theobalds.

On the ground floor of the south-east corner was the Great Parlour. To the east of the parlour, physically part of Middle Court, was Burghley's chapel; to the west, in Conduit Court, a great staircase leading up to the rooms on the upper floors. Here were the Great Chamber, which measured about 30 feet by perhaps 60 feet; a room known as the Privy Chamber, with a great marble chimneypiece and panelled walls decorated with hangings; and a withdrawing room.

Elizabeth had seen Theobalds for the first time in 1564. She visited every year from 1571 to 1573, and returned again in late May of 1575. She must have seen a great difference each year, as the house was always growing. She liked to lodge in rooms on the upper floor in the south front of Middle Court, overlooking the Great Garden. These gardens were twice the size of Henry VIII's at Hampton Court. There was a great marble fountain at their centre, as well as an ornamental pool, and statues of the twelve Roman emperors. We can be sure that Burghley, the passionate gardener, planned his Great Garden with meticulous care. It was planted with sycamore, lime and elm as well as fruit trees. The garden was, quite simply, magnificent, and it became a model for the gardens of other important Elizabethan courtiers.[10]

When Elizabeth visited Theobalds the house had to function as one of her palaces. She took over a whole suite of rooms. Her bedchamber was under the tower at the centre of the southern range of Middle Court. The Great Parlour became the royal Presence Chamber, where the cloth of estate, the tapestry of the arms of England, hung, and where Elizabeth met her subjects. Middle Court would have bustled with her servants as well as Burghley's own. Government, too, carried on during progress, so the Privy Council met at Theobalds just as it would at, say, Whitehall or Greenwich or Hampton Court, its papers carried in an elegant wooden chest.

To entertain the court like this was a huge undertaking. Burghley's kitchen staff, for example, could not cope on their own with feeding hundreds of people. Temporaries were taken on: cooks, 'turnspits', women for the scullery and labourers. The expenses of the royal visit of 1575 were carefully accounted for. It cost Burghley £340 17s. 4d. This was huge sum: he spent that much in three years maintaining and improving Cecil House on the Strand.

Much of the money was spent on food, over £42 on beef alone. The tables were laid with every dish possible. The list of ingredients is very long indeed: veal, mutton, lamb, capons, chickens, green geese, quails, pheasants, bacon, calves' feet, sea fish and river fish, butter, eggs, cream, salt, yeast, oatmeal, herbs and salads. The final bill for food came to £53 18s. 10d.

Burghley and his steward were careful to budget for everything, even down to the gifts that were given to the Queen's officers. Few expenses were spared. Elizabeth was a frank and at times a critical guest: she said exactly what she thought about how she had been entertained. She had to be impressed; and so too, at Theobalds in 1575, had the earls of Sussex, Leicester and Warwick, Lord Admiral Clinton, Sir Francis Knollys, Sir James Croft, Sir Thomas Smith and Sir Francis Walsingham. Burghley had to maintain the very highest standards of hospitality.[11]

For Burghley, of course, there was no escape from business. In the weeks after the royal visit of 1575 he went with the court to Hatfield, and then back to Cecil House. It was here that he wanted to work quietly on public business and 'in doing some little things of mine own'. Since Elizabeth had left Theobalds, he wrote to Walsingham, 'I assure you I have done little or nothing in mine own poor private causes'. He seemed in an especially melancholy mood, as 'greatly oppressed in debt' as he was 'many times in winter oppressed with sickness'. Perhaps he was coming to terms with the expenses of the royal visit. Certainly he was thinking of Theobalds. He had three or four days of work to do in the Exchequer, he explained to Walsingham, 'and those done I would covet but three or four for myself at my house at Theobalds, where though my wife and my children are, yet have I not been two nights there since Her Majesty went from thence. A hard case to bridle my desire.'[12]

These summer weeks were the last of Lady Anne de Vere's pregnancy, and she gave birth on 2 July to a baby girl, Elizabeth. Sir Walter Mildmay, who days before had been working with Burghley in the Exchequer, wrote with his congratulations: 'I thank God heartily with your Lordship for the good delivery it hath pleased him to give my Lady of Oxford. . . . I trust God shall make her a glad mother of many children.' Nothing at all was said of Lady Anne's husband, the Earl of Oxford, many hundreds of miles away on the continent.[13]

In late summer Burghley wrote to Walsingham to forewarn the Secretary of his movements. They did business by post. Burghley seldom rested. On 28 July he was working at Theobalds; the next day he planned to be in London 'for Her Majesty's service'. This was his familiar journey, travelling the fourteen miles or so up and down the Great North Road between Hertfordshire and the Strand, attended by a small team of servants. But by the beginning of August he broke the routine and travelled to Derbyshire for the sake of his health.[14]

Burghley went to take the waters of St Anne's well in Buxton. The baths at Buxton were not as large or as popular as those in Bath, but by the 1570s they were attracting impressive clients like the Earl of Leicester and the Earl of Sussex; indeed Sussex was at Buxton with Burghley on 6 August. The baths were also used in summer by the Queen of Scots, held securely close by at Tutbury Castle.[15]

Burghley was an old hand in self-diagnosis and treatment, and a great collector of books on medical matters. By the 1570s he had been at the mercy of eminent physicians for years, treated with all kinds of pills and medicines. His great complaint was what he called gout, the first attack of which he had during the difficult parliament of 1566. This may or may not have been the disease today popularly called gout; certainly it can be a risky business trying to diagnose a disease or complaint at a distance of 450 years. We can say that Burghley's joints in his legs and hands were often affected, making him lame (as he had been just a few months before) or forcing him to dictate letters to his secretaries, something he hated to have to do. Interesting, too, is the timing of Burghley's illnesses. As Elizabeth's Secretary, sickness often came on him at times of political emergency. But even without the terrible anxieties of politics in the secretariat, Burghley's health was not improving with age.

Buxton had all kinds of healthful benefits. One expert on the baths there, John Jones, wrote that Buxton was especially good at 'assisting the animal, vital, and natural faculties' of those who took its waters. The air was clear and pure, but cold in the Derbyshire peaks. The waters were cooler than those of Bath, where, Jones wrote, the temperature was something like that of two pints of cold water added to a gallon of boiling water; at Buxton it was the other way round. The wellspring, he explained, was in a valley, very close to a running brook. At the meeting of these two flows of water one could feel hot water on one side of the river and cold on the other. This was the perfect mix, 'very excellent, and beneficial for divers distemperatures, griefs* and sicknesses'.

At Buxton the Earl of Shrewsbury, the local power in Derbyshire, had built a fine health complex. Near the spring was 'a very goodly house, four square, four stories high', with thirty lodgings for bathers. The baths themselves, some little way off, were also 'bravely beautified with seats round about: defended from the ambient air: and [with] chimneys for fire, to air your garments in the baths' side, and other necessaries most decent'. It was here, under medical supervision, that Lord Burghley came for his cure in the late summer of 1575.

What Burghley would not have experienced was a relaxing break at a health spa. He would have been subject to a strict medical regimen suited to the state of his health and fitness and the nature of his disease. A physician like John Jones, or a considerably more distinguished medical expert like Dr William Turner, sometime physician to the Duke of Somerset, would apply himself very carefully to a patient's bathing. It was a complicated business. The weather had to be taken into account, as well as astronomical calculations of the positions of the planets. Food had to be strictly regulated. Turner, the great herbalist, wrote at length about this. The stomach of a patient at the baths, he wrote, was in danger. He should confine himself to chicken or lamb, and sprinkle these meats with a powder blended of cinnamon, ginger, cloves,

* An injury or ailment, a disease or sickness.

fennel, saffron and other spices. Before meat, aniseed comfits, sweetmeats preserved with sugar, could be taken; after food, coriander comfits. Any bread eaten should be a day or two old. Drink was to be white wine. Raw herbs, fruit and fish, buttermilk and cheese, pies and pastry crusts and unleavened bread were all to be avoided.[16]

Exercise was also prescribed, but what kind and how much of it depended on the health and strength of the patient. This aided the 'evacuation of excrements' and conserved the state of the body. Jones suggested four physical pursuits: bowling and archery, both very familiar to Burghley; 'wind ball' or 'yarn ball'; and training with weights. This was all part of the careful regimen of exercise, meat, drink and sleep.

There had to be two or three days of rest before a patient entered the water. He or she could bathe morning or evening, but only after exercise and purging, or the cleansing of the body 'by nature or artificially'. At Buxton the patient could stay in the water for two to three hours. When he or she came out of the baths, it was very important for clothes to be aired (hence the chimneys in the bath-house at Buxton) and for the body, and especially the head, to be well dried.

Burghley stayed at Buxton for at least a week in August. His physicians advised a fortnight, for by 9 August Burghley had not made the recovery he had hoped for. He looked a few days ahead, consulting the 'gests', the itinerary for that summer's royal progress. He had wanted to be with the court in Dudley in Staffordshire, and he asked Walsingham to send his letter on to Lord Dudley 'in my excuse for not coming thither'. It was, he wrote, too dangerous for him to travel back so soon: the counsel of his doctors was that 'I should have come with my harm'. He was keen to know how long the Queen was going to be in Worcester.[17]

Burghley may have met the court in Worcester, where Elizabeth stayed between 13 and 20 August, but it is perhaps more likely that he spent a little time longer away on leave. On the 30th he was at Theobalds. A few days later he was securely back in harness. On 8 September Burghley, the Earl of Leicester and Sir Francis Walsingham met the French ambassador in Oxford. On the 12th, however, he was back at Theobalds again, it seems for a few days at least, expecting the Earl of Sussex as a guest later that week.[18]

Burghley would not have been resting at Theobalds: his desk was always piled high with work. But one of the reasons he may have wanted to be at home was his little granddaughter. Elizabeth de Vere was by now nine months old. Her uncle, Burghley's son Thomas, wrote in the middle of September with his best wishes to 'the little lady to continue her good growing'. Thomas was struggling with an injury. For ten days, he wrote to his father, he had not been outside, 'neither am not able to put on a boot by reason I have hurt my leg again, upon an old hurt I had this progress and being then careless of it'. He took no other surgery, he said, than his wife's, 'which I hope will mend it'.

Thomas Cecil was prospering: indeed now he was Sir Thomas, knighted at Kenilworth in July, and comfortably established in the Cecils' parsonage at Wimbledon. He was, at thirty-three, a distinguished soldier. The memories of his adolescent misdemeanours in Paris were perhaps fading. He ended his letter as Burghley's 'most loving and obedient son', and he closed with an oddly familiar signature. It was quite different to the way he had signed his name as a very young man. It was, in fact, a precise facsimile of his father's signature before 1571, but of course 'Tho. Cecill' rather than 'W. Cecill'. It was a salute by Thomas to his father.[19]

In the last days of September Burghley was again at Theobalds. The great power-broker complained to the Earl of Sussex about criticisms of the way he, Burghley, influenced the Queen in matters of patronage. Once again we hear the injured tone of the public servant doing only what was best for Elizabeth: 'And this have I well felt in sundry things past, that when I have sought to stay such unconvenient grants, my doings have been interpreted as diminutions of Her Majesty's prerogative.' This was a serious charge indeed, though probably in late September 1575 it was merely a minor irritation to Burghley. But it was commonly associated by many people with his great wealth. Only days later, Thomas Bellot, Burghley's steward, put the finishing touches to his master's household accounts for the year which Burghley, with characteristic attention, went through very carefully. In a single year, Michaelmas to Michaelmas, Burghley had spent nearly £955 on Theobalds, of which £148 had gone on his gardens. His riches easily matched his political authority in Elizabeth's government.[20]

*

For the two years after October 1575 we have a wonderful source that can tell us all kinds of things about life in Lord Burghley's household: his comings and goings and those of his family; how guests were entertained and what they ate; and the challenge for Thomas Bellot, the man who left us this source, of keeping up with a family who generally moved between two but sometimes three houses. It is the keen eye of his steward that allows us to see something of how Burghley lived.

The first thing to say is that Burghley and his wife and daughter, Lady Anne, were on the move almost every day. They rarely stayed in one place for very long. Burghley, of course, often had to be at court, which could be anywhere from Whitehall to Greenwich or Richmond. He also had to preside in the Court of Wards. For his time in Westminster, Cecil House on the Strand was his base. But it is clear that he tried to be at Theobalds as often as he could.

Lady Anne and Lady Mildred were just as busy travelling to and from London. They were inseparable: the young mother whose husband was abroad and Lady Mildred who, as the wife of Elizabeth's Lord Treasurer, had a high profile at court. She was now in her early fifties and doubtless as formidable as ever. Sir Thomas Cecil, the respectful and dutiful son, was keen for his mother and sister to visit him at Wimbledon, and wrote a very elaborate letter on this subject to his father in October 1575: 'I trust your Lordship will be my mean unto my Lady my mother and my Lady of Oxford, coming so near, not to overpass Wimbledon, which I desire as a comfort unto my wife and me, and an honour to my poor parsonage.'[21]

In October and November of 1575 Burghley spent a good amount of time away with the court and Council at Windsor. Sometimes Lady Mildred went to court (as, for example, she did on 29 October), just as Burghley would often return home to dine in the evenings in his own apartments at Theobalds. On 5 November he ate a supper of fish (ling and haberdine, a sort of cod often salted or sun-dried), mutton, pheasant, snites (small birds akin to snipes), butter and cheese. The next day Burghley had dinner with his wife and daughter, and then went off to London with Lady Mildred. He travelled on to Windsor, but his wife returned home on the 7th. Both of the Burghleys were at Theobalds on 19 November to dine that evening with Lady Mildred's brother, Richard Cooke, and his wife Anne.

What is clear from Thomas Bellot's meticulous accounts is that Burghley kept an open house for guests. Neighbours dined regularly, and were given hospitality and perhaps a chance, if he was at home, of eating with the Lord Treasurer. Whether the family was at home or not did not much matter: there were still guests to feed. But those visitors who did dine with Burghley probably had business to discuss with him, like Roger Manners, the brother of the Earl of Rutland, in the first days of December; or indeed Laurence Chaderton, a canon of Westminster, Andrew Perne of Cambridge and Clarenceux King of Arms a few days later. Roger Ascham once wrote of Burghley, at dinner, putting aside business of state and preferring to talk of some matter of learning. Even so, Burghley's power and influence surely meant that even a little time at his table could be put to very good use by a visitor.

In the new year of 1576 Burghley had to deal with the business of his son-in-law, the young Earl of Oxford. Oxford was by now in Siena, from where he wrote to his father-in-law in early January. He had written a couple of months earlier, and on the same topic, the sale of his lands to settle (as he put it) 'the greatness of my debt and greediness of my creditors'. Burghley had counselled against the disposal of lands but Oxford was resolute. In November he had said very plainly, 'I shall desire your Lordship to make no stay of the sales of my land.' He issued the same direction again in January. Burghley let the earl know how hard his fortunes were, though this phrasing is Oxford's, not Burghley's.

Now Oxford restated the authority he was giving to Burghley to sell his lands, and Burghley, ever careful, made sure to note this in the margin of the letter. Oxford felt very hard done by. The inconvenience of it all, he said, meant that he would continue travelling till he could 'better settle' himself at home; 'the which thing', Oxford wrote rather sharply to his father-in-law, 'in no wise I desire your Lordship to hinder'. The young earl ended his letter of January on a bitter and resentful note. Any prospect he had of prospering by royal service was finished. 'For', he wrote, 'having made an end of all hope to help myself by Her Majesty's service, considering that my youth is objected unto me and for every step of mine a block is found to be laid in my way, I see it is but vain.'[22]

It would have taken some time for Oxford's letter to arrive in Burghley's hands. It probably had not reached him just over three weeks later when, from Cecil House, Burghley complained to Sir Francis Walsingham of pain he had had on his coming from court. 'And therefore I have entered this day into another loathsome pain by physic with pills.' He was 'assailed' by business; if his health continued poor, he wrote, he intended to withdraw himself from suitors.[23]

But perhaps the Earl of Oxford's letter had arrived by 3 February, when Arthur Golding and his brother Henry dined with Burghley. The Goldings knew Oxford very well. Henry had been steward to the earl's father, and Arthur had taught him as Burghley's ward at Cecil House in the 1560s. This was certainly one of those occasions on which Burghley could have spoken to the Goldings about scholarship and learning, for Arthur was a writer and classical scholar, a translator of Ovid. But it is likely, too, that they spoke about the young earl, and Burghley perhaps considered their advice on the sale of Oxford's lands. In any case, it seems, from later twists and turns in the tale, that Burghley went ahead and did what the earl wanted. He received few thanks for it.

If Oxford's relationship with Burghley had been prickly before and during his absence abroad, his home-coming was made in even worse humour. Burghley recorded it as tersely and bluntly as he could: 'The Earl of Oxford arrived, being returned out of Italy; he was enticed by certain lewd persons to be a stranger to his wife.' Oxford's ship had been boarded by pirates in the English Channel and most of the prizes he had brought from Italy were taken from him. There was a diplomatic effort to restore Oxford's property when in the middle of April Robert Beale, a clerk of the Privy Council, was sent on a mission to Holland. But worse for Lady Anne and Burghley was the fact that on his return Oxford had deliberately avoided meeting his wife. Something was wrong.[24]

A few days after Beale's departure, Burghley tried to make sense of it all. He wrote a narrative which began, as so much did when it came to the Earl of Oxford, with money.

The financial arrangements between Oxford and Lady Anne had been strained. She had been ill for a long time before becoming pregnant, and the earl had left her, Burghley wrote, 'in debt for lack of relief', bearing the costs of food and drink for herself and her female servants. Still, there had been, he continued, no sign of any unkindness between Anne and her husband when he left for the continent. Before he departed she told him that she thought she might be pregnant. When he arrived in Paris he sent her his picture 'with kind letters and messages', as well as two coach horses. After Elizabeth was born, Oxford thanked Burghley for sending him the news.

The first Burghley heard of the earl's 'misliking of anything' came in a letter from Paris dated 4 April 1576. (This is interesting: it suggests that Burghley read nothing in Oxford's frosty letter of January that he felt was out of the ordinary.) Burghley immediately sent for his son, Thomas, to meet the earl on his return to Dover. Thomas spoke to Oxford a few hours after he had landed, carrying with him the commendations of Burghley and Lady Anne. Thomas 'did not understand from him any point of misliking'.

Burghley's advice to Anne was to wait for her brother's report of Oxford's 'contentation'. But she was too impatient, and so went off to meet her husband with Oxford's sister, Lady Mary. Meanwhile, Burghley had written twice to the earl to invite him to use Cecil House as his lodging, letters to which he had no reply. Thomas reported that he thought Oxford wanted 'to keep himself secretly two or three days in his own lodging', but there was news, while the earl was on his way to Gravesend, that he would indeed go to Cecil House, 'Whereupon', wrote Burghley, 'I was very glad but his wife gladder.'

Once he arrived at Gravesend, Oxford took a wherry to the house of his companion, Rowland Yorke, in London. Again Burghley invited the earl to stay at Cecil House. This time Oxford replied, saying that 'he meant to keep himself secret there in his lodging two or three days'; then the earl would speak to Burghley. Lady Anne sent a messenger to her husband 'with request that if he should not come that night to her father's house, that then she would come to him, for she desired to be one of the first that might see him'. His reply, according to Burghley, was terse: 'Why? I have answered you.' The messenger took this to mean that the earl had already made it clear that he wanted to be alone for two or three days. Burghley's advice to his daughter was to wait to see who went to him. Within two hours Burghley had reports that his son-in-law was happy to entertain visitors, even to dine out in London.[25]

The earl wrote to Burghley two days later. It was a sharp, cold, dismissive letter, very much in Oxford's style. He had found faults in his wife, though he would not say what they were. 'I must let your Lordship understand this much, that is, until I can better satisfy or advertise myself of some mislikes I am not determined, as touching my wife, to accompany her. What they are, because some are not to be spoken of or written upon as imperfections, I will not deal withal.' He was no longer prepared, he said, to weary his life with 'such troubles and molestations' as he had already endured; 'nor will I', he wrote icily, 'to please your Lordship only, discontent myself.' Anne, wrote Oxford, could stay with her parents. Burghley had already offered to take his daughter back into his own house. Burghley and Lady Mildred could take care of her and Oxford would be 'rid of the cumber thereby'. He said that his wife had sufficient money for her maintenance. Anne and her family were completely bewildered.[26]

And this is precisely what happened, for by May Lady Anne was living at Theobalds and travelling with her mother, as she had done for many months. Burghley, like Oxford, was at the court at Greenwich.

But Oxford's letter was by no means the end of the business. The rumours were that little Elizabeth de Vere was not the earl's child, rumours that were both shaming for Lady Anne and damaging at court for Anne's father. In the months following, Oxford's friends even whispered about Burghley's mismanagement of the earl's money.

In the early years of the marriage, it must have seemed to Burghley a wonderful dynastic match between the Cecils and the de Veres. The painful fact by the early summer of 1576 was that Anne's marriage to Oxford had almost completely unravelled and that it was fast becoming a court scandal.

*

It was also in the summer of 1576 that Sir Anthony Cooke, Lady Mildred's father, died at Gidea Hall in Essex. Sir Anthony had made his will a few weeks before, appointing as executors his sons, Richard and William, and his sons-in-law Sir Nicholas Bacon and Burghley. Bacon and Burghley were each to receive £200 for their 'pains and travail' in executing the provisions of the will. Cooke carefully set out the bequests to his daughters, of silver and also of books: two volumes of Greek and one of Latin from his library, their choice alone, first to Mildred, then to Anne, Elizabeth and Katherine. These were fitting gifts from a knight-scholar to his clever daughters.

A will is such a formulaic thing; and yet it is also a very personal document which can tell us all kinds of things about a family. All the daughters were equal, though ranked by age, Mildred first and Katherine last. Sir Anthony's eldest son, Richard, naturally inherited the bulk of his estate, but he made careful provisions for Richard's wife, Anne, and for his second son William and William's wife Lady Frances. Richard Cooke's legitimate sons would inherit unless he died without issue, in which case the estate would pass to William and his sons. In default of these, Lady Mildred would inherit.

Sir Anthony left various legacies. To his granddaughter, the Countess of Oxford, £50; to the Earl of Leicester the choice of two horses in Havering Park; to his grandson Robert Cecil, by now nearly thirteen years old, £20; and to Robert's younger sister, Elizabeth, the same amount. The sons of Sir Nicholas Bacon, Anthony and Francis, each received, like their Cecil cousins, £20; Sir Anthony's Hoby grandsons, Edward and Posthumous, were left £10 apiece.

Cooke confirmed his will on 7 June in the presence of seven witnesses. Burghley was one of them, Sir Anthony's daughter Katherine and his daughter-in-law Anne two others. Gabriel Goodman, the Dean of Westminster, close to the Cecils and Cookes for many years, was also in attendance. On the same day Burghley, Lady Mildred and their daughter Lady Anne travelled back to Theobalds with a party of sixteen servants. Sir Anthony died two days later.[27]

He was buried on 21 June at St Andrew's Church in Romford. Sir Anthony had asked to be buried 'with convenient and not excessive charges'. It would have been a simple ceremony according to the Prayer Book. In his will Sir Anthony had committed his soul to God through his saviour, Jesus Christ. It was a trust confirmed by the Prayer Book's Order for the Burial of the Dead. 'Almighty God, with whom do live the spirits of them that depart hence in the Lord, and in whom the souls of them that be elected, after they be delivered from the burden of the flesh, be in joy and felicity. We give thee hearty thanks, for that it hath pleased thee to deliver . . . our brother out of the miseries of this sinful world. . . .' It was an appropriate hope for a man who eighteen years before had been one of the architects of Elizabeth's Reformation.[28]

Burghley, with ten servants, returned home from the funeral that same day. He may have reflected on what Cooke had meant to him over the years. If Burghley had glanced round the church, he would have seen in its east window the stained glass of St Edward the Confessor and a tale of pilgrimage that had to do with St John the Evangelist, the saint of Burghley's old college in Cambridge. Nearby was the monument to Avery Cornburgh, a servant to Henry VII, and his wife Beatrice, with an elaborate explanation of the chantry that was set up to pray for their souls. Sir Anthony Cooke, like Burghley, had helped to sweep all this away: pilgrimages, saints, prayers for the dead, the old superstitions.

There was Burghley's early political career, too. Sir Anthony had been a major figure in the courts of Henry VIII and Edward VI, a committed religious reformer and, unusually for a country gentleman, a respected scholar. Cooke had taken Cecil, just twenty-five when he married Mildred, under his wing. Now, over thirty years later, Burghley had lost one of his connections with a fading past. It was all a lifetime ago.[29]

Soon enough Burghley was back at court at Greenwich, where the business of the Earl of Oxford and his daughter rumbled on. It caused Burghley great pain; he had always been close to Anne, and the family had idolised her from a baby. But her very public separation from her husband was quickly becoming a problem at court. The rumours were irritating. There was a whispering campaign against Burghley at court. He blamed 'liars and malicious backbiters', 'the maintainers and devisors' of untruths and 'secret reports'. He was deliberately vague about who these people were. Perhaps they were Oxford's friends, like Lord Henry Howard; or perhaps the source of the tales was the earl himself, whose malicious blend of self-regard and self-pity could be withering. Burghley surely knew, or thought he knew, but he was not about to give a hostage to fortune by naming names, at least on paper.

A tussle like this was damaging for Burghley. It was not a political danger, in the sense that when a colleague disagreed on a matter of policy it could be thrashed out in the Council chamber. Instead this was pure scandal; it was corrosive and, to a man whose position in the Queen's service rested on what he liked to think was unimpeachable integrity, it hurt sorely. Indeed he did what in the end he felt he had to do. He went to Elizabeth to explain himself.

Burghley asked the Queen for her help. Having had proof of her favour 'in causes not so important', he wrote, 'I doubt not but to find the like influence of your grace in a cause so near touching myself as your Majesty will conceive it doth'. He did not know why things stood as they did between the Earl of Oxford, himself and his daughter. He said he had only ever seen Anne use herself 'honestly, chastely and lovingly' towards her husband, and she had been filled with joy at the prospect of his return home from Italy. Burghley requested Elizabeth's favour in seeking 'my just defence for me and mine'. He desired that either Oxford should yield to Anne 'that love that a loving and honest wife ought to have' or that he should 'notify some instant cause of her not deserving such favour and that she may be permitted to make her answer'.[30]

Oxford wrote to Burghley a month later. It was hardly a cheering letter. The earl agreed to Burghley's request, and the Queen's, that Anne be brought to court by her father. But there were conditions. Anne could not come to her husband. She could not at any time talk to him. Finally, Burghley should do nothing more in her cause. Oxford understood that Burghley meant that day, 13 July, to bring Anne to St James's Palace and to continue to plead her case. Oxford insisted that his father-in-law should do nothing of the kind.[31]

It was, of course, a catastrophe; it is hard to imagine a more embarrassingly public display of a family falling to pieces. Burghley was determined to defend himself and his daughter as robustly as he could: his reputation depended on it. Only days before Oxford's letter, he had answered some particularly nasty rumours that he had deliberately sought to sabotage the earl's financial arrangements, first by subverting an entail of Oxford's property, and secondly by starving the earl of money when he was in Italy. These were serious allegations of financial malfeasance, calculated to get under Burghley's skin. 'I will always be ready to try my honesty with confusion of all liars', he wrote with great passion.[32]

It may be easy to see in all of this a daughter's happiness sacrificed to a father's dynastic ambitions. For the most part we have Burghley's side of the story, though it is hard not to notice the coldness of Oxford's letters and how reluctant he was to bend, even when pushed hard by a father-in-law as powerful as Lord Burghley and by the Queen herself. If we believe Burghley's account, there was no forewarning of the separation Oxford insisted on when he returned to England. Oxford doubtless had his own reasons. Perhaps he genuinely believed Elizabeth de Vere was not his daughter, though he was pleased enough when he heard the news of her birth. Perhaps, in all that self-confidence and in his resentment at being passed over for court office and royal favour, he was bored. Certainly he had an exaggerated capacity for self-pity. He was a poet, after all.

*

Daily life went on for Lord Burghley, as it had to do. On the surface little had changed. But for Burghley his standing and reputation with the Queen, the honesty and dignity of his royal service, were everything. The 'poorest lord in England' may have reflected that a marriage that at first had brought great credit to his family had turned to a cost he could not afford to pay for very much longer.

15

A Gaping Gulf

Burghley kept one of the finest tables in England. The kitchens at Theobalds hummed with activity. The ever-efficient Thomas Bellot, Burghley's steward, was equal to anything. The guests could be as grand as the Earl of Leicester, the Earl of Warwick and Sir James Croft of the Council who dined at Theobalds in spring 1577. Bellot made sure that they had everything they wanted: rice pottage, ling, whiting, eel, carp, mutton, veal, pullets, rabbit, and salad, always a favourite with Leicester. Grand as this meal was, Burghley was away at Westminster with Lady Mildred and their daughter Anne.

The record we have of Burghley's guests at table is a Who's Who of Elizabethan elite society. A man as powerful as he was drew people to him like a magnet. Grand churchmen, university academics, lawyers, royal heralds, neighbours and of course family all ate with the Burghleys. Sometimes Burghley dined alone in his apartments, sometimes with his wife and daughter. Often either he or Mildred was away at court or in Westminster. Lady Anne regularly ate with her little brother, Robert, and sister, Elizabeth, and with the royal wards.

Some guests were very young. In Lent 1577 Robert Devereux, the second Earl of Essex whose father had died while fighting in Ulster, dined with Mildred, Anne and the children. Essex was eleven years old and he was, like so many noblemen before him, temporarily in the care of Burghley as Master of the Court of Wards. A man who would grow up to be a very influential courtier indeed had dinner with Lord Burghley as a boy. He also knew young Robert Cecil. The foundations of friendships and enmities of the future were being set down in Burghley's household.

We can see something of Burghley's patronage in the names of those who were invited to dinner. It just so happened that when the Earl of Essex ate with Burghley for the first time, on 7 March 1577, a great celebrity happened to be dining too. Burghley's guest was John Foxe, the compiler of *Actes and*

Monuments, the great 'Book of Martyrs', who brought as a gift a salmon for Burghley's kitchens.

Foxe and Burghley had known each other for a very long time, and Burghley was perhaps his principal patron. The first English edition of *Actes and Monuments*, printed in 1563, has a fascinating woodcut of Burghley, Foxe and Foxe's printer, John Day, standing bareheaded before Elizabeth's imperial throne. Day, of course, was the printer who had worked so hard at producing the propaganda pamphlets against the Duke of Norfolk and Mary, Queen of Scots. He was also the printer who had worked secretly on Burghley's land in Mary Tudor's reign. The world of Elizabethan politics and religion was a very small one indeed.

Burghley's interest in John Foxe and his *Actes and Monuments* tells us something important about Burghley's religion. He had ducked and weaved his way through the treacherous religious politics of the 1540s and 1550s. The great supporter of godly King Edward VI survived Mary's reign; he even prospered. He came to Elizabeth's reign with a mission to return England to the 'true religion'. He hated the Pope, the Catholic Church and the works of Antichrist. How he made sense of all this, and the psychological gymnastics he performed in Mary's reign, we can only wonder at. But Burghley believed in England's true religion and in Elizabeth's office as Supreme Governor of the Churches of England and Ireland next under God, as the familiar formula had it. He believed that she had care of her subjects' souls. He wanted reform. And he was keen, too, for Elizabeth's people to understand God's providence as it worked in England. Here *Actes and Monuments* was essential. It told the story of the terrible martyrdoms of Protestants at home and abroad. It celebrated Elizabeth's rule. It revealed the blessings of God in the preservation of his people. So important was this message that the Privy Council instructed that *Actes and Monuments* be placed in every parish church in the kingdom. It was to be made public 'and come to the hands and knowledge of all Her Majesty's good subjects generally'. Foxe's great work was given to the people, and with it the notion that England was one of God's nations blessed by true religion. Mary Tudor was demonised as the wicked persecutor of her subjects. Burghley, and friends like the Earl of Leicester and the Earl of Bedford, pulled off a propaganda coup that shaped the writing of English history for centuries.[1]

*

Burghley was forever on the move. As the winter of 1577 gave way to the spring of 1578 he travelled between home and court. Family and friends dined at Theobalds: Lady Anne Bacon, Lady Mildred's sister, one day; Frances

Windebank, the wife of Burghley's former secretary Thomas, another. There was a great dinner in April on the eve of St George's Day. The young Earl of Essex was at home with Robert and Elizabeth Cecil but Lady Mildred took him to Elizabeth's court on 30 April.

In May the court came to Theobalds. It was, as ever, a huge operation. Even the alert and hawk-eyed Bellot had to run to keep up with the arrival of hundreds of guests. Every detail had to be just right. Elizabeth had ferociously high standards and she was not afraid to make her feelings plain.

To entertain the court was a great honour for Burghley. He, his family and his house were on display. He spared no expense. On a visit of three days he spent £337 7s. 5d.; this was as much as it had cost him to entertain Elizabeth for a fortnight in 1576. He was not left entirely out of pocket: many of the Queen's courtiers paid for their stay in kind with gifts of food. There was also blatant lobbying of Burghley by special interest groups who did their best to seek favour with the great man. The Mayor and aldermen of Cambridge, like the Mayor and burgesses of Stamford and the German merchants of the Steelyard in London, sent gifts to remind Burghley of his friendship to them. Even some of his humble tenants clubbed together to raise £3 3s. 4d. to give to Bellot. For the men and women on Burghley's estates this was a huge amount of money. The gift came to about as much as Burghley would spend on a single dinner for his colleagues in the Privy Council.

Burghley knew exactly how society worked. He policed the landed class as Master of the Wards. He had an instinctive feel for social rank and degree. He also understood his duties. These were just as clear to him when he was Elizabeth's powerful Lord Treasurer in the later years of the 1570s as they had been fifty years before in Stamford. His mother, Jane, by now well into her seventies, continued to leave him in no doubt as to his obligations, especially to family. She expected her son to help his sister's husband, Robert Wingfield, in what Jane called Wingfield's 'just cause' against another gentleman. Jane, quiet and determined, used her son's influence to protect the interests of her family. She was, as we will see later in this chapter, a quiet kind of matriarch.[2]

Burghley was, as ever, caught up in the tough slog of government business. Early May in 1577 was cold and wet and it was no better in the first week of June. We find him doggedly making his way up and down the Great North Road from Theobalds to court and back again. Some of his guests dined with him; others did not. Lord Admiral Clinton had supper with Burghley in late May, Master Seckford of the Queen's Privy Chamber the next day. Edward Baeshe, another guest, was a Hertfordshire neighbour as well as an official of the Queen's navy, and he dined at Theobalds in early June. William Cooke, Lady Mildred's brother, was there the following Sunday when the hall must have been packed. As well as Cooke and his servants, the kitchens prepared food for workmen, labourers and their wives. In a single sitting of dinner 144 people were fed.[3]

In late summer Burghley set out once again for the baths at Buxton. He left Theobalds on 22 July, probably in the company of Dr Julio, a London physician with many clients at court, who had dined at Burghley's table a couple of days before. Doctors of physic were regular guests of the Lord Treasurer. Only a few months before, on the eve of St George's Day, one of the Queen's physicians, Dr Richard Master, and his wife Elizabeth had had supper with the Burghleys.

Gout was still Burghley's old enemy. In fact it was troubling him more than ever. Dr Master may have been something of an expert on the gout, at least if one piece of questionable verse is anything to go by, for it was dedicated to him. The poet offered his sympathy to the sufferer:

> Diseased sore he lies and able,
>> not to stir a limb:
> So hath the wretch venomed his joints
>> and so hath plagued him.
> That still he is enforced to keep his house,
>> as doth a snail:
> O piteous hap and great mischance,
>> that each man ought to wail.
> It grieves me to the heart to see,
>> the torments that he bears . . .

Here was someone who seemed to understand Burghley's pain. While Burghley usually worked through his gout, by summer it was time once again to seek relief and perhaps a cure.[4]

This time Burghley's arms were affected. The pain had eased by 21 July, but he was still sore. And so he went off to Buxton in a series of tactical bounds, at Burghley House on the 24th, with a pause of a day or two for his servants to gather provisions; and then the journey into Derbyshire through Derby and Ashbourne and the Peak District.[5]

Burghley was an old hand at taking the waters. But Elizabeth's courtiers loved nothing more than to swap cures and advice. This explains why the Earl of Leicester insisted on giving his fellow Garter Knight the full wisdom of his last cure. Leicester and his brother Ambrose, Earl of Warwick, had observed a very strict regimen at the baths. At meal times they had eaten only a dish or two of the many they could have chosen. They had exercised moderately either on foot or on horseback. Leicester knew full well that at Burghley's last going to the baths the Lord Treasurer had over-exerted himself, taking daily journeys out from Buxton of ten or twelve miles. This, Leicester suggested, was no way to go about taking the waters.[6]

Burghley went off to Buxton that summer with special instructions from the Queen. It was Leicester who gave Burghley the full story: Elizabeth wanted a hogshead of water from the spring, to be sent back to the court in specially prepared barrels. Burghley did exactly as he was told, as careful in this mission as he was in his other services to the Queen. He had the 52 gallons of spring water transported off to court. When the barrels arrived, Leicester wrote to Burghley to thank him.

But Leicester was mystified. He, like Burghley, had carried out Elizabeth's commands very carefully. The Queen had pestered him about the water: twice or thrice she had commanded Leicester to write to Burghley at Buxton, and she often asked him whether he had remembered to do it. But when the barrels finally arrived, she wanted nothing to do with them. In fact she was annoyed, and told Leicester so. She held him responsible for spreading a rumour at court that she was suffering with a sore leg. Leicester doubtless shrugged at the ways of princes. He wrote to Burghley that Elizabeth's health was good but now and again she had her 'old aching' when she took cold in her legs. He trusted that Burghley's pain had eased.[7]

It was a short visit that year to Buxton: it should come as no surprise that even Burghley's cures were tightly timetabled. He was on the move by 15 August, the same day that Lady Mildred set out from Theobalds for Burghley House. Together they spent about a week at Burghley before returning home down the Great North Road.

There were probably two things that Burghley wanted to do that summer. The first was to see his mother. The second was to view the new building work on his father's old house.

By this time Jane Cecil had been a widow for twenty-four years. She was now living at Burghley House 'for altogether', that is permanently. She was about seventy-seven years old. Peter Kemp, the senior servant at Burghley, had a responsibility to look after Jane. In 1573 Kemp said that she had wept for joy at her son's care of her. A chamber was furnished. Burghley had sent her dresses. She valued one so much that she said she would wear it only on special occasions. Kemp's advice to his master was that he should probably have another one made up of silk and cloth with clear instructions from Burghley that Jane should wear it every day.[8]

Jane Cecil always stayed close to Stamford. She never dined at Theobalds, at least in the 1570s. She was a modest kind of matriarch, always attentive to the needs of those of her children who did not have the influence of her son. Certainly she was not afraid to write very plainly to Lord Burghley for his help. Once this was for Lady Stafford, a friend, to whom Burghley was asked by his mother to give his 'lawful favour'. In the same letter Jane wrote that she had to trouble him with his sister Elizabeth 'who hath small friends to trust unto, only desiring you to be good unto her'.[9]

Jane Cecil's letters give the impression that she moved very much within her family circle. On the day she wrote to Burghley about Lady Stafford and his sister Elizabeth, Jane was at the house of her son-in-law, Roger Cave, and this because 'God hath taken my sight from me'. There is a hint of frailty in her letters. Peter Kemp made an interesting observation in her first days back at Burghley House in 1573. When Burghley had sent the gown to his mother, Kemp reflected that her habit was to wear 'base apparel' which was not fit even for someone beneath her rank in society. Dress had to match social status: there were acts of parliament to forbid some people from wearing certain clothes. So Jane was making a statement. Why is harder to fathom. Perhaps her rejection of ostentation had something to do with her religion, which she was careful to practise. In 1573 Jane wanted to have a minister at Burghley House to allow her to worship twice daily.[10] What seems strange indeed is that this elderly and pious woman lived in one of the grandest houses in the kingdom. At Burghley the glamour of the architecture was in severe contrast to the modesty of the house's principal occupant.

Burghley was ambivalent about the magnificence of his houses. He was a determined and passionate builder who spent a vast fortune on Cecil House, Theobalds and Burghley House. But he was very sensitive indeed to the charge that he built and kept houses fitter for kings than for subjects. He defended himself vigorously. If Theobalds was large and comfortable, he said, it was because the Queen visited the house so regularly and her standards were very high. Cecil House was so old it was hardly worth bothering about. At Burghley, he once wrote, 'I have set my walls but upon the old foundations; indeed I have made the rough stone walls to be of square, and yet one side remaineth as my father left it.' If this was strictly true, it was by no means the whole story.[11]

Burghley was a family inheritance, and William Cecil wanted it to pass to his son, Thomas. He called it his 'principal house'. In Hertfordshire, even twenty years after buying Theobalds, he counted himself a 'new-feathered gentleman', an outsider. From the manor of Burghley he took the title of his barony, a mark of proud belonging. Burghley was family business, pure and simple: it was in his blood.[12]

From what Burghley wrote, it sounds as though he did little more than tidy up the little bit of building done by his father. This is a very modest appraisal of Burghley's commission to his master masons. He did what he had done at Theobalds: he took the old manor house and built out. Certainly he took his time. The rough chronology of Burghley's building projects looks something like this: first of all work at Burghley House between about 1556 and 1561, remodelling the original house inside and building new kitchens; then in the early 1560s the building of the mansion on the Strand; from 1564 all the way up to the middle 1570s Theobalds; and then back to Burghley House from about 1575. But the effect at Burghley, as at Cecil House and even more obviously at Theobalds, was spectacular.

Burghley House in the 1560s was arranged around a court. It was a house that looked in on itself, rather as Cecil House did. To the east of the courtyard on the ground floor was a range of buildings with the great hall at the centre. To the north of the hall were the kitchens; to the south were rooms for the family, the parlours, which led to a loggia on the south range of the house overlooking gardens. Lady Mildred's suite of rooms was on the first floor of the north-east corner of the house. The chapel, the family's great chamber and the privy chamber were set out along the southern range. Probably on the western side was the set of rooms used by Sir Thomas Hoby and his wife, Elizabeth, when they stayed at Burghley after their wedding in 1558.[13]

By the 1570s Burghley had decided on change. He wanted his house to look outward, not inward. It was to be magnificent, a bold, confident affirmation in stone of Burghley's nobility. As ever, he spared no expense. The master mason was John Symonds, who drew up a 'plat' for building at Burghley in 1578. But work had already begun. The west entrance was finished by 1577. Probably by the time Lord and Lady Burghley visited the house in the summer of that year the gatehouse was complete. Certainly it would not have looked out of place at the Queen's palaces of Hampton Court and St James's: only a subject as important as Burghley could afford the kind of architecture commissioned by princes. Over the coming years the west of the house, with all its grand windows designed to catch the sun and use light to best effect, and the eastern side too, would be rebuilt to express so much about its owner: his riches, his taste, his devotion to family.[14]

That summer the Burghleys spent about ten days together in Northampton-shire. They were back at Theobalds in time for supper on 28 August. Burghley House, the peaceful retreat from business, faded as a memory quickly enough. After dinner with Lord Hunsdon and Sir William Fitzwilliam on the 30th the Baron of Burghley set out on the old familiar road to court.

*

There was little change for Burghley over the following months. He moved between home and the royal court, which came, in May 1578, to Theobalds.

If entertainment and business were two constants in Burghley's life, sickness was a third. He was ill in early October. He wrote to Walsingham that he did not know what reports there were of his health; he hardly expected that 'so small a matter' would hold any place 'amongst causes of court'. Yet to Walsingham, his 'very friend', he was bold to give a report. He was still weak, in spite of having kept to a strict diet for five or six days and taken physic that had made him very sick. 'But now am at quiet,' he continued, 'hoping that if physic will not diminish the humour . . . yet time will spend it, and bring me to an ebb, when the flux is spent.'

Burghley wanted to know from Walsingham whether he was needed at court. If he was, he was content to be a 'lodger' in his chamber there. Too much work, however, would lengthen his infirmity. 'And therefore I commend my case to your advice. Hoping that without good cause you will rather advise me to that which might recover me, than to overthrow me.'

Burghley was not of course idle. He was working that day, even from his couch, investigating the Queen's debts in Ireland, and 'in suspense of many cogitations' till he heard confirmation of the reported death of Don John of Austria, the captain-general of Spain's military campaign in Flanders. If a constant in Burghley's life was his fragile health, then just as certain in the politics of western Europe was the threat of Spain and its military efforts to destroy Protestantism in the Low Countries. Sick or well, Burghley kept as close an eye on news from abroad as he had ever done. This is exactly what he did over the next fortnight, carefully reading the reports of Elizabeth's ambassador and those of an intelligence source he referred to only as 'IR', 'a man', he wrote to Walsingham, 'very meet to be continued in service'.[15]

Burghley was fifty-eight years old that autumn. He was not an old man, and he may have reflected that his predecessor as Lord Treasurer, the first Marquess of Winchester, had died in office at the age of about ninety-seven. But Burghley was feeling his age just a little. Life in the sixteenth century was uncertain at the best of times. Illness always lurked, and here Burghley was certainly not alone.

On the day Burghley wrote to Walsingham about the intelligence reports on the Low Countries, 25 October 1578, the Queen had what John Dee called a 'fit' from nine o'clock in the evening till one o'clock the next morning. Days before, Dr Bayley had spoken to Dee about Elizabeth's health, 'Her Majesty's grievous pangs and pains by reason of the ache and the rheum, &c.' On 28 October the Earl of Leicester and Sir Francis Walsingham conferred together. The Queen was sick again with a 'sore fit' for three hours the next afternoon. On 4 November Leicester and Walsingham spoke to Dee and 'directed' him to his voyage abroad, the purpose of which (he recorded rather grandly) was 'to consult with the learned physicians and philosophers beyond the seas for Her Majesty's health-recovering and preserving'.[16]

Elizabeth was now forty-five years old. She was still not married, and it was clear to anyone who thought about it that her child-bearing years were quickly disappearing. She was her kingdoms' security, still the best hope, as wife and mother, for the future. However complicated her choice of husband, and however unwilling the Queen herself might be to marry, this was a fact of Elizabethan politics. There was neither room nor time for complacency. Elizabeth's enemies waited for their chance. Spanish armies were just across the water. Mary, Queen of Scots was still alive and living in hope. The old fears that Burghley had articulated as Elizabeth's Secretary still haunted the Queen's advisers.

Fear was a constant of Elizabethan politics, and with fear uncertainty, anxiety, even despair. Yet all the time the court was changing. It was, as Burghley himself wrote, a small world: intense, competitive, inward-looking, and always fluid. There were old problems to be faced by new figures of authority at court, and some fresh problems confronted by men of long-established position like Burghley and the Earl of Leicester. The court was a place of power, display, culture, riches and government. Temper, fallings out, heightened emotions were all parts of its life; so were friendship, collegiality, common interest and the shared codes and behaviours of nobility.

Two very different courtiers and royal servants were Sir Christopher Hatton and Sir Nicholas Bacon. In the autumn of 1578 Hatton, fairly recently appointed Vice-Chamberlain of the royal household, was in his late thirties: Bacon, the Lord Keeper of the Great Seal and Burghley's brother-in-law, was thirty years older than Hatton. Sir Christopher was a courtier proper: his rise from the Privy Chamber to a seat in the Privy Council came about because of a close personal friendship with Elizabeth. Her nickname for him was 'Lids'; and if Hatton's letters to his colleagues were brisk, articulate and businesslike, those he wrote to the Queen were richly expressive of his love and devotion to her.[17]

In late 1578 Burghley was still coming to an appreciation of Hatton. Certainly he had known him for a long time, but now Hatton was a serious force, the young councillor close to the Queen. One letter Burghley wrote to Hatton on 15 December tells us a lot about how the two men came to terms with each other.

Burghley said that he was comforted to hear from Sir Christopher after a morning of being 'tormented with my familiar enemy, the gout'. What follows in the letter is vintage Burghley: very carefully worded, just a little guarded, sensitive to any offence given by the older man to the younger. Burghley paid close attention to the niceties of correspondence, sending the letter to Hatton 'In possession of all friendship'. There had been a falling out over some matter of patronage, but Burghley was quick to say that Hatton had 'satisfied my careful mind, having been perplexed with many heavy cogitations rising upon conceit all this night'. 'I find you surely by your writing readier to change offence taken, than any other with whom I have had like occasion.' Hatton had acknowledged Burghley's intention to serve Elizabeth 'carefully'. Burghley intended to do his best for Hatton in the matter of the suit. He ended by saying how satisfied he was by Sir Christopher's 'wise, modest and friendly letter' and gave his 'recontinuance of my former devotion to love and esteem you'.[18]

So much of this letter was in code. It was to do with place and standing at court, with Burghley's power and Hatton's influence. It was a careful, delicate, deliberate effort to test another courtier: to understand and make sense of Hatton. This was a game Burghley knew very well. Many years before he had been just like Sir Christopher, the young man who packed a terrific punch in the competitive world of Tudor politics, even if he had not quite played the elaborate courtly game Hatton thrived on.

Burghley professed to be the plain servant, though there was little either simple or straightforward about his service to Elizabeth. Still, he stood for solidity and plain dealing, in speaking truth to the Queen on matters of policy and patronage. This was probably the cause of the delicate encounter with Hatton: as Burghley had once put it, his efforts to squash unsuitable grants of royal patronage were interpreted by some as 'diminutions' of the Queen's rule.[19]

Burghley was an oak of his own generation: solid, dependable, trustworthy. He would have said the same, no doubt, of his brother-in-law, Sir Nicholas Bacon. Again we can contrast Bacon and Hatton. Bacon, like Burghley, was a servant plain and simple. He had few of the courtly arts. He was a poet, certainly, and wrote verse for his wife, Anne, Lady Mildred Burghley's sister. But he was before everything else the upright public servant who decorated the long gallery of his house near St Albans with texts from the works of the Roman philosopher and writer Seneca. Above the doorway of this house, Gorhambury, visitors could read of Bacon's service to the Queen set out with his family motto: '*Mediocria firma*', 'Safety in moderation', taken from Seneca – not quite the text a glittering young courtier like Hatton would have chosen. In the orchard at Gorhambury was a banqueting house decorated with the liberal arts of grammar, arithmetic, logic, music, rhetoric, geometry and astronomy, each subject with its celebrated authors. The Bacons, Cookes and Cecils prided themselves on their scholarship and learning and valued the depth this gave to their royal service.[20]

Two days before Christmas in 1578, and a week after Burghley's letter to Sir Christopher Hatton, Bacon made his will. He appointed Burghley as the overseer of his executors, and gave his brother-in-law a great standing cup garnished with crystal. To his sister-in-law, Lady Mildred, he left a deep bowl with a cover marked with the heraldry of the Bacon family. He died two months later.[21]

Like the death of Sir Anthony Cooke nearly three years before, that of Nicholas Bacon was the passing of a political career, with all of its ups and downs, successes and failures, as well as the passing of a life. Bacon was devoted to his family, and he was sadly missed. Burghley had known him for nearly forty years, from his arrival at Gray's Inn, where Bacon was already a senior figure. They had seen so much together in politics and government, but they had not always seen eye to eye on policy: they were used to speaking to each other plainly and frankly. Occasionally they had fallen out.

Bacon was buried in early March at St Paul's Cathedral. His tomb, carefully prepared, was ready and waiting for him. His family and servants all wore black mourning clothes. In the first provisions of his will he set out the legacies for his wife, Lady Anne. He left £193 6s. 8d. to the poor and to the prisoners of Bury St Edmunds and St Albans. He gave rings worth 26s. 8d. each to members of his family, to lawyers, judges, churchmen and physicians, and to old colleagues. These were the old campaigners of Elizabethan politicians, men close to Bacon's generation, who had sat with him in hundreds of meetings of the Privy Council: Lord Admiral Clinton, the Earl of Sussex, the Earl of Leicester, Sir Walter Mildmay and Sir Ralph Sadler.

In the early spring of 1579 Sir Nicholas Bacon, Elizabeth's first Keeper of the Great Seal, could wait quietly in his grand tomb for the Day of Judgment. The old colleagues who wore his rings were granted no such rest.

*

In the weeks and months following Bacon's death, Elizabeth's councillors debated a question that was, on the face of it, simple enough. Should the Queen marry Francis, Duke of Anjou, the son of Catherine de Medici and the younger brother of the King of France?

It was a question that had been debated since Anjou was Duke of Alençon, and for years there was no resolution. There was little clear cut about it. Some of the councillors believed that Anjou was a good candidate. He was a Catholic, certainly, but there was just the chance that as Elizabeth's husband his resources could be brought to help the Dutch in their struggle against Spain. Those councillors who disagreed could not bring themselves to sanction an alliance with the Catholic enemy, however pliant or politically useful he might turn out to be. Anjou's religion was a serious factor to be taken into account. But the old dynastic impulse was difficult to suppress, that desire for Elizabeth to marry and to produce an heir, something which, even in her middle forties, it was felt her body would still allow her to do.

So it is no wonder that talk of the match between Francis and Elizabeth had rumbled on for a long time without any great hope of resolution. But in the new year of 1579 the duke sent an envoy to London. He was Jean de Simier, the Master of his Wardrobe, and Simier was just the sort of charmer Elizabeth liked: 'a choice courtier, a man thoroughly versed in love-fancies, pleasant conceits and court dalliance', a Leicester perhaps, or a Hatton. Elizabeth even had a nickname for him, a play on his name in Latin: she called him her 'Ape'. He came from his master with money and jewels and courtly grace. But behind Simier's simpering was hard politics.[22]

The Council worked tirelessly on the Anjou question from the spring of 1579. Elizabeth was keen to marry, or so it appeared. She received a number of letters from the duke in March and Burghley set to work analysing the case for and against the match. For it, for example, were arguments of protection by France and help for fellow Protestants abroad, as well as the benefits of marriage for the Queen. Against the match were the old fears of international Catholic conspiracy against England and the destruction of Protestantism.[23]

At first only a small group of councillors considered the Anjou match: Burghley, the Earl of Sussex, the Earl of Leicester and Sir Christopher Hatton. In May they were instructed to brief the whole Council, whose members soon wanted to interview Simier. There were all kinds of positive signals. In June Anjou himself was granted a passport to visit England which he did, secretly, two months later. The debates continued into autumn but with a newly focused sense of uncertainty.

By now many people were deeply worried by the prospect of the Anjou match, both within the Privy Council and outside it. Burghley was not convinced; neither were the Earl of Leicester, Sir Christopher Hatton, Sir Francis Walsingham and others. The great proponent of the marriage was the Earl of Sussex. Strains were beginning to show at court, in the writings of Edmund Spenser and Philip Sidney. There was a fierce popular reaction, too, with horrific consequences for the writer of one important pamphlet, John Stubbs.

Stubbs, who believed himself to be a loyal subject of the Queen and a good Protestant, wrote *The discoverie of a gaping gulf*. It was a robust and passionate attack on the Anjou marriage, strident in its criticism of the duke, of the French more generally, and of the certain destruction the match would bring to God's true religion in England. There was pure shock at how hard the Queen came down on Stubbs. In a royal proclamation Elizabeth told her subjects that she could not 'but detest greatly and condemn such a seditious author with his fardel of false reports, suggestions, and manifest lies forged against a prince of a royal blood, as Monsieur, the French King's brother is'. There was a sense of numbness and horror when after he was found guilty of disseminating seditious writings Stubbs's right hand was publicly removed with a cleaver in Westminster.[24]

It was clear as day that Elizabeth was in no mood to compromise. But the debate still rumbled on. In early October 1579 Burghley read a statement of the Council's position to Elizabeth. Some councillors continued to support the marriage, others strongly opposed it. The Queen was blunt. She met Burghley, Lord Admiral Clinton, the Earl of Sussex and the Earl of Leicester that same afternoon: 'then she began to show her great misliking of such as she thought would not prefer her marriage before any device of surety, and with a great number of arguments seemed to reprove them'. She understood that they were greatly concerned by Anjou's religion but told them that 'she did marvel that any person would think so slenderly for her, as that she would not for God's cause, for herself, her surety and her people, have so straight regard thereto'. It was the familiar message: no one knew as well as she did what was right for her people.[25]

Nothing, of course, was resolved. The Council was divided, just as Elizabeth was mystified that such an opportunity for safety and security at home and abroad could be missed. Many of the Queen's advisers, Burghley among them, remained unconvinced by her great hope for the Anjou match. The hopes for old-fashioned dynasty were fading very quickly, and experienced men like Burghley were terrified by what might lie ahead. God's punishment seemed all too near.

*

On a Wednesday in the first week of April 1580, just before six o'clock in the evening, there was an earthquake that had people in London running from their supper, shook ships at Sandwich in Kent, and sent part of the cliffs at Dover crashing into the sea.[26]

There was a rush to print to explain what had happened. To show off their wit and learning two scholars, Edmund Spenser and Gabriel Harvey, published elegant letters on the earthquake. A third writer, Arthur Golding, sometime tutor in the household of Lord Burghley and no mean classical scholar himself, produced a pamphlet that was a good deal more robust than the courteous exchange of clever letters between Spenser and Harvey. Golding saw the earthquake as a warning of doom. God had shaken his rod in anger. Golding's thesis was this: 'God never poured out his grievous displeasure and wrath upon any nation, realm, city, kingdom, state or country, but he gave some notable forewarning thereof by some dreadful wonder.'

The earthquake was a call to repentance for a society in moral and spiritual crisis. Everything was turned upside down. Servants had become like masters. Men had taken to wearing 'garish attire' and now affected the behaviour of women, just as women had 'gotten up the apparel and stomachs of men'.

Young gentlemen practised hatred, malice, disdain and desire for revenge. Idleness, pride and usury ruled. Faithfulness was fled into exile and falsehood vaunted itself in its place. Too many people spent the sabbath 'taverning, tippling, gaming, playing, and beholding of bear-baitings and stageplays'. Golding suggested that this was a society on the slide, in mortal danger of itself and its own sin, and at risk from the civil wars of its neighbours.[27]

Lord Burghley would not have disagreed with one of his occasional dinner guests. He knew in his fear of God that Elizabeth's kingdoms walked with death and destruction, as though they were their companions.

*

Cartography was one of Burghley's great passions. He had a very precise mind and a love of detail. Survival, he may have reflected, was knowledge: Burghley had to know who and where his enemies, and his allies, were. Maps, plans, charts, lists and notebooks gave him the information he needed to keep Elizabeth's government ahead of the game. His was a strongly visual sense of where Queen and realm stood in the greater scheme of things.

Burghley made sure that he had the latest cartography. In the 1560s Laurence Nowell had given him a map of the British Isles and the coasts of continental Europe, an essential piece of kit for a royal Secretary. Burghley supervised the work of Christopher Saxton in his ground-breaking cartography of England. He also owned the best world atlas of the day, Abraham Ortelius's *Theatrum orbis terrarum* (1570), which Burghley carefully signed on its title-page and annotated in great detail. Beautiful as it was, this was a working volume, and over the years Burghley wrote in it all kinds of information: the details of Martin Frobisher's expedition of 1576 to find the north-west passage to China; the names of French ports and their governors; a royal genealogy for Poland; a list of the Ottoman sultans; and, much closer to home, hand-drawn maps of Cornwall and Wales.[28]

One of the most delicate and beautiful maps tipped into Burghley's Ortelius was, in all kinds of ways, entirely fanciful. It was of the north-east passage to China, and it was made in 1580 by John Dee. Dee had his ups and downs at Elizabeth's court, in good part because of his confidence in the route to China which, had it existed in the way Dee thought it did, would have been a triumph for Elizabethan commerce. Dee was a natural scholar: brilliant, polymathic, prickly, difficult and temperamental; he was also spectacularly well connected, giving his advice to the Queen on all kinds of subjects, and meeting courtiers as powerful as Sir Christopher Hatton and Sir Francis Walsingham. He was a friend of Abraham Ortelius and Gerardus Mercator. He knew the young geographer, Richard Hakluyt, and taught navigation to Martin Frobisher.

John Dee was also a great believer in English sea power and Elizabeth's imperial claims in the north, which had their foundation, he said, in the conquests of King Arthur. This was a project he had been working on for some years, encouraged by courtiers like Leicester and Hatton. His book *General and Rare Memorials* (1577) began with 'a necessary advertisement' to readers who looked to 'the prosperous state of the commonwealth of this British kingdom, and the political security thereof'. Imperial Britain was Dee's passion. He saw that a strong kingdom, and especially a strong navy, would bring to England commercial wealth as well as military security. The *Memorials* was only the first part of a book he called *The Brytish Monarchy*. It was this work that brought Dee to the court at Richmond to meet Burghley on Monday, 3 October 1580.[29]

Burghley had a strong interest in British history, and it was a subject he wrote on himself in the 1580s. That October he took it upon himself to read Dee's historical account of the 'British empire'. Dee had put all his researches into two great rolls which he delivered to the Queen in her garden at Richmond at eleven o'clock on the morning of the 3rd. A few hours later, Dee was invited into Elizabeth's Privy Chamber 'to hear further of the matter'. Burghley was there, and he gave Dee the strong impression that he was not at all convinced by Dee's account of Elizabeth's title. Dee was instructed to tell Burghley about his researches 'more plainly and at his leisure', which he did in Burghley's chamber for the next two days.

On Friday Dee was jittery. He had come to see Burghley, and Burghley had been told that Dee was outside. When Burghley came out of his chamber, Dee was standing right in front of him, but the Lord Treasurer, he wrote, 'did not or would not speak to me. I doubt much of some new grief conceived.'

Dee need not have worried. When he spoke to Elizabeth a few days later, she told him that Burghley 'had greatly commended my doings for her title, which he had to examine (which title in two rolls he had brought home two hours before)'. A few weeks later, Burghley sent Dee a haunch of venison in salutation.[30]

*

At sixty years old Burghley was the great scholar-statesman of his generation, or so perhaps he would have imagined himself. He was as busy as ever, in parliament in early 1581 working on bills against recusants who refused to conform to the Elizabethan Church, or weeks later hosting a grand banquet for visiting French diplomats. As usual he had a single concern in everything he did: the political security (to use John Dee's coining) of Elizabeth's throne. 'The will of God be done to maintenance of his glory, and the preservation of that crown fast upon Her Majesty's head, where it ought by justice only to stand.'[31]

At Cecil House on 30 April Burghley, the Earl of Sussex, Lord Admiral Clinton and other councillors spoke over dinner to a visiting delegation of French commissioners. Every detail of the banquet was planned, with teams of servers and their assistants assigned to the great chamber and the gallery. Servants were instructed to fetch beer and wine, to guard the doors, to take away napkins and spoons and to wash plates. The most senior of Burghley's household servants, including his secretaries Vincent Skinner and Henry Maynard, were in attendance on the diners. Eight men were given the task of translating for the French guests: among them were Francis Bacon, Burghley's twenty-year-old nephew, Thomas Cecil, and a young secretary called Michael Hickes.[32]

Family and household, politics and business: there were so few clear boundaries between these aspects of Burghley's life. He was, as I have written elsewhere in this book, an instinctive dynast. Burghley's family was public business. One family marriage had, of course, been a catastrophe. When Arthur Golding wrote of what passed for virtues to modern young gentlemen – hatred, malice, disdain and desire for revenge – perhaps he had in mind his former pupil, the Earl of Oxford.

Oxford and his wife, Lady Anne, were still estranged in 1581. For two years before that the earl had lurched from crisis to crisis, falling out violently with Philip Sidney, denouncing his own friends, the Earl of Arundel and Lord Henry Howard as Catholic sympathisers but finding himself put in the Tower instead, and finally, in 1581, fathering a child with his mistress, Anne Vavasour, one of the Queen's maids of honour. For this, once again, he was sent to the Tower.

We can imagine that Burghley was at his wits' end with his son-in-law. Oxford was a standing rebuke to everything Burghley professed to believe in: moderation, probity, age, wisdom, experience, the values of the philosophers and politicians of ancient Rome. But Oxford and his daughter were married, and that was that; and so, ever the pragmatist, Burghley wondered whether it was possible to effect their reconciliation. When Sir Francis Walsingham wrote to Burghley from court in July 1581 to explain that 'Her Majesty is resolved [. . .] not to restore the Earl of Oxford to his full liberty before he hath been dealt withal by his wife', Burghley wrote ambiguously in the margin: 'This is more easier to be done, than courtiers do think.'

Walsingham indicated that in the case of Oxford Sir Christopher Hatton was working hard for Burghley's cause. Walsingham was, too, but on the day he wrote to Burghley he had to deal with a spectacular falling out between the Earl of Sussex and the Earl of Leicester in Elizabeth's Privy Chamber at

Greenwich. But soon enough Walsingham 'dealt very earnestly' with the Queen 'touching the Earl of Oxford's liberty', putting her in mind of the promise she had made to Burghley and Lady Mildred.[33]

What Elizabeth's promise was to the Burghleys that summer is not precisely clear: probably it was her royal favour in bringing about the reconciliation of Oxford and Lady Anne, perhaps with some royal leniency towards the earl. Reconciliation was something Burghley himself worked hard at. In early December Anne wrote to her husband. Within a few days she even had a reply to her letter.

But here is the fact of the matter. Anne's letters were written, not by the countess herself, but by her father. For all his heavy workload, Burghley drafted them personally. He was as careful in composing these letters from a wife to a husband as he ever was in writing papers for the Queen or Privy Council. For Burghley, for his daughter and family, it was essential to establish something like a stable marriage between Oxford and Anne.

Anne reminded Oxford that in the summer he had 'renewed some part' of his favour towards her; but 'now, after long silence of hearing anything from you', Burghley wrote, 'at the length, I am informed . . . that your Lordship is entered into some misliking of me without any cause indeed or thought'. Anne was in misery: 'I beseech you in the name of that God that knoweth all my thoughts and my love towards you, notwithstanding your evil usage of me, let me know the truth of your meaning towards me, upon what cause you are moved to continue me in this misery, and what you would have me do in my power to recover your constant favour.'[34]

Oxford's reply gave cold comfort. He was, Burghley's letter tells us, 'unquieted with the uncertainty of the world': in other words, he was fed up with the royal court, Oxford's usual lament. Anne offered to help him as much as she could: 'I would bear the greater part of your adverse fortune and make it my comfort.' Her father, she assured Oxford, wished him well, whatever the earl had heard from 'practices at court'. 'Good, my Lord, assure yourself, it is you whom only I love and fear, and so am desirous above all the world to please God, wishing that I might hear oftener from you until better fortune will have us meet together.'[35]

And eventually they were indeed reconciled, at least after a fashion. Even so, the cost to Anne's happiness, and her father's, was incalculable.

It just so happened that while the business of Oxford and his wife was rumbling away, Burghley's youngest daughter, Elizabeth, now seventeen years old, fell in love with a young man of about twenty-six called William Wentworth. William, like Elizabeth, was the son of a baron. Burghley knew his father, Thomas, second Baron Wentworth, very well. Wentworth was a cousin, through the Seymours, of Edward VI and of Burghley's old master,

Protector Somerset, who had knighted Wentworth after the battle of Pinkie. As well as Somerset and Pinkie, Burghley and Wentworth had Cambridge in common: both men had studied at St John's College at much the same time. The Wentworths were good, solid, reliable Tudor nobility.

Lord Wentworth had written to Lord Burghley about the marriage of their children in June 1581. He professed to know nothing of their love: 'truly, my Lord, for this liking of my son of your daughter I never thought of it or knew anything of it till [he] himself opened the matter unto me'. He thoroughly applauded the match, rejoicing, he wrote, 'that my son did make so honourable a choice and in so good a house'. They set to drawing up the necessary agreements about money and property, and Wentworth made all the appropriate noises of self-deprecation: 'The marriage is to be solemnised in your Lordship's house,' he wrote to Burghley, 'for my cottage being very little is not fit for such a purpose.'[36]

Everything was in place by February 1582. Burghley was sick in bed on the 25th when he wrote an effusive letter to his 'dear friend' Walsingham. He was proud of the match between his daughter and William Wentworth. It had been blessed that day by the Queen, who had shown great favour to both Burghley and Wentworth. Burghley was surely relieved, too, that in spite of the shame of Anne's estrangement from her husband Elizabeth still favoured him 'above my deserts'.

Wentworth had come that day to Burghley's bedside and told him what the Queen had said: 'for, as he reporteth, Her Majesty in commending of the matching with my daughter, used so gracious speeches of me, my wife and my daughter in such effectual sort, as thereby she hath increased and stablished his liking, as could not by my purse be redeemed; and therefore Her Majesty therein hath increased my daughter's value above my hability.'

Here at last was a son-in-law Burghley could value: 'yet both I, my wife, and specially my daughter, esteem Her Majesty's favours towards him'. The demands of dynasty, love and reputation were, at last, in something like perfect balance.[37]

Elizabeth Cecil and William Wentworth were married the next day. It was to be all too short a union.

16

The Execution of Justice

In the late March of 1582, almost a month to the day after the wedding of Elizabeth Cecil and William Wentworth, Thomas Norton wrote a letter to Sir Francis Walsingham. Both men are already familiar characters in this book, Norton as Burghley's hired pen and propagandist, Walsingham as Elizabeth's Secretary and Burghley's protégé.

Norton's letter was an apologia, a defence against certain allegations made about the part he had played in interrogating two Jesuit priests, Edmund Campion and Alexander Briant. Campion had been questioned, sometimes under torture, for three months before being tried in November 1581 and executed at Tyburn, along with Briant and another priest, Ralph Sherwin, in early December. Their crime was treason.

Norton's tone was one of injured innocence. His Catholic enemies had denounced him as 'the rack master', the priests' principal torturer. He felt he had to defend himself, and so he listed five reasons why it was unfair that Catholics had specially criticised him. First, he said, he had not conducted torture himself. Secondly, torture was applied only with a warrant signed by at least six members of the Privy Council. Thirdly, only the guilty were tortured, those 'known to the Council to be guilty of treason'; the innocent were not put to torment. Fourthly, no man was tortured for his faith, only for the purposes of discovering treason. Fifthly, any prisoner who had sworn to tell the truth on his allegiance to the Queen escaped torture.

Norton put the arguments as clearly and tersely as that: the tone of his letter bristles with righteous indignation that Catholics could say anything so dreadful about what he had done. This was a private defence of his actions; but he told Walsingham that he would be prepared to write a paper for Lord Burghley 'to use as it pleaseth him', particularly if Norton could in any way help to answer the seditious writers of anti-government books who infected the minds of Elizabeth's subjects.

Some months later Thomas Norton did indeed write a public defence of how the Queen's commissioners had interrogated Catholic priests. It was printed with a pamphlet written by Burghley himself. The title of this work was *The Execution of Justice in England*.[1]

The Elizabethan state was at war with secret enemies who wanted to destroy it. This is what men like Norton, Walsingham and Burghley believed in their bones. Western Europe was in a state of ideological cold war. It was an unsettling, febrile time. In the Low Countries, where the war machine of Philip II was grinding down Protestant resistance, there was real war, just as there had been on and off in France for years. Elizabeth's England was in terrible danger. The great powers of continental Europe plotted against it. Agents and spies were at work on all kinds of conspiracies: some were disaffected Englishmen, others diplomatic representatives of foreign powers.

So in the view of the English government, the English priests who were being trained abroad at continental seminaries were not innocent holy men: they were traitors who stirred rebellion against the Queen and sought to overthrow England's true religion; they were agents of the Catholic powers. If like Campion they were captured and interrogated, it was because of their treason, not because of their religious beliefs: this was the official line. But to Catholic Englishmen like William Allen, whose job it was to train the shock troops of the Catholic faith, the priests who suffered terrible execution were simply martyrs.

Allen likened the persecution of Catholic priests by Elizabeth's government to the persecution of the early Christians by Rome. In 1582 he wrote *A briefe historie of the glorious martyrdom* of twelve English priests, in which he explained how 'by colour of contrived treason and conspiracy (the cause indeed being religion) the enemies of the Christian faith have shed their innocent blood to the infinite shame of our nation'. This was 'a spectacle of heretical cruelty and Machiavellian practices' put on by a gang of 'atheists' and 'politiques' in government who pretended that the priests had committed treason. In fact, Allen wrote, everyone knew full well that the priests suffered for faith and conscience. Worse still, this persecution was carried out like the heathen persecutions of the early Church. Priests were tortured on Sundays and holy days, and prisoners were exposed to the 'pitiful sighs, groans and complaints' of their comrades 'proceeding of infinite pains'.[2]

Who was right, Norton or Allen? Were Burghley and his colleagues atheist persecutors who sought the blood of innocent priests? Or were they merely dutiful public servants who were doing their best to protect the realm against rebel insurgents? The answers to these questions were anything but clear, and they depended (and depend still, perhaps) very much on one's point of view. But one fact is beyond any doubt. This was the great ideological battle of

Elizabeth's reign – conscience set against the state, treason against martyrdom – and Burghley was right at the heart of it.

*

Burghley dominated the Elizabethan scene. The great clash of absolutes, between faith and the state, between Protestant England and Catholic Europe, was a central part of the architecture of his life and career. Already we are on the road to Mary Stuart's doom, for what Mary did above all was to evoke in Burghley a terrible fear of England's destruction. The Queen of Scots, rebellion, conspiracy, the missions of Jesuits and seminary priests, the fear of Spain: all were in some way connected. It was as early as this that Burghley began to put the pieces in place for Mary's execution at Fotheringhay in 1587. There is no bigger story than this in the history of Britain in the sixteenth century.

So here we have Burghley the great player, standing on the world stage, determining policy and affecting many thousands of lives. But the public and the private can sit together awkwardly. Draw the curtain back just a little, and in early 1582 we find a sixty-one-year-old man struggling with health, with grief, with providence, and with the question of loyalty.

For Burghley 'the doubtful opinions of the physicians' were nothing new, and in late March he was finding them a distraction while working at Cecil House on the royal revenues. It was the same that summer when from his bed he wrote of the Queen's health and of the benefits of Buxton baths. He was no better the next day; he sought some comfort in writing but instead had to dictate a letter to Walsingham 'using . . . my man's hands and my own tongue'. He was still in Westminster, he wrote, but his mind was at Theobalds. It was in Hertfordshire that he spent at least a few days in August while the court was on progress near Oatlands.[3]

It was at Theobalds, too, that William Wentworth, Burghley's son-in-law for just eight months, died that November. His last illness came quickly. He made his will three days before his death on 7 November. He was in his middle twenties; he left his wife, Elizabeth, a widow at the age of eighteen.

There was shock at court. The next day Walsingham wrote to Burghley: 'It was my hap immediately afore my arrival at this my poor cottage to receive your Lordship's doleful letter'. Already Walsingham had sent this on to Sir Christopher Hatton, who told the Queen of Wentworth's death. Walsingham believed that the loss of a man of his virtue was 'a manifest argument of God's displeasure towards us'. He prayed for God's grace to give Burghley patience to bear the cross. The Queen heard the news the same day. She was, wrote Hatton, 'so much inclined with your sorrowful letters as she findeth herself much more fit to accompany you in your grief than to comfort you in this your irrecoverable loss'.

The letters sent to Burghley by Walsingham, Hatton, the Earl of Sussex and the Earl of Leicester were all very similar in tone and substance: sadness, condolence, exhortations to patience. Hatton wrote at length: Burghley, so 'well exercised with the mutable accidents of this wretched world, will call reason to your relief: with thankfulness that God the creator of us all hath called this his virtuous and zealous creature to the participation of his heavenly inheritance'. He wrote of Wentworth's 'most glorious exchange' of a frail and sinful life for an everlasting one.[4]

Beyond these few pieces of correspondence, and our knowledge of the 'doleful letter' Burghley sent to Walsingham on the day of William Wentworth's death, there is nothing, either of Burghley's grief or of his daughter Elizabeth's. We have something here of loss and sadness: Leicester wrote of Wentworth as his good friend whose death meant as much to him as the death of a near kinsman. Pain, loss and grief: but also the patient acceptance of God's will in corrupt times.

So life went on, and by the middle of November Burghley was ferociously busy. He was asked by the Queen, through Walsingham, to compile an account of all the dealings they had had over the years with Mary, Queen of Scots. It was meant to be exhaustive, and former ambassadors to Scotland like Henry Killigrew and Thomas Randolph were interviewed about what they remembered of their embassies. Here Walsingham relied on Burghley's memory as well as his formidable archive of papers: the 'greatest part of the proceedings', he wrote, 'remain in your Lordship's hands'. This became something of a pattern in business on Scotland: if men like Walsingham or Sir Christopher Hatton did most of the routine work, then Burghley was brought in to advise them. He was never far away from the most secret counsels of Elizabeth and her Secretary.[5]

Burghley always worked closely with Walsingham, advising, directing, commentating and annotating. There was a constant flow of paper between the two men, even when Burghley was away from court. The topics were diverse, from the politics of the French court ('I pity to see so weak a government in so mighty a kingdom') to the day-to-day mechanics of Elizabethan government.[6]

As the winter months of 1582 turned into the spring of 1583 Burghley was concerned, as ever, by business and providence. He could never quite escape from work, even in retreat in Hertfordshire. At his 'dark house at Theobalds' in the week before Christmas he read and returned letters sent to him by Walsingham about Scotland. He thought of the Queen: 'God save her and give her his graces to understand his blessings, by whose life and being we here are worldly saved.'

Burghley believed in the providential workings of God. This was obvious to him in all kinds of ways: in war and famine, in the sicknesses of the Queen, in natural disasters like the great earthquake of 1580, or, in January 1583, when many were killed and injured at Paris Garden on the south bank of the Thames. The Lord Mayor of London wrote urgently to Burghley about Paris Garden the next day. The stage had collapsed at the bear-baiting. It was taken as a sign of God's anger: the accident had happened on a Sunday and, as John Dee wrote, 'The godly expound it as a due plague of God for the wickedness there used, and the sabbath day so profanely spent.' Burghley would have understood this notion instinctively. In matters as diverse as the deaths of family, the Queen's policies at home and abroad, and the collapse of a stage at one of London's pleasure spots, God intervened directly in the world.[7]

And yet few things were simple, particularly when God's truth was tangled up in the politics of the Elizabethan state. Was it possible, for example, to be a good and loyal subject and a Catholic? Strictly it was not. Even without the complication of *Regnans in excelsis*, the papal bull that had excommunicated and condemned Elizabeth in 1570, the willing acceptance in conscience of the Queen's governorship of the English Church was an essential element in the architecture of the Elizabethan state; so were worship according to the Prayer Book and regular attendance at church. If in the early years of Elizabeth's reign her government had turned a blind eye to offenders, then by the 1570s and 1580s there were some very tough laws on treason and recusancy which it was hard to ignore.

The matter of loyalty set against religion was even more testing for men of the ruling elite. This was territory Burghley himself had navigated years before in Mary's reign, when he had eventually conformed and worshipped as a Catholic. So it would be fascinating to know what he made of the case of Lord Vaux of Harrowden, a convinced Catholic and recusant, who was interviewed by Burghley and Sir Walter Mildmay in early February 1583. The evidence we have of the encounter comes from Burghley: first a short note of the conversation with Vaux, and then a longer statement by Vaux to the Queen written entirely in Burghley's hand.

What is striking about Burghley's interview with Lord Vaux is how sympathetic it was. We have to remember Burghley's passionate hatred of the Roman Catholic Church. Later on in this chapter we will see how he viewed obedience to Rome as treason against Elizabeth. There was no doubt that Vaux was a committed Catholic who had been accused of sheltering Edmund Campion (indeed of engaging Campion as tutor to his children), and who had served time in the Fleet prison for his offence. Vaux's interview with Burghley and Mildmay was about his rehabilitation and his humble submission to be restored to Elizabeth's favour. This involved an admission of the grievous offence of refusing to disclose the truth to the Privy Council. Vaux, through Burghley's pen, besought Elizabeth 'to be my gracious Lady and to forgive and pardon me for the same'. He also asked for her compassion in sparing him his fine for recusancy.

But most telling of all was Vaux's request to be allowed to stay away from church. This, once again, came from Burghley's pen, which makes it all the more remarkable a statement. Vaux 'required most humbly to be forborne to be compelled to come to the church, not for that I should so do in contempt of Her Majesty or of her laws, but that my conscience only and nothing else as not thereto well persuaded did stay me'. He offered to hear 'any instruction whereby my conscience may be better informed and satisfied'. This would show that he did not refuse to attend church 'upon a contemptuous meaning but only for offence of my conscience'.[8]

For years, in spite of all his sympathies, Vaux had been considered loyal. Although his association with Campion caused him trouble, it was as if Elizabeth's government could see beyond it: as if, indeed, there was a quite different standard which could be applied in his case. Was this because of his rank and position in society? Was it something to do with Lord Vaux himself, either the fact that he had already served time in the Fleet or any personal connection he may have had with Burghley and Mildmay, two men of his own country of Northamptonshire? Was it even respect, or what was described as the humility of his statement to Burghley and Mildmay? It is hard to be sure. What is clear, however, is that in the strange and difficult world of Elizabethan politics and religion, loyalty and treason, we can take nothing for granted.

*

Sir Francis Walsingham was at court in April 1583 when he wrote to Burghley with condolences on another death in his family. This was Elizabeth Wentworth, Burghley's youngest daughter: she was just eighteen years old, and she had survived her husband, William, by only a few months. 'It is very hard for the weakness of flesh in parents to yield with that Christian patience that appertaineth unto the loss of children', wrote Walsingham. When such an affliction was laid upon any Christian, he continued, it was his duty to kiss the rod. Burghley should thank God for his daughter's life: 'in that the young gentlewoman before her departure left so good testimony unto the world that she is departed from a transitory unto a life eternal she hath left an earthly father to be with a celestial where instead of misery she enjoyeth unspeakable bliss'. This was not, Walsingham wrote, 'a common hap to all parents', so Burghley had just cause to be thankful to God.[9]

In the few days that followed, the Queen moved between Richmond and

Greenwich, and Burghley was given leave to stay away from court. But five days after Walsingham's letter of the 15th, his time to come to terms with Elizabeth's death was up. 'My very good Lord,' Walsingham wrote, 'Her Majesty hath willed me to signify unto your Lordship that as she hath been pleased for a time to permit you to wrestle with nature', so she assumed that both wisdom and religion had brought resolution to a man of Burghley's place and calling. If his health permitted it, the Queen thought he should do better to occupy himself 'in dealing in public causes' than by 'secluding himself from access to give yourself over a prey to grief'. She needed his advice on the weighty matter of the Queen of Scots.[10]

This was in so many ways the cost of Burghley's service to the Queen: in the end the public always came before the private. When in May Burghley's eldest daughter, Anne, gave birth to a son, styled Lord Bulbeck, who died within four days, it was a dynastic matter as well as a family loss. Grief once again, to be borne patiently: Burghley had to kiss the rod of unquestioning service and submission to God and Queen.

There was never for Burghley a clear boundary between family and home and the business of government. When the court stayed at Theobalds in very late May, the visit was planned to the last detail. Theobalds was a statement of power and riches, of the ambitions of dynasty and service: a statement of the public as much as of the private.

It was Burghley's job, as a loyal servant, to remain vigilant, particularly in matters of security. Throughout 1583 he paid close attention to Mary, Queen of Scots and to the political state of Scotland and the rule of young James VI. England relied on a friendly and pliable Scotland for security: affairs there were carefully weighed and considered. But Burghley also involved himself in the covert work of protecting Elizabeth from her enemies. While Mary Stuart protested loyalty, Burghley and Walsingham knew, from secret sources, that the plotting on her behalf continued. Mary had always been a danger, the stirrer of rebellion and the kinswoman of Elizabeth's old enemies, the Guises. Burghley had always recognised that the Scottish Queen had many supporters in England and, as ever, he was a keen advocate of a tough policy on domestic security.[11]

It was clear to Burghley that there was a war going on between the Catholic powers of Europe and beleaguered Protestants, between the forces of Antichrist and the professors of true religion. Burghley would never forget the outrage of the Massacre of St Bartholomew in 1572. His seventeen-year-old grandson, the second William Cecil, put it very well in a letter he wrote from Paris: 'Upon St Bartholomew's day, we had here solemn processions, and other tokens of triumphs, and joy, in remembrance of the slaughter committed this time eleven years past. But I doubt they will not so triumph at the day of judgement.'[12]

*

It was on 17 December 1583, from the press of Christopher Barker, the Queen's printer, that a short pamphlet appeared called *The Execution of Justice*. There was no mention of an author anywhere in the work, but we know for certain that it was written by Burghley.[13]

An early draft had not sounded very promising. Burghley had called it 'An advertisement meet for all persons, that is for good subjects to continue in their duties'. This was too pedantic and clumsy a title for the sharp effective defence of Elizabeth's government it had to be. In his private letters Burghley used wonderfully vivid language and he loved metaphor and simile, but in his public works he was inclined to write rather stodgy mandarin prose. Probably 'An advertisement' was given to an experienced pamphleteer for polishing, perhaps to Thomas Norton, whose defence of the torture of Catholic priests was printed with *The Execution of Justice*.[14]

For all this, what we have in *The Execution of Justice* is a defence of Elizabeth's government in Burghley's own words, and this is precious indeed. Certainly the arguments are very important if we want to understand Burghley's thought in the 1580s; but so, too, is the passion of his pamphlet, its expression of intense loyalty to faith and Queen as well as its hatred of the Church of Rome. There is little doubt that he had at least some advice in writing *The Execution of Justice*, perhaps from Norton and almost certainly from Dr John Hammond, Norton's colleague in interrogations, who wrote a briefing paper on the authority of the Pope. But Burghley knew his church history well enough. And he knew, too, that the Church of Rome and the Catholic powers of Europe sought to destroy England and its religion. It is his passion that we have to be alert to when we read *The Execution of Justice*.[15]

Burghley hated rebels, as all Tudor politicians and political theorists did: they upset the delicate order of society, they threatened orderly government, and they were an offence to God. He began *The Execution of Justice* with a frontal assault on the pretensions of rebels. 'It hath been in all ages and in all countries a common usage of all offenders . . . to make defence of their lewd and unlawful facts by untruths and by colouring and covering their deeds (were they never so vile) with pretences.' Rebels were traitors; and it was obvious that rebellion and treachery in England and Ireland had been 'stirred up by the Devil, the father of rebels' against Elizabeth. Burghley's argument was uncompromising right from the beginning: there was no matter of conscience or belief here, certainly none of innocence: those who stood up against the Queen were traitors.[16]

It was clear to Burghley that behind the rebellions of the last years was the Pope, who had authorised Elizabeth's subjects to take up arms against her. She was denounced as God's anointed servant, and her subjects were threatened on pain of excommunication to break their natural ties of allegiance to her. For a long time traitors had engaged in all kinds of unsavoury enterprises, some gathering men and weapons for rebellion, others plotting to murder 'the GREATEST', as Burghley called Elizabeth, yet others publishing 'public infamous libels, full of despiteful terms and poisoned lies, altogether to uphold the foresaid anti-Christian and tyrannous warrant of the Pope's bull'.[17]

Within a few pages, Burghley came to the priests who had professed as their defence the Catholic faith. He denounced them in the strongest possible terms. They were nothing more than 'seedmen in their tillage of sedition'. He explained how the priests, seminarians and Jesuits came secretly into England, 'bringing with them certain Romish trash, as of their hallowed wax, their Agnus Dei, their grains and many kinds of beads and suchlike'. Still in secret they laboured to persuade the people of the Pope's bulls 'and of his absolute authority over all princes and countries, and striking many with pricks of conscience to obey the same'. They threatened to provoke 'an horrible uproar and a manifest civil destruction of both the realms' of England and Ireland or, as the line appeared in print, 'a manifest bloody destruction of great multitudes of Christians'. Elizabeth's kingdoms faced open civil war because of these rebel priests.[18]

So it was ridiculous to Burghley, in *The Execution of Justice*, to imagine that Catholic priests like Campion were simply unworldly holy men: they were the Queen's mortal enemies. Thankfully Elizabeth had been protected by providence from terrible treasons: 'But God's goodness, by whom kings do rule and by whose blast traitors are commonly wasted and confounded, hath otherwise given to Her Majesty, as to his handmaid and dear servant ruling under him, the spirit of wisdom and power, whereby she hath caused some of these seditious seedmen and sowers of rebellion to be discovered.'[19]

Burghley developed two important arguments in *The Execution of Justice*. The first was that the way Elizabeth's government had gone about prosecuting rebels, by the ancient law of treason, proved that the priests who had been tried and sentenced to death were so dealt with because of their treason, not because of their faith. The second was that Elizabeth had dealt fairly with men who had refused to submit to her religious settlement. It was a subtle argument, from a certain point of view, but in many ways also an effective one. *The Execution of Justice* gave a long account of senior clergy in the English Church who had not been persecuted for resisting the new ways. One of these men was Thomas Watson, Burghley's old teacher at St John's College, whom he described as being of nature 'altogether sour'. He may have thought, too, about his interview earlier that year with Lord Vaux of Harrowden, not mentioned by name, but perhaps one of the 'men of good credit in their countries, manifestly of late time seduced to hold contrary opinions in religion for the Pope's authority'.[20]

The Execution of Justice was written to convince and confute; it was a work of passionate loyalty to Queen and religion; it was a statement of self-evident truth just as much as it was a piece of carefully crafted propaganda. It had the dignity of anonymity, for it appeared with neither excuse nor attribution from the press of the Queen's printer; it was official without being partisan, and perhaps those who read or heard it sensed that it came corporately from Elizabeth's government. In fact it spoke with a voice that was distinctively Burghley's. *The Execution of Justice* was, and was intended to be, many things at once.

Burghley's pamphlet did not convert the enemy. Probably he had never supposed it would. Instead it provoked a Catholic response in the form of a much longer book by William Allen, called *A True, Sincere, and Modest Defence of English Catholics*, which mocked Burghley's position. Allen said again, and with more force, what he had been saying for some time: the English priests who had died were martyrs; the prosecutions under treason law were mere show; men were being persecuted for their faith in the manner of the first Christians. If Burghley had attacked popes who presumed to usurp God's princes on earth, Allen argued that it was right and proper for temporal monarchs to acknowledge the spiritual supremacy of Rome.[21]

Who was right, Burghley or Allen? It is impossible to know: both men wrote with a passion for absolutes, for clear rights and wrongs, truth against lies; they were utterly sure of themselves. Burghley ended *The Execution of Justice* with a short verse from the first book of Esdras (4:41): 'Great is truth, and she overcometh'. On the title-page of his *Defence* Allen fired back with two verses from Psalms: 'That the mouth may be stopped of such as speak unjustly' (Psalm 62:12); and 'Thy mouth hath abounded in malice, and thy tongue hath cunningly framed lies' (Psalm 49:19).[22] There was no common ground here, no shared understanding of the world; Burghley and Allen saw nothing the same way.

But arguments on paper can be clear where life is not. Already Burghley had had to make his way on the hard ground of life and loyalty. Given that in *The Execution of Justice* he wrote with passion about the horror of Queen Mary's burnings, dismissed by Allen merely as rightful punishment for heretics, we may wonder about Burghley's comfortable life in Mary's reign. Catholics taunted Burghley with the memory of his conformity: how, they said, he had 'bestirred himself to get credit with the Catholics, frequented Masses, said the Litanies with the priest, laboured a pair of great beads which he continually carried, preached to his parishioners in Stamford, and asked pardon of his errors in King Edward's time'. When Burghley wrote *The Execution of Justice* he was addressing more than the treason of rebels: perhaps he was also setting to rights his own past.[23]

*

In January 1584, the month of the printing of a corrected edition of *The Execution of Justice*, Lord Henry Howard was interviewed by Robert Beale. Beale questioned Howard about letters that had passed to and from Charles Paget, an English Catholic exile in Paris who was a supporter of Mary, Queen of Scots. Howard was 'enjoined in Her Majesty's name' to talk about his conversations and correspondence with Paget. Secret sources said Lord Henry Howard was one of Mary Stuart's men in England. Another supporter of Mary was Francis Throckmorton, arrested a couple of months earlier in possession of a list of English Catholic gentlemen and a note on harbours suitable for military landings.

Robert Beale was a clerk of the Privy Council and Sir Francis Walsingham's brother-in-law. He was very much of Walsingham's and Burghley's mindset, a firm Protestant and, by the 1580s, an experienced royal servant. His name will appear every so often in this and the following chapters.

Lord Henry Howard was a dangerous man. He possessed serious social clout. He was clever, a graduate of Cambridge, where in his twenties he had taught rhetoric. He was also the younger brother of Thomas Howard, fourth Duke of Norfolk, who had lost his head for treason in 1572, and a friend of Burghley's son-in-law, Edward, Earl of Oxford. Burghley had kept a close eye on Lord Henry Howard for many years and in recent months it had become clear to Burghley and to Walsingham, through an agent they had in the French embassy, that Howard was tangled up in plots against Elizabeth.[24]

Beale's examination of Howard appeared to establish a number of facts. The first was that Lord Henry had communicated with Paget 'touching the Queen of Scots: Charles Paget justifying all her doings, he told him that if she could acquit herself of the marriage with Bothwell it might serve for her defence'. Howard was careful to suggest to Beale that both he and Paget believed that Mary 'had not sufficiently cleared herself thereof'. Still, Paget had promised to show Howard 'such matter as should satisfy him'.

Lord Henry told Beale about the arrangements they had made for the delivery of Paget's letters to London. When the letters began to arrive, there was nothing to suggest where they had come from: Howard said they were completely blank on the outside. One contained a sheet and a half from Paget on the subject of Mary's marriage to Bothwell. Howard had no idea who had delivered the letter, and even the two or three seals which had been used to secure the packet gave him no clue. But he remembered that another letter which had been handed to him one day in St James's Park 'was sealed with a seal having a St Andrew's cross'. Howard seems to have admitted to Beale that this letter may have come indirectly from the Queen of Scots, but he denied ever having received correspondence from her directly. Everything, he said, came from Charles Paget.[25]

It is easy to be seduced by the glamour of Howard's secret correspondence: the mysterious letters delivered by he knew not whom, Paget the exile working on behalf of the imprisoned queen. There is no way to tell whether we should trust what Howard said to Beale. This was not the first interview with Howard, for he had been under arrest since the middle of November. It may have been the fifth or sixth or seventh; there is little context to go on. Howard's story seems plausible enough, but often even apparently convincing examinations were at most versions of the truth which could take experienced interrogators a very long time to test. Howard was an exceptionally bright man, and probably he put up all kinds of defences in his interview with Beale, able to make half-truths sound plausible, to give enough to satisfy his interrogator without revealing everything he knew. So we have to be careful.

Yet for all this, Howard's examination was significant. It was a single fragment in a puzzle of conspiracy which Sir Francis Walsingham, Burghley and others were trying to put together: it involved Mary Stuart, certainly, and Francis Throckmorton and Don Bernardino de Mendoza, the Spanish ambassador. It was proof of conspiracies by foreign powers and by English subjects who had renounced their natural allegiances in favour of Rome. Surely *The Execution of Justice* was right. Of the seriousness of the danger Burghley would have been in little doubt: he saw it in 1584, just as he had seen it with the Ridolfi plot twelve years earlier and would again before too long.

We have to try to put ourselves in Burghley's shoes. There was evidence, from all kinds of sources, of plots and conspiracies at home. He knew that the Catholic superpowers of Europe were quite able by 1584 to launch an invasion of England: it was simply a matter of time. So it should come as no great surprise that Burghley began to think about how to defend England against the invasion which was bound to come soon enough. By early February 1584 he was engaged in detailed war planning, and with Henry Maynard, one of his private secretaries, he set out a paper 'of sundry things to be executed within the realm to withstand perils'. One of his concerns was money, which, as Lord Treasurer, was naturally his business. England's defence by land and sea would cost in the region of £35,000 for three months – a staggering sum of money to protect Elizabeth's kingdoms.

Burghley understood that the greatest military threat to the kingdom came from a seaborne invasion. He believed the enemy would make for one of three points on the English or Welsh coasts: either Essex or Sussex or near Milford Haven in Pembrokeshire.

The plan of defence was something like this. Three 'companies' of Elizabeth's navy would sit off the coast, twelve thousand men in all. Most of the fleet would be in the west, where Burghley supposed the enemy would try to land. But just in case the Spanish fleet came from the west and moved up the English Channel, it would be followed and finally met by all the companies of the navy near the Sussex Downs. If an invading force was able to get to the coast, Burghley considered the digging of trenches to give cover for gunners 'to impeach landing'. He also, that February, wanted men of the coastal counties to muster for training three days a week. He believed that any invasion would come that summer.[26]

For a week Burghley made further plans. He considered the money that would be needed to repair forts and support garrisons. He thought about munitions and protection for the Queen's navy. He anticipated a parliament in the spring. He also wrote 'to have regard to Sheffield', by which he meant Sheffield Castle and so Mary, Queen of Scots. Mary, the most dangerous woman in Europe, was always part of Burghley's calculations.[27]

*

It was a quiet enough spring in Burghley's household. Lady Mildred was ill in late March. Her malady was treated by two physicians, Dr Hector Nunes and Dr Bayley, who prescribed over four days a strict diet and a recipe for barley cream. Within weeks there was good news about Burghley's daughter, Anne: she and her husband, the Earl of Oxford, temporarily reconciled, had a second child, Bridget, born in early April.[28]

Life carried on as ever: family, friends, home and court. In that summer of 1584 the Earl of Leicester thanked Burghley for the hospitality offered to him at Theobalds. Burghley had been away from home, and Leicester and his companions had arrived at the house at three o'clock on a long summer's afternoon 'without any jot of warning'. They wanted to see Burghley's garden walks and the new buildings at Theobalds. But they also found 'both meat and good drink of all sorts there, too much for such sudden guests' and were 'most kindly used by all your servants'. The party had even hunted in Burghley's park: 'I have been bold to make some of your stags afraid but killed none; if I had your Lordship should have been presented with our good fortune, yet had I very good sport and killed a young hind.' These were the ties of nobility and friendship.[29]

Yet for Lord Burghley, and for the Earl of Leicester too, the fear of disaster was never far away, and this had everything to do with the tricky geopolitics of

western Europe in the 1580s. Already in the early months of 1584 Burghley
had set out plans to withstand invasion, no doubt mindful of the plotting of
Francis Throckmorton and others. In April the Duke of Parma recovered
Ypres from the Dutch, evidence that Protestants in the Low Countries were
being put under serious military pressure by the Spanish. By June the Duke of
Guise presided over a Catholic League in France to oppose Henry of Navarre's
claim to the throne after the death of the Duke of Alençon. At the same time,
Elizabeth's government was trying to determine how to deal with James VI of
Scotland, just turned eighteen and a young king with a mind of his own: for
England the politics of Scotland was, as ever, a snake pit. Ireland was exposed
and an obvious route for the invasion of Elizabeth's realms, as Burghley had
made plain in *The Execution of Justice*. At home the government wrestled with
the old and thorny problem of what to do with Mary, Queen of Scots. The
future of Mary was tied to Elizabeth's relations with her son, and this kept
councillors busy till autumn.[30]

In May the government went public on Francis Throckmorton's plot. At
the time of Throckmorton's trial for treason, Christopher Barker, the Queen's
printer, produced a pamphlet giving every detail of the great conspiracy. It was
anonymous, and whoever composed it (perhaps Burghley or Walsingham or
an experienced writer like Thomas Norton) introduced it with the common
device of a fabricated letter, this time from one 'Q.Z.' of Lion's Inn.

*A discoverie of the treasons practised and attempted against the Queenes
Majestie* shone a penetrating light on a Europe-wide conspiracy. It was alleged
that Throckmorton was a 'privy conveyor and receiver' of letters to and from
Mary Stuart, and when his papers had been searched investigators found a list
of English Catholic noblemen and gentlemen, an account of ports 'for landing
of foreign forces', and twelve pedigrees of the English royal line defending the
'pretended title of the Scottish Queen' to Elizabeth's crown, these by the
Bishop of Ross, John Lesley, Burghley's old adversary.[31]

The pamphlet gave an account of Throckmorton's torture, administered, it
was suggested, both reluctantly and moderately. Elizabeth's councillors were
'constrained' to give Throckmorton 'to such as are usually appointed in the
Tower to handle the rack, by whom he was laid upon the same, and somewhat
pinched, although not much'. It took a second racking to get him to confess
the truth. And the truth, now set out by the government in careful detail, was
shocking.[32]

It was revealed that Francis Throckmorton was one man in a spidery
network of conspirators. Another was Sir Francis Englefield in the Low
Countries, 'who daily solicited the Spanish king in Spain, and his governors in
the said Countries, to attempt the invading of the realm'. Also there were
Thomas Throckmorton, Francis's brother, and Thomas Morgan. At the heart

of the plan to invade England was the Scottish Queen 'and her confederates in France and in other foreign parts, and also in England'. The plan itself would be executed by Mary's kinsman, the Duke of Guise. Their pretext was to free the Queen of Scotland and force Elizabeth to grant toleration in religion. But their real intention 'should be upon the Queen's Majesty's resistance, to remove Her Majesty from her crown and state'.[33]

The pamphlet revealed that the conspirators had been well advanced in their planning. The Duke of Guise had his forces. He had sent to Rome and Spain for money; the Spanish ambassador in England said that King Philip 'would bear half the charge of the enterprise'. The Guises had sent an agent into England in the summer of 1583 to brief an English fifth column of Catholic sympathisers. Throckmorton was the conspiracy's link man in England, helped by Philip's ambassador, Don Bernardino de Mendoza. Meanwhile, the Duke of Guise planned precisely where he would invade: it was to be on the Sussex coast near Arundel. Every detail was covered, even the contingency of the loss of Thomas Throckmorton on a mission from France to England. His replacement would be Lord Henry Howard's correspondent, Charles Paget, who went under the wonderful names of Mope *alias* Spring.[34]

And so the treason of Francis Throckmorton and others was revealed to the reading public of London, as well as to those who attended his trial in London's Guildhall. In a sense it does not matter whether the great conspiracy explained with so much care by the government existed in this form or not: Burghley and his colleagues believed it. We know, for example, that Philip of Spain was reluctant to support French plans for an invasion of England. But Philip did commission a report on a possible Spanish invasion and some of his generals were enthusiastic supporters of such a venture. And Elizabeth's government was afraid of Spanish power. Invasion was surely inevitable: the Throckmorton plot, whatever it was or was not, merely confirmed the deepest fears of Elizabeth's councillors.[35]

It is with all this in mind, and the knowledge of the assassination of the Dutch Protestant leader, William of Nassau, Prince of Orange, in July 1584, that we can make sense of Burghley's plan to mobilise the English political elite in common cause. Orange's killing had been commissioned by Philip of Spain. England was already tangled up in the long-running Spanish campaign against Dutch Protestants: as if the death of Orange was not bad enough, that September Ghent surrendered to Philip's general, the Duke of Parma. It was a grim, panicky time for the English government, and disaster loomed.

Burghley and Secretary Walsingham considered appropriate responses. First of all, Burghley prepared a statement of self-defence in the face of Spanish aggression: Elizabeth could help to protect Holland and Zeeland from King Philip for her own safety. She had 'many just causes to think that the King of

Spain mindeth to invade her realm and to destroy her person'. So, he wrote, Elizabeth was bound by God's law to defend herself and her realm against Philip.[36]

Burghley drafted this statement of self-defence on 10 October 1584. Two days later, in his study at Cecil House, he was hard at work on a joint project with Walsingham, a second response to the dangers facing England. By the 12th they had written what was known a week later as the 'Instrument of an Association'. Burghley wanted the document to be in Latin, but probably there was no time to have it properly translated from English. He also thought, on 12 October, that he had found a better statement in a 'confederation of the nobility' of the Low Countries against the Inquisition from 1568, which, he wrote to Walsingham, 'if I had seen before, I would have followed some form thereof'. But however imperfect he thought it to be, the Association was a hugely important document.[37]

It was at Hampton Court exactly a week later, on Monday, 19 October, that the Privy Council signed Burghley and Walsingham's Association. This was a very large document indeed, beautifully written on a single sheet, very probably the work of Thomas Windebank, a clerk of the Signet and formerly a gentleman servant in Burghley's household: it was graceful and daunting at the same time; and to this text of nearly eight hundred words Elizabeth's councillors put their names and appended their seals.

The language of the Association was intentionally robust. It proceeded from the plain fact that Elizabeth's death had been 'most traitorously and devilishly sought' for the 'furtherance and advancement of some pretended titles' to her crown. Those who entered into this 'bond of one firm and loyal society' swore vengeance on anyone who in any way tried to harm the Queen. It was the firmest of resolutions: 'And we shall never desist from all manner of forcible pursuit against such persons to the uttermost extermination of them, their counsellors, aiders and abettors.'[38]

Burghley and Walsingham were careful not to mention Mary Stuart by name; but anyone who swore the Association swore in effect to destroy Mary's agents and even Mary herself. The Instrument was, in this sense, a critical document, designed to protect Elizabeth from her mortal enemies. We can take it as no accident that within months the Queen of Scots herself was encouraged to put her hand and seal to the Association. It was the ultimate guarantee of her good behaviour, a knife pressed to her own heart. Needless to say, this was a document Walsingham kept very safe indeed.[39]

Lord Burghley was in a self-congratulatory mood on the evening of 19 October. Once he had returned to Cecil House from Hampton Court he wrote to Walsingham 'late at night'. Everything was running smoothly: the Association would be made public to 'many sorts of persons by degrees of offices and callings'. The next day Walsingham agreed: 'The more public the matter is made the better effect it is like to work.' Copies of the Instrument were delivered to local officers, who were given clear instructions on getting subscriptions. And the exercise was hugely successful, for many thousands of men across England signed it. But the Association was really only the beginning.[40]

*

Elizabeth's fifth parliament met towards the end of November. Burghley wanted to leave nothing to chance: the law had to be used to protect the Queen, her title and her realm and to threaten England's enemies in the strongest possible way.

What followed over the next weeks and months unfolded in a familiar way. First of all the Queen's councillors gave an unmistakable steer to the Commons. Sir Walter Mildmay explained, in a passionate speech, how all subjects could worship freedom and liberty. He spoke about the administration of law to all. Their 'mortal and capital enemy' was the Pope, 'that both hateth us and the very soil that we tread on'. He referred to Pius V's bull, the invasion of Ireland, the international conspiracy to destroy Protestantism 'in all places but especially in this kingdom'. He spoke about the Jesuits and about the plotting of Francis Throckmorton and his fellow conspirators. It was almost scripted from *The Execution of Justice*.[41]

And so parliament set to work that same afternoon on a bill for the Queen's safety. Burghley applied himself to it with his usual care, and over the weeks it assumed a variety of forms. He experimented with an old idea he had had over twenty years earlier, the creation of a great council to govern England in the event of Elizabeth's death. In the end the Act for the Queen's Surety was limited to the pursuit of anyone who sought the harm of Elizabeth's person. Like the Instrument of Association it did not mention Mary Stuart by name, but its meaning was clear enough. It was the act of parliament under which she was eventually tried at Fotheringhay Castle.

The Act for the Queen's Surety set out exactly what would happen if, in the language of the statute itself, 'anything shall be compassed or imagined tending to the hurt of Her Majesty's person' by any person with or without the knowledge of anyone who pretended title to the English crown. Commissioners would then meet to examine the offences and their commission would pass a sentence on the offenders. This judgment would be declared by proclamation under the Great Seal of England and 'all persons against whom such a sentence or judgement shall be so given and published' would be prevented from having any claim to the English throne.

If all this sounds very restrained, then the act also confirmed the Association: all subjects would, by virtue of the Act for the Queen's Surety, be able 'by all forcible and possible means [to] pursue to death every [one] of such wicked persons, by whom or by whose means assent or privity any such invasion or rebellion shall be in form aforesaid denounced to have been made, or such wicked act attempted, or other thing compassed or imagined against Her Majesty's person'.

The long and short of all this was that Mary Stuart could be prosecuted under the Act for the Queen's Surety for the actions of anyone plotting in her name with or without her knowledge. She could also be hunted down and brought to justice by Elizabeth's subjects. Mary was caught in a cat's claws: whichever way she moved, she could not escape.[42]

*

One of the reasons why parliament framed such an uncompromising law was the 'horrible fact' (as Sir Walter Mildmay put it) of the conspiracy of Dr William Parry. Of all the plotters, conspirators and fantasists of these years of cold war, no one better illustrates the conflicting loyalties of Elizabeth's reign: faith against the state, treason and religion.[43]

For many years Parry had written letters to Burghley. He had got to know William Cecil and William's uncle Robert, two young men of much the same age, when they had been travelling and studying abroad in the early 1580s. Parry had presented himself to Burghley as the perfect secret agent against the Catholics; in return he had hoped for patronage and favour. Seriously in debt, he offered to spy for Elizabeth's government for money. In the end it is hard to know whose side he was on – probably he had no clear idea himself. But it does seem that he got tangled up with a man called Thomas Morgan in a plot to kill the Queen.

William Parry made his confession to Elizabeth from the Tower of London on St Valentine's Day in 1585. He began with what may have been extra-ordinary self-insight: 'Your Majesty may see by my voluntary confession the dangerous fruits of a discontented mind.' Morgan, he wrote, could not be touched: he was safe in France and could be left to God. And so Parry sought to counsel his Queen. She could, he said, ease her Catholic subjects and restore relations with her princely neighbours. 'There is possibility to repair all', he wrote. 'The Queen of Scotland is your prisoner, let her be honorably entreated but yet surely guarded. She may do you good.' 'Cherish and love her,' he continued, 'she is of your blood and your undoubted heir in succession. It is so taken abroad and will be found so at home.'

Parry ended this extraordinary document with a startling goodbye.

Everything is packed into these words: the conflicting loyalties of this testing time, when nothing was obvious or constant or dependable. Whether he knew it or not, Parry spoke for a generation.

And so farewell, most gracious and the best natured and qualified Queen that ever lived in England. Remember your infortunate Parry, overthrown by your hard hand. Amend that in the rest of your servants, for it is past with me if your grace be not greater than I look for. And last and ever, good madam, be good to your obedient Catholic subjects. For the bad I speak not.[44]

17

The Commission

It was in December 1585 that a young man called Gilbert Gifford took lodgings in London with one Thomas Phelippes. This seems an unremarkable fact to record in a biography of the great Lord Burghley. But it was the secret work of Phelippes and Gifford that gave Burghley his opportunity less than a year later to stand face to face with Mary Stuart at Fotheringhay Castle and tell her plainly that she had plotted to kill her royal sister Elizabeth.

What unfolded over the next months and years was an intelligence and security operation of subtlety and cunning. Phelippes was the technician, the artist of counter-espionage work; Sir Francis Walsingham, Elizabeth's Secretary, was in overall charge; Gifford was the double agent they had to keep on the straight and narrow; and Lord Burghley watched and waited.

Gilbert Gifford was the best possible weapon Walsingham and Phelippes could use against Mary. The parallels between Gifford and the agents of double-cross deployed against the German *Abwehr* by the British Security Service in the Second World War are hard to ignore. He operated under control against his former masters. His pedigree was perfect. He was twenty-seven years old and the son of a family of Catholic recusants from Staffordshire. He had been educated at Douai College in Rheims and then at the English College in Rome. His sympathies were with Mary, at least before his recruitment by Walsingham. In December 1585 he had only just returned to England with a letter of recommendation from Mary's agent in Paris, Thomas Morgan.

Thomas Phelippes remains a shadowy figure. He was a mystery even to his own father, who reflected on his son's 'staid and secret nature'. Phelippes was about thirty, 'of low stature, slender every way, eaten in the face with small pocks, of short sight': the description is Mary Stuart's, into whose confidences Phelippes had tried to manoeuvre himself before Christmas 1585. He was a graduate of Trinity College in Cambridge, a talented linguist and mathematician and a gifted code-breaker. He was a true citizen of the secret world.[1]

Phelippes possessed all the gifts needed to run a security operation of great complexity and subtlety. Gifford was prickly and highly strung, a man of divided loyalties and competing emotions. But slowly, and with the careful handling of Gifford, Phelippes and Walsingham managed to ready Mary Stuart's neck for the block.

The trick was to intercept Mary's post without Mary or her correspondents knowing. She had to be able to read only what Walsingham had read first; and if she was able to send letters, Walsingham had to have copies. But this principle of close observation, as Walsingham and Phelippes well knew, could be extended easily to what might be called a more interventionist mode of operation. They could exercise control over the Queen of Scots without her knowing; they could even, through the clever use of interception and forgery, shape Mary's correspondence with her supporters. They could, quite simply, entrap Mary Stuart.

And so it was that from January 1586 Mary began to receive letters secretly from Thomas Morgan. They arrived in sealed tubes hidden inside beer barrels brought to the place of Mary's keeping, Chartley in Derbyshire, by a brewer from Buxton. In a terrible slip of security, though of course a deliberate one, Mary's guards apparently did not bother to look inside the barrels. She could at last speak to the world and the world could speak back, all in secret – or so she thought.

The trap was set with care and imagination by Thomas Phelippes. Gilbert Gifford was an essential element in the chain; Mary still believed him to be loyal. The brewer was in the pay of the government. Phelippes made copies of the ciphered letters and sent the deciphered documents on to Walsingham. With a talented man like Phelippes running the show, and Mary and her men believing that Gilbert Gifford was for them, Sir Francis could control Mary's correspondence and keep an eye on any plotting she was dabbling in. In April 1586 Elizabeth told the French ambassador very plainly: 'Monsieur Ambassador, you have much secret intelligence with the Queen of Scotland. But, believe me, I know everything that is done in my kingdom.' She had some very good reasons to be so confident.[2]

It was in this way that Sir Francis Walsingham was able to nourish the conspiracy against Elizabeth that we know as the Babington plot. This was a complicated conspiracy, a coming together of a number of young Catholic men with all kinds of ideas of how to free Mary Stuart, defend Catholics from government persecution and kill the heretic Elizabeth. It was a plot, then, of many strands – a confusion of conspiracies – that would culminate in the summer of 1586.

Anthony Babington, eventually the leader of this group, was a young man of twenty-four born in Derbyshire. He was acquainted with Thomas Morgan,

Mary's man in Paris, where they had met in 1580. By 1586 Babington was in touch with John Ballard, a Catholic priest and visitor to Rome in 1584. Ballard had connections with the leading Catholic powers of Europe and was known to the Spanish ambassador in Paris, Don Bernardino de Mendoza. There were other plotters, whose names may or may not appear later in this chapter: Antony Tyrell, who had been in Rome with Ballard; William Gifford and John Savage, two other associates; Thomas Salisbury, a young Welshman and graduate of Oxford; and others. In 1586 these men plotted: in 1586 many also died traitors' deaths.

*

In the early summer of 1586 the government was jittery. There were rumours of plots and rebellions. On the south coast the Earl of Sussex wrote of the intelligence brought to him 'of certain mutiny and assembly to be shortly practised'. Sussex was genuinely worried. His further investigations revealed that this 'conspiracy of rising and tumult' was to be started by the firing of beacons. Sussex's information was simple: there was to be a rebellion across the whole kingdom. Sussex said it would be 1549 all over again, a rebellion Burghley would have well remembered. Burghley would have thought too of more recent invasions of Ireland. The conspirators, said Sussex, were Catholic recusants in England, supported by foreign rebels and fugitives.[3]

Burghley had expected an invasion since 1583. He knew that the rumours of rebellion meant something. He probably understood, too, that Phelippes and Gifford were getting close to extracting from Mary Stuart evidence of her involvement in the Babington plot. In July Walsingham and Phelippes knew for sure.

It was in July that Mary wrote a letter to Babington which for Walsingham proved that she was part of a treasonable conspiracy against Elizabeth. Phelippes knew, too: it is why, when he sent his copy of the letter to Walsingham he drew a gallows on the outside of the packet. It was partly on the evidence of this letter that Burghley confronted Mary, and because of what she had written in it that she knelt down at the executioner's block in February 1587.[4]

If we want to understand Burghley's case against Mary, Queen of Scots, we have to understand something of how this letter was composed, of what it said, and in what form it survived for the government to be able to use it to condemn Mary. Walsingham's trap had sprung neatly and cleanly; but the letter was a subtle document indeed.

It was written by Mary's secretaries, Jacques Nau and Gilbert Curll: she was too clever to leave any evidence in her own hand. In it she thanked Babington and his fellow conspirators for their 'common desire to prevent in time the designments of our enemies for the extirpation of our religion out of this realm with the ruin of us all'. She appeared to endorse the 'enterprise' of an invasion of England by the great powers of Catholic Europe and their efforts to free her from captivity.[5]

The letter was written over ten days. It was finished on 17 July and posted a day later by Gilbert Curll. That same night it arrived in the hands of Phelippes, who deciphered it and sent his copy, with its gallows mark, to Walsingham on the 19th. Phelippes kept the original letter for another ten days. On 29 July, a Friday, he arrived in London with it. The letter was handed to Babington by one of Phelippes's couriers that same evening.

But Phelippes had by now forged a postscript to Mary's letter using her cipher. She – or rather Walsingham and Phelippes – wanted to know the names of Babington's fellow conspirators, 'as also from time to time particularly how you proceed, and as soon as you may, for the same purpose, who be already, and how far everyone [is] privy hereunto'. It was an incredible risk for Walsingham and Phelippes to take: either they would discover everything or Babington would know that he had been discovered. Success or disaster depended on the quality of Phelippes's forgery. But would Anthony Babington fall for it?

A day later, on Saturday, 30 July, Babington and Chidiock Tichborne, a fellow conspirator, dutifully deciphered Mary's letter and Phelippes's postscript. The question now was whether Babington would write an answer to the Scottish Queen that told her all about the conspiracy. Or perhaps he would go silent, aware that Walsingham's hand was on his shoulder.[6]

It was one of the most delicate moments of Walsingham's distinguished career as an intelligence operator. He was ready to pounce. By 2 August a proclamation was ready in draft to order the arrest of Babington and Tichborne. Walsingham's first instinct was to arrest Babington and John Ballard 'and such as are noted to be his familiars' and hold them at his house for interrogation. He fought his instinct. A day later, on the 3rd, he thought that he had miscalculated. Everything appeared to be unravelling. He received information that Babington was running, on the way, Walsingham supposed, to Mary. But at least Ballard could still be pulled in. He gave strict orders to Phelippes that Ballard was to be apprehended only as any other Jesuit priest would be: nothing was to reveal the government's suspicions about his conspiracy with Babington.[7]

Walsingham believed on 3 August that Phelippes's forged postscript had given the game away. 'And so praying God to send us better success than I look for,' he wrote to Phelippes that day, 'I commit you to his protection.' But the same evening Phelippes learned that Babington was actually still in London. He was hiding in the garden of Robert Poley, another of Walsingham's agents who had posed to Babington as a Catholic conspirator.[8]

Between 3 and 4 August Walsingham had some fine judgements to make. He was in a stronger position than he had imagined. Should he let Babington run for a little while longer? On the 3rd he was still inclined to have Babington brought in. He explained his view to Phelippes. 'I think if your messenger received not answer this day at Babington's hands then it were not good to defer the apprehension of him lest he should escape.' Everything rested on whether Phelippes thought Babington would post a reply to Mary's letter of 17 July: if this was likely, 'then were it a great hindrance of the service to proceed over hastily to the arrest'. 'These causes are subject to so many difficulties as it is a hard matter to resolve.' But Walsingham was as clear as Burghley would have been: 'Only this I conclude: it were better to lack the answer than to lack the man.'[9]

Phelippes showed remarkable coolness under pressure, if we assume that the decision to let Babington run was his. When John Ballard was arrested the next day, 4 August, at Robert Poley's house, Babington, also there, was left alone. To protect his value as Walsingham's agent, Poley was sent to the Tower. But the raid rattled Babington. He knew he had to act. He wrote a remarkable letter to Poley: 'The furnace is prepared wherein our faith must be tried. Farewell till we meet, which God knows when.'

Babington ate later that day with a man he knew full well to be another of Walsingham's agents, one Scudamore. During their meal a note arrived from the court for Scudamore. Babington suspected it was an order for his arrest, so he went off to the bar to 'pay the shot'. In fact he slipped out of the inn and ran to Westminster as fast as he could to meet two of his associates. Knowing for sure they were now being hunted by Walsingham's men, they went into hiding, first in St John's Wood and then eventually in Harrow, where after a few days they had to beg for food.[10]

Burghley was involved in the hunt for Babington only indirectly. On 10 August, a Wednesday, he wrote to Walsingham about a strange encounter he had had on his way home from the court to Theobalds. It is a wonderful letter, in which the dialogue, all Burghley's, deserves to belong to a short scene in a Tudor comedy. Still, it was comedy with a flinty edge to it.

It rained for most of Burghley's journey that day, at least till Enfield, which is why he had not thought too much about the groups of ten or twelve men standing together in every town he had passed through in his coach. He had imagined that either they were sheltering from the rain or else they were going to drink 'at some ale house'. But it was dry in Enfield, so he stopped the coach and called to the men there to explain themselves.

They said they were watchmen who were there to apprehend three young men. Burghley asked how they would recognise the men they were looking for. 'Marry, my Lord,' they said, 'by intelligence of their favour.'

'What mean you by that?' Burghley replied.

'Marry,' they said, 'one of the parties hath a hooked nose.'

'And have you no other mark?' Burghley persisted. They said they had not: this was the only description they had of one of the men. The Lord High Treasurer of England was underwhelmed by their performance.

Of course Burghley knew exactly how hard Walsingham had worked to trap Babington and his conspirators: the fine judgements of character, the intricate timing; everything that was balanced and intelligent thrown away by the incompetence of watchmen who only half knew what they were doing. Burghley had been there before and he saw the danger. As soon as he arrived at Theobalds, he wrote to Walsingham and sent his letter by urgent courier: 'And if they be no better instructed,' he wrote of the watchmen of Enfield, 'but to find three persons by one of them having a hooked nose, they may miss thereof, and thus I thought good to advertise you, that the justices that had the charge as I think may use the matter more circumspectly.'[11]

Babington and his associates were captured four days later: the watchmen of Enfield were never given their chance to discover the young man with a hooked nose. On 15 August the conspirators were sent to the Tower. On the 18th Burghley was at Cecil House before he went off to Ely Place for the first of Anthony Babington's nine interrogations. In the next days and months Burghley would get to know Babington's plot inside out.[12]

Anthony Babington told his story over three days to Burghley, Lord Chancellor Bromley and Sir Christopher Hatton. If Burghley had left the operational handling of Phelippes, Gifford and Babington to Walsingham, the time had come for him to master Babington's confession and the evidence against Mary Stuart. He had done this many times over the years, and by now he was very practised at unpicking the stories and conspiracies of the Queen's enemies.

Babington's confession went back as far as 1580, when in Paris he had met Chidiock Tichborne, Thomas Morgan and Mary Stuart's ambassador at the French court, the Bishop of Glasgow. He, like them, soon came to believe in Mary's 'undoubted title' to the English crown. He recounted his meetings with like-minded men. Through John Ballard he became aware of the Catholic League of European powers and the League's 'enterprise' against Elizabeth. Slowly but surely a conspiracy came together.

Even as late as June 1586, Babington explained, this committed band of men had debated what they were about to do: the risks to themselves and their lives, and the effects of foreign invasion on England. Babington said he had resolved to leave the kingdom; and it was at this time, in late June and early July, that he had had two interviews with Walsingham about securing a royal licence to travel. At these meetings Babington said he gave Walsingham an offer of service 'in general terms'. If this is true, it tells us two things. First, Walsingham believed the best way to trap Mary was to allow Babington's conspiracy to flourish. Secondly, Walsingham knew his man.

This was Babington's crisis. In the first week of July he made his choice: after talking again to Ballard, Babington, young as he was, became the leader of the conspiracy. This was still in flux: Babington thought that John Savage's proposal to assassinate the Queen should be rejected; and he listened to a plan to kidnap Elizabeth and to force her to grant toleration in religion. There were ways of freeing the Queen of Scots from captivity. Robert Poley said that the Earl of Leicester could be killed 'by poison and violence', and Babington agreed that there were the men and the means to do this. Poley suggested also the murders of Burghley and Walsingham.

Over three days Babington gave his narrative of the plot: how true it all was only time would tell. Already Burghley and his colleagues were cross-examining him and checking the details. They wanted to know about Babington's correspondence with Mary Stuart. He said that he had sent one letter to her by an unknown boy. In this letter Babington told her about Ballard and the Catholic League; about the six men who would 'undertake somewhat upon the Queen's person'; and about the plans for her own freedom.

Babington had a reply from Mary delivered by a serving man in a blue coat who brought the letter from his master. Babington proceeded to tell Burghley, Bromley and Hatton about the 'tenor' of its contents. 'And so willing me to assure the gentlemen of all that should be required of her for their good,' Babington related, 'she ended, requiring to know the names of the six gentlemen: that she might give her advice thereupon.'

Burghley would have known the instant he said it. Babington the clever conspirator had fallen completely for Walsingham's operation, and it seemed from his interrogations that he still had no idea how his secret correspondence was compromised. The unknown boy was Phelippes's messenger; Phelippes himself was the supposed master of the servant in the blue coat; and the postscript to the letter from Mary which Babington read as coming entirely from the Scottish Queen was Phelippes's forgery.[13]

Burghley, Walsingham and their colleagues knew that they were close to Mary's treason. They acted quickly, first to crack down on known Catholic recusants, and secondly to gather as much evidence against the Scottish Queen as they could. In late August a list was drawn up of thirty houses to be searched in and around London. Three at least were the homes of knights, many others those of gentlemen. It promised to be a mass raid, the full weight of the Elizabethan state brought down hard on plotters and Catholic sympathisers. Walsingham and Phelippes prepared questions for the interrogation of the conspirators.

Councillors were desperate to do as much as they could. Sir Christopher Hatton, who had helped to question Babington, wrote to Burghley: 'Is it not possible that with the eye of Her Majesty's wisdom these most horrible and dangerous practices may be thoroughly looked into? Surely, sir,' he continued, 'if she did there would be no days given from the prevention of them. God hath mightily defended us.'[14]

By early September Burghley was carrying the weight of the investigations. Hatton was at his house in Northamptonshire, sick with a fever and coughing up blood: 'I must commit myself to God and this physician for a while', he wrote to Burghley: he could not return to court. Walsingham, too, was ill, suffering from an inflamed right leg. Even Burghley was struggling with an 'evil foot'. But it was Burghley, still in Westminster, who set to work on Mary's secretaries, Nau and Curll, and who sought the conclusive evidence of her authorship of the all-important gallows letter.[15]

On 3 and 4 September Burghley questioned Nau. He went at him too hard. Nau confessed quickly that Mary's draft of her letter survived in her papers. Walsingham's response to this was 'I would to God these minutes were found.' But it was soon clear that there was no copy in Mary's hand. Nau, terrified, had told Burghley what Burghley wanted to hear, not the truth.[16]

All that Burghley and Walsingham had was Phelippes's copy of the gallows letter. They did not even have the original in Curll's hand, never mind a draft or a copy in Mary's. Babington had destroyed the letter once he had committed it to memory. Phelippes's copy would be difficult to produce as evidence, particularly if someone with sharp eyes realised that the postscript was a later addition, even a forgery. Phelippes's copy of the gallows letter was a remarkable document: in so many ways it was everything, the proof at last of Mary's treasonable conspiracies; but at the same time it was nothing, almost without value as material evidence against the Scottish Queen.

Burghley knew this full well. It may explain why, for all the pain of his foot, he threw himself into the investigation: he had to find out everything. On 4 September he read a paper prepared by Phelippes on the Jesuits in England: their names and short biographies, the gentry houses they stayed in, and so on. The information came from the interrogations of one of Babington's accomplices, Antony Tyrell. From his bed at Cecil House Burghley wrote to Hatton to give him the latest news. Henry Dunne, 'that lay so long in the mire' with Babington in early August, was confessing everything Burghley knew him to be guilty of, but shifting as much of the blame as he could. Two conspirators had been captured in rural Herefordshire. Burghley was still applying pressure to Nau and Curll and was keen for Hatton to bring back to court any of Mary's writings that would 'serve us better and spare our threatenings to them'.[17]

*

Claude Nau and Gilbert Curll were means to an end: that end, simply, was the prosecution of Mary Stuart under the terms of the Act for the Queen's Surety. Mary Stuart was going to be tried for treason. That much was clear by the beginning of September. But Elizabeth was, as ever, petrified of proceeding against her cousin.

So Elizabeth dithered. On her fifty-third birthday, 7 September, she 'flatly refused' to have Mary's case heard in the Tower of London. The next day Burghley thought that Elizabeth would have to settle either on Mary's removal to Fotheringhay in Northamptonshire or to Hertford Castle. But nothing looked likely to be resolved quickly: 'We are occupied with many offers to and fro in words,' Burghley, still sick, wrote to Walsingham, 'but I cannot certify you what shall be determined.'

At least Elizabeth had decided on the composition of the Commission that would hear the evidence against Mary: nine earls who were not privy councillors and eight or nine barons. 'We stick upon parliament,' Burghley added, indicating his desire for Elizabeth to summon Lords and Commons, 'which Her Majesty misliketh to have, but we all persist, to make the burden better borne and the world abroad better satisfied.'[18]

Two days later little had been settled. 'Sir,' he wrote to Walsingham, 'here we are still in long arguments, but no conclusion do last, being as variable as the weather.' Elizabeth was raising more problems than her advisers could answer to her satisfaction. For three days there had been arguments about the place of the trial. Elizabeth had agreed to Hertford Castle; she changed her mind after a day. 'And so even with weariness by talk, Her Majesty hath left all off till a time I know not when.'

Burghley was deeply frustrated. He had planned every detail of any number of options for Mary's removal from Chartley; he had even written to Sir Walter Mildmay about the provisions of beer and coal for Mary's trial. But nothing was settled. Burghley did not know when to summon the earls and barons to hear the case or when to arrange matters for parliament. It was made worse by his lameness. 'And yet I will refuse no labour that my evil legs will afford, for Her Majesty's service most important at this time.'[19]

Elizabeth was jumpy, for reasons we can well understand. Reports were passing to and fro between the Council and the Earl of Sussex of a Spanish fleet gathering off the coast of Brittany 'and of some suspicion to be had of their invasion of England'. It took a week for the reports to be discounted.[20]

At Windsor Elizabeth was getting nervous, too, about the trials of Babington and his accomplices. She was sure that if anything was said in evidence about the Scottish Queen 'whereby it might be thought she should be criminally touched for her life, it might be perilous to Her Majesty's person'. Burghley did not understand why this should be a problem and why the fact of the gallows letter should not be acknowledged in Babington's arraignment. He told Elizabeth on 12 September that he thought Babington's letter was actually mentioned in the indictment. Elizabeth wanted to know 'with all speed' whether this was really so, and Burghley was instructed to write to Hatton about it. She 'had a mind' to have nothing said about the evidence against Mary, 'a thing to me very strange', wrote Burghley. But if Elizabeth wanted to shield the Scottish Queen, she was determined to make an example of Babington. The judge, she insisted, was to refer the traitors' punishments to her and her Council.[21]

Burghley had his instructions from the Queen at ten o'clock in the morning of the 12th. Eleven hours later he was able to thank Hatton for all his work that day in sending Babington's indictment. Elizabeth was indeed unhappy with it: 'She seemeth to mislike that the particularities' of the Scottish Queen's letters were contained in the indictment. There was no time to change it, but Elizabeth very clearly said that there was to be no 'enlargement' of Mary's crime, and indeed no 'sharp speeches to be used in condemnation or reproof' of the Queen of Scots. Elizabeth's only reason for this, she said, was to protect herself from supporters of the Queen of Scots who feared for Mary's life. Burghley must have been shaking his head in wonder at the ways of princes.[22]

There was nothing to do but for Hatton and the Crown's lawyers to obey the Queen. And on the first day of the Babington trial, Tuesday, 13 September, Elizabeth made very sure that Hatton was doing exactly what he was told. In the end she was satisfied; and so, just, was Burghley, who made some allowances for what he must have regretted as a chance missed to advertise Mary Stuart's crimes. 'And so,' he wrote to Hatton that day, 'wishing your ready proceeding without these kind of stops that cannot but engender unconvenient opinions, although Her Majesty seemeth to have no other meaning but a foresight for surety of her own person, which God preserve above all ours.'[23]

At least Burghley was making some progress in the arrangements for Mary's trial. On 15 September he knew that Elizabeth would not have Mary held at Woodstock 'and any other place but Fotheringhay'. Ever in hope, he had already sent instructions to Sir Amias Paulet and Sir Walter Mildmay, 'the one to carry her away, the other to provide for her bestowing'. Perhaps it was on this day that he sent his agent to Fotheringhay to measure the great hall there ready to plan the seating arrangements for the trial. Yet for the optimism of his letters to Paulet and Mildmay, which had certainly gone out by the 15th, experience had taught Burghley that things could change very quickly: 'How long this determination will last I know not, but I have set it onward.'[24]

Burghley was by now supervising the whole business of Mary's trial. With Walsingham away from court still, he was, he wrote to Hatton on 15

September, 'constrained to scribble in haste'. He dealt with the practical arrangements and set out the timetable for the trial. By the 16th he knew for certain that the evidence against Mary would be heard by Elizabeth's nobility at Fotheringhay. The Council would be at Westminster on 27 September and the Scottish Queen at Fotheringhay two days later; Burghley and his colleagues could be there on 5 October.[25]

The proceedings at Fotheringhay would be Burghley's best chance yet to show Mary Stuart for what he believed her to be, a determined and dangerous conspirator against Elizabeth. So he was still hard at work in late September assembling the case. Of course Mary denied everything: 'The Queen of Scots sweareth by her faith . . . that it is not true that she sent any letters to Babington, and if Nau and Curll say so, it is by constraint of the rack.' This protestation of innocence made little difference to Burghley.

He wrote the same day to the Earl of Leicester. There would be a Commission according to the Act for the Queen's Surety, and a parliament to take order with Mary 'according to part of her deserts'. Both he and Leicester had been 'very good motes in the traitors' eyes'. They were to have been killed (of course Burghley had heard this from Babington's own lips in August): 'After us two gone they purposed Her Majesty's death. But God our defender hath graciously prevented their matter.'[26]

Burghley and the Crown's lawyers were working to a very tight deadline in late September. On the 25th John Popham, Elizabeth's Attorney-General, was hard at work on the royal commission which set out the Queen's authority for the trial to go ahead. From his chambers on Chancery Lane at eight in the morning he wrote to Burghley about the important matter of how to address Mary in the document. This was not a trivial matter: every detail had to be correct and the process completely watertight. Popham thought he could borrow wording from the Treasons Bill against Mary which both houses of parliament had passed in 1572 but Elizabeth had failed to assent to; and so Robert Beale was sent off to find it. Popham gave the draft of the royal commission to Burghley: they had to work quickly. Popham made it very clear to Burghley that any mistakes would put the whole trial at risk.[27]

In fact the lawyers worked right down to the wire, and not always to Burghley's satisfaction. As late as 3 October Attorney-General Popham and Solicitor-General Egerton were still unsure about how to draw up the royal commission. Even after a morning conference with the judges who would sit at Fotheringhay, they still did not know what to call Mary. Nothing had been resolved by the 4th, when Burghley grumpily wrote to Walsingham from his bed 'not so well as need requireth'. He had seen the Attorney-General last evening. The royal commission was still peppered with mistakes, with councillors' names left out and Mary's title of 'Queen of Scots' needing something like the formula 'commonly called'. Burghley had instructed that the whole document be written out again. This would take a day to do.[28]

If the law officers seemed jittery, it was entirely understandable. These were completely uncharted waters. After all, Mary Stuart was not a mere subject. She was an anointed queen, ordained by God. She would say she was answerable to no one but her maker. Burghley begged to differ. Mary was a traitor to Elizabeth. She could be tried according to English law. And so Burghley, on the mission of his life, prepared himself for the trial of a monarch.

On 4 October he was working through the papers for the trial, just as the Queen's Serjeant, John Puckering, had done a few days before. He wanted to examine everything and to be as certain of the evidence as he could be. He wanted attested copies of some of Mary's correspondence. Here he knew he had to rely on affirmations by Claude Nau and Gilbert Curll, which were, as he realised only too well, the best he could get by way of evidence. He still hoped for something written by Mary personally: 'If there be any papers to be had of the Scottish Queen's own hand concerning any of these matters they should serve for great purpose.' Here he was to be disappointed.[29]

Mary's trial at Fotheringhay was fast approaching. Once again Elizabeth was getting jumpy. She was not entirely satisfied with the royal commission, in part for the way that Mary's royal title was set out. Walsingham wrote to Burghley with little patience: 'I would to God Her Majesty would be content to refer these things to them that can best judge of them, as other princes do.' Elizabeth imagined also that Mary would want to speak to the commissioners privately, so she set out instructions for Burghley.[30]

The time had come at long last. Elizabeth wrote to Mary from Windsor on 6 October to let her know that she would be tried at Fotheringhay. The Queen was 'given to understand' that Mary had conspired against her in a 'most horrible and unnatural attempt' on her life, for Elizabeth a cause of 'great and inestimable grief'. Mary's case would be heard by Elizabeth's commissioners, and the Queen advised and required Mary 'to give credit and make answer' to them.[31]

Burghley was absolutely sure of what he and his fellow commissioners were going to Fotheringhay to do. He wrote of it to the Earl of Leicester on 1 October, twelve days after Babington and his associates were executed:

... [T]he greatest matter here in hand we find cause so manifest against the party, the party so dangerous to our Queen, our country and that is of most importance to the whole cause of God's Church throughout Christendom, as without a direct and speedy proceeding it had been less danger to have concealed than revealed this great conspiracy. I hope that God which hath given us the light to discover it will also give assistance to punish it. For it was intended not only Her Majesty's person, and yours and mine, but utterly to have overthrown the glory of Christ's Church and to have erected the synagogue of Antichrist. I need not to debate this argument.

Elizabeth had insisted that Babington and the other conspirators should suffer particularly horrible punishments for their treasons. Burghley was just as determined to make Mary Stuart pay for her crimes.[32]

*

The commissioners were at Fotheringhay Castle to hear a morning sermon on Wednesday, 12 October 1586. After this they settled down to plan their business.

Burghley, the longest-serving of Elizabeth's councillors, gave them all Mary's story from the beginning. It was a story he knew very well, that indeed he had helped to fashion: the claim by Mary and her first husband, Francis, to the royal arms of England; Mary's failure to ratify the treaty of Edinburgh; and the terrible conspiracies of the Guises. This was the architecture of his political career. Mary, commonly called the Queen of Scots, was Burghley's business.[33]

The same day Sir Walter Mildmay, Sir Amias Paulet and Edward Barker, a notary, delivered Elizabeth's letters to Mary. Once she had read them she said that 'she was very sorry that the Queen her good sister was so evil informed of her'. She then did what she would try to do for the next few days: talk about her rights and immunities and claim that they had no right to do what they were doing:

I allow not her [Elizabeth's] commissioners my lawful peers, and therefore am not to be dealt withal, but by such as myself (absolute princes) . . . . I never have done anything against her person, by what suggestion soever the Queen may be misinformed, but notwithstanding that I am an absolute prince, and not within the compass [of] your laws, nor to be examined or tried to yield to but only to God, for that I am equal to any prince of Europe.

It was an impressive statement. But Burghley and his fellow commissioners were determined to press on regardless. They knew very well that Mary would try to argue this point. On 13 October a small delegation led by Burghley went to meet Mary privately. Burghley told her that they had every right to hear her case: in 'very large and ample sort' he declared 'that neither her pretended captivity nor her claim of privilege of being born a sovereign prince could exempt her from answering . . . to a crime of that nature'. He added that they could quite properly execute their commission with or without her presence.

Mary was torn: either she could stick to her principles or she could risk, as she said, 'being drawn within the danger of many other laws and statutes of this realm, and namely for matter of religion'. She wanted time to think. She asked to see the names of the commissioners and the 'principal effect' of their commission. She would give her 'determinate answer' that afternoon.[34]

Mary decided to appear before the whole Commission. It was the next day, Friday, 14 October, that her trial really began.

It may be as well to set the scene more fully than I have done so far. The hall in Fotheringhay Castle measured twenty-three yards by seven. The seating of the commissioners and their assistants, and of Mary herself, was very carefully arranged. Burghley himself made a sketch of the hall with all its dimensions and set out where exactly he wanted the benches, chairs and table to be put.[35]

Burghley sat with Lord Chancellor Bromley, ten earls and one viscount, Lord Montague, in strict order of rank and precedence. Facing them on the other side of the room were the barons, all twelve of them. These were the two long sides of the chamber. At one end, between Lord Chancellor Bromley and Lord Abergavenny, ran the wall on which hung Elizabeth's cloth of estate. In this wall, near to the earls' bench, was the door through which Mary was brought.

At the opposite end of the hall, flanked by Viscount Montague and Lord Cheyne, were the officers of Elizabeth's household and privy councillors. At the centre of the chamber was a table, on either side of which sat the various law officers and the two notaries who recorded the Commission's proceedings. The Queen of Scots was placed near to the cloth of estate on the barons' side, next to Lord Abergavenny. Her chair was on a carpet and she was able to rest her feet on a cushion. She sat slightly inclined towards the earls.[36]

So Burghley at last faced his greatest enemy after nearly thirty years of hard politics. They were not as young as they had been. In 1587, just before her execution, Mary was described as being 'of stature tall, of body corpulent, round shouldered, her face fat and broad, double chinned and hazel eyed'. She was now forty-five years old, faded and aged prematurely by her long imprisonment. But she was still subtle, sharp and clever and she used everything she could to defend herself.[37]

Her two great opponents, Burghley and Walsingham, were sixty-six and fifty-four years old respectively. Both men had been in ill health for weeks, but still they had worked ferociously to prepare for their chance to confront the Queen of Scots. Burghley had soaked himself in the evidence: he knew its strengths and its weaknesses. He was passionate about the justice of the case against Mary; and so, though it was Lord Chancellor Bromley, Serjeant Puckering and Serjeant Gawdy who put the main points of the case to the Scottish Queen, it was Burghley who in effect presided over the trial.

When Mary came at last before the commissioners, the Lord Chancellor announced the case against her. The Queen of England understood that the Queen of Scots had contrived her death and had laid 'divers and sundry plots' against her. The purpose of the assembly was to hear and examine whether Mary had compassed and imagined Elizabeth's death: whether, in short, she had committed treason.

When Bromley had finished, the royal commission and the Act for the Queen's Surety were read out loud. At once Mary dug in her heels: 'I protest', she said, 'that this law is insufficient and therefore [I] cannot submit myself to it.' It was Burghley, not Bromley or any of the other lawyers, who spoke to this. He stated the law to be sufficient and said that Mary could be tried in this way. She countered that this law was made against her.

'We have commission to proceed,' said Burghley, 'and if your grace will not hear we will proceed therein.' The facts were clear: Mary could stay or she could be tried in her absence: the choice was hers and it made no difference.

'Then,' said Mary, 'I will hear and answer.'[38]

The law officers began to give the substance of the evidence against her. They began with the confession of Anthony Babington. They alleged that Mary had received a letter from Babington in which he wrote of his plot to kill Elizabeth. What is more, they said, Mary had replied by writing a letter to Babington. Her response, quite simply, was that she did not know Babington. The fact that Babington had written a letter to her, she continued, was no proof of her conspiracy. These matters were, said Mary, 'not to the purpose nor answerable by her'. But immediately Burghley challenged her. They were absolutely to the purpose, he suggested: the Babington plot was entirely relevant to the case against her. All the pieces of evidence presented to her so far 'were necessary inducements to the proof of the matter wherewith she was charged, and they were so woven and interlaced one with another, as without the showing of this the other could not appear'.[39]

So the law officers persisted. Babington's confession, which proved his correspondence with Mary, was read out again. She stuck to her argument about the relevance of this so-called evidence. 'There be some that send me letters and I know them not, nor from whence they come.' Babington's confession was read for a third time. Mary replied: 'I never wrote of any such letter.' More correspondence was read to the Commission, to which she responded acidly: 'If Anthony Babington and all the world say it, they lie of it.' And then, cleverly, she said: 'I would see my own handwriting.' And that, of course, was the point.[40]

Burghley must have known this was coming. As he had said only ten days earlier: 'If there be any papers to be had of the Scottish Queen's own hand concerning any of these matters they should serve for great purpose.' But to

Mary Burghley simply stated that she had indeed received Babington's letter and that she had replied to it. He produced her answer in the form of a letter that had been delivered to Babington by a serving man in a blue coat. What Burghley had in his hand was Thomas Phelippes's copy of the gallows letter. So much rested now on how Mary would respond.

She did not try to expose the fabrication straight away. Both Mary and the commissioners were on decidedly uneven ground, she because she had of course exchanged letters with Babington, and they because of the absence of any evidence in her handwriting. Mary simply wept. Either these were genuine tears of anger or frustration at knowing that the first line of her clever defences had been breached; or they were pure diversion. She did not admit guilt; but she did state the obvious: 'I confess that for the Catholics' delivery from their persecution I have sent and will work. And if I could with my blood save them from destruction I would; and if it might be so I pray you lay it upon me.'

'Madam,' Burghley replied, 'the Queen putteth no man to death for his conscience, but they might own the liberty of their conscience if they live as dutiful subjects; and therefore, Madam, refrain your opinion therein.'

Mary said that she had read it in a book, by which she meant one of the works of the Catholic exiles. 'They that wrote so, Madam,' Burghley said very clearly, 'wrote also that the Queen of England is no queen.'[41]

Mary knew full well that if Burghley possessed a copy of the gallows letter, it was made covertly. She must have imagined that Babington had destroyed the original, as she had instructed; probably she knew, too, that there was no draft of it in her papers. And if there was a secret copy of her letter, the man who must have had it made was Secretary Walsingham. She now told Walsingham that he had been her great enemy and had worked with certain persons against her. 'But Master Walsingham,' she said, 'I think you are an honest man. And I pray you in word of an honest man whether you have been so or no.'

Walsingham stood up from his seat at the opposite end of the chamber to Mary and walked towards the lawyers' table. 'Madam,' he said, 'I stand charged by you to have practised something against you. I call God and all the world to witness I have not done anything as a private man unworthy of an honest man; nor as a public man unworthy of my calling. I protest before God that as a man careful of my mistress's safety I have been curious*.'[42]

It was a fabulously elusive answer. Mary wept again and protested that she would not make a shipwreck of her soul in conspiring against her good sister Elizabeth.

The Commission broke for lunch at one o'clock. Burghley told Mary that she had sat for too long and that he was sure that some of the noblemen there

* Anxious, concerned, solicitous.

were not used to fasting for this length of time. She agreed; but she made a point of saying that she would break 'not for herself, but for the nobility's ease'.[43]

When they reconvened at three o'clock Serjeant Puckering rehearsed the morning's proceedings. He went back to the gallows letter, which was read out loud. In response Mary said she wanted one of two things: either a copy of the letter or legal counsel. Burghley told her that she knew whether or not she had written the letter, so to have a copy of it, or to have the help of lawyers, served no purpose. To this Mary said that the laws of England were strange 'that would neither permit her counsel, witness nor copy of that she was accused of', and she prayed to God that if there were such laws to protect her from them.[44]

Mary still knew that the weakness of the case against her was that there was no evidence actually in her handwriting. Instead the Commission had to present the sworn statements of Claude Nau and Gilbert Curll, which proved, they said, that she did write to Babington. Once again Mary disputed that she had had anything to do with the conspiracy.

At this point in the proceedings there was an electric exchange between Mary and Burghley about money she had given to two conspirators against Elizabeth, Thomas Morgan and William Parry. The Queen of Scots said again that she did not know Anthony Babington. 'No, Madam,' said Burghley, appearing to agree with her: 'I will tell you whom you know: Morgan that hired Parry to kill the Queen. And after you knew it, you gave him a pension. You give pensions, Madam, to murderers.'[45]

These few words capture so much: Mary's injured innocence and Burghley's disciplined anger; above all, the deadly seriousness of the proceedings and the sense in which the Commission was there to determine whether or not Mary Stuart should live.

It had been a remarkable day. On the surface the proceedings were calm and polite. All the social niceties had been observed. The lawyers had called Mary 'madam' and 'your grace' and she had called them 'my lords'. But under the surface there was the hostility of twenty-seven years. Mary, lying to protect herself, knew that everything was stacked against her. This was a trial at which there were no witnesses; in which she was not allowed legal counsel; and for which much of the evidence came from secret sources which could not be disclosed.

That same day, at Windsor, Secretary Davison wrote to Sir Francis Walsingham. Elizabeth ordered the commissioners to come to her royal presence to make a report of what they had done at Fotheringhay. Nothing could happen till they had acquainted the Queen with their 'reasons and opinions' on the matter of the Queen of Scots. It is likely that by the end of

Friday Burghley had read the 'few hasty and scribbled lines' written hours before by Davison: there was to be a stay of the sentence. But there was nothing in these letters to say that the Commission could not continue to hear the evidence against Mary.[46]

The Queen of Scots came before the Commission again on the morning of Saturday, 15 October. After the passionate exchanges of Friday, her intention was to hear the case against her in dignified silence. She declared that 'she would not answer to anything that should be objected'. She ascended to the moral high ground. When Mary came into the chamber, she made a statement. She said she had been 'very hardly dealt with'. She had always kept her word. Promises made to her when she first arrived in England had not been kept, and here she appealed to the consciences of Burghley, the Earl of Shrewsbury and others. Since then she had been encouraged to go out hunting while her chests had been rifled for papers; her servants had been arrested. She had been told that the purpose of the Commission was to examine her touching the conspiracy against her dear sister Elizabeth. But now she realised that it was 'a plot laid long and advisedly premeditated of'. At this point she mentioned Burghley's name.[47]

It was a very controlled performance. Mary made a distinction between any conspiracy against Elizabeth and her own legitimate efforts to escape from captivity. She compared herself to women of the Old Testament. She would never be, she said, 'a Judith to kill Holofernes for the delivery of her people, but an Esther to pray for them'. She was 'certainly persuaded' that the Commission 'was a matter to entangle her and to make a record against her'. Therefore she would not answer any further. She finished by making a clever reference to Elizabeth's time in the Tower of London in the 1550s: Elizabeth had not been 'dealt withal when she was holden suspected of Wyatt's conspiracy'.[48]

All of this was very well done. The tone of dignified injury was just right; the arguments were effective. It was everything we should expect of a subtle and clever politician like Mary. But Burghley was having none of it. When the Queen of Scots ended by saying that she was 'altogether unexperimented in the laws', and so would consider herself more 'indifferently [impartially, without bias or prejudice] dealt withal' if her lawyers could speak for her, Burghley simply said that the Commission had been called to hear her matter fully. If she would not answer then she could go and leave them to their business. The choice was hers: either she could sit still and listen or go back to her chamber to take her ease. Pointedly she replied that she would not sit still, but that they should proceed at their pleasure.

Mary stayed to hear Serjeant Puckering deliver what remained of the case: that she had pretended title to Elizabeth's crown since the making of the Act for the Queen's Surety; and that this fact was proved by her correspondence. Mary, unable to stay silent, said this was false. She spoke privately to Burghley. Then she left the hall. As she did so, she turned to the law officers and said to them: 'God bless me and my cause from your laws.' Then she called across the room to Sir Christopher Hatton and Sir Francis Walsingham and asked Hatton to deliver her petition to the Queen.[49]

And with that she was gone: Mary Stuart's trial at Fotheringhay Castle was over.

18

To Kill a Queen

Who had won at Fotheringhay? Was it Mary Stuart, who had played the part of the wronged queen to perfection? Or was it the Commission, who with care and determination had set out to Mary the evidence of her treason? On Saturday, 15 October 1586 the answers to these questions were not at all obvious.

Sir Francis Walsingham was absolutely clear in his own mind. The Scottish Queen was, he wrote to the Earl of Leicester, 'charged not only to have been privy and assenting to the murder of Her Majesty but also an encourager of those that should have been executioners'. The sworn evidence of her secretaries was beyond doubt: 'she had no other defence but a plain denial'. It was only Elizabeth's 'secret countermand' that had prevented the Commission from passing sentence. Walsingham's frustration showed in his letter: God, he told Leicester, was punishing them for their sins.[1]

As Walsingham well knew on 15 October, the Commission was adjourned for ten days. Burghley was at Burghley House the next day wrestling with the technical problems of the adjournment: wrestling, that is, with Elizabeth's delay. Nothing could be done, he thought, before the 25th. But he hoped that when the Commission did meet it could transact its business in no more than two days. The matter that really had to be sorted out was Mary's allegation 'that we came thither with a prejudgement. And that as she said it was so reported commonly.'[2]

Burghley was at Royston on the 19th and at Theobalds the day after that. All the way back to Westminster he read what Elizabeth had to say about the proceedings at Fotheringhay as well as the reports of conversations between the Queen of Scots and her custodian, Sir Amias Paulet. 'If there be any matter that hath passed from that Queen worth knowledge,' he wrote to Walsingham, 'I pray you advertise me.'[3]

The commissioners met as planned on Tuesday, 25 October in the Star Chamber in Westminster Palace. Only the Earl of Shrewsbury and the Earl of Warwick, both of them sick, were absent. The Commission interviewed

Claude Nau and Gilbert Curll, whose sworn testimony had helped to prove Mary's guilt at Fotheringhay. All the papers previously affirmed to be accurate by the two secretaries were shown to them again. Both men 'did then eftsoons voluntarily acknowledge and affirm all that to be true which they had before so confessed and subscribed'. They confirmed that they did this without any threat or constraint. Curll went even further, saying that Babington's letter to Mary and the draft of her reply to him were both burned by her command-ment. Curll explained to the Commission that after he had deciphered Babington's letters and read them to Mary he had 'admonished her of the danger of those actions, and persuaded her not to deal therein, nor to make any answer thereunto'. She had ignored him.[4]

And so at last Mary's guilt was clear, and the Commission pronounced sentence on her. 'By their joint assent and consent, they do pronounce and deliver their sentence and judgement . . . divers matters have been compassed and imagined within the realm of England, by Anthony Babington and others . . . with the privity of the said Mary, pretending title to the crown of this realm of England, tending to the hurt, death and destruction of the royal person of our said Lady the Queen.'

All that was left was for the sentence of execution to be carried out. But before that could be done, Burghley and his colleagues had to convince Elizabeth that Mary should die.[5]

*

From the start Burghley had known that there would have to be a parliament. It was part of his meticulous planning for Mary's prosecution under the Act for the Queen's Surety. As early as 8 September he had written that 'the judgement of the noblemen', when it was arrived at, 'shall be affirmed by parliament'. For Burghley this confirmation of the sentence against the Scottish Queen was absolutely essential. The realm had to speak as one.[6]

From early November he was engaged in tactical warfare with Elizabeth over Mary's future. If Elizabeth by now knew that the Scottish Queen should die, which is what she said, she believed that Mary should be quietly killed by someone acting on the oath of the Instrument of Association. Burghley believed, by contrast, in a judicial process that could be held up to Europe as fair dealing. He wanted to be seen to do the right thing. It had to be a judicial killing, not a backroom assassination. Neither Queen nor Lord Treasurer was willing to give way. It was a tussle which led both to Mary's death and to the near breakdown of Burghley's relationship with Elizabeth.

Parliament was carefully choreographed by Burghley and his colleagues. On Thursday, 3 November Sir Christopher Hatton delivered a vicious attack on

Mary Stuart in the House of Commons. 'The manner of the Queen of Scots' life', he said, 'and her practices from the beginning [are] most filthy and detestable; if you look well into them you shall well find that her ambitious mind, grounded in papistry, hath still thirsted after this crown of England, and our overthrow.' He recounted the plots and conspiracies of late years. When he sat down, Sir Walter Mildmay and Sir Ralph Sadler stood in turn to support him. So once again parliament was going to be used against Mary, and from the beginning Elizabeth's privy councillors marshalled what would be in the end the last and fatal attack.[7]

The next day committees of the Lords and Commons were appointed, to be chaired by the Speaker of the Lower House, John Puckering. On the 5th, a Saturday, Lord Chancellor Bromley gave an account to the Lords of Mary Stuart's 'obdurate' malice towards Elizabeth and explained the work of the Commission. Over the weekend Burghley did two things. First he, Secretary Walsingham and Secretary Davison discreetly arranged for Claude Nau to be able to walk freely in Walsingham's garden, a mark that Nau had done his job. The second thing was much more important and it was deathly secret, even from the Queen: Burghley went to work on a petition to move Elizabeth to execute Mary.[8]

The first draft of the petition was written by Speaker Puckering, and it did the job well enough. But Burghley was leaving nothing to chance, so he went through Puckering's text word by word. He did everything he could to make the case against Mary as watertight as possible. He made it crystal clear that the Scottish Queen was personally responsible for the plots against Elizabeth's life. He emphasised how carefully the commissioners had weighed the evidence against Mary in her own presence. And he struck out a long reference to the Association that could have given Elizabeth just the excuse she needed to remind her subjects of their sworn duty to destroy the Queen of Scots. Burghley wanted Mary to die, not by a piece of private enterprise, but on Elizabeth's direct orders.[9]

Puckering's joint committee met to consider the petition on Monday, 7 November. Quickly, with the help of Thomas Egerton, the Solicitor-General, they had a text Burghley was happy to present to Elizabeth. The next day the Lords heard the Commission's sentence against Mary. They considered the evidence put before the Commission and considered 'all the process and proceeding' at Fotheringhay and in Star Chamber. The Lords came to their conclusion with 'one assent': the Commission's sentence and judgment was 'honourable, just and lawful'. The same careful procedure was followed in the House of Commons. On 9 November Lords and Commons agreed to 'join together in most humble and instant petition' to Elizabeth to proclaim the sentence against Mary publicly 'and thereupon to give direction for further speedy proceeding against the said Scottish Queen'.[10]

It may have been that the joint committee of parliament considered Burghley's corrected text of the petition in its meeting at three o'clock on the afternoon of the 9th. Certainly it was finished by the next day when it was read to the Commons. MPs were moved 'with one full consent . . . [to] resolve and conclude that the ground and matter of the said petition was in all things most just and true'. They believed the dangers facing Queen and realm to be so great that they wanted to present the petition to Elizabeth as soon as they could. Elizabeth agreed, sending her message through Vice-Chamberlain Hatton. Together Hatton and Burghley carefully chose the day of the presentation.[11]

Naturally there were some wrinkles still to iron out. The first was whether the archbishops and bishops should come with the temporal Lords to present the petition. Burghley felt there was no reason why they should not be there – he may have believed that they would lend moral weight to the petition – but he thought the choice should be Elizabeth's.

He was less flexible, however, on a much more important point. The Queen had seen an advance text of the petition and she was not keen on it: in particular she wondered why there was no reference to the oath of Association. Burghley, of course, had scrubbed out the reference: he knew that for Elizabeth it could be a kind of escape clause, and he had no intention of altering the petition. So he made excuses: 'Her Majesty's meaning cannot be performed', he wrote to Secretary Davison, for the Lords had temporarily adjourned. Burghley thought 'Her Majesty's meaning' could be supplied instead by a speech from Speaker Puckering. Sir Christopher Hatton agreed. Burghley did not mind a spoken reference to the Association, but he would not allow anything to be set down on paper.[12]

On Saturday, 12 November the great day arrived. Lords and Commons went to meet the Queen at Richmond. John Puckering delivered a passionate speech against Mary. To spare her, he said, would be to give courage to Elizabeth's enemies and to drive loyal subjects to despair. The cause was Queen, religion and realm. If Elizabeth failed to act, there could be no doubt that God's judgment on her would be a terrible one: princes who spared the wicked had been deprived of their kingdoms. Then the petition, so carefully crafted by Burghley, was read out.[13]

Elizabeth's reply to Puckering's speech and parliament's petition was beautifully controlled: passionate in its own way, but careful, reflective, even wistful. 'I have had good experience and trial of this world', she said. 'I know what it is to be a subject, what to be a sovereign, what to have good neighbours, and sometime meet evil willers. I have found treason in trust.' She accepted the fact of Mary's crimes. But she told the Lords and MPs packed into the royal

Presence Chamber that she had to be exceptionally careful. '[W]e princes I tell you are set on stages, in the sight and view of all the world. . . . It behoveth us therefore to be careful that our proceedings be just and honourable.' So it was that in the Act for the Queen's Surety parliament 'had laid an hard hand on me that I must give direction for her [Mary's] death, which cannot be but most grievous and an irksome burden to me'. She reminded them, pointedly, of the Association and of the oaths they had sworn. But in the end she decided to wait for the time being and to pray for God's guidance. Sir Thomas Bromley was commanded to tell the House of Lords that Elizabeth took great comfort from the love of her subjects but was 'greatly grieved that she should be occasioned for the safety of herself and her realm to use so severe and sharp a course contrary to her own disposition and nature'.[14]

Burghley was sick, forced on 16 November to keep to his chamber as a 'lame fool'. Still, he hoped to be up and about 'to celebrate the blessed day' of the 17th, the twenty-eighth anniversary of Elizabeth's accession. That day, and those following, the matter of Mary rumbled on. The Earl of Shrewsbury, like Burghley sick and immobile, wrote to thank him for his account of 'the proceeding of the foul matters of the Scots Queen'. Shrewsbury prayed that God would inspire the Queen to act for her own safety, 'which in my counsel cannot be without speedy execution'. Debates continued in the House of Lords along much the same lines: there was no alternative but to publish the sentence against Mary.[15]

Elizabeth was still stalling. On 24 November she once again met a delegation of Lords and Commons. She spoke less concessively than she had done nearly a fortnight before, knowing that it would be hard for her to say the right thing: 'I have strived more this day than ever in my life whether I should speak or use silence. If I speak and not complain I shall dissemble. If I hold my peace your labour taken were full vain.' She was worried about her reputation abroad and defended herself against any charge of tyranny and cruelty.

And yet, as ever, she had a good practical reason for pausing before giving sentence on Mary. 'I am not so void of judgement as not to see mine own peril,' she said, 'nor yet so ignorant as not to know it were in nature a foolish course to cherish a sword to cut mine own throat.' She had of course recognised the dreadful consequences of signing away Mary's life. Catholics would have little compunction in killing her. But she also realised the terrible precedent that would be set by the judicial killing of an anointed monarch by act of parliament, by proclamation, and by royal letters patent. She deliberately chose not to give plain answer: 'Your judgement I condemn not, neither do I mislike your reasons, but pray you to accept my thankfulness, excuse my doubtfulness, and take in good part my answer answerless.'[16]

If Elizabeth was still determined to resist the clever mechanisms of

Burghley's trap for Mary, very probably in the hope that a private subject would in the meantime quietly kill the Queen of Scots, then Burghley was just as determined to proceed to his objective. Certainly everything hung in the balance in the last week of November. On the evening of the 28th Burghley and Lord Chancellor Bromley received word from the court that the Queen wanted parliament to be prorogued. Burghley grumpily complained about short notice and the time it had taken the courier to bring him the letter. His real worry was that parliament would end without any resolution being taken by the Queen on Mary.[17]

But in the end an understanding was reached: the circle was squared. Burghley would have his proclamation and Elizabeth would be able to tell the world of the terrible predicament she was in. In the closed world of Whitehall politics the Commission met again in the Star Chamber on 29 November to 'subscribe the sentence' against Mary. Burghley already had the text of the all-important proclamation, which he sent the next day to Secretary Davison at Richmond. Burghley was at Cecil House, and with him that afternoon were Sir Thomas Bromley, Sir Christopher Hatton and Sir Walter Mildmay. They knew that Elizabeth's enemies would carefully examine every sentence of the proclamation. 'We all that are here', Burghley wrote to Davison, 'do think it will ask some time, to alter the proclamation as your letter doth make mention. For that will require a declaration of the fact by the Scottish Queen, and of Her Majesty's grief for the same etc.'[18]

Doubtless Elizabeth insisted on this public declaration of royal grief. And she went one step further in allowing her two speeches of 12 and 24 November to be published. In fact she carefully edited them herself, and they were introduced by a fictitious letter from young Robert Cecil to the Earl of Leicester, just home from the Low Countries, as an account of the Queen's gracious dealings with parliament. Of course they presented Elizabeth in the best possible light, and she was praised to the skies by twenty-three-year-old Robert. It was certainly no accident that the Queen's reference to the oath of Association was left intact.[19]

The pieces were almost in place. *The Copie of a Letter* cast Elizabeth as the thoughtful and sympathetic queen reluctantly forced by circumstance to do a terrible thing. For Burghley the pamphlet was simply a useful way to outrage public opinion with Mary Stuart's crimes. Yet he was still nervous, even if the proclamation of the sentence was effectively in the bag. In the hours before parliament was prorogued, Burghley wanted Lords and MPs to go away with 'some demonstration to proceed from Her Majesty' on Mary's fate. If there was not, he wrote, 'the realm may call this a vain parliament or otherwise nickname it a parliament of words'. The sentence against Mary was still 'dumb': 'It were full time it should also speak.'[20]

Burghley travelled to Richmond Palace before dawn on 1 December. He need not have hurried: the Queen did not rise out of her bed till ten o'clock. But eventually he was able 'to please her fully to all respects' with the vitally important proclamation, and this in the presence of the Earl of Leicester and Secretary Davison. Nevertheless, the Queen's late rising had thrown Burghley's plan off track. There was no time that day for Elizabeth to sign the document. Burghley was disappointed, for he wanted the proclamation to be read the following day. The Queen, however, did not: she would not have it published before Saturday, the 3rd. It was released on Sunday.[21]

At ten o'clock on the morning of Tuesday, 6 December the proclamation of Mary's sentence was read in the presence of the Lord Mayor of London and 'divers earls and barons, the aldermen in their scarlet gowns', other gentlemen and 'fourscore of the most grave and worshipfulest citizens in coats of velvet and chains of gold, all on horseback'. The proclamation was delivered at the Cheapside Cross, where Fleet Street met Chancery Lane; at the corner of Leadenhall; and at St Magnus near London Bridge. While the document was being read, noblemen, 'gentlemen of good account', local sheriffs and justices of the peace conducted 'great solemnities' at Whitehall Palace, near Temple Bar and in Holborn. It was quite a show.[22]

The following facts were made public by the proclamation. The Commission at Fotheringhay had investigated the charge that Mary had acted contrary to the clauses of the Act for the Queen's Surety. The commissioners had demonstrated Mary's complicity in the plot of Anthony Babington. The Commission's judgment had been endorsed by parliament. Elizabeth was 'greatly and deeply grieved' to think that these unnatural and monstrous acts had been 'either devised or willingly assented unto' by Mary, 'her being a princess born, and of our sex and blood and one whose life and honour we had many times before saved and preserved'. These were the words that Burghley and his colleagues had known were so important: as he had put it, 'Her Majesty's grief for the same etc.' Mary's crimes were now public. There was no turning back.[23]

Burghley had spent more than a week carefully preparing the proclamation. Now he applied himself to the production of a document of even more weight and importance. Within six days of the public proclamation of her guilt Mary's death warrant was ready. The words Burghley set down on paper, nearly eight hundred of them, were the most significant so far of his public career.

Mary's death warrant was at once a legal document which had to be absolutely watertight and an affirmation of the rightness of Elizabeth's case against her cousin. It confirmed the sentence given against Mary by the Commission. Burghley made a point of emphasising the urgency of parliament's petition for swift justice against a woman who was an 'undoubted danger' to Elizabeth and the 'public state of this realm', as well as to 'the cause of the Gospel and the true religion of Christ'.

Burghley explained that Elizabeth was now 'overcome with the evident weight' of wise counsel on Mary Stuart. She had at last 'condescended to suffer justice to take place'. The earls to whom the warrant was addressed in the Queen's name – Kent, Derby, Cumberland and Pembroke – were commanded to go to Fotheringhay and 'cause execution to be done upon her person' in the presence of Sir Amias Paulet, Mary's custodian. The warrant, 'these letters patent sealed with our Great Seal of England', was sufficient authority to end the life of the Scottish Queen.[24]

When Burghley had finished writing the warrant, he drafted a covering letter for Sir Amias Paulet. With Elizabeth's knowledge, he gave the death warrant to Secretary Davison. Davison would keep the document till his royal mistress called for it. It was worthless without Elizabeth's sign manual and the Great Seal of England.

Elizabeth did nothing for six weeks.[25]

*

In early 1587 it was clear to everyone except the Queen that Mary had to die for the safety of Elizabeth's kingdom. Burghley and his colleagues at last saw their chance and took it. With care, secrecy and precision Burghley engineered the Scottish Queen's death. What followed was a terrible fracture in Burghley's relationship with Elizabeth. This was a defining moment in his political career.

The great problem is evidence. The truth about Mary's execution, too painful to be faced properly at the time, was buried away from prying eyes. We have, for example, Elizabeth's story, told by her Attorney-General a few weeks after Mary's death. We have also the account given by William Davison, who in the end went to the Tower of London for his part in the execution of the Scottish Queen. Elizabeth's and Davison's accounts, as we might expect, do not agree with each other. And there are other claims, counter-claims and stories written by those who in the weeks after the execution struggled to come to terms with what they had done.[26]

It is 1553 all over again: bias, perception, memory and distortion affect everything. The critical reader takes nothing in the sources at face value. But there are two facts that are incontrovertibly true. The first is that Mary Stuart's head was removed from her body by the executioner's axe. The second is that Lord Burghley played a leading role in the judicial killing of an anointed monarch.

Elizabeth signed her cousin's death warrant on Wednesday, 1 February 1587. She made the decision to do this herself. On Candlemas eve, she commanded Lord Howard of Effingham to bring Davison, with the warrant, to her presence. She applied her sign manual, 'Elizabeth R', to Burghley's document. Then she instructed Davison to take it to the Lord Chancellor, Sir Thomas Bromley, and to Sir Francis Walsingham, ill and away from court, 'to whom', she added with bitter gallows humour, 'it would be a great cordial to heal him of his sickness'.[27]

Davison thought he understood his instructions very clearly. He was to take the signed warrant to Bromley to have the Great Seal of England applied to it. Then he was to send it to the commissioners on Mary's case. Davison remembered that Elizabeth had told him not to trouble her any more with the matter till the Scottish Queen was dead, 'she for her part having (as she said) performed all that in law or reason could be required of her'. The thing was done. Or was it?[28]

Secretary Davison's version of events is clear enough. Elizabeth signed the warrant on 1 February. It was sealed that day. If Davison disobeyed the Queen, it was only to give her time to think about what she had done. He held on to the warrant overnight and took it to Elizabeth again on the 2nd. She was, he remembered, still 'resolved to proceed therein according to her former directions'. But by 2 February it was clear to Davison that Elizabeth was wobbling, 'yet desirous to carry the matter so as she might throw the burthen from herself'. Davison was 'absolutely resolved to quit his hands' of the death warrant as quickly as he could.[29]

Elizabeth's story was quite different from Davison's. She said that she had indeed signed Mary's death warrant on 1 February and commanded Davison to take it to the Lord Chancellor to be sealed with the Great Seal. But she had changed her mind by the next day, and so she sent a gentleman of her Privy Chamber, William Killigrew, to find Davison. If Davison had not yet been to see Lord Chancellor Bromley, then Killigrew was to stop Davison's going 'till he knew Her Majesty's further meaning'. Killigrew could not find Davison. When the Secretary came into Elizabeth's presence he told her that the warrant had already been sealed. Her reply to this was 'What needed so much haste?'

The official interpretation of what Elizabeth meant by this question was either that she did not want the warrant to be sealed or that it should not have been sealed so quickly. If Davison's account is right, then Elizabeth had done a complete about-turn and as early as 2 February was blaming Davison for preventing it from being known. But Davison's greatest mistake in those two days was to leak the news of the fact that Elizabeth had signed Mary's death warrant. As well as going to Bromley and Walsingham, Davison also told Sir Christopher Hatton, and Hatton in turn told Burghley. Now there was no time to lose: by 2 February Burghley, Hatton and

Walsingham had decided to send the death warrant, signed and sealed, to Fotheringhay.

Why did Burghley act so quickly? He was, naturally, desperate to see Mary die: this was the moment he had been waiting for for months. But going on behind the scenes was an even murkier game. A formal execution was only one way to get rid of Mary Stuart. From the start, Elizabeth had preferred the notion of a secret killing under the terms of the Instrument of Association. And it was probably no surprise to Burghley that at some time on 1 February, the very day she signed Mary's death warrant, Elizabeth had instructed Davison and Walsingham to write to Sir Amias Paulet and Sir Dru Drury at Fotheringhay suggesting that very thing. Her Majesty, wrote her secretaries, was indisposed to shed blood. Paulet and Drury could save her the trouble; indeed in the light of the Scottish Queen's obvious guilt the oath of Association actually obliged them to take Mary's life. It was a great disappointment to Elizabeth that they had not already acted. Walsingham and Davison explained that they had written the letter after hearing a speech 'lately uttered by Her Majesty'. They made no mention of Mary's death warrant.[30]

So Burghley had no time to lose. More than this, some of his colleagues appeared to agree with Elizabeth. Robert Beale, who was to play such a big part in what happened over the next few days, explained the notion: 'Then others should have smarted, as Sir Amias.' The sentiment, according to Beale, was the Earl of Leicester's. Archbishop Whitgift, Walsingham, Davison, Paulet and Drury opposed the plan to do away with Mary on Paulet's watch. Paulet in particular was appalled. When he received the Secretaries' letter at Fotheringhay at five o'clock on the afternoon of the 2nd he wrote back an hour later: 'God forbid that I should make so foul a shipwreck of conscience, or leave so great a blot to my poor posterity, to shed blood without law or warrant.'[31]

All of this may help to explain why Burghley, Hatton, Walsingham and Davison acted together as swiftly and efficiently as they did. For two days they ran the show: they planned every detail. They had the warrant at last, and Mary could be executed by justice; it had to be put into action as quickly as possible. They arranged everything, even their choice of courier to take the warrant to Fotheringhay.

It was Burghley into whose hands Davison delivered the death warrant. Davison said he did this late in the day on 2 February once he had heard from Elizabeth her final resolution that Mary should die: quite whether she meant by the warrant or by assassination is unclear. We can imagine that it was an agreeable exchange for both men: for Davison because he could at last get rid of the responsibility of keeping the warrant; and for Burghley because this was the document he had been desperate for Elizabeth to sign for weeks. The exchange took place in Burghley's chamber in the presence of Hatton. Davison said later that the warrant never left Burghley's possession till it was sent off to Fotheringhay.[32]

At home on Seething Lane Walsingham had already begun to set out how everything was going to happen, from the delivery of the death warrant to the Earl of Kent, to the matter of where Mary's body would be buried after her execution. He sent the paper to Burghley at Greenwich.

Burghley read Walsingham's paper very carefully on 2 February. At last he knew that Mary was going to die. He even wrote the last words she would ever hear, a crib for the earls of Kent and Shrewsbury. They had a judicial finality to them: 'To express her many attempts both for destruction of the Queen's person, and the invasion of this realm . . . she is justly condemned to die, the whole realm hath often time vehemently required that justice might be done which Her Majesty cannot longer delay.'[33]

That same Thursday, probably in the evening, Burghley, Hatton and Davison chose Robert Beale to carry the warrant to Fotheringhay. Beale was in London, having not long recovered from a serious illness. He was a good choice: dependable, competent and able, trusted by all. He was also Walsingham's brother-in-law. Davison was sent off to tell Walsingham what they had decided. Sir Francis agreed.[34]

At eleven o'clock that Thursday night, Beale, asleep in bed, received word from Davison that he should be at Walsingham's house the next morning. Beale was there at nine o'clock on Friday, 3 February to meet Walsingham and Davison. He was called in by Sir Francis, who showed him the death warrant. This was the authentic document bearing the Great Seal with Elizabeth's sign manual at the top. Probably Davison had brought it to Walsingham's house that morning from Greenwich; he must have borrowed it from Burghley. The idea, we have to suppose, was to make a powerful impression on Beale, to impress upon him the gravity of his mission.

At Seething Lane Walsingham told Beale that 'Her Majesty was contented' the warrant 'should forthwith be dispatched'. He explained to Beale that the Privy Council had specially chosen him to 'carry it down' and that their pleasure was for him to go with Secretary Davison to Greenwich 'there to attend their lordships' further pleasure'.[35]

Sir Francis explained to Beale that he would send one of his servants, George Digby, to go with the hangman to Fotheringhay. They would travel separately from Beale, going by way of Baldock in Hertfordshire to Sir Walter Mildmay's house close to Fotheringhay. Walsingham wrote to Sir Amias Paulet: 'I send down the executioner by a trusty servant of mine who will be at Fotheringhay upon Sunday at night.' He was to travel secretly, posing as a serving man; he would carry his axe in a trunk. 'There is great care taken to have the matter pass in secrecy,' he added, 'but there are so many councillors made acquainted withal, as I hold it a matter impossible.' In fact everything ran like clockwork.[36]

Davison and Beale went off to Greenwich where, after a time, they were taken into Burghley's inner chamber. By now Burghley had squared the whole Council: they knew Mary could die by royal authority. In the room were the Earl of Derby, the Earl of Leicester, Lord Howard of Effingham, Lord Cobham, Lord Hunsdon, Sir Francis Knollys, Sir Christopher Hatton and John Wolley: a formidable array of councillors indeed. Burghley spoke for them all. He told Beale that the carrying of the warrant to Fotheringhay required both speed and secrecy, for if news of what was happening got out the Queen's life would be in great danger. Burghley handed the death warrant to Beale. Beale, he said, would also carry letters to the Earl of Kent, the Earl of Shrewsbury and Sir Amias Paulet. The councillors told Beale to go first to the Earl of Kent and show him the warrant; Kent would inform Shrewsbury; and finally Beale would take the warrant to Sir Amias.[37]

The letters were prepared for Beale to carry. In them Burghley and his colleagues set out the official line: the Queen now directed her commission 'for the special service, tending to the safety of her royal person and universal quietness of her whole realm'. The privy councillors impressed upon Kent, Shrewsbury and Paulet the need to keep all their proceedings secret. Once the letters were ready, each councillor in Burghley's chamber signed them.[38]

The next day, Saturday, 4 February, Beale was in Bedfordshire at the Earl of Kent's house. He was at Fotheringhay with Paulet and Drury on Sunday; from them he heard about the proposal to kill Mary secretly. Paulet was unable to ride, so on Monday, the 6th, Drury and Beale set off to see the Earl of Shrewsbury. The same day Paulet, Drury and Beale wrote a letter to one of the deputy lieutenants of Northamptonshire, who was to be at Fotheringhay Castle by eight o'clock on the morning of Wednesday, 8 February to 'understand Her Majesty's further pleasure'. It was now clear that this was the day on which the Scottish Queen would die. Mary heard the news of her approaching execution from Lord Buckhurst and Beale together either on Monday or Tuesday. Soon after this Paulet and Drury pulled down her cloth of estate, a symbolic act indeed. The earls of Kent and Shrewsbury arrived at Fotheringhay on the 7th. Within twenty-four hours Mary Stuart was dead.[39]

While all this was going on at Fotheringhay, Burghley calmly considered some matters of security. The news of Mary's execution would be out soon enough: it was time to detain subversives. He began to set out plans for the mass arrest of Catholic recusants, their detention in houses across six counties in the south and south-east of England, and their examination by special teams of royal commissioners. He looked also to the kingdom's sea defences and to the military musters in each county. He knew that an invasion of England could not be long in coming.[40]

The calmness with which Burghley set out the provisions for the defence of the realm was utterly deceptive. A storm was about to break such as he, or any of his colleagues, had never seen before. For the next few weeks even experienced Burghley was thrown by the Queen's fury. Their relationship came as close as it ever did to breaking down.

Burghley told Elizabeth of Mary's execution on the evening of Thursday, 9 February. Even so he may not have volunteered the intelligence. This was why Elizabeth was so angry with him: in audiences following the secret dispatch of the death warrant he had said nothing at all about Mary: 'at such time as I was called to her [Elizabeth's] presence for matters of the Low Countries', he explained later, 'myself not minding nor giving any occasion by speech of the matter of the Scots Queen until Her Majesty did charge me therewith'. For the one man who for twenty-eight years had spoken his mind bluntly, whether Elizabeth liked it or not, this was a curious reticence.[41]

When she did find out, Elizabeth exploded with rage. But did she really believe that Davison would hold back from telling the Council? Or that councillors who had been pressing her for weeks to sign Mary's death warrant would not have some way of finding out that she had at last done so? Maybe she did, or maybe she did not. Perhaps Davison's indiscretion in telling Hatton of the signed warrant was just the excuse she needed. The thing was done, but it was not her fault; she had countermanded her orders of 1 February; she had chastised Davison for acting so quickly. She had been disobeyed, sidestepped, betrayed. Her conscience was clear.

Still, Elizabeth lashed out. Her first thought, according to Robert Beale, was to punish Burghley. She must have been livid even to have contemplated such a spectacular punishment: 'But Her Majesty thought that to commit him to the Tower would kill him.' Instead he was to be denied access to the Queen's presence. He was ignored: for Burghley this was almost as terrible as the Tower.

He began to feel Elizabeth's displeasure soon enough. 'Most mighty and gracious sovereign,' he wrote, 'I know not with what manner of words to direct my writing to your Majesty. To utter anything like a councillor, as I was wont to do, I find myself barred so to do by your Majesty's displeasure.' This letter to the Queen was delivered personally by Hatton. Elizabeth may even have refused to read it. Burghley had never experienced anything like this before in his career.[42]

Someone had to suffer for Mary's execution. Whoever it was had to be senior enough to be made an example of but not too important to endure the indignity of imprisonment. Burghley, sixty-six years old and always in delicate health, was too fragile; but in the end he was probably also too grand. The other principal ringleader, Walsingham, called to court from London, was suitably penitent. Hatton, Burghley's intermediary with the Queen, appears to have escaped censure. The man who took the blame was William Davison. Robert Beale thought it was the Earl of Leicester's idea to put Davison in prison: 'Therefore Master Davison must bear the burden.'[43]

Davison's colleagues knew that he had to suffer, but they tried at the same time to moderate his punishment. Walsingham wrote to Burghley from London on 13 February. 'Tomorrow I mean with the leave of God to be at the court and to see your Lordship. In the mean time I humbly beseech your Lordship to use all good means you may to remove Her Majesty's heavy displeasure from Master Secretary Davison, who as I am informed is greatly dejected.' Davison had every right to be depressed: for two days he had known that he was going to the Tower of London. Burghley had already written on Davison's behalf. It would be a sorrowful example to the Queen's servants and a joy to her enemies, he said, if Davison was put in the Tower. It did no good. The Queen's junior Secretary went to prison on 14 February.[44]

For all the evasions, contradictions, omissions and fabrications in the accounts given by Elizabeth and Secretary Davison of the events leading to Mary's execution, there is really no doubt that Burghley and his colleagues acted in effect on their own authority. The fact that they did this with a death warrant signed by the Queen and sealed with the Great Seal of England makes little difference. Burghley had known full well what he was doing.

But had Burghley foreseen the depth of Elizabeth's fury? Had he calculated that it was a price worth paying for the death, at long last, of her mortal enemy? Did he think that he would just weather Elizabeth's temper? It is hard to be sure. He had worked closely with the Queen for nearly thirty years, and he had known her for ten years before that. He had a very shrewd appreciation of Elizabeth, as shrewd, no doubt, as hers was of him. They had disagreed about policy before: he had confronted her head on; and as the years passed by she had developed some effective ways to block efforts by Burghley and his colleagues to make her do things she did not want to do. Delay and indecision were two of her great tactical weapons. But on 1 and 2 February 1587 there came the crisis. She tried to block and delay but she was ignored. Burghley forced her, and he went too far.

For many years Burghley had given his service to Elizabeth on their shared understanding that he was indispensable in the execution of her rule. What he did in early February nearly wrecked the intricate system of a whole way of balancing the absolute rule of God's lieutenant on earth with the tough practical politics of preserving and protecting a kingdom under attack by its enemies. Elizabeth fought her councillors as hard as they had tried to fight

Mary Stuart and Mary's agents. Burghley saw danger and conspiracy everywhere. But in spite of these radically different perspectives on the world, they had made government work. Now, for a time, the great Lord Burghley had to get used to changed conditions.

Burghley may not have recognised straight away that he had come close to breaking the delicate mechanism of Elizabeth's government, but he quickly knew he was in trouble with the Queen. Instinctively he went on the attack. He began to do two things that were very important to him. First, he wrote, on behalf of the Council, a humble apology for what they had done; this, as we might expect, was not so much an apology as an apologia, a justification and a defence. Secondly, he began to frame an official account of Mary's execution: even temporarily out of favour he tried to determine the government's line. For this purpose he had specially commissioned a first-hand narrative of the Scottish Queen's death at Fotheringhay.

Burghley had spoken for the Council in the secret meeting with Beale at Greenwich; now, nine days later, on Saturday, 12 February, he wrote a defence of what they had done. Through Burghley's pen the councillors prayed Elizabeth to suspend her heavy censure of them till they had explained why they had sent Beale on his mission to Fotheringhay. 'We confess that we are most heartily sorry . . . to the bottom of our hearts to hear that your Majesty is so deeply grieved in your mind.' Burghley laboured over his text; he tested every word and phrase; the details had to be right. The Council's resolution recognised that all good and wise men in the realm saw the dangers to Elizabeth growing daily. When they found out that the Queen had put her hand to Mary's death warrant, which was shown to them by Secretary Davison, they wanted to lose no time. They had concluded, Burghley wrote, 'that it was most necessary to use all secrecy herein for fear of great danger'.[45]

Within a few days Burghley had his eyewitness account of Mary's execution. By 17 February he had set to work on what should be said officially about the execution; he may also have begun his own narrative of Beale's mission to Fotheringhay. The justification began, naturally enough, with Mary's part in plots to destroy Elizabeth. It emphasised Elizabeth's mercy. It referred to the hostility to England of French and Scottish diplomats. 'And Her Majesty, beholding all these former causes of dangers like to arise to her own person and her realm, did yield to think it needful' to act.

Burghley, the master of words, gave a subtle account of how the Queen's warrant came to be sent to Fotheringhay: 'which writing being so signed was in the custody of her Secretary, Master Davison, who did carry the same to the Lord Chancellor to put the Great Seal thereto, which was done very secretly; and afterwards did declare the same to certain of the lords and others of Her Majesty's Privy Council, who seemed glad thereof'. This was breathtaking understatement. And of course it squarely blamed Davison for breaching counsel to Elizabeth by leaking to Hatton and Burghley.[46]

Burghley was already trying to smooth over the rough politics and hard facts of February. But his words did not calm Elizabeth. For weeks there was nothing he could do to effect his reconciliation with the Queen. By the middle of March he was exasperated; he may even have been desperate.

Burghley had to use intermediaries to plead his case. On 15 March he sent a note to Sir Christopher Hatton. Five days later Burghley gave another letter to William Killigrew of the Privy Chamber, to which he received no answer. By this time Burghley had at least seen Elizabeth – he wrote on the 15th that in her 'princely compassion' she had permitted him 'to her presence a few days past' – though she had had nothing to say either to or about him except 'sharp and piercing speeches', and these in front of the Earl of Leicester and Sir Francis Walsingham. Five weeks after Mary's execution, Elizabeth was still livid because Burghley had not told her about it when she had met him in audience, and instead of volunteering information she had had to drag it out of him.

The letter to Hatton is a remarkable document. It tells us all we need to know about Burghley's predicament. He felt lost, alone and vulnerable. Although he did his best to make a case for Elizabeth's forgiveness, using his considerable powers as a wordsmith, his prose was forced and awkward. Self-importance, self-pity, suspicion, paranoia: they are all present.

'Since regarding in great anguish of heart the weight of Her Majesty's displeasure so settled and increased,' he wrote, 'and mine own humility not able to abide the continuance of such Her Majesty's displeasure, I am therefore most careful how by any means possible I may shun all increase of the weight hereof.'

Already he had begun to worry that he had secret enemies at court. But in one of the most telling sentences he ever wrote, he wondered how anyone could possibly be his enemy: 'I cannot imagine that any person is my enemy for any private act of mine own, but only in respect of my services for Her Majesty, wherein I have certainly felt of long time many sharp effects for doing my duty.' Service and duty, never for power, never for personal gain: the consummate public servant, loyal and disinterested.

But the public servant was also the politician, desperately conscious of his reputation and of his position at court. He wrote that he could tolerate the 'sharp effects' of many years when he had had Elizabeth's favour. But now it was common knowledge that the Queen was grievously offended with him, and his enemies were taking full advantage of this, presuming that her ears were open 'to any sinister calumniatum to be devised against me'. Now he came close to making a threat. The only thing he felt he could do in the circumstances was to withdraw from all 'public actions of state whereunto I am not expressly commanded by Her Majesty' – till of course he was accepted back into her presence.[47]

This was not the first time a councillor had been banished from Elizabeth's presence. Even the Earl of Leicester, a close friend of the Queen, had been disciplined this way. But for Burghley it was the greatest shock of his career. He had never before received such treatment. This indeed was Leicester's analysis in April: Burghley's offence to the Queen was exactly the same as that of all of those who sent the warrant off to Fotheringhay. But it was Burghley's 'place and credit heretofore' that made it heavier for him to bear 'and more noted to the world than to all the rest'. Leicester was calmly hopeful of reconciliation. He trusted that God would direct and preserve the Queen.[48]

In the weeks after Mary's execution Burghley had to lay himself bare. We might think that it was all an act. For Burghley words were means to be used for practical ends, and if that meant throwing himself on the mercy of the Queen to restore him to her counsels then really anything he set down on paper was worth it. We might think that Burghley, ever the canny politician, merely did what had to be done. But to anyone who reads his letters very closely the tone is unmistakable. When Elizabeth refused him access to her royal person, she struck at what made Burghley Burghley, the great servant and counsellor. In his first letter to Elizabeth after Mary's execution he drew back, just, from writing that he was now able only 'to speak like a common subject', not a councillor. It is a very telling comment. He believed he was more than an ordinary subject.

By March 1587 Burghley felt annoyance, self-pity, irritation and vulnerability. For years he had written about the demands made of him, the strains of his work and his enemies at court. But then he had been at the heart of things, overworked but secure and close to the Queen. Now it was different. His entire career – his political soul even, if that is not putting it too grandly – was being exposed. What he revealed were some deep anxieties about being away from the Queen and from power. He thought about his enemies: and how real did he believe they were? For a time he may even have had to confront the notion that his service had come to an end. And that, as he well knew, would have robbed his life of its purpose.[49]

So the execution of Mary, Queen of Scots was a bitter-sweet victory for Burghley. He had at last succeeded in obtaining one of the objectives of his career, the security of the kingdom through the death of Mary Stuart. But this achievement came at a heavy personal cost. It threatened the delicate instrument of Elizabethan government. Above all, it caused him to consider his relationship with the Queen. Things would never be quite the same again.

19

Burghley Triumphant

In his later years Lord Burghley looked to the future. He knew as well as anyone that life was fragile. His hope in the end was for deliverance from the burdens of the flesh and the miseries of a sinful world: these were words he had heard intoned many times at the burial services of family and colleagues.

Burghley was painfully aware of his mortality. For years he had struggled with his health, the physic of pills as much of a trial as the pain that treatment sought to ease. He was often lame and unable to write. Sometimes he wrote or dictated letters from his couch or his bed. He could be frail. And yet his work, whether in the Court of Wards or the royal Exchequer in Westminster, or at Elizabeth's court, or at Cecil House on the Strand, rarely eased. He was still a politician of power and instinct, compelled to direct and control. Here little changed, even if the world around him did.

Burghley had planned a tomb for his family as early as 1562. In the few years after 1579 he carefully attended 'many times' to his last will and testament. He had 'perfected' it in July 1583 but then revisited it in 1586. His revisions became more frequent as time went on. He looked death straight in the face: or at least he made sure that he saw to his affairs and to his posterity and made the sensible dispositions of a careful man.

These were years in which Burghley began to look to his legacy and to the provisions he intended to make for his dynasty. He completed his houses of Theobalds and Burghley, two grand statements in stone of service, family and rank. Burghley's family grew. There were marriages and alliances, grand-children and great-grandchildren. There was also the early blossoming of the career of Burghley's youngest son, Robert. But there was grief too, in the deaths of Burghley's mother, his second daughter, Anne, and his wife Mildred. In this last decade of Lord Burghley's life there were beginnings and there were endings: and that, after all, is the way of things.

*

We can only imagine what it felt like for Burghley to achieve the objective of nearly thirty years at the highest levels of Elizabethan politics. Mary Stuart was dead: Burghley had even commissioned a personal account of her execution at Fotheringhay Castle. He knew in his bones that Mary was the greatest threat to Elizabeth's throne. He and his colleagues were clear in their minds and consciences that she had to die.

That absolute certainty had nearly ruined Burghley's long relationship of trust with Elizabeth. It was a long road back to any kind of normality between these two complex personalities. Motives, ends and outcomes were mixed and jumbled together: Burghley was determined and resolute and showed not even limited evidence of regret at what he had done; Elizabeth, the queen who had after all signed her cousin's death warrant, was content to blame everyone except herself. Burghley's part in Mary Stuart's execution was slow to be forgiven by the Queen, but then so it had to be; she could hardly accept responsibility directly. In long investigations in March and April Burghley was questioned by a commission of enquiry. As subtle and supple as ever, he claimed that he and his colleagues did not actually order Mary's death: they dispatched the letters 'without directing any point for the execution'. This was at best a creative reading of the facts, and it hardly suggested an attitude of contrition. William Davison was thrown to the wolves. From February till June Elizabeth was given to periodic outbursts of temper against Burghley. She protested her innocence of any hand in the affair, even to Mary's son, King James. There was no single, inspirational moment when Elizabeth forgave Burghley; instead there was a slow thawing of the frostiness between them, and by June her tone was changing. In late summer Burghley entertained Elizabeth and her court at Theobalds. He was, after all, one of her oldest servants; the stormy waters settled. The Earl of Leicester had been right: it was precisely because of Burghley's rank and importance that the Queen was especially furious with him, but this meant that eventually he was accepted back into favour. In a sense he had won; but what had been exposed in his winning was his own political mortality. Here was the fact of absolute rule. In the end everything rested on the Queen's favour, and that could never be taken entirely for granted.[1]

Mary Stuart was escorted to her resting place in Peterborough Cathedral at the end of July 1587. She was accorded all the ceremony due to a queen. Elizabeth's representatives and Mary's old servants laid her to rest in the cathedral's choir. The careful and sombre rituals of royal burial were performed. But it was all deeply ambiguous. Also in the cathedral's choir lay the tomb of Katherine of Aragon, that other un-queened queen. And there was no mistaking the secrecy of Mary's burial, for the cortège had set out from Fotheringhay at ten o'clock at night on 30 July and arrived in Peterborough at two o'clock the next morning. Burghley was not there but Sir Thomas Cecil, his forty-five-year-old son, was present, temporarily accorded the rank of baron. The father saw to Mary's execution: the son held one of the four corners of a pall of black velvet over her coffin. With Sir Thomas was his wife, Lady Dorothy Cecil. They were attended by ten servants dressed in mourning black.[2]

So Mary was gone, her body safely sealed in lead and neatly put away for the time being in Peterborough Cathedral. But some of the old fears persisted. The execution of the Queen of Scots did not bring peace and security for Elizabeth. Quite the opposite: enemies still lurked who now seemed more likely to strike than ever. Burghley had expected there to be a seaborne invasion since the early 1580s. Here his instincts were dead right. As we will see later in this chapter, Burghley had to fight with weapons he knew very well, the arts of intelligence and the skills of propaganda.

*

Burghley was a dynast. His family ambitions were measured by the number of his descendants and by the rhythm of the generations. If he was more conscious by the day of his own mortality, then he knew also that his name and title would live on, and this was quite as important to him as anything in the business of day-to-day politics at court. As Master of the Court of Wards he presided over the proper ordering of landed society; he did no less for his own family, enforcing the codes of behaviour that governed how his children and grandchildren looked to him for advice and guidance. He was the rule by which all things were measured. His family deferred to him, and rightly so.

It is with this in mind that we have to understand the terrible shame of his daughter's failed marriage. But by the later years of the 1580s Anne and her husband, the Earl of Oxford, were reconciled, at least after a fashion. They had two more daughters, Bridget born in 1584, and Susan in May 1587. In children there was hope, even if Anne's marriage was still terribly unhappy.

Only a few months after the birth of Lady Susan de Vere, Sir Thomas Cecil wrote to his father with good news about his daughter, Lucy, the wife of Lord St John. Lucy was of 'great belly'. Thomas had sent word to the Marquess of Winchester, Lord St John's father, and his wife, 'next ourselves not knowing who will congratulate the good hap than your Lordship and they'. He ended his 'present scribbling' with his humble commendations and those of his wife and daughters.

When Sir Thomas Cecil wrote to his father with news of Lucy's pregnancy he was at Burghley House. It may seem incredible that Lord Burghley spent so much money on a house he visited only occasionally. And yet all the work to turn Burghley into one of the most magnificent houses in the realm would have made perfect sense to its owner, just as it did to his son, who hoped in August 1587 that his noble father would soon see the 'perfection' of all the 'long and costly buildings' there. Burghley House was for both present and future. It was a mark of Lord Burghley's taste and his love of beautiful architecture. It was about order, about grandeur, and about authority. Like other great Tudor houses and palaces, the house had a long gallery in which it was possible to walk and talk privately: this was the setting for conversations of power. We should not be surprised to find that the setting and lighting of the long gallery were subjects Burghley was keen to read about. He had specially instructed that the latest book on the subject, Philibert de l'Orme's *Nouvelles Inventions*, should be sent to him from Paris.[3]

Everything about Burghley House was carefully contrived to impress the visitor. The house made certain statements about its builder. Here was Lord Burghley the classical scholar, the Roman senator even, with references to Medea, Jason, Hector and Cassandra. The great Roman staircase in the north range of the house looked to the French styles of Paris, as well as to Burghley's family in its carved coats of arms. Busts of two of the greatest political figures of the sixteenth century, Emperor Charles V and Suleiman the Magnificent of the Ottoman Empire, were carved in relief in the courtyard: here was someone who understood power and rule. It was clear, too, that the builder of Burghley was a Christian Knight of the Most Noble Order of the Garter, for the badge of the Garter appeared on the outside of the house, and up the grand stairs in the south range were the names and arms of some of Burghley's fellow knights. One of the chambers in this range had as its theme St George, the patron saint of the Order.[4]

But Burghley House also looked back to the past and forward to the future. If the first Baron of Burghley had beautified it, he had done so using the walls and foundations of his father's house. At Burghley William Cecil was Richard Cecil's heir. The house belonged to the family, to Burghley's line and posterity; it was an investment that stretched well beyond the first Lord Burghley's life. All of this goes a good way to explaining why in 1587 Thomas offered to pay half the cost of some fine tapestries for Burghley. He was not entirely sure that his father would want to bear their full cost. Thomas Bellot, Lord Burghley's steward, had the accounts, and Sir Thomas must have been in no doubt that his father, who watched every penny, would look through them carefully. Still, he hoped that Burghley would help to buy them, for they were fine pieces of work and had already been fitted for the house.[5]

The future was as certain as it could be. Burghley had an heir, and Sir Thomas himself had two sons. The eldest was the second William Cecil, born at Burghley House and now twenty-one years old. The line of David and Richard Cecil was assured, the rhythm of inheritance uninterrupted. Richard's old house was now fit for a baron, a humble servant of the Queen. It was the best expression of the fact that this nook of Northamptonshire was the Cecils' 'country', their native homeland, where their roots ran deep.

Thomas Cecil was Lord Burghley's eldest son and heir. But Burghley had another son to provide for, young Robert Cecil. Robert was now twenty-four years old and he was beginning to make his way in the world of Elizabethan politics. He was different from Thomas in all kinds of ways: a born scholar, like his father and mother, and not at all physically robust. If Thomas was the tough and experienced soldier, Robert was the scholar-statesman in the making. Even so, the two brothers, with twenty-one years' difference in their ages, genuinely liked each other.

Robert was given the best foundation possible for a public career. As a boy he studied Latin, Greek, French, Spanish and Italian, as well as mathematics, music and cosmography. He was taught at home, as Thomas had been years before, by the best tutors from Cambridge. Burghley's household was as ever a place of scholarship and learning. Burghley owned a fabulous library and he encouraged learned discussions over meals. In 1580 Robert was admitted, as his father had been forty years before, to Gray's Inn to study the common law. He was in Paris in 1583 and 1584 with his uncle William, Thomas's heir, who was actually much the same age; and we know that Robert attended lectures at the Sorbonne, the theological school of the University of Paris. Robert returned to England to sit in the House of Commons for Westminster. His name had even appeared in print in 1586 in Burghley's campaign for the execution of Mary Stuart. It was fair warning that Robert Cecil was on his way. As Robert's Latin motto would one day put it, *Sero sed serio*: 'Late but in earnest'.[6]

By the late summer of 1587 the Queen had granted Robert the reversion of all his father's offices in the county of Hertfordshire: that is, Robert would hold those positions of responsibility once Burghley relinquished them. This had been done at the mediation of the young Earl of Essex, who ten years earlier had sat with Robert for meals at Theobalds. Essex, twenty-one years old and something of a war hero after his service abroad with his stepfather, the Earl of Leicester, had well and truly arrived at Elizabeth's court. But Robert was establishing himself, too, and in Hertfordshire, a county where Burghley had only ever claimed to be a 'new-feathered' gentleman.

In late August Robert thanked Burghley for the favour he had shown to him and asked for his 'advice and fatherly direction' in offering appropriate thanks to the Earl of Essex. Already Robert Cecil was used to the important and delicate rituals of Elizabeth's court. He ended his letter at eleven o'clock that Friday morning 'desiring God to give me no longer breath than while I carry an obedient heart to your Lordship, craving your daily blessing'. He was in London but on his way to Theobalds.[7]

If Burghley was Thomas Cecil's inheritance, then Theobalds was Robert's. Like Burghley House, Theobalds was built to make a statement: it advertised Burghley's power, wealth and his special relationship with the Queen. To the 'backbiters' who accused him of building at Theobalds a palace fit for kings, he had a simple and entirely reasonable explanation. The house was 'begun by me with a mean measure, but increased by occasions of Her Majesty's often coming, whom to please I would never omit to strain myself to more charges'. Elizabeth had found fault 'with the small measure of her chamber, which was in good measure for me'. What could he do but make it bigger?

In the same letter Burghley defended Theobalds. 'If my buildings mislike them,' he wrote of his enemies, 'I confess my folly in the expenses, because some of my houses are to come, if God so please, to them that shall not have land to maintain them.' Robert Cecil was a second son, but his father wanted to provide for him as grandly as he would for Thomas. In this sense Theobalds was Robert's patrimony.[8]

Burghley built Theobalds in part to educate his son in matters essential to the service of the crown. Burghley had spent many years studying all the subjects that any politician needed to know, with maps, plans and charts of Europe and the world; using genealogies of noble and royal families at home and abroad; and knowing the geography and topography of England, Ireland and Scotland. These were the practical tools of the royal Secretary and the privy councillor. In being trained in all of this, Robert Cecil was his father's apprentice.

Robert, like everyone else in the family and household, would have seen Theobalds grow. Doubtless he knew the rooms of the house and their decoration off by heart. There was the Green Gallery, looking out into Dial Court one way and into Middle Court the other, where the arms of the English nobility were set out on fifty-two painted trees. Burghley was passionate about genealogy, and he was keen for Robert, and for visitors to Theobalds, to know his own, which was set out on the north side of a loggia facing out to the Great Garden. There was the pedigree of the Cecil family, as well as the family trees of other ancient families and the genealogy of the kings of England. This was a place of historical reference, with paintings of castles and battles.[9]

Robert Cecil's apartments at Theobalds were in Conduit Court, at the centre of which was a great fountain of Venus and Cupid. In the west range of the court, near to Robert's rooms, was the Great Gallery of Theobalds, and it was probably here, more than anywhere else, that Lord Burghley impressed upon visitors his standing as a great European politician and at the same time educated his son in the history of Europe. Many admired the sumptuousness of the decoration, the marble tables and the great landscapes of European cities. The gallery was also something like an instructional manual for classical and contemporary history. There were portraits and busts of Roman emperors. There was a great terrestrial globe: this was the history of the world, from Rome to the Habsburgs, with their knights of the royal Order of the Golden Fleece, some of whose portraits were on display.

Also in the gallery hung pictures of all the English kings of the fifteenth century, from Henry IV to Henry VII, whose servant David Cecil had been. Across from the kings were portraits of some of the great figures of contemporary Europe, enemies as well as friends: Don John of Austria, Philip II's general in the Low Countries; that other great man of Spanish politics, the Duke of Parma; the Count of Egmont, executed by Parma in 1568; the Admiral of France; the distinguished Huguenot leader, Louis de Bourbon, Prince of Condé; and Maurice, Duke of Saxony. If on one side of the gallery there was a reminder of the Wars of the Roses in England, on the other were unmistakable references to the forces that shaped the Europe Burghley knew, the wars of religion in France and the Spanish conquest of the Low Countries.

This remarkable statement of history and politics, from the ancient to the contemporary, was contrived to show Burghley's mastery of the past and present, his command of global affairs: he was showing himself to be, as Robert Cecil's cousin Francis Bacon put it, 'the Atlas of this commonwealth'. It was this knowledge and authority that Burghley wanted to pass on to Robert.[10]

At Theobalds, just as at Burghley, William Cecil celebrated his family. There was the genealogy of the Cecils in the loggia under the Great Chamber; and downstairs from the Great Gallery there were portraits of Burghley's forebears, each one with an account of his service to the Tudor monarchs. Perhaps here was another clever device: the Cecils were like those august political families of ancient Rome who displayed the death masks of their forebears in order to advertise their lineage. Burghley's enemies claimed that Master Cecil, 'for divers years after his coming to credit, went about to derive his name of Cecil from Cecilius the Roman name'. Maybe there was just the tiniest grain of truth in their satire.[11]

*

On 6 March 1588 Jane Cecil, Richard Cecil's widow and Burghley's mother, added a memorandum to her will. She died four days later in Stamford at the age of about eighty-seven, a widow for nine days short of thirty-five years. In looking back over her life, the first Baron of Burghley would have seen that his family had come a very long way from the house in Lincolnshire where he was born, which had been left to Jane by her father seventy-six years before.[12]

In a lifetime the world had changed. The will of Jane's father, William Hekington, had set out with great care the various bequests he wanted to make to local monasteries, churches and religious guilds. Those days had gone: his grandson had helped to see to that. Jane Cecil made sure that her charitable bequests were untainted by any Catholic superstition. She left some money to local churches. The 'poor artificers and occupiers and other inhabitants' of Stamford and St Martin's parish received £50, and she gave £30 to the poor of Burghley's birthplace, Bourne. She left a further £3 to buy black cloth to make gowns for the poor of whichever parish she was to be buried in. There were to be mourning clothes, too, for Lord and Lady Burghley, for Sir Thomas Cecil and his wife Lady Dorothy, for Burghley's sisters and their husbands, and for Jane's nephews.

Jane Cecil had been well known for charity and modesty. But she still wanted a fine tomb to be set up for her by her son. She had thought well ahead, making sure that Burghley had £120 'to cause such a monument for to be made at the place of my burial for me and my late husband as he shall think good'. Jane and Richard's monument, in St Martin's Church in Stamford, is that of a knight and his lady: like the tomb Burghley had imagined for himself and Mildred in 1562, they face each other kneeling at prayer over a small lectern. Burghley's sisters are similarly at prayer beneath them. Above are the coats of arms of Richard and Jane and Burghley's motto, *Cor unum, via una*: 'One heart, one way'.[13]

What Jane Cecil was able to express in her will was a powerful sense of family and place. She was of Stamford: the town and her family were her world. There were obligations, even for someone as powerful as Lord Burghley, who was required in his mother's will 'to deliver and give unto my Lady his wife and unto Robert their son £20 apiece as of my gift of such money as he doth owe unto me'. In leaving £20 for her godson Richard Cecil, one of Thomas's younger sons, she honoured the memory of her late husband. The greatest part of her estate in land and property went to her son Burghley and 'his heirs and assigns' for ever. But there was plenty more for Jane to do in her will and she made sure to set out her bequests with great care, from the £60 to be divided between Thomas's children when they married or reached the age of twenty-one, to the salts, bowls and spoons of silver and silver gilt she left to her daughters. No member of the family was forgotten: Jane's command of detail was as powerful as her son's, and twice she went back to her will to bring it up to date, missing no change in situation or circumstance.

Jane Cecil bequeathed her soul 'unto the hands of Almighty God, hoping and believing steadfastly that through the only merits of our Lord and Saviour Jesus Christ I shall be saved'. She left her estate in the care of her executrix, Burghley's sister Elizabeth Alington, with the help and supervision of Thomas Cecil. Elizabeth was by now married to Hugh Alington, Burghley's nephew on the Cheke side of his family, his former confidential secretary and now his brother-in-law. This was a family held together by old bonds of love, duty and service. Jane had taken care of all the details. She had made her peace with God after what, in the sixteenth century, was an exceptionally long life.

The life of Anne, Countess of Oxford, was neither as long nor probably as happy as her grandmother's. Lord Burghley's daughter, his 'little Nan Cecil', died in June. She was thirty-one years old. In the space of three months Burghley had lost his mother and his second daughter.

Anne's marriage to the seventeenth Earl of Oxford was a private catastrophe for her, a troublesome inconvenience for her husband, and a cause of grief to her father. A union that had promised to be a great dynastic *coup*, an alliance between the Cecils and one of the most distinguished noble families in the kingdom, instead turned out to be the occasion of open hostility between the young earl and his father-in-law. For years there had been all kinds of ructions at court: the Oxford marriage was a blot on the reputations of Burghley and his daughter.

Anne professed to love a husband who for years had refused even to talk to her and could barely stand to have her in his presence. He had nourished a resentment against his wife which he could not bring himself to state plainly and which she was unable to comprehend. There had, it was true, been something like a reconciliation after 1582, and the couple had even had two more children after Elizabeth, both daughters, Bridget and Susan. But little had really changed for Anne and her husband. As late as May 1587 Burghley had complained to Sir Francis Walsingham that Oxford, who was as suspicious and dismissive of his father-in-law as ever, was failing to support his wife and children properly and that he, Burghley, was having to bear the burden of her household.[14]

Anne died at Greenwich on 5 June. She was buried twenty days later in Westminster Abbey. Burghley became guardian to her three daughters. If he had borne the burden privately before Anne's death, he did so now more publicly, taking her girls into his household. At the age of sixty-seven Burghley began to care for eleven-year-old Elizabeth, three-year-old Bridget, and baby Susan, just a year old.[15]

Burghley would give his daughter a grand tomb in Westminster Abbey. That was some time away in the summer of 1588. It was a tomb Anne would share with Lady Mildred Burghley, the mother who had been her constant companion during some of the most wretched times of her marriage.

*

When Anne's sister, Elizabeth, had died in 1583 the Queen had given their father about five days to grieve for his loss, to 'wrestle with nature'. A man like

Burghley was expected to exercise discipline and self-control. Public service came before everything else. As Sir Francis Walsingham had put it in the dark days following Elizabeth Wentworth's death, the Queen imagined that wisdom and religion had wrought in Burghley the resolution fitting for a man of his place and calling. Better to work than to be 'a prey unto grief'. The advice would have been the same in 1588. In times of affliction it was the duty of Christians to kiss the rod.[16]

Business never went away for Burghley. His desk was always piled high with work: the Wards, the Exchequer, the Council, letters to colleagues, officials and ambassadors abroad, queues of petitioners at Cecil House – he read a vast acreage of paper every day of his life. Even in the calm times there was little peace to relax and to be. But the summer of 1588 was neither calm nor peaceful. The seas looked rough: invasion was on the way.

Burghley had never doubted that one day war would come. For twenty years he had been deeply pessimistic about England's security. He watched as France was torn apart by religious civil war and Spain, the global superpower of its day, sought methodically to crush the Protestant Dutch. He believed that England's true religion was a standing offence to Catholic Europe, but he seriously wondered whether, when the time came, the realm could stand up to the terrible power of the enemy.

Burghley knew as well as anyone the diplomacy of European war. He read the letters and reports and paid for the English forces abroad. He knew the personalities, friends and enemies, some of whose portraits were on the walls of his Great Gallery at Theobalds. The greatest names in European politics wrote private letters to him: powerful men, princes even, signed themselves his true friends. But he was never in any doubt that the foreign powers of Catholic Europe were, as he wrote in 1569, making 'great wastes of their own people by bloody battles and persecutions'. Persecution was sure to come eventually to England, brought by 'the Pope's tyrannous, bloody and poisoning persecutors'. Europe was being turned upside down by war and misery. England's situation was, and had been from the beginning of Elizabeth's reign, perilous.[17]

Burghley had perceived that Mary, Queen of Scots was at the heart of an international conspiracy to seize the English throne from Elizabeth. Her execution was necessary; but it was never going to be some kind of magic wand to make the dangers disappear. It merely hastened the inevitable. A long cold war with Philip II's Spain had been warming for some years. Elizabeth had already committed land forces to the Low Countries. The actions of English privateers antagonised the Spanish; a trade war looked as if it would become a real war. It was surely only a matter of time. The execution of Mary was the last straw.[18]

There was nothing particularly surprising about this. King Philip believed he was on a divine mission to bring Elizabeth's heretic kingdom back to the true Catholic faith. At the end of 1585 he committed himself to the invasion. Burghley would have known this from intelligence reports of the utmost secrecy and sensitivity. The English government had some very effective spies close to the heart of Spanish war planning. And anyway, Spain's Armada was one of the worst-kept secrets in Europe.[19]

We know exactly what Burghley made of the Spanish threat for in February 1588 he put his thoughts down on paper. As a blunt account of the enemy's power with some confidence in an English victory it has a Churchillian ring about it. The enemy was the King of Spain, Burghley wrote, helped by the Pope. Their aim was to subvert the true Christian religion. Philip's ambition would not be satisfied by mere conquest: he wanted to subdue religion and to enlarge his powers as king. Burghley did not doubt that Philip's resources were great indeed. 'He is the mightiest enemy that ever England had, yea mightier than ever his father the Emperor Charles or any other monarch of Christendom was these many years.'

Burghley tried to predict how Philip would organise his invasion. The attack would be made on England and Ireland 'jointly and at an instant'. He would need a great navy of ships to carry a large army. He might send, Burghley thought, some of his skilful captains and soldiers to Scotland with money to bribe King James to help. If Philip were successful in this, invasion could come from the northern border as well as from the southern sea coasts. But even if James refused to help, there was still the worry of a party of English noblemen who were 'devoted papists and sworn enemies to England'.

Ships were the key, and Burghley had some confidence in Elizabeth's navy: 'For ships of England Her Majesty is of her own proper ships so strong as the enemy shall not be able to land any power where Her Majesty's navy shall be near to the enemy's navy.' In number, in strength and in personnel, Burghley believed, Elizabeth's navy was stronger than it had ever been: but still he looked for help to ships from Denmark and Scotland.

Burghley recognised that it would cost a vast amount of money to fight off the power of Spain: he estimated that Elizabeth would have to budget for many tens of thousands of pounds. But even for a practical man like Burghley, there was more to defeating Spain than cash and tactics. It was a holy war: England was fighting for religion. He trusted to God:

> The first and last comforter for Her Majesty to take hold on is the Lord of Hosts, for whose cause only her enemies are risen with might and fury to overthrow the Gospel of Christ and the professors thereof. . . . And so with a firm hope of God's assistance in his own cause . . .[20]

The test came, famously, in July 1588. This book will not tell the story of the Gran Armada. Burghley was not a hero in the front line: he was, after all, Elizabeth's sixty-seven-year-old Lord Treasurer, and the last battle he had seen at first hand was Pinkie, near Edinburgh, in 1547. Burghley fought from Westminster, with his secretary Henry Maynard at his side, looking to the supply of munitions and money. Lord Howard of Effingham, Lord Henry Seymour and Sir Francis Drake, the navy's commanders, were happy at sea: Burghley was more suited to the corridors of power.

Moments of emergency bring fine words from leaders. Everybody knows that Elizabeth addressed her troops in the camp at Tilbury in Essex on 30 July with rousing words: 'I know I have the body but of a weak and feeble woman, but I have the heart and stomach of a king.' They are as famous as the words Shakespeare later gave to John of Gaunt on his deathbed and to Henry V on the eve of the battle of Agincourt, just as patriotic and just as expressive of grit, determination and heroism. Elizabeth's words at Tilbury may be just as fictional: there is no hard evidence that she ever spoke them.[21]

Soon enough a whole Armada industry grew up to celebrate England's providential protection from the horrors of Spanish invasion. Medals were cast to celebrate England's preservation. The beautiful 'Armada Portrait' proclaimed Elizabeth as 'great empress of the world' in ways that John Dee, the great empire man, would have applauded. The Queen, fabulously dressed and beautifully serene, rests her right hand on a globe. Her crown imperial, rich with jewels, sits next to her. Over her right shoulder the ships of her navy sail in calm waters. Over her left shoulder the Spanish fleet is dashed against rocks. And if historians today think that the weather may have been as responsible for the Armada's defeat as the prowess of English sailors, then Elizabeth had her answer in two lines of a song that was sung in the procession to the service of thanksgiving at St Paul's Cathedral. The victory was God's: 'he made the winds and waters rise / to scatter all mine enemies'. Philip II of Spain was not the only monarch of Europe to believe in the divine assurance of his cause.[22]

Behind all this glitz and glamour was a tough, gritty propaganda war. Burghley was an old hand at this. Catholic writers had had him in their sights for years: he was the power behind Elizabeth's throne, the atheist *politique* who persecuted Catholics. In *The Execution of Justice* Burghley had given a defence of the mildness of Elizabeth's government in prosecuting priests for their treachery, not for their faith. The very notion of this was mocked by William Allen in his *True, Sincere and Modest Defence of English Catholics*. By the time of the execution of the Queen of Scots Allen was the spiritual leader of English Catholics and he had the ear of Pope Sixtus V.

In *A Declaration of the Sentence and deposition of Elizabeth, the usurper and pretensed Quene of Englande* Sixtus confirmed that the Queen was a bastard heretic schismatic. She and her government needed to be removed from power. And so it was that the 'mighty and potent King Catholic of Spain' would 'employ those forces which Almighty God hath given him, to the deposition of this woman, and correction of her complices, so wicked and noisome to the world, and to the reformation and pacification of these kingdoms'. There was no doubting the identity of one of the Queen's most prominent 'accomplices'. For Elizabeth this was poison: Burghley applied himself to the antidote.[23]

In the later months of 1588 a short book appeared in London which claimed to be the copy of a letter sent by one Richard Leigh, an English Jesuit priest, to Philip II's former ambassador to Elizabeth's court, and Burghley's old enemy, Don Bernardino de Mendoza. Copies of Leigh's letter had been found 'by good hap' in his study. It was a heart-rending piece, now published for all to read with the most important passages indicated in the book's margins.

Leigh explained to Mendoza how English Catholics had waited a long time for the Duke of Parma's great invasion and the speedy conquest of England. But in eight or nine days in July the Spanish forces had fallen to pieces. 'And herewith I am astonished what I may best think of such a work so long time in framing', Leigh wrote, 'to be suddenly overthrown, as by no reason could proceed of man, or of any earthly power, but only of God.' Leigh attacked the works of Cardinal Allen. He also described for Mendoza the careful preparations made by Elizabeth and her subjects for the defence of England. He related to Mendoza how Drake and Howard with only a few ships 'furiously pursued the whole navy of Spain'. England had been protected by providence and preparation. The people sang psalms to thank God for their victory.[24]

There was no such letter, of course: it was pure fabrication, written by Burghley and printed with all kinds of other documents to give it authenticity: various reports from Ireland, the examinations of Spanish sailors wrecked and driven ashore, an account of the Spanish ships and men lost in the sea battle and on the coast of Ireland. This was raw propaganda: not showy, like medals or portraits, but a classic ruse by Burghley: low-key, believable in its detail. Over the years, and particularly in the long battle against the Queen of Scots, he had produced similar books and pamphlets. The dark arts of politics never left him. He always fought with the weapons that were available to him. So often those weapons were words.[25]

*

On 4 April 1589, a Friday, Lady Mildred Burghley died at Cecil House on the Strand in Westminster. Five days later, stricken by grief, her husband made sense of his loss.

In the days before her funeral he tried to come to terms with one plain fact: he could never have her back. 'There is no cogitation to be used with an intent to recover that which never can be had again, that is to have my dear wife to live again in her mortal body.' Body and soul would come together again only by the power of God on the day of resurrection, but when that happened it would be 'an everlasting and unspeakable joy, such as nothing can express, nor heart conceive'.

Burghley tried to comfort himself with memories of their lives together. He also wanted to make a record of Mildred's 'sundry charitable deeds, whereof she determined to have no outward knowledge whilst she lived'. Burghley had known little of this: it was her secret. But now after her death he talked to those people who had helped her to give money to the poor and he saw the writings in her own hand to prove the fact. With his characteristic eye for detail, he set out what charitable deeds Lady Mildred had done, and he did so 'for my comfort in the memory thereof, with assurance that God hath accepted the same in such favourable sort, as she findeth now the fruits thereof in Heaven'.

Proudly, Burghley gave an account of his wife's charity. Later he made sure that it was carved in marble on her tomb for all to see. She had given money to the poor of Romford in her father's county, Essex; meat and bread and money for drink for the poor of Cheshunt and Waltham in Hertfordshire; money to four hundred men and women in London four times a year to buy bread, cheese and drink. She had sent shirts and smocks to the needy of Cheshunt and London, and given wool and flax to the poor women of Cheshunt parish, 'willing them to work the same into yarn and to bring it to her to see their manner of working'.

Lady Mildred long supported learning too, in Cambridge, where she helped to build new lecture halls and donated books, one of them a 'Great Bible in Hebrew'; and in Oxford, at Christ Church and St John's College. St John's College in Cambridge, her husband's old college, received her special attention. There she gave money for scholarships and preaching, and donated 'very many books in Greek, of divinity and physic and of other sciences'. But Lady Mildred had been concerned about bodies as well as minds. She had given a sum of money to the Master of St John's to pay for fires in the college's hall on Sundays and holy days in the freezing winter months between All Saints and Candlemas 'when there were no ordinary fires of the charge of the college'. All this she had done with the secret advice and help of the Dean of Westminster, Gabriel Goodman, an old family friend; and Dean Alexander Nowell of St Paul's. To both men she gave 'some small pieces of plate to be used in their chambers, as remembrances of her good will for their pains'.[26]

It was Nowell who preached Mildred's funeral sermon. Burghley made his wishes plain. There was to be no great pomp. Nothing about the funeral should suggest that its ceremony could in any way 'procure of God the relief or the amendment of the state of her soul, who is dead in body only'. Burghley was 'fully persuaded' by the graces bestowed on Lady Mildred in life and of her 'continual virtuous life and godly death' that God had received her soul into a place of blessedness. He wrote once again that nothing could bring her back to him, that hard fact he had been dwelling on for days.

For all this, Burghley celebrated Lady Mildred's funeral 'as a testimony of my hearty love which I did bear her, with whom I lived in the state of matrimony forty and two years, continually without any unkindness'. It was an act of homage. It was also to be done 'for the assembly of our friends', to show them the estimation, love and reverence that Burghley bore to Mildred's father and mother. Her ancestry and connections would be shown 'by the sundry coats of noble houses joined by blood with hers'. This was not 'for any vain pomp of the world, but for civil duty towards her body'.[27]

Modesty and nobility, the secret acts of charity and the ties of land and kinship: this was the circle Burghley was trying to square. The old days of superstition had gone. This was clear in the rhythm of generations, in the great contrast between the will of his grandfather Hekington and Hekington's daughter, William's mother, Jane. No act of piety and charity could hope, as Burghley put it, to 'procure of God' the relief of the soul. The old bequests to religious houses, to chantries, to religious guilds had long gone. But the charity of the rich to the poor would surely be taken into account by God, even though Lady Mildred had been saved by divine grace through the death of Christ, 'whereof', Burghley wrote, 'she was a professor from her youth'. Faith, not actions: but good deeds counted.

If Lady Mildred Burghley's funeral was a fittingly modest affair, the tomb her husband provided for her in Westminster Abbey became her rank in society and the excellence of her family. It was a tomb to a mother and her daughter: Mildred and Anne shared in death as they had spent so much time together in life. It was a magnificent monument, described with beautiful precision in the late seventeenth century:

On each side of this pedestal are two canopies, supported by some little Corinthian columns, curiously painted with azure, and gilt with gold, underneath each of which is a death's-head encased in crystal ... by the latter, at the head of their mother and grandmother are three little images of female children kneeling, the Lady Elizabeth, the Lady Bridget, and the Lady Susan de Vere, and by the former, at the feet of his mother and sister the figure only of a youth kneeling, for Robert Cecil.

The inscriptions on the tomb gave fulsome praise to Anne and Mildred. Lady Mildred's support of learning and her gifts to the poor, which Burghley had discovered only in the days after her death, he commemorated in stone. And now the young de Vere girls, any observer would have noted, were in the care of their affectionate grandfather.[28]

*

In little over a year Lord Burghley had lost his mother, his wife of forty-two years, and his little Nan Cecil, for whom he had written poems when she was a girl. The world of politics was changing too. The Earl of Leicester died a couple of months after the victory over the Armada. Leicester had been one of the great men of Elizabeth's reign, an architect of thirty years of her rule. Sir Francis Walsingham, Burghley's old comrade, died in April 1590. But, as Walsingham had once told Burghley, it was a Christian's duty to kiss the rod, to believe that body and soul would one day be joined together again at the resurrection: of this Burghley had had to remind himself in the weeks following Mildred's death. 'Give sorrow words,' says Shakespeare's Malcolm: 'the grief that does not speak / Whispers the o'er-fraught heart, and bids it break.'[29]

And yet the business of dynasty carried on. Twenty-six-year-old Robert Cecil married a few months after his mother's death. Robert's wife was Elizabeth Brooke, the daughter of the tenth Lord Cobham. They married at Cobham's house in London. It was, naturally, a political alliance. Cobham was a privy councillor and like Burghley a member of the elite club of the Order of the Garter. He claimed descent from the Pole family with its Plantagenet blood. Cobham's wife, Lady Frances, had offered to intercede with the Queen when Elizabeth had refused to see Burghley in the weeks after Mary Stuart's execution. She was close to the Queen in her Privy Chamber, which Robert's new wife Elizabeth had entered in the 1580s. Lady Frances had been the chief mourner at the funeral of Anne de Vere and a principal mourner for Lady Mildred. The marriage of Robert and Elizabeth was one of clever politics and dynastic alliance.[30]

Burghley sought to observe all the social rules that governed noble families. He could be tough when he wanted to be. In May 1590, for example, William Cecil, Sir Thomas's son, wrote to his grandfather Burghley. The knot William was trying to unpick was the naming of his young son. William's mother-in-law, the Countess of Rutland, thought that the name Edward, 'for her honourable husband's sake, was the name she most liked'.

The story here is that the countess was a widow. Her husband, Edward, third Earl of Rutland, who as a royal ward was educated in Burghley's household, had died in 1587. But Burghley was his great-grandson's godfather, and the convention was that the baby should take his Christian name. Burghley had made this plain in a letter to the countess who, wrote William, 'was conformable unto your Lordship'.

But there had been another breach of protocol. William's wife, Elizabeth, had let slip that she also liked the name Edward. For this William and Elizabeth were sorry 'to give your Lordship occasion to think we know not our duties, as to wish anything to our child before by your direction we should know what would best stand with your liking'. William looked to his grandfather for instructions on the 'decorum' to be observed in the baby's baptism. The child was, he wrote, 'well liking every day more and more, the mother gathereth strength'. In early June he was baptised at Newark and named William Cecil.[31]

This William Cecil never knew his mother. Elizabeth Cecil, Lady Rous died in April 1591 at the age of fifteen, and was buried a month later in St Nicholas's Chapel in Westminster Abbey. The generations ebb and flow. A month before Elizabeth died, Robert Cecil and his wife, also Elizabeth, had a son. He was born in Westminster. They named him William.[32]

Burghley's dynasty was established. His eldest son's son was William Cecil and this William was the father of a third boy of the same name: Burghley's posterity stretched out before him, amply provided for: it was no accident that Burghley had attended to his will early in 1590. Robert, too, was on his way. His wife was in the service of the Queen in her Privy Chamber, and now he had an heir. He was his father's son, a more natural successor to his father in the business of government than Thomas; and it was precisely this point that Burghley wanted to impress upon the Queen when she came to Theobalds for ten days in May 1591.

It was a visit that cost Burghley at least £1,000. Over £600 was spent on supplies for the pantry, buttery, cellar and kitchen: the best food and the best wine, with all the other expenses of hiring cooks, labourers, turnspits and bakers. There were rewards of £44 15s. 2d. for the Queen's musicians, the yeomen of the guard and the footmen attending the officers of the royal household. Burghley presented Elizabeth with a gown worth £100.[33] Burghley had a special purpose in entertaining the Queen so grandly. He wanted to recommend Robert to her. He also suggested that it was perhaps time for him to stand back from service in her government. He wanted peace and quiet in his old age. His reason was grief, and it was time to look to his failing health.

When the Queen arrived at Theobalds that May she was met by an actor dressed as a hermit. The hermit explained to her how Lord Burghley, overtaken with excessive grief, 'betook him to my silly hermitage, /And there hath liv'd two years and some months, /By reason of these most bitter accidents'. This was the time that had passed since Lady Mildred's death. But there were more Cecils to serve the Queen. 'I wish for my good founder's sake,' the hermit continued, 'That [Robert] may live with this his first-born son, / Long time to serve your sacred Majesty, /As his grandfather faithfully hath done.' A mock charter was read out loud by one of Elizabeth's retinue. It was addressed to the hermit; but it also suggested that Lord Burghley was the new hermit of Theobalds.[34]

How seriously Burghley entertained the notion of retirement is far from clear. Till almost the day of his death his desperate need for leisure was matched only by his compulsion to work: the old habit of control was a hard one to break. We will see much more of this in the next chapter. For years now, Theobalds had been both a retreat for Burghley and a house where he applied himself to the business of royal government.

But perhaps Burghley really had made some kind of mental break with the past. Robert was nearly twenty-eight, and he was knighted as Elizabeth left Theobalds after breakfast on 20 May. Weeks later Sir Robert was sworn a member of the Privy Council at Nonsuch. The circle was complete. If Elizabeth had made Sir William Cecil Baron of Burghley for his painful service to her, then surely she could sanction his retirement from the hard business of government by a document that was produced to look something like the beautiful charter of his barony. The lavish entertainment at Theobalds would have been a neat conclusion to a long and distinguished career in Elizabeth's service of thirty-two years. Too neat by half: seldom are lives that tidy.

*

In the year of the Theobalds entertainments a short volume of musical settings for the Psalms was dedicated to Burghley by one William Swayne. The music was by William Daman, who had died in March. Daman had been one of the Queen's musicians.

With Swayne's effusive dedication is a beautiful woodcut of Burghley's coat of arms, and his motto, *Cor unum, via una*, 'One heart, one way'. The same arms could be found on the monument to his mother and father at Stamford and on the tomb of his wife and daughter in Westminster Abbey. This was the badge of his dynasty.

Swayne believed that 'this simple work' would serve to the glory and praise of God. He hoped Burghley could enjoy it in times of peace and relaxation, 'at some times for the recreation of your mind, after your worthy and great travail from day to day taken in the most weighty affairs of this commonwealth'.

The second of the several verses before the Psalms was 'The humble suit of a sinner'. Perhaps in 1591 it spoke particularly to Lord Burghley's condition:

Lord of whom I do depend, behold my careful heart:
and when thy will and pleasure is, release me of my smart.
Thou seest my sorrows what they are, my grief is known to thee: and there
is none that can remove, or take the same from me.[35]

20

'Better for Heaven than for the World'

If Burghley craved retirement it was for the very good reason that he was horribly overworked. At the age of seventy-one he carried the burden of two jobs, as Elizabeth's Lord Treasurer and also, after the death of Sir Francis Walsingham, her acting Secretary. He was being worked to the bone. That he complained about it is no great surprise: what seems incredible is that he was able to do so much while he struggled with such poor health.

In 1592 Burghley carried with him a tiny notebook of matters of official things to do. This was an old habit. He had done the same forty years before as Edward VI's Secretary. The book was filled with notes in Burghley's small, neat, educated hand. The piles of paper grew on his desk. Letters to foreign powers, commissions for lieutenants in the counties, ordnance for Elizabeth's troops, commissions for Catholic recusants and investigations of their wives – every day there was more to do, a bureaucratic machine to run as well as a network of informants and intelligencers and a whole system of patronage. Little wonder that Burghley was so keen for Sir Robert Cecil to carry on the family business.[1]

The 1590s was not an easy decade. These were war years, when heavy fighting abroad caused all kinds of strains and discontents at home; it was a time of dearth, famine and illness; politicians feared uprisings and disorder; the politics of the royal court were competitive and strained. So much had changed since the early days of Elizabeth's reign. Then of course there had been emergencies, panics and failed policies at home and abroad, as well as a queasy feeling of the imminence of disaster, of war, plots, rebellion or invasion. Back then Secretary Cecil and his colleagues had fallen out in the Council chamber and sometimes argued at court. There were tussles and temper tantrums: there was a queen who at once knew her mind and yet was temperamentally averse to making it up, a paradox councillors like Leicester, Burghley and Walsingham struggled with almost every day of their working lives. But for all this – in fact we might say because of this – Burghley and his colleagues had been able to work together most of the time with a feeling of common purpose.

It was different in the 1590s. Almost a whole generation of politicians had gone, along with old friendships, obligations and common memories of the early days. Burghley was the last of the men who had been at Hatfield in November 1558. No one else remembered the hard times of the middle Tudor years. Of his boyhood at St John's College in Cambridge he wrote that he was 'the only person living of that time and education'. He could say the same about all the things he had heard and seen in the early decades of Elizabeth's rule.[2]

Burghley was the great survivor of Elizabeth's government and his enemies hated him for it. There was something about his longevity that to Catholics made his crimes even more dastardly. In 1592 Richard Verstegan, an Oxford-educated intelligencer, wrote a pamphlet about the men around Elizabeth who had ruined England. It was the *Guilty Men* of its day. They were the Earl of Leicester, Sir Nicholas Bacon, Sir Christopher Hatton, Sir Francis Walsingham, all dead. Burghley was their principal, the base-born nobleman who had brought the realm to perdition, who all but held Elizabeth I captive, and who made himself rich and powerful at the expense of the Queen and her subjects. Verstegan dipped his pen in bitter ink to condemn Burghley's destruction of England and his persecution of God's people. Verstegan's book was known by the popular title of 'Burghley's Commonwealth'.[3]

And so Burghley, the seasoned campaigner, the loyal councillor, the old enemy, survived. He now sat in Council with friends' sons. It was a comfort to him that his own son was there too: if he was determined that his dynasty should survive at Burghley House and in his estates, he was quite as keen to look to his political legacy. But other new men were on the rise, like the second Earl of Essex, Robert Devereux, young enough to be Burghley's grandson. The twenty-seven-year old earl who was appointed by the Queen to her Council in February 1593, brimming with ideas and self-confidence, had eaten at Burghley's table as a boy, a royal ward, his father dead in Ireland. All about Burghley were new men and new fashions. But before everyone there was Essex, a powerful force to be reckoned with.

*

How much longer would Burghley live? That, bluntly, was a question Essex and others were beginning to ask in 1593.

Burghley was 'dangerously sick' at the beginning of January, slightly improved by spring, given a special dispensation by Elizabeth to stay away from Garter celebrations on St George's Day: 'we are pleased to accept your reasonable excuse in that behalf, and by these presents* do pardon you for your absence'. In the odd symmetry of life, this was the fortieth anniversary of the sickness that had threatened to keep thirty-two-year-old Sir William Cecil away from the Garter solemnities of Edward VI. Then he had been an official of the Order confined to his bed at Wimbledon and worried about what kind of gown he should wear: now he was a Garter Knight and the Lieutenant of the Order.[4]

Spring brought little relief, either in health or in politics. The Earl of Essex was already pushing hard for a shift in policy on France. Sick or not, Burghley stood his ground in Council. He wrote to Robert Cecil on 21 May: 'The great haste that the lords made yesterday in the morning showed a great difference betwixt their humours and mine, for though they were quick as marshal men are . . . Her Majesty misliked not my slowness, whereby I am the better confirmed in my opinion.' It was imperative that the Queen should hear her oldest councillor. He spoke through Robert, who was to tell Elizabeth that though his body was in pain, his mind was comforted by her kind speeches.[5]

Here Burghley was being neither sentimental nor sycophantic. This was calculated politics. The Queen had rarely taken the advice of any of her councillors without at least some travail on their part. But before everything she had to listen to advice. It followed, then, that councillors had to be able to give counsel. To be cut off from Elizabeth was to be slowly asphyxiated. Burghley had said as much in the early months of 1587 when Elizabeth had refused to admit him to her presence. His long absences from court in 1593 evoked that same anxiety, the sense of control slipping away. No wonder that Burghley carefully briefed Sir Robert on what he should say to the Queen. The old councillor who wanted to retreat to his hermitage in his last years could not afford to be forgotten.

For years Theobalds had been Burghley's retreat. Now, feeling sick and wretched, he was hiding away at Cecil House. Sir Robert and Lady Elizabeth were at court, Burghley's grandchildren at Theobalds. He thought of Pliny, who reported an authority which held that owls shut themselves away for sixty days in winter. He was like an owl, he wrote to Robert, though besieged by suitors.[6]

Over the next days life and business went on. Burghley presided at the Court of Wards and worked from Cecil House. On 27 May he sent Robert a letter about the important business of the moment, the adjournment of part of the Trinity law term because of plague. In spite of reports of infection in London and Westminster, Burghley worked on. He believed he was dying. He added a postscript to his letter to Robert: 'I find myself so decaying in strength as I find

* i.e., this document.

it more needful for me to be occupied about my last will and other establish-
ments for my children etc.'[7]

The next day Burghley was determined to drag himself to court: 'I am weak
and uncertain how I shall be able to come to the court, yet I am in mind to
come tomorrow . . . with the opinion that [in] one or two days Her Majesty
will licence me to return to seek my amendment.' He gave a strong hint that
he felt a journey to the grave would be more fitting. And yet he was still
working. 'Until this dinner time,' he wrote to Robert, 'I have had neither kin
nor inward friend to see me or salute me but multitude of suitors that only
come for their own causes.'[8]

And that was the state of things in the late spring of 1593. Elizabeth's Lord
Treasurer, by now seventy-two years old, was sick, burdened with business
and minded to embrace death. But Burghley's Commonwealth was not
finished yet.

*

Burghley did not revise his will in May 1593 but he did review and change it a
few months later in November. He was preoccupied by the great military slog
in Ireland in December ('I cannot but continue my care for Ireland', he
wrote to Sir Robert Cecil) but was still sick, though well enough to make a
witticism to entertain the Queen. On Saturday, he said, his head and neck had
'seemed to be made of lead, and yesterday somewhat lighter as of iron'. He
wrote in pain and so the letter was not fit to be shown to Elizabeth. He hated
not to be able to write for himself. He was very proud of the scholarly italic
handwriting he had learned all those years before from two masters of
penmanship, John Cheke and Roger Ascham. Burghley's gout interfered with
one of the trademarks of his service to Elizabeth.[9]

He spent the next few days on Ireland, an acknowledged area of his
expertise on which he gave his 'simple opinion'. He was also occupied with
France, and asked Robert to talk to the Earl of Essex about it and to 'give the
request your best furtherance with Her Majesty at your best opportunity'. Late
that same night he wrote to Robert again, this time using a secretary to ease his
hand. Robert was well and truly serving his apprenticeship. His father directed
him to a big folio book he had at Windsor called 'Matters of France' in which,
over the years, Burghley kept his archive carefully indexed.[10]

This was one of the reasons why Burghley was so formidable: he simply
knew so much, all that experience and knowledge both in his memory and in
his papers. It was no wonder that Elizabeth looked for his presence at court the
following week. But for Robert it was an exacting apprenticeship to a father
whose only standard was perfection. Even nestled away like an owl at

Theobalds, Burghley complained when he had not heard from Robert about important business by five o'clock in the afternoon.[11]

Knowledge was power for Burghley: the knowledge of years of diplomacy and government business, and knowledge, too, from secret sources of the dangers to Elizabeth's crown. Burghley was an old master of intelligence work. Even when he was sick, in January 1594, 'not in tune to write' and not fit to rise from his couch, he was reading transcripts of letters of English Jesuit priests to William Allen in Rome. He looked back to the execution of Richard Hesketh of Lancashire who had been tangled up in a Catholic plot to put the fourth Earl of Derby on the English throne. For Burghley the dangers to realm and religion never went away.[12]

Elizabeth's councillors employed their own freelance agents and intelligencers, so it was no wonder that intelligence work had a sharp political edge to it. Now the Earl of Essex, keen to show how zealous he was for the Queen's safety, happened to find a terrible plot laid against her life. The supposed assassin was Dr Roderigo Lopez, one of Elizabeth's physicians, a Portuguese Jew who had practised medicine in London since the beginning of the reign. Lopez had treated some of the most powerful men in the kingdom, like the Earl of Leicester and Essex himself. He fell foul of Essex by revealing details of the earl's medical treatments.

Essex went on the attack in late January. He named Lopez in a desperate treason. The Queen was to be killed by means of poison. At first Essex's accusations were laughed at, but the earl was no fool and he persisted. Lopez was arrested and interrogated. His covert links to Spain were revealed. There were no surprises here; Lopez was after all one of Burghley's sources. But in the politics of ambition and legacy Lopez was thrown to the wolves. Burghley and Sir Robert Cecil parried Essex, not by seeking to save Dr Lopez, but by denying the earl the clear and acknowledged glory of his kill. Lopez was tried, found guilty of treason, and hanged, drawn and quartered at Tyburn in June 1594. Burghley did not protect Dr Lopez. Quite the opposite: Lopez was sacrificed to the hard politics of Elizabeth's court.[13]

Burghley wanted to have the last word in the Lopez affair: this was a habit he had formed over many years. Now, once again, he practised his old skills of propaganda. Using his secretary, Henry Maynard, Burghley wrote a long 'publication of certain treasonable attempts against the Queen's Majesty, whom God defend from the same'. This became the official published account of Lopez's horrible treason, the revelation of King Philip of Spain's part in the outrage. The conspiracy was, Burghley wrote, 'very happily discovered by the great diligence and carefulness of one of the Lords of Her Majesty's Privy Council'. It was a form of words he had spent some effort crafting. He did not say who Elizabeth's diligent councillor was. Probably indeed he meant himself, not young Essex; Burghley was the Queen's oldest servant, ever watchful of her safety.[14]

*

Burghley was sick in February 1594. 'I am not in so good health as to write with mine own hand', he wrote to Robert. Naturally he was still hard at work, particularly on the business of money for Ireland, and he sent Robert a long list of matters to deal with. But before the packet was closed up with Burghley's red wax seal of his arms and the Garter, a letter from Robert arrived. Burghley gingerly added another paragraph of his own. 'Even now I received your letter,' he wrote, 'wherein you report Her Majesty's care for my health for the which I most humbly thank her, hoping that her good wishings shall help to return me to strength for her service which I esteem the service of God, whose place she holdeth in earth.' He was, he said, three-quarters of a man whole, a quarter sick.[15]

Burghley was torn between Theobalds and court, work and rest: these were the tensions of his final years. He fought daily to do the Queen's business. In April he proposed to look to his health. For a whole Thursday he had been in the Wards and Exchequer listening to cases. That evening he conferred with his physicians about what he called a 'pilgrimage' to the waters at Bath. They prescribed 'only exercise of body and idleness of mind', and 'for these two', he explained to Robert, 'I have none to further me but Her Majesty'. He wanted to make himself better. But he wrote that evening 'almost in the dark' and he marvelled that he had not heard from Robert about some official letters to be sent to Ireland 'whither I have in readiness some from myself'. It was the old compulsion: Burghley's Commonwealth could hardly run itself. In his last years he doggedly worked himself towards the grave.[16]

Elizabeth visited all the Cecil men on her summer progress in 1594: Sir Thomas Cecil at Wimbledon, Burghley some weeks later, and Sir Robert Cecil at his house on the Strand, close to Cecil House. This was the time of Dr Lopez's execution at Tyburn and the Cecils were prospering. Robert was absorbed by business at court and exchanged letters sometimes thrice daily with his father. Burghley presided, over the Wards, over the Exchequer, over his second son's career. Always Burghley offered a commentary for Robert on political affairs at home and abroad, and Robert, now thirty-one years old, was a careful and attentive pupil.[17]

Autumn brought little relief for Burghley, either in health or in business. He wrote to Robert in late September about money and munitions for the war in Ireland. 'I am rather worse than better,' he said, 'but better for heaven than for the world.' He was in Westminster days later, making clear to Elizabeth, through Robert, his views on the archbishopric of York, which had been vacant since the death of John Piers four weeks earlier. Archbishops or minor government officials: the distinction hardly mattered to Burghley, who always had a view and generally a candidate in mind. Days later the Queen wanted him at court. 'I see how desirous Her Majesty is to have me there; now I have a mind to come thither tomorrow, but you shall not be known thereof until I shall come. Cause my chamber to be made ready.' In doing this, he added, he would venture his life: 'but I remit all to God'.[18]

Burghley went to court but it left him feeling wretched. 'My great weakness increased upon me since I came from the court', he wrote to Robert. He had wanted to go back that day but could not. If the Queen still intended to remove to Richmond Palace, he said, he would try to see her there. It was clear that she wanted to see him. This was eleven o'clock at night and the Chancellor of the Exchequer, Sir John Fortescue, had only just told him that Elizabeth 'looked for me this night which he said he thought I was unable to do'. 'I have thought good in this my perplexity,' he said to Robert, 'to satisfy Her Majesty's mind, to require you to understand what Her Majesty shall herein direct for me to do. And I will obey the same.' He was willing to serve her whatever the cost, he wrote, even if it was death, 'and thereby enter into the eternal service of Almighty God'. But some time later he received one royal instruction he felt he was not able to obey. Elizabeth wanted him to be at court to dance. He was ready to dance with all his heart, he said, yet he could dance in mind only.[19]

What comes across forcefully in Burghley's many letters to Robert is how for all his physical frailty his mind was as sharp as ever. He felt the daily frustrations of not being able to do everything he wanted to do: to work, to serve, to influence the direction of Elizabeth's mind, to control. His compulsion to work was matched only by his determination every day to counsel the Queen through Robert. But there were some days when the physical pain in his joints was too much. 'Out of my bed being not able to sign any better', he wrote to Robert one day. 'I have no hope to amend towards the world', he said on another. 'I am more fitter for an hospital than to be a party for a marriage', he wrote the day before the wedding of his granddaughter, Lady Elizabeth de Vere, and the sixth Earl of Derby.[20]

Burghley hated to surrender control, either over his letters by using Henry Maynard to write them for him, or over his own body, having to force himself to write the same words over and over again: 'Your loving father, W. Burghley'. His body became his enemy, conspiring against him; it was not the finely balanced instrument of service it had been once. His hand, he wrote shakily in late January 1595, was unable to fight and his right eye, troubled by a 'flux', could not take a level.[21]

Burghley was fighting long, hard, debilitating pain. There was no cure for him, only relief. He hated the winter for the good reason that it caused him misery. His old enemy, he once wrote, was the gout, and it had stalked him for many years. It was likened in the seventeenth century to a sly and subtle serpent that crept even into the courts of the greatest princes of the world and tormented their officers in church and commonwealth. It crept up silently on its victim, catching him unawares. But the pain in Burghley's joints was such a constant companion that he knew his enemy well enough.[22]

He lived with pain and worked through it, as he told Robert almost daily. 'I find no ease of pains, nor increase of strength,' Burghley wrote in February, 'and yet I assure you I expedite more poor suitors than I think any judge or minister of law doth in this term.' His health tended to improve with good, dry and fair weather, but he could still find travelling in his coach a painful business, and even in spring he was sometimes confined to his bed: 'I cannot yet get out of my bed; what I shall be able to do tomorrow I know not.' He scribbled this last letter 'not without pain'. But there was always work. He read papers in his coach when he was able to, and often worked from his couch at Theobalds. One of his secretaries was always nearby: twenty-nine-year old John Clapham, perhaps, a translator of Plutarch who had attended on Burghley since about 1591; or often Henry Maynard, a former lawyer of the Middle Temple in his middle forties.[23]

Burghley's mind was generally clear and sharp, his command of information powerful. Sometimes he slipped on dates, only by a day, but enough to have him writing a letter of correction and explanation to Robert. On what he thought was 12 September 1595 he looked forward to his birthday 'within forty hours'. But he had made a mistake. The day he had identified as 12 September was in fact the 13th, and so he wrote as quickly as he could to explain himself to Robert. 'I mistook yesterday to have been the 13th so as this to have been but 13 and tomorrow the 14, my birthday, the sun entering into Libra. God send you to live so many,' he continued, 'within which time many accidents shall happen to all astrologers.' A long life in politics had shown him many things which he distilled, Polonius-like, into sayings to edify friends and family. His lawyer's eye for detail never left him, even if just occasionally a day or two passed him by.[24]

*

In 1595 Queen Elizabeth declared war on her Lord Treasurer's fingers. It is a little-known conflict which consumed neither the money nor the lives of the battles against Spain or the counter-insurgency operations in Ireland. But Lord Burghley wrote to Sir Robert Cecil about it on the first Tuesday in December.

The fault was Robert's in reading Burghley's latest letter to Elizabeth. If his father had instructed him not to show the letter to the Queen, embarrassed by his shaky writing, Robert disobeyed him, or else Elizabeth insisted. 'I perceive you have read and showed my letter of my handwriting to Her Majesty, who saith that she will have a battle with my fingers.' He thought that Elizabeth would win. Burghley remembered King David's words from Morning Prayer a few days before. The Queen, he wrote, was allowed to say as David said in Psalm 144: 'Blessed be the Lord my strength, which teacheth my hands to war, and my fingers to fight.' He believed the next verse properly belonged to Elizabeth: 'My hope and my fortress, my castle and deliverer, my defender in whom I trust: which subdueth my people that is under me.' 'And if Her Majesty's hands or fingers were to fight, I durst match her with King Philip and overmatch him.'[25]

Burghley performed wonderful acts of ventriloquism through Robert. He made himself live at court in the character of the loyal old councillor, whether he was actually able to attend Elizabeth or not. When he likened the Queen to King David he was, or had been, at the court at Whitehall sitting with the Privy Council. He played the part of the wise old councillor to perfection. Sometimes he used his remote grandeur to good effect. If being away from Elizabeth's presence had its risks, he could, when his mood was right, step naturally into his role of grandee. 'I bethink with myself of so many things meet to be considered by Her Majesty, and by her authority to her Council for her affairs in respect of the noise from Spain, as though I cannot, without conference with such councillors as Her Majesty shall please to name, do or further such things to execution by myself.'

From the grand eloquence of a wise councillor he moved in the blink of an eye to his infirmity. He loved to play with words and images: 'I am willing to come thither to be near Her Majesty, though I am not able to make access to her person, but of force;* without more amendment in strength [I] must presume to keep my chamber, not as a potentate, but as an impotent aged man.' He used self-deprecating humour: he was, he said, in body not half a man but in mind passable to the muster of the rest of the Queen's councillors and his good friends. These lines were addressed to Robert, but it is as clear as day that they were meant for Elizabeth.[26]

The rhythm of the days and months was well established. Burghley moved between sickness and health just as often as he went from Theobalds to Westminster and the court. He spent a lot of time working on Ireland, and in the law terms he was absorbed in the business of the Wards and Exchequer. He also looked back to his boyhood and to the College of St John the Evangelist

---

* Full of strength, vigorous; only when he was strong again.

in Cambridge. He well knew his obligations to St John's, 'having been wholly brought up there from my age of fourteen years'. He gave the college silver communion vessels, and the senior fellows wrote to him of their joy at his gift. No one else living could remember Mass in the college chapel, or the calculated destruction of Bishop Fisher's tomb, or Thomas Cromwell's revolutionary injunctions for teaching in the university. Burghley was the last of a generation, and he was very conscious of that fact. His memories were now unique.

Looking back he may have been frustrated by the disparity between youth and age, between the bright young student and the old man of seventy-four who was at the 'beginning of a lesson' all over again, 'that is, to hold my pen in order to write'.[27]

It was in these last years that Burghley tried to make sense of his life of royal service. He had done so before many times, often when he could no longer contain the frustrations and anxieties of working at the highest level of government in times of emergency. More than once he had criticised Elizabeth's course of action in policy, her delays and her misjudgements. He had fumed in private. To colleagues he had raised his eyebrows and shaken his head. He had even threatened to resign, though how seriously he meant these offers of resignation we will never know. He had worked for years to build a relationship with the Queen that was marked by his careful, sober and painful dedication to duty: this was a pose, and it was one he was able to maintain till the day he died. He was not a gadfly of the court: he was a councillor whose job it was to speak the truth plainly.

For years the great political paradox Burghley had wrestled with was how to serve a monarch whose rule was absolute. Elizabeth was God's lieutenant on earth. Burghley's trick was to speak to her public body, to her duty; if he gave counsel it was for the public good, the commonwealth, the state; if he told Elizabeth things she did not want to hear, then he was doing it for the good of her people. He spoke to her sacred duty, and felt he had to do so because he was a councillor, her servant and God's.

In March 1596 Burghley imparted to Robert the secret of his long service. Only a few months later Elizabeth appointed Robert her Principal Secretary. He understood his father's political creed. He had served his apprenticeship.

Burghley used words like precision instruments: for well over forty years they had been the weapons he fought with at court or in Council. But for all its precision, his account of his service was still wonderfully subtle and elusive. As long as he was allowed to give advice, he wrote to Robert, he would never bend his opinion merely to suit Elizabeth's wishes, 'for that were to offend God, to whom I am sworn first'. As a servant he would obey the Queen's commandments 'and in no wise contrary the same, presuming that she, being

God's chief minister here, it shall be God's will to have her commandments obeyed; after that I have performed my duty as a counsellor'. He wished the Queen's commandments 'to have such good successes, as I am sure she intendeth'.

'You see,' he continued, 'I am in a mixture of divinity and policy, preferring in policy Her Majesty afore all others on the earth, and in divinity the King of Heaven above all, betwixt alpha and omega.'

There is nothing sentimental or easy here. It was the old paradox. Any councillor was caught between God and Queen. This was a fact of counsel Burghley had known for a lifetime.[28]

A few months later, when he asked God to 'send me some good hours, for I have no good days', he wrote that news from Robert of the Queen's best wishes for his return to health filled his heart 'to full'. He was courtly and effusive. 'Your large reports of Her Majesty's allowance of my insufficiencies as sufficient and of her superabundant care and desire of my amendment' had so moved him that he could not 'contain in the flowing of my heart'. He sent to Elizabeth, through Robert, a portion of the comfort of his heart 'by way of most humble thankfulness to Her Majesty, with a portion also of my sacrifice to Almighty God by my hearty prayers for the continuance of her happiness, wherein she exceedeth all her equals in body and government'.[29]

These were the words of someone who had tried many times to force Elizabeth's hand; who had practised all the dark arts of politics; who could be ruthless in obtaining his political objectives; who had engineered the execution of Mary Stuart, a monarch ordained by God. He always said that everything he did was for religion, realm and monarch. Now Burghley had made some kind of peace with the paradox of his service.

*

For a very long time Lord Burghley had looked to his legacy, at Burghley House, at Theobalds and in politics. In the summer of 1597 he set out ordinances 'for the order and government' of thirteen poor men in a hospital, or almshouse, in Stamford Baron, on the south bank of the River Welland facing up the hill to St Mary's Church where Burghley had been taught as a boy by Libeus Byard. To found such an institution was a very natural thing for him to do. For thirty years, after all, Burghley had lived across the Strand from one of the great royal hospitals for the poor, the Savoy Palace.

When Lady Mildred died in 1589 and Burghley, grief-struck, tried to make some sense of his loss, he had consoled himself by putting down on paper all her works for the poor in London and Hertfordshire. Burghley's establishment in Stamford was going to be more public than his wife's secret charity:

the ordinances of the hospital were printed by the royal printer and available for anyone to read in London. But that was the point. Burghley was rich, powerful and had deep roots in Northamptonshire. His hospital would show to the world his allegiance to his native 'country', just as it would help him to discharge his obligations to the poor.

Burghley set out the ordinances of the hospital with great precision. Of the thirteen poor men to be cared for, Burghley would choose and admit the first five. That right would pass to his heirs at Burghley House. The other poor men would be elected by the vicar of St Martin's Church, various local church-wardens, the Alderman of Stamford (the office his grandfather, David, had held), and various town officers. The records of the hospital would be kept in the vestry of the chancel of St Martin's, the parish church long associated with the Cecil family. Duplicate copies would be held by the Alderman.

The warden of the hospital, chosen by Burghley himself, would have an allowance of cloth each year for his gown, and so would his twelve fellows. The cloth would be the same colour as the livery coats worn by Burghley's servants. The poor men had to be 'of honest Christian profession': once nominated for a place, each man had to present himself on a Sunday morning to the vicar of St Martin's to recite aloud the Lord's Prayer and the Apostles' Creed and to begin to learn the Ten Commandments.

They were to be local men who for seven years had lived no more than seven miles from Stamford. None was to be under thirty years of age. Lepers could not be appointed, and no man diseased with the pox. Lunatics, drunkards, adulterers, thieves and fraudsters were not welcome either. Ideally the poor men were to be honest soldiers or workmen, masons, carpenters or other artisans, labourers or servants who were 'by sickness, age or other impediment unable to get their living by their handiwork or by daily service as beforetime they have done'.

With Burghley's charity came the discipline of community life. We should expect nothing less. Burghley valued the cohesion of common endeavour, especially of common worship, whether in a Cambridge college or in his own household. Cards and dice were to be strictly forbidden in the hospital. Every Sunday, Wednesday, Friday and holy day the men would go in their livery gowns to Morning and Evening Prayer at St Martin's. They would sit or kneel in the place indicated to them by the churchwardens. Failure to attend church without good reason would cost an offender sixpence out of his week's wages; these wages were set at 3s. for the warden and 2s. 4d. for the others, to be paid every Sunday by the vicar and local bailiff after Evening Prayer.

The poor men were to do honour to Burghley's family. Within the parish of St Martin's they were always to wear their livery gowns. Every first Sunday in each quarter of the year they would, if Lord Burghley kept household, go to

Burghley House to eat in the hall. If Burghley's heir at Theobalds came to Burghley House or to Stamford, then the thirteen poor men were to 'present themselves dutifully unto him, and shall offer any service they can do to him, in memory of the founder William Lord Burghley, ancestor of the said owner of Theobalds'.[30]

Burghley Hospital, as much as Burghley House or Theobalds, was part of a Lord Treasurer's legacy, an act of obligation to Stamford, and a remembrance of his family.

*

So much of Lord Burghley's life had to do with paper and parchment. His life was littered with documents: memoranda and letters, reports from ambassadors, the papers of the royal bureaucracy, financial accounts, official records of law courts, humble letters from suitors or poor students – a vast acreage of animal skins and watermarks. This was daily business for Burghley, and in much of it there was little that was remarkable. The indenture for Burghley Hospital, witnessed by Henry Maynard, Michael Hickes, Walter Cope and John Clapham, all trusted servants, was yet another piece of parchment; the paper with the names of the thirteen poor men nominated, carefully read and annotated by Burghley, another piece of business, brought to him by a secretary, perhaps Maynard, perhaps Clapham, who had only ever known him as an old man.[31]

But there was no document more important, or more final, than Burghley's last will and testament, which he revised for the last time on 1 March 1598. This most Protestant of Tudor royal servants made his peace with God and a disposition of his earthly goods on Ash Wednesday, the old day of Catholic penitence.

Burghley recorded the facts of his birth and remembered how by the order of his parents he was brought up and instructed in good religion in his young years; 'after that,' he said, 'I did come to the years of discretion to have knowledge of the Gospel of our Saviour Jesus Christ, the knowledge whereof began about that time to be more clearly revealed here in England.'

With the assistance of the Holy Spirit he hoped 'to have grace during this frail life to continue in that mind, and to have a desire to obey his will and commandments, in living religiously and virtuously as far forth as the infirmity of my flesh will suffer'. He did not know when or where or how he would die, but he knew that his worldly end could not be too far away. The signs were clear, 'by increase of years and other infirmities of my body grown for a great part by continual public services'. Whatever he had enjoyed in life, he said, had been given by the goodness of Almighty God. He wanted now to bequeath his earthly goods, 'being at this time occupied with the cogitation of my mortality'. He wished to be buried in St Martin's Church in Stamford 'with convenient comeliness according to the degree of baron and a lord of parliament'. The cost of his burial was not to exceed £1,000.

His son, Robert, came first in the will. He was to have his father's estates in Hertfordshire and Middlesex. Thomas Cecil would inherit Burghley House and lands nearby. To his sister, Anne White, Burghley left the interests he had in land in Rutland and a small annuity. For the will of such a powerfully connected politician it is very much a family affair: Burghley looked first to his sons and his sister, to his granddaughters, Lady Susan and Lady Bridget de Vere, to his daughter-in-law, to grandchildren and great-grandchildren, to his nephews and nieces. Burghley was scrupulous in the fairness of the division of his goods between Robert and Thomas.

Burghley's political archive, 'all my writings concerning the Queen's causes either for her revenue or for affairs of counsel or state', went to Robert, which was only to be expected. The rolls of family pedigrees were for Thomas, though Robert was to have use of them for two or three months to take copies. The two sons would share his Garter chains, collars and badges of St George. Thomas would inherit his father's 'best greatest collar with the George there-unto pendant', and Robert the second collar. These were remembrances for posterity, not glittering jewels of ostentation: they would remind Thomas, Robert and their sons' sons that the first Baron of Burghley had the honour to be a Knight of the Most Noble Order of the Garter. And Burghley wanted his two sons and their heirs to be conscious of their common heritage, of their shared blood. To Robert he gave the manor in Rutland which had been given by Richard Cecil to his parents before their marriage as a place for Robert and his heirs, or the daughters of Robert's sister, Anne, 'to resort unto where my eldest son's livelihood doth lie, to continue familiarity and acquaintance in blood betwixt them'.

Burghley made sure that his de Vere granddaughters were well provided for. They were children still, Lady Bridget twelve years old and Lady Susan nine. He left them the furniture and household stuff from the chambers, school-rooms and nurseries they occupied at Cecil House and at Theobalds, and each could choose one of their grandfather's coaches with two coach horses. Burghley's gold and silver plate would be used to guarantee their marriage money. How much would depend on a future husband's rank: £4,000 for an earl or his heir; £3,000 for a baron or his heir; and £2,000 for any man under the degree of baron.

And that was nearly that: a family provided for, the wages of servants protected, rewards of plate, an annuity of £20 for life to Thomas Bellot, Burghley's loyal old steward, and a few other arrangements.

When it was drawn up to his satisfaction, Burghley signed his will. It was witnessed by four men: William Wade, a clerk of the Privy Council; Henry Maynard; George Coppin, a trusted servant and a clerk in Chancery; and John Clapham. Burghley appointed as his executors Thomas Bellot and Gabriel Goodman, the Dean of Westminster, who over forty years before had served in Burghley's household as Thomas Cecil's schoolmaster. Two men would oversee the administration of the estate: Sir Thomas Egerton, the Lord Keeper of the Great Seal; and Thomas Owen, Justice of the Court of Common Pleas.[32]

How long Lord Burghley had to live only God knew.

*

In April 1598 Burghley was licensed to be absent from the Garter feast of St George by reason of his 'want of health and weak estate of body yet remaining' from his 'late great sickness'. He was not much better by the summer, when his health began to fail for the last time.[33]

Burghley left Cecil House for Theobalds at the end of the first week of June. He wanted to escape the oppressive air of Westminster, 'forced', as he wrote to Robert, 'to seek a resting place, but without rest'. The appetite he had lost was returning slowly. On the evening of 8 June he ate five or six artichoke leaves, doubtless hoping that they would help his stomach; and also a small panada, bread boiled in water and flavoured with sugar and spices. He was trying to work but felt wretched: 'And so I will prove all good means either to amend or to make a good end.'[34]

The next day he tried to work on Irish affairs. He wrote to Robert with 'as ill a stomach to write of these matters as I have to my meat, which is hitherto fitter for fasting than for feasting; and the weather so cold as I am fitter for the fire than for the garden'. He thought on the 11th that he was 'without hope of amendment' and asked Robert to present his humble thanks to the Queen 'for Her Majesty's frequent messages, for which I knowledge my debt greater than I am able to acquit, but yet I will gage* my heart to be thankful with prayer'.[35]

Burghley's servants had nothing to be cheerful about. Henry Maynard wrote to Michael Hickes from Theobalds on 16 June. 'A more melancholy time was never seen by any than this hath been here by my Lord without any comfort; what will become of it God knoweth.' Burghley was sleeping well but eating very little. He wanted to go neither to court nor to London, 'and for aught I see', Maynard thought, 'we may stay here I know not how long'. Burghley asked for no other servants. 'Business he hath none to speak of,' wrote Maynard, 'nor will

* To pledge or pawn.

be troubled with any. I conceive the world conceiveth him to be secluded from business.' Hardly any suitors were at Theobalds.[36]

But for all Maynard's gloominess, and his master's wretched health, Burghley went a few days later to Council, and on 21 June he gave his advice on a small matter of patronage. He was still poorly: 'I can make no boast of amendment, though Her Majesty's comfortable wishings feed me with hope.' For the next fortnight he struggled to more of the Privy Council's meetings.[37]

On 10 July, in a very shaky hand, Burghley wrote to Robert. 'Though I know you count it your duty in nature so continually to show you careful of my state of health, yet were I also unnatural if I should not take comfort thereby, and to beseech Almighty God to bless you with supply of such blessings as I cannot in this infirmity yield you.' He asked Robert 'diligently and effectually' to tell the Queen how her singular kindness overcame his power to acquit it. Burghley alluded to a visit he had had from the Queen. He said that she would never be a mother, 'yet she showeth herself, by feeding me with her own princely hand, as a careful nurse'. For Burghley old age became childhood once again: 'if I may be weaned to feed myself, I shall be more ready to serve her on the earth; if not, I hope to be in heaven a servitor for her and God's church'. He thanked Robert for his gift of partridges.

Burghley ended his letter with a remarkable statement. With a very weak hand he wrote one of the most arresting sentences of his life, directly, forcefully to Robert: 'Serve God by serving of the Queen, for all other service is indeed bondage to the Devil.' He closed as Robert's 'languishing father'.[38]

In fiction those would have been Burghley's last words, utterly expressive of who he was and what the purpose of his life had been. And so they are in one way, for this is the last of Burghley's surviving letters. But he did not die.

Burghley managed to get to the Council again but he must have been very frail. His fellow councillors wrote to him on 21 July to ask for his advice in 'a cause of some weight', though they were loath to trouble him, 'your health not serving you so well as we do wish'. By now he had returned to Cecil House on the Strand. His throat had begun to trouble him. Three nights later he could not sleep and stayed in bed till three o'clock in the afternoon of the 25th. He tried to get out of bed but was too weak to sit up. His legs and hands were very painful. At dinner he found it impossible to swallow without pain and he was also finding it difficult to speak.[39]

On 26 July, a Wednesday, Burghley asked Robert, through George Coppin, to call two of Elizabeth's surgeons, George Baker and Master Goodroose, as quickly as he could. Burghley's throat was swollen and sore. He had had a terrible night and was much worse than he had been the day before. He was unable to sit up in bed. Later the same day he was visited by Goodroose and a physician, Dr Gilbert.[40]

He rallied a little. On Thursday he ate a little broth and a dish of blanc-mange, minced meat with cream, rice, sugar, eggs and almonds. He had a quiet night without pain and was able to rest. At seven o'clock the next morning he asked for a drink of asses' milk, and his servants hoped that he would be able to eat a full meal of meat.[41]

Of what happened in the next few days there is no reliable account. His first biographer described Burghley's last few hours: his children gathered round his bed; his prayer for the Queen; his words to Thomas Bellot, 'I have ever found thee true to me and now I trust thee with all'; the prayers of his chaplains; his last words, 'Lord receive my spirit; Lord have mercy on me'. There is no way to tell whether Burghley's life really ended like this; the best we can say is that it may have done.

What we do know for certain is that he died at Cecil House at about seven o'clock on the morning of 4 August, a Friday. He was seventy-seven years old.[42]

In life William Cecil had known and understood the words of the Prayer Book: 'We brought nothing into this world, neither may we carry anything out of this world. The Lord giveth, and the Lord taketh away. Even as it hath pleased the Lord, so cometh things to pass: blessed be the name of the Lord.'[43]

Epilogue

Numbness, a sense of unreality, feelings of dislocation: all these quickly follow any death. Surely Burghley's was no different. In a moment, a last breath, everything changed. The physical presence of the most powerful and capable politician of his generation, his memory and experience, were all gone. In death there are ends and beginnings, losses and gains, wrenching changes and deep continuities. For Burghley's family and servants there was a new world to get used to.

Within hours of his death old colleagues began to send letters of condolence, doubtless to Thomas, his heir, and also to Sir Robert Cecil; those to Robert survive. Sir Thomas Egerton wrote with what he called a message of love and affection. He said he wanted to leave off formalities and ceremonious compliments, but he condoled with both Robert and the commonwealth. Fulke Greville, courtier, poet and friend of Philip Sidney, wrote the following day to offer comfort to Robert in his grief.[1]

For two of Burghley's secretaries, Henry Maynard and John Clapham, the painful business of tidying up the affairs of the dead began properly on 6 August. Maynard quickly requested a leave of absence to go to his house in Essex. He heard nothing from Sir Robert for two days. On the 8th he was busy compiling an inventory of 'principal things' in the gallery at Cecil House. That day he again asked Robert to be allowed to attend to his private affairs. Maynard had been with Burghley for weeks before he died. He surely wanted a break from what must have been a melancholy service. He knew his future was secure. Like Walter Cope, Maynard was a tenant of one of Burghley's houses in Westminster, and Burghley left each man an estate in those houses. Soon enough it was being said in Westminster that if Sir Robert was to be appointed either Lord Treasurer or Master of the Court of Wards, Maynard would be Secretary. Burghley had been a demanding master but he rewarded long and honest service.[2]

We can imagine the busyness at Cecil House in the days after Burghley's death: inventories to be compiled, records found, books to be sorted through – the early instructions of Sir Robert and Thomas, second Baron of Burghley, and of Thomas Bellot and Gabriel Goodman, too. And yet for all this activity Burghley had been clear that he did not want Thomas to take possession of Cecil House for six weeks after his death. Bellot, the trusted steward, was to preside over Burghley's household in the old way. There was to be a pause. Lady Bridget and Lady Susan de Vere kept their lodgings on the Strand and lived there as they had done when their grandfather was away from Westminster. For a month and a half time stood still at Cecil House.

Gabriel Goodman, the Dean of Westminster, wrote to Robert on 10 August. Burghley's death, he said, was a public loss and calamity. One of the blessings of providence had been that, just as King David had seen the succession of his son Solomon, Robert's good father had had Robert succeed him in his place. Goodman remembered a favourite verse of Robert's mother, Lady Mildred, from Psalm 55: 'Cast thy burden upon the Lord'.[3]

Four days later the preparations for Burghley's funeral were well under way. Thomas had set out the charges for black mourning clothes. He proposed to ask Anthony Watson, the Bishop of Chichester and the Queen's almoner, to preach the funeral sermon. The ceremony had to be just right for a man of Burghley's rank and importance. He had been a stickler for form and tradition. For years he had policed the nobility and landed society as Master of the Court of Wards and Liveries and as a Garter Knight. It was highly appropriate that one man busily working on the great funeral was William Camden, Clarenceux King of Arms and an antiquary, and Burghley's official historian.[4]

While the great and the good prepared for Burghley's funeral, Thomas Bellot quietly fulfilled some of his old master's wishes. Burghley wanted money to be given within a month of his death to the poor of Westminster, Hertfordshire and Northamptonshire: £10 for each parish of St Clement's the Savoy, St Martin-in-the-Fields, Cheshunt, and St Martin's in Stamford. He also bequeathed money to be shared between the prisoners of Newgate, Ludgate and the Gatehouse in London. With great rank and power came charity and a remembrance for the poor. These were the old duties.[5]

It was the grandest of funerals, a vast procession that moved on Tuesday, 29 August from Cecil House on the Strand to Westminster Abbey. Over five hundred mourners attended. The choreography was superb, almost the whole of Elizabethan society set out in careful order to celebrate the longest career in royal service in a century. The poor of Westminster went first with their beadles. The officers of the royal bureaucracy came next, and then the judges, Burghley's old servants, and royal officials. Sir Robert Cecil and Thomas, Baron of Burghley walked behind their father's servants. They were followed a little way back by Goodman and Bellot, Burghley's executors, and then

Bishop Watson of Chichester. Watson was followed by the royal heralds who carried Burghley's helm, crest, sword, shield and coat armour.

Burghley's body was carried by eight gentlemen. They walked with four assistants who each held a corner of the velvet pall. Behind them came the Queen's councillors, all on horseback and dressed in black: the Earl of Essex, Earl Marshal; Sir Thomas Egerton, Lord Keeper of the Great Seal; the Lord Admiral, the Earl of Nottingham; the Earl of Shrewsbury; and the Earl of Worcester. The ancients of Gray's Inn followed them, and then the people. It was, as one eyewitness wrote, a 'sorrowful solemnity'. After the funeral service was done, the mourners went back along the Strand to dine at Cecil House.[6]

Burghley wished to be buried in St Martin's Church in Stamford Baron, and within weeks his sons and executors had arranged for this to happen. Westminster Abbey was held as a reserve, a spot near to the spectacular tomb of Mildred and Anne. But Burghley had wanted above all to return to his ancestors, to the place in St Martin's specially chosen and prepared by him for the bodies of his grandfather, father and mother, himself and his posterity.

Burghley had given special instructions for the return of his body to Stamford. He was to be carried without pomp in a coach covered with black. Twelve men should accompany the cortège up the Great North Road from Westminster to Burghley House. His coffin would rest in a church for each night of the journey, and the poor of those parishes which received his corpse would receive 40s. Of the twelve men some would be gentlemen 'and the rest yeomen and grooms'. This was to keep costs down, 'for avoiding of an unnecessary charge, in a long carriage of a dead carcase'. The poorest lord in England, the builder of Cecil House, Burghley House and Theobalds, was keen to economise to the very end. John Clapham was probably one of the gentlemen who travelled with the cortège. He wrote to Sir Robert on 3 September that he was desirous to accompany his lord's corpse back to Stamford.[7]

And so it was in this way that Sir William Cecil, Knight of the Most Noble Order of the Garter, Baron of Burghley and Lord Treasurer of England, returned home to his country to wait in his tomb for Judgment Day.

Reflections

The dead live on in the memories of those they leave behind. Sometimes these memories are clear and vivid, sometimes they are not. Sometimes they are fragments of memories, perceived only for a second or two, bright flashes of recollection, stimulated perhaps by one of the senses; sometimes they are reflections of reflections, rearranged or embellished or even manufactured for purposes we cannot or do not want to understand.

Even the clearest memories can deceive us. The conditions which allow us to remember can be created by others. Sometimes the dead, if they have been powerful men, want to set down what precisely people will remember of them; sometimes it is the living who establish the boundaries, say what can and cannot be remembered, what it is proper or improper to speak of those who have gone.

What follow are some fragments of William Cecil as he was remembered in the few years after 1598.

*

In the month Burghley made his final journey to Stamford, Thomas and Robert Cecil presented Sir John Stanhope with a jewel in the figure of their father's heart. Stanhope was a kinsman of Protector Somerset, Lord Burghley's first master, and so by marriage a kinsman of King Edward VI. He was also a cousin to Lady Mildred, a shade older than Thomas, and as a boy in Mary's reign he had lived with the Cecils at Wimbledon before going off to study at Cambridge. When Thomas and Robert wrote to cousin Stanhope in 1598 he was an officer of the Queen's household.

The jewel was for Elizabeth. Thomas and Robert presented it together: they were, they wrote, children of an undivided spirit. They cherished their father's words, which were engraved on the back of the jewel. They were those of Burghley's motto, *Cor unum, via una*, 'One heart, one way'. The golden sheaf of corn above the heart, the garb of the Cecils that appeared on Burghley's coat of arms, was to remind the Queen that their father had always wished her, as they put it, a harvest of felicities to accompany her infinite virtues. The heart celebrated the life and service of the first Baron of Burghley, but it left Elizabeth in no doubt that his sons honoured her too.[1]

Robert had perhaps been meditating on his father's heart for some weeks. Days after Burghley's death Gabriel Goodman reminded Robert of the origins of his father's motto, the inspiration for the Burghley jewel. The words came from the prophet Jeremiah, which Robert would have known as well as the venerable Dean of Westminster. They were the words of God to his people:

> Behold, I will gather them out of all countries, wherein I have scattered them in mine anger, & in my wrath, and in great indignation, and I will bring them again unto this place, and I will cause them to dwell safely.
>
> And they shall be my people, and I will be their God.
>
> And I will give them one heart & one way that they may fear me for ever for the wealth of them, & of their children after them.[2]

*

'O what a heart is this that will not let me die! – Come, Lord Jesu! – One drop of death, Lord Jesu!' Burghley's first biographer records these as some of William Cecil's last words.

The writer explains that Burghley spoke about his heart because he complained of a pain in his chest before he took to his bed for the last time. The physicians who examined him believed that the cause of this pain was a humour of the gout. They found nothing wrong with Burghley's pulse, and said that it was impossible that he could be heartsick. So in fact it was a strong heart that prevented Burghley from dying as quickly as he would have liked to have done in his last days: *Cor unum, via una.*[3]

The author of this biography of Burghley wrote a long deathbed scene which is clearly observed and compellingly graphic. The detail is arresting: twenty friends and servants round Burghley's bed, the wailing and the prayers, the quiet slipping away. But it is also a highly stylised and crafted account of a great man's death. So the problem we have here is to establish whether this account is reliable, a question we can ask of the biography, the so-called 'Anonymous Life', more generally.

From the first paragraph the writer puts us on our guard. His purpose is a moral one: it is to excite the admiration of his readers for Burghley as an exemplar of virtue and selfless service. And from the start the biographer sets out to impress. He tells us how Henry VIII was amazed by the penetrating intelligence of young Master Cecil brought to the royal court by his father, Richard. At St John's College in Cambridge he was a brilliant student, so keen to learn that every day the bell-ringer woke him at four o'clock in the morning. In Mary's reign he was a man of grit and principle: 'Here was no turn-coat, nor seller of his soul, nor renouncer of his faith for ambition of a councillor's place, as many would do upon so fair an offer.'

Yes, he was powerful: 'He grew now to some greatness, carrying a reputation to bear such sway and rule in the commonwealth and state as it was thought nothing was done without him.' But everything he did was tempered by justice and integrity. He always showed father-like care for poor tenants and litigants. As a judge he was blind to the power of the rich. In his habits he was frugal and modest. He put his service to the crown before his own comfort and health. He seldom played games but instead read books to relax and rode in his gardens on his little mule. He was a model master and public servant who grew 'to the height and perfection of a grave and great councillor by his infinite, continual study, care and practice'.[4]

Some of what the 'Anonymous Life' tells us rings true enough. There is, for example, a very expressive portrait of white-bearded Burghley on his mule holding a pink and a honeysuckle. We know he loved books, though in his younger days he did not hate games quite as much as his biographer suggests. The sayings recorded in the 'Anonymous Life' sound like Burghley. 'That counsel without resolution and execution was but wind.' 'A good prince must hear all but strive to follow the best counsel.' 'Good princes ought first to prefer the service of God and his Church, and next of the commonwealth, before their own pleasure or profit.' The author gets the architecture of Burghley's life and career approximately right, even if he wobbles on some of the details. He writes in clear, direct, vivid prose: the 'Anonymous Life' is an entertaining read. But should we believe any of it?[5]

First, perhaps, we should find out about the author, if we can. If we are able to trust the biographer then maybe we can trust the biography. Here we seem to be on solid ground. From what the biographer tells us, he was one of Burghley's servants, a man of a certain rank and age. Obviously he was educated, which narrows the field. In fact a convincing case has been made for the candidacy of Michael Hickes. Hickes entered Burghley's service in the 1570s, and in 1598 Hickes was one of his master's secretaries. We can even establish that Hickes, if indeed he was our mystery biographer, wrote his life of Burghley within only a few years of Burghley's death.

But the plain fact is this. The 'Anonymous Life' was not a scholarly biography of Burghley. Michael Hickes did not test all his sources. He wrote a version of Burghley's life for a purpose we can guess at but which in the end we cannot really know for sure. We should note that it was never printed.

Certainly the biographer saw in Burghley's great life a moral example. This was, after all, the purpose of history. Thomas Norton, Burghley's expert propagandist, wrote of works of history as mirrors in which the present day could be understood and the future discerned. In the 'Anonymous Life' we are looking at a reflection of a reflection.[6]

The book is all the richer for this. It tells us something about what Michael Hickes knew, or thought he knew, of his old master's story. Perhaps it says something, too, of the image Burghley cultivated for himself. This was a trick that powerful men then, as now, were very good at.

We can only guess at what Hickes did or did not know about Burghley's early life. When we read the 'Anonymous Life', we can ask questions. Who was around to tell Hickes about all of this? Was it Burghley himself, over dinner or supper, or travelling to court in his coach? Did Hickes speak to an old servant, or a member of the family, or someone with a long memory, like Gabriel Goodman? Was Hickes really such a star-struck admirer of Burghley, or did he also see faults in his master? The questions could go on and on. We may even begin to worry that what we have in the 'Anonymous Life' is merely an idealised version of Burghley's life: set down in celebration, using well established modes of structure and expression to give the life of a great man. But in the end it is a simple heroic story, with many of the contradictions and difficulties of character smoothed away for the sake of the reader's moral edification.

All of this may sound difficult and confusing. Many people like a good plain tale with simple facts everybody can understand: objective, no-nonsense history, just the way it was, without sleights of hand and hidden agendas. Seldom is history that simple. But in a way it is the opacity of the 'Anonymous Life' that makes it an interesting book. If we take it at face value, comparing what Hickes wrote to what we do know and can prove to be some of the facts of William Cecil's life, the 'Anonymous Life' is a sadly deficient book, full of all kinds of mistakes or misrepresentations. In the end we have to enjoy the 'Anonymous Life' for what it is: earnest, passionate and in places a wonderful narrative. We have to thank Hickes, or whoever the author was, for taking the time and trouble to write the first substantial biography of Lord Burghley. But we do not have to believe him.

*

Books are often important for what they do not quite tell the reader. Here we may have stumbled on one of the secrets of the 'Anonymous Life'. Michael Hickes was bothered about Burghley's reputation for honesty and fair dealing. He set out the official position. Burghley's qualities were simply beyond question: he was zealous for law and justice, a man of integrity, loyalty and charity; he was full of pity for the poor and never partial to the rich. He was neither corrupt nor mean. In fact Hickes used the examples of Theobalds, Burghley House and Cecil House to demonstrate, not Lord Burghley's extravagance, but his generosity to queen and state.

In matters of law Burghley was scrupulous in his honesty. He refused gifts of plate at New Year, said Hickes, and even the odd buck. His saying was, 'I will take nothing of you, having a cause depending before me'. He was careful as Master of the Wards to look to the Queen's benefit, not his own. He was as straight in his dealings as he was generous in his gifts to learning and to the poor, whether in his donations to St John's College, Cambridge or in the foundation of Burghley Hospital in Stamford. What Hickes was very keen to squash was the notion that Burghley was covetous: he was instead generous and open in his charity.[7]

Burghley's scrupulous care of money and his dispassionate execution of justice: the anonymous biographer does not distinguish very greatly between them. Burghley was loved by his tenants and praised by everyone for his fairness of mind and passion for justice. But on these matters not everyone agreed with Michael Hickes.

For almost his whole career Burghley fought off critics and enemies who hated his power and the way he used it. He was attacked in pamphlets published abroad from the 1570s all the way through to the 1590s. William Herle, Burghley's agent and intelligencer, heard the gossip on the streets of London, near the wharves of Billingsgate, in the taverns. Prisoners said that Burghley wanted to murder the Duke of Norfolk in the Tower. Ordinary men and women said that he was in secret league with Spain. People pointed at his great mansion on the Strand, or at Theobalds, and said he built houses fit for kings. He was a subject who overreached himself. Old friends tried to console him. 'Your conscience shall be your testimony to Almighty God; it is no new matter for such as take pains for the good government of the commonwealth to be reviled on.' That was Archbishop Parker of Canterbury. But it still rankled.

Tudor officials did not receive very large salaries from the Queen. Instead they relied on patronage, on grants of land and more offices. Over the years Burghley built up an enormous portfolio of property throughout England. He was a landed nobleman and this was his income. But there were other fees and payments. As Master of the Court of Wards and Liveries, a subject on which Michael Hickes was rather sensitive, it is clear that Burghley made a vast amount of money. In one wardship from the 1580s, payments were made by the Court to Lady Mildred and to one of Burghley's secretaries, Barnard Dewhurst. In that case Burghley came away with more money than the Queen.

This was not an isolated example. Perhaps it was not open corruption: we might say that it was the oil applied to make a whole system of government and patronage run more smoothly. But many of Burghley's contemporaries were less forgiving.[8]

In the last weeks of his life Lord Burghley, barely able to hold his pen properly, wrote to Sir William Peryam, Chief Baron of the Exchequer. Peryam was family, the husband of Burghley's niece, Elizabeth Bacon, the sister of Francis Bacon. Burghley had been slandered by some of the poor tenants of Claxby, a little village in the wilds of Lincolnshire. At Cecil House Burghley had pored over the examinations of the tenants taken by a local gentleman. He had identified the culprit, one Johnson, 'who hath made this lewd report of me'. The slanders were to do with bribery and corruption. Burghley's letter was sealed. The seal bore an impression of the Garter and its motto, *Honi soit qui mal y pense*, 'Shame be to him who evil thinks.'[9]

Somehow we have to reconcile all this with Michael Hickes's passionate defence of his old master. It perhaps makes us wonder, too, about the great marble tomb in St Martin's Church under which (as the inscription puts it) Burghley waits for the second coming of Christ. Here his memory was carefully protected by his heirs. He was, the inscription says,

> entrusted with the greatest & most weighty affairs of this kingdom, & above all others approved; in promoting the true religion, & providing for the safety & honour of the commonwealth; by his prudence, honesty, integrity, & great services to the nation he obtained the highest honours: & when he had lived long enough to nature, long enough to glory, but not long enough to his country, quietly fell asleep in Christ.[10]

*

If it was Burghley's duty to God to advise the Queen, then it was also his responsibility as a father to counsel his sons. In this he was on a hiding to nothing with young Thomas on his travels in France in the early 1560s, though relations between Burghley and his heir eased considerably over the following years. Robert was counselled almost every day of the 1590s. Burghley gave his thoughts on life, on business and on service: 'This my cogitations you may use to your own good', he wrote to Robert in 1596, muddling his singulars and plurals just a little bit.

Burghley was a dynast. He saw to his posterity. He guarded the reputation of his family as carefully as he could, no easy thing when his son-in-law, one of the most elegant noblemen of the court, spent a decade spreading damaging rumours about him. Burghley policed family protocol and made sure that sons and daughters, grandchildren and great-grandchildren, behaved properly. All of this came very naturally to a man who had an instinct for nobility and whose responsibility it was, as Master of the Wards and as Elizabeth's councillor, to preserve and sustain a landed society of rank and degree.

In the seventeenth century Burghley was known for his wise sayings to Robert. *The Counsell of a Father to his Sonne, in ten severall Precepts* was printed as a single large folio sheet in 1611. Nothing indicated the author of the *Precepts*, nor the identity of the son, though the observant reader would have noticed three things: first, the father was dead; secondly, the son's mother was held by his father to be 'matchless', a careful and godly governor of the boy in his infancy and a woman of 'virtuous inclination'; thirdly, the son was as yet unmarried. This is not the place for a long dissertation on the *Precepts*, but if it was really Burghley's, it was written before Robert married Elizabeth Brooke in 1589. There may be something significant, too, in the fact that it was not till 1637, twenty years after the *Precepts* was printed for the second time, that Burghley was revealed as the author. At best the *Precepts* was Burghley's; at worst it was perceived to be his, reflections of a reflection, made more opaque still by its anonymity.

Whatever the *Precepts* was or was not, it spoke to the son, and to readers on the streets of London, with wonderful directness. The precepts were about how a gentleman should conduct himself, from his choice of wife ('Make not choice of a dwarf or a fool') to the running of a house, the government of children, hospitality, the treatment of kinsmen, friendship, deportment, conversation and behaviour. In places the advice is truly heartfelt: 'Suffer not thy sons to pass the Alps, for they shall learn nothing but pride, blasphemy and atheism.' Was Burghley (if it was Burghley) thinking here of his famously foppish son-in-law Oxford in Italy?

This last example captures something of the tone of the precepts. They are, for the most part, conservative enough; but there is an edginess to them, too, which nicely matches the sort of thing Burghley wrote to Thomas Cecil during his catastrophic stay in Paris: catastrophic for Burghley, of course, but not for Thomas, who really rather enjoyed himself.

As early as the second precept, Burghley wrote about a father and his children and the rhythm of posterity: 'Bring thy children up in obedience and learning, yet without austerity; praise them openly; reprehend them secretly; give them good countenance, and convenient maintenance according to thy ability, for otherwise . . . what portion thou shalt leave them, they may thank death and not thee for it.'[11]

*

In the great labyrinth of Shakespeare scholarship it used to be thought by some, and robustly denied by others, that Burghley was the model for Polonius, the grave councillor of King Claudius in *Hamlet*.

This is a problem that is as knotty as one chooses to make it. For some it is no problem at all. Polonius was Lord Chamberlain, Burghley was Lord Treasurer: but Polonius's office at court was not mentioned at all in Shakespeare's first folio of 1623. Polonius's son, Laertes, wishes to go to France, and Polonius grudgingly agrees, his son, he says, having 'wrung from me my slow leave /By laboursome petition'. Was Laertes Thomas Cecil? Polonius has a daughter, Ophelia, who is seriously in danger of falling prey to love, of being caught like a woodcock in a trap. 'Marry thy daughters betimes lest they marry themselves', Burghley said to Robert in his *Precepts*; and he had been as worldly-wise as Polonius in making sure that the marriages of his children were about dynasty, not love. Was Ophelia Anne, Countess of Oxford? The *Precepts* has also been used in evidence. Burghley advised Robert that 'if thou imprint them in thy mind, thou shall reap the benefit': Polonius speaks to Laertes of 'these few precepts in thy memory'. But surely we know that Burghley's friends and colleagues gave similar advice to their sons, and that Shakespeare's words are close to a text by the Greek rhetorician Isocrates.[12]

In this way we can chase our own tails, a pastime which suits some people more than it does others. Brilliant writers and dramatists do not need to have characters ready made for them, like mannequins to be dressed for a shop window: they come out of imagination and experience, from a deep creative resource. William Shakespeare did not need to study the life of Lord Burghley to write the character of Polonius.

Yet it is still highly likely that Shakespeare knew Burghley: not personally, perhaps, but certainly by reputation. Anyone who lived and worked in London, and who was as close to the court as Shakespeare was by the 1590s, must have known something of the most powerful man in England. Shakespeare's literary patron from about 1594, Henry Wriothesley, third Earl of Southampton, was brought up and educated by Burghley as a royal ward. Ferdinando Stanley, fifth Earl of Derby, was the patron of a very successful theatrical company of which Shakespeare may have been a member. Ferdinando's brother, William, the sixth earl, married Burghley's grand-daughter, Lady Elizabeth de Vere, in 1595.[13]

These are, of course, associations and speculations. To them we should add something about the stock image of a councillor. True and honest councillors were men of gravity, wisdom and education. They were old men, for age brought wisdom. To trust the counsels of the young was to invite flattery, and flattery brought destruction to commonwealths.

So it was very easy for Shakespeare to cast royal councillors as rather dull men out of touch with the wit and energy of the young. John of Gaunt, in *Richard II*, is too serious by half, at least for his nephew the King. Gonzalo, the honest old councillor of *The Tempest*, is mocked by Sebastian and Antonio. Gonzalo's fantasy for the strange island he and his king have landed on is Tudor society turned upside down. 'No sovereignty', he says, to which the riposte comes 'Yet he would be king on't.' The audiences of London theatres could laugh at Gonzalo, and perhaps more cruelly at Polonius being run through by Hamlet's sword. The perfumed young noblemen of Elizabeth's court, more absorbed in their poetry than in matters of policy and counsel, would have been just as amused by these hulking old dinosaurs of government.[14]

Perhaps for some in the early years of the seventeenth century there was a memory of Burghley in the character of Polonius, a fragment, a reflection: probably for others there was not. Audiences are not, after all, literary scholars or historians of politics. We cannot even expect them to be experts on the news of the day. They are there to enjoy themselves.

And so in the end the test is really an imaginative one. When King Claudius asks Polonius for his judgement on Hamlet's psychological state, the grave councillor replies as a grave councillor should. Can we imagine old Lord Burghley speaking these lines?

> I assure my good liege
> I hold my duty as I hold my soul,
> Both to my God and to my gracious king;
> And I do think, or else this brain of mine
> Hunts not the trail of policy so sure
> As it hath us'd to do, that I have found
> The very cause of Hamlet's lunacy.[15]

*

Francis Bacon, lawyer, philosopher and insinuating career politician, was Burghley's nephew, the son of Sir Nicholas and Lady Anne Bacon. Bacon was a brilliant essayist who was caught up in the rhythm of his own prose and captivated by his own cleverness. But in playing with words, Bacon said some remarkable things about the human condition.

Bacon, like Shakespeare, is a bridge between our world and Burghley's. So much of what Burghley knew is gone, either emptied of meaning or changed beyond all recognition. Old institutions, like parliament or the Privy Council or even the monarchy, survive for reasons we may or may not understand. Our language is the language Burghley spoke and yet it, too, has changed by being spoken in different ways and for different purposes for over four hundred years. Anything that can help us to make some kind of connection with the Elizabethan past is useful. Bacon helps us to think particularly about politics.

Tudor courtiers were not professional politicians. Throughout this book I have, for reasons of economy and simplicity, used words like 'politician' and 'government' in ways that are familiar to most people today. But they are approximations only. Burghley called himself a servant, a minister and a counsellor; he advised a monarch who was understood to be God's lieutenant on earth; he saw the direct intervention of God in the world around him. The politics of Tudor England existed in a world quite removed from our own. Yet for all this difference there are things we recognise about Burghley's time. Pompous Polonius, dull and old-fashioned, belongs to Shakespeare; but so do the ruthless ambition of Richard III and the detached self-absorption and complacency of divinely ordained Richard II. Politics was a tough game in the sixteenth century and then, as now, to play that game came with some costs.

This is what Francis Bacon describes in one of his essays, 'Of Great Place', printed in 1612. What follows is a very long passage from the essay. It seemed more appropriate to consider the whole passage, which is beautifully written, than to read it in fits and starts of quotation.

Men in great places are thrice servants: servants of the sovereign or state; servants of fame; and servants of business. So as they have no freedom, neither in their persons, nor in their actions, nor in their times. It is a strange desire, to seek power and to lose liberty; or to seek power over others and to lose power over a man's self. The rising unto place is laborious, and by pains men come to greater pains; and it is sometimes base, and by indignities men come to dignities. The standing is slippery; and the regress is either a downfall, or at least an eclipse, which is a melancholy thing. *Cum non sis qui fueris, non esse cur velis vivere.* [When you are no longer the man you have been, there is no reason why you should wish to live.] Nay, retire men cannot when they would; neither will they when it were reason; but are impatient of privateness, even in age and sickness, which require the shadow. . . . Certainly, great persons had need to borrow other men's opinions, to think themselves happy; for if they judge by their own feelings, they cannot find it: but if they think with themselves what other men think of them, and that other men would fain be as they are, then they are happy as it were by report, when perhaps they find the contrary within. For they are the first that find their own griefs, though they be the last that find their own faults. Certainly, men in great fortunes are strangers to themselves, and while they are in the puzzle of business they have no time to tend their health, either of body of mind. *Illi mors gravis incubat, qui notus nimis omnibus, ignotus moritur sibi* [Death lies heavily on the man who, too well known to others, dies a stranger to himself].

There is passion here, and empathy; self-knowledge and ruthless diagnosis. What really concerns Bacon is the personal cost of power. The psychological effect of holding great office, he seems to be saying, is the obliteration of the private man. The 'puzzle of business' steals time and wrecks health. The young man works hard for office and once he has it the only way is down. The old man knows that he is not what he once was, but still he clings to power and cannot let go of it. He cannot stand to be alone. He no longer knows himself. The only reflection he sees or wants is in the distorted opinions of others. He cannot recognise his own faults but he is quick enough to feel sorry for himself.[16]

We cannot say that Francis Bacon had uncle Burghley in mind when he wrote his essay: he knew many other powerful men, and he spent much of his life trying himself to climb the slippery pole of politics. But still Bacon helps us in a couple of ways. For a start, he makes a connection between the fact of having power and the idea of being a servant. To some this will be an odd notion even in a modern democracy where senior members of the government are called ministers. Secondly, he is not afraid to use the word power: 'power over others'. Service to sovereign and state was power and authority. But service to fame and to business was a trap from which there was no escape.

These are themes and preoccupations we find over and over again in Burghley's letters. He was merely a servant, merely a minister; he could never give up his service to the Queen; he was trapped by the business of service, pitifully overwhelmed by paper and suitors. Perhaps this is why the most powerful man in Elizabeth's government wrote so often of his powerlessness. When he was sick and old he wanted release and retirement; and yet he still went through Sir Robert Cecil's letters annotating and correcting; he could never quite let go. He felt alone in his work in Westminster and he wanted to see a reflection of himself, the great dynast, in the old and young 'descended of my body'.

For Bacon the pieces would have fitted. Perhaps Burghley knew they did too.

*

It is surely only to be expected that a man as powerful as Burghley should commission the first official history of Elizabeth's reign. A year or two before he died he asked William Camden, antiquary and Clarenceux King of Arms, to write the book. Camden was deeply troubled by his commission. When part of the *Annales* was published in scholarly Latin in 1615, and then again when Camden's book was translated into English twenty years later, Camden recalled the almost physical anxiety he suffered when he began the project:

> For I light upon most thick piles and heaps of writings and instruments of all sorts, reasonably well digested in respect of the times; but in regard of the variety of the arguments most confused. In rigging and searching whereof, whilst I laboured till I sweat, being covered over with dust, and gathered fit matter together (which was diligently sought for, but more rarely found than I expected), both he died and my industry waxed very cold.

Many historians of Elizabeth's reign know exactly how Camden felt.[17]

Burghley left us with these first *Annales* of Elizabeth's reign. He did so indirectly, of course, through Camden who, from 1598, was free to write what he wanted to write from Burghley's papers – or almost: Camden was, after all, a servant of Mary, Queen of Scots' son, James VI and I. But there is at least a fragment here of Burghley, a reflection of a reflection. Camden's book was a standard and unimpeachable source on Elizabeth's reign for centuries: it told the official story.

William Camden was effusive in praise of his old patron. For the year 1598 he recorded Burghley's death. He gave an account of a fine public career over many decades. He echoed the inscription on Burghley's tomb in St Martin's Church in Stamford. But he also said something about the man, of his gout and sickness and the grief of the last years.

Like Michael Hickes, or Burghley's sons, Camden's purpose was to write of Burghley as an ideal. I suspect – in fact I hope – that my Burghley is a much more ambivalent character, but that is only to be expected: Camden wrote in his day and I write in mine. But even at a distance of four centuries it is hard not to be impressed by the scale of Burghley's life and the power of his personality. He was a man who believed with a terrifying intensity. He saw his world in black and white. He thought in absolutes. And so, for all of the contradictions and complexities of William Cecil's character, the strains of life in government, the great talents as well as the darker skills of the ruthless political operator, the discipline and the control, William Camden's encomium says so much about a minister, a humble functionary, a man of controlled passion:

> Certainly he was a most excellent man, who (to say nothing of his reverend presence and undistempered countenance) was fashioned by nature and adorned with learning, a singular man for honesty, gravity, temperance, industry and justice. Hereunto were added a fluent and elegant speech (and

that not affected, but plain and easy), wisdom strengthened by experience, and seasoned with exceeding moderation and most approved fidelity; but above all, singular piety towards God. To speak in a word, the Queen was most happy in so great a counsellor, and to his wholesome counsels the state of England forever shall be beholden.[18]

Notes

Abbreviations

Add. MSS	Additional Manuscripts, British Library, London
APC	*Acts of the Privy Council of England*, ed. John Roche Dasent *et al.*, new series, 46 vols (London, 1890–1964)
Bod.	Bodleian Library, Oxford
CA	*The Compleat Ambassador*, ed. Sir Dudley Digges (London, 1655)
CJ	*Journals of the House of Commons*
Cott. MSS	Cotton Manuscripts, British Library, London
CP	Cecil Papers, Hatfield House, Hertfordshire
CPR	*Calendar of the Patent Rolls preserved in the Public Record Office*, Henry VII–Elizabeth I, multiple vols (London, 1914—)
CSPF	*Calendar of State Papers, Foreign: Edward VI, Mary, Elizabeth I*, ed. J. Stevenson *et al.*, 25 vols (London, 1861–1950)
CSPV	*Calendar of State Papers and Manuscripts Relating to English Affairs Existing in the Archives and Collections of Venice and in Other Libraries of Northern Italy*, 38 vols (London, 1864–1947)
CUL	Cambridge University Library
Eg. MSS	Egerton Manuscripts, British Library, London
f(f.)	folio(s)
Harl. MSS	Harley Manuscripts, British Library, London
Haynes	Samuel Haynes, ed., *A Collection of State Papers* (London, 1740)
HMC *Salisbury*	Royal Commission on Historical Manuscripts, *Calendar of the Manuscripts of the Most Hon. The Marquis of Salisbury*, 24 vols (London, 1883–1973)
Lans. MSS	Lansdowne Manuscripts, British Library, London
LJ	*Journals of the House of Lords*
LP Henry VIII	*Letters and Papers, Foreign and Domestic, of the Reign of Henry VIII*, ed. J.S. Brewer, J. Gairdner, R.H. Brodie *et al.*, 21 vols and *Addenda* (London, 1862–1932)
Murdin	William Murdin, ed., *A Collection of State Papers* (London, 1759)
NA	National Archives, London
Oxford DNB	*Oxford Dictionary of National Biography*, ed. H.C.G. Matthew and Brian Harrison, 60 vols (Oxford, 2004)
PCC	Prerogative Court of Canterbury
PROB	Prerogative Court of Canterbury, Will Registers
RCHME	Royal Commission on the Historical Monuments of England
Royal MSS	Royal Manuscripts, British Library, London

SC	*Scrinia Ceciliana: Mysteries of State & Government in Letters of the Late Famous Lord Burghley* (London, 1663)
sig(s).	signature(s)
SP	State Papers, National Archives, London
SR	*Statutes of the Realm*, ed. A. Luders, T.E. Tomlins, J. Raithby *et al.*, 11 vols (London, 1810–28)
STC	*A Short-Title Catalogue of Books … 1475–1640*, ed. W.A. Jackson, F.S. Ferguson and Katharine F. Pantzer, 3 vols (London, 1986–91)
VCH	Victoria County History of England

Correspondents

ER	Queen Elizabeth I
MQS	Mary, Queen of Scots
PC	Privy Council
RC	Robert Cecil
TC	Thomas Cecil
WC/WB	William Cecil/Lord Burghley

1. The Cyssylls of Stamford

1 PROB 1/3, WB's will, 1 Mar. 1598, f. 1; WB to RC, 13 Sept. 1595, CUL MS Ee.3.56 no. 59; Add. MS 6059 f. 9*v*.

2 PROB 11/16 (PCC 24 Bennett).

3 RCHME *Cambridge*, vol. 1, 102; Birkbeck, *Bourne*, 38–9.

4 Feb. 1519, *LP Henry VIII*, vol. 3, pt 1, 32 (102.18).

5 1520, *LP Henry VIII*, vol. 3, pt 1, 244 (704); Starkey, *Henry VIII*, 50–3.

6 15 Mar. 1517, *LP Henry VIII*, vol. 2, pt 2, 967 (no. 3013). On King's Cliffe Park, see VCH *Northampton*, vol. 2, 581.

7 David Cyssyll to Thomas Cromwell, 28 June [1532], Cott. MS Vespasian F.13 f. 267*r*–*v*; David Cyssyll to Thomas Cromwell, 4 Nov. [?1532], Cott. MS Titus B.1 f. 356*r*–*v*; David Cecyll to Thomas Cromwell, 8 Apr. [1532], Cott. MS Vespasian F.13 f. 266*r*–*v*. The spelling WC used in writing his own name in 1545 is from CUL shelf-mark Rel.d.52.17, a reference I owe to the kindness of Richard Rex. Spellings for the Cecils of Allt Yr Ynys can be found in *CPR* for the reign of Edward VI, 1547–53; and in Jones, *Monmouthshire Wills*, 191–2.

8 There is a copy of the will of Richard Philip Seyceld, Oct. 1508, annotated by WC, in CP 141 f. 28*r*–*v*; *STC* 19885, 38–9. The best accounts of the Cecils of Stamford and the Cecils of Allt Yr Ynys are by Barron, *Northamptonshire Families*, 21–2; and by Rowse, 'Alltyrynys and the Cecils', 54–76. Much else that has been written, particularly in the nineteenth century, is suspect. On Allt Yr Ynys see RCHME *Herefordshire*, vol. 1, 247.

9 *LP Henry VIII*, vol. 1, pt. 1, 65 (no. 132.49); and *LP Henry VIII*, vol. 1, pt. 2, 1114 (no. 2535.13); Barron, *Northamptonshire Families*, 23, 25.

10 PROB 11/15 (PCC 13 Adean); *CPR, 1494–1509*, 515.

11 RCHME *Stamford*, 118–19; Rogers, 'Late Medieval Stamford', 30.

12 Gonville and Caius College, Cambridge, MS 266/670 ff. 49*v*, 51*r* (Lady Margaret); MS 266/670 f. 39*v* (David and Alice Cecil).

13 Gonville and Caius College, Cambridge, MS 266/670 ff. 1*v*–2*r* (Smith and Smith, *English Gilds*, 188–9).

14 PROB 11/29 (PCC 3 Spert).

15 Barron, *Northamptonshire Families*, 25; *Survey and Antiquities … of Stamford*, 27.

16 Sir Thomas Audley to [Thomas Cromwell,] 4 Nov. [1532], *LP Henry VIII*, vol. 5, 640 (no. 1518); *LP Henry VIII*, vol. 4, pt 1, 692 (no. 1540).

17 Charlton, *Burghley*, 160–1; Barron, *Northamptonshire Families*, 26–7.
18 Leach, *English Schools*, pt. 1, 7–55; pt 2, 132–2, 138–9; VCH *Lincolnshire*, 479.
19 David Cecil to Thomas Cromwell, 14 Oct. [1532], *LP Henry VIII*, vol. 5, 603 (no. 1424); Deed, *Stamford School*, 103–6.
20 Deed, *Stamford School*, 108.
21 RCHME *Stamford*, 23; Pevsner and Harris, *Lincolnshire*, 694–5; Leland, *Itinerary*, vol. 4, 91.
22 *STC* 18094, sig. +5*v*.

2. St John the Evangelist

1 WB to RC, 7 Dec. 1595, CUL MS Ee.3.56 no. 66.
2 On Window 4 of King's College Chapel see Wayment, *Windows*, 55–6; and King, *Tudor Royal Iconography*, 85–6.
3 Miller, *Portrait*, has a short history of St John's College, but see also Howard, *Finances*; Leader, *University of Cambridge*, 284–91; and Scott, *Notes*; *STC* 832, sigs Q1*v*–Q2*r*.
4 *STC* 832, sig. Q2*r*; Torry, *Founders and Benefactors*, 2–6.
5 RCHME *Cambridge*, vol. 2, 187–8; Leader, *University of Cambridge*, chs 2, 3; Miller, *Portrait*, 8–15.
6 WB to RC, 7 Dec. 1595, CUL MS Ee.3.56 no. 66; the gatehouse of St John's is described in RCHME *Cambridge*, vol. 2, 189.
7 Mayor, *Early Statutes*, 104–8; Torry, *Founders and Benefactors*, 4; Leader, *University of Cambridge*, ch. 5; Scott, *Notes*, fourth series, 258; Leedham-Green, *Cambridge Inventories*, vol. 1, 15–17.
8 Computus Roll, 1534–5, St John's College, Cambridge, MS SB3.10; Bursars' Book, 1534–5, St John's College, Cambridge, MS D106.14 ff. 35–45; Bursars' Book, 1535–6, St John's College, Cambridge, MS D106.15 ff. 31–4.
9 Mullinger, *University of Cambridge*, 54–61; Goldhill, *Who Needs Greek?*, ch. 1.
10 Ryan, *Roger Ascham*, chs 2, 3; *STC* 832, sig. Q1*r*.
11 John Cheke to Matthew Parker, 6 Feb. 1553, Corpus Christi College, Cambridge, Parker MS 106 f. 609.
12 Porter, *Tudor Cambridge*, ch. 3; Leader, *University of Cambridge*, ch. 13; Lamb, *Collection*, 14–18; Leedham–Green, *Cambridge Inventories*, vol. 1, 17–18, 19.
13 *STC* 832, sigs Q1*v*–Q3*r*; Lamb, *Collection*, 19, 20–5, 37–9; Leader, *University of Cambridge*, ch. 13.
14 Underwood, 'John Fisher', 40; Leader, *University of Cambridge*, 332–41.
15 Scott, *Notes*, third series, 332.
16 Miller, *Portrait*, 15–17; Baker, *History*, 115–26.
17 Foster, *St Mary the Great*, 31, 32, 43, 57, 63, 66.
18 7 Jan. 1530, CUL, Vice-Chancellor's Court Wills, vol. 1, 1501–58, f. 50*v*.
19 Roger Alford to WC, 9 Apr. 1553, CP 151 f. 91*v*.
20 *STC* 832, sigs B1*r*–B2*r*.

3. London and Court

1 Prockter and Taylor, *Elizabethan London*, 5, 7, 20; Douthwaite, *Gray's Inn*, xii–xvi.
2 Colvin and Foister, *Panorama*, esp. drawings 1, 3, 5, 7, 9, 11.
3 Wriothesley, *Chronicle*, vol. 1, 134–5, 137, 152; MacLure, *Paul's Cross*, 23–7.
4 27 July 1540, *LP Henry VIII*, vol. 15, 454 (no. 917).
5 9 July 1540, *LP Henry VIII*, vol. 15, 471 (no. 942.46).
6 Fisher, *De veritate*, CUL shelf-mark Rel.d.52.17, a reference I owe to the kindness of Richard Rex.

7   PROB 1/3, WB's will, 1 Mar. 1598, f. 1.
8   Fisher, 'Inns of Court', 129.
9   Fletcher, *Pension Book*, 48; Douthwaite, *Gray's Inn*, 153–4.
10   Foster, *St Mary the Great*, 101.
11   Roger Alford to WC, 9 Apr. 1553, CP 151, fol. 91*v*.
12   Lans. MS 118 f. 35*v*; Nov. 1545, *LP Henry VIII*, vol. 20, pt 2, 455 (no. 910.82).
13   McIntosh, 'Sir Anthony Cooke', 237–40.
14   NA, E/23/4; 30 Dec. 1546, *LP Henry VIII*, vol. 21, pt 2, 634 (no. 634.1, 10). See also
     Ives, 'Henry VIII's Will'.

4. Servant and Secretary

1   Alford, *Kingship and Politics*, 80–1; Bush, 'Requests', 451–64.
2   Earl of Shrewsbury to WC, 9 Apr. 1548, College of Arms, London, Talbot MS 3193
     ff. 55, 56.
3   *STC* 19476.5, sigs P4*v*–P5*r*.
4   Alford, *Kingship and Politics*, 81.
5   Lans. MS 118 f. 35*v*; *STC* 4827 (5 Nov. 1547); *STC* 4828 (28 Mar. 1548).
6   Royal MS 17 B 18 f. 2*v*.
7   *STC* 10089, sig. a2*r*.
8   Deed, *Stamford School*, 107–9.
9   *STC* 11222, 805–6.
10   *STC* 11222, 770–6.
11   Alford, *Kingship and Politics*, 77.
12   Alford, *Kingship and Politics*, 49, 65.
13   Duchess of Suffolk to WC, 16 Nov. 1549, Lans. MS 2 f. 58*r*; Brigden, 'Richard
     Scudamore', 94.
14   Brigden, 'Richard Scudamore', 98, 104.
15   *APC, 1547–50*, 372; Brigden, 'Richard Scudamore', 114.
16   Hoak, 'Privy Chamber', 92–4; Edward VI, *Chronicle*, 26.
17   Richard Scudamore to Sir Philip Hoby, 26 Apr. 1550, Brigden, 'Richard Scudamore',
     130.
18   Duchess of Suffolk to WC, 9 May 1550, SP 10/10 ff. 10*r*–11*v*; Scudamore to Hoby, 1
     June 1550, Brigden, 'Richard Scudamore', 134.
19   Richard Whalley to WC, 26 June 1550, SP 10/10 ff. 21*r*–22*v*.
20   Edward VI, *Chronicle*, 38–40.
21   Alford, *Kingship and Politics*, 139–40.
22   *APC, 1550–52*, 118; WC to Sir Thomas Smith, 11 Jan. 1564, Lans. MS 102 f. 56*r*;
     Duchess of Suffolk to WC, 2 Oct. 1550, SP 10/10 ff. 83*r*–84*v*.
23   Richard Goodrich to WC, 30 Sept. 1550, SP 10/10 ff. 78*r*–79*v*.
24   *APC, 1550–52*, 348.
25   Duchess of Suffolk to WC, Sept. 1551, SP 10/13 ff. 107*v*–108*v*; Alford, *Kingship and
     Politics*, 124–32. On 'the sweat', see *STC* 4343.
26   Corpus Christi College, Cambridge, Parker MS 102 ff. 253–8, 259–66.
27   Edward VI, *Chronicle*, 86.
28   Edward VI, *Chronicle*, 88.
29   SP 10/14 ff. 115*r*–122*v*.
30   Sir Anthony Cooke to WC, 20 Aug. 1552, SP 10/14 f. 138*r*–*v*.
31   Richard Goodrich to WC, 22 Aug. 1552, SP 10/14 f. 144A*r*.
32   Lans. MS 118 f. 1*r*; Machyn, *Diary*, 32.
33   Roger Alford to WC, 9 Apr. 1553, CP 151 ff. 91*r*–93*r*; HMC *Salisbury*, vol. 1, 116; 5
     June 1553, *CPR, 1547–53*, 6.

34 Nicholas Wotton to WC, 21 June 1553, CP 151 f. 16r (Haynes, 152); John, Lord Audley to WC, 9 May 1553, SP 10/18 f. 36r–v.
35 WC to Duke of Northumberland, 14 May 1553, Inner Temple Library, London, Petyt MS 538, vol. 47, f. 529r–v.
36 Loach, *Edward VI*, ch. 12.

5. Conscience or Treason?

1 *SR*, vol. 3, 955–8.
2 Roger Alford to WB, 4 Oct. 1573, Cott. MS Titus B.2 f. 374r.
3 Nichols, *Chronicle*, 89–90 (Inner Temple, Petyt MS 538, vol. 47, f. 317).
4 Cott. MS Titus B.2 ff. 374v–375r.
5 Fuller, *Church-History*, bk 8, 1–2.
6 Fuller, *Church-History*, bk 8, 2.
7 Fuller, *Church-History*, bk 8, 2–3; Cott. MS Titus B.2 f. 375r; MacCulloch, 'Vita Mariae', 248.
8 Lans. MS 104 f. 1r.
9 Lans. MS 104 ff. 3r, 4v.
10 Fuller, *Church-History*, bk 8, 3.
11 Cott. MS Titus B.2 f. 375r–v; Fuller, *Church-History*, bk 8, 3–4.
12 Nichols, *Chronicle*, 90–1 (Inner Temple, Petyt MS 538, vol. 47, f. 316).
13 Cott. MS Titus B.2 ff. 375v–376r.
14 Nichols, *Chronicle*, 90–1 (Inner Temple, Petyt MS 538, vol. 47, f. 316).
15 Nichols, *Chronicle*, 91–100.
16 8 July 1553, Wriothesley, *Chronicle*, vol. 2, 85; Mary to the PC, 9 July 1553, STC 13569, 1084–5; Cott. MS Titus B.2 f. 377v; MacCulloch, 'Vita Mariae', 253; STC 13569, 1084–5.
17 10 July 1553, Lans. MS 1236 f. 24r–v. The proclamation of Jane as queen is STC 7846. See also Wriothesley, *Chronicle*, vol. 2, 85–6; Cott. MS Titus B.2 f. 377v; PC to Mary, [9] July 1553, STC 13569, 1084–5.
18 12 July 1553, Lans. MS 3 ff. 48r, 49r.
19 Cott. MS Titus B.2 f. 376r–v; Harl. MS 6222 ff. 2r–16r.
20 Lans. MS 104 f. 1r–v.
21 STC 20188, quotation at sig. A7v; Wriothesley, *Chronicle*, vol. 2, 87–8; STC 13569, 1087.
22 Cott. MS Titus B.2 f. 376r–v.
23 Harl. MS 6222 ff. 11r–12v.
24 PC to Lord Rich, 19 July 1553, Lans. MS 3 f. 50r.
25 Wriothesley, *Chronicle*, vol. 2, 88–9.
26 Nichols, *Chronicle*, 109; Wriothesley, *Chronicle*, vol. 2, 89–90; MacCulloch, 'Vita Mariae', 265.
27 Cott. MS Titus B.2 f. 377v.
28 MacCulloch, 'Vita Mariae', 270.
29 Lans. MS 104 ff. 1r–2r; Cott. MS Titus B.2 f. 377v.
30 MacCulloch, 'Vita Mariae', f. 377r; Cott. MS Titus B.2 f. 377v.

6. 'Some Fruit Made of an Evil Time'

1 7 Aug. 1553, Lans. MS 118 f. 86v.
2 *Archaeologia*, 12 (1796), 334–96; Loach, *Edward VI*, 167–9.
3 Thomas Cranmer to WC, 14 Aug. 1553, Longleat House, Portland Papers 1 f. 79r.
4 Evenden, 'Michael Wood', 383–94.
5 Lans. MS 118 f. 41v; Evenden, 'Michael Wood', 385–6.

6   Lans. MS 118 f. 36r.

7   Lans. MS 118 ff. 37r (diet), 40v (transport).

8   Lans. MS 118 ff. 35v, 36r.

9   Hodgett, *Chantry Priests*, 24, 48.

10   For example, 22 Oct. 1554, Lans. MS 118 f. 70r; Starkey, *Elizabeth*, 236–7.

11   23 Apr. [1554], Lans. MS 118 f. 67v.

12   Rodriguez-Salgado and Adams, 'Feria's Dispatch', 323, 332.

13   Lans. MS 118 ff. 35v (Goodman), 67r (Seres); *STC* 832, sig. B1r.

14   Lans. MS 118 f. 36r.

15   22 Oct. 1554, Lans. MS 118 f. 70r.

16   Sir John Mason to Sir William Petre, 7 Dec. 1554, *CSPF, 1553–8*, 142; 27 Dec. 1554, Lans. MS 118 ff. 59v, 70v; 1 Jan. [1555], Lans. MS 118 f. 70v.

17   *CPR, 1554–5*, 55–9; 24 Mar. 1555, Lans. MS 118 f. 71v; 25 Mar. 1555, Lans. MS 118 f. 34v; 5 Apr. 1555, Lans. MS 118 f. 27r.

18   Machyn, *Diary*, 86; Loades, *Mary Tudor*, 232, 234, 248–51.

19   May 1555, Lans. MS 118 ff. 72r–v, 81r, 83r–v.

20   Lans. MS 118 f. 32v.

21   Lans. MS 118 ff. 62v, 73v; servants' bills, 1 Sept.–1 Oct. [1555], CP Bills 1.

22   Servants' bills, 15–19 Oct. 1555, CP Bills 1; 28 Oct. 1555, Lans. MS 118 f. 74r; 4 Nov. 1555, *CJ*, vol. 1, 43; 13 Nov. 1555, *CJ*, vol. 1, 44, 45.

23   26 Nov. 1555, *CJ*, vol. 1, 45; Loach, *Parliament*, 138.

24   Emmison, *Tudor Secretary*, 197; Loach, *Parliament*, 139–43, 155.

25   Ralph Baldwin's bills, 12 Sept.–22 Dec. 1555, CP Bills 1; 14 Dec. 1555, Lans. MS 118 f. 63v; Quentin Sneynton's bills, 16–27 Dec. 1555, CP Bills 1.

26   Servants' bills, 9–16 Feb. 1556, 23 Feb.–1 Mar. [1556], 22–29 Mar. 1556, CP Bills 1.

27   Easter Book, Wimbledon, 5 Apr. 1556, SP 11/8 ff. 1r–2v.

28   Servants' bills, 7–14 June [1556], CP Bills 1.

29   Roger Warde to WC, 13 June 1556, SP 11/9 ff. 7r–8v.

30   Sir Philip Hoby to WC, 1 July 1556, Lans. MS 3 f. 113r.

31   5 July 1556, Add. MS 32091 f. 149r–v.

32   Sir John Cheke to WC, 18 Feb. 1556, Lans. MS 3 ff. 130r–131r.

33   Sir Thomas Benger to WC, 24 Oct. 1556, CP 151 f. 152r (Haynes, 202); Sir Roger Cholmley to WC, 28 Oct. 1556, SP 11/9 f. 88r–v; Countess of Bedford to WC, 31 Oct. 1556, CP 151 f. 153r.

34   William Cayworth's accounts, 8 Nov.–30 Dec. 1556, SP 11/9 ff. 107r–108v; 5 Dec. 1556, CP 140 f. 13v; Emmison, *Tudor Secretary*, 200; Hoby to WC, [10] Dec. 1556, CP 152 f. 2r. See also Cripps, *Old English Plate*, 313–22.

35   Ralph Baldwin's bills, 29 Dec. 1556–5 Jan. 1557, CP Bills 1; Hoby to WC, 2 Jan. 1557, CP 151 f. 140r; Sir Anthony Cooke to WC, 10 Jan. 1557, CP 151 f. 141r.

36   Ralph Baldwin's bills, 29 Dec. 1556–5 Jan. 1557, CP Bills 1; CP 151 f. 141r.

37   William Cayworth's bills, 17–21 Jan. 1557, CP Bills 1; servants' bills, 12–19 Jan., 19–26 Jan., 2–9 Feb. 1557, CP Bills 1; Hoby to WC, 21 Feb. 1557, CP 151 f. 144r.

38   Lord John Grey to WC, 26 Feb. 1557, CP 151 f. 145r; servants' bills, 28 Feb.–[8] Mar. 1557, CP Box 1; household accounts, Mar. 1557, CP Bills 1.

39   Lord Wentworth to WC, 16 Jan. 1557, CP 151 f. 142r; Sir Thomas Cornwallis to WC, 5 Mar. 1557, CP 151 f. 146r (Haynes, 203).

40   Servants' bills, 4–11 Apr. 1557, CP Bills 1.

41   Servants' bills, 11–18 Apr. 1557, CP Bills 1; William Cayworth's bills, 21–26 Apr. 1557, CP Bills 1; servants' bills, 25 Apr.–2 May 1557, CP Bills 1; Machyn, *Diary*, 132–3.

42   Servants' bills, 11–18 Apr., 7–9 June, 24–27 June 1557, CP Bills 1; Machyn, *Diary*, 139.

43   Servants' bills, 9–16 Feb. 1557, 24–27 June [1557], CP Bills 1; Hoby, 'Travels', 126.

44   Earl of Bedford to WC, 26 July 1557, CP 152 f. 14r; Countess of Bedford to WC, 9 Aug. 1557, CP 152 f. 17r; 13 Aug. 1557, CP 152 f. 18r.

45   Sir Nicholas and Lady Anne Bacon to WC, 18 Aug. 1557, CP 152 f. 19r; Aug. 1557, Lans. MS 118 f. 27r.
46   Servants' bills, 23–30 Jan. 1558, CP Bills 1.
47   Machyn, *Diary*, 162–3; Cooke to WC, 24 Jan. 1558, CP 152 f. 6r (Haynes, 205).
48   Machyn, *Diary*, 166–7; Starkey, *Elizabeth*, 221.
49   Quentin Sneynton's bills, 27 Feb.–6 Mar. 1558, CP Bills 1.
50   Loades, *Mary Tudor*, 306–11, 370–83.
51   Rodriguez-Salgado and Adams, 'Feria's Dispatch', 323, 332.

7. Master Secretary's Device

1   Starkey, *Elizabeth*, ch. 15.
2   17 Nov. 1558, SP 12/1 f. 3r–v; 18 Nov. 1558, SP 12/1 f. 4r–v.
3   SP 12/1 f. 4r–v.
4   Cott. MS Caligula E.5 f. 56r.
5   *APC, 1558–70*, 3.
6   SP 12/1 f. 3v.
7   SP 12/1 f. 12r–v.
8   Sir Nicholas Throckmorton to ER, 18 Nov. 1558, SP 12/1 f. 7r–v.
9   John Eyre to WC, 4 Dec. 1558, SP 12/1 f. 48r.
10   SP 12/1 ff. 156r–158r.
11   The 'Device' survives in two manuscripts copies only, Cott. MS Julius F.6 ff. 167r–169v, and Add. MS 48035 ff. 141r–146v. It is the second copy, in the papers of Robert Beale (*d.* 1601), which may be the more reliable text. Beale noted that his copy came 'out of a book' belonging to Sir Thomas Smith (*d.* 1577). Beale worked for Smith in the royal secretariat between 1572 and 1577. It may be that Beale's copy of the 'Device' was made at this time or in the years after Smith's death. There is no conclusive proof from Beale's text that WC wrote the 'Device', but its form, structure and style suggest strongly that he did.
12   Hoak, 'Coronations', 123–4; Machyn, *Diary*, 185.
13   *CSPV, 1558–80*, 11; Chambers, *Elizabethan Stage*, vol. 1, 155–6.
14   Hughes and Larkin, *Proclamations*, vol. 2, 102–3; Bowers, 'Chapel Royal', 325–6.
15   Machyn, *Diary*, 186; *STC* 7590; *CSPV, 1558–80*, 12–16.
16   *CSPV, 1558–80*, 16–18; Hoak, 'Coronations', 148–50.
17   Hoak, 'Coronations', 150.
18   Hartley, *Proceedings*, vol. 1, 33–9, quotation at 34.
19   Jones, *Faith by Statute*, 94.
20   Machyn, *Diary*, 189; MacLure, *Paul's Cross*, 40–1.
21   Jones, *Faith by Statute*, 88–90; Bowers, 'Chapel Royal', 334; Machyn, *Diary*, 189; *CSPV, 1558–80*, 30–1.
22   Jones, *Faith by Statute*, 89–99, quotation at 94; Bowers, 'Chapel Royal', 334–6.
23   Hartley, *Proceedings*, vol. 1, 7–11; Jones, *Faith by Statute*, 97–100.
24   Hartley, *Proceedings*, vol. 1, 12–17; Jones, *Faith by Statute*, 102–3.
25   Jones, *Faith by Statute*, 102–3, 117–24.
26   William Day to ?Matthew Parker, 31 Mar. 1559, Corpus Christi College, Cambridge, Parker MS 118 f. 383r–v.
27   *APC, 1558–70*, 77; Jones, *Faith by Statute*, 127.
28   *APC, 1558–70*, 78–9; MacLure, *Paul's Cross*, 41; Machyn, *Diary*, 194.
29   Jones, *Faith by Statute*, 130, 132.
30   Hartley, *Proceedings*, vol. 1, 27–32.
31   Act of Supremacy 1559 (1 Elizabeth I c. 1), *SR*, vol. 4, pt 1, 350–5; Act of Uniformity 1559 (1 Elizabeth I c. 2), *SR*, vol. 4, pt 1, 355–8.

8. 'This Famous Isle'

1   Minute of WC to Sir Nicholas Bacon, 21 July 1563, Lans. MS 102 f. 70v.
2   20 May 1559, CP 5 f. 35r.
3   PC to Sir Nicholas Throckmorton, 13 June 1559, SP 70/5 f. 31r–v.
4   Add. MS 48035 ff. 141r–143r; Cott. MS Julius F.6 ff. 167r–169v.
5   WC to Sir Henry Percy, 4 July 1559, SP 52/1 ff. 99r–101v; WC to Sir James Croft, SP 52/1 f. 105r–v.
6   WC to Earl of Shrewsbury, 12 July 1559, Lambeth Palace Library, Shrewsbury Papers MS 709 f. 1r–v.
7   Throckmorton to ER, 27 July 1559, Cott. MS Caligula E.5 f. 107v; PC to Congregation, 28 July 1559, SP 52/1 f. 148v.
8   WC to Sir Ralph Sadler, 24 Aug. 1559, Add. MS 33591 f. 50r–v; Alford, *Early Elizabethan Polity*, 55, 59.
9   Lans. MS 4 ff. 26r–27v (Alford, *Early Elizabethan Polity*, 223–4).
10 WC to Sadler, 5 Sept. 1559, Add. MS 33591 f. 83r; WC to Sadler and Croft, 11 Sept. 1559, Add. MS 33591 f. 102r.
11 WC to Sadler, 27 Sept. 1559, Add. MS 33591 f. 139r; WC to Sadler and Croft, 3 Oct. 1559, Add. MS 33591 f. 170r.
12 WC to Sadler and Croft, 31 Oct. 1559, Add. MS 33591 f. 249r–v; 3 Nov. 1559, Add. MS 33592 ff. 1r–2r.
13 Alford, *Early Elizabethan Polity*, 64–5.
14 Harl. MS 253 ff. 83v–92v; Harl. MS 398 ff. 12v–21r; Folger Shakespeare Library, MS V.a.143.
15 WC to Sadler and Croft, 23 Dec. 1559, Add. MS 33592 f. 212r; WC to Shrewsbury, 26 Dec. 1559, Lambeth Palace Library, MS 3196 f. 57.
16 SP 12/7 ff. 185r–190v.
17 27 Dec. 1559, SP 12/7 f. 191v; 28 Dec. 1559, SP 52/1 f. 318r.
18 Lans. MS 102 f. 1r.
19 29 Jan. 1562, Lans. MS 103 ff. 3r–4r; 23 Mar. 1560, SP 12/11 ff. 75r–78v; Cott. MS Caligula B.10 ff. 89r–92v.
20 Minute of WC to Earl of Huntly, 18 Mar. 1562, CP 152 f. 68r–v.
21 Lans. MS 103 f. 5r–v.
22 Throckmorton to ER, 6 Dec. 1560, *CSPF, 1560–1*, 423–4.
23 10 Jan. 1561, *CPR, 1560–3*, 44.
24 13 May 1561, *CPR, 1560–3*, 165–6
25 R. Jones to Throckmorton, 4 July 1561, Add. MS 35830 f. 141r; Husselby and Henderson, 'Cecil House', 161.
26 Hugh Alington to Thomas Windebank, 10 Feb. 1562, SP 12/21 f. 96r.
27 WC to Thomas Randolph, 30 June 1561, Harl. MS 6990 f. 13r.
28 Hartley, *Proceedings*, vol. 1, 44.
29 WC to Throckmorton, 14 July 1561, Add. MS 35830 ff. 158r–159v.
30 WC to Earl of Sussex, 25 July 1561, Cott. MS Titus B.13 f. 48r–v.
31 Throckmorton to ER, 11 Aug. 1561, Add. MS 35830 ff. 175v–176v.
32 WC to Sussex, 12 Aug. 1561, Cott. MS Titus B.13 f. 50r–v.
33 Duchess of Somerset to WC, Aug. 1561, SP 12/19 f. 64r–v; WC to Sussex, 12 Aug. 1561, Cott. MS Titus B.13 f. 50r–v.
34 Windebank to WC, 4 Aug. 1561, SP 12/19 f. 14r; WC to Windebank, 17 Aug. 1561, SP 12/19 f. 48r.
35 WC to Sussex, 21 Aug. 1561, Cott. MS Titus B.13 f. 54r–v.
36 WC to Windebank, 17 Aug. 1561, SP 12/19 f. 48r; WC to TC, 27 Aug. 1561, SP 12/19 f. 73r.
37 WC to Windebank, 10 Sept. 1561, SP 12/19 ff. 92r–93r.

38 WC to Windebank, 3 Oct. 1561, SP 12/20 f. 1r.
39 WC to Sussex, 17 Sept. 1561, Cott. MS Titus B.13 f. 60r–v; 7 Oct. 1561, Cott. MS Titus B.13 f. 62r–v.
40 WC to Windebank, 4 Nov. 1561, SP 12/20 f. 55r.
41 WC to Windebank, 14 Nov. 1561, SP 12/20 f. 61r–v.
42 Windebank to WC, 26 Nov. 1561, SP 12/20 f. 69r–v; WC to Windebank, 14 Nov. 1561, SP 12/20 f. 61r–v.
43 WC to Sussex, 28 Nov. 1561, Cott. MS Titus B.13 f. 68r; 14 Dec. 1561, Cott. MS Titus B.13 f. 71r.
44 WC to Throckmorton, 22 Dec. 1561, Add. MS 35830 ff. 228r–229v.
45 WC to Windebank, 27 Dec. 1561, SP 12/20 f. 95r; WC to TC, 27 Dec. 1561, SP 12/20 f. 96r.
46 STC 18684. See also James and Walker, 'Gorboduc', 109–21.
47 Throckmorton to WC, 6, 9, 14 Mar. 1562, CSPF, 1561–2, 549, 552–4.
48 WC to Throckmorton, 24 Mar. 1562, Add. MS 35831 ff. 22r–23r.
49 Guy, 'My Heart is My Own', 159–62; Alford, Early Elizabethan Polity, 93–6.
50 MacCaffrey, 'Newhaven Expedition', 1–21.
51 WC to [Sir Thomas Chaloner], 11 Oct. 1562, Cott. MS Vespasian C.7 ff. 224r–225r.
52 WC to Sir Thomas Smith, 29 Oct. 1562, Lans. MS 102 f. 35r–v; WC to Throckmorton, 11 Nov. 1562, Add. MS 35831 f. 87r. See also Doran, Elizabeth, 85.
53 WC to Smith, 4 Dec. 1562, Lans. MS 102 f. 45r.
54 STC 18684, sigs E3v–E4r.

9. 'As Sheep without a Shepherd'

1 Strong, Portraits, vol. 1, 28, of National Portrait Gallery 2184.
2 Guy, 'My Heart is My Own', 168; WC to Sir Thomas Smith, 14 Jan. 1563, Lans. MS 102 f. 18r.
3 Nowell, Catechism, 223–8; Alford, Early Elizabethan Polity, 104–5.
4 Alford, Early Elizabethan Polity, 106, 107–9.
5 Alford, Early Elizabethan Polity, 108–9.
6 Alford, Early Elizabethan Polity, 110.
7 SP 12/28 ff. 68r–69v (Alford, Early Elizabethan Polity, 225–8).
8 Oxford DNB, vol. 10, 746.
9 Matthew Parker to WC, 23 July 1563, Lans. MS 6 f. 154r.
10 Edmund Grindal to WC, 30 July 1563, Lans. MS 6 ff. 156r–157r.
11 Grindal to WC, 30 July 1563, Lans. MS 6 ff. 156r–157r; 1 Aug. 1563, Lans. MS 6 f. 160r; Parker to WC, 6 Aug. 1563, Lans. MS 6 f. 162r; STC 16506.7.
12 WC to Maitland of Lethington, 20 Aug. 1563, Add. MS 32091 ff. 199r–200r.
13 WC to Parker, 25 Aug. 1563, Royal MS 7 B.11 f. 3v; Lord John Grey to WC, 29 Aug. 1563, Lans. MS 6 f. 92r; Countess of Hertford to WC, 3 Sept. 1563, Lans. MS 6 f. 92r; Hertford to WC, 7 Nov. 1563, Lans. MS 6 f. 100r; Grey to WC, 7 Nov. 1563, Lans. MS 6 f. 102r; 15 Nov. 1563, Lans. MS 6 f. 105r.
14 WC to Smith, 11 Jan. 1564, Lans. MS 102 f. 55r.
15 WC to Smith, 27 Apr. 1564, Lans. MS 102 f. 89v.
16 Lans. MS 102 f. 89v; WC to Smith, 1 May 1564, Lans. MS 102 f. 93r.
17 Macauley, 'Matthew Lennox', ch. 5.
18 Guy, 'My Heart is My Own', ch. 12; Dawson, 'Mary Queen of Scots', 1–24.
19 WC to Smith, 12 Sept. 1564, Lans. MS 102 f. 98r–v; 23 Sept. 1564, Lans. MS 102 f. 100r–v.
20 ER to WC, 23 Sept. 1564, SP 52/9 no. 48; Guy, 'My Heart is My Own', 202; WC to Smith, 4 Oct. 1564, Lans. MS 102 f. 102r.
21 WC to Smith, 26 Nov. 1564, Lans. MS 102 ff. 103r–104r.

22 WC to Smith, 15 Dec. 1564, Lans. MS 102 f. 105r.
23 WC to Smith, [25]–30 Dec. 1564, Lans. MS 102 ff. 107r–109r.
24 Lans. MS 102 ff. 107r–109r.
25 Harl. MS 6990 ff. 68r–69v; SP 52/10 ff. 91r–92v.
26 Alford, *Early Elizabethan Polity*, 134–7; 24 Sept. 1565, Cott. MS Caligula B.10 ff. 358r–359v.
27 24 Sept. 1565, Cott. MS Caligula B.10 f. 350v.
28 WC to Sir Henry Sidney, 24 June 1566, SP 63/18 f. 62r–v.
29 WC to Marquess of Winchester, 29 July 1566, Cott. MS Caligula B.13 ff. 173r–174r; Murdin, 762; RCHME *Stamford*, 33.
30 Alford, *Early Elizabethan Polity*, 145.
31 Alford, *Early Elizabethan Polity*, 148.
32 Hartley, *Proceedings*, vol. 1, 154.
33 SP 12/41 ff. 38r–40v; 15 Nov. 1566, SP 12/41 ff. 41r–44v; 16 Nov. 1566, SP 12/41 ff. 45r–48v.
34 WB to RC, 13 Mar. 1596, CUL MS Ee.3.56 no. 85; Alford, *Early Elizabethan Polity*, 156.
35 Alford, *Early Elizabethan Polity*, 156.
36 Alford, *Early Elizabethan Polity*, 154–5.
37 Cott. MS Charter 4.38 f. (2)r. See also Lans. MS 1236 f. 42v.
38 Lynch, 'Queen Mary's Triumph', 1–21; Guy, '*My Heart is My Own*', 284–5.
39 WC to Sir Henry Norris, 10 Feb. 1567, *SC*, 105.
40 WC to Norris, 19 Feb. 1567, *SC*, 108.
41 WC to Norris, 20 Feb. 1567, *SC*, 107–8.
42 WC to Norris, 5 Mar. 1567, *SC*, 109–10.
43 WC to Sidney, 23 Apr. 1567, SP 63/20 f. 144r.
44 WC to Norris, 12 May 1567, *SC*, 112; 27 May 1567, *SC*, 113.
45 WC to Norris, 26 June 1567, *SC*, 114.
46 WC to Norris, 19 Aug. 1567, *SC*, 116–17.
47 WC to Norris, 3 Sept. 1567, *SC*, 118; 12 Feb. 1568, *SC*, 125.

10. Household and Family

1 Much of what follows is derived from the superb article by Husselby and Henderson, 'Cecil House'.
2 WC's proclamation as Steward in March 1563 is *STC* 16704.9.
3 Husselby and Henderson, 'Cecil House', 172–3; *STC* 18635, 44–6.
4 Henderson, 'Tudor Garden', 54–72.
5 *STC* 13485, 24.
6 Husselby and Henderson, 'Cecil House', 183. See also Lans. MS 118 f. 38r, 8 Nov. [?1555]; and Knight, 'Wimbledon', 50–51.
7 Husselby and Henderson, 'Cecil House', 179–81.
8 CP Box G/16; Read, 'Household Accounts', 344–5.
9 WB to William Herle, 18 July 1585, SP 12/181 f. 158r.
10 Summerson, 'Theobalds', 107–10.
11 Murdin, 755.
12 Lans. MS 104 f. 193r; WC to Nicholas White, 15 Apr. 1569, Lans. MS 102 f. 141r.
13 Minute of WB to Alexander Nowell, 21 Apr. 1589, Lans. MS 103 f. 167r.
14 Croft, 'Matriarch', 284–8.
15 *STC* 24324, 61.
16 Croft, 'Matriarch', 284, 288–91.
17 Hoby, 'Travels', 127; Murdin, 745, 761–2.
18 Murdin, 756.

19   WC to Nicholas White, 8 Sept. 1569, Lans. MS 102 f. 149*r–v*.
20   WC to Smith, 2 Feb. 1564, Lans. MS 102 f. 61*r*; Murdin, 764.
21   Memorial for the Earl of Rutland, 12 Jan. 1571, SP 12/77 ff. 10*r–11v*; PROB 1/3, WB's will, 1 Mar. 1598, f. 1.
22   Flower, 'Laurence Nowell', esp. 4–10; Kiernan, *Beowulf*, 121–2.
23   Laurence Nowell to WC, June 1563, Lans. MS 6 f. 135*r*; Add. MS 62540. See also Skelton and Summerson, *Maps*, esp. 3–39.
24   For example, 18 June 1566, CP Bills 2. See also Read, 'Household Accounts', 343.
25   PROB 1/3, WB's will, 1 Mar. 1598, f. 1.
26   CP Maps II/14.

11. Conspiracy and Rebellion

1   WC to Earl of Leicester, 15 May 1568, Magdalene College, Cambridge, Pepys MS 2502 f. 799; 20 June 1568, Cott. MS Caligula C.1 ff. 139*r–140v*; WC to Sir Henry Norris, 13 July 1568, *SC*, 132–4.
2   WC to Norris, 25 July 1568, *SC*, 134–6; 27 Aug. 1568, *SC*, 138–9.
3   For a compelling forensic examination of the surviving copies of the Casket Letters, see Guy, *'My Heart is My Own'*, chs 25, 26.
4   WC to Norris, 16 Nov. 1568, *SC*, 145–6.
5   Guy, *'My Heart is My Own'*, 418–28.
6   WC to Norris, 14 Dec. 1568, *SC*, 148–9.
7   WC to Norris, 3 Jan. 1569, *SC*, 149–50.
8   7 Jan. 1569, Cott. MS Caligula C.2 f. 373*r–v*.
9   WC to Norris, 3 Jan. 1569, *SC*, 149.
10   CP 157 ff. 2*r–7v* (Haynes, 579–88).
11   Francis Walsingham to WC, 20 Dec. 1568, SP 12/48 f. 165*r*.
12   WC to Norris, 30 Jan. 1569, *SC*, 152–4.
13   WC to Norris, 27 Mar. 1569, *SC*, 159.
14   WC to Norris, 6 Apr. 1569, *SC*, 157–8; WC to Nicholas White, 15 Apr. 1569, Lans. MS 102 f. 141*r*.
15   WC to Norris, 27 Apr. 1569, *SC*, 159–60; 1 May 1569, Cott. MS Caligula C.1 ff. 410*r–411r*.
16   WC to White, 6 June 1569, Lans. MS 102 f. 143*r–v*.
17   WC to Earl of Sussex, 30 May 1569, Cott. MS Appendix L f. 121*r*.
18   'A necessary consideration of the perilous state of this time', June 1569, SP 12/51 ff. 9*r–13v*; WC to Norris, 3 July 1569, *SC*, 164–5.
19   WC to Norris, 11 July 1569, *SC*, 165.
20   WC to Norris, 20 July 1569, *SC*, 166.
21   WC to Norris, 13 Aug. 1569, *SC*, 169.
22   WC to White, 8 Sept. 1569, Lans. MS 102 f. 149*v*.
23   *STC* 13869.
24   WC to ER, 6 Oct. 1569, Cott. MS Caligula C.1 f. 456*r–v*.
25   WC to Norris, 3 Oct. 1569, *SC*, 171–2.
26   Earl of Huntingdon and Viscount Hereford to WC, 27 Sept. 1569, Haynes, 532; Earl of Shrewsbury and Huntingdon to ER, 29 Sept. 1569, Haynes, 537–8; ER to Shrewsbury and Huntingdon, 1 Oct. 1569, Haynes, 538–9.
27   WC's copy of the earls' proclamation, [28 Nov.] 1569, is Harl. MS 6990 f. 89*r–v*; Duke of Norfolk to ER, 3 Dec. 1569, Haynes, 567; Earl of Pembroke to ER, 5 Dec. 1569, Haynes, 568; Earl of Arundel to ER, 5 Dec. 1569, Haynes, 569.
28   Earl of Oxford to WC, 24 Nov. 1569, Lans. MS 11 f. 121*r*; TC to WC, 2 Dec. 1569, SP 15/15 f. 127*r*.
29   Harl. MS 6990 f. 89*r–v*; *STC* 18679.5–18682. Thomas Norton, *To the Queenes*

Majesties poore deceived subjectes of the northe contreye, drawne into rebellion by the Earles of Northumberland and Westmorland ([London:] Henry Bynneman for Lucas Harrison, 1569).

30   Earl of Sussex to WC, 16 Nov. 1569, SP 15/15 f. 49r; WC to Norris, 24 Dec. 1569, *SC*, 176.

31   31 Dec. 1569, SP 15/15 ff. 239r–v, 241r–242r, 243r–v; and SP 12/66 f. 129r–v.

32   WC to Norris, 3–7 Feb. 1570, *SC*, 179–80.

33   WC to Norris, 6 Feb. 1570, *SC*, 181.

34   *SC*, 181; Sir Nicholas Throckmorton to WC, 25 Feb. 1570, Haynes, 577; 10 Mar. 1570, Haynes, 579.

35   7 Mar. 1570, SP 12/67 ff. 7r–12v.

36   18 Apr. 1570, Haynes, 594–6.

37   23 Apr. 1570, *CA*, 9–17.

38   29 Apr. 1570, Cott. MS Caligula C.2 ff. 63r–65r.

39   WC to Norris, 4 May 1570, *SC*, 183–4; 23 May 1570, *SC*, 189. Lesley's book was *The defence of the Honour of … Marie Queene of Scotlande* (*STC* 15506), early elements of which WC may have seen in the fragments preserved by Robert Beale, Add. MS 48027 ff. 284r–91r. On Lesley's *Defence*, see Beckett, 'John Lesley', 61–3.

40   Elton, *Tudor Constitution*, 425–8; WC to White, 26 May 1570, Lans. MS 102 f. 154r; WC to Norris, 8 June 1570, *SC*, 189–90.

41   WC to Norris, 22 June 1570, *SC*, 190–1; 24 June 1570, *SC*, 191.

42   Norfolk to WC, 14 July 1570, Haynes, 596; WC's statement, 12 July 1570, Cott. MS Caligula C.2 f. 33r.

43   Sir Ralph Sadler to WC, 1 Aug. 1570, SP 12/73 f. 3r; WC to Norris, 26 Sept. 1570, *SC*, 192.

44   WC's and Mildmay's instructions of 25 Sept. 1570 are Cott. MS Caligula C.2 ff. 39r–41v; WC to Norris, 26 Sept. 1570, *SC*, 192.

45   5 Oct. 1570, Haynes, 608–14; Cott. MS Caligula C.2 ff. 49r–53v.

46   Norfolk to WC, Oct. 1570, SP 12/74 f. 71r.

47   Cott. MS Caligula C.2 ff. 82r–83r.

48   Cott. MS Caligula C.2 ff. 84r–85v.

49   Memorial for the Earl of Rutland, 12 Jan. 1571, SP 12/77 ff. 10r–11v.

50   19 Feb. 1571, Cott. MS Caligula C.2 ff. 88r–92v, 93r–96v; 20 Feb. 1571, Cott. MS Caligula C.2 ff. 97r–98v; 21 Feb. 1571, Cott. MS Caligula C.2 f. 99r–v.

51   SP 14/89 f. 23r.

52   WB to White, 14 Mar. 1571, Lans. MS 102 f. 152r.

12. Vomiting up a Poison

1   Robert Beale, 'A treatise of the office of a councillor and principal secretary to her Majesty' (1592), in Read, *Walsingham*, vol. 1, 427, 428.

2   By far the best introduction to the Ridolfi plot is Parker, 'Messianic Vision'; see also Edwards, *Marvellous Chance*.

3   From WB's official narrative of the Ridolfi plot, SP 12/84 f. 35r.

4   WC to Francis Walsingham and Francis Rowe, 26 Jan. 1570, SP 12/66 f. 92r–v; WB's narrative, Jan. 1572, SP 12/84 f. 35r–v.

5   On Charles Bailly and his career, see Edwards, *Marvellous Chance*, esp. ch. 1.

6   SP 12/84 ff. 35v–36r.

7   CP 5 ff. 107r–108v (Murdin, 4–5); SP 12/82 f. 36r; the ciphered letters of Apr. 1571, and the deciphered copies that were eventually made of them for WB, are CP 5 ff. 108r–118r.

8   Charles Bailly to John Lesley, 20 Apr. 1571, CP 5 ff. 107r–108v (Murdin, 4–5); Bailly to Lesley, 24 Apr. 1571, CP 5 f. 113r–v; William Herle to WB, 26 Apr. 1571, Cott. MS

Caligula C.3 f. 68r; Herle to Lesley, 27 Apr. 1571, Cott. MS Caligula C.3 ff. 69v–70r; Herle to Lesley, 28 Apr. 1571, Cott. MS Caligula C.3 f. 70r–v; Herle to WB, 29 Apr. 1571, Cott. MS Caligula C.3 ff. 70v–71v.

9   CP 157 f. 114r; Langbein, *Torture*, 102–3.

10   Bailly to Lesley, 26 Apr. 1571, Murdin, 7–8; Bailly to Lesley, 29 Apr. 1571, CP 5 ff. 118r–119v (HMC *Salisbury*, vol. 1, 496).

11   Lesley to Bailly, 1 May 1571, CP 5 ff. 121r–123v (Murdin, 9); Herle to WB, 1 May 1571, Cott. MS Caligula C.3 f. 71v.

12   Bailly to WB, 2 May 1571, CP 5 f. 125r–v (Murdin, 9–10).

13   Bailly to WB, 5 May 1571, CP 6 ff. 1r–v, 2r–3v (Murdin, 11–12).

14   WB's notes, 1574, CP 164 f. 130v (Murdin, 771).

15   CP 157 f. 115r (Murdin, 13).

16   CP 6 ff. 4r–5v (Murdin, 14–15); SP 12/84 ff. 36v–37v.

17   SP 12/84 f. 37r.

18   SP 12/84 f. 38r; WB's notes, 1574, CP 164 f. 131r (Murdin, 772).

19   Murdin, 67.

20   WB to Sir Thomas Smith, 3 Sept. 1571, Cott. MS Caligula C.3 ff. 255r, 270r; Smith and Thomas Wilson to WB, 3 Sept. 1571, Murdin, 68.

21   Smith and Wilson to WB, 3 Sept. 1571, Murdin, 68; Smith and Wilson to WB, 4 Sept. 1571, Murdin, 69.

22   Sir Ralph Sadler to WB, 5 Sept. 1571, SP 12/81 ff. 14r, 15v.

23   SP 12/81 f. 15v; SP 12/81 ff. 16r–17v; CP 164 f. 131r.

24   WB to Earl of Shrewsbury, 5 Sept. 1571, Lambeth Palace Library, MS 3197 ff. 33, 36.

25   Duke of Norfolk to ER, 12 Dec. 1569, CP 156 f. 141r (Haynes, 571); WB to Smith and Wilson, Cott. MS Caligula C.3 f. 240r; WC to Sir Henry Norris, 20 Feb. 1567, *SC*, 108.

26   Smith and Wilson to WB, 2 Sept. 1571, SP 12/81 f. 1r; CP 6 f. 17r.

27   Murdin, 87–92; WB to Sadler, [Smith and Wilson], 9 Sept. 1571, Cott. MS Caligula C.3 f. 268r.

28   Norfolk to ER, 10 Sept. 1571, CP 6 f. 19r–v; Heath, *Torture*, 232; WB to Smith, 16 Sept. 1571, Cott. MS Caligula C.3 f. 253r.

29   WB to Smith, 16 Sept. 1571, Cott. MS Caligula C.3 f. 253r; WB to Smith and Wilson, 16 Sept. 1571, Cott. MS Caligula C.3 f. 254r.

30   PC to Smith and Wilson, 21 Sept. 1571, Cott. MS Caligula C.3 f. 271r; CP 6 ff. 20r, 21r–v (21–22 Sept. 1571).

31   Wilson to WB, 1 Oct. 1571, CP 6 f. 22r–v; 4 Oct. 1571, HMC *Salisbury*, vol. 1, 533; 10–11 Oct. 1571, SP 12/81 f. 107r; Bailly to WB, 12 Oct. 1571, CP 6 ff. 23r–24v (Murdin, 15–17).

32   *STC* 11504–11506; *STC* 11506, sig. B2r.

33   *STC* 11506, sig. A1r–v.

34   *STC* 11506, sigs A2r–A3v.

35   *STC* 11506, sig. A4r.

36   14 Oct. 1571, Murdin, 18.

37   WB to Francis Walsingham, 19 Oct. 1571, *CA*, 146; Cott. MS Caligula C.3 ff. 107r–110v; WB to the Earl of Bedford, 23 Oct. 1571, HMC *Salisbury*, vol. 2, 552; Lesley to MQS, 8 Nov. 1571, CP 6 ff. 136r–137v (Murdin, 55).

38   26 and 27 Oct. 1571, Murdin, 19.

39   Murdin, 24–5.

40   Murdin, 32–4, 35–8; 3 Nov. 1571, CP 6 ff. 109r–110v, 111r–112v (Murdin, 41–3, 45); 6 Nov. 1571, Murdin, 46–51, quotation at 49–50. See also Parker, 'Messianic Vision', 216.

41   WB to Walsingham and Henry Killigrew, 1 Nov. 1571, *CA*, 151.

42   Guy, '*My Heart is My Own*', 467–8.

43   Wilson to WB, 8 Nov. 1571, Murdin, 57; Guy, '*My Heart is My Own*', 388–95; Mahon, *Indictment*, 23–6; *STC* 3981, sig. Y3r.

44 Lesley to WB, 16 Nov. 1571, CP 6 ff. 144r–145v (Murdin, 58–60); Lesley to WB, 30 Nov. 1571, CP 7 f. 3r (Murdin, 61); Norfolk to WB, 10 Nov. 1571, CP 6 f. 138r; 'A brief declaration of those things which I have omitted', Cott. MS Caligula C.3 ff. 198r–203r; WB's paper of charges against Norfolk, Nov. 1571, SP 12/83 f. 57r–v.

45 Taviner, 'Robert Beale', 192; 'A consideration of the case of Scotland' by WB, 10 Dec. 1571, Cott. MS Caligula C.3 ff. 222r–225v, quotation at f. 222r; Margaret, Countess of Lennox to WB, 4 Nov. 1571, SP 12/83 f. 7r; WB's minute of ER to the Duke of Alba, 15 Dec. 1571, CP 7 f. 7r.

46 WB to Walsingham, [19] Dec. 1571, *CA*, 163–4.

13. To Kill a Duke

1 4 Jan. 1572, CP 5 f. 61r (Murdin, 194).
2 Edwards, *Marvellous Chance*, 246.
3 13 Jan. 1572, Murdin, 194–200; 15 Jan. 1572, Murdin, 200–1.
4 28 Jan. 1572, CP 5 ff. 82r–83v (Murdin, 202–3); WB to Sir Francis Walsingham, 23 Jan. 1572, *CA*, 164.
5 Murdin, 205; Edwards, *Marvellous Chance*, 251–2.
6 Walsingham to WC, 20 Dec. 1568, SP 12/48 f. 165r.
7 Taviner, 'Robert Beale', 192–3; *STC* 17565.
8 *STC* 17565, sigs A4r–v; quotation at sig. B2r.
9 *STC* 17565, sig. A4r.
10 Cobbett, Howell and Howell, *State Trials*, vol. 1, cols 957–8, 959; Add. MS 48027 f. 84r–v.
11 Add. MS 48027 f. 84v; Cobbett, Howell and Howell, *State Trials*, vol. 1, col. 966; Thomas Howard to ER, 22 Jan. 1572, CP 5 f. 70r (see also Howard to ER, 23 Jan. 1572, CP 5 ff. 72r–73v).
12 WB to Walsingham, 23 Jan. 1572, *CA*, 164.
13 *CA*, 164.
14 WB to Walsingham, 2 Feb. 1572, *CA*, 165; Cobbett, Howell and Howell, *State Trials*, vol. 1, cols 1042–50.
15 WB to Walsingham, 11 Feb. 1572, *CA*, 165–6.
16 *CA*, 166; Doran, *Elizabeth*, 219.
17 *CA*, 166; 'The perils growing by forbearing to do justice', [Feb. 1572], Cott. MS Caligula C.2 ff. 86r–87v.
18 Cott. MS Caligula C.2 ff. 86r–v.
19 Lord Hunsdon to WB, 12 Apr. 1572, SP 15/21 f. 65r; WB to [Walsingham], [4 Apr. 1572], Cott. MS Vespasian F.6 f. 6r–v.
20 Cott. MS Vespasian F.6 f. 7r.
21 Cott. MS Caligula C.3 ff. 457r–459r.
22 Henry Skipwith to WB, 1 May 1572, SP 12/86 f. 155r.
23 12 May 1572, *LJ*, vol. 1, 706; *CJ*, vol. 1, 94–5; 13 May 1572, Hartley, *Proceedings*, vol. 1, 270–2.
24 14 May 1572, Hartley, *Proceedings*, vol. 1, 319–23; 15 May 1572, *CJ*, vol. 1, 95; Hartley, *Proceedings*, vol. 1, 273, 324.
25 19 May 1572, *CJ*, vol. 1, 95–6; Hartley, *Proceedings*, vol. 1, 327; 21 May 1572, *CJ*, vol. 1, [96].
26 21 May 1572, Hartley, *Proceedings*, vol. 1, 327–8; WB to Walsingham, 21 May 1572, Cott. MS Vespasian F.6 f. 64r.
27 23 May 1572, *CJ*, vol. 1, 97; Hartley, *Proceedings*, vol. 1, 331, 374.
28 23 May 1572, *CJ*, vol. 1, 97; 24 May 1572, *CJ*, vol. 1, 97–8. The MPs who wrote down their reasons for Thomas Howard's execution were Thomas Digges and Thomas

Dannet (Hartley, *Proceedings*, vol. 1, 294–8; Add. MS 48027 ff. 108*r*–111*v*) and Thomas Norton (Add. MS 48027 ff. 112*r*–114*r*).

29   [26 May 1572,] Hartley, *Proceedings*, vol. 1, 274–7.
30   28 May 1572, *CJ*, vol. 1, 98–9; *LJ*, vol. 1, 712–13.
31   Earl of Leicester to Walsingham, 21 May 1572, *CA*, 203; 31 May 1572, *CJ*, vol. 1, [99]; Hartley, *Proceedings*, vol. 1, 313; Skipwith to WB, 31 May 1572, SP 12/86 f. 228*r*; Skipwith to WB, 1 June 1572, SP 12/88 f. 2*r*.
32   2 June 1572, Hartley, *Proceedings*, vol. 1, 333; Sir Owen Hopton to Leicester and WB, 2 June 1572, SP 12/88 f. 3*r*; WB to Walsingham, 6 June 1572, *CA*, 212.
33   2 June 1572, *LJ*, vol. 1, 715; 4 June 1572, *LJ*, vol. 1, 716–17; 5 June 1572, *LJ*, vol. 1, 717; 6 June 1572, *CJ*, vol. 1, 100–1; Hartley, *Proceedings*, vol. 1, 333–5; 7 June 1572, *CJ*, vol. 1, 101; 9 June 1572, *CJ*, vol. 1, 101; 10 June 1572, *LJ*, vol. 1, 720–1; *CJ*, vol. 1, 101–2; 'Certain articles containing matters wherewith the Queen of Scots may be charged', 11 June 1572, CP 7 ff. 38*r*–40*v* (Murdin, 218); Read, *Bardon Papers*, 6–8; WB's notes, 1574, CP 164 f. 132*v*; WB to Walsingham, 6 June 1572, *CA*, 212; MQS's protestation, 17 June 1572, Read, *Bardon Papers*, 8–9; WB's notes, 1574, CP 164 f. 132*v*.
34   SP 12/88 ff. 47*r*–50*r*.
35   WB to Walsingham, 24 June 1572, *CA*, 218; 24 June 1572, *CJ*, vol. 1, 102; 25 June 1572, *CJ*, vol. 1, 102–3; Hartley, *Proceedings*, vol. 1, 307–15.
36   WB to Walsingham, [?30 June 1572,] *CA*, 219.
37   WB to Walsingham, 27 July 1572, Cott. MS Vespasian F.6 f. 131*r*.
38   Thomas Bellot's accounts for 1572, CP Box G/16.
39   WB to Walsingham, 23 Apr. 1572, Cott. MS Vespasian F.6 f. 49*r*.
40   WB to [Walsingham], 11 Sept. 1572, Cott. MS Vespasian F.6 f. 148*r*–*v*; *STC* 16511.
41   Add. MS 48049 ff. 340*r*–357*v*; Cott. MS Titus F.3 ff. 302*r*–308*v*.
42   'T.G.' to Christopher Hatton, 25 June 1573, Murdin, 256; *STC* 23617.5, sig. **v*; Beckett, 'John Lesley', ch. 5.
43   *STC* 23617.5, quotation at sig. **4r*; Thomas Wilson to WB, 31 July 1573, SP 15/23 f. 58*r*–*v*.
44   Matthew Parker to WB, 11 Sept. 1573, Murdin, 259.

14. 'The Poorest Lord in England'

1   WB to White, 14 Mar. 1571, Lans. MS 102 f. 152*r*.
2   John Dee to WB, 3 Oct. 1574, Lans. MS 19 f. 81*r*–*v*.
3   WB to Sir Francis Walsingham, 15 May 1575, SP 12/103 f. 111*r*.
4   CP 9 ff. 8*r*–9*r*.
5   *Oxford DNB*, vol. 56, 286–9; Murdin, 775; 16 Aug. 1574, Add. MS 5754 f. 136*r*; 21 Aug. 1574, Murdin, 776; Martin, 'Sir Francis Walsingham', 20.
6   WB to Walsingham, 11 Apr. 1575, SP 12/103 f. 56*r*.
7   WB to Walsingham, 19 Apr. 1575, SP 12/103 f. 65*r*.
8   Till, 'Burghley House', esp. 16–19.
9   What follows is taken from Summerson, 'Theobalds', esp. 116–22. See also Sutton, *Theobalds*, 2–9; and Sutton, 'Decorative Program'.
10   Andrews, 'Theobalds', esp. 135–7.
11   June 1575, CP Box G/16.
12   WB to Walsingham, 25 June 1575, SP 12/103 f. 139*r*.
13   Sir Walter Mildmay to WB, 3 July 1575, CP 8 f. 35*r*.
14   WB to Walsingham, 28 July 1575, SP 12/103 f. 148*r*.
15   WB to Sir Thomas Smith and Walsingham, 6 Aug. 1575, SP 15/24 f. 89*r*; Guy, '*My Heart is My Own*', 442, 447–8.
16   *STC* 24366, sig. D2*r*.
17   WB to Walsingham, 9 Aug. 1575, SP 12/105 f. 57*r*.

18 WB to Henry Bosseville, 30 Aug. 1575, SP 15/24 ff. 93r, 94v; Martin, 'Sir Francis Walsingham', 24; Earl of Sussex to WB, 12 Sept. 1575, CP 8 f. 60r.
19 TC to WB, 12 Sept. 1575, SP 12/105 f. 94r–v.
20 WB to Sussex, 27 Sept. 1575, Cott. MS Titus B.2 f. 233r–v; Thomas Bellot's accounts, CP Box G/16.
21 TC to WB, 3 Oct. 1575, CP 8 f. 72r.
22 Earl of Oxford to WB, 2[7] Nov. 1575, CP 8 f. 76r; Oxford to WB, 3 Jan. 1576, CP 8 ff. 12r–13r.
23 WB to Walsingham, 27 Jan. 1576, SP 12/107 f. 64r–v.
24 Murdin, 778.
25 CP 160 ff. 99r–110v (HMC Salisbury, vol. 2, 131–2)
26 Oxford to WB, 27 Apr. 1576, CP 9 f. 1r.
27 PROB 11/59 (PCC Daughtry); APC, 1575–7, 124–5; Bellot's accounts, 7 June 1576, CP 226.
28 STC 16305a, sig. x8v.
29 For the windows and tombs in Romford Church, see STC 25223, 647–50.
30 12 June 1576, CP 9 ff. 8r–9r.
31 Oxford to WB, 13 July 1576, CP 9 f. 15r.
32 CP 157 ff. 131r–132v.

15. A Gaping Gulf

1   Evenden and Freeman, 'Propaganda', esp. 1292–3.
2   Jane Cecil to WB, 20 Apr. 1577, Lans. MS 104 f. 162r.
3   7, 8 May 1577, Fenton, John Dee, 2; 22, 23 May 1577, CP 226; 8 June 1577, Fenton, John Dee, 2.
4   STC 13127, sig. B1r.
5   WB to Earl of Sussex, 21 July 1577, Cott. MS Titus B.2 f. 235r–v.
6   Earl of Leicester to WB, 13 June 1577, CP 160 f. 129r–v.
7   Leicester to WB, 23 July 1577, CP 160 f. 139r–v (HMC Salisbury, vol. 2, 157); Leicester to WB, 8 Aug. 1577, CP 160 f. 144r–v (HMC Salisbury, vol. 2, 159).
8   Peter Kemp to WB, 26 May 1573, CP 202 f. 108r (HMC Salisbury, vol. 2, 52); Kemp to WB, 7 June 1573, CP 7 f. 103r (HMC Salisbury, vol. 2, 52–3).
9   Jane Cecil to WB, 12 Dec. 1574, Lans. MS 104 f. 160r.
10 Kemp to WB, 7 June 1573, CP 7 f. 103r.
11 WB to William Herle, 14 Aug. 1585, SP 12/181 ff. 157v–158r.
12 WB to [Sir Francis Walsingham], 10 Sept. 1586, SP 12/193 f. 76v.
13 Husselby, 'Burghley House', 26–8.
14 Girouard, 'Elizabethan Architecture', 27; Pevsner, Lincolnshire, 121–30, esp. 126; Husselby, 'Burghley House', 31.
15 WB to Walsingham, 12 Oct. 1578, SP 12/126 f. 14r; WB to Walsingham, 25 Oct. 1578, SP 12/126 f. 29r.
16 Fenton, John Dee, 4, 18.
17 Doran, Elizabeth, 89.
18 WB to Sir Christopher Hatton, 15 Dec. 1578, SP 15/25 f. 225r.
19 WB to Sussex, 27 Sept. 1575, Cott. MS Titus B.2 f. 233r–v.
20 STC 25223, 583–4; Collinson, 'Sir Nicholas Bacon', 258–64.
21 PROB 11/61 (PCC Bakon).
22 Doran, Monarchy & Matrimony, ch. 7. See also Mears, 'Gaping Gulf', esp. 634–7.
23 CP 148 (HMC Salisbury, vol. 2, 234–54).
24 STC 23400; Hughes and Larkin, Proclamations, vol. 2, 445–9, quotation at 447.
25 7 Oct. 1579, Murdin, 336–7.
26 Fenton, John Dee, 8–9, 19.

27   *STC* 11987, sig. A3*r*, C1*v*–C2*v*, C5*r*.
28   WB's Ortelius is in the Burghley House Collection. See Doran, *Elizabeth*, 46–7.
29   Doran, *Elizabeth*, 142–3, 154–7.
30   Fenton, *John Dee*, 11.
31   WB to Nicholas White, 3 Jan. 1581, Lans. MS 102 f. 176*r*–*v*.
32   Lans. MS 31 ff. 118*r*–121*v*. See also Martin, 'Sir Francis Walsingham', 42.
33   Walsingham to WB, 12 July 1581, SP 12/149 f. 155*r*–*v*. See also Fenton, *John Dee*, 13.
34   WB's minute of Countess of Oxford to Earl of Oxford, 7 Dec. 1581, Lans. MS 104 f. 164*r*.
35   WB's minute of Countess of Oxford to Earl of Oxford, 12 Dec. 1581, Lans. MS 104 f. 166*r*.
36   Lord Wentworth to WB, 8 June 1581, SP 12/149 f. 83*r*. See also Wentworth to WB, 20 June 1581, SP 12/149 f. 114*r*.
37   WB to Walsingham, 25 Feb. 1582, SP 12/152 f. 87*r*.

16. *The Execution of Justice*

1   Thomas Norton to Sir Francis Walsingham, 27 Mar. 1582, SP 12/152 f. 124*r*–*v*. See also *STC* 4901.
2   *STC* 369.5, sigs a2*v*–a3*r*, *a3v*, a4*r*, b3*r*–*v*.
3   WB to Walsingham, 29 Mar. 1582, SP 12/152 f. 126*r*; WB to Walsingham, 16 July 1582, SP 12/154 f. 105*r*; WB to Walsingham, 27 July 1582, SP 12/154 ff. 111*r*–112*r*; 8 Aug. 1582, SP 12/155 f. 10*r*; 12 Aug. 1582, SP 12/155 f. 25*r*; Chambers, *Elizabethan Stage*, vol. 4, 99.
4   Walsingham to WB, 8 Nov. 1582, Lans. MS 36 f. 25*r*; Sir Christopher Hatton to WB, 8 Nov. 1582, Lans. MS 36 f. 27*r*; Earl of Sussex to WB, 10 Nov. 1582, Lans. MS 36 ff. 29*r*, 30*v*; Earl of Leicester to WB, 13 Nov. 1582, Lans. MS 36 f. 33*r*.
5   Walsingham to WB, 16 Nov. 1582, Cott. MS Caligula C.7 ff. 89*r*–90*v*; Henry Killigrew to WB, 18 Nov. 1582, Cott. MS Caligula C.7 f. 93*r*–*v*.
6   WB to Walsingham, 21/22 Nov. 1582, SP 12/155 f. 184*r*–*v*.
7   WB to Walsingham, 19 Dec. 1582, SP 12/156 f. 36*r*; 13 Jan. 1582, Fenton, *John Dee*, 52; 14 Jan. 1583, Thomas Blanke to WB, 14 Jan. 1583, Lans. MS 37 f. 8*r*.
8   6 Feb. 1583, Lans. MS 103 ff. 25*r*, 27*r*–*v*.
9   Walsingham to WB, 15 Apr. 1583, Lans. MS 38 f. 154*r*–*v*.
10   Fenton, *John Dee*, 67–8; Walsingham to WB, 20 Apr. 1583, Lans. MS 38 f. 156*r*.
11   Bossy, *Embassy Affair*, chs. 1, 2; 5 Aug. 1583, 'Memorial for Scotland' by WB, SP 12/162 ff. 5*r*, 32*r*, 33*v*; 10 Aug. 1583, WB's instructions for Walsingham's mission to Scotland, Cott. MS Caligula C.7 ff. 312*r*–313*v*; 16 Aug. 1583, Earl of Shrewsbury to ER, Lans. MS 37 f. 122*r*–*v*. See also Basing, 'Robert Beale', 68–70.
12   William Cecil to WB, 26 Aug. 1583, Lans. MS 104 ff. 168*r*–*v*; 169*v*.
13   *STC* 4902 (17 Dec. 1583); Christopher Barker's second, corrected edition of Jan. 1584 is *STC* 4903.
14   SP 12/73 ff. 112*r*–117*r* (Kingdon, *Execution of Justice*, 3–10, 23–4, 25); SP 12/153 ff. 145*r* (Kingdon, *Execution of Justice*, 15–19); Norton's *Declaration* is *STC* 4901 (Kingdon, *Execution of Justice*, 44–50).
15   John Hammond's paper on the authority of the Pope is Add. MS 48063 ff. 65*r*–74*v*.
16   SP 12/73 f. 112*r*; *STC* 4903, sig. A2*r*–*v* (Kingdon, *Execution of Justice*, 3–4).
17   SP 12/73 f.113*v*; *STC* 4903, sig. A3*r* (Kingdon, *Execution of Justice*, 5).
18   *STC* 4903, sig. A3*v* (Kingdon, *Execution of Justice*, 6–7); SP 12/73 f. 114*v*–115*r*.
19   *STC* 4903, sig. A4*r* (Kingdon, *Execution of Justice*, 7).
20   *STC* 4903, sigs B1*r*–B2*v* (Kingdon, *Execution of Justice*, 9–12); SP 12/73 f. 116*v*.
21   *STC* 373.
22   The verses are from the Douai Bible (1609–10): *STC* 2207, second tome, 98 (Psalm 49:19), 116 (62:12).

23   *STC* 19885, 16.
24   Bossy, *Embassy Affair*, ch. 2.
25   Cott. MS Caligula C.7 ff. 361*r*–362*r*.
26   3 Feb. 1584, SP 12/168 ff. 4*r*–7*v*. Henry Maynard's fair copy is SP 12/168 ff. 8*r*–10*v*,
       endorsed by WB on f. 11*v*.
27   3 Feb. 1584, SP 12/168 f. 6*r*–*v*; 10 Feb. 1584, SP 12/168 ff. 22*r*–23*v*.
28   22 Mar. 1584, Lans. MS 40 ff. 64*r*, 65*v*; 26 Mar. 1584, Lans. MS 40 ff. 62*r*–63*v*.
29   Leicester to WB, 31 July 1584, SP 12/172 f. 50*r*.
30   On Scotland, see Read, *Bardon Papers*, 21–4.
31   *STC* 24050.5, sigs A1*v*–A2*r*.
32   *STC* 24050.5, sigs A2*v*–A3*r*.
33   *STC* 24050.5, sig. A3*r*–*v*.
34   *STC* 24050.5, sigs A3*v*–A4*r*.
35   Parker, *Grand Strategy*, 169–72.
36   10 Oct. 1584, SP 12/173 f. 102*r*.
37   WB to Walsingham, 12 Oct. 1584, SP 12/173 f. 111*r*. Some drafts of the Association
       with Walsingham's additions and corrections are SP 12/173 ff. 130*r*–133*v*.
38   SP 12/174 no. 10.
39   Add. MS 48027 f. 249*r* is an apograph of MQS's subscription to the Association on 5
       Jan. 1585. Robert Beale had seen the original: 'This have I, Robert Beale, seen under
       the hand and seal of the Scottish Queen, remaining with Master Secretary
       Walsingham.'
40   WB to Walsingham, 19 Oct. 1584, SP 12/173 f. 134*r*; Walsingham to WB, 20 Oct.
       1584, SP 12/173 f. 135*r*. Cressy, 'Binding the Nation', 217–26. See also Collinson,
       'Monarchical Republic', 51–6; and Collinson 'Exclusion Crisis'.
41   Hartley, *Proceedings*, vol. 2, 132–8.
42   Act for Surety of the Queen's Person 1585 (27 Elizabeth I c. 1), *SR*, 4, pt 1, 704–5.
43   15 Feb. 1585, Hartley, *Proceedings*, vol. 2, 176.
44   Lans. MS 43 no. 47.

17. The Commission

1   *Oxford DNB*, vol. 43, 992.
2   Pollen, *Babington Plot*, lxiv.
3   Earl of Sussex to WB, 4 June 1586, Lans. MS 50 ff. 43*r*, 44*v*; Sussex to WB, 13 June
       1586, Lans. MS 50 ff. 45*r*, 46*v*, 47*r*.
4   SP 53/18 no. 55 (Richards, *Secret Writings*, 54–5). See also Guy, 'My Heart is My
       Own', 482–4.
5   Pollen, *Babington Plot*, 38–46.
6   Pollen, *Babington Plot*, 27, 45–6.
7   Hughes and Larkin, *Proclamations*, vol. 2, 525–6; Sir Francis Walsingham to
       [Thomas Phelippes,] 2 Aug. 1586, Cott. MS Appendix L f. 140*r*–*v*; Pollen, *Babington
       Plot*, 131–2; Walsingham to Phelippes, 3 Aug. 1586, Cott. MS Appendix L f. 144*r*;
       Pollen, *Babington Plot*, 132–3.
8   Walsingham to Phelippes, 3 Aug. 1586, Cott. MS Appendix L f. 144*r*; Pollen,
       Babington Plot, 132–3.
9   Walsingham to Phelippes, 3 Aug. 1586, Cott. MS Appendix L f. 141*r*; Pollen,
       Babington Plot, 134.
10   Pollen, *Babington Plot*, clxx–clxxii.
11   WB to Walsingham, 10 Aug. 1586, SP 12/192, f. 28*r*.
12   Pollen, *Babington Plot*, clxxii, 49–66; WB to Earl of Leicester, 18 Aug. 1586, Cott. MS
       Galba C.9 ff. 368*r*–370*r*.
13   My account of Babington's first confession is from Pollen, *Babington Plot*, 49–66.

14 List of houses to be raided, SP 12/192 ff. 76*r–v*, 77*r–v*, 78*v*; Sir Christopher Hatton to WB, 2 Sept. 1586, SP 12/193 f. 7*r*.

15 Hatton to WB, 2 Sept. 1587, SP 12/193 f. 7*r*; Walsingham to WB, 5 Sept. 1586, Read, *Bardon Papers*, 50; WB to Hatton, 4 Sept. 1586, Eg. MS 2124 f. 26*r* (Read, *Bardon Papers*, 42–4).

16 Pollen, *Babington Plot*, 27–8.

17 Antony Tyrell, SP 12/193 ff. 20*r–22v*; WB to Hatton, 4 Sept. 1586, Eg. MS 2124 f. 26*r* (Read, *Bardon Papers*, 42–4).

18 WB's 'Memorial', 8 Sept. 1586, Lans. MS 103 ff. 62*r–63v*; WB to Walsingham, 8 Sept. 1586, Cott. MS Caligula C.9 f. 448*r*.

19 Lans. MS 103 ff. 62*r–63v*; WB to Walsingham, 8 Sept. 1586, Cott. MS Caligula C.9 f. 448*r*; WB to Walsingham, 10 Sept. 1586, SP 12/193 ff. 75*r–76v*.

20 9 Sept. 1586, Read, *Bardon Papers*, 48; Sussex to WB, 10 Sept. 1586, Lans. MS 50 f. 55*r–v*; WB to Hatton, 13 Sept. 1586, Eg. MS 2124 f. 32*r* (Read, *Bardon Papers*, 48).

21 WB to Hatton, 12 Sept. 1586, Eg. MS 2124 f. 28*r–v* (Read, *Bardon Papers*, 45–6).

22 WB to Hatton, 12 Sept. 1586, Eg. MS 2124 f. 30*r* (Read, *Bardon Papers*, 46–7).

23 WB to Hatton, 13 Sept. 1586, Eg. MS 2124 f. 32*r* (Read, *Bardon Papers*, 47–8).

24 WB to Hatton, 15 Sept. 1586, Eg. MS 2124 f. 34*r* (Read, *Bardon Papers*, 49–50).

25 WB to Hatton, 15 Sept. 1586, Eg. MS 2124 f. 34*r* (Read, *Bardon Papers*, 50); WB to Hatton, 16 Sept. 1586, Eg. MS 2124 f. 36*r* (Read, *Bardon Papers*, 51).

26 WB to Hatton, 15 Sept. 1586, Eg. MS 2124 f. 34*r* (Read, *Bardon Papers*, 49–50); WB to Leicester, 15 Sept. 1586, Cott. MS Galba C.10 ff. 19*r–20v*.

27 John Popham to WB, 25 Sept. 1586, Lans. MS 50 ff. 59*r–60r*; Beale to Walsingham, 25 Sept. 1586, Cott. MS Julius F.6 ff. 30*v–32v*; Popham to WB, 1 Oct. 1586, Lans. MS 50 ff. 61*r–62r*.

28 Popham and Thomas Egerton to WB, 3 Oct. 1586, Lans. MS 50 ff. 63*r–v*, 64*v*; WB to Walsingham, 4 Oct. 1586, Cott. MS Appendix L, f. 146*r–v*.

29 John Puckering's notes, 29 Sept. 1586, Read, *Bardon Papers*, 53–64; WB to Walsingham, 4 Oct. 1586, Cott. MS Appendix L, f. 146*r–v*. See also Pollen, *Babington Plot*, 29; and Walsingham to [Phelippes], 6 Oct. 1586, Cott. MS Caligula C.9 f. 460*r*.

30 Walsingham to WB, 6 Oct. 1586, SP 12/194 f. 34*r*; ER to WB, 7 Oct. 1586, Harl. MS 290 f. 188*r–v*; Davison to Walsingham, 8 Oct. 1586, SP 12/194 f. 47*r*.

31 Harl. MS 290 f. 187*r* (Steuart, *Trial*, 135–6).

32 WB to Leicester, 1 Oct. 1586, Cott. MS Galba C.10 f. 49*r*.

33 CP 15 f. 14*r*; CP 15 ff. 74*r–75v*; Murdin, 584–6.

34 MQS's protestation, 12 Oct. 1586, Harl. MS 290 f. 191*r*; Davison to Walsingham, 15 Oct. 1586, SP 12/194 f. 70*r*; MQS's protestation, 13 Oct. 1586, Harl. MS 290 ff. 194*r–195r*. On whether MQS could or should be tried in England, see the legal briefing paper by John Hammond, Add. MS 48027, ff. 380*r–397v*; and Steuart, *Trial*, 104–31.

35 Cott. MS Caligula C.9 f. 635*r* (Steuart, *Trial*, 48–9).

36 Add. MS 48027 f. 570*r*.

37 'RW' (?Ralph Warcup or ?Robert Wingfield) to WB, 11 Feb. 1587, Bod. MS Eng. hist. b. 117 f. 76.

38 Bod. MS Eng. hist. b. 117 f. 55*r*.

39 Cott. MS Caligula C.9 f. 632*v*.

40 Bod. MS Eng. hist. b. 117 f. 55.

41 Bod. MS Eng. hist. b. 117 f. 56.

42 Bod. MS Eng. hist. b. 117 f. 56.

43 Cott. MS Caligula C.9 f. 633*r*.

44 Cott. MS Caligula C.9 f. 633*r*.

45 Bod. MS Eng. hist. b. 117 f. 57.

46 ER to WB, 12 Oct. 1586, Cott. MS Caligula C.9 f. 467*r*; William Davison to Walsingham, 14 Oct. 1586, SP 12/194 f. 69*r*.

47 Cott. MS Caligula C.9 f. 633*v*.
48 Add. MS 48027 f. 573*v*; Cott. MS Caligula C.9 ff. 633*v*–634*r*.
49 Cott. MS Caligula C.9 f. 634*r*.

18. To Kill a Queen

1 Sir Francis Walsingham to Earl of Leicester, 15 Oct. 1586, Cott. MS Caligula C.9 f. 543*r*.
2 WB to Walsingham or Sir Christopher Hatton, 16 Oct. 1586, SP 12/194 f. 71*r*.
3 WB to Walsingham, 19 Oct. 1586, SP 12/194 f. 77*r*.
4 25 Oct. 1586, Cott. MS Caligula C.9 f. 693*r*.
5 Steuart, *Trial*, 61.
6 8 Sept. 1586, Lans. MS 103 f. 62*r*.
7 Hartley, *Proceedings*, vol. 2, 214–21, quotation at 214. See also Hatton's notes in Read, *Bardon Papers*, 66–73, 82–93.
8 5 Nov. 1586, Neale, 'Proceedings', 107–8; William Davison to Walsingham, 6 Nov. 1586, SP 12/195 f. 7*r*.
9 Heisch, 'Lord Burghley', 216–23; Heisch, 'Arguments', 594, 597–8.
10 Neale, 'Proceedings', 108–9.
11 Neale, 'Proceedings', 109; WB and Hatton to Davison, 10 Nov. 1586, SP 12/195 f. 10*r*.
12 WB to Davison, 11 Nov. 1586, SP 12/195 ff. 17*r*, 18*r*; Heisch, 'Arguments', 595.
13 Hartley, *Proceedings*, 239–43.
14 12 Nov. 1586, Hartley, *Proceedings*, 249–52; 14 Nov. 1586, Neale, 'Proceedings', 111.
15 Earl of Shrewsbury to WB, 17 Nov. 1586, CP 165 f. 4*r* (Murdin, 572). WB to Davison, 16 Nov. 1586, SP 12/195 f. 21*r*; 19 Nov. 1586, Neale, 'Proceedings', 111.
16 Hartley, *Proceedings*, 266–70.
17 WB to Davison, 28 Nov. 1586, SP 12/195 f. 34*r*; WB to Davison, 29 Nov. 1586, SP 12/195 f. 34*r*.
18 WB to Davison, 29 Nov. 1586, SP 12/195 ff. 34*r*, 35*r*; 30 Nov. 1586, SP 12/195 f. 37*r*.
19 *STC* 6052; Heisch, 'Arguments', 599–603.
20 WB to Davison, [1 Dec. 1586,] SP 12/195 f. 30*r–v*.
21 WB to Walsingham, 1 Dec. 1586, SP 12/195 f. 81*r*.
22 Hughes and Larkin, *Proclamations*, vol. 2, 528; *STC* 13569, 1586.
23 Hughes and Larkin, *Proclamations*, vol. 2, 528–9; *STC* 8160; Cott. MS Caligula C.9 ff. 602*r*–607*r*; *STC* 13569, 1586–7.
24 Robert Beale's copy of the death warrant is Add. MS 48027 ff. 645*r*–646*r*.
25 CP 165 f. 10*r–v* (Murdin, 574–5); Cott. MS Caligula C.9 f. 648*r–v*.
26 WB's narratives are CP 165 ff. 20*r*–21*v*; and CP 164 ff. 17*r*–18*r*; see also Beale's account, Add. MS 48027 ff. 636*r*–641*r*; Davison's defence of his actions, Cott. MS Caligula C.9 ff. 648*r*–649*v*; and the Crown's case against Davison in Mar. 1587, Add. MS 48027 ff. 398*v*–403*r*. For more on these weeks of Feb. 1587, especially the parts played in the execution of MQS by William Davison and Robert Beale, see the important work of Taviner, 'Robert Beale', ch. 8.
27 Add. MS 48027 f. 636*r*.
28 Cott. MS Caligula C.9 f. 648*r–v*.
29 Cott. MS Caligula C.9 f. 648*r–v*.
30 Morris, *Letter-Books*, 359–60.
31 Add. MS 48027 f. 402*v*; Read, 'Mary Queen of Scots', 234–5; Morris, *Letter-Books*, 360–2.
32 Cott. MS Caligula C.9 f. 648*v*.
33 CP 164 f. 9*r–v*.
34 Add. MS 48027 f. 636*r*.

35   Add. MS 48027 f. 636*v*.
36   Walsingham to Sir Amias Paulet, 3 Feb. 1587, Add. MS 48027 f. 644*v*; Beale's narrative, Add. MS 48027 f. 636*v*.
37   Add. MS 48027 f. 637*r*.
38   Beale's copies of the letters are Add. MS 48027 ff. 643*r* (Earl of Kent), 643*v* (Paulet), 644*r* (Shrewsbury). See also Sotheby & Co., *Catalogue*, 3–4 June 1946, 40.
39   Add. MS 48027 ff. 636*v*–637*r*; WB's narrative, CP 165 f. 20*r*; Cott. MS Caligula D.1 f. 137*r*; Read, 'Mary Queen of Scots', 235; Bod. MS Eng. hist. b. 117 ff. 76–83; Guy, *'My Heart is My Own'*, ch. 29.
40   SP 12/198 ff. 38*r*–39*v*, 60*r*–61*v*, 62*r*.
41   WB's draft, 15 Mar. 1587, Lans. MS 102 f. 10*r*.
42   Lans. MS 102 f. 6*r*.
43   Add. MS 48027 f. 402*v*.
44   Walsingham to WB, 13 Feb. 1587, SP 12/198 f. 78*r*; Lans. MS 102 ff. 6*r*–7*v*.
45   CP 164 f. 15*r*–*v* (HMC *Salisbury*, vol. 3, 220–1); CP 164 f. 10*r*–*v* (HMC *Salisbury*, vol. 3, 218–19).
46   'RW' [?Ralph Warcup] to WB, 11 Feb. 1587, Bod. Eng. hist. b. 117 ff. 76–83, of which there is a copy in Cott. MS Caligula B.5 ff. 174*r*–179*v*. WB's narrative of Beale's mission is CP 165 ff. 20*r*–21*v*; WB's defence of 17 Feb. 1587 is CP 164 ff. 17*r*–18*r* (HMC *Salisbury*, vol. 3, 223–4).
47   Lans. MS 102 ff. 10*r*–*v*, 11*v*.
48   Leicester to WB, 9 Apr. 1587, CP 165 f. 57*r* (Murdin, 586–7).
49   Lans. MS 102 f. 6*r*.

19. Burghley Triumphant

1   Add. MS 48027 ff. 702*r*–703*v*; Marcus, Mueller and Rose, *Collected Works*, 296–7.
2   Bod. MS Eng. hist. b. 117 ff. 84–6.
3   Coope, 'Long Gallery', 52.
4   Husselby, 'Burghley House', 34–42; Till, 'Burghley House'.
5   TC to WB, 27 Aug. 1587, CP 165 f. 95*r*.
6   *STC* 6052; *Oxford DNB*, vol. 10, 746–50.
7   William Herle to Earl of Leicester, 8/9 Sept. 1587, Cott. MS Titus B. 7 f. 57*r*–*v*; RC to WB, 25 Aug. 1587, CP 165 f. 94*r*.
8   WB to Herle, 14 Aug. 1585, SP 12/181 ff. 157*v*–158*r*.
9   For this, and what follows, Sutton, 'Decorative Program'; Sutton, *Theobalds*, ch. 2.
10   *SC*, 1.
11   *STC* 19885, 38.
12   PROB 11/72 (PCC Rutland).
13   Peck, *Antiquities*, vol. 1, 271–2. See also Barron, *Northamptonshire Families*, 41; Jessopp, Gotch and Fox–Davies, *William Cecil*, 107.
14   Payne, 'Cecil Women', 267–8.
15   Payne, 'Cecil Women', 268–9.
16   Walsingham to WB, 20 Apr. 1583, Lans. MS 38 f. 156*r*.
17   'A necessary consideration of the perilous state of this time', June 1569, SP 12/51 ff. 9*v*, 10*v*. For a fine collection of letters to WB by foreign leaders in the 1570s, see Bod. MS Rawl. Letters 88.
18   Rodriguez-Salgado and Adams, *Gran Armada*, esp. chs 1, 2, 9.
19   Parker, *Grand Strategy*, ch. 7; Parker, 'Messianic Vision', 209–15; Rodriguez-Salgado and Adams, *Gran Armada*, chs 8, 10.
20   Cott. MS Vespasian C.8 ff. 12*r*–16*v*.
21   Doran, *Elizabeth*, 235–6; Frye, 'Tilbury'.

22 Doran, *Elizabeth*, 230–40. See also Daultrey, 'Weather', 113–41.
23 *STC* 22590; Add. MS 48035 ff. 135r–136v.
24 *STC* 15413, quotations at 3, 17.
25 Lans. MS 103 ff. 134r–163v.
26 Murdin, 790; Lans. MS 103 ff. 117r–118v.
27 Lans. MS 103 ff. 159v, 167r.
28 *Monumenta Westmonasteriensia*, 76–7, 253–60; Payne, 'Cecil Women', 268–71.
29 Shakespeare, *Macbeth*, Act IV, scene iii, line 209.
30 *Oxford DNB*, vol. 7, 917–20.
31 HMC *Salisbury*, vol. 5, 71; William Cecil to WB, 21 May 1590, Lans. MS 104 f. 179r–v; Barron, *Northamptonshire Families*, 29–30; Murdin, 794.
32 HMC *Salisbury*, vol. 5, 71.
33 SP 12/238 ff. 237r–239r; Murdin, 796.
34 Sutton, 'Retiring Patron', 159–79; Sutton, *Theobalds*, ch. 3.
35 *STC* 6221, quotation at 1.

20. 'Better for Heaven than for the World'

1 Royal MS Appendix 67.
2 WB to RC, 7 Dec. 1595, CUL MS Ee.3.56 no. 66.
3 *STC* 19885.
4 Fenton, *John Dee*, 258; ER to WB, 22 Apr. 1593, Lans. MS 94 f. 112r.
5 WB to RC, 21 May 1593, CUL MS Ee.3.56 no. 2; HMC *Salisbury*, vol. 4, 318.
6. WB to RC, 22 May 1593, HMC *Salisbury*, vol. 4, 319. For Pliny the Elder on owls, see Seager, *Natural History*, 226; and *STC* 20029, 278.
7 WB to RC, 27 May 1593, CUL MS Ee.3.56 no. 4; Hughes and Larkin, *Proclamations*, vol. 3, 118–20.
8 WB to RC, [28] May 1593, CUL MS Ee.3.56 no. 5.
9 WB to RC, 1 Dec. 1593, CUL MS Ee.3.56 no. 7.
10 WB to RC, 7 Dec. 1593, CUL MS Ee.3.56 nos. 10, 12.
11 WB to RC, 7 Dec. 1593, CUL MS Ee.3.56 no. 14; and 9 Dec. 1593, CUL MS Ee.3.56 no. 13.
12 WB to RC, 23 Jan. 1593, CUL MS Ee.3.56 no. 15.
13 *Oxford DNB*, vol. 34, 429–31; Green, *Doctor Lopez*, esp. chs 13–16.
14 CP 139 ff. 41r–48v, quotation at f. 43r; *STC* 7603.5, quotation at 11; *STC* 7603.5.
15 WB to RC, 10 Feb. 1594, CUL MS Ee.3.56 no. 17.
16 WB to RC, 25 Apr. 1594, CUL MS Ee.3.56 no. 19.
17 Chambers, *Elizabethan Stage*, vol. 4, 108; Fenton, *John Dee*, 266; Murdin, 804.
18 WB to RC, 5 Oct. 1594, CUL MS Ee.3.56 no. 28; and 13 Oct. 1594, CUL MS Ee.3.56 no. 31.
19 WB to RC, 19 Oct. 1594, CUL MS Ee.3.56 no. 32; and 2 Dec. 1594, CUL MS Ee.3.56 no. 33.
20 WB to RC, 14 Dec. 1594, CUL MS Ee.3.56 nos 35, 36; and 28 Dec. 1594, CUL MS Ee.3.56 no. 37.
21 WB to RC, 14 Jan. 1595, CUL MS Ee.3.56 no. 38; and 25 Jan. 1595, CUL MS Ee.3.56 no. 39.
22 *STC* 12539, sigs A2r–A3r.
23 WB to RC, Feb. 1595, CUL MS Ee.3.56 no. 44; and 1 May 1595, CUL MS Ee.3.56 no. 47.
24 WB to RC, [12] Sept. 1595, CUL MS Ee.3.56 no. 58; and 13 Sept. 1595, CUL MS Ee.3.56 no. 59.
25 WB to RC, 2 Dec. 1595, CUL MS Ee.3.56 no. 73. The English of WB's Latin in Psalm 144 is from the Bishops' Bible (1568), *STC* 2102, f. 201.

26   WB to RC, 6 Dec. 1595, CUL MS Ee.3.56 no. 68.
27   WB to RC, 7 Dec. 1595, CUL MS Ee.3.56 no. 66; senior fellows of St John's College,
      Cambridge, to WB, 21 Jan. 1596, Lans. MS 80 f. 145r; WB to RC, 21 Feb. 1596, CUL
      MS Ee.3.56 no. 81.
28   WB to RC, 13 Mar. 1596, CUL MS Ee.3.56 no. 85.
29   WB to RC, 26 May 1596, CUL MS Ee.3.56 no. 93; and 31 May 1596, CUL MS Ee.3.56
      no. 97.
30   STC 4908.
31   The indenture for Burghley Hospital, 20 Sept. 1597, is Burghley House, MS Ex
      76/109; 'The names of the poor men to be in Burghley Hospital', c. Sept. 1597, is
      Burghley House, MS Ex 1/76.
32   PROB 1/3, WB's will, 1 Mar. 1598.
33   CP 204 f. 70r.
34   WB to RC, 7 June 1598, CUL MS Ee.3.56 no. 131; and 9 June 1598, CUL MS Ee.3.56
      no. 131. On the 'physic, benefits and helps of the artichoke', see STC 13485, 53.
35   WB to RC, 10 June 1598, CUL MS Ee.3.56 no. 134; and 11 June 1598, CUL MS
      Ee.3.56 no. 135.
36   Henry Maynard to Michael Hickes, 16 June 1598, Lans. MS 87 f. 71r.
37   18 June 1598, APC, 1597–8, 525; WB to RC, 21 June 1598, CUL MS Ee.3.56 no. 136;
      WB to Sir William Peryam, 27 June 1598, Lans. MS 87 f. 75r; 29, 30 June 1598, APC,
      1597–8, 553, 556; 9 July 1598, APC, 1597–8, 564.
38   WB to RC, 10 July 1598, CUL MS Ee.3.56 no. 138.
39   15 July 1598, APC, 1597–8, 576; PC to WB, 21 July 1598, APC, 1597–8, 601; George
      Coppin to RC, [24] July 1598, CP 63 f. 34r; and 25 July 1598, CP 62 f. 85r.
40   Coppin to RC, 26 July 1598, CP 62 ff. 87r, 88r.
41   Roger Houghton to RC, 28 July [1598], CP 213 f. 46r.
42   Harl. MS 36 ff. 385v–386r.
43   STC 16292, sig. P3v.

Epilogue

1   Sir Thomas Egerton to RC, 4 Aug. 1598, CP 63 f. 26r; Fulke Greville to RC, 5 Aug.
     1598, CP 63 f. 27r.
2   Henry Maynard to RC, 6 Aug. 1598, CP 63 f. 30r; and 8 Aug. 1598, CP 63 f. 38r;
     PROB 1/3, WB's will, 1 Mar. 1598, f. 9; John Chamberlain to Dudley Carleton, 30
     Aug. 1598, SP 12/268 f. 54r.
3   Gabriel Goodman to RC, 10 Aug. 1598, CP 63 f. 43r.
4   Thomas, Baron Burghley to RC, 14 Aug. 1598, CP 63 f. 52r.
5   PROB 1/3, WB's will, f. 9.
6   SP 12/268 ff. 52r–53r; R. Lytton to Dudley Carleton, 29 Aug. 1598, SP 12/268 f. 51r.
     See also Chamberlain to Carleton, 30 Aug. 1598, SP 12/268 f. 54r; RC's diary, 29 Aug.
     1598, Harl. MS 36 f. 386r.
7   John Clapham to RC, 3 Sept. 1598, CP 63 f. 92r.

Reflections

1   Minute of Thomas, Baron Burghley and RC to Sir John Stanhope, Sept. 1598, CP 64
     f. 66r.
2   Jeremiah 32:36; Geneva Bible (1560), where the verses are 37–39, STC 2093, f. 321r.
3   Smith, Anonymous Life, 131–3, quotation at 133.
4   Smith, Anonymous Life, 53, 65, 70.
5   Strong, Portraits, vol. 1, 32; vol. 2, pl. 56; Smith, Anonymous Life, 142–5.
6   STC 785, sigs A2r–A3v.

7   Smith, *Anonymous Life*, 79, 80, 84–7, 95–7.

8   Hurstfield, *Queen's Wards*, 260–70. See also Hurstfield, *Freedom, Corruption & Government*, ch. 5.

9   WB to Sir William Peryam, 27 June 1598, Lans. MS 87 ff. 75r, 76r. See also Lans MS 87 ff. 73r, 74v.

10   Peck, *Antiquities*, vol. 1, 273.

11   *STC* 4900.5; *STC* 4897; *STC* 4900.

12   Phillips, *Lord Burghley*, ch. 4; Bennett, 'Advice', 3–9; Bowers, 'Polonius', 362–4; Bennett, 'Precepts', 275–6; Wilson, 'Polonius', 83–5; Davis, 'Advice', 85–6; Tyrrell, 'Advice', 122; *Hamlet*, Act I, scene ii, lines 58–9; Act I, scene iii, lines 88–136; Act II, scene 3, lines 58–81.

13   Cooper, *Shakespeare*, 123, 127.

14   *The Tempest*, Act II, scene i, lines 148–57; *Hamlet*, Act III, scene iv, lines 23–6.

15   *Hamlet*, Act II, scene ii, lines 43–9.

16   *STC* 1141, 37–40. The first Latin quotation is from Cicero, *Letters to Friends*, VII.3.4; and the second is from Seneca, *Thyestes*, 401–3. See Bacon, *Of Empire*, 17–18.

17   *STC* 4501, sig. c2r. See also *STC* 4496, sig. A3r–v. On Camden more generally, see Collinson, 'William Camden', 79–98.

18   *STC* 4501, 494–5, quotation at 494.

Select Bibliography

Manuscripts

British Library, London
Additional Manuscripts
Cotton Manuscripts and Charters
Egerton Manuscripts
Harley Manuscripts
Royal Manuscripts
Stowe Manuscripts

National Archives, London
E 23, Exchequer, Treasury of the Receipt, Royal Wills
PROB 1, Prerogative Court of Canterbury, Wills of Selected Famous Persons
PROB 11, Prerogative Court of Canterbury, Will Registers
SP 10, State Papers, Domestic, Edward VI
SP 11, State Papers, Domestic, Mary I
SP 12, State Papers, Domestic, Elizabeth I
SP 14, State Papers, Domestic, James I
SP 15, State Papers, Addenda, Elizabeth I
SP 52, State Papers, Scotland, Elizabeth I
SP 53, State Papers, Mary, Queen of Scots
SP 63, State Papers, Ireland, Elizabeth I
SP 70, State Papers, Foreign, Elizabeth I

College of Arms, London
Talbot Manuscripts

Inner Temple Library, London
Petyt Manuscripts

Lambeth Palace Library, London
Shrewsbury Papers

London Guildhall Library
Peter Osborne's papers (MS 21607)

Hatfield House Library, Hertfordshire
Cecil Papers

Burghley House, Lincolnshire
Exeter Manuscripts

Longleat House, Wiltshire
Portland Papers

Cambridge University Library
Two-letter Manuscript classes
Vice-Chancellor's Court Wills

Corpus Christi College, Cambridge
Parker Manuscripts

Gonville and Caius College, Cambridge
Papers of St Katherine's Guild, Stamford (MS 266/670)

King's College, Cambridge
Commons Books
Mundum Books
Protocollum Books

Magdalene College, Cambridge
Pepys Manuscripts

St John's College, Cambridge
Bursars' Books
Computus Rolls

Bodleian Library, Oxford
Carte Manuscripts
MSS Don.
MSS Eng.

MSS Rawlinson
MSS Tanner

National Library of Scotland, Edinburgh
Advocates Manuscripts

Huntington Library, San Marino, California
Ellesmere Collection

Folger Shakespeare Library, Washington, DC
Bagot family papers
Burghley's papers

Printed Primary Works

1. *Short-Title Catalogue*

STC 369.5 [William Allen,] *A briefe historie of the glorious martyrdom of xii. reverend Priests* ([Rheims: J. Foigny?] 1582).

STC 373 [William Allen,] *A true, sincere and modest defence, of English Catholiques that suffer for their faith both at home and abrode* ([Rouen, 1584]).

STC 785 Thomas Norton, *Orations of Arsanes agaynst Philip the trecherous kyng of Macedone* (London: John Day, [1560?]).

STC 832 Roger Ascham, *The Scholemaster* (London: John Day, 1570).

STC 1141 Sir Francis Bacon, *The essaies of Sr Francis Bacon Knight, the Kings Solliciter Generall* (London: John Beale, 1612).

STC 1145 Sir Francis Bacon, *The essaies of Sr Francis Bacon Knight, the Kings Attorney Generall* (London: I.D. for Elizabeth Jaggard, 1614).

STC 2093 [Geneva Bible] *The Bible and holy scriptures* (Geneva: Rouland Hall, 1560).

STC 2102 [Bishops' Bible] *The Bible in English* (London: Richard Jugge & John Cawood, 1568).

STC 2207 [Douai Bible] *The Holy Bible Faithfully Translated out of the Authentical Latin* (Douai, 1609–10).

STC 3981 [George Buchanan,] *Ane detectioun of the duinges of Marie Quene of Scottes thouchand the murder of hir husband, and hir conspiracie, adulterie, and pretensed mariage with the Erle Bothwell. And ane defence of the trew Lordis, mainteineris of the Kingis graces actioun and authoritie. Translatit out of the Latine quhilke was written by G.B.* ([London: John Day, 1571]).

STC 4343 John Caius, *A boke, or counseill against the desease commonly called the sweate, or sweating sicknesse* (London: Richard Grafton, 1552).

STC 4496 William Camden, *Annales rerum Anglicarum, et Hibernicarum, regnante Elizabetha* (London, 1615).

STC 4501 William Camden, *Annals, or, The historie of the most renowned and victorious princesse Elizabeth, late Queen of England Containing all the important and remarkable passages of state both at home and abroad, during her long and prosperous reigne* (London: Thomas Harper for Benjamin Fisher, 1635).

STC 4827 Queen Katherine Parr, *The lamentation of a sinner* (London: Edward Whitchurch, 1547).

STC 4828 Queen Katherine Parr, *The Lamentation of a sinner* (London: Edward Whitchurch, 1548).

STC 4897 [?William Cecil, first Baron of Burghley,] *Certaine precepts or directions, for the well ordering and carriage of a mans life* (London, 1617).

STC 4900 [William Cecil, first Baron of Burghley,] *The counsell of a father to his sonne, in ten severall precepts left as a legacy at his death* (London: Joseph Hunt, [1611]).

STC 4900.5 William Cecil, first Baron of Burghley, *Precepts, or, directions for the well ordering and carriage of a mans life, through the whole course thereof: left by William, Lord Burghly, to his sonne, at his death, who was sometimes Lord Treasurer of this kingdome* (London: [Thomas Harper] for Thomas Jones, 1637).

STC 4901 [Thomas Norton,] *A Declaration of the favourable dealing of her Majesties Commissioners appointed for the Examination of certaine Traitours* ([London: Christopher Barker,] 1583).

STC 4902 [William Cecil, first Baron of Burghley,] *The execution of Justice in England for maintenaunce of publique and Christian peace* ([London: Christopher Barker,] 1583).

STC 4903 [William Cecil, first Baron of Burghley,] *The Execution of Justice in England for maintenaunce of publique and Christian peace* ([London: Christopher Barker,] 1584).

STC 4908 William Cecil, first Baron of Burghley, *Ordinances made by Sir William Cecill, Knight of the Order of the Garter, Baron of Burghley, for the order and government of xiij. Poore men, whereof one to be the Warden of the Hospitall at Stanford Baron in the Countie of Northampton* ([London: deputies of Christopher Barker, 1597]).

STC 6052 *The Copie of a Letter to the Right Honourable the Earle of Leycester* (London: Christopher Barker, 1586).

STC 6221 William Daman, *Bassus. The second booke of the musicke of M. William Damon, late one of her maiesties musitions conteining all the tunes of Dauids Psalmes, as they are ordinarily soung in the Church* ([London:] T. Este, the assigné of W. Byrd, 1591).

STC 7590 *The passage of our most dread Soveraigne Lady Quene Elyzabeth through the citie of London to Wesminster the daye before her coronacion* (London: Richard Tottill, 1559).

STC 7601 *A treatise of treasons against Q. Elizabeth, and the Croune of England, divided into two Partes* ([Antwerp, 1573]). See also *STC* 23617.5.

STC 7603.5 *A True report of sundry horrible conspiracies of late time detected to have (by barbarous murders) taken away the life of the Queenes Most Excellent Majestie whom Almighty God hath miraculously conserved against the treacheries of her rebelles, and the violences of her most puissant enemies* (London: Charles Yetsweirt, 1594).

STC 7846 *Jane, by the grace of God quene of England, Fraunce and Ireland, defendor of the faith, & of the Church of Englande, & also of Irelande under Christ in earth the supreme head* (London: Richard Grafton, [1553]).

STC 10089 *Injunccions geven by the moste excellent prince, Edward the sixte* (London: Richard Grafton, 1547).

STC 11036 William Fleetwood, *The effect of the declaration made in the Guildhall by M. Recorder of London, concerning the late attemptes of the Quenes Majesties evill, seditious, and disobedient subjectes* (London: John Day, [1571]).

STC 11222 John Foxe, *Actes and Monuments of these latter and perilous dayes* (London: John Day, 1563).

STC 11504–11506 [William Cecil, first Baron of Burghley,] *Salutem in Christo* ([London: John Day, 1571]).

STC 11987 Arthur Golding, *A discourse upon the Earthquake* (London: Henry Binneman, 1580).

STC 11997 Reginald Montanus, *A discovery and playne Declaration of sundry subtill practises of the Holy Inquisition of Spayne*, trans. Vincent Skinner (London: John Day, 1569).

STC 12539 Philemon Holland, *Gutta podrica: a treatise of the gout* (London: Thomas Harper, 1633).

STC 13127 Christopher Arbaleste, *The overthrow of the Gout* (London: Abraham Veale, 1577).

STC 13485 Thomas Hill, *The Gardeners Labyrinth* (London: Henry Bynneman, 1577).

STC 13569 John Holinshed, *The Third volume of Chronicles*, ed. John Hooker (London: [Henry Denham,] 1587).

STC 13869 Thomas Norton, *A discourse touching the pretended match betwene the Duke of Norfolke and the Queene of Scottes* ([John Day, 1569]).

STC 13870 Thomas Norton, *A discourse touching the pretended match between the Duke of Norfolke and the Queene of Scottes* ([London: John Day, 1569]).

STC 15413 [William Cecil, first Baron of Burghley,] *The copie of a letter sent out of England to Don Bernardin Mendoza* (London: J. Vautrollier for Richard Field, 1588).

STC 15506 [John Lesley,] *A treatise concerning the defence of the honour of the right high, mightie and noble Princesse, Marie Queene of Scotland, and Douager of France* ([Rheims, 1569]).

STC 16292 *The booke of common praier, and administration of the Sacramentes, and other rites and ceremonies in the Churche of Englande* (London: Richard Jugge & John Cawood, 1559).

STC 16305a *The Booke of common prayer* (London: Richard Jugge, [1575]).

STC 16506.7 *A Fourme to be used in Common prayer twyse a weke, and also an order of publique fast ... duryng this tyme of mortalitie* (London: Richard Jugge & John Cawood, [1563]).

STC 16511 *A fourme of common prayer to be used, and so commaunded by aucthoritie of the Queenes Majestie, and necessarie for the present tyme and state. 1572. 27 Octob.* (London: Richard Jugge, [1572]).

STC 16704.9 *Wyllyam Cecill knight, high stewarde of the citie of Westminster, and Ambrose Caue, knight, chauncelour of the duchye of Lancaster ... greeting knowe ye that our sayde soueraigne lady the quene, hauyng compassion of the estate of that her citie, because of the long visitation thereof with the plague* (London: Richard Jugge, 1564).

STC 17565 [William Cecil, first Baron of Burghley,] *The copie of a letter written by one in London to his frend concerning the credit of the late published detection of the doynges of the Ladie Marie of Scotland* ([London: John Day, 1572]).

STC 18635 John Norden, *Speculum Britanniae. The first parte an historicall, & chorographicall discription of Middlesex* ([London: Eliot's Court Press, 1593]).

STC 18679.5 Thomas Norton, *To the Queenes Majesties poore deceived subjectes of the northe contreye, drawne into rebellion by the Earles of Northumberland and Westmerland* ([London:] Henry Bynneman for Lucas Harrison, 1569).

STC 18684 Thomas Norton and Thomas Sackville, *The tragedie of Gorboduc* (London: William Griffith, 1565).

STC 19476.5 William Patten, *The Expedicion into Scotlande* (London: Richard Grafton, 1548).

STC 19885 [Richard Verstegan alias Rowlands,] *An advertisement written to a secretarie of my L. Treasurers of Ingland* ([Antwerp, 1592]).

STC 20029 Pliny the Elder, *The historie of the world*, trans. Philemon Holland (London: Adam Islip, 1601).

STC 20188 *The copie of a pistel or letter sent to Gilbard Potter in the tyme when he was in prison for speakinge on our most true queens part the Lady Mary before he had his eares cut of* ([Richard Jugge for] Hugh Singleton, 1553).

STC 22590 Sixtus V, *A Declaration of the Sentence and deposition of Elizabeth, the usurper and pretensed Quene of Englande* ([Antwerp: A. Conincx, 1588]).

STC 23095 Edmund Spenser and Gabriel Harvey, *Three proper, and wittie, familiar Letters* (London: H. Bynneman, 1580).

STC 23400 John Stubbs, *The discouerie of a gaping gulf vvhereinto England is like to be swallowed by another French mariage, if the Lord forbid not the banes, by letting her Majestie see the sin and punishment thereof* ([London: H. Singleton for W. Page,] 1579).

STC 23617.5 *A table gathered owt of a booke named A Treatise of treasons against Q. Elizabeth, and the Croune of England* [Antwerp: J. Fowler 1573]. See also *STC* 7601.

STC 24050.5 *A discoverie of the treasons practised and attempted against the Queenes Majestie and the Realme, by Francis Throckmorton* ([London: Christopher Barker,] 1584).

STC 24324 George Turberville, *The Booke of Faulconrie or Hauking, for the onely delight and pleasure of all Noblemen and Gentlemen* (London: for Christopher Barker, 1575).

STC 24366 William Turner, *The seconde part of William Turners herbal* (Cologne, [1562]).

STC 25223 John Weever, *Ancient funerall monuments* (London: Thomas Harper, 1631).

2. Collections or editions of primary sources

Acts of the Privy Council of England, ed. John Roche Dasent *et al.*, new series, 46 vols (London, 1890–1964).

Archaeologia, 12 (1796), 334–96.

BACON, Francis, *Of Empire* (London, 2005).

BAKER, Thomas, *HISTORY of the College of St John the Evangelist, Cambridge* [1740], ed. J.E.B. Mayor, 2 vols (Cambridge, 1869).

BEALE, Robert, 'A TREATISE of the Office of a Councillor and Principal Secretary to Her Majesty' (1592), in Read, *Walsingham*, vol. 1, 427–43.

BRIGDEN, Susan, ed., 'The Letters of RICHARD SCUDAMORE to Sir Philip Hoby, September 1549–March 1555', *Camden Miscellany 30*, Camden Society, fourth series 39 (London, 1990), 67–148.

COBBETT, William, T.B. HOWELL and T.J. HOWELL, eds, *Cobbett's Complete Collection of STATE TRIALS and Proceedings for High Treason*, 33 vols (London, 1809–28).

The Compleat Ambassador, ed. Sir Dudley Digges (London, 1655).

EDWARD VI, *CHRONICLE and Political Papers*, ed. W.K. Jordan (London, 1966).

ELTON, G.R., ed., *The TUDOR CONSTITUTION* (Cambridge, 1982).

FENTON, Edward, ed., *The Diaries of JOHN DEE* (Charlbury, Oxfordshire, 1998).

FLETCHER, Reginald James, ed., *The PENSION BOOK of Gray's Inn ... 1569–1669* (London, 1901).

FOSTER, J.E., ed., *Churchwardens' Accounts of ST MARY THE GREAT Cambridge from 1504 to 1635* (Cambridge Antiquarian Society; Octavo Series, 35; Cambridge, 1905).

FULLER, Thomas, *The CHURCH-HISTORY of Britain* (London, 1656).

HALL, Spencer, *Documents from SIMANCAS relating to the Reign of Elizabeth* (London, 1865).

HARTLEY, T.E., ed., *PROCEEDINGS in the Parliaments of Elizabeth I*, 3 vols (Leicester, 1981–95).

HAYNES, Samuel, ed., *A Collection of State Papers* (London, 1740).

HOBY, Sir Thomas, 'The TRAVELS and Life of Sir Thomas Hoby, Knight', ed. Edgar Powell, *Camden Miscellany 10*, Camden Society, third series, 4 (London, 1902).

HODGETT, G.A.J., ed., *The State of the Ex-Religious and Former CHANTRY PRIESTS in the Diocese of Lincoln 1547–1574* (Lincoln Record Society, 53; Hereford, 1959).

HUGHES, Paul L. and James Francis LARKIN, eds, *Tudor Royal PROCLAMATIONS*, 3 vols (New Haven, CT and London, 1964–69).

JONES, Judith, ed., *MONMOUTHSHIRE WILLS Proved in the Prerogative Court of Canterbury, 1560–1601* (South Wales Record Society; Cardiff, 1997).

Journals of the House of Commons.

Journals of the House of Lords.

KINGDON, Robert M., ed., *The EXECUTION OF JUSTICE by William Cecil and A True, Sincere, and Modest Defense of English Catholics by William Allen* (Folger Documents of Tudor and Stuart Civilization; Ithaca, NY, 1965).

LAMB, John, ed., *A COLLECTION of Letters, Statutes, and Other Documents ... Illustrative of the History of the University of Cambridge* (London, 1838).

LELAND, John, *The ITINERARY of John Leland in or about the Years 1535–1543*, ed. Lucy Toulmin Smith, 5 vols (London, 1907–10).

Letters and Papers, Foreign and Domestic, of the Reign of Henry VIII, ed. J.S. Brewer, J. Gairdner, R.H. Brodie *et al.*, 21 vols and *Addenda* (London, 1862–1932).

MacCULLOCH, Diarmaid, ed., 'The *VITA MARIAE Angliae Reginae* of

Robert Wingfield of Brantham', *Camden Miscellany 28*, Camden Society, fourth series, 29 (London, 1984), 181–301.

MACHYN, Henry, *The DIARY of Henry Machyn*, ed. John Gough Nichols (Camden Society, 42; London, 1848).

MAHON, R.H., *The INDICTMENT of Mary Queen of Scots* (Cambridge, 1923).

MARCUS, Leah S., Janel MUELLER and Mary Beth ROSE, eds, *Elizabeth I: COLLECTED WORKS* (Chicago and London, 2000).

MARTIN, C.T., ed., 'Journal of SIR FRANCIS WALSINGHAM, from December 1570 to April 1583', *Camden Miscellany 6*, Camden Society, 104 (London, 1871).

MAYOR, J.E.B., ed., *EARLY STATUTES of the College of St John the Evangelist in the University of Cambridge* (Cambridge, 1859).

MORRIS, John, ed., *The LETTER-BOOKS of Sir Amias Poulet Keeper of Mary Queen of Scots* (London, 1874).

MURDIN, William, ed., *A Collection of State Papers* (London, 1759).

NEALE, J.E., 'PROCEEDINGS in Parliament relative to the Sentence on Mary Queen of Scots', *English Historical Review*, 35 (1920), 103–13.

NICHOLS, John Gough, ed., *The CHRONICLE of Queen Jane* (Camden Society, 48; 1849).

NICHOLS, John Gough, ed., *The Diary of Henry MACHYN, Citizen and Merchant-Taylor of London, from AD 1550 to AD 1563* (Camden Society; London, 1848).

NOWELL, Alexander, *A CATECHISM written in Latin*, ed. G.E. Corrie (Parker Society; Cambridge, 1853).

POLLEN, John H., ed., *Mary Queen of Scots and the BABINGTON PLOT* (Scottish History Society, third series, 3; Edinburgh, 1922).

READ, Conyers, ed., *The BARDON PAPERS: Documents relating to the Imprisonment & Trial of Mary Queen of Scots* (Camden Society, third series, 17; London, 1909).

READ, Conyers, ed., 'Lord Burghley's HOUSEHOLD ACCOUNTS', *Economic History Review*, new series 9 (1956), 343–8.

READ, Conyers, ed., 'The Proposal to Assassinate MARY QUEEN OF SCOTS at Fotheringhay', *English Historical Review*, 40 (1925), 234–5.

RICHARDS, Sheila R., *SECRET WRITINGS in the Public Records: Henry VIII–George II* (London, 1974).

RODRIGUEZ-SALGADO, M.J. and Simon ADAMS, eds, 'The Count of FERIA'S DISPATCH to Philip II of 14 November 1558', *Camden Miscellany 28*, Camden Society, fourth series, 29 (London, 1984), 302–44.

SCOTT, R.F., *NOTES from the Records of St John's College, Cambridge*, first to third series (Cambridge, 1889–1913).

Scrinia Ceciliana: Mysteries of State & Government in Letters of the Late Famous Lord Burghley (London, 1663).

SMITH, A.G.R., ed., *The ANONYMOUS LIFE of William Cecil, Lord Burghley* (Lampeter, 1990).

SMITH, Toulmin and Lucy Toulmin SMITH, *English Gilds* (Early English Text Society; London, 1870).

Sotheby & Co., *CATALOGUE of Fine Illuminated Manuscripts, Valuable Printed Books, Autograph Letters and Historical Documents etc.* 3–4 June 1946.

Statutes of the Realm, ed. A. Luders, T.E. Tomlins, J. Raithby *et al.*, 11 vols (London, 1810–28).

STEUART, A. Francis, ed., *TRIAL of Mary Queen of Scots* (London, Edinburgh and Glasgow, 1951).

Survey and Antiquities ... of Stamford, ed. A. Rogers and J.S. Hartley (Wakefield, 1979).

WILLIAMS, C.H., *English HISTORICAL DOCUMENTS ... 1485–1558* (London, 1967).

WRIOTHESLEY, Charles, *A CHRONICLE of England during the Reigns of the Tudors*, 2 vols (Camden Society, new series 11, 20; London, 1875, 1877).

SECONDARY WORKS

1. Works of reference

BARNETT, Richard C., *Place, Profit, and Power: A Study of the SERVANTS of William Cecil, Elizabethan Statesman* (Chapel Hill, NC, 1969).

BARRON, Oswald, *NORTHAMPTONSHIRE FAMILIES* (Victoria County History; London, 1906).

Calendar of the Patent Rolls preserved in the Public Record Office, Henry VII–Elizabeth I, multiple vols (London, 1914–).

Calendar of State Papers, Foreign: Edward VI, Mary, Elizabeth I, ed. J. Stevenson *et al.*, 25 vols (London, 1861–1950).

Calendar of State Papers and Manuscripts Relating to English Affairs Existing in the Archives and Collections of Venice and in Other Libraries of Northern Italy, 38 vols (London, 1864–1947).

CHAMBERS, E.K., *The ELIZABETHAN STAGE*, 4 vols (Oxford, 1951).

COLVIN, Howard and Susan FOISTER, eds, *The PANORAMA of London circa 1544 by Anthonis van den Wyngaerde* (London Topographical Society, 151; London, 1996).

The Complete Peerage, ed. Vicary Gibbs *et al.*, 13 vols (London, 1910–40).

CRIPPS, Wilfred Joseph, *Old English Plate* (London, 1967 edn).

The History of the King's Works, ed. H.M Colvin *et al.*, 6 vols (London: HMSO, 1963–82).

LEEDHAM-GREEN, E.S., ed., *Books in CAMBRIDGE INVENTORIES*: Booklists from Vice-Chancellor's Court Probate Inventories in the Tudor and Stuart Periods, 2 vols (Cambridge, 1986).

London County Council, *Survey of London*, 18 vols (London, 1900–37).

MacLURE, Millar, *Register of Sermons Preached at PAUL'S CROSS, 1534–1642*, rev. Peter Pauls and Jackson Campbell Boswell (Ottawa, 1989).

Monumenta Westmonasteriensia (London, 1683).

Oxford Dictionary of National Biography, ed. H.C.G. Matthew and Brian Harrison, 60 vols (Oxford, 2004).

PECK, Francis, *ANTIQUITIES of Stamford and St Martin's*, ed. W. Harrod, 2 vols (Stamford, 1785).

PEVSNER, Nikolaus, *Cambridgeshire* (Buildings of England; Harmondsworth, 1982).

PEVSNER, Nikolaus, *Northamptonshire* (Buildings of England; Harmondsworth, 1961).

PEVSNER, Nikolaus and John HARRIS, *Lincolnshire*, rev. Nicholas Antram (Buildings of England; Harmondsworth, 1991).

PROCKTER, Adrian and Robert TAYLOR, eds, *The A to Z of ELIZABETHAN LONDON* (London Topographical Society, 122; London, 1979).

Royal Commission on Historical Manuscripts, *Calendar of the Manuscripts of the Most Hon. The Marquis of SALISBURY*, 24 vols (London, 1883–1973).

Royal Commission on the Historical Monuments of England, *City of CAMBRIDGE*, 2 vols (London, HMSO, 1959).

Royal Commission on the Historical Monuments of England, *An Inventory of the Historical Monuments in HEREFORDSHIRE*, vol. 1, South-West, 3 vols (London, HMSO, 1931–34).

Royal Commission on the Historical Monuments of England, *An Inventory of the Historical Monuments in LONDON*, 5 vols (London, HMSO, 1924–30).

Royal Commission on the Historical Monuments of England, *An Inventory of Historical Monuments: the Town of STAMFORD* (London, HMSO, 1977).

SEAGER, H.W., *NATURAL HISTORY in Shakespeare's Time* (London, 1896).

A Short-Title Catalogue of Books ... 1475–1640, ed. W.A. Jackson, F.S. Ferguson and Katharine F. Pantzer, 3 vols (London, 1986–91).

SKELTON, R.A. and John SUMMERSON, eds, *A Description of MAPS and Architectural Drawings in the Collection made by William Cecil First Baron of Burghley now at Hatfield House* (Roxburghe Club; Oxford, 1971).

STRONG, Roy, *Tudor & Jacobean PORTRAITS*, 2 vols (National Portrait Gallery; London, HMSO, 1969).

Victoria County History of England, *A History of the County of LINCOLNSHIRE* (London, 1906).

Victoria County History of England, *A History of the County of NORTHAMPTON*, 5 vols (London, 1902–2002).

Wayment, H.G., *The WINDOWS of King's College Chapel Cambridge* (London, 1972).

2. Books, articles and unpublished dissertations

ADAMS, Simon, *Leicester and the Court: Essays on Elizabethan Politics* (Manchester, 2002).

ADAMS, Simon, ed., *Household Accounts and Disbursement Books of Robert Dudley, Earl of Leicester, 1558–1561, 1584–1586* (Camden Society, fifth series, 6; Cambridge, 1995).

ALFORD, Stephen, *The EARLY ELIZABETHAN POLITY: William Cecil and the British Succession Crisis, 1559–1569* (Cambridge, 1998).

ALFORD, Stephen, *KINGSHIP AND POLITICS in the Reign of Edward VI* (Cambridge, 2002).

ANDREWS, Martin, 'THEOBALDS Palace: The Gardens and Park', *Garden History*, 21 (1993), 129–49.

BASING, Patricia, 'ROBERT BEALE and the Queen of Scots', *British Library Journal*, 20 (1994), 65–81.

BECKETT, Margaret J., 'The Political Works of JOHN LESLEY, Bishop of Ross (1527–96)', PhD dissertation, University of St Andrews (2002).

BENNETT, Josephine Waters, 'Characterization in Polonius' ADVICE to Laertes', *Shakespeare Quarterly*, 4 (1953), 3–9.

BENNETT, Josephine Waters, 'These Few PRECEPTS', *Shakespeare Quarterly*, 7 (1956), 275–6.

BIRKBECK, J.D., *A History of BOURNE* (Bourne, 1970).

BOSSY, John, *Giordano Bruno and the EMBASSY AFFAIR* (New Haven, CT and London, 1991).

BOWERS, R.H., 'POLONIUS: Another Postscript', *Shakespeare Quarterly*, 4 (1953), 362–4.

BOWERS, Roger, 'The CHAPEL ROYAL, the First Edwardian Prayer Book, and Elizabeth's Settlement of Religion, 1559', *Historical Journal*, 43 (2000), 317–44.

BUSH, M.L., 'Protector Somerset and REQUESTS', *Historical Journal*, 17 (1974), 451–64.

CHARLTON, W.H., *BURGHLEY: The Life of William Cecil, Lord Burghley* (Stamford, 1847).

COLLINSON, Patrick, 'The Elizabethan EXCLUSION CRISIS and the Elizabethan Polity', *Proceedings of the British Academy*, 84 (1994), 51–92.

COLLINSON, Patrick, 'The MONARCHICAL REPUBLIC of Queen Elizabeth I', in his *Elizabethan Essays* (London, 1994), 31–57.

COLLINSON, Patrick, 'SIR NICHOLAS BACON and the Elizabethan *Via Media*', *Historical Journal*, 23 (1980), 258–64.

COLLINSON, Patrick, 'WILLIAM CAMDEN and the Anti-myth of Elizabeth: Setting the Mould?', in Susan Doran and Thomas S. Freeman, eds, *The Myth of Elizabeth* (London, 2003), 79–98.

COOPE, Rosalys, 'The "LONG GALLERY": Its Origins, Development, Use and Decoration', *Architectural History*, 29 (1986), 43–84.

COOPER, Tarnya, *Searching for SHAKESPEARE* (London, 2006).

CRESSY, David, 'BINDING THE NATION: The Bonds of Association, 1584 and 1696', in GUTH and McKENNA, eds, *Tudor Rule and Revolution*, 217–34.

CROFT, Pauline, 'Mildred, Lady Burghley: The MATRIARCH', in Croft, *Early Cecils*, 283–300.

CROFT, Pauline, ed., *Patronage, Culture and Power: The EARLY CECILS* (Studies in British Art, 8; New Haven, CT and London, 2002).

DAULTREY, S., 'The WEATHER of Northwest Europe during the Summer and Autumn of 1588', in P. Gallagher and D.W. Cruickshank, eds, *God's Obvious Design* (London, 1990), 113–41.

DAVIS, O.B., 'A Note on the Function of Polonius' ADVICE', *Shakespeare Quarterly*, 9 (1958), 85–6.

DAWSON, Jane E.A., 'MARY QUEEN OF SCOTS, Lord Darnley, and Anglo-Scottish Relations in 1565', *International History Review*, 8 (1986), 1–24.

DAWSON, Jane E.A., 'RESISTANCE AND REVOLUTION in Sixteenth-Century Thought: The Case of Christopher Goodman', in J. Van Den Berg and P.G. Hoftijzer, eds, *Church, Change and Revolution* (Leiden, 1991), 69–79.

DEED, B.L., *A History of STAMFORD SCHOOL* ([Stamford,] 1982).

DENNIS, G. Ravenscroft, *The House of Cecil* (London, 1914).

DORAN, Susan, *MONARCHY & MATRIMONY: The Courtships of Elizabeth I* (London, 1996).

DORAN, Susan, ed., *ELIZABETH: The Exhibition at the National Maritime Museum* (London, 2003).

DOUTHWAITE, William Ralph, *GRAY'S INN: Its History and Associations Compiled from Original and Published Documents* (London, 1886).

EDWARDS, Francis, *The MARVELLOUS CHANCE: Thomas Howard, Fourth Duke of Norfolk, and the Ridolphi Plot, 1570–1572* (London, 1968).

EMMISON, F.G., *TUDOR SECRETARY: Sir William Petre at Court and Home* (London, 1961).

EVENDEN, Elizabeth, 'The MICHAEL WOOD Mystery: William Cecil and the Lincolnshire Printing of John Day', *Sixteenth Century Journal*, 35 (2004), 383–94.

EVENDEN, Elizabeth and Thomas S. FREEMAN, 'Print, Profit and PROPAGANDA: The Elizabethan Privy Council and the 1570 Edition of Foxe's "Book of Martyrs"', *English Historical Review*, 119 (2004), 1288–307.

FISHER, R.M., 'The INNS OF COURT and the Reformation 1530–1580', PhD dissertation, University of Cambridge (1974).

FLOWER, Robin, 'LAURENCE NOWELL and the Discovery of England in Tudor Times', in E.G. Stanley, ed., *British Academy Papers on Anglo-Saxon England* (Oxford, 1990), 1–27.

FRYE, Susan, 'The Myth of Elizabeth at TILBURY', *Sixteenth Century Journal*, 23 (1992), 95–114.

GIROUARD, Mark, 'ELIZABETHAN ARCHITECTURE and the Gothic Tradition', *Architectural History*, 6 (1963), 23–39.

GOLDHILL, Simon, *WHO NEEDS GREEK? Contests in the Cultural History of Hellenism* (Cambridge, 2002).

GREEN, Dominic, *The Double Life of DOCTOR LOPEZ* (London, 2003).

GUTH, DeLloyd J. and McKENNA, eds, *Tudor Rule and Revolution* (Cambridge, 1982).

GUY, John, *'MY HEART IS MY OWN': The Life of Mary Queen of Scots* (London, 2004).

HEAL, Felicity, 'What can King LUCIUS do for you? The Reformation and the Early British Church', *English Historical Review*, 120 (2005), 593–614.

HEATH, James, *TORTURE and English Law* (Westport, CT and London, 1982).

HEISCH, Allison, 'ARGUMENTS for an Execution: Queen Elizabeth's "White Paper" and Lord Burghley's "Blue Pencil"', *Albion*, 24 (1992), 591–604.

HEISCH, Allison, 'LORD BURGHLEY, Speaker Puckering, and the Editing of HEH Ellesmere MS 1191', *Huntington Library Quarterly*, 51 (1988), 211–26.

HENDERSON, Paula, 'The Architecture of the TUDOR GARDEN', *Garden History*, 22 (1999), 54–72.

HIGHAM, C.S., *WIMBLEDON under the Cecils* (London, 1962).

HOAK, Dale, 'The CORONATIONS of Edward VI, Mary I, and Elizabeth I, and the Transformation of the Tudor Monarchy', in C.S. Knighton and Richard Mortimer, eds, *Westminster Abbey Reformed 1540–1640* (Aldershot and Burlington, VT, 2003), 114–51.

HOAK, Dale, 'The King's PRIVY CHAMBER, 1547–1553', in GUTH and McKENNA, *Tudor Rule and Revolution*, 87–108.

HOWARD, Henry Fraser, *An Account of the FINANCES of the College of St John the Evangelist in the University of Cambridge 1511–1926* (Cambridge, 1935).

HUME, Martin, *The Great Lord Burghley (William Cecil): A Study in Elizabethan Statecraft* (London, 1906).

HURSTFIELD, Joel, *FREEDOM, CORRUPTION & GOVERNMENT in Elizabethan England* (London, 1973).

HURSTFIELD, Joel, *The QUEEN'S WARDS: Wardship and Marriage under Elizabeth I* (London, 1958).

HUSSELBY, Jill, 'The Politics of Pleasure: William Cecil and BURGHLEY HOUSE', in Croft, *Early Cecils*, 21–45.

HUSSELBY, Jill and Paula HENDERSON, 'Location, Location, Location! CECIL HOUSE in the Strand', *Architectural History*, 45 (2002), 159–93.

IVES, E.W., 'HENRY VIII'S WILL – A Forensic Conundrum', *Historical Journal*, 35 (1992), 779–804.

JAMES, Henry and Greg WALKER, 'The Politics of *GORBODUC*', *English Historical Review*, 110 (1995), 109–21.

JESSOPP, Augustus, J.A. GOTCH, James L. CAW and A.C. FOX-DAVIES, *WILLIAM CECIL, Lord Burghley* (London, 1904).

JONES, Michael K. and Malcolm G. UNDERWOOD, *The KING'S MOTHER: Lady Margaret Beaufort, Countess of Richmond and Derby* (Cambridge, 1992).

JONES, Norman L., *FAITH BY STATUTE: Parliament and the Settlement of Religion 1559* (London, 1982).

KIERNAN, Kevin S., *BEOWULF and the Beowulf Manuscript* (New Brunswick, NJ, 1981).

KING, John N., *TUDOR ROYAL ICONOGRAPHY: Literature and Art in an Age of Religious Crisis* (Princeton, NJ, 1989).

KNIGHT, Caroline, 'The Cecils at WIMBLEDON', in Croft, *Early Cecils*, 47–66.

LANGBEIN, John H., *TORTURE and the Law of Proof: Europe and England in the Ancien Régime* (Chicago, 1977).

LEACH, Arthur F., *ENGLISH SCHOOLS at the Reformation 1546–8* (Westminster, 1896).

LEADER, Damian Riehl, *A History of the UNIVERSITY OF CAMBRIDGE … to 1546* (Cambridge, 1988).

LOACH, Jennifer, *Edward VI*, ed. G.W. Bernard and Penry Williams (New Haven, CT and London, 1999).

LOACH, Jennifer, *PARLIAMENT and the Crown in the Reign of Mary Tudor* (Oxford, 1986).

LOADES, David, *MARY TUDOR: A Life* (Oxford and Cambridge, MA, 1990).

LYNCH, Michael, 'QUEEN MARY'S TRIUMPH: The Baptismal Celebrations at Stirling in December 1566', *Scottish Historical Review*, 69 (1990), 1–21.

MACAULEY, Sarah, 'MATTHEW Stewart, Fourth Earl of LENNOX and the

Politics of Britain, *c.*1543–1571', PhD dissertation, University of Cambridge (2006).

MacCAFFREY, Wallace, *Elizabeth I* (London, 1993).

MacCAFFREY, Wallace, 'The NEWHAVEN EXPEDITION, 1562–1563', *Historical Journal*, 40 (1997), 1–21.

MacCULLOCH, Diarmaid, *Thomas Cranmer: A Life* (New Haven, CT and London, 1996).

McINTOSH, M.K., 'SIR ANTHONY COOKE: Tudor Humanist, Educator, and Religious Reformer', *Proceedings of the American Philosophical Society*, 119 (1975), 233–50.

MEARS, Natalie, 'Counsel, Public Debate, and Queenship: John Stubbs's *The Discoverie of a GAPING GULF*, 1579', *Historical Journal*, 44 (2001), 629–50.

MILLER, Edward, *PORTRAIT of a College: A History of the College of Saint John the Evangelist Cambridge* (Cambridge, 1961).

MULLINGER, James Bass, *The UNIVERSITY OF CAMBRIDGE from the Royal Injunctions of 1535 to the Accession of Charles the First* (Cambridge, 1884).

PARKER, Geoffrey, *The GRAND STRATEGY of Philip II* (New Haven, CT and London, 1998).

PARKER, Geoffrey, 'The Place of Tudor England in the MESSIANIC VISION of Philip II of Spain', *Transactions of the Royal Historical Society*, sixth series, 12 (2002), 167–221.

PAYNE, Helen, 'The CECIL WOMEN at Court', in Croft, *Early Cecils*, 265–81.

PHILLIPS, G.W., *LORD BURGHLEY in Shakespeare: Falstaff, Sly and Others* (London, 1936).

PORTER, H.C., *Reformation and Reaction in TUDOR CAMBRIDGE* (Cambridge, 1958).

READ, Conyers, *Lord Burghley and Queen Elizabeth* (London, 1960).

READ, Conyers, *Mr. Secretary Cecil and Queen Elizabeth* (London, 1955).

READ, Conyers, *Mr. Secretary WALSINGHAM and the Policy of Queen Elizabeth*, 3 vols (Oxford, 1925).

RODRIGUEZ-SALGADO, M.J. and Simon ADAMS, eds, *England, Spain and the GRAN ARMADA 1585–1604* (Edinburgh, 1991).

ROGERS, Alan, 'LATE MEDIEVAL STAMFORD: A Study of the Town Council 1465–1492', in Alan Everitt, ed., *Perspectives in English Urban History* (London and Basingstoke, 1973), 16–38.

ROWSE, A.L., 'ALLTYRYNYS and the Cecils', *English Historical Review*, 75 (1960), 54–76.

RYAN, L.V., *Roger Ascham* (Stanford, CA and London, 1963).

SMITH, A.G.R., *Servant of the Cecils: The Life of Sir Michael Hickes* (London, 1977).

STARKEY, David, *ELIZABETH: Apprenticeship* (London, 2000).

STARKEY, David, ed., *HENRY VIII: A European Court in England* (London, 1991).

SUMMERSON, John, 'The Building of THEOBALDS, 1564–85', *Archaeologia*, 97 (1954), 107–26.

SUTTON, James M., 'The DECORATIVE PROGRAM at Elizabethan Theobalds: Educating an Heir and Promoting a Dynasty', *Studies in the Decorative Arts*, 7 (2000), 33–64.

SUTTON, James M., *Materializing Space at an Early Modern Prodigy House: The Cecils at THEOBALDS, 1564–1607* (Aldershot and Burlington, VT, 2004).

SUTTON, James M., 'The RETIRING PATRON: William Cecil and the Cultivation of Retirement, 1590–98', in Croft, *Early Cecils*, 159–79.

TAVINER, Mark, 'ROBERT BEALE and the Elizabethan Polity', PhD dissertation, University of St Andrews (2000).

TILL, Eric, 'Fact and Conjecture: The Building of BURGHLEY HOUSE 1555–1587', *Northamptonshire Past and Present*, 52 (1999), 15–20.

TORRY, A.F., *FOUNDERS AND BENEFACTORS of St John's College, Cambridge* (Cambridge, 1888).

TYRRELL, R.Y., 'The ADVICE of Polonius to Laertes', *Classical Review*, 6 (1892), 122.

UNDERWOOD, Malcolm, 'JOHN FISHER and the Promotion of Learning', in Brendan Bradshaw and Eamon Duffy, eds, *Humanism, Reform and Reformation: The Career of Bishop John Fisher* (Cambridge, 1989), 25–46.

WILSON, Elkin Calhoun, 'POLONIUS in the Round', *Shakespeare Quarterly*, 9 (1958), 83–5.

Index